FOR WORKERS' POWER

THE SELECTED WRITINGS OF MAURICE BRINTON

Maurice Brinton circa 1968

PRESS

EDINBURGH · OAKLAND · WEST VIRGINIA

For Workers' Power
The Selected Writings of Maurice Brinton
Edited by David Goodway
Copyright 2004 Christopher Pallis
Introduction Copyright 2004 David Goodway
ISBN 1-904859-07-0

AK Press
674-A 23rd Street
Oakland, CA 94612
USA
www.akpress.org
akpress@akpress.org
510-208-1700

AK Press
PO Box 12766
Edinburgh, EH8, 9YE
Scotland
www.akuk.com
ak@akedin.co.demon.uk
(0131) 555-5165

The addresses above would be delighted to provide you with the latest AK
Press catalog, featuring several thousand books, pamphlets, audio and video
products, and stylish apparel published and distributed by AK Press.
Alternatively, visit our websites for the complete catalog, latest news and
updates, events and secure ordering.

Library of Congress Control Number: 2004115248

Printed in the USA.

AK Press would like to thank Ken Weller and the Solidarity Group for their
contribution to the publishing of this book.

Cover design by Chris Wright
Cover photograph circa 1967 by Bob Potter

TABLE OF CONTENTS

INTRODUCTION

Maurice Brinton was the principal writer, translator and thinker of the Solidarity Group, which was at its most active and exerted greatest influence in Britain during the 1960s and the first half of the 1970s. It was a section of the Old Left which broke away to become, it can now be seen, part of the New Left, although it has never been accepted as such - especially since it almost immediately passed beyond any recognizable Marxism to a fully left-libertarian position, while largely holding back from the self-description of "anarchist". Brinton, in particular, has always been extremely critical of anarchism and the anarchists, denying that he himself is an anarchist, only being comfortable with the appellation of "libertarian socialist". Because of the way in which his writing has fallen between the poles of Marxist humanism and anarchism; because it overwhelmingly appeared in cyclostyled publications, never being reprinted by mainstream publishers; and because of his own pseudonymous existence, Maurice Brinton has never received the recognition that the quality of his political output deserves. It is the intention of this ample sampling of his work to begin to rectify this deplorable state of affairs.

Although in the late sixties and early seventies Solidarity's ambition was to inspire by its example a major movement - and indeed, at one time or another, at least 25 groups existed in London and elsewhere - in terms of numbers its membership was never appreciable. Solidarity's significance lay not in its size but in the excellence of its publications. The group was initially called "Socialism Reaffirmed" and its journal first appeared in October 1960 under the title of *Agitator* (redolent of the Trotskyist origins of most of the group's founding members); but from the sixth issue (May 1961) it became *Solidarity*. It seems significant that both the IWW and the Shop Stewards' and Workers' Committee Movement - with their very similar industrial politics - had published journals with the same name. *Solidarity*, with the striking sub-title of *For Workers' Power*, came out every two to four months until 1977 when there was a merger with the *Social Revolution* group, resulting in *Solidarity: For Social Revolution*. Around 1982 the original London group resumed publication of *Solidarity*, eventually adopting the sub-title of *A Journal of Libertarian Socialism*, yet after 31 issues of the new series the paper folded in 1992; and the group is now defunct.

In parallel to the journal there were more than sixty impressive pamphlets and four important books. It was through the circulation of the pamphlets in particular that a wider radical readership was aware of the group's ideas; and it was through the excellence of its journal, pamphlets and books in general that *Solidarity* exerted significant influence in the 1960s and 1970s amongst anarchists and libertarian socialists.

Yet for a few months in the early 1960s *Solidarity* exercised a key role on the national level in shaping the outlook of the most militant section of the nuclear disarmament movement. CND (Campaign for Nuclear Disarmament) had been launched in 1958, but by autumn 1960 dissatisfaction with its legal methods and constitutional action spawned within it the direct-action Committee of 100.

Unequivocally opposed to all nuclear weapons, unlike Soviet sympathizers embedded in CND's leadership or the Trotskyist Socialist Labour League (SLL) with its risible defence of the "workers' bomb", the Committee of 100 was the most important anarchist – or at least near-anarchist – political organization of modern Britain.[1] The two best-known anarchists of the time, Herbert Read and Alex Comfort, were among its approximately one hundred members, while two more anarchists, Augustus John and George Melly, were also members and another influential libertarian, A.S. Neill, a supporter.

The Committee of 100 called for mass civil disobedience against the preparations for nuclear war and its sit-downs in central London reached their peak in September 1961 when, with Bertrand Russell, its 89-year-old president, and 31 other members in prison, 12,000 sat down in Trafalgar Square and 1,300 were arrested.

The failure of the demonstration at the Wethersfield airbase in December, however, led to the decentralization of the Committee into thirteen regional Committees (several of which were already existent). Although there was a nominal National Committee of 100, the dominant body was to be the London Committee of 100 (set up in April 1962). It was now that the Solidarity group became "one of the most important influences…in the Committee of 100": "in 1962, 1963, and beyond". The most authoritative historian of the nuclear disarmament movement concludes: "It was in practice a combination of *Solidarity* and anarchistic activists who constituted the militant hard core of the Committee in this period".[2]

The long, harsh winter of 1962-3, one of the twentieth century's worst, saw renewed crisis, now acted out within the London Committee of 100. The radicals, mainly from or close to Solidarity, circulated the arrestingly titled discussion document, "Beyond Counting Arses", advocating radical subversive action: "We must attempt to hinder the warfare state in every possible way".[3] It was essentially this group who constituted the Spies for Peace, locating and breaking into the Regional Seat of Government (RSG) at Warren Row, Berkshire, and producing the pamphlet, *Danger! Official Secret: RSG-6*. Thereby many of us on the Aldermaston March of Easter 1963 were diverted to explore the sinister surface buildings of the subterranean bunker.

The anarchist Nicolas Walter was the only member of the Spies for Peace ever to declare himself or herself publicly (of the eight, two were women).[4] For a short time he was very close to Solidarity, attending its group meetings and writing Pamphlet 15, *The RSGs, 1919-1963*, which detailed the historical development of the Regional Seats of Government.

The distinctiveness of Solidarity's politics was primarily twofold. There was its irreverent, humorous iconoclasm of all Left orthodoxies, the importance and novelty of which cannot be stressed too much, since the self-important ideologues of the far left have little sense of the comic. This was combined with the publication of the writings of "Paul Cardan":

1   Cf. Colin Ward, "The Future of the Committee of 100: An Anarchist View", *Peace News*, 26 January 1962.

2   Richard Taylor, *Against the Bomb: The British Peace Movement, 1958–1965* (Oxford: Clarendon Press, 1988), pp. 249–50.

3   "Beyond Counting Arses", reprinted in *Solidarity*, II, 11 [1963], p. 12.

4   Walter did so unambiguously as early as 1968, remarkably, and on the radio at that (Richard Boston, "Conversations about Anarchism", *Anarchy*, no. 85 (March 1968), p. 68); but in general see his unattributed accounts, "The Spies for Peace Story", *Inside Story*, nos. 8 (March–April 1973) and 9 (May–June 1973), and "The Spies for Peace and After", *Raven*, no. 5 (June 1988).

...we are ourselves and nothing more. We live here and now, not in Petrograd in 1917, nor Barcelona in 1936. We have no gods, not even revolutionary ones. Paraphrasing Marx ("philosophers have only interpreted the world; what is necessary is to change it"), we might say that "revolutionaries have only interpreted Marx (or Bakunin), what is necessary is to change them".

We are the products of the degeneration of traditional politics and of the revolt of youth against established society in an advanced industrial country in the second half of the twentieth century. The aim of this book is to give both purpose and meaning to this revolt and to merge it with the constant working–class struggle for its own emancipation.

This is from the introduction, printed in full below, to Solidarity's second book, Cardan's *Modern Capitalism and Revolution* (1965). In addition to texts by him in the journal, Solidarity also brought out nine pamphlets by Cardan: *Socialism Reaffirmed* (1960); *The Meaning of Socialism* (no. 6, September 1961); *Socialism or Barbarism* (no. 11, 1962?); *The Crisis of Modern Society* (no. 23, 1966); *From Bolshevism to the Bureaucracy* (no. 24, 1967); *History and Revolution: A Revolutionary Critique of Historical Materialism* (no. 38, 1971); *Workers' Councils and the Economics of a Self-Managed Society* (no. 40, 1972); *Redefining Revolution* (no. 44, 1974); and *History as Creation* (no. 54, 1978).[5] With the publication of the last, "Paul Cardan" was finally revealed as one of the pseudonyms of Cornelius Castoriadis (Pierre Chaulieu and Jean-Marc Coudray were two others).

Kornelios Kastoriades had been born in 1922 in Istanbul (or Constantinople as it was still called), grown up in Athens, joined the Greek Communist Party as a teenager, but moved to Trotskyism during the Second World War and was involved in the resistance against the German occupation. Under threat of death from both Fascists and Stalinists he escaped to France in 1945 and, as a statistical economist, became a high-ranking official of the OEEC (Organization for European Economic Co-operation), superseded in 1961 by the OECD (Organization for Economic Co-operation and Development).

In 1949 Castoriadis was a founding editor of *Socialisme ou Barbarie*, which ran until 1965. With Situationism *Socialisme ou Barbarie* was to be a prime influence in the events of May 1968: Daniel Cohn-Bendit in particular gladly acknowledged his "plagiarism".[6] Although the future postmodernist, Jean-François Lyotard, was also a member of the group, the other principal theorist in *Socialisme ou Barbarie* was Claude Lefort until he broke in 1958 to form with others *Informations et Liaisons Ouvrières* (later transformed into *Informations et Correspondance Ouvrières*), which was to be another influence on Cohn-Bendit. For Solidarity, *Socialisme ou Barbarie* were "our French co-thinkers".[7]

Castoriadis not only considered that Western capitalism was becoming increasingly authoritarian through a process of bureaucratization which would eventually lead to totalitarianism: a process that impelled its working classes to revolt. He also believed that in the Soviet Union the bureaucracy had formed a new ruling class - what was crucial was not who *owned* the means of production, but who *controlled*

5   A tenth pamphlet, *The Fate of Marxism* (n.d.), published by Solidarity (Clydeside), reprinted a text that had originally appeared in *Solidarity*, IV, 3 (August 1966).

6   Gabriel Cohn-Bendit and Daniel Cohn-Bendit, *Obsolete Communism: The Left-Wing Alternative* (Harmondsworth: Penguin, 1969), pp. 18–19, also: (Oakland, AK Press, 2000), pp. 19–20.. Maurice Brinton's review of this book is reprinted below.

7   See, for example, *Solidarity*, II, 2 (June 1962), p. 28, and V, 12 (July 1969), p. 16.

them. Russian capitalism was a higher form into which Western capitalism was developing.

The proletariat "never frees itself completely", *outside of production*, "from the influence of the [capitalist] environment in which it lives"; on the other hand: *"In the course of production* the class constantly creates the elements of a new form of social organization and of a new culture". So Castoriadis came to advocate a society self-managed by autonomous workers – a prescription that was central to *Solidarity*'s politics – and in France his notion of *autogestion* did come to exercise some considerable appeal in the 1970s.

> The Commune of 1871, the Soviets of 1905 and 1917, the Russian factory committees of 1917-1918, the German workers' councils of 1919 and 1920, the Italian factory committees of 1921, the councils set up by the Spanish workers in 1936-37 and the Hungarian workers' councils of 1956 were at one and the same time organs of struggle against the ruling class and its State – *and* new forms of social organization, based on principles radically opposed to those of bourgeois society.

These quotations are taken from Castoriadis's *"Prolétariat et organisation, I"*, which first appeared in *Socialisme ou Barbarie* in 1959, and was translated as "Working Class Consciousness" in *Solidarity* in 1962.[8] Solidarity regarded it as so "basic [a] statement of our views" that they broke with custom by reprinting it seven years later.[9] "…organs of struggle against the ruling class and its State…new forms of social organization, based on principles radically opposed to those of bourgeois society": this is the kind of potential Solidarity conceived the Committee of 100 as having.[10] It should also be apparent that Castoriadis's position in this article is indistinguishable from anarchism.

In 1970 Castoriadis retired from the OECD, becoming a French citizen and then (in 1974) a psychoanalyst. He began to reprint his early political writings and for the first time to write books, now using his real name. Rather than advocating "socialism", by the end of the seventies he had come instead to use the term "autonomous society" but *Solidarity*, which had otherwise followed in his theoretical wake, did not do likewise. He died in Paris in 1997.[11]

While an American Solidarist called Owen Cahill did some of the earlier Cardan translations, these were always revised by Maurice Brinton who in any case wrote all the introductions and translated the bulk of the texts. It was Brinton and Ken Weller who were – and remained – the principal figures in a talented group. Weller was a young London engineer and AEU (Amalgamated Engineering Union) shop steward.

---

8   *Solidarity*, II, 2 (April 1962), p. 26, and II, 3 (May 1962), p. 26. See Cornelius Castoriadis, *Political and Social Writings* [hereafter *PSW*], ed. David Ames Curtis (Minneapolis: University of Minnesota Press, 3 vols., 1988–93), II, pp. 193–222 (esp. pp. 198, 200). Cf. Paul Cardan, *Modern Capitalism and Revolution* (London: Solidarity, 1965), pp. 3–4.

9   *Solidarity*, VII, 12 (July 1969), p. 8.

10   Cf. Taylor, pp. 252–3.

11   The secondary literature, at least in English, on *Socialisme ou Barbarie* and Castoriadis is limited and unreliable. It got off to a bad start with George Lichtheim, *Marxism in Modern France* (New York and London: Columbia University, 1966), pp. 132n, 183n, witheringly reviewed by Brinton in *Solidarity*, IV, 10 (November 1967). The first edition of Dick Howard, *The Marxian Legacy* (Basingstoke and London: Macmillan, 2nd edn., 1988), chaps. 7 and 8, and pp. 306–33, is even more decisively dismissed by E.P. Thompson, *The Poverty of Theory and Other Essays* (London: Merlin Press, 1978), p. 396 n167. There is also Richard Gombin, *The Origins of Modern Leftism* (Harmondsworth: Penguin, 1975), pp. 32–9, 97–105, 112–17; Mark Poster, *Existential Marxism in Postwar France: From Sartre to Althusser* (Princeton, NJ: Princeton University Press, 1975), pp. 172–3, 202–5; Richard

It was he who was largely responsible for *Solidarity*'s extensive industrial coverage and analysis, for which, in the 1960s, it seemed most likely the group would be principally remembered.

Brinton is an immensely gifted intellectual, whose career is similar to Castoriadis's at several points. He was born in India in 1923 to a distinguished Anglo-Greek family. When his father decided to retire and return to Europe, he chose to settle in Switzerland and in consequence Brinton received most of his schooling there, becoming fluent in not only English and Greek but also French. He went up to Oxford University in 1941 to read medicine and instantly joined the CPGB (Communist Party of Great Britain), but was almost immediately expelled on account of his criticism of its policy on the Second World War. He therefore moved on to Trotskyistm and support of the Revolutionary Communist Party (RCP) until 1946. The pursuit of his medical career then led to a temporary cessation of all political activity.

In 1957 he was appointed as a consultant at a London teaching hospital and he then made contact with the group that became the SLL two years later. Under the autocratic leadership of Gerry Healy, this soon began to haemorrhage with the loss of many of its most able members. Reflecting on the bizarreries of the SLL, the Marxist historian John Saville comments: "Trotskyism was anti-Stalinist, of course, but their creeds were dogmatic, inflexible and sectarian to a quite remarkable degree..."[12] In 1960 Brinton, as a member of the SLL's national committee, took part in the expulsion of a group that contained Ken Weller, but within several months he too had seceded. Brinton was already familiar with *Socialisme ou Barbarie* and together with Weller, more ex-SLL members and some other dissident socialists formed, on the basis of the French journal's critique of Bolshevism, the libertarian Socialism Reaffirmed group, which was to be renamed Solidarity.

"Maurice Brinton" is a pseudonym. He had carried over the name of "Martin Grainger" from his SLL activism - and as such contributed the diary to the pamphlet on the Belgian General Strike of 1960-61 and jointly wrote the long article on the Paris Commune with Philippe Guillaume (of *Socialisme ou Barbarie*). In summer 1961, however, a right-wing press campaign led to his exposure; and thereafter, abandoning "Martin Grainger", all his political writings and translations have been either anonymous or signed "Maurice Brinton" or "M.B."[13] Unusually, I think, neither "Martin Grainger" nor "Maurice Brinton" was chosen for any particular association, both

---

Gombin, *The Radical Tradition: A Study in Modern Revolutionary Thought* (London: Methuen, 1978), pp. 41–3; Alex Callinicos, *Trotskyism* (Minneapolis: University of Minnesota Press, 1990), pp. 66–72; and Sunil Khilnani, *Arguing Revolution: The Intellectual Left in Postwar France* (New Haven and London: Yale University Press, 1993), esp. pp. 67–9, 128–30, 149–51, 181–3. Much more rewarding are André Liebich, "*Socialisme ou Barbarie*: A Radical Critique of Bureaucracy", *Our Generation*, XII, 2 (Fall 1977); Alex Richards, "The Academicization of Castoriadis", *Edinburgh Review*, nos. 78–9 (1988); and above all two primary texts: "An Interview with C. Castoriadis", *Telos*, no. 23 (Spring 1975), and "An Interview with Claude Lefort", *Telos*, no. 30 (Winter 1976–7). Obituaries of Castoriades appeared in *Guardian*, 31 December 1997; *The Times*, 28 January 1998: *Freedom*, 2 February 1998; *Anarchist Studies*, VI, 1 (March 1998), pp. 93–4; *Revolutionary History*, VII, 2 (1999), pp. 219–21. See also the assessment by Takis Fotopoulos, "Castoriadis and the Democratic Tradition", *Democracy and Nature*, no. 10 (1998).

12   John Saville, *Memoirs from the Left* (London: Merlin Press, 2003), p. 114. For the SLL (which was to become the Workers' Revolutionary Party) and its origins, see Terry Brotherstone and Geoff Pilling, *History, Economic History and the Future of Marxism: Essays in Memory of Tom Kemp (1921–1993)* (London: Porcupine Press, 1996), chap. 12, and also pp. 9–10, 359n4.

13   A robust defence by "Martin Grainger" of his activities was published in *Tribune* (21 July 1961). The first appearance of "Maurice Brinton" is as author of "Danger! Party Hacks at Work" in *Solidarity*, II, 10 (April 1963).

composites probably being assembled through a random search in the telephone directory. And unlike Cornelius Castoriadis he has no wish to resort to his real name.

Although Brinton's writings for *Solidarity* and its associated publications extend over a quarter of a century, he does not consider that he personally contributed theoretically, regarding himself as merely the translator and transmitter of Castoriadis's ideas, as well as an activist who sought their practical application. In what then does Brinton's achievement consist?

First, he has been assessed (by Richard Taylor) as "the most dominant individual" within Solidarity and, by someone even better placed to know, Nicolas Walter, its "main leader" or "leading figure".[14] All this is acknowledged by Ken Weller, regarded by Brinton as not just his closest political friend but his best friend *tout court*, sentiments that are entirely reciprocated.

Second, Brinton was the *creative* translator of Castoriadis, thereby introducing him, when he known as Paul Cardan, to the Anglophone world (and indeed beyond). With the exception of the four items (articles and/or pamphlets) drawn from "Marxism and Revolutionary Theory", which came to form Part 1 of the major book, *L'Institution imaginaire de la société* (1975)[15], all of Brinton's translations have been utilized in David Ames Curtis's massive three-volume edition – though covering only 1946 to 1979 – of the *Political and Social Writings*. Curtis goes so far indeed as to dedicate his very substantial and useful *Castoriadis Reader* to Brinton.[16] But Brinton both added and subtracted to Castoriadis's dense and frequently obscure texts, making them accessible to political militants, not only working-class but middle-class. His translations were, as Walter commented, "often improvements on [Paul Cardan's] originals".[17] Brinton himself once explained:

> Our text is a close (but not always literal) translation of the French original. The milieu in which our pamphlet will be distributed and discussed differs from that of the 1957 article. Throughout, our main concern has been with getting essential concepts over to as wide (and unspecialized) an audience as possible. To a great extent this has influenced our choice of wording and sentence structure. Paragraphs have been shortened. A number of sectional and chapter headings have been added. Some additional footnotes have been inserted (clearly indicated as *Solidarity* footnotes). One or two of the original footnotes have been omitted, and one or two others incorporated into the text proper, which has been slightly shortened.[18]

In contrast Curtis has dropped Brinton's popularizing elements and reverted to the originals, despite their frequent turgidity.

Thirdly, Brinton writes very well: he is lively, his style is punchy and accessible, and he possesses a wicked sense of humour. Especially noteworthy are his vivid eyewitness reports from upsurges of popular self-activity: the Belgian General Strike of

---

14   Taylor, p. 250; NW, "Obituary: Cornelius Castoriadis", *Freedom*, 7 February 1998; NW, "Cornelius Castoriadis", *Freedom*, 15 August 1998.

15   Translated by Kathleen Blamey as Cornelius Castoriadis, *The Imaginary Institution of Society* (Cambridge: Polity Press, 1987). See C. Castoriadis, *History as Creation* (London: Solidarity, 1978), p. 2, for the publication details. In addition, there is P. Cardan, "Listen, Psychiatrist", *Solidarity*, VIII, 7 (August 1977).

16   David Ames Curtis (ed.), *The Castoriadis Reader* (Oxford: Blackwell, 1997), p. xvi.

17   NW, "Cornelius Castoriadis", *Freedom*, 15 August 1998.

18   "Our Preface", [Pierre Chaulieu] *Workers' Councils and the Economics of a Self-Managed Society* (London: Solidarity, 1972), p. 2n. For obvious reasons this footnote has been omitted from the text of the preface as reprinted below.

1960-61, Paris in May 1968, and rural and urban Portugal in 1975 and 1976. He is a merciless reviewer and polemicist. And although in controversy he can seem to get bogged down in finicky detail – as in "France: The Theoretical Implications", "*Solidarity* and the Neo-Narodniks" and "Factory Committees and the Dictatorship of the Proletariat" – he always moves on to such bold and arresting generalization that the effort of following his argument is fully rewarded.[19] A definite limitation, though, is the repetitiveness of Brinton's prose. For example, in three of the articles reprinted here, as well as in *The Irrational in Politics*, he quotes Spinoza's tag, "neither to laugh nor to weep, but to understand", and the splendid passage already cited from the introduction to Cardan's *Modern Capitalism and Revolution*, reappears in *As We Don't See It* as:

> We want no gods, not even those of the Marxist or anarchist pantheons. We live in neither the Petrograd of 1917 nor the Barcelona of 1936. We are *ourselves*: the product of the disintegration of traditional politics, in an advanced capitalist country, in the second half of the twentieth century.

It must be recalled that Brinton was following a crowded and successful career as a medical scientist, all his political writings being the product of his spare-time. In this (and other defining ways, such as his concern with sexuality and with the application of scientific method to the socio-political realm) he resembles his anarchist contemporary, Alex Comfort. For Comfort was also a great recycler of previously published material and repeater of well-turned phrases.[20] It needs to be insisted too that Brinton wrote with no thought of eventual republication in a volume of the present kind. If he had been able to edit it himself, it would have been of considerable interest to see how much cutting and rewriting he would have subjected his prose to.

Finally, despite his disclaimer, Brinton *was* responsible for original work, in certain areas going beyond Castoriadis. *The Irrational in Politics*, a booklet originally published in 1970 and considered by one reviewer as Solidarity's best work to date, explores the role of sexual repression and authoritarian conditioning in generating socio-political conformity.[21] While derivative of Wilhelm Reich (as Brinton fully acknowledges), he is here probing at that central matter of the proletariat, outside of production, never freeing itself "completely from the influence of the environment in which it lives". He is able, very convincingly, to point to the sexual permissiveness of the 1960s as a major breakthrough in the "undermining of tradition" and terminating a vicious cycle. Whereas "for Reich any large scale sexual freedom was inconceivable within the framework of capitalism": "The change in traditional attitudes is both gaining momentum and becoming more explicit in a manner which would have surprised and delighted [him]".[22] On the other hand, the pessimism only four years later of his review (in which there is a rare glimpse of his professional expertise) of George Frankl's *The Failure of the Sexual Revolution* needs to be taken into consideration.

---

19 "Factory Committees and the Dictatorship of the Proletariat" is a reply to Chris Goodey's criticisms in "Factory Committees and the Dictatorship of the Proletariat (1918)", *Critique* (Glasgow), no. 3 (Autumn 1974), pp. 36–9.

20 See David Goodway (ed.), *Against Power and Death: The Anarchist Articles and Pamphlets of Alex Comfort* (London: Freedom Press, 1994), pp. 14–15.

21 *Socialist Leader*, 27 June 1970. See also *Anarchy*, 2nd series, no. 1 (February 1971) for an appreciative, though critical, review by Marshall Coleman.

22 The original pamphlet had the title of *Authoritarian Conditioning, Sexual Repression and the Irrational in*

Also dating from 1970 is Brinton's *chef d'oeuvre*, which Castoriadis was rightly to assess as "remarkable".[23] This is *The Bolsheviks and Workers' Control, 1917-1921: The State and Counter-Revolution*, which originally appeared as a 100-page book, tracing the obliteration of the Russian Factory Committees of 1917-18 so that by 1921 Russian factories and trade unions had been subordinated to the new Bolshevik state and the party:

> In 1917 it had been proclaimed that "every cook should learn to govern the State".
> By 1921 the State was clearly powerful enough to govern every cook!

Extraordinarily, but significantly, this very necessary task had not previously been attempted and the (anarchist) conclusions properly drawn are:

> *The basic question: who manages production after the overthrow of the bour-geoisie? should therefore now become the centre of any serious discussion about socialism.* Today the old equation (liquidation of the bourgeoisie = workers' state) popularized by countless Leninists, Stalinists and Trotskyists is just not good enough.

In his stimulating *Rethinking the Russian Revolution* the highly regarded Russianist, Edward Acton, reviewing the libertarian interpretation of the Revolution, cites *The Bolsheviks and Workers' Control* more times than any of Berkman, Voline, Arshinov or Maximov. This is quite a tribute.[24]

Brinton is well known in libertarian circles for *Paris: May 1968, The Irrational in Politics* and *The Bolsheviks and Workers' Control*, three publications that have been widely read and admired and each has gone through a number of editions. In the case of *The Irrational in Politics*, in the five years after its first appearance it had been translated into French, German, Swedish and Greek and been published in the USA, Canada and Australia.[25] Within little more than three years *The Bolsheviks and Workers' Control* was translated into French, Dutch, German, Swedish, Spanish, Greek and Japanese.[26] *Paris: May 1968* was not only the first pamphlet (or book) to be pub-lished - as early as June 1968 - but remains one of the best participant accounts there is of "the events in France", a reviewer later that year acclaiming it for giving:

> the clearest possible picture of what was actually happening. It managed to somehow capture the very flavour and essence of the inspiring movement taking place. Like no other publication…it carries with it the very smell of tear gas, the very guts of revolution.[27]

Since the three areas covered in these three works are so central in Brinton's output, related articles, reviews and, in one case, a leaflet are here reprinted. It should be noted, though, that "France: The Theoretical Implications" was considered sufficient-ly important by Solidarity for it to be appended in 1973 to the second edition of *Paris: May 1968*, while the introduction to the 1975 edition of *The Irrational in Politics*

Politics. For Castoriadis on sexuality and child rearing, see *PSW*, III, pp. 15–16, 56–63.

23   *PSW*, III, p. 105 n17.

24   Edward Acton, *Rethinking the Russian Revolution* (London: Edward Arnold, 1990), pp. 177–81. See also *ibid.*, p. 43.

25   Maurice Brinton, *The Irrational in Politics* (London: Solidarity (London), 1975 edn), pp. 2–3. In "On the Solidarity Wavelength" Brinton surveyed the translations up to the early 1970s of Solidarity Pamphlets into Swedish and Japanese (*Solidarity*, VII, 4 (December 1972) and VII, 5 [1973]).

26   *La Quinzaine Littéraire*, no. 178 (1–15 January 1974). For an enthusiastic review of the Spanish edition, see *Frente Libertario*, no. 29 (March 1973).

27   *Guerilla* (Manchester), no. 2 (17 October 1968).

referred readers to the two reviews of Wilhelm Reich and, particularly, to that of George Frankl's book.

This still leaves a very considerable corpus of items for potential selection. A provisional check-list of Brinton's post-Trotskyist political publications has come up with at least 108 items, whether articles, pamphlets, book and film reviews, or translations (and in addition there are many anonymous articles that, decades later, it is not possible to assign with certainty as well as fugitive leaflets).[28] Many of these would not be entirely his work. *Solidarity* editorials, statements such as *As We See It* and *As We Don't See It*, and introductions would all be circulated within the group for criticism and rewriting: for Solidarity not merely advocated libertarian ultra-democracy but actually practised it. This is a major reason for Brinton wishing to maintain his pseudonym and, in a very real sense, his anonymity, regarding himself as merely the communicator of the group's collective position and analysis. But all the same he was the primary author of all the texts included in this selection - with the exception of the co-written *The Commune, Paris 1871*.

***

In 1960 Brinton abandoned the SLL and rejected Trotskyism, proceeding to draft the leaflet, "Socialism Reaffirmed", dated October 1960 and the initial item reprinted here. That this document should be fully libertarian may seem extraordinary until it is recalled that he was already familiar with *Socialisme ou Barbarie*; and indeed at the same time an article by Castoriadis from *Socialisme ou Barbarie*, no. 1, was published with the identical title, *Socialism Reaffirmed*, as the new group's first pamphlet.[29] In the leaflet "the fundamental contradiction of contemporary society" is identified as "its division into those who own, manage, decide and direct, and the majority who…have to toil and are forced to comply with decisions they have not themselves taken". What the working class requires is "a revolutionary organization, not as its self-appointed leadership but as an instrument of its struggle". This organization "should anticipate the socialist future of society rather than mirror its capitalist past", the three criteria being that "local organs have the fullest autonomy", "direct democracy is practised wherever possible", and "all central bodies having power of decision involving others should be constituted by *delegates*, these being *elected* by those they represent and *revocable* by them, *at any time*". These points, as well as others in the leaflet, were to be reiterated in the years that followed and reappear constantly in the reprinted texts.

In "Socialism Reaffirmed" Brinton quotes for the first time one of his favourite dicta of Marx's: "The emancipation of the working class is the task of the workers themselves". He also counters Lenin's insistence, to which he is continually to return, that "the workers can only develop a trade union consciousness", contending that the working class is "capable of rising to the greatest heights of revolutionary consciousness, and challenging the very basis of all exploiting regimes" by pointing to its achievements in the Paris Commune, the Russian Revolutions of 1905 and 1917, the Spanish Revolution and the Hungarian Revolution, a catalogue that he was to repeat and to extend.

---

28   I am, though, much indebted to assistance from Ken Weller on this as well as other matters.

29   I have not been able to locate a copy of this pamphlet – even Brinton has not retained one in his files – but the text is included in Castoriadis, *PSW*, I, pp. 76–106 (although Curtis's attribution of the English translation is erroneous).

Another major theme which Brinton touches on in "Socialism Reaffirmed" is not only that working-class trade-union and political organizations have now degenerated , expressing "non-proletarian social interests", but that this degeneration has "a subjective basis in the imposition of capitalist methods of thinking and organization into the ranks of the labour movement". This he developed the following year in "Revolutionary Organization":

> Exploiting society consciously encourages the development of a mass psychology to the effect that the ideas or wishes of ordinary people are unimportant and that all important decisions must be taken by people specially trained and specially equipped to do so…. All the ruling groups in modern society encourage the belief that decision taking and management are functions beyond the comprehension of ordinary people. All means are used to foster this idea. Not only do formal education, the press, the radio, television and the church perpetuate this myth, but even the parties of the so-called opposition accept it and, in so doing, lend it strength. All the political parties of the "left"…oppose the present order only by offering "better" leaders, more "experienced" and more capable of solving the problems of society than those who mismanage the world today.

And so:

> The Labour Party, Communist Party and the various Trotskyite and Leninist sects all extol the virtues of professional politicians or revolutionaries. All practice a rigid division within their own organizations of leaders and led. All fundamentally believe that socialism will be instituted from above and through their own particular agency.

> Each of them sees socialism as nothing more than the conquest of political power, and the transformation, by decree, of economic institutions. The instruments of socialism, in their eyes, are nationalization, state control and the "plan".

Fifteen years later, introducing Phil Mailer's *Portugal: The Impossible Revolution*, Brinton reflected gloomily on:

> the risk of genuinely radical upheavals being deviated into state capitalist channels. It is the danger that any new creation (in the realm of ideas, relationships or institutions) will immediately be pounced upon, penetrated, colonized, manipulated – and ultimately deformed – by hordes of power-hungry "professional revolutionaries"…These people bring with them attitudes and patterns of behaviour deeply (if not always consciously) moulded by Lenin's notion that the workers, left to themselves, "can only develop a trade union consciousness". Their current organizational practices and their prescriptions for the future are bureaucratic to the core…. Their preoccupation with leadership destroys initiative. Their concern for the correct line discourages experiment. Their obsession with the past is a blight on the future. They create around themselves a wasteland of cynicism and disgust, of smashed hopes and disillusion, that buttresses the deepest dogma of bourgeois society, namely that ordinary people are incapable of solving their own problems, by themselves and for themselves.

His prediction was that "in future upheavals the traditional revolutionaries will prove 'part of the problem, not part of the solution'". In contrast, revolutions in the past could either be defeated by those whose privileges they sought to destroy – as with the Paris Commune, Germany in 1918-19, Spain and Hungary – or "they could be destroyed from within, through bureaucratic degeneration (as happened to the Russian Revolution of 1917)".

It is with the latter – the degeneration of the Russian Revolution – that Brinton is obsessed in his writing (and when I first encountered him back in 1963, inviting him to speak to the Oxford Anarchist Group, this was the topic he chose). In 1961 he introduced for *Solidarity* the section on Kronstadt from Victor Serge's *Memoirs of a Revolutionary* (a major work not then available in English), and this was later published as a pamphlet, *Kronstadt, 1921*. There followed in 1962 his impressive edition of Alexandra Kollontai's *The Workers' Opposition* (Pamphlet 7), reprinted for the first time in English since its original appearance in 1921 in Sylvia Pankhurst's *Workers' Dreadnought* as "a contribution to the great discussion now taking place concerning 'what went wrong'". Brinton next produced the first English translation of Ida Mett's *The Kronstadt Commune* (Pamphlet 27). Finally, in 1970, came the outstanding and very original *The Bolsheviks and Workers' Control*, his study of how the Bolsheviks defeated the Revolution in the factories.

This relentless preoccupation with the Russian Revolution – whereas the achievement of the Spanish Revolution is only ever mentioned in passing – may perplex readers only familiar with world politics since the collapse of Communism, but those who recall any part of the period between 1917 and 1989 will attest how central analysis of the apparently "actually existing socialism" of Russia, China and their satellite slave states was not just to Stalinists, Trotskyists and other Marxist-Leninists, but even to anarchists and social democrats. All the same, Brinton's Trotskyist past and his belief during those years that the Soviet Union was a "deformed workers' state" clearly moulded his mindset – and range of reference – for many years to come. As late as the early 1970s a publicity leaflet for *The Bolsheviks and Workers' Control* addresses those who were still Trotskyist:

COMRADES,
YOU HAVE (more or less) SEEN THROUGH STALINISM
NOW SHED YOUR LAST ILLUSIONS
YOU CAN'T FIGHT BUREAUCRACY BY BUREAUCRATIC METHODS
WHY CLING TO THE LENINIST AND TROTSKYIST MYTHS?
LET THE DEAD BURY THE DEAD
ONE MORE EFFORT TO TOTAL DEMYSTIFICATION
...AND TO BECOMING REAL REVOLUTIONARIES[30]

An article he wrote, as "Martin Grainger", for the group which would shortly become the SLL in the issue of its weekly celebrating the fortieth anniversary of the Bolshevik Revolution illustrates well the intellectually impoverished automatism that was requisite. "How They Took Power in Petrograd" is a breathless chronology "from February to October".[31]

Only three years separates the unthinking piety of this fourth-rate piece from the subversive radicalism of "Socialism Reaffirmed". Yet the passage from the parrot-cry orthodoxy of Trotskyism to an innovative libertarianism is not peculiar to Brinton and some of his fellow Solidarists in Britain. In France Castoriadis, Lefort and *Socialisme ou Barbarie* had led the way to libertarian socialism; and Daniel Guérin was later to move to an outright anarchism. In the United States Murray Bookchin, previously a Trotskyist for many years, became an excitingly original anarchist thinker. Also in the States C.L.R. James, Raya Dunayevskaya and their Johnson-

---

30   *Trotsky Revisited* (London: Solidarity [1972?]).

31   *Newsletter*, 7 November 1957. See also the long letter from "Martin Grainger" on Freud in the sister publication, *Labour Review*, III, 3 (May–July 1958).

Forrest Tendency moved to a distinctive libertarian socialism (as James continued to do after being deported to Britain in 1953). Indeed there were close relations between *Socialisme ou Barbarie* and the Johnson-Forrest Tendency for ten years, Castoriadis contributing with James and Grace Lee to *Facing Reality* (1958).[32] So Trotskyism has possessed an impressive capacity for generating some of the most outstanding modern anarchists and libertarian socialists, notable for not only their fresh thinking but also their theoretical rigour.

There can be no doubt that Brinton's primary intellectual influence is that of Castoriadis and only secondarily their mutual indebtedness, great though it is, to Marx. Between 1961 and 1964 Castoriadis published in *Socialisme ou Barbarie* "Marxism and Revolutionary Thought" in which he broke decisively with Marxism. Brinton translated in 1966 a first instalment of this substantial text as "The Fate of Marxism", which initially appeared in *Solidarity* and was later reprinted by Solidarity (Clydeside) as a pamphlet of the same title. In "The Fate of Marxism" Castoriadis argues that:

> for the last forty years Marxism has become an *ideology* in the full meaning that Marx himself attributed to this word. It has become a system of ideas which relate to reality not in order to clarify it and to transform it, but on the contrary in order to mask it and justify it in the abstract.

He concludes: "we have now reached the stage where a choice confronts us: to remain Marxists or to remain revolutionaries". Brinton's comment is that this text is "bound to infuriate those who have never had a new idea of their own", alluding to one of his favourite aphorisms, applied throughout to all sections of the left (not least the anarchists) and only attributed in "Capitalism and Socialism: A Rejoinder" to the Victorian writer, Walter Bagehot: "one of the greatest pains to human nature is the pain of a new idea".[33]

One of Brinton's major strengths is his ability to relish "the pain of a new idea"; but it was not until 1972 that he published another extract from "Marxism and Revolutionary Thought" - and in which this time Castoriadis ditched historical materialism - as the pamphlet *History and Revolution*. Brinton defended this "revolutionary critique of historical materialism", declaring that

> I have enjoyed writing this article. Firstly because the discarding of an illusion is like the shedding of a load - one moves about more freely without it.. Secondly because to help demystify others, far from being "barren", is...a fruitful activity in itself.[34]

He explains:

> In both *Modern Capitalism and Revolution* and *History and Revolution* Cardan demands that revolutionaries apply to Marxism itself one of the most profound of Marx's insights...that the dominant ideas of each epoch are the ideas of its ruling class. Marx wrote in a period of full bourgeois ascendancy. It would have been a miracle...if some bourgeois ideas had not permeated his own writings.[35]

---

32   See Cornelius Castoriadis, "C.L.R. James and the Fate of Marxism" and "Three Letters", in Selwyn R. Cudjoe and William E. Cain (eds.), *C.L.R. James: His Intellectual Legacies* (Amherst: University of Massachusetts Press, 1995); also Kent Worcester, *C.L.R. James: A Political Biography* (Albany, NY: State University of New York Press, 1996).

33   Paul Cardan, "The Fate of Marxism", *Solidarity*, IV, 3 (August 1966), pp. 15–16, 19.

34   Maurice Brinton, "On Unhistorical Materialism", *Discussion Bulletin*, no. 1 (Solidarity [1971?]), p. 6.

35   *Ibid*, p. 7.

While Brinton continues to believe in the continuing validity of such features of Marxism as "the class struggle, the concept of surplus value, the theory of alienation, the importance of economic factors in historical development, the need ruthlessly to demystify all ideologies", Marxist economics and the materialist conception of history are in contrast "suspect".[36] He concurs with the identification of "the alien (bourgeois) element" in the Marxist interpretation of history. For Castoriadis

> sees it in the attempt by Marx and Engels to apply to the whole of human history certain categories and relationships which are *not* transcendental...but which are *themselves* the product of historical development and more particularly of the rise of the bourgeoisie. Among such *historical* (non-transcendental) categories and relationships, [he] stresses two: the notion of the primacy of the economy and the concept of a certain pattern of interaction (determination) between economic "infrastructure" and ideological "superstructure". The retrojection of these categories and patterns on to others areas of history - with a view to constructing a universal and "scientific" theory of history...can only be achieved...through a systematic rape of the facts.[37]

Introducing *Redefining Revolution* in 1974, Brinton explained: "In a chemical reaction there is no element of choice... The water in the kettle cannot choose not to boil when the kettle is placed on the fire". "Social development", however, "cannot be brought down to the level of a chemical reaction....*There is a choice* wherever people are concerned". Positivism, determinism and Marxism are all replaced by a philosophical and postmodern libertarianism.

> If a "scientific" theory of history can predict history, there is no such thing as genuine choice. If it cannot, then "scientific" interpretations of the past are subject to the same limitations as similar prediction of the future.

This is from the introduction to the fourth instalment of "Marxism and Revolutionary Thought", published as *History as Creation* in 1978. What is now central for Brinton (and Castoriadis) is "genuine creation": "the act of producing...affairs". "Such creation plays a major role in history", by "its very nature" defying "the dictates of predetermination".

As Brinton is increasingly emancipated from the shackles of Marxism-Leninism - in the form of Trotskyism - and eventually indeed from any form of Marxism, he becomes correspondingly creative and daring in his writing. While fully revealed during the 1970s, this was becoming apparent by the late 1960s. As early as 1965 he can celebrate "The Balkanization of Utopia":

> There is no one road to utopia, no one organization, or prophet, or Party, destined to lead the masses to the Promised Land. There is no one historically determined objective, no single vision of a different and new society, no solitary economic panacea that will do away with the alienation of man from his fellow men and from the products of his own activity.

He even concludes that this is "the sole guarantee that 'utopia', if we ever get near to it, will be worth living in", a pluralist belief remote from Trotskyism or, indeed, "class-struggle" anarchism.

While he continued to believe that "in modern industrial societies socialist consciousness springs from the real conditions of social life" (*As We Don't See It*, 1972),

---

36   *Ibid*, p. 13.
37   *Ibid*, p. 8.

he came to emphasize the importance of the non-economic realm of exploitation, as in "Capitalism and Socialism" 1968:

> ...a society in which relations between people are based on domination will maintain authoritarian attitudes in relation to sex and to education, attitudes creating deep inhibitions, frustrations and much unhappiness...From his earliest days man is subjected to constant pressures designed to mould his views in relation to work, to culture, to leisure, to thought itself...*the socialist revolution will have to take all these fields within its compass, and immediately, not in some far distant future*. The revolution must of course start with the overthrow of the exploiting class and with the institution of workers' management of production. But it will immediately have to tackle the reconstruction of social life in *all* its aspects. If it does not, it will surely die.

And in 1970 he introduces in the concluding section, "Limits and Perspectives", of the title essay of *The Irrational in Politics*, the extremely important concept of recuperation which had originated with the Situationists, explicating it more fully two years later in "The Malaise on the Left":

> Over the last few decades – and in many different areas – established society has itself brought about a number of the things that the revolutionaries of yesterday were demanding. This has happened in relation to economic attitudes, in relation to certain forms of social organization, and in relation to various aspects of the personal and sexual revolutions.

It is legitimate, he says, to refer to this adaptation as "recuperation" when it actually benefits the established society, contributing to its continuance as an exploiting hierarchy.[38]

Brinton's politics are fully anarchist: in his analysis of existing society, in his vision of a socialist society, and in the means he advocates in order to get from here to there. On the other hand, he has resolutely rejected much of anarchism and refused to describe himself as any sort of anarchist. The affiliation that satisfies him is rather "libertarian socialism". A raft of issues fill him with scorn for most varieties of anarchism. Whereas he highlights the need both to take on board new ideas and to supplement emotion with understanding, he comments acidly in his note on Kropotkin that "anarchist abstentionism in both...areas seem...to be as old as the hills". Fifteen years later, in "About Ourselves 2", one of the final texts in this collection, he returns to the first charge:

> ... it is necessary to break decisively with the anti-modernism of the traditional anarchist milieu. It is no longer relevant to rely on the experience of the Spanish Revolution as the paradigm of revolutionary practice; and it is pointless today to centre our theoretical discussions on the debates of the anarchist movement of the late nineteenth and early twentieth centuries. The world has changed since then.

The second criticism he develops by arguing that it is also

> necessary to counter the blind actionism found in many anarchists. To change the world it is necessary to interpret it: the "refusal of thought" so prevalent in the anarchist milieu – which is closely related to its predilection for outdated models of revolution – has done untold harm to the cause of libertarian social revolution.

Most anarchists incline to either the insurrectionism of Bakunin or the communism of Kropotkin, but Brinton, in his review of Paul Avrich's *The Russian Anarchists*,

---

38   Compare also the penultimate paragraph of *Paris: May 1968*.

has no time for either man, regarding the former as "muddleheaded" and an author-itarian conspirator and the latter as a romantic visionary who pined for a pastoral utopia, "oblivious of the complex forces at work in the modern world".[39] In contrast, he approves of the anarcho-syndicalist, G.P. Maximov, and also Ida Mett, the Platformist author of *The Kronstadt Commune*, who represents "what is best in the revolutionary tradition of 'class-struggle' anarchism": "She thinks in terms of a col-lective, proletarian solution to the problems of capitalism" as opposed to "the rejec-tion of the class struggle, the anti-intellectualism, the preoccupation with transcen-dental morality and with personal salvation that characterize so many of the anar-chists of today..."[40]

Finally there is the central matter of organization. In his introduction to Murray Bookchin's *On Spontaneity and Organization*, Brinton equates Bookchin's under-standing of "spontaneity" with his own notion of "autonomy" – as developed in *"Solidarity" and the Neo-Narodniks* – concurring that "spontaneity does not preclude organization and structure" but that it "yields non-hierarchical forms of organiza-tion". While it is, of course, a fallacy that anarchism and organization are incompat-ible, some anarchists have always opposed organization; and it is understandable, highly regrettable though it is, that Bookchin, who after many years contesting anti-organizational and "life-style" anarchists – and sharing very similar theoretical and political perspectives (as well as background) to Brinton – has now ceased to call himself an anarchist.

It has already been mentioned that some of Brinton's best writing consists of his first-hand descriptions of major upsurges of popular self-activity. He was pres-ent for the opening days of the Belgian General Strike of 1960-61 and from the end of the decade comes the widely-read *Paris: May 1968*. It is remarkable that it was through chance that he happened to be already in France for other reasons and hence was able to produce the two pamphlets. On the other hand, he was obliged to take holidays to visit Portugal in 1975 and 1976 in order to write "Portuguese Diary 1 and 2". It was virtually automatic that he should cover Solidarnosc in 1980 (in "Suddenly This Summer"), but he did not visit Poland to do so. The common themes are admiration for the creativity of ordinary people in struggle and contempt for the degeneration, Stalinism and political irrelevance of the Communist Parties, the van-guardist presumption of the Trotskyists and Maoists, and the corruption and bureaucracy of the social democratic parties and trade unions.

There is much reference to "bureaucracy" and the "bureaucratic" in Brinton's writing. Bureaucratization is defined, in the introduction to Cardan's *Modern Capitalism and Revolution* as "the organization and control of activity *from the out-side*" and, in "Factory Committees and the Dictatorship of the Proletariat", an article of 1975, a bureaucracy is "a group seeking to manage *from the outside* the activities of others".[41] If that is bureaucracy, it is a perennially recurring feature of human soci-eties and equally to be perennially resisted. But by what is it to be replaced? It is in "The Malaise on the Left" that Brinton defines socialism as "the creation of forms of living that will enable all – free from external constraints or internalized inhibitions –

---

39   In "The Irrational in Politics", section 6, Proudhon is also described as "muddleheaded".

40   For Nicolas Walter's reviews of *The Kronstadt Commune* and its "eccentric" preface, see *Freedom*, 18 November 1967 ("The *Solidarity* School of Falsification"), and 20 November 1971. For further spats between *Freedom* and *Solidarity*, see "Listen, Solidarist!" (*Freedom*, 12, 26 September, 24 October 1970), and *Freedom*, 17 April 1971.

41   But cf. Cardan, *Modern Capitalism and Revolution*, p. 3.

to rise to their full stature, to fulfil themselves as human beings, to enjoy themselves, to relate to one another without treading on anybody..." Introducing *Portugal: The Impossible Revolution?* he asks "can one imagine any socialism worth living under without self-managed individuals, collectivities and institutions?" And in the concluding text, "About Ourselves 4", he explains:

> Socialism is not just common ownership and distribution: it means equality, real freedom, the end of oppression based on restrictive male-female social roles, reciprocal recognition and a radical transformation of all human relationships. It is people's understanding of their environment and themselves, their domination over their work and such social institutions as they may need to create. These...are essential parts of the whole process of social transformation, for without them no genuine social transformation will have taken place. A socialist society can therefore only be built from below. Genuine freedom will only be possible when our lives are no longer the object of economic, cultural and political forces which we experience as external to ourselves, and which constantly tend to regenerate capitalist or authoritarian social relations.

Since that was written in 1985 there have been vast economic, social and political changes throughout the world. Brinton's vision of a non-hierarchical and free society, however, remains as valid and as necessary as it ever was.

David Goodway

1. SOCIALISM REAFFIRMED.

We here outline certain ideas which might form a basis for a regroupment of revolutionary socialists.

None of the traditional working class organizations express the interests of the class. Their degeneration and bureaucratization have been accompanied by a profound decay of socialist theory, of concepts of struggle and organization and even of fundamental notions concerning the nature of socialism. Agreement must be reached on what socialism is, if revolutionary practice is genuinely to assist the working class and is not to result in further confusion and demoralization. The following points are, in our opinion, quite basic:

(1) "The proletarian movement is the *self-conscious, independent* movement of the immense majority, in the interest of the immense majority". Some of the "revolutionary" tendencies pay lip-service to this idea. None take it seriously, or even seem to understand its implications. "Self-conscious" implies that the class itself must understand the full significance of its actions. 'Independent' implies that the class itself must decide the objectives and methods of its struggle.

(2) "The emancipation of the working class is the task of the workers themselves". The working class cannot entrust its historical task to anyone else. No "saviours from on high" will free it. The class will never achieve power, *its* power, if it entrusts the revolutionary struggle to others. Mass socialist consciousness and mass participation are essential. The revolutionary organization must assist in their development and must ruthlessly expose all illusions that the problem can be solved in any other way.

Moreover the working class will never *hold* power unless it is prepared consciously and permanently to mobilize *itself* to this end. All previous attempts by the working class to delegate power to specific groups, in the hope that such groups would exert power "on its behalf" have resulted in the formation of bureaucracies and in the economic and political expropriation of the working class. Socialism, unlike all previous forms of social organization, requires the constant, conscious and permanent participation of the great majority.

(3) The fundamental aspect of all class society is that a specific social group assumes a dominant position in the relations of production. In this position it firstly "disposes of the conditions of production" (i.e. organizes and manages production) and secondly determines the distribution of the total social product. Individual ownership of the means of production is but one of several possible ways in which a ruling class can legitimize its domination.

Every ruling class strives to perpetuate its privileged status in society through its control of the instruments of coercion, i.e. the State machine. No ruling class in history has ever surrendered its dominant position in the economy and its control of the State without ferocious struggle.

(4) The fundamental contradiction of contemporary society is its division into those who own, manage, decide and direct, and the majority who, because they are deprived of access to the means of production, have to toil and are forced to comply with decisions they have not themselves taken. This contradiction is the basis of alienation, of the class struggle and of the deep going crises which affect both bourgeois and bureaucratic societies.

The objective of the class struggle is to ensure, through the revolutionary accession to power of the working class, the abolition of all antagonistic divisions within society and of all the limitations these divisions impose upon men's lives.

(5) By its everyday struggle in capitalist society, the working class develops a consciousness which has an essentially socialist content. The class struggle is not only a struggle for surplus value (as "vulgar" Marxists would have us believe). It is also a struggle for completely different conditions of existence. This struggle takes place at the point of production, where it challenges both bourgeois and bureaucratic prerogatives of management.

It is in the factory and the workshop that the workers counterpoise their wishes and aspirations to the bureaucratic decisions of the bosses, and attempt to assert their own forms of organization against those imposed upon them from above. This aspect of the class struggle has the most profoundly revolutionary implications, for who manages production manages, in the last analysis, society itself. The revolutionary organization must stress, in its agitation and propaganda, this particular aspect of the working class struggle and underline its fundamentally socialist content.

(6) The working class has repeatedly attempted to solve the basic question of its status as an exploited class. It is untrue that workers are only capable of achieving "trade union consciousness". The Paris Commune of 1871, the revolutions of 1905 and 1917, the Spanish Revolution of 1936-38 and the Hungarian Workers' Council's of 1956, all prove that the working class is capable of rising to the greatest heights of revolutionary consciousness, and of challenging the very basis of all exploiting regimes.

(7) Between its great revolutionary upsurges, the working class has attempted to create political and trade union organizations to fight for both its immediate and long-term interests. These organizations have all degenerated and now express non-proletarian social interests. This degeneration has an objective basis, in the changing structure of capitalist society, and a subjective basis in the imposition of capitalist methods of thinking and organization into the ranks of the labour movement. Both facts therefore reflect the persistence of capitalism.

The struggle of the working class for its social emancipation is not just a simple, day-by-day struggle against capitalist exploitation. It also takes place within the working class itself, against the constant rebirth of capitalist ideas and reformist illusions. The fight of the revolutionary organization against all forms of ideological mystification – and against those who disseminate them – is both essential and inevitable.

(8) Socialism means workers' management, both at the level of the factory and of society as a whole. If the working class does not hold economic power firmly in its

own hands, its political power will at best be insecure. As long as the working class holds economic power, its political power cannot degenerate. Factory committees and workers' councils are the probable forms through which the working class will exert its rule.

"Nationalization" and "planning" can only have a socialist content if associated with workers' management of production and working class political power. In and of themselves, they can solve nothing. If the workers do not themselves manage society, "nationalization" and "planning" can become ruthless instruments of exploitation.

(9) The class needs a revolutionary organization, not as its self-appointed leadership but as an instrument of its struggle. The organization should assist workers in dispute, help through its press to generalize working class experience, provide a framework for linking up autonomous organs of working class struggle and constantly stress the ideas and revolutionary potentialities of *independent mass action*.

The structure of the organization should reflect the highest achievements of working class struggle (i.e. workers' councils) rather than imitate capitalist types of organization. It should anticipate the socialist future of society rather than mirror its capitalist past. In practice this means:

that *local organs have the fullest autonomy*, in relation to their own activities, that is in keeping with the general purpose and outlook of the organization;

that *direct democracy* (i.e. the collective decision of all those concerned) is resorted to wherever materially possible;

that all central bodies having power of decision involving others should be constituted by *delegates*, these being *elected* by those they represent and *revocable* by them, *at any time*.

SOCIALISM REAFFIRMED LEAFLET, OCTOBER 1960.

2. THE BELGIAN GENERAL STRIKE: DIARY, DECEMBER 28–31, 1960

THE BACKGROUND:

In 1950 a general strike had led to the abdication of King Leopold. In 1958-59 workers, and in fact whole villages, had taken part in widespread strikes and struggles in protest at the closing of the nationalized Borinage coalfields. The strike of 1960-61 was the culmination of a growing movement of social protest that had been building up over many years. The economic situation of Belgium had been slowly deteriorating. The last and most drastic attempt to improve it, at the expense of the working class, was the introduction of the loi unique, which cut into workers' purchasing power and threatened their conditions of work. On December 14, 1960, a one-day demonstration was called by the Socialist Party and the trade unions to protest against this law. It met with tremendous success. On December 20, the day the debate on the law began in Parliament, the municipal workers came out on official, nationwide, strike. While most of the other unions were discussing what to do next, a spontaneous movement of unparalleled extent swept the country like a tidal wave. The official strike call, which came a few days later, was the endorsement of an accomplished fact. Within a week nearly a million workers were out.

BRUSSELS, WEDNESDAY, DECEMBER 28

11.00 am. This is the seventh day of the struggle.

At the Air Terminal, the escalator is not moving. Current, says the Government, must be economized. Buses and trams have stopped. Refuse blows along pavements that have not been swept for days. The weather is clear and sunny, but very cold. A few people hurry about their business. There seem to be plenty of cars. Petrol distribution is not seriously affected. In the Air Terminal windows, an enormous portrait of the recently married royal couple. This is a bit provocative, I feel, and unlikely to endure.

The Central Railway Station is almost deserted. Out of curiosity, I walk in. Well provided with light weapons, small groups of soldiers in green and brown camouflage uniform stand disconsolately about. In the poorly lit central hall an enormous blackboard announces: "In view of the social conflict, no communications can be ensured in any direction". People walk up to it, stare, read it once, twice, three times …and walk silently away. One ticket kiosk is open. "A train to Liège?" "No, Sir. We have no information, Sir. If you would call again in a couple of hours, Sir, we may know something more. We cannot guarantee that you will arrive, Sir". I wonder whether the man behind the counter is obsequious because he is a scab or whether it's the other way around.

***

At a little kiosk I buy a copy of *Le Peuple*, the official organ of the Belgian Socialist Party (PSB). It announces a big demonstration for that morning. At the Maison du Peuple, the party headquarters, I am told the direction the procession has moved. After an hour I catch up as it is about to disperse. About two or three thousand people are still thronging a broad crossroads. A tram has been surrounded and its front windows smashed. The crowd is swarming around another tram. Posters proclaim, "No, to the New Law" and "Why must *we* always pay?". "Eyskens, resign", chants the crowd in rhythm. Other groups are shouting, "Eyskens, to the gallows". There are masses of young people there.

Two hefty-looking lads, one about 25, the other older, tell me they are tram drivers. This is the first day of a token strike of the Brussels tramwaymen. All the tram workers belonging to the Brussels FGTB[42] have been called out. The Catholic trade union has instructed its members to remain at work. For psychological reasons, they tell me, all the scabs have been concentrated on the 6.00 am shift, "to give the public an impression that many trams are still running". "Look", they say, "they have taken out the smallest trams they could and the ones in the worst state of repair. They would never allow an old tram like that on the lines in ordinary times. They won't run them for long. There's a rule that if, for any reason, a tram window is broken, the vehicle must return to the depot". "If it can", chipped in the other, laughing.

The crowd starts marching down one of the main shopping streets, singing the *Internationale*. The police half-heartedly throw a cordon of about thirty men across it. They are only one deep. Good-humouredly the crowd turns the edges of the cordon, or even walks straight through it, and proceeds down the boulevard, singing, laughing and shouting. I see the banners of the Socialist Youth. They are very interested to learn how closely some people in Britain have been following their struggle. Fraternal bonds are established within minutes. "This is something", one of them says, "that neither your rulers nor ours will ever understand".

2.00 pm.
The Socialist Youth (Jeunes Gardes Socialistes) are very helpful. Mobilized since the struggle began, their working headquarters is a long, dark room in a little side street just behind the Maison du Peuple. It is a constant hive of activity. One of the comrades accompanies me to their official office in the party headquarters. I am given my passport to Socialist Belgium: a letter of introduction from the Jeunes Gardes.

The comrade then takes me to the national FGTB headquarters, a massive modern well-equipped building, just like "official" trade union headquarters anywhere else. The walls are hung with large portraits of the aged and bearded founders of the Belgian labour and trade union movement. I am introduced to André Renard's secretary. Renard is assistant secretary of the FGTB and is generally regarded as the official spokesman of its "left" wing, a kind of Belgian Frank Cousins, with a big following in the industrial region around Liège.

I explain my purpose to her. Our interview is constantly interrupted by incoming and outgoing telephone calls, themselves a time consuming procedure. The conversations are constantly interrupted or branched on to wrong numbers. The gross-

---

42 The Fédération Générale des Travailleurs Belges is the equivalent of the Trade Union Congress. It differs however in that it has a number of semi-autonomous regional organizations, each comprising the representatives of various trades and occupations in a given area.

ly restricted staff of scabs at the Central Telephone Exchange must be having an exhausting time. At the FGTB the delays are accepted with patience and a sort of amused pride. "In Brussels, everything is normal", the wireless has just announced. I reflect on the multiple aspects of a telephonists' strike in a period of mass social upheaval.

Finally I meet André Renard for a few minutes. Here is the "anarchist", the "revolutionary", the actual villain in the eyes of the screaming bourgeois press. Looking younger than his years, an immensely self-confident man, he is obviously aware of the tremendous strength of several hundred thousand miners and metal workers in the Walloon area. At least for the time being they seem to speak one language and he appears to be the embodiment of their will to struggle.

He assures me that I will encounter no difficulties from the strike pickets and trade unions in the Walloon area and wishes me good luck in my tour. "Tell your readers that we will fight this to the end", he says. His secretary appends a few lines to my "pass" which is now an open-sesame to strike-bound Belgium. We leave.

"No applications in writing! No referral of the matter to this or that sub-committee!", I comment to my young friend, delighted at the informality and helpfulness just encountered. "They have to…now", he answered.

9.00 pm.

With the picket, outside the Brussels Main Post Office and Sorting Station. This is an enormous modern building, some 300 yards long and perhaps ten storeys high. Half an hour ago the postmen's delegate had called at the Socialist Youth Headquarters asking for reinforcements. A dozen comrades quickly go there. Soon we are joined by other hastily summoned reinforcements.

The majority of the 2,000 postal workers attached to the office have been on strike for about a week. The scabs are still working, protected by tommy-gun carrying parachutists and gendarmes. All the sorting of incoming and outgoing mail for the Brussels area takes place here. Only one entrance is in use, for both pedestrians and vehicles. This leads under an arch and into a small yard and is very heavily guarded. Between 9.00 and 9.30 pm the shifts change. Work at the office goes on around the clock. The authorities seem well aware of the importance of maintaining even a skeleton staff. Fast-moving, heavily guarded lorries carry the scabs in and out. They are loudly booed. The picket, which numbers perhaps fifty people, is not allowed within eighty yards of the entrance to the depot and contact, verbal or physical, with the scabs is not possible. Such is the present relation of forces. At the moment, little can be done to alter it. The lads on the picket seem however just as aware as the authorities of the necessity to maintain a substantial picket. I am repeatedly told it is one of the key points of the strike in the Brussels area.

It is extremely cold. We walk up and down, along the pavement, between the arrival and departure of the scab lorries. Only a small minority of the picket seem to be post office workers. The rest are militants from other unions, the Socialist Party and the Jeunes Gardes.

I interview a young postal worker, who has worked for five years at this depot. He tells me that for the first few days there was a massive picket of post-office workers. "But there were too many troops. We now only send a token picket. We know who's working".

I question him about the organization of the post office workers at this depot (Bruxelles X - Bureau de Tri). About fifty percent apparently belong to the Centrale Générale des Services Publics, an affiliate of the FGTB. About thirty percent belong to the Catholic Confédération Syndicale Chrétienne. The others are either not in unions or are members of the *syndicats neutres*.

He tells me that in the FGTB, to which he belongs, there are no regular branch meetings for the workers in his department. Every so often, when important decisions have to be imparted on the men, the union leaders convene a meeting. Such meetings may be attended by up to eighty percent of the men. "The leaders tell us what we have to decide. Then they take the temperature of the meeting. If there is massive opposition, things are modified". I ask him if there are ever mass meetings of all the workers employed in a given department or section, irrespective of their particular union affiliation. No, he says. He agrees it would be a good idea. "We are very divided. It weakens us". He had been in the Socialist Youth movement but now concerns himself exclusively with trade union matters. He has heard of and is interested in the British Shop Stewards' Movement.

He tells me how union delegates are elected at his place of work. There are yearly elections to determine the distribution of delegates, between the various unions "catering" for post office workers. "In a given office, the elections may show that FGTB will be allocated three delegates, the Christians two, the others one. The FGTB will then assemble its supporters separately, to elect its three delegates". These are not revocable during their tenure in office. "We don't see as much of them as we would like".

At this stage a platoon of about twenty gendarmes marches past us on the pavement. They are greeted with a resounding *Internationale*. They glare at us as they march by.

10.30 pm.

General Assembly at the Socialist Youth Headquarters. About forty young comrades are present, sitting on crates and chairs in various states of disrepair. About a third of them are girls. No one seems much over thirty. A single light. The corners of the room are in darkness. On one side a big stove. On the walls posters of the Algerian Revolution, posters relating to their own activities and a portrait of Lenin. Earlier that afternoon they had met and discussed what they would do the following day. Certain slogans had been collectively decided upon: "Eyskens to the gallows" - "For a strike to the finish" - "The bankers must pay" - "The soldiers are with us" - "The factories to the workers". Two comrades had been delegated to contact Communist Youth to explore the possibilities of united action for Thursday.

The Communist Youth, the delegates report, had agreed to all the slogans except the last one. The delegation had thereupon agreed to omit the "offending" slogan. When they announced this to the Assembly there was an unholy rumpus. "Mandate exceeded", they were told again and again. An overwhelming vote was taken dissociating the meeting from the actions of its delegates and pledging support for the controversial slogan. The delegates were instructed to contact the Communist Youth again, informing them of the decision: "We will march separately, if necessary. We will carry the slogans of our choice".

The posters were made. Next day the slogan, "The factories to the workers", was taken up again and again by the crowd. Various papers carried pictures of comrades carrying this poster. It was shown on the television newsreel. The message had been taken into tens of thousands of working class homes.

***

Today, there has been a further extension of the strike. 35,000 metal workers in the Senne valley have downed tools. The strike has spread to the engineering works of Peugeot, Raguenau, Metallurgia, Rateau, Acomal and Standard Triumph. It also spread at Ypres, at Courtrai and at Alost. The furniture workers at Malines and both boot and shoe operatives and textile workers at Termonde have joined the strike.

There have been massive demonstrations at Bruges and at Ghent, where 10,000 demonstrators paraded in the streets. There were several violent scuffles with the police. At Namur a gendarme told the strikers: "You can have another Grace-Berleur, if you want one!"[43]

At Herstal, an industrial suburb of Liège, 5,000 strikers assembled to hear Lambion, the secretary of the local metal workers federation. At Liège 2,000 railway workers walked through the streets and then paraded in front of the railway station singing the *Internationale*, 15,000 workers assembled in the industrial town of Huy, 8,000 at Waremme.

At Charleroi, a recently arrived comrade tells us, the strikers had formed enormous queues outside the Post Office, where a few scabs are still working, under heavy police protection. Any genuine customers arriving had been sent to the end of the queue, where they soon lost patience. One by one, the strikers had entered the Post Office to buy ten centime (halfpenny) stamps, each holding out a bank note and telling the scab to hurry up and give them change. "That's what you're there for, isn't it?", they had asked.

BRUSSELS, THURSDAY, DECEMBER 29.

10.00 am.

By 10.00 am, an enormous crowd has already assembled in front of the Maison du Peuple, the headquarters of the Socialist Party, of the Cooperatives and of the Mutual Aid Societies. Together with the FGTB unions these three organizations constitute the Action Commune which is "running" the strike.

Here are the working people of Brussels in their thousands: metal workers and engineers from the "red" suburb of Forest, railway workers, Government and municipal employees, shop girls and white collar workers from all over the city, old and young, seasoned veterans and people participating in this sort of thing for the first time, all of them in their opposition to the latest Government proposals, all of them determined to say, "No! It will not always be at *our* expense that they solve *their* problems". It is an impressive sight. The crowd swarms over the pavements, overflows into the neighbouring streets. Vendors selling *Le Peuple* (journal of the Socialist Party), *La Wallonie* (journal of the socialist trade unions of the Liège area), *Le Drapeau Rouge* (journal of the Communist Party) and *La Gauche* (journal of the Socialist Party "left") are all doing a roaring trade. The crowd is in good humour. People buy all the papers they can lay their hands on, discuss them, avid for news, happy at the sight of their own multitude.

---

43   At Grace-Berleur, near Liège, three striking workers were shot dead by the gendarmerie in 1950, during the massive agitation against King Leopold.

Loudspeakers are fitted on the window-sills of the Maison du Peuple, Trade Union and Party leaders address the crowd, assure it that *they* will fight to a finish, that *they* will not compromise, that the iniquitous law cannot be amended, that it must be rejected wholesale, that Government propaganda is spreading, that victory is assured and that the Government cannot but be impressed at the numerical strength and self-discipline of the thousands of demonstrators. The crowd listens happily in the pale winter sunshine. Contingents from some of the big cities (Ghent, Antwerp, Liège) march up the street, singing the *Internationale*, and are loudly applauded. Finally the procession sets off, socialist parliamentarians and provincial delegations in the lead, a broad river of red flags and posters denouncing the law in Flemish, overflowing its banks, lapping up small streams of demonstrators joining it at various points.

Slowly the procession proceeds to the fringes of the so-called neutral zone, where Parliament is situated and within which demonstrators are not permitted. The zone is guarded by barbed wire and crammed with mounted police, troops in jeeps, detachments of gendarmerie, water-lorries with pressure hose equipment, etc. A very small delegation of the Action Commune is allowed to enter the zone and is received by the Prime Minister. The main procession continues through the main streets, growing in volume from minute to minute.

It passes in front of a number of big banks and finance houses. The slogan, "The bankers must pay", is taken up by thousands of demonstrators and must be heard in the most remote offices or crypts. The windows of several banks are bombarded with stones and large bolts, with which many demonstrators seem extraordinarily well supplied. The police lining the pavement look on, quite helpless. On one occasion two policemen advance towards a demonstrator carrying a large brick. An angry growl from the crowd sends them scurrying back, as fast as their legs can take them. Some of the missiles thrown do not reach their targets, but hit the masonry between the windows and fall back on to the pavement. So confident is the crowd in its numbers that demonstrators come and pick up their projectiles at the feet of the policemen, pocketing them for later use. The relation of forces is rather different than last night, outside the Post Office.

The official socialist press commented as follows: "After ten days of an extremely hard strike, Thursday's demonstrators had no particular bad feelings towards the shopkeepers in the city centre. If the windows were broken of a few enterprises representing big business, it's because the demonstrators were fully aware whence was coming the aggression threatening their social conquests". Which, from the mouthpiece of social democracy, is quite an admission!

The procession proceeds joyfully through a number of lesser streets to emerge into an enormous boulevard, the Botanique, where it turns sharply to descend into the centre of the city. The sight is unforgettable. Marching twenty or thirty abreast, occupying the whole width of the boulevard, the procession extends as far back as the eye can see. The *Internationale* rends the air again and again. Many young people are now in the very front rows. They sing as if they mean every word of it. Here is the answer, I cannot help thinking, to those who assert that youth is non-political, that the proletariat no longer exists, that it has suffered disintegration through capitalist prosperity or assimilation into the structure of capitalist society. The slogan, "The factories to the workers", is taken up again and again encountering each time a growing echo. The most popular slogan however is undoubtedly "Eyskens, to the gallows"!

After a further hour of marching through the shopping area, bedecked with forlorn looking Christmas decorations, the procession reaches the Place Fontainas, where a mass rally was to have taken place. The speakers are already waiting, all smiles, with their microphones and their flags, on an elevated dais. The continuation of the street is barred by a double row of stewards: this is intended to be the dispersal point.

The head of the procession has now been taken over by the Socialist Youth and a number of young militants from Liège and Antwerp. They have been discussing for the last two hours. More marches? More speeches? What next? How can *we* intervene? What does the crowd really want? Is it one crowd or several crowds? Half a mile further on, beyond the barrage of stewards, lies the main Post Office with its two or three hundred massively protected scabs.

A new slogan bursts forth: "*A l'action! A l'action!*" Enough speeches! The procession ignores the call to stop coming from the loudspeakers but marches right up to the stewards, cutting through them as if they did not exist. Three hundred, four hundred, now five hundred people have broken the barrier. The stewards, helped by the trade union officials and parliamentarians, succeed in re-establishing it. Twenty or thirty comrades from the cut off section at the head of the procession are promptly dispatched behind the cordon. Again the slogans ring out and again the crowd swarm through the barrier. The flood can no longer be contained. Thousands of people turn their backs on the Place Fontainas and surge towards the Post Office.

The following day the socialist press was to describe the incident as follows: "The demonstrators, having reached the Place Fontainas, did not stop as had been anticipated but carried on towards the Midi, which was guarded by powerful gendarmerie detachments". In fact such was the pressure from the rank and file that the paper even had to endorse what happened: "This was not the result of activities of excited agitators. The flood tide, which although it may at times take on violent forms, is always inspired by legitimate motives".

The procession raggedly advances on the Post Office. A "black" tram is spotted in a side street by some demonstrators who immediately give chase to it, disrupting the procession still further. The conductor accelerates, fleeing for his life and, disregarding all safety regulations, hurtles along the rails, nearly running over several people in the process. He just escapes.

The comrades in front then stop. The ranks reform. A crowd can show immense self-discipline when striving for objectives of its own choice. The stragglers and those who had given chase to the tram are reabsorbed. The compact procession moves on. The police have obviously been taken as much by surprise as have the organizers of the demonstration. Only some thirty mounted gendarmes and a few dozen on foot line the front of the building. Boos greet the gendarmes. The horses rear and throw off two of their riders as the crowd shower bolts and thunder-flashes into the ranks of the police. The crowd cheers ironically. The gendarmes do not attempt to disrupt the procession at this stage and are left alone by the crowd. At the Post Office every window is broken at street level and many on the first floor. The stones rain into the building for at least ten minutes. Under the impotent gaze of about fifty extremely frightened policemen, demonstrators seize bins, full to the brim with the uncleared refuse of a week, and discharge their content through the broken windows into the offices and onto the desks of the scabs.

Some of the demonstrators then disperse, but other contingents march through side streets, rejoining the tail of the procession and thus coming in front of the Post Office a second time.

A postal bus, of the kind used to escort scabs into the depot, is turned over. Finally, hastily summoned reinforcements of mounted and foot police appear and succeed in clearing the street. It requires drawn swords and the threatening display of loaded guns to achieve this end. The crowd straggles back to the Place Fontainas where they are addressed by Gedhof, the trade union delegate from Sabena airline.

The speaker tells the demonstrators that sixty-five percent of the Sabena personnel are on strike but that Mr. Dieu, the manager, has just issued an instruction to the staff announcing the strictest measures against the strikers. "Mr. Dieu still thinks himself in the Congo", the speaker said. "For years he has been ordering coloured people about there; now he thinks he can do the same with us".

The speaker announced a demonstration, for the following day, to go to Sabena headquarters. This was the demonstration in which the first fatal casualty of the strike was to occur.

LIÈGE, THURSDAY DECEMBER 29.

Arrived here about 5.00 pm. The strike is far more widespread than in Brussels. All public transport has been at a standstill for several days. Many of the big stores are closed. Others are obeying the "request" of the FGTB and are opening only 10.00 am to 1.00 pm. Groups of about a dozen policemen scurry about the streets. Groups of strikers congregate in tight little knots arguing. Many people have gathered outside the offices of the local FGTB paper, *La Wallonie*. Some read the latest issue pasted on the boards. Others examine the front window of the premises, damaged a few nights ago when right-wing hooligans smashed the panes with a bottle.

La Wallonie has played an important role in the strike. It has been the mouthpiece of the most militant section of the trade union apparatus. It has given publicity and support to the strike, describing in considerable detail and with many pictures the main meetings of strikers, and has reported in full all the statements of the Socialist Party and FGTB leaders. It has attempted, from above, to co-ordinate the struggle, announcing meetings and places where socialist papers may be collected. It has repeatedly denounced and exposed the falsifications of the bourgeois press.

On December 24 the paper printed a special call to the troops: to fraternize with the strikers, to refuse to be used as blacklegs, and not be traitors to their class. This appeal, one of the most dramatic documents to have emerged from the great struggle of the Belgian working class, truly enraged the Government. That same evening, on orders from Brussels, officers of the judicial police accompanied by the judge and a royal attorney (*procureur du roi*) were busy in the most undignified task of tearing down posters, forcing the locks of display panel boxes, etc. An order had gone out for the paper to be "seized". The officers then erupted into the paper's offices and took all the issues they could find. In the early hours of Christmas Day visits and searches of homes were ordered. Accompanied by gendarmes, parties set out to raid the homes of trade union officials and militants; others descended on trade union premises and bookshops seizing copies of the December 24 issue.

In its next issue the paper spoke up quite boldly: "*La Wallonie* has no intention of keeping quiet. It will continue, as before, to fight for the good cause. It will not be dissuaded from doing its duty, even if threatened by seizure".

The seizure had interesting repercussions. The "forbidden" article was taken up by two other socialist papers, *Le Monde du Travail* and *Le Peuple*, which published it in full – and were thereupon promptly "seized" in their turn! Teams of young socialists and trade unionists then plastered the walls and hoardings of the city with leaflets reproducing the appeal. Some of these had been scraped off by officialdom but many remained.

***

I am beginning to learn my way about. I ask for "*La Populaire*" (the colloquial term for the Maison du Peuple). At this stage of the struggle I sense it will be a focal point. The ground floor is an enormous restaurant, run on co-operative lines, where free coffees are served to strikers at all times of the day or night. Groups of comrades from the unions and the Socialist Party are in permanent session in the various offices upstairs. An enormous red flag hangs from the first floor windows.

I tell them my business. Several comrades kindly agree to take me to various places. While waiting I talk to several people at the tables downstairs. First a refuse collector, a strapping great man with a keen sense of humour. "We stopped work on the very first day. In a sense we started all this. But they couldn't take it. Dirt frightens them. We were requisitioned on the fourth day. An armed gendarme on a motorbike called at each of our homes with a summons. We had to report next day at our usual depot. And I'd told the missus not to open the door! The cop barged in and just dumped the paper on the table. If he doesn't come we'll lock him up, he said. They passed a law in 1789 entitling them to do this. We discussed it amongst ourselves. We don't want to be in clink on great days like this. Sort of an unsanitary place, we felt. We couldn't be much help behind bars. So we went to work next day…wearing these!" He showed me the posters they had slipped over their dungarees. One said "Requisitioned by force", the other "Solidarity with the strikers", "No to the *loi unique*". The photos were published next day in all the socialist press.

I next spoke to a professional man employed by the municipality. "This is the most vicious onslaught on rights and conditions which it has taken us years of struggle to acquire. This law is the last straw. Why should ordinary people always have to foot the bill? They will agree no longer. In a country like Belgium no government can rule without the consent of the working class. We will win!" His quiet assurance, I thought, promised untold difficulties for anyone trying to sell out the struggle.

A young metal worker from the industrial suburb of Seraing tells me of interesting developments in his area. Old people are short of coal. It is a bitterly cold winter. The coal merchants have no stocks. The union now looks after all cases of hardship. The coal merchant comes to the union. They issue him with a permit, allowing him to collect a given quantity of coal from authorized persons. Without this certificate no deliveries can take place. "A good idea for after the strike", he muses, "we have accounts to settle!"

A railway worker tells me of the events that morning outside the Gare des Guillemins, the main Liège railway station. In the very early hours a scab postal van had arrived, bringing in large bundles of rightwing papers from Brussels. The van had intended to discharge its contents into a strike-bound militarily guarded postal depot at the station. It had been spotted by the railwaymen's picket, before it could reach the depot. Its contents had made an enormous bonfire at which the pickets had been able to warm themselves.

6.30 pm.

A comrade collects me and we proceed to the *Wallonie* premises. The streets are poorly lit. Current is scarce and supplies may fail, we are told, at any moment. A few young comrades are guarding the side entrance to the building, the only one in use. They each hold an iron bar. They anticipate further trouble. Some people, I am told, have been whipped into a white rage against the strikers and their press, by the incitements of the bourgeois papers. *Le Matin* (of Antwerp) and *Flandre Liberale* had called on the Government to become even tougher in relation to "the riot". *Le Libre Belgique* had screamed, "Down with Collard, Major and Leburton" (moderate socialist and trade union leaders). The wireless must no longer be put at the disposal of the revolutionaries. Daily these papers were exhorting their readers to be ruthless with the strikers, who were presented as the scum of the earth.

The young guards were taking no chances. My escort was fortunately known to them. Upstairs one of the editors gave me some photos and a file of back numbers of the paper. With a chuckle he went to a cupboard and produced a copy of the "seized" issue! "Look after this one", he said, "it could become a historical number". "Tell your friends what you have seen. This is a magnificent movement. Every working man and woman in this area is involved in this struggle. I am now well over fifty. I never thought I would see anything like it. Working people in Britain must be told the true facts". I promised to do my best. We went downstairs again. We found it considerably easier to leave the building than to enter it!

8.00 pm.

In the car of one of the comrades of the Liège Socialist Party, we visit a number of the Maisons du Peuple around Liège. These are very similar to the Working Men's Clubs in Britain. Almost overnight they became local strike headquarters. Here the strikers check in each day, or alternate days, according to region or occupation. Here the strike benefits are paid. Although they vary from area to area the average is around £2 per week. Solidarity funds are pouring in on an increasing scale from all over the country and free food is distributed here to families in need. The clubs are also distribution centres for the working class papers. Picket rotas are planned and other important local decisions are taken in these halls. Before the strike the clubs had mainly a recreational function. Many ran football teams or had teams of pigeon fanciers. Some showed "socialist" films regularly. In the Maison du Peuple of Saint-Gilles, which we are now visiting, the film *Salt of the Earth* had just been shown. This had inspired the idea of the women's picket, walking silently round and round in front of the Liège Post office from 7.00 to 9.00 am every morning.

A great welcome meets us at all these places. Everyone is anxious that the British working class get to know the facts. "The papers will all tell lies about us", I am told again and again. Naturally I agree. The Belgian wireless and television are violently opposed to the strike. I am just in time to see a TV version of the events I had personally witnessed in Brussels that very morning. Slick editing ensured that the rowdiest episodes were shown in a very fragmentary manner. No pictures appeared showing the enormous size of the demonstration and discreet cutting had ensured that the brutality of the gendarmerie did not appear on the screen. I have a short discussion with a local trade union militant, a lorry driver. "The movement must develop. We have done well so far. But we cannot stop. *Il faut aller jusqu' au bout*".[44]

A local Socialist Party official tells me the Party will fight to the end. Another comrade informs me that even Senator Dehousse is on their side. He is a local boy who has made good in a big way. He is apparently well known in the United Europe movement. His speeches at Strasbourg are very polished ones. I point out that Europe is not united now. Half of it is backing Eyskens. The other half is on the side of men like themselves. They all agree.

A little way from there, at the bottom of the Rue St. Laurent, we pass over a bridge, spanning the Brussels-Liège railway line. A lone soldier is sitting on the stone parapet, a tommy gun on one side and a thermos flask on the other. He is talking to a group of three railwaymen, who have just brought him hot soup. When the men have left I walk up to him. I tell him who I am. He seems quite friendly. He is about 28, fair-haired, Flemish. He told me that he spoke to the local people every night. He was called back from Germany three days ago. No, he is not a conscript. He has done his time, but re-enlisted. His father is a bricklayer, now working at Namur. What he thinks of the strike? "They must see no other way!" Has he heard of the appeal, in the seized issue of *La Wallonie*? Of course! Well? He looks me straight in the eyes: "*Je ne tirerai jamais sur pareil à moi!*"[45] All, after this, is anti-climax. Yes, they discuss the strike in his mess. Some are for, some against. The officers? As you'd expect! I've orders to speak to no one, he suddenly says, abruptly changing his tone, as a military lorry appears at the other end of the bridge.

Léo Collard, leader of the Socialist Party, told a Press Conference today that "the strike will last as long as necessary, even if trade union resources dry up. Common Action will itself start strike payments on Saturday. This will be a first instalment, the extent of which will vary…according to the man's occupation and to the number of days he has been on strike. The *loi unique* cannot be the basis of a solution. The government has conceived of this law as an organic whole . . .we cannot see how a compromise could be reached by amending its details. We are struggling, quite simply, for its withdrawal".[46]

Bold words. But verbal assaults hardly topple governments.

Also today: a gigantic rally of 50,000 workers in Antwerp. The procession, headed by hundreds of red flags, had crossed the town and paraded through the working class districts followed by all available local police. All shops had shut. One of the main slogans had been "Catholic workers, join us". A convoy of gendarmes hastily dispatched from Brussels had then arrived and had attacked the tail of the procession with tear gas grenades as it was beginning to disperse.

LIÈGE, FRIDAY, DECEMBER 30.

6.00 am.

With the picket, outside the Vuillemins station. The postal sheds are the key points. At least eighty lads are picketing. They are cheerful: yesterday morning's events warmed both hearts and hands!

---

44   "We must go to the very end of the road".

45   "I will never shoot at my own kind!"

46   *La Wallonie*, December 30, 1960.

Nothing very much happens. No postal van is likely to run the gauntlet again. And it's very early for Messieurs the Gendarmes to be out.

The picket is again of very mixed composition: postmen, railwaymen, engineers, even a miner. I speak to him. He works in a small pit, at Milmort, employing 450 men at the face and 150 on top. They joined the strike on Wednesday, December 21 - as soon as they heard that the municipal employees in Liège had walked out."Nothing could stop us. Agitation against the Law had been building up for weeks. The men were all prepared for action. The union leaders were dithering about when, and how, and for how long…It was like a tidal wave. Within hours the whole coalfield was out. The official decision came 24 hours later!"

Other pickets gave the same story: immediate and massive solidarity action of the rank and file, then hasty "official" decisions, ratifying the established fact. Nevertheless once the official machinery got moving it gave a further impetus to the struggle. The Liège-Huy-Waremme Regional Congress of the FGTB, meeting on December 22, called for "total and immediate cessation of work in all sectors, in production and distribution and in both private and public enterprises". It pledged that the local FGTB organizations would remain united "until final victory was assured".

8.00 am.

Over a hundred women are picketing outside the Liège main Post Office. They walk in silent procession up and down the pavement in front of a small main entrance through which the scabs must pass. Twenty yards away stand the menfolk, ominously watching lest they be molested. Three large policemen and two armed soldiers stand in front of the door. They look extremely stupid and quite embarrassed as the girls circle round them, as if they did not exist. The picket seems effective. Few scabs confront the cold irony of these determined women.

On the first day, about thirty of the sixty women pickets had been arrested and roughly thrown into two black Marias. There was an unholy rumpus because one of them was the deputy Fontaine-Borguet. They were all promptly released. . . and proceeded straight back to the picket line. Next day, over a hundred women were picketing. Today, about 130. My thoughts went to other pickets. There women had been arrested, none of whom had enjoyed the benefits of parliamentary immunity!

10.30 am.

A mass meeting is being held in the big hall of the Maison du Peuple, which is packed with about 1,200 local government personnel, postmen, clerks from the births and deaths registry, tramwaymen, road sweepers, girls from the public library, the manual and white-collar staff of innumerable departments of local government, both large and small. The speakers on the platform look self-important and self-satisfied. The meeting starts half-an-hour late. The crowd waits patiently. The audience are flattered about their "heroic struggle, their unity, their discipline", but no plan is developed. They listen in silence. Three passages evoke applause: reference to a possible march on Brussels, a statement that "although calm and dignified today each one of us is prepared for more active forms of struggle tomorrow", and a peroration "that Belgium had been misruled for long enough and that it was high time the working class took Belgium's fate into its own hands".

At the end of the lengthy meeting, many of the audience drift down to the "gents" in the basement. Money-boxes adorn the walls with the inscription: "Now remember that strike fund!"

12.30 pm.

After the meeting, several hundred of the audience drift to the Place St. Paul, a secluded square in front of the FGTB headquarters. Here they are joined by about a thousand strikers who had previously been aimlessly strolling through the town. A crowd of about 2,000 is soon waiting for something to happen. But nothing happens. In the trade union headquarters, the discussion is doubtless proceeding along its orderly course. The situation calls for some kind of lead, the absence of which is painfully obtrusive. Suddenly a group of quite young workers start chanting rhythmically: "*A l'action!*" The slogan spread. In minutes the whole square is resounding to its echo. Startled heads pop out of windows of the trade union building. Some thirty youngsters rush the front door shouting: "We'll shake them up". Part of the audience cheers. Others laugh. Others loudly disapprove. A minor official, standing on the steps, improvises a discourse on…discipline. A leading official appears and skillfully endorses the crowd's desire for action. "It must be united action though. . . Let us march to the railway station". The crowd agree enthusiastically. Their idea of a march on to the station obviously differs from that of their leaders. They set off shouting: "*A l'action*" and "The parachutists to the factory bench". One can feel the temperature rising. The procession advances for about a mile. It is then overtaken by an official trade union van, complete with loudspeaker equipment. The van draws up. The procession stops. Posters and banners are handed down to the demonstrators. "No, to the Law", "Eyskens, resign", "The Walloon country has had enough", the banners of a week ago. The lads in the front ranks sheepishly take them. The "leaders" launch their slogans into the loudspeaker. The crowd takes them up half-heartedly. They cannot really compete. The procession reaches the large open space in front of the station, circles round it twice - well away from the gendarmes lining the pavement - and proceeds, in confused and perplexed silence, to disappear into a small street, leading *away* from the station.

3.00 pm.

A young comrade has agreed to drive me to Seraing, the big industrial suburb of Liège. This is Renard's home ground, the much publicized "heart of the strike". Here live thousands of steel workers and engineers who work at the giant Cockerill-Ougrée industrial complex. We drive past miles of plant - enormous sheds, deserted furnaces, pressing rooms and smelting ovens. I was later to learn that many factories in this area had in fact been closed down by employers, as soon as they had seen how widespread the strike was going to be.

Too bad for the odd scab who might have wished to work. Too bad for their sacred "right to labour". But much safer, no doubt, from the employers' point of view. There is danger to valuable equipment when a town is full of strikers and the plants all have pickets at their gates. This is a sort of strike-cum-lockout, by mutual consent.

A thin plume of smoke still emerges from some chimneys. By mutual consent, too, the maintenance men had been kept at work.

The threat to withdraw the maintenance staff is Renard's trump card, the high point of his industrial strategy. The weapon however is a double-edged one. Several workers viewed its use with misgiving. "We may win the strike and inherit a desert". Cockerill–Ougrée employ over 25,000 men. If the furnaces went out thousands would be out of work for months.

The strike in Seraing is total. Only food shops are open – and this only at times allowed by the unions. Everything is extraordinarily quiet. Not a policeman, not a picket in sight. No women or children in the streets. Here and there groups of men stand at the crossroads, doing nothing.

We reach the Maison du Peuple which at least shows some signs of activity. My friend and I are brought into a tiny office where we meet three members of the Strike Committee, all three union officials. Elected committees are exceptional.

They look at us cagily. "Yes, the strike is quite solid. Hadn't I read the papers?" "Everything is quite orderly in Seraing. What did I expect?" Would the present methods of struggle be sufficient to make the Government capitulate? "Well, we'd have to see about that. To each day its tasks, however!" A march on Brussels? "Well, that would have to be a national decision. They were just holding the fort at Seraing!"

A significant paradox? The strike at its most complete and the streets as quiet as early on a Sunday morning. On the home ground of the FGTB "left", the apparatus is in full and undisputed control. I have an uneasy impression that the wheels seem to be turning in the air.

***

5.00 pm.

We return from Seraing along another route, close to the river, and enter Liège through the densely populated suburbs of Outre-Meuse. As we turn sharply on to the *quai* along the river Ourthe, an unforgettable sight suddenly meets our gaze. Three hundred yards on, a bridge spans the river. A procession is crossing the bridge, three enormous red flags at its head. Half the bridge is empty, half is black with people. The strains of the *Internationale* can be heard in the distance.

We quickly join up with the procession. It was unlike any other I had seen, being composed almost solely of young people. It had formed spontaneously as soon as the news had reached Liège, of the death that morning in a Brussels demonstration, of a young painter. It was entirely "unofficial". A single, hastily made poster was carried at its head: "Eyskens, assassin. In Brussels today: one dead, ten wounded". Within twenty minutes the procession had doubled its size. Through the narrow streets of the working class quarters it wound its angry way. A single slogan fiercely chanted by twelve or fifteen hundred youngsters: "Eyskens, assassin! Eyskens, assassin!" A single song, sung with more passion than I have ever heard: the *Internationale*.

The procession reaches the square where stands the statue of Tchantchès, the famous puppet of Walloon folklore. It stops. A youngster gets on to the base of the statue, and speaks his mind. "This is their real face... This is what faces us. What can we do? How can we make our will effective? In the Party and Union headquarters, they talk. The Government waits. Time is not on our side. I have marched so much I have holes in my shoes. We should do something more". Others follow him. The idea of a march on Brussels is greeted with applause. But who will organize it? The Party and the Unions? But they don't want such a march. Or they only use one as a safety valve. "What can we do, here? We can disseminate the idea of the March. We must ourselves contact other young people, in other towns. No one will do it for us".

Others speak in the same vein. "The Government's hands are red with blood. The hands of our leaders are crippled with arthritis".

The procession returns to town, lodges a protest at the town hall, "the only practical thing we can do just now, comrades", and disperses. Heavy rain begins to fall.

***

Today there have been mass meetings at Mons and Charleroi. At Mons a meeting announced the previous evening was attended by 10,000 workers. Many had had to walk for hours to get to the town, most roads having been either unpaved by the strikers or blocked by tree trunks. A socialist leader, Marcel Busieau, stated, "it is alleged we might be ready to negotiate with the Government on the basis of a withdrawal of parts of the *loi unique*. This is false. We will fight to the end for its complete withdrawal". The *Monde du Travail* described this speech as "wildly applauded". So much for the record. The strikers then "visited" a bank where scabs were still at work. There was no scuffle. The manager agreed to close down immediately.

At Charleroi, a gigantic rally of 45,000 strikers shouts, "To Brussels, to Brussels". The speaker Josse van Eynde asks them, "only heed the official slogans of the Action Commune".[47] A resolution, in which readers will detect interesting undertones, is read over the microphone and "approved by acclamation":

> Today, Friday, December 30, 45,000 workers who, for the past ten days have of their own free will left their factories, building sites, mines, schools and offices…proclaim:
>
> a) their firm opposition to the *loi unique*;
>
> b) their demand that it simply be withdrawn;
>
> c) that they have absolute confidence in their trade union organizations and in the Action Commune;
>
> e) that they mandate their leaders to express their wishes and defend their interests;
>
> d) that they reject with contempt the campaign of lies, intimidation and diversion launched by the Government, "its" radio, "its" Press, "its" television and "its" valets of the Confédération Syndicale Chrétienne.

To all this we oppose the following slogan: "The Strike Continues".

Why did the "leaders" need reassuring?

LIÈGE, SATURDAY, DECEMBER 31.

10.00 am.

Theo Dejace, Communist Party deputy for Liège, is addressing an open air meeting in the Place de la République Francaise. Leaflets were distributed the previous day. About 600 people listen. The speaker calls for daily public meetings of the organizations leading the strike, whence clear directives could be issued and where comments from the rank and file might be heard. There is too little contact he says, between the official organizations and the strikers. This he believes is regrettable. He warns the crowd against rowdies, drunkards, and "leftists". The main task apparently is to prevent the new law from being voted on January 3. Between now and then

---

47   *Le Monde du Travail*, December 31, 1960.

assemblies of strikers should daily send deputations to the homes of all Social-Christian deputies "to impress upon them that they should comply with the wishes of their electors rather than obey the orders issued by the Banks and Government". An official Communist Party leaflet (*Two Communist Proposals for a Total and Rapid Victory*) is distributed at the meeting. It ends as follows:

> If despite the popular will, the reactionary majority in Parliament were to continue its support for the *loi unique*, the struggle would continue. Let the Government have no doubt on this matter!

> A Parliament which opposed itself in so flagrant a manner to public opinion would have to be dissolved without delay!

> The strike is powerful. Let there be no irresponsible acts, that might weaken it!

The crowd listens without great enthusiasm. The labels are different. The medicine tastes the same.

***

The Communist Party has played no important role in the present upsurge of the Belgian working class. Its rank-and-file members have doubtless fought shoulder to shoulder with Socialist Party militants and with thousands of struggling workers who do not belong to either organization, but its leadership and in particular its press have played, to say the least, a ludicrous role.

On December 20 the Communist Party had issued a call for a 24-hour general strike (having previously demanded only a national demonstration on that day). The self-appointed "leadership" proved quite out of touch with the militancy of the rank and file. The movement has now lasted four weeks!

On December 27 the Communist Party deputy Gaston Moulin addressed a letter to Mr. Kronacker, President of the Chamber of Deputies, in which "he sought permission to question the Prime Minister of the Interior. . . on the utilization of the Army and on the recall of reservists. . . on the arbitrary arrests of strikers and militant workers, on the arbitrary 'seizures' of leaflets and papers and on the dissemination of false news through official channels".

Does it really take a general strike to make the Communists aware of the class nature of the Capitalist State, and to drive them to "protest" about it. . . in Parliament?

On December 28, the *Drapeau Rouge* splashed on its front page that the Liège demonstrations demanded of the Liberal and Social-Christian deputies that they "obey the will of their electors". The paper hoped that in the next few days closer contacts would be established between the population and the (right-wing) deputies, "who had become isolated from their electors".

The paper reported that the Liège Federation of the Communist Party considered that "the Liège deputies Harmal, Herbiet, Olislaeger, Deslenay and Jeunehomme must answer the call addressed to them by the demonstrators and must finally understand that their stubbornness is an obstacle to the rapid and democratic solution to the conflict".

On December 29 the *Drapeau Rouge* was even more explicit: it titled in big letters "An Essential Objective of the Strikers: To Recall to the Liberal and Christian Deputies that they are in Parliament to Accomplish the Popular Will!" Well, well! And we, around the *Agitator*, who always thought they were in Parliament to defend the class interests of the bourgeoisie...

And what does the Belgian Communist Party see as the outcome of the strike? This is made quite explicit in a draft law submitted to Parliament by Communist Party deputies Gaston Moulin and Theo Dejace. This demanded:

a) the control of the banks, of the insurance companies and of big business [no specification as to who does the "controlling"];

b) the creation of a Committee for National Investment; and

c) the creation of a National Investment Fund to allow the rapid and harmonious development of the economy, to ensure full employment and to permit a rapid rise in the material and cultural level of the people.

Somehow I doubt the Borinage miners are struggling as they are for ends of this kind.

LIÈGE, SATURDAY, DECEMBER 31.

10.00 am.

A procession to mourn the death of the Brussels painter has been hastily arranged by the Action Commune. Instructions go out that the procession is to be a silent one. No posters. No slogans. Only red flags draped with black will be allowed. "This is a heaven-sent opportunity for them", a young bank clerk tells me. "It will enable them to contain the movement a little longer. Without this excuse for a silent march there would have been real violence today".

December 31 is usually a bumper day for the big stores. They were to have been allowed (in agreement with the FGTB) to remain open from 10.00 am to 6.00 pm. But when the news reached Liège yesterday that a man had been killed in Brussels, the Liège FGTB immediately issued a request: all shops were to remain closed the following day as a sign of mourning.

Today all the big stores are shut. Some have big posters in their windows: "In agreement with the FGTB and as a sign of mourning, we will not open on Saturday, December 31". The solicitude of the multiple store millionaires for a humble Brussels painter is truly touching. And the size and temper of the crowd in the streets is impressive.

The procession sets off in silence – about 6,000 strong. For the first half-hour no slogans are shouted, no songs sung. People exchange experiences, discuss the events of the past few days.

I meet a young worker from Cockerill-Ougrée, the big steel works outside Liège. Lucien works on the night shift, in one of the tin-plating shops. He gives me the most vivid account of the onset of the movement I have yet heard.

The unions had first called a national demonstration for December 15. This was the day of the royal wedding. It had officially been decreed a paid holiday. Under pressure from the ranks the demonstration had been brought forward to December 14. A massive strike took place that afternoon. Fifty thousand workers assembled at the Place St.-Lambert, in Liège. Many of the posters demanded a general strike.

Renard had spoken. He had concluded with the ambiguous statement: "Consider yourselves mobilized on a war footing. . . and wait for official directives". The meeting had been noisy and at times angry. A member of the Socialist Youth had then climbed on to the balcony and attempted to address the crowd. He had been prevented from doing so by Party officials. PSB deputy Simon Paque had seized the microphone from him and had again addressed the crowd. "Remain ready for action. The meeting is closed".

I asked Lucien what had happened where he worked, on that famous Tuesday, December 20. "Things moved immediately. Hundreds of workers left the central shops. They went from shop to shop, getting the lads to down tools. Three thousand men gathered in the new Thomas steel plant among valuable equipment! It was dangerous but it's one of the biggest available places. Several fights took place with the trade union delegates. They were trying to get the men back to work until official instructions had been received. Meetings were promised for the next day. Why not now, the men had asked. Many remained on the premises to prevent the night shift from coming on. Only half the factory worked that night. By Wednesday morning it had come to a complete standstill. The Metal Workers Federation of the Liège FGTB called us all out officially as from the Thursday".

The procession has now crossed the river. The first incidents occur as we pass a large store that has not complied with the FGTB request. A group of angry demonstrators enter threateningly. Stewards hastily intervene. *They* will talk to the manager. The demonstrators reluctantly walk out, but wait outside. After a few minutes, the shutters are closed. The manager has decided to participate in the mourning.

A little further on we pass a shop displaying a poster of the "Union of the Middle Classes". This is headed "FREEDOM FIRST". The freedom referred to is the freedom of scabs to work and of the Government to use all means to break the strike. The owner of the shop is instructed to remove the poster. He takes one look at the crowd and immediately obeys. Further on other shopkeepers start arguing. But not for long. If the offending posters do not disappear, the window-panes do. Noisily. The whole atmosphere gradually changes. The demonstrators are now on the lookout for hostile posters and for open shops of any size. Small shops are left strictly alone. Some of the stewards - notably those of the socialist students - object to the transformation taking place. "Remember, comrades, this is a silent procession. You must obey the official instructions". But their protests are of little avail. The police lining the pavements are powerless, as in Brussels on Thursday morning. The Union of the Middle Classes is in for a bad day. Instinctively the crowd is becoming aware of its terrific strength.

1.00 pm.

I am with a group of comrades associated with the weekly *La Gauche*. They have no illusions on the limitations of the present leadership of both Party and Unions. But they still seem to think that genuine solutions are possible within the framework of these organizations. The idea that they should themselves get together and issue a leaflet saying quite openly what they think strikes them as sectarian.

Ernest Mandel, editor of *La Gauche*, writes in a special issue of the paper (December 24):

> The workers fear that if the Government fell as a result of the present social crisis the Socialist Party would enter a new coalition "so that the country should not become ungovernable". The immense majority of the strikers will only tolerate such a reversal of the (parliamentary) alliances on two conditions:
>
> a) that the new government abandon the *loi unique*, i.e. not only the austerity measures in the social field but also the increases in indirect taxation;

b) that the new ministerial programme should retain the essential features of the *"réformes de structure"*.[48]

If these two conditions are not fulfilled one must be resolutely opposed to any socialist participation in the Government in order to end the strike.

Mr. Mandel believes that these objectives might even be achieved through the bourgeois deputies. Under the heading "Decisive Moments" he writes: "A new parliamentary majority in relation to the questions of withdrawing the *loi unique* and voting a law on fiscal reform and the *'réformes de structure'* could well emerge. It would only require that the Christian-Democrat deputies listen to the voices of their electors and, under the pressure of the strike, align themselves on the aspirations of those they represent".

Thus speaks Trotskyism, at the height of a general strike…

3.00 pm.

We are driving back to Brussels in a tiny Citroen. Episodes too numerous to record still jostle in my mind: the sympathy with the strikers shown by innumerable small shopkeepers and café owners; the farmers supplying free vegetables to the Maisons du Peuple, for the communal soup kitchens; thousands of ordinary people discovering within themselves unlimited reserves of energy, initiative and devotion; men, women and children, many seriously short of sleep, active from dawn to dusk on the picket lines, as couriers, organizing relief, participating in meetings, marches and demonstrations, all imbued with an indomitable determination to assert their collective will, all feeling for once that what they do, feel, think, really matters, all dragged out of the anonymity and isolation of their daily lives and suddenly confronted with the heart-warming image of their numbers, their cohesion, their strength…

I remembered what a postman told me, on the picket line at Brussels. "Each Christmas we sell calendars to the people in our areas. They give generously. We often get, at this time, what amounts to two months' pay. We decided nevertheless to launch this fight on December 20. We knew we would not fight alone".

He was right, of course. Solidarity action was massive and not confined to other workers. Early in the course of the strike, the Minister of the Interior had issued orders to all local *bourgmestres* (mayors) instructing them to report to the authorities all absences from work of local government employees. On December 26, the 62 socialist *bourgmestres* from the Liège district met and unanimously decided "to take no account of the orders of the minister". They proclaimed their complete solidarity with the strikers. Similar statements were made by meetings of the socialist *bourgmestres* of the Verviers, Nivelles, Charleroi, Namur, Borinage and other districts.

At Huy the Common Action Committee had even concluded an agreement with the local shopkeepers' federation, who had declared itself against the *loi unique* and had made financial contributions to the local strike fund. In Seraing, even the priests had, on Christmas day, read messages in their Churches expressing solidarity with the strikers. These messages were in marked contrast to the appeal of Cardinal van Roey, Archbishop of Malines, exhorting the strikers to return to work.

---

48   By *"réformes de structure'"* are meant a series of "transitional" demands. These, it is alleged, would without overthrowing capitalism wrest from it some of its commanding heights. Among these "reforms" are the control of the holding banks, the nationalization of power industries, a national economic plan and the constitution of a public National Investment Fund. We see no basic socialist content in any of these demands.

I recall how in a street in Liège, working men had been repairing a burst main. On their van a large poster: "We are strikers. We are working of our own free will, with the permission of our union, and out of consideration for the local population".

Local Government had broken down. Local initiative and self-reliance had replaced it. Here was the true face of the working class - the harbinger of a new society.

I recall above all a discussion with two young comrades one evening in Liège. One worked in a machine tool factory, the other at the Ateliers Jaspar, making lifts. "The leaders tell us do this, do that. We don't know any longer. We, the workers, ought to decide. We are the ones that get shot and wounded. We are the ones they put in gaol. There will be no sell out if we decide how we should struggle".

[Editor's note: The general strike lasted until 21 January, when the 120,000 metal workers from the Liège and Charleroi regions finally returned to work. The Eyskens government was compelled to dissolve Parliament and in the ensuing election the governmental coalition was defeated. Important sections of the loi unique were never implemented and there was no decline in the real wages of the working class. On the other hand, the new government was a coalition of the Social Christians (Parti Social Chrétien), not only the majority in the previous administration but Eyskens's own party, and the Socialists (PSB); and not even any of the réformes de structure that had been envisaged by Ernest Mandel and the left-wing of the PSB materialized. For further details see Ernest Mandel, "The Dialectic of Class and Region in Belgium", New Left Review, no. 20 (Summer 1963), esp. pp. 24-6; and Serge Simon, "The Belgian General Strike: The General Strike Day by Day", Revolutionary History, VII, 1 (1998).]

FROM *BELGIUM: THE GENERAL STRIKE*, AGITATOR/ NEW GENERATION PAMPHLET (JANUARY 1961)

3. REVOLUTIONARY ORGANIZATION

1. "What is not to be done"

The term "rethinking" is often used as an excuse for not thinking at all. One hesitates to use it. Much rethinking has nevertheless to be done by revolutionary socialists. A cursory glance at the Labour movement in Western Europe today should convince anyone of this dire need. More and more ordinary people show an indifference bordering on contempt for the mass Labour and Communist Parties of yesterday. The old men of the "left" attempt to resolve this crisis by repeating in ever more strident tone the dogmas and concepts that were good enough for their own grandads.

We here wish to examine one of the most fervently adhered to dogmas of the "Left": the need for a tightly centralized socialist party, controlled by a carefully selected leadership. The Labour Party describes this type of organization as an essential feature of British democracy in practice. The Bolsheviks describe it as a "democratic centralism". Let us forget the names and look below the surface. In both cases we find the complete domination of the party in all matters of organization and policy by a fairly small group of professional "leaders".

As none of these parties has ever been successful in achieving a society where the great mass of people control and manage their own destinies, both their politics and their organizational methods must be considered suspect. It is our opinion that the type of organization required to assist the working class in its struggle for socialism is certainly a matter for serious thought.

Post-war capitalism has certainly provided more jobs and better paid ones than many may have thought possible. But its drive to subordinate people to the process of production has intensified at an enormous rate. At work, people are reduced more and more to the role of button-pushing, lever-pressing machines. In the "ideal" capitalist factory human beings would perform only the most simple, routine tasks. The division of labour would be carried to its extreme. Managers would decide. Foremen would supervise. The workers only comply.

In the body politic, omnipotent social institutions similarly decide all issues: how much production will be "allowed" to increase or decrease, how much consumption, what kind of consumption, how many H-bombs to produce, whether to have Polaris bases or not, etc., etc. Between those who rule and those who labour there exists a wide and unbridgeable gulf.

Exploiting society consciously encourages the development of a mass psychology to the effect that the ideas or wishes of ordinary people are unimportant and that all important decisions must be taken by people specially trained and specially equipped to do so. They are encouraged to believe that success, security, call it what you will, can only be achieved within the framework of the accepted institutions. The rebel, the militant, the iconoclast may be admired, even envied, but their example must be shunned. After all no one can really challenge the powers that be. Just look at what happens to those who try!

Ironically enough the very organizations that have set themselves up as the liberators of the working class and the champions of their cause have become facsimile replicas of the very society they are supposedly challenging. The Labour Party, the Communist Party and the various Trotskyite and Leninist sects all extol the virtues of professional politicians or revolutionaries. All practice a rigid division within their own organizations of leaders and led. All fundamentally believe that socialism will be instituted from above and through their own particular agency.

Each of them sees socialism as nothing more than the conquest of political power, and the transformation, by decree, of economic institutions. The instruments of socialism, in their eyes, are nationalization, state control and the "plan". The objective of socialism is to increase both productivity and consumption. The elimination of economic anarchy and the full development of the productive forces are somehow equated with the millennium.

Labour's nationalized industries are proof of the attitude of the Social Democrats. The Bolsheviks would replace the Robertsons and Robens with people loyal to the Party. The Soviet experience makes this quite clear. As early as 1918 Lenin had stated "the Revolution demands, in the interests of socialism, that the masses *unquestioningly obey the single will* of the leaders of the labour process".[49] By 1921 he was saying: "It is absolutely essential that all authority in the factories should be concentrated in the hands of management…under these circumstances all direct interference by the trade unions in the management of factories must be regarded positively harmful and impermissible."[50]

Trotsky wanted to militarize the trade unions. Is it very far from this to the statement, issued by Stalin's Central Committee in September 1929, that "Soviet Union Communists must help to establish order and discipline in the factory. Members of the Communist Party, union representatives and shop committees are instructed not to interfere in questions of management".[51]

None of them argued for the working people themselves managing and organizing industry and the affairs of society, now. That was a carrot to be nibbled in a distant future.

This conception of socialism spawns the bureaucratic parties that today constitute the traditional political organizations of the "left". To all of them the determination and application of policies are a matter for experts. Gaitskell scorns the Scarborough decisions because they were made by people whom he considers to be intellectually incapable of comprehending matters of international importance. The Communist Party and the Socialist Labour League oppose British H-bombs but support Russian ones. Their leaders consider the millions of people who want to end *all* H-bombs as being sentimental and uninformed. They have obviously not read the appropriate volumes that would "clarify" them and make them see how essential Russian bombs really are.

The businessmen insist on the importance of their managerial rights. So do the leaders of the political organizations of the "Left". This rigid control from above creates not efficiency but the very reverse. Whenever decisions are taken at higher levels and simply transmitted to the lower orders for execution a conspiracy against

---

49   "The immediate tasks of the Soviet government", *Isvestiya of the All-Russian Central Executive Committee*, No.85 (April 28, 1918). (Emphasis in original.)

50   "The role of the Trade Unions under the N.E.P."

51   Reported in *Freiheit*, German language paper of the American Communist Party, September 9, 1929.

both leaders and orders arises. In the factory the workers devise their own methods of solving work problems. If bonus can be made in five hours well and good. Work is skilfully spread over eight-and-a-half hours. Supervisors lie to departmental managers. These, in turn, lie to works' managers, who lie to the directors and shareholders. Each seeks to preserve his own niche. Each seeks to hide wastage, error, and inefficiency. In the hierarchical organization of the modern factory where work is not a matter for common decision and responsibility, and where relations are based on mistrust and suspicion, the best "plan" can never be fulfilled in life.

This is repeated in the political parties. Officials have an existence to justify. Members who are nothing more than contributors to party funds, and sellers of party literature are regularly called to order to explain how many papers they have sold and how many contacts they have visited with their leader's latest line. Those who attempt to discuss reality or to think for themselves are denounced as either "sectarians" or "opportunists" or just "politically immature". The factory managers never really know what is happening in their factories. The political "leaders" really don't know either what is taking place in their own organizations. Only the leaders, for instance, believe the membership figures issued.

Bolsheviks argue that to fight the highly centralized forces of modern capitalism requires an equally centralized type of party. This ignores the fact that capitalist centralization is based on coercion and force and the exclusion of the overwhelming majority of the population from participating in any of its decisions. The most highly specialized and centralized bodies under capitalism are its means of enforcing its rule - its military and its police. Because of their bureaucratic centralism these organizations produce a special breed of animal noted for its insensitiveness, brutality and other moronic qualities.

The very structure of these organizations ensures that their personnel do not think for themselves, but unquestionably carry out the instructions of their superiors. Trotsky, as far back as 1903, believed that the Marxist movement should have a similar structure. He told the Brussels Conference that the statutes of the revolutionary organization should express "the leadership's organized distrust of the members, a distrust manifesting itself in vigilant control from above over the Party".[52]

Advocates of "democratic centralism" insist that it is the only type of organization which can function effectively under conditions of illegality. This is nonsense. The "democratic centralist" organization is particularly vulnerable to police persecution. When all power is concentrated in the hands of the leaders, their arrest immediately paralyses the whole organization. Members trained to accept unquestioningly the instruction of an all-wise Central Committee will find it very difficult or impossible to think and act for themselves. The experiences of the German Communist Party confirm this. With their usual inconsistency, the Trotskyists even explain the demise of their Western European sections during World War II by telling people how their leaders were murdered by the Gestapo!

The overthrow of exploiting society is not a military operation to be planned by a secretariat of amateur generals, armed with a library of Marxist textbooks and an outdated military manual. A social revolution can only take place providing the working class itself is conscious of the need to change society and is prepared to struggle. Its success is dependent on the disintegration of the capitalist institutions

---

52   See Isaac Deutscher, *The Prophet Armed*, p.76.

more than on their military overthrow. Unless whole sections of the military can either be won over or neutralized, then the taking of power is impossible.

Because of their basically reactionary ideas and methods of organization neither social democracy nor Bolshevism are able to understand or express the real needs of people. The dynamic of any socialist movement is the desire of people to change the conditions of their lives. The Hungarian Revolution was more than a struggle for an extra ten bob a week. It was not a struggle for an extension of nationalization or for more "efficiency" in Government departments. Millions of Hungarian people rose against their oppressors because *they* wanted to determine the conditions of their own lives and to manage their own affairs. For a brief, heroic period they replaced the society of rulers and ruled with direct democracy, where every representative was not only elected by direct vote but was revocable at any time. The ideas of committees appointed from above and of "panels' commissions" would have been quite alien to them. Surely political tendencies whose organizational methods are the very antithesis of what the working class has demonstrated, in practice, that it wants, should re-examine all their ideas and previously held theories.

2. Why?

All the ruling groups in modern society encourage the belief that decision taking and management are functions beyond the comprehension of ordinary people. All means are used to foster this idea. Not only do formal education, the press, the radio, television and the church perpetuate this myth, but even the parties of the so-called opposition accept it and, in so doing, lend it strength. All the political parties of the "left" – whether social democratic or Bolshevik – oppose the present order only by offering "better" leaders, more "experienced" and more capable of solving the problems of society than those who mismanage the world today.

All of them, bourgeois and "radicals" alike, distort the history of the working class and attempt to draw a discreet veil over the immense creative initiative of the masses in struggle. For the bourgeois, the Russian revolution was the conspiracy of organized fanaticism. To Stalinists and Trotskyists, it is the justification for their right to lead. For the bourgeois, the Hungarian Revolution of 1956 showed how capitalist rulers were better than Stalinist ones. For the Stalinists, it was a fascist conspiracy. The Trotskyists wrote pamphlets showing how badly the Hungarians needed their own services. Over every revolution and struggle the parties compete in the squalid business of seeking to justify both themselves and their dogmas. They all ignore the efforts, the struggles, the sacrifices and the positive achievements of the participants themselves. Every attempt by people to take control of their own destiny by instituting their own rule has been buried beneath a million official tracts and a welter of "expert" interpretations.

It is now almost impossible to learn what actually happened in Italy during the early 1920s when the workers occupied and managed the factories. The Asturian Commune of 1934, the May Days in Barcelona in 1937, the sit-down strikes in France and the U.S.A. during the late thirties and the events of Budapest in 1956 have become closed books.

If the myth that people are unable to manage, organize and rule society themselves is to be debunked, workers must be made aware that on several occasions other workers have in fact managed society. They have done so both more humanely and more effectively than it is managed at present. To us who publish *Agitator* there can be no thought of socialism unless the working class establishes its own rule. Socialism for us implies the complete and total management of both production and government. The essential precondition for this is a rise in mass consciousness and the development of a confidence within people that they are able not only to challenge the old society but build the new one.

Making these past experiences available to people is one of the primary tasks of revolutionary socialists. All channels of information are in the hands of capitalists, bureaucrats, or self-appointed saviours with special axes to grind. We disagree with those who argue that there is no need for a revolutionary organization. The production of a truthful and a serious history requires the conscious and organized association of revolutionary socialists.

The revolutionary organization must also bring to workers' notice the common interests that they share with other workers.

On the one hand the concentration of capital has led to an increasing concentration of workers in giant factories often linked with one another in various kinds of monopolies. On the other hand the new productive techniques have led to greater division between the producers. The labour process has been so broken down that workers are not only separated by national, regional and sectional boundaries, but also by artificial divisions within factories and departments. The increasing tempo of production and introduction of piecework has fostered the idea that the interests of workers in one section are quite different from those of men in other sections.

The trade union officials help the employers to maintain these divisions. Separate and often widely differing wage and piece-rates are negotiated. Workers in one factory or shop are pitted against workers in other factories and shops. The employers and the union officials unscrupulously use the men's short-term interests – or apparent short-term interests – to sabotage their real needs. The very presence of different unions competing against one another for members illustrates how sectional interests are promoted above general requirements. Clerical workers are today being reduced to mere cogs in the impersonal machine of production. The increase in union membership among these workers shows that they are becoming aware of this fact. The union bureaucracies organize them into separate unions for white-collar workers, or into special sections of the industrial unions.

The revolutionary organization must help break down the false divisions between workers. With its paper and publications and through its militants the revolutionary organization should bring to people's notice the struggles that are taking place in society. It must truthfully report what these struggles are about and show how they affect the lives and interests of other workers.

Most people do not at present see the need for socialism. If by socialism is meant what currently passes as such - both East and West of the Iron Curtain - we can scarcely blame them. There is no doubt, however, that vast numbers of people are prepared to struggle on real issues, on issues that really concern them, and against the innumerable and monstrous social injustices and social frustrations of contemporary society. At an elementary level, they are prepared to fight against rent increases, against changes in piecework rates and against changes in job organization about which they have not even been consulted. At a higher level, they are prepared to campaign against the production of nuclear weapons. They are constantly challenging the various "solutions" to these problems, imposed upon them from above. How can this challenge be generalized? How can it be transformed into one directed against the very society which perpetuates the division of men into order-givers and order-takers?

The revolutionary organization must assist people engaged in a struggle against exploiting society to understand the need to act in an organized class way and not as isolated groups with limited or sectional objectives.

***

Is the socialist society a utopian dream? The answer depends on how one sees the development of socialist consciousness. The Bolsheviks - Stalinists and Trotskyists - both endorse Lenin's statement: "The history of all countries shows that the working class, exclusively by its own efforts, is able to develop only trade union consciousness."[53]

The adherents to this theory, quite logically, consider it the job of professional revolutionaries to *plan* the strategy, *organize* the taking of power and take all the decisions for the instituting of the "socialist" society. Lenin, the firmest advocate of this reformist and reactionary idea which was borrowed from Kautsky[54] went so far as to applaud the Webbs' ironical and scornful comments about the attempts of the British workers to manage their own trade unions.[55]

We completely reject this idea. First, because it attempts to impose upon workers a relationship to "their" leadership which is a replica of the relation already existing under capitalism. The effect would only be to create apathy and the alienation of the masses - conditions which powerfully assist the growth of decision-taking groups, which rapidly assume increasing managerial functions and which however "well-intentioned" originally, rapidly start settling matters in their own interests and become exploiting groups and bureaucracies.

We believe that people in struggle *do* draw conclusions which are fundamentally socialist in content. Industrial disputes, particularly in Britain, frequently take on the character of a challenge to managerial rights. Workers constantly dispute the bosses' right to hire and fire. Strikes regularly take place over employers' attempts to reorganize and "rationalize" production. In these workers counterpoise their own conceptions and ideas of how production should be organized to those of the employers. Such disputes not only undermine the whole authoritarian, hierarchical structure of capitalist relations, they also show quite clearly that people are repeatedly seeing the need to organize production - which is the basis of all social life - as *they* think best.

During the Hungarian Revolution of 1956 the Workers' Councils demanded drastic reductions in wage differentials, called for the abolition of piecework and introduced workers' management of industry. These organizations of political and

---

53   V.I. Lenin, *What Is To Be Done?* (London: Lawrence and Wishart, 1944), p.33.

54   In *Neue Zeit*, 1901–1902, XX, No.3, p.79, Kautsky wrote: "...socialist consciousness is represented as a necessary and direct result of the proletarian class struggle. This is absolutely untrue...Modern socialist consciousness can arise only on the basis of profound scientific knowledge...the vehicles of science are not the proletariat but the bourgeois intelligentsia..." Lenin, in *What Is To Be Done?* (p.40), quotes Kautsky in full and refers to his views as "profoundly true and important utterances".

55   Lenin wrote (*ibid.* p.125): "In Mr. and Mrs. Webb's book on trade unionism, there is an interesting chapter entitled 'Primitive Democracy'. In this chapter, the authors relate how, in the first period of existence of their unions, the British workers thought it was an indispensable sign of democracy for all the members to do all the work of managing the unions; not only were all questions decided by the votes of all the members but all the official duties were fulfilled by all the members in turn. A long period of historical experience was required to teach these workers how absurd such a conception of democracy was and to make them understand the necessity for representative institutions on the one hand, and *for full-time professional officials on the other*".

industrial rule - far more important than the Nagy government - were based on elected and immediately revocable delegates.

The Hungarian Revolution followed the tradition first established by the Commune of 1871. But the aims of the Hungarian workers went further than those of any previous revolution. In the anti-bureaucratic nature of their demands the Hungarian workers showed that they were fighting for something which will become the fundamental feature of all workers' struggles in this epoch. Such a programme is far more revolutionary and more profoundly socialist in character than anything advocated by any of today's so-called socialist parties.

The Social Democrats and Bolsheviks look either to war or economic misery as means of converting to socialism. It is primitive and insulting to believe that people are unable to oppose exploiting society unless their bellies are empty or their heads about to be blown off.

That this is untrue is shown by the innumerable disputes which take place in the motor industry. Car workers - despite their relatively high wages - fight back against employers' attempts to establish an ever more rigid control over workshop conditions. Often employers are prepared to pay more money if workers will give up their hard-won rights in the workshops. Workers often reject this bribery.

Capitalist and bureaucratic societies both seek to subordinate the great majority to the needs of their ruling groups. The rulers attempt to impress the stamp of obedience and conformity on to every aspect of social life. Initiative, intellectual independence, creativeness are crushed and despised. Unless man can develop to the full these - his most precious qualities - he lives but half a life. Men want to be something more than well-fed servants. The desire to be free is not a pious liberal phrase, but the most noble of man's desires. The pre-condition of this freedom is, of course, freedom in the field of production - workers' management. There can be no real freedom and no real future for humanity in an exploiting society. The path to freedom lies through the socialist revolution.

The resentment of people today against the stifling and degrading relations imposed upon them by class society provides the strongest driving force towards the socialist future.

3. How?

What type of organization is needed in the struggle for socialism? How can the fragmented struggles of isolated groups of workers, of tenants, of people opposed to nuclear war be co-ordinated? How can a mass socialist consciousness be developed?

In parts 1 and 2 we were quite emphatic about what we *didn't* want. We looked at all the traditional organizations and found both in their doctrine and in their structure mirror images of the very society they were allegedly fighting to overthrow. We would like now to develop some of our conceptions of what is needed.

Our suggestions are not blueprints. Nor are they intended as the ultimate and final word on the matter. The methods of struggle decided by the working class will to a large extent mould the revolutionary organization - that is, provided the organization sees itself as the instrument of these struggles and not as a self-appointed "leadership". "Elitist" conceptions lead to a self-imposed isolation. Future events may show us the need to modify or even radically alter many of our present conceptions. This does not worry us in the least. There is nothing more revolutionary than reality, nothing more reactionary than an erstwhile revolutionary idea promoted to the rank of absolute and permanent truth.

Exploiting society constantly seeks to coerce people into obeying its will. It denies them the right to manage their own lives, to decide their own destinies. It seeks to create obedient conformists. The real challenge of socialism is that it will give to men the right to be masters of their fate.

It seems quite obvious to us that the socialist organization must be *managed* by its members. Unless it can ensure that they work together in a spirit of free association and that their activity is genuinely collective it will be useless. It will appear to people as no different from any other organization or institution of capitalism, with its rigid division into order-givers and order-takers.

Without democracy the revolutionary organization will be unable to develop the required originality of thought and the vital initiative and determination to fight upon which its very existence depends. The Bolshevik method of self-appointed and self-perpetuating leaders, selected because of their ability to "interpret" the teachers' writings and "relate them to today's events" ensures that no one ever intrudes with an original idea. History becomes a series of interesting analogies. Thought becomes superfluous. All the revolutionaries need is a good memory and well-stocked library. No wonder the "revolutionary" left is today so sterile.

Struggle demands more than a knowledge of history. It demands of its participants an understanding of today's reality. During strikes, workers have to discuss in a free and uninhibited way how best to win. Unless this is made possible the ability and talent of the strikers is wasted. The loyalty and determination that strikers display – often referred to by the press as stubbornness or ignorance – derives from the knowledge that they have participated in the decisions. They have a feeling of identification with their strike and with its organization. This is in marked contrast to their general position in society where what they think and do is considered quite unimportant.

During strikes, representatives of the various political groups gain control of the Committee. Demands entirely unrelated to the dispute then make their appearance. The outcome is inevitable. A lack of interest, a diminution of activity, sometimes even a vote to return to work. The feeling of identification disappears and is replaced by a feeling of being used.

When the direct management of an organization by its members is replaced by an alien control from above, vitality is lost, the will to struggle lessens. Many will ask what do we mean by "direct management"? We mean that the organization should be based upon branches or groups, each of which has the fullest autonomy, to decide its own activities, that is in keeping with the general purpose of the organization. When possible decisions should be collective ones. Branches should elect *delegates* to any committees considered necessary for the day-to-day functioning of the organization. Such delegates are not elected for three years, for twelve months…or even twelve days. They are, *revocable, at any time* their fellow members consider it necessary. This is the only way that the membership can effectively ensure that their representatives carry out their jobs properly. We lay no claims to originality in proposing this. In every revolution, during most strikes and daily at the level of workshop organization the working class resorts to this type of direct democracy.

It is rather amusing to hear Bolsheviks argue that this may be all right for everybody else – but not for themselves. Apparently the same workers who are expected to have determination and consciousness sufficient to overthrow capitalism and to build a new society do not possess sufficient know-how to put the right man in the right place in their own organization.

The same arguments against direct democracy repeatedly raise their bald heads! We are reminded that you cannot have a mass meeting to discuss every single issue - true, but not very profound. Of course certain committees are needed. They must however be directly responsible to the membership, and their duties must be clearly defined. They must be charged with placing *all* the facts of any matter under discussion before all the members. The withholding of essential information from members is a powerful factor reinforcing the division between leaders and led. It lays the basis for bureaucracy within the organization. Genuine democracy does not only imply an equality of rights…it implies the fullest possible dissemination of information, allowing the rational use of those rights.

We reject the idea that matters of great importance require split second decisions by a central committee, with "years of experience" to its credit, meeting in a secret conclave. If the social conflict is so intense as to require drastic action, the need for such action will certainly have become apparent to many workers. The organization will at best be the expression of that collective will. A million correct decisions are quite useless unless they are *understood* and *accepted* by those involved. People cannot fight blindly in such situations, their unthinking actions projected by a group of revolutionary theoreticians - if they do the results are liable to be dangerous.

When important decisions have to be taken they must be placed before the members for approval or otherwise. Without this there can be no understanding of what is involved. And without understanding there can be no conviction, and no genuinely effective action. There will only be the usual frantic appeals to "discipline". And as Zinoviev once put it: "discipline begins where conviction ends".

Our critics will ask us about differences of opinion within the organization. Should not the majority decisions be binding on all? The alternative, we are informed, is ineffectiveness. Again there are precedents to which we may refer: the real experiences of workers in struggle. During strikes and even more so during revolutions, big issues are at stake. Fundamental decisions have to be taken. In these circumstances the members will automatically expect of each other full and active participation. Those who do not give it will cut themselves off from the movement, will have no desire to remain members. It is quite another matter, however, to insist on the absolute acceptance of a party line on matters not calling for immediate decision and action. Those who wish an organization to be run on these lines have clearly assigned to themselves a divine right of interpretation. Only they know what is "correct", what is "in the best interest of the movement".

This attitude is very widespread and is an important factor in the utter fragmentation of the revolutionary left today. Various sects, each claiming to be the elite, the one-and-only "genuine" Marxist group, fight furiously with one another, each quite certain that the fate of the working class, and of humanity at large, is tied up with "finding the correct solution" to each and every doctrinal squabble. Faction fights and the "elite" conception of the Party (the "brain" of the working class) are but different sides of the same coin. This conception profoundly underestimates the creative abilities of the working class. No wonder they reject this type of organization…and this type of politics.

What should the activity of the revolutionary organization be? Whilst rejecting the substitutionism of both reformism and Bolshevism, we also reject the essentially propagandist approach of organizations such as the Socialist Party of Great Britain. We consider it important to bring to workers information and reports of the struggles of other workers – both past and present – reports which emphasize the fact that workers *are* capable of struggling collectively and of rising to the greatest heights of revolutionary consciousness. The revolutionary press must help break down the conspiracy of silence about such struggles. It must bring to the working class the story of its own past and the details of its present struggles. But it must do more than merely disseminate information. When strikes occur, when tenants oppose rent increases, when thousands protest against the threat of nuclear war, we feel it our responsibility to provide the maximum support and assistance. The revolutionary organization or its members should actively participate in these movements, not with the idea of "gaining control" or "winning them over" to a particular line – but with the more honest objective of helping people in struggle to win.

This does not absolve conscious revolutionaries from arguing for their own ideas or from the need to try and convince people of the wider implications of their struggles. We do not "bow to spontaneity".[56] We believe we have something positive to say but also that we must earn our right to say it. The revolutionary organization must see its job as serving the working class, not leading it, helping co-ordinate its struggles, not imposing methods of struggle upon it, learning from the struggles that are taking place, not ramming *its* learning down the throat of others. It must realize that correct as its ideas may be, they are dependent on workers agreeing with them.

AGITATOR, I, 4 AND 5 (MARCH AND APRIL 1961); *SOLIDARITY*, I, 6 (MAY 1961)

---

56   Most discussions on this theme are quite meaningless. All mass struggles have both immediate and remote causes and all are influenced to a greater or less degree by the experiences of previous struggles.

4. THE COMMUNE, PARIS 1871 (*JOINTLY WITH PHILIPPE GUILLAUME*)

The Commune…from Marx to Trotsky

"Each time we study the history of the Commune we see something new in it, thanks to the experiences gained in later revolutionary struggles…" Thus wrote Trotsky in 1921, in his preface to a book by Talès[57] which was to become basic reading for a whole generation of French revolutionaries.

The "tricks of History", as Marx delighted to call them, *have* amply confirmed the correctness of Trotsky's statement. We can now examine the Paris Commune in a new light - in the light precisely of the rich experience of Bolshevism and of Trotskyism. We mean, more specifically, in the light of their failure. Stated more concretely, the proletarian revolution of 1871 must now be re-evaluated in the light of the degeneration of the Russian Revolution and of the positive lessons of the revolutionary struggle of the Hungarian Workers' Councils in 1956 against bureaucratic society in which the means of production were completely "nationalized".

Trotsky could hardly have forseen these developments when he wrote his prophetic words in the heroic days of 1921. This however in no way detracts from their absolute correctness.

For Trotsky and Talès the great defect of the Commune was the absence of a revolutionary leadership. "The Commune", Trotsky emphasized, shows us "the incapacity of the masses to choose their own path, their indecision in the leadership of the movement, their fatal inclination to stop after the first successess…" How can this be overcome? Trotsky is quite explicit: "It is only through the help of the Party, basing itself on the whole history of the past, theoretically forseeing the paths of development and all its stages, and extracting from them the necessary formulas for action, that the proletariat frees itself from the need constantly to restart its own history…" He summarizes his views with his usual logic: "We can look, page by page, through the history of the Commune. We will find in it *only a single lesson*: there must be a strong Party leadership" (our emphasis).

The present generation of revolutionaries have lived through or studied the history of the last forty years, and have experienced all the ills that have flown from the hypertrophy and subsequent degeneration of such a "leadership"- even when it has proved victorious in its struggle against the bourgeoisie. They have witnessed its gradual separation from the masses and its steady conversion into a ruling group, as fundamentally opposed to the basic wishes of the masses themselves to administer society as any previous ruling group in history. For revolutionaries in 1961 the Paris Commune of 1871 should be seen as an historical precursor of the essentially anti-bureaucratic mass movement that swept through Hungary in 1956. The measures taken by the Communards to prevent the emergence of a bureaucracy from within their own ranks were to be taken up again by the Budapest workers in 1956. Both revolutions posed the question of who was in reality to manage both production and society in no uncertain terms.

---

57   C. Talès, *La Commune de 1871* (Paris: Librairie du Travail, 1924).

It is interesting to contrast the Bolshevik appreciation of the Commune with that of the Commune's great contemporaries, Marx and Engels. In his *Civil War in France*, written as the last Communards were being slaughtered by the forces of the victorious Versaillese, Marx does not once attribute the defeat to the absence of a "strong Party leadership". He is vastly impressed by its great positive achievements. He describes the Commune as "essentially a working class government, the produce of the struggle of the producing against the appropriating class, the political form, at last discovered, under which to work out the economic emancipation of Labour". He does not say that it was the Party who discovered this particular form, a form which neither he nor any other member of the First International had either forseen or prepared for. The masses in struggle *themselves* created this form of organization, just as in 1905 they were themselves to create the Soviets, at first denounced by the Bolsheviks as "sectarian organizations". There is no question of the Party, or anyone else for that matter, "theoretically foreseeing the paths of development and all its stages…" Twenty years later, in 1891, Engels was to write, "what is still more wonderful is the correctness of much that was done by the Commune, composed as it was of Blanquists and Proudhonists".[58] In other words the everyday experience of the masses impelled them to take measures of a class character. They generated their own socialist consciousness, assisted but not dictated to by conscious revolutionaries of various kinds.

The Commune was militarily crushed, having held power for just over two months. Its defeat was an extremely bloody one. It is scarcely surprising that Trotsky, president in October 1917 of the Revolutionary War Committee in Petrograd, brilliant military strategist and creator of the Red Army, should have been exasperated by the Commune's lack of military success, by its vacillations, by the "inefficiency" of a number of its leaders and by its total lack of a clearly thought-out military policy, when confronted by a cynical bourgeoisie prepared ruthlessly to destroy it and "to restore order for a generation".

What is less permissible however is that the same Trotsky should have lent military authority to Talès's effort systematically to denigrate the most creative and positive aspects of the Paris Commune. But the real culprit here is not even Talès. It is Bolshevism and Trotskyism themselves. If, as they tell us, "the crisis of society is the crisis of the revolutionary leadership", it is easy to equate the history of the Commune with the history of its leadership. From this postulate everything flows quite logically…and in particular the defeat of the Commune! Or so they would have us believe!

History, on this basis, becomes an easy subject. The social composition and the prevailing ideologies of the Central Committee of the National Guard[59] and of the Commune itself were extremely diverse. The predominating influence was that of the radical, patriotic, anti-clerical petty-bourgeoisie. The members of the First International lacked ideological clarity. The Blanquists, the most determined revolutionaries and the ones most prepared to struggle, lacked any positive social conceptions. To these facts should be added the backward structure of the Parisian proletariat of the time. Industrial concentration, which had been achieved many years previously in the textile mills of Manchester and which was to be achieved some

---

58   Introduction to K. Marx's *Civil War in France* (Marx-Engels Selected Works, vol. I, (Moscow, 1958), p.481).

59   A soldiers' council of elected and revocable representatives which took over the defence of Paris, first against the armies of Bismarck, then against those of Thiers, the most class conscious leader the French bourgeoisie has produced for generations.

decades later by the Russian proletariat in the great Putilov works in Petrograd, was only just beginning in Paris.[60]

But such an emphasis on the leadership of the Commune immediately leads to an insoluble contradiction. If history is an account of the achievements or short-comings of revolutionary leaderships, how can we explain that the Commune, with its petty-bourgeois leadership, was capable of introducing to the modern world the most advanced conceptions of proletarian democracy? Why did Marx refer to it as "the glorious harbinger of a new society"? Why did Engels state that the measures taken by the Communards would, in the last resort, have led "to the abolition of class antagonism between capitalists and workers"? Why did he taunt the Social-Democratic philistines with his famous "Look at the Paris Commune. That was the Dictatorship of the Proletariat!"

The Commune introduced the eligibility and revocability of all officials and the payment to them of working men's salaries. These are profoundly revolutionary measures. Their application will inevitably undermine and destroy any bourgeois (or bureaucratic) state machine. These demands introduce complete popular domina-tion of the civil administration, of the army and of the judiciary. They lead to the cre-ation, from below, of a completely new kind of social organization. The October Revolution, in its early days, sought to implement these demands. The developing Stalinist bureaucracy sought ruthlessly to destroy them. Nearly a century after they were first put forward by the Communards, they still form the basis of all genuinely revolutionary struggles.

Marx stated that the Communards had "stormed heaven". Talès explains that the story of the Commune is the story of the failure of a radical-anarchist-petty-bourgeois leadership! His "explanation" is also peddled today by the crudest of Stalinists. This is no accident. In March 1961, during the ninetieth anniversary cele-brations in Paris, Garaudy, Stalinist senator for the Seine department and university pen-pusher in the cause of Stalinism (completely unknown in England…and rightly so), declared: "The great lesson of the Commune is that the working class can only overcome its enemies under the leadership of a revolutionary party. It is essential to grasp this fundamental precondition of revolutionary victories at a time when some people under the pretext of a creative development of Marxism-Leninism are lead-ing us back to the worst illusions of pre-Marxist socialism, to petty bourgeois anar-chism, to Proudhonism, or to Blanquist adventurism…" Sundry Trotskyists and non-Trotskyist Leninists would agree with every word of this.[61] In so doing they reveal themselves worthy successors of those Marx castigated as "mere bawlers, who by dint of repeating year after year the same set of stereotyped declamations…have sneaked into the reputation of revolutionists of the first water".

How did it come about, we would ask these gentlemen (or at least those of them who refuse to accept that Russia is not in any sense a socialist society) that in

---

60   "In 1886, at the apogee of Parisian expansion in this period, the total population was 1,825,274. There were 570, 280 workshops (as against 64,816 in 1847 and 101,171 in 1860), owned by 65,987 masters, employing only 442,310 workers (besides 34,846 clerks and 23,251 servants). This meant that the average number of workers per shop was only 7.7 sinking from 13 in the building and metal trades to 1.4 in the food industry. By far the largest numbers were employed in the garment industry: 306,567 (208,675 women); building, owing to Baron Haussmann's reconstruction of the capital, employed most men, 125,371 (63,675 women); and the various luxury industries, upon which the repute and prosperity of Paris mainly depended, employed 63,617 workers. In all, workers (468,337) and their dependents (286,670) made up about 40 per cent of the population of Paris" (F. Jellinek, The Paris Commune of 1871 (London: Gollancz, 1937).

61   See, for instance, any article, in any issue of the Workers' News Bulletin, any week, in the last ten years.

the twentieth Century *all* revolutionary movements, despite their repeated victories over and expropriations of the bourgeoisie, and despite the drastic changes they have introduced in the *property relations,* have failed to bring about socialism, that is a fundamental change in the *relations of production,* in the relation of man to man in his labour and in his social life?

To answer this question one needs a very different conception of history than that of Talès or of the Bolsheviks. A serious study of the Commune, which we cannot here undertake in full, will suggest some of the answers. The real history of the Commune is the history of the masses themselves, struggling for fundamentally different conditions of existence, and not primarily the history of leadership. Seen in this light the history of the Commune has still to be written.

The Commune: A creation of the people.

The workers, artisans and ordinary people of the period did not conceive of social life, least of all their own, in terms of universal concepts, but in terms of action. Nine workers out of ten still do so today. Action is their language. It is in fact the only language of which they have acquired complete mastery. For intellectuals words are often a substitute for action. For workers, actions are a form of speech. To add to revolutionary theory in the course of revolutionary action is the essential task of the revolutionary proletariat.[62] This was the immortal contribution to revolutionary theory of the Parisian workers in 1871 and of their successors, the Hungarian workers of 1956. Such was the language of the Commune, which socialists must now attempt to decipher.

The decisive date in the history of the Commune is March 18, 1871. Thiers sees the armed workers of Paris as his main obstacle to the conclusion of a peace treaty with Bismarck, and as a potential danger for the whole of bourgeois France. He decides to send "loyal" battalions to remove the cannons held by the National Guard at Montmartre, Buttes Chaumont and Belleville, cannons bought by public subscription during the siege. The operation starts successfully in the early hours of the morning. After a little firing the guns at Montmartre are captured. But time passes. The operation has been bureaucratically and inefficiently planned. The necessary gun-carriages don't arrive to remove the captured guns. The crowd begins to grow. Women, children, old people mingle with the troops. The National Guard, hastily summoned, arrives. An extraordinary confusion reigns. Some soldiers of the 88th Regiment start talking to the Guard. When General Lecomte, losing his head, orders his troops to open fire, it is already too late. The soldiers refuse to fire, turn their rifle butts up, join with the people. The language of acts has been heard. Soldiers and civilians have fraternized.

But acts have a logic of their own. The soldiers have compromised themselves. They take General Lecomte as a hostage. A little late General Thomas, "the butcher of 1848", is spotted in the crowd. Tempers mount. Both generals are shot by their own soldiers.[63]

---

62   The idea that revolutionary theory is something static, enshrined once and for all in the writings of the four great teachers, something to be derived from the study of books, and the idea that socialist consciouness has to be brought to the proletariat "from outside" (Lenin) by the bourgeois intelligentsia, which is "the vehicle of science" (Kautsky), are both profoundly reactionary and profoundly anti-dialectical, in the deepest sense of the term.

63   As Marx so clearly put it: "the inveterate habits acquired by the soldiery under the training of the enemies of the working class, are not of course likely to change, the very moment these soldiers change sides".

Thiers orders the withdrawal from the town of the standing Army. There is a precipitous retreat, in complete confusion, to Versailles. The major part of the civilian administration, government officials, senior officials in charge of food supplies, of the post, of lighting, of sewerage, of public assistance, of public health and of the thousand and one other aspects of life in a big city, leave Paris precipitously in the course of the next few days. An enormous social vacuum is created. Everything has to be created anew, from next to nothing, from below. And a war has to be fought at the same time.

We must dispose of the myth, which has gained much credence in Bolshevik circles, that alone a revolutionary Party would have had the "correct answers" at such a moment. "If there had been in Paris a Party leadership", Trotsky wrote, "it would have incorporated in the retreating armies...a hundred or a few dozen devoted workers giving them the following directives: work up the discontent of the soldiers against their officers and take advantage of the first psychologically favourable moment to break the soldiers from their officers and bring them back to Paris to unite with the people".

Trotsky speaks here with the wisdom of hindsight and somewhat distorts the real facts. Talès himself tells us that "March 18...started by the collective and anonymous action of the masses and ended in acts of individual initiative, isolated militants rallying the support of (local) committees of the National Guard". On March 19 leading Blanquists such as Eudes and Duval "proposed an immediate march on Versailles" but their proposals "encountered no echo on the Central Committee". A far-sighted minority *had* a fairly clear idea of what was required. That the majority were not at that stage prepared to follow their advice was a regrettable fact, but was also an objective element in the real situation. To argue that "if there had been a revolutionary Party, this or that would have followed" is like arguing that "if my aunt had...she would be my uncle".

What of the creative activity of the Commune? What were its prevailing moods and the level of consciousness of it participants? These are clearly enumerated in Engeis's 1891 introduction to Marx's *Civil War in France*. We don't apologize for reproducing the relevant passage, in full:

> On March 30 the Commune abolished conscription and the standing army, and declared the sole armed force to be the National Guard, in which all citizens capable of bearing arms were to be enrolled. It remitted all payments of rent for dwelling houses from October 1870 until April, the amounts already paid to be booked as future rent payments, and stopped all sales of articles pledged in the municipal loan office. On the same day the foreigners elected to the Commune were confirmed in office, because "the flag of the Commune is the flag of the World Republic". On April 1 it was decided that the highest salary to be received by any employee of the Commune, and therefore also by its members themselves, was not be exceed 6,000 francs... On the following day the Commune decreed the separation of the church from the state, and the abolition of all state payments for religious purposes as well as the transformation of all church property into national property; as a result of which, on April 8, the exclusion from the schools of all religious symbols, pictures, dogmas, prayers – in a word, "of all that belongs to the sphere of the individual's conscience" – was ordered and gradually put into effect. On the 5th, in reply to the shooting, day after day, of captured Commune fighters by the Versailles troops, a decree was issued for the imprisonment of hostages, but it was never carried into execution. On the 6th, the guil-

lotine was brought out by the 137th battalion of the National Guard, and publicly burnt, amid great popular rejoicing. On the 12th, the Commune decided that the Viceroy Column on the Place Vendôme, which had been cast from captured guns by Napoleon after the war of 1809, should be demolished as a symbol of chauvinism and incitement to national hatred. This was carried out on May 16. On April 16 it ordered a statistical tabulation of factories which had been closed down by the manufacturers, and the working out of plans for the operation of these factories by the workers formerly employed in them, who were to be organized in co-operative societies, and also plans for the organization of these co-operatives in one great union. On the 20th it abolished night work for bakers, and also the employment offices, which since the Second Empire had been run as a monopoly by creatures appointed by the police - labour exploiters of the first rank; these offices were transferred to the mayoralties of the twenty *arrondissements* of Paris. On April 30 it ordered the closing of the pawnshops, on the ground that they were a private exploitation of the workers, and were in contradiction with the right of the workers to their instruments of labour and to credit. On May 5 it ordered the razing of the Chapel of Atonement, which had been built in expiation of the execution of Louis XVI.

Thus from March 18 onwards the class character of the Paris movement, which had previously been pushed into the background by the fight against the foreign invaders, emerged sharply and clearly. As almost only workers, or recognized representatives of the workers, sat in the Commune, its decisions bore a decidedly proletarian character.

The Commune was born of the exasperation provoked by the prolonged siege of Paris and of the disgust engendered by its capitulation without a fight. Nationalist or even chauvinist feeling might have been strong in the Paris of 1871. Yet the Commune "admitted all foreigners to the honour of dying for an immortal cause" and made a German working man, Leo Frankel, its Minister of Labour. It "honoured the heroic sons of Poland[64] by placing them at the head of the defenders of Paris" (Marx).

Much has been made by the advocates of the "hegemony of the Party" of the fact that few, if any, of the social measures taken by the Commune were *consciously socialist* ones. To accept that they were would of course deny the exclusive function of the Party, that of bringing "socialist consciousness" to the working class. What did the Communards think of their own activities? The very first proclamation of the Central Committee of the National Guard, on March 18, said: "The proletarians of Paris, amidst the failures and treasons of the ruling class, have understood that the hour has struck for them to save the situation, *by taking into their own hands* the direction of public affairs…they have understood that it is their imperious duty and their absolute right *to render themselves masters of their own destinies*, by seizing upon the governmental power". We would suggest that this reveals an extremely high degree of political consciousness, a degree which was to be achieved again by the Hungarian workers of 1956. One of the essential reasons of the degeneration of the Russian revolution was that the Russian masses were unable to sustain this degree of revolutionary consciousness for more than a few months. Under the mistaken idea that they could "leave it to the Party" which they themselves had created out of their flesh and blood, they retreated from the historical arena. The bureaucratic degeneration set in, with the Party as its nucleus.

---

64   Dombrowski and Wroblewski.

Marx himself was aware of the importance of self-conscious activity. He refers to "the new era of history" which the Commune "was conscious of initiating". The great positive achievements of the Commune were no isolated or artificial gestures, but were measures reflecting the popular will and determined by it. Talès, our "Bolshevik" historian, makes fun of the love of the masses, at the time, for what he calls "symbolic acts". To illustrate his point he quotes the destruction of the monuments. This is because he has never understood this language of acts, through which ordinary people express themselves. When it pulled down the Vendôme column, which Marx referred to as a "colossal symbol of martial glory", the crowd was expressing in actions the very notion which completes internationalism, namely anti-militarism.

The Meaning of the Commune

Almost every measure taken by the Commune can be explained through an understanding of the deepest daily experiences of the masses. Such was the decree limiting to 6,000 francs a year the top salary paid to any member of the revolutionary government (incidentally, such a salary was in practice never received by anyone). Such also was the decree stipulating that workshops abandoned by the employers should be taken over by the working class organizations and run by them, for the workers themselves.

These two measures were among the most characteristic taken by the Commune. Bolsheviks have argued interminably on the compensation clause. Today we realize how academic such a discussion really is. What the workers felt at the time was the importance of themselves *managing* production and distribution. As long as *they* managed what mattered indemnity to the previous owners, an indemnity whose effects would be restricted in time anyway? Ninety years later the Chinese bureacracy was to discover all this anew...and in its own interests. Having bureaucratically ensured to itself the effective management of industry, it allowed itself the luxury of compensating – and even at times even of employing – the previous owners as salaried executives!

Marx was quite conscious of these deep-going aspects of the Commune. "When the Paris Commune took the *management* of the revolution in its own hands", he wrote, "when plain working men for the first time dared to infringe upon the governmental privilege of their 'natural superiors' and under circumstances of unexampled difficulty performed their work modestly, conscientiously and efficiently...the old world writhed in convulsions of rage at the sight of the Red Flag, the symbol of the Republic of Labour, floating over the Hôtel de Ville". The distance separating *this* evaluation of the role of the Commune and that of Trotsky who saw the "only lesson" of the Commune to be the need for " a strong Party leadership" could hardly be greater!

As for the strivings of the Commune towards an equalization of wages, and its demands for the eligibility and revocability of all representatives, they reflect a fundamental preoccupation with the question of destroying *at its very roots* the hierarchical organization of society.

Since then much has been written and said about "soviets" and about "workers' councils". But it would seem that the real nature of these new forms of social life has been forgotten by those who stand in admiration before their bureaucratic caricatures. Discussing the Commune, Marx wrote:

Instead of deciding once in three or six years which member of the ruling class was to misrepresent the people in Parliament, universal suffrage was to serve the people, constituted in Communes, as individual suffrage serves every other employer in the search for workmen and managers in his business. And it is well known that companies, like individuals, in matters of real business generally know how to put the right man in the right place, and, if they for once make a mistake, to redress it promptly... Nothing could be more foreign to the spirit of the Commune than to supersede universal suffrage by hierarchic investiture.

"Hierarchic investiture"! Here is the hub of the whole problem. How is the hierarchical structure of society to be destroyed and superseded? The Commune showed in its *acts* how this was to be done. At *all* levels, *all* officials and functionaries were to be elected. And *all* were to be removable by those who elected them!

Direct election and permanent revocability are clearly not panaceas for the solution of all problems. But in themselves they carry the seed of the most profound transformation of society. An officer or a magistrate whom one elects and whom one controls *at all times* is already no longer fully an officer or a magistrate. This is the yardstick by which one can begin to measure the "withering away of the state". The real content of this withering away is precisely the progressive elimination of hierarchical investiture and of hierarchical institutions.

Engels was quite emphatic on this question. Again referring to the Commune he stated "the working class must...safeguard itself against its own deputies and officials, by declaring them *all, without exception*, subject to recall at any moment" (our emphasis).

There has been much misunderstanding about the significance of the "communal" regime, some of it patently dishonest. Thus Trotsky, correctly criticizing some of the leaders of the Commune, could give vent to his sarcasm: "Paris, you see, is but one commune among many others. Paris does not wish to impose anything on anyone. Paris does not struggle for a dictatorship other than 'the dictatorship of example'". But he continues quite wrongly: "The Commune was but an attempt to replace the developing proletarian revolution by a petty-bourgeois reform: communal autonomy. This idealist chatter, of the type indulged in by parlour anarchists, was in reality a cover for cowardice when confronted with revolutionary action, which needed to be carried out ceaselessly and to the end..."[65] Marx had seen deeper than this. He pointed out that the Commune had (already in May 1871!) been subjected to a "multiplicity of interpretations" but that its essential features were that it was "a working class government" and "a thoroughly expansive political form, while all previous forms of government had been emphatically repressive".

The most significant aspect, however, of the Paris Commune is that it created social forms which in a sense define socialism itself, social forms which serve as yardsticks for proletarian revolutions passed, present and to come. These forms provide criteria for analyzing the social nature of any particular regime. Nearly a century later, societies can still be looked at according to categories established by the Paris Commune. And it is most revealing how clearly things fall into proper perspective when one confronts the Russian or Chinese realities of today with the first, short, hesitant experience in 1871 of a genuinely proletarian revolution and of genuine working class power.

---

65   Introduction to Talès's *La Commune de 1871*.

Paris 1871–Hungary 1956

The Hungarian Revolution of 1956 is seen in a completely new light when looked at with the proletarian experience of 1871 in mind.

There are both superficial and deep analogies. The central facts of the Hungarian Revolution were firstly the active participation of the masses and secondly the anti-bureaucratic and anti-hierarchical character of the most spontaneous and deepest-going demands of the working class, demands which emerged more and more clearly as the Workers' Councils became the sole revolutionary force, in the later stages of the struggle.

In the first stages of both revolutions one sees the civilian crowds, women, children, old people, massively erupt on to the scene. Their total participation paralyzes for a while the intervention of the enemy. In both revolutions temporary conditions exist for genuine fraternization.

The Hungarian workers in 1956 immediately put forward demands for workers' management of the factory, for a drastic reduction in the wage differential and for the abolition of piece-rates. Like the Parisians they get straight down to essentials. Managers are elected and submitted to continuous, direct control. It matters less, in this respect, that a number of the previous managers were re-elected. What is essential is the radical transformation of all existing relations between men.

On a more tragic plane, in their fate each revolution resembles one another. In both cases it is a desperate, bitter struggle, fought out street by street, to the last drop of blood, without compromise, without submission, as only men can fight who know what they are fighting for and who have themselves determined the objectives of their struggle. Despite military defeat, which the revolutionaries in both circumstances came to see as more or less inevitable, it was a timeless ideal they fought for, an ideal to be defended unconditionally, in a fight in which inevitable death was almost welcomed as a release.

In both revolutions the threatened classes resorted to bloody repression. This was done with the calculated ferocity which ruling classes only resort to when their most fundamental prerogative is threatened, namely their right to rule. The iron fist then emerges from the velvet glove. Class society reveals itself in its true colours - as the perpetual, systematized, organization of violence by the minority against the immense majority. That Thiers was "more liberal" than Napoleon III is about as relevant in this respect as the fact that Khrushchev was "more liberal" than Stalin.

During both civil wars moreover, bystanders stood cynically on the side lines (Bismarck and Eisenhower) protesting at the use of so much violence, and forgetting that this class violence was but an image of their own.

The tragic defeat of the Hungarian Revolution, like the tragic defeat of the Commune, both call for reflection. Their lessons are innumerable. The need for an efficient co-ordination and for an organization capable of ensuring it should be obvious to all. But what kind of organization? How is it to be evolved? What are its relationships to the masses? *This* is the whole question. When we speak of organization we mean an organization evolved through struggle by the communes, by the soviets, by the workers' councils themselves.

In his preface to the book by Talès, mentioned at the beginning, Trotsky wrote:

> Before the broad masses of the soldiers can acquire the experience of well choosing and selecting commanders, the revolution will be beaten by the enemy, who is guided in the choice of his commanders by the experience of centuries. The

methods of amorphous democracy (*simple eligibility*) *must be supplemented and to a certain degree replaced by measures of selection from above*. The revolution must create an organ composed of experienced, reliable organizers in which one[66] can have absolute confidence, and give it full powers to choose, designate and educate the command.

In this last quotation from Trotsky two little words epitomize, in a way, the whole subsequent degeneration of the great proletarian revolution of 1917: the words "from above". No one denies the need for selection, particularly in so crucial a field as the field of armed struggle, to which the whole fate of the revolution is tied. Obviously the command must be selected. Training, aptitudes, experiences vary enormously. The proletarian heritage is heterogeneous in the extreme. But it is a question of selection *from below*.

Selection from above has a remarkable tendency to transform itself from the exception to the rule. It is carried over, by its own momentum, from wartime into peace time. It spreads from the regiment into the factory. From the barracks it invades the factories involved in war work and the workers' councils themselves. From the military "High Command" it takes a brisk step into the "High Command" of the Party. It becomes systematized. It becomes the "hierarchic investiture" of which Marx spoke and which is one of the essential features of all class society. And as the principle proceeds on its way the masses soon retreat from the historical arena, leaving it to others who "are more efficient", who "know better" to act "on their behalf". The degeneration has begun. The seeds of the Stalinist regime are sown: the co-option of bureaucracy by the bureaucracy itself. Engels was almost prophetic in his foresight when he insisted that "*all* officials, *without exception*, must be subject to recall *at any moment*".

A new generation of young revolutionaries must now seriously turn the lessons of the Paris Commune and the lessons of the great contemporary analogue, the Hungarian Revolution of 1956. Scattered, misinterpreted, deliberately misused for ends that are not the ends of the Revolution, the basic documents of both are to be found[67] by those wishing to find them. They should be studied. Both revolutions are of fundamental importance to the socialist movement, and to an understanding of the class struggle in our epoch.

SOLIDARITY, I, 6 (MAY 1961)

---

66   Who is this anonymous and mysterious "one"? Who is to bestow "absolute confidence" in the revolutionary organ and the revolutionary organizers? Is it the masses? Is it the Party "acting in the interests of the masses"? Is it the Party leaders "acting in the interests of the Party" as a whole? Is Trotsky's ambiguity on this point entirely accidental?

67   See R.W. Postgate, *Revolution from 1789–1906* (London: Grant Richards, 1920) and *Socialisme ou Barbarie*, Vol. IV, Nos. 20 and 21.

5. INTRODUCTION TO PAUL CARDAN, *THE MEANING OF SOCIALISM*

The following text originally appeared - in a somewhat different form - in the Spring 1961 issue of *International Socialism*. It was written by Paul Cardan, one of the editors of the French magazine *Socialisme ou Barbarie*.

A fundamental restatement on the objectives of the socialist movement is, we believe, imperative. The "left" today is not noted for the originality of its thought, the intelligibility of its message or for its mass appeal. Its main features are in fact its conservatism, its antiquated, almost ritualistic jargon and its utter isolation. Its adherents "whistle in the dark". Followers are consoled with assurances that the stagnant years are only temporary. The capitalist crisis will sooner or later descend upon us. The day of the sects will then arrive.

Meanwhile influence wanes. Circulation of papers and magazines dwindles. The jargon becomes more rarefied, more obscure and more irrelevant. Few have the temerity to challenge the hallowed concepts. Those who do are quickly excluded as pariahs or "agents of the counter-revolution". Or they are accused of "throwing the baby away with the bath water". But what is it really that is going down the drain? Is it a viable infant or is it some putrefying abortion that has been poisoning the water for several decades?

Forty-four years after the Russian Revolution and sixteen years after World War II, the infallible dogmas of yesterday still serve as good coin. The fact that people display an ever-increasing indifference is scarcely noticed by the self-appointed repositories of "revolutionary" rust.

The decay of the "Marxist" left is due, we believe, to its refusal to recognize the new reality. We are reminded of some of the leaders of the Paris Commune of 1871, who tragically attempted to garb that essentially proletarian movement in the phrases of the petty-bourgeois radicals of 1793.

The crises and contradictions of exploiting society have not lessened. They express themselves however in forms that differ from those accepted in the "classical" left. The standard of living of the working class has not worsened under capitalism. In this respect, John Strachey is right and the "orthodox" Marxists wrong. But other, more important changes have taken place. Proletarianization has proceeded relentlessly. Thousands of jobs and professions formerly requiring skill and training and offering their occupants status and satisfaction have today been stripped of their specialized nature. Not only have they been reduced to the tedium and monotonous grind of any factory job, but their operatives have been degraded to simple executors of orders, as alienated in their work as any bench hand. Marxists would be better employed analyzing the implications of this important change in the social structure rather than waving their antiquated economic slide-rules at Strachey.

Both the ruling and the working classes have amassed a whole new historical experience. It is ludicrous to assume that only the proletariat is capable of learning. The wholesale nationalization of the means of production in Russia and increasing State intervention in economic affairs in the West have shown that the abolition of private ownership and state planning do not of themselves lessen exploitation or bring socialism any nearer. Such measures may in fact strengthen the grip of the rulers and save their economies from the recurrent slumps which were once such a common feature of capitalism. They are accepted by "progressive" capitalism and bureaucracy alike. All this necessitates a complete change in emphasis in socialist propaganda. Precisely what we mean is well illustrated in Cardan's article.

A number of urgent questions confront us. What is the nature of exploitation in the contemporary world? How do people struggle against it? How do they show *their* alternative to the present society? How will people build the new one?

Cardan's article does not provide all the answers to these questions. No blueprint ever will, of course. But it boldly sweeps aside the accumulated theoretical cobwebs of a generation. It attempts to discuss real problems and avoids the fruitless and endless arguments about interpretations of socialist Holy Writ. In our opinion, this is reason enough why it should be widely read.

SOLIDARITY PAMPHLET 6 (SEPTEMBER 1961)

6. PREFACE TO PAUL CARDAN, *THE MEANING OF SOCIALISM*

In September 1961 *Solidarity* first published this text in pamphlet form. Several hundred copies were sold within a few weeks. In the course of the last four years we have had to reprint on four occasions and the total number of copies "out" is now nearly 2,000. The sustained interest in and demand for this pamphlet has encouraged us to reprint yet again, this time on a much larger scale.

The slow disintegration of traditional socialist ideology has produced an enormous theoretical vacuum. The ideas outlined in this pamphlet are a contribution, however small, to filling this void.

The return of a Labour Government, now seeking "efficiently" to administer capitalist society (in the interest of those who own the means of production and manage the productive machine), the collapse of the Young Socialists movement (the best illustration to date of the "participation-exclusion" dilemma confronting the bureaucratic organizations in their relations with "their" members), the increasing campaign (jointly waged by management and the trade union bureaucracies) against "unofficial" action in industry, the 'betrayal' of layer after layer of reformist, Stalinist, or Trotskyist supported "leaders", all highlight the need for a basic restatement of socialist objectives and for a rethinking of socialist strategy and methods of action.

The pamphlet is not a blueprint for a socialist society. The content and form of such a society will be determined by the masses themselves - in struggle - and not through theoretical speculation by even the most "revolutionary" of revolutionary theoreticians. We hope however that the pamphlet will play its part in the development of the consciousness necessary for this gigantic task of social transformation.

The pamphlet is aimed primarily at those breaking with the organizations of the "traditional" left. We think it will provide them with a whole new system of ideas with which to analyze, comprehend and challenge the all-pervasive bureaucratic society around them. It argues in terms with which they will be familiar. It will, we hope, assist them to purge themselves of the hangover of "traditional" ideas and concepts which are almost inevitably carried over, following a sudden organizational break with a traditional organization (whether reformist or Bolshevik).

We are confident that these ideas, denounced as "premature", "utopian" and "sectarian" when they were first published, will continue to make headway in the months and years to come. The fact that they correspond to today's reality - and that they are seen to correspond to it - is the best guarantee of their ultimate success.

SOLIDARITY PAMPHLET 6, 2ND EDITION (NOVEMBER 1965)

7. INTRODUCTION TO PAUL CARDAN, *MODERN CAPITALISM AND REVOLUTION*

This small book is an attempt to describe the main features and to analyze the dynamic of modern, fully industrialized, capitalist societies from a revolutionary socialist point of view. It attempts, for the world of 1965, what Marx attempted a hundred years ago, in relation to the world around him.

What are the dominant features of modern societies? In what respect do they resemble and in what respect do they differ from the capitalist societies of the nineteenth century? How have they altered over the last few decades, not only in their economic structure, but in the content of their ideologies and in the function of their institutions? What are the attitudes within them of both rulers and ruled and what has moulded these attitudes? In what respect do these societies differ from the mental image most revolutionaries still have of them? What ensures their apparent cohesion? And what are the sources of their crises? Does their development, finally, still create the conditions of a socialist revolution?

Many of the ideas discussed will be new to those nurtured, ideologically, in the traditional left (whether "Marxist" or "anarchist"). The main text has therefore been prefaced with a short synopsis of the argument as a whole, which is then amplified in the following chapters.

The first few chapters define the areas to be discussed. Starting from the phenomenon of political apathy (bemoaned and misunderstood by professional politicians, trade union officials, entrist Trots and the anti-bomb movement alike), Cardan seeks to document the profound changes in economic framework and prevailing ideology, brought about by the last hundred years of continuous working class struggle. The analysis is extrapolated, as the author seeks to outline the economic and political relationships which would pertain in a society of total bureaucratic capitalism.

But these early chapters go even further. They seek to clear the ideological decks, to break decisively with a method of thinking that has wrought havoc in the ranks of the "left". Taking Marx's profoundly true statement that "the dominant ideas of each epoch are the ideas of its ruling class", Cardan seeks to apply this concept to Marxism itself. Marxism was not born and did not develop in a political vacuum, but in the capitalist society of the nineteenth century. Cardan attempts to discover what it was in traditional revolutionary theory which led (and still leads) successive generations of revolutionaries to make such absurdly false prognoses and to equate the essence of capitalism with the features of a society that capitalism had not yet sufficiently permeated and controlled. He tries to unearth the "unmarxist" in Marx, the bourgeois kernel that has corrupted the revolutionary fruit. And whether one agrees or not with this analysis, one must concede that it is at least a serious attempt – the only serious attempt we know of – to grapple with this major theoretical problem, which most contemporary "Marxists" are either blissfully unaware of or prefer to ignore.

The next few chapters define, describe and analyze the bureaucratic phenomenon. They show how, starting in the process of production, bureaucratization (the organization and control of activity *from the outside*) gradually invades all aspects of social life, destroying the meaning of work, creating mass irresponsibility, corroding the content of politics, disrupting the channels of communication (not only between rulers and ruled, but within the ranks of both rulers and professional revolutionaries), corrupting all traditional values (including the revolutionary ones), and rendering the rational management of modern industrial societies by bureaucratic "elites" increasingly difficult.

The book then examines the crises of bureaucratic society and discusses why the bureaucratic project is likely to fail. The bureaucratization of society is seen as preparing the ground for a libertarian resurgence, deeper in socialist content and closer to fundamental human aspirations than any previous revolution in history. And because action is what distinguishes the conscious revolutionary from the philosopher or sociologist, the text concludes by defining some principles which should form the basis of meaningful revolutionary activity today. These are the ideas which have guided *Solidarity* since its inception and which are now recognized as relevant by increasingly numerous people, often starting from very different premises.

There is finally an appendix, for those whose blind (but usually uninformed) loyalty to Marxist economics prevents them from seeing the world as it is. We urge these comrades to read this appendix carefully, for it not only takes the economic analysis of state capitalism further than Marx did (or could), but it does so using Marx's own categories. Having completed this task, it then puts the whole problem where it belongs, well in the background. We have deliberately placed these comments at the very end of the book. Socialism is not fundamentally about production or about productivity. It is not even fundamentally about consumption. It is about freedom. It is about the relations between people, both in production and out of it. It is about the relation between man and his work and between man and the social institutions he creates. Control of the economy is but a means to these ends.

In a sense this book is ahead of its time. It describes phenomena which are not as yet universal, which in many places only manifest themselves as tendencies, which do not yet apply in many areas of the world, but which in the absence of *socialist* revolutions will almost certainly become the dominant pattern in years to come. At first these ideas may only be accepted by a small minority. But we are confident they will make their way.

Spinoza's motto, "neither to laugh nor to weep, but to understand", epitomizes the purpose of the work as a whole. Some will doubtless weep – at the systematic demolition of their cherished beliefs. Others will snigger – at this attempt to challenge revolutionary Holy Writ and to rethink socialist ideology from rock bottom. We are confident however that the main message will be understood by those who have seen the inadequacy of traditional politics or those who have never been embroiled in them. (There will, of course, always be those who, blinkered by their respective orthodoxies, incapable of an original thought of their own, will never understand. They will remain the repositories of revolutionary rust.)

We expect the book will be denounced as revisionist. In a world where everything is changing, where every field of knowledge and of technology is being revolutionized more completely than at any other period of human history, it is necessary to run, if we are merely to keep pace. Only the "revolutionaries" mark time. A constant ideological renewal is needed in order even to understand the world around us, let alone to grapple with it or change it. In this respect Cardan's text is unashamedly revisionist. It is revisionist in the sense that Galileo was revisionist when he asserted, against the tenets of the Church and of Aristotelian doctrine, that the Earth revolved around the Sun and not vice versa.

The text and its publishers will be labelled "anarcho-Marxist" by those who like ready-made tabs for their ideological wares. The cap fits insofar as we stand in a double line of fire, denounced as anarchists (by the Marxists) and as Marxists (by the anarchists). It is true insofar as we appeal to the libertarian ideals of *some* Marxists and to the need – clearly felt by some anarchists – for a self-consistent and modern ideology going further than the slogan "politics: out!" Basically, however, we are ourselves and nothing more. We live here and now, not in Petrograd in 1917, nor in Barcelona in 1936. We have no gods, not even revolutionary ones. Paraphrasing Marx ("philosophers have only interpreted the world; what is necessary is to change it"), we might say that "revolutionaries have only interpreted Marx (or Bakunin), what is necessary is to change them".

We are the product of the degeneration of traditional politics and of the revolt of youth against established society in an advanced industrial country in the second half of the twentieth century. The aim of this book is to give both purpose and meaning to this revolt and to merge it with the constant working class struggle for its own emancipation.

SOLIDARITY **BOOK (APRIL 1965)**

8. THE BALKANIZATION OF UTOPIA

"Until he has witnessed an Easter march, the average citizen can have no idea of the number of groups hell-bent on the balkanization of Utopia and the diversity of magazines and badges which they produce. Yesterday Ilford Liberation Group, the Fellowship Party, and the Anarchists were groups for the connoisseur, while the Young Communist League, the district committees of London area Communist parties, and the Young Socialists provided more familiar forms of dissent" (Guardian, April 19, 1965).

The Press, the police, and representatives of the established political parties must share a certain incredulous surprise on occasions like Aldermaston. For there, surfacing into broad daylight, emerging from the anonymity of their daily lives, are literally dozens of different political (or anti-political) groupings, scores of rank-and-file papers, subversive to various degrees of the Established Order, and thousands upon thousands of individuals – with strongly felt opinions of their own – united in their opposition to the Bomb and in their determination to take responsibility for their own actions.

What vision of the future do these people hold? The categories of traditional politics are quite inadequate to define them. These crowds are unlikely to be demonstrating for either Mr. Wilson's or Mr. Gollan's "alternatives" to the established order. This mass of humanity on the road, "hell-bent on the balkanization of utopia", must be a bureaucrat's nightmare.

The procession – as is well-known – is filmed and photographed from every angle, dissected, enlarged, submitted to the most refined technologies of identification known to the Special Branch. This rabble, this horde of potential troublemakers must be identified, their affiliations established, the files kept accurate and up to date. How much easier it would be to treat them all as "reds" or "pacifists", as "communists" or "anarchists", without having to worry about the finer shades of doctrinal difference, without having to document this massive dissent.

But that wouldn't do in this scientific age! The clerks and computers must be kept busy. Tagged, the rebels must be. Who is "dangerous" and who is "daft"? Who owes allegiance to Moscow and who to Transport House? Who lives in the past and who in the present? Who believes in non-violence and who doesn't? Who believes in Parliament and who does not? Who are the "resolutionaries" and who the "revolutionaries"? And how the hell can we make sure their beliefs remain static, and that they won't split, and shift allegiance, and bugger up the card index? Who are sheep? Who are goats? And in which pigeonhole do we put the hybrids?

The politicians must view it much as the police does. Why don't all these people just stay at home and leave it to us? Why don't they trust their elders and betters? Why aren't they happy just to vote for us every few years? Why do they argue so much – and in the streets too?

And is all this just the top of the iceberg? How many others, today, think as they do? How many will, tomorrow? Could this scruffy lot be the "don't knows" of the

Gallup polls? Are these the solid core of non-voters? How often does their "don't know" mean "won't tell"? And how often does "won't tell" mean "fuck the lot of you"?

Why, oh why, won't all these people accept our "realistic", parliamentary alternatives? Why don't they leave complicated things – like their own life and death – to the professional politicians? If they must have their utopias, why can't they accept our standard models, prefabricated, provided and priced by official society itself? We may bemoan their apathy, but surely this is better than having them turn up in hundreds at May Day and shout us down, or make awkward comments about "Vietnam" or "MPs'salaries" or "old age pensioners" or other unpleasant subjects.

The press – although aware of the newsworthiness of the esoteric – is less concerned about getting facts straight. They worship at the altar of power. They are the mouthpieces of those who have arrived. And these marchers are getting nowhere. They are all "weird" anyway. Why bore our readers (and tax our own grey matter) by going into their beliefs more fully? Our political vocabulary is limited, our knowledge of sects' anatomy more limited still. We have so consistently got things wrong when venturing to the left of the Communist Party that we had better keep to safe ground. So let's tidy up reality a little. Let's just call them all "beatniks", "anarchists", the "lunatic fringe". After all Gaitskell called them "peanuts".

And what about the demonstrators themselves? The "balkanization" of their respective utopias is too obvious to deny. Geography and history get muddled. For some Mecca is Moscow, for others Peking. Some live in Petrograd (in 1917) – others in Barcelona (in 1936). Internationals and ideologies interpenetrate. Revolutionary Gods (Marx, Bakunin, Luxemburg, Malatesta, de Leon, Lenin and Trotsky) jostle one another on the narrow summits of a revolutionary Olympus. The truly godless are also clamouring for room to breathe.

For some, this fragmentation has solely negative aspects. These groups echo the views of the powers-that-be: dissent should be centralized, co-ordinated, channeled along the lines of one particular revolutionary development, which they alone, of course, have grasped. Everything else is diversion and irrelevance. They alone are the conscious agents of an Almighty Historical Providence. They alone have understood the "laws" of history. They alone are carried forward by the historical floodtide. Such groups are elitist to the core. They (and they alone) are potential leaderships. Other groups are dangerous competitors in the permanent auction for revolutionary clientele. The masses, by themselves, can do nothing. They are but an amorphous infantry at the disposal of a self-appointed general staff of revolutionary generals. That ordinary people could themselves make history – and could make it in ways unforeseen and unsuspected by the professional revolutionaries – would never occur to the residual legatees of Bolshevism. History is thus turned upside down. Monolithic conceptions of the road to "utopia" foreshadow utopias in their own image, i.e. monolithic to the core.

For others in the movement "men make their own history" – and in ways much wider and fuller than is usually conceded. There is no one road to utopia, no one organization, or prophet, or Party, destined to lead the masses to the Promised Land. There is no one historically determined objective, no single vision of a different and new society, no solitary economic panacea that will do away with the alienation of man from his fellow men and from the products of his own activity.

For groups holding such views the "balkanization of utopia" need convey no disparaging overtones of incapacity or futility. Established society is being corroded at many points, in many ways, *here* and *now*. Hundreds of thousands are contributing to the process, both consciously and otherwise: brick-planting policemen and lying Labour politicians, young people rejecting traditional sexual morality and students questioning the categorical imperatives of death "for Queen and Country", train robbers and "Spies for Peace" evading arrest month after month, and well-paid trade union officials pontificating about the merits of an "incomes policy" for their members. All are playing a worthy part in a vast and essential process of demystification.

So are South Bank clergymen de-godding God and Catholic priests acting as salesmen for Durex. So are Trots still building left-wings in the Labour Party and calling on Labour leaders to *legislate* for workers' control, while Labour MPs vote themselves a £30 a week wage increase and thunder against those who "rock the boat". So are French Stalinists supporting de Gaulle and Chinese Stalinists supporting the suppression of the Hungarian Revolution, Negroes exposing the whole fraudulent nature of the American judicial system and White House politicians showing the world their notion of the "rule of law" in the Dominican Republic. So too, finally, are workers at Paisley using sit-in tactics and having to be carried out by the police, while Labour leaders lambast latent Luddites, confer baronetcies on the Brockways and Sopers of this world and encourage the half-pissed platitudes of "brother" Brown.

For those who hold that mass consciousness rather than a change of leadership is an essential precondition of social change, the events of the last few years can be viewed with reasonable satisfaction. Starting from very different premises, various groups are making fundamental critiques of established society. Some have been through the mill of traditional "left" politics, others not. Some start from their experience in production, others from their experience in the anti-Bomb movement, some from the total crisis of culture and values in the admass society, and others still from the void of their own daily lives. These critiques are slowly converging. They are literally ploughing up every acre of established thinking, including the so-called revolutionary ideologies. They are preparing a resurgence of libertarian thought and action, based on more genuinely socialist objectives than at any previous period of history. The era of closed ideologies (including totalitarian "revolutionary" ideologies) is slowly coming to an end. The cults of efficiency, of hierarchy, of production for production's sake, of consumption for consumption's sake, of organization for organization's sake, of "ever more" (of the same) are slowly being subverted and replaced by genuinely human values.

The "balkanization of utopia" bemoaned by bourgeois and Bolsheviks alike is therefore neither tragedy nor farce. It is the sole guarantee that "utopia", if we ever get near to it, will be worth living in.

SOLIDARITY, III, 9 (JUNE 1965).

9. FOR WORKERS' POWER

The standard of living of workers has improved considerably during the last century. The impoverishment predicted by Marx has not taken place. But capitalism remains an inhuman system where the vast majority are bossed at work and manipulated in consumption and leisure. Increased wages are balanced by speed-up and the creation of artificial needs. Both East and West, society is still dominated by ruling classes who control the means of production, use the state in their own interests and who are prepared to risk the destruction of humanity to defend these interests.

The decay of the trade unions and of the traditional parties has gone much further than is generally admitted. They cannot be reformed. They have come to terms with the existing system, of which they are now a key part. The degeneration of working class organizations, itself the result of the failure of the revolutionary movement, has been a major factor in creating working class apathy.

The same applies to the Communist Parties. They are equally impotent and although they seek to create a superficially different kind of society (namely state capitalism on the Russian or Chinese model) their aims can hardly be called socialist.

The road to socialism - and socialism itself - means the conscious and independent action of workers. It means the end of the division between leaders and led. By their rigid, hierarchical structure most "revolutionary" organizations encourage precisely those divisions. A socialist society will be one in which decisions will be taken by workers' councils, composed of elected and revocable delegates, and where the workers themselves will manage production.

The class struggle today takes mainly "unofficial" forms. Revolutionaries should be active in these struggles rather than attempting to take over the traditional organizations. Working class resistance to the employers and the union leaders is as strong as ever. But these struggles are mainly reflex actions: their aims are inevitably limited. If the working class is to learn and generalize its experiences and if it is to struggle for socialism it must form revolutionary organizations. These must be instruments of struggle, not a general staff imposed from the outside.

The idea that socialism can be achieved by an "elite" party, however "revolutionary" acting on behalf of the working class, is both absurd and reactionary. *Solidarity* does not present itself as yet another "leadership" but merely as a tool of struggle.

SOLIDARITY, III, 9 (JUNE 1965)

10. PREFACE TO IDA METT, *THE KRONSTADT COMMUNE*

The fiftieth anniversary of the Russian Revolution will be assessed, analyzed, celebrated or bemoaned in a variety of ways.

To the peddlers of religious mysticism and to the advocates of "freedom of enterprise", Svetlana Stalin's sensational (and well-timed) defection will "prove" the resilience of the respective doctrines, now shown as capable of spouting on what at first sight would appear rather barren soil.

To incorrigible liberals, the recent, cautious reintroduction of the profit motive into certain sectors of the Russian economy will "prove" that laissez-faire economics is synonymous with human nature and that a rationally planned economy was always a pious pipe-dream.

To those "lefts" (like the late Isaac Deutscher) who saw in Russia's industrialization an automatic guarantee of more liberal attitudes in days to come, the imprisonment of Daniel and Sinyavsky for thought-crime (and the current persecution of those who stood up for them) will have come as a resounding slap in the face.

To the "Marxist-Leninists" of China (and Albania), Russia's rapprochement with the USA, her passivity in the recent Middle East crisis, her signing of the Test Ban Treaty and her reactionary influence on revolutionary developments in the colonial countries will all bear testimony to her headlong slither into the swamp of revisionism, following the Great Stalin's death. (Stalin, it will be remembered, was the architect of such revolutionary, non-revisionist, measures as the elimination of the Old Bolsheviks, the Moscow Trials, the Popular Front, the Nazi-Soviet Pact, the Teheran and Yalta Agreements and the dynamic struggles of the French and Italian Communist Parties in the immediate post-war years, struggles which led to their direct seizure of power in their respective countries.)

To the Yugoslavs, reintegrated at last after their adolescent wandering from the fold, the re-emergence of "sanity" in Moscow will be seen as corroboration of their worst suspicions. The 1948 "troubles" were clearly all due to the machinations of the wicked Beria. Mihajlo Mihajlov now succeeds Djilas behind the bars of a people's prison…just to remind political heretics that, in Yugoslavia too, "proletarian democracy" is confined to those who refrain from asking awkward questions.

To the Trotskyists of all ilk - at least to those still capable of thinking for themselves - the mere fact of the fiftieth anniversary celebrations should be food for thought. What do words mean? How "transitional" can a transitional society be? Aren't four decades of "Bonapartism" in danger of making the word a trifle meaningless? Like the unflinching Christians carrying their cross, will unflinching Trotskyists go on carrying their question mark (concerning the future evolution of Russian society) for the rest of their earthly existence? For how much longer will they go on gargling with the old slogans of "capitalist restoration or advance towards socialism" proposed by their mentor in his *Revolution Betrayed*…thirty years ago! Surely only the blind can now fail to see that Russia is a class society of a new type, and has been for several decades.

Those who have shed these mystifications – or who have never been blinded by them – will see things differently. They will sense that there can be no vestige of socialism in a society whose rulers can physically annihilate the Hungarian Workers' Councils, denounce equalitarianism and workers' management of production as "petty-bourgeois" or "anarcho-syndicalist" deviations, and accept the cold-blooded murder of a whole generation of revolutionaries as mere "violations of socialist legality", to be rectified – oh so gingerly and tactfully – by the technique of "selective posthumous rehabilitation". It will be obvious to them that something went seriously wrong with the Russian Revolution. *What was it? And when did the "degeneration" start?*

Here again the answers differ. For some the "excesses" or "mistakes" are attributable to a spiteful paranoia slowly sneaking up on the senescent Stalin. This interpretation (apart from tacitly accepting the very "cult of the individual" which its advocates would claim to decry) fails, however, to account for the repressions of revolutionaries and the conciliations with imperialism perpetuated at a much earlier period. For others the "degeneration" set in with the final defeat of the Left Opposition as an organized force (1927), or with Lenin's death (1924), or with the abolition of factions at the tenth Party Congress (1921). For the Bordigists the proclamation of the New Economic Policy (1921) irrevocably stamped Russia as "state capitalist". Others, rightly rejecting this preoccupation with the minutiae of revolutionary chronometry, stress more general factors, albeit in our opinion some of the less important ones.

Our purpose in publishing this text about the Kronstadt events of 1921 is not to draw up an alternative timetable. Nor are we looking for political ancestors. The construction of an orthodox apostolic succession is the least of our preoccupations. (In a constantly changing world it would only testify to our theoretical sterility.) Our occupation is simply to document some of the real – but less well-known – struggles that took place against the growing bureaucracy during the early post-revolutionary years, at a time when most of the later critics of the bureaucracy were part and parcel of the apparatus itself.

The fiftieth anniversary of the Russian Revolution presents us with the absurd sight of a Russian ruling class (which every day resembles more its Western counterpart) solemnly celebrating the revolution which overthrew bourgeois power and allowed the masses, for a brief moment, to envisage a totally new kind of social order.

What made this tragic paradox possible? What shattered this vision? How did the Revolution degenerate?

Many explanations are offered. The history of how the Russian working class was dispossessed is not, however, a matter for an esoteric discussion among political cliques, who compensate for their own irrelevance by mental journeys into the enchanted world of the revolutionary past. An understanding of what took place is essential for every serious socialist. It is not mere archivism.

No viable ruling class rules by force alone. To rule it must succeed in getting its own vision of reality accepted by society at large. The concepts by which it attempts to legitimize its rule must be projected into the past. Socialists have correctly recognized that the history taught in bourgeois schools reveals a particular, distorted, vision of the world. It is a measure of the weakness of the revolutionary movement that *socialist* history remains for the most part unwritten.

What passes as socialist history is often only a mirror image of bourgeois historiography, a percolation into the ranks of the working class movement of typically bourgeois methods of thinking. In the world of this type of "historian" leaders of genius replace the kings and queens of the bourgeois world. Famous congresses, splits or controversies, the rise and fall of political parties or unions, the emergence or degeneration of this or that leadership replace the internecine battles of the rulers of the past. The masses never appear independently on the historical stage, making their own history. At best they only "supply the steam", enabling others to drive the locomotive, as Stalin so delicately put it.

> Most of the time, "official" historians don't have eyes to see or ears to hear the acts and words which express the workers' spontaneous activity…They lack the categories of thought - one might even say the brain cells - necessary to understand or even to perceive this activity as it really is. To them an activity that has no leader or programme, no institutions and no statues, can only be described as "troubles" or "disorders". The spontaneous activity of the masses belongs by definition to what history suppresses."[68]

This tendency to identify working class history with the history of its organizations, institutions and leaders is not only inadequate - it reflects a typically bourgeois vision of mankind, divided in almost preordained manner between *the few* who will manage and decide, and the *many*, the malleable mass, incapable of acting consciously on its own behalf, and forever destined to remain the object (and never the subject) of history. Most histories of the degeneration of the Russian Revolution rarely amount to more than this.

The Stalinist bureaucracy was unique in that it presented a view of history based on outright lies rather than on the more usual mixture of subtle distortion and self-mystification. But Khrushchev's revelations and subsequent developments in Russia have caused official Russian versions of events (in all their variants) to be questioned even by members of the Communist Party. Even the graduates of what Trotsky called "the Stalin school of falsification" are now beginning to reject the lies of the Stalinist era. Our task is to take the process of demystification a little further.

Of all the interpretations of the degeneration of the Russian Revolution that of Issac Deutscher is the most widely accepted on the Left. It echoes most of the assumptions of the Trotskyists. Although an improvement on the Stalinist versions, it is hardly sufficient. The degeneration is seen as due to strictly conjunctural factors (the isolation of the revolution in a backward country, the devastation caused by the Civil War, the overwhelming weight of the peasantry, etc.). These factors are undoubtedly very important. But the growth of the bureaucracy is more than just an accident in history. It is a worldwide phenomenon, intimately linked to a certain stage in the development of working class consciousness. It is the terrible price paid by the working class for its delay in recognizing that the true and final emancipation of the working class can only be achieved by the working class itself, and cannot be entrusted to others, allegedly acting on its behalf. If "socialism is Man's total and positive self-consciousness" (Marx, 1844), the experience (and rejection) of the bureaucracy is a step on that road.

The Trotskyists deny that early oppositions to the developing bureaucracy had any revolutionary content. On the contrary they denounce the Workers' Opposition and the Kronstadt rebels as basically counter-revolutionary. Real opposition, for

---

68   Paul Cardan, *From Bolshevism to the Bureaucracy* (Solidarity Pamphlet 24).

them, starts with the proclamation - within the Party - of the Left Opposition of 1923. But anyone in the least familiar with the period will know that by 1923 the working class had already sustained a decisive defeat. It had lost power in production to a group of managers appointed from above. It had also lost power in the soviets, which were now only ghosts of their former sleves, only a rubber stamp for the emerging bureaucracy. The Left Oppostion fought within the confines of the Party, which was itself already highly bureaucratized. No substantial number of workers rallied to its cause. Their will to struggle had been sapped by the long struggle of the preceding years.

Opposition to the anti-working-class measures being taken by the Bolshevik leadership in the years immediately following the revolution took many forms and expressed itself through many different channels and at many different levels. It expressed itself *within* the Party itself, through a number of oppositional tendencies of which the Workers' Opposition (Kollontai, Lutovinov, Shlyapnikov) is the best known.[69] Outside the Party the revolutionary opposition found heterogenous expression, in the life of a number, often illegal groups (some anarchist, some anarcho-syndicalist, some still professing their basis faith in Marxism).[70] It also found expression in spontaneous, often "unorganized" class activity, such as the big Leningrad strikes of 1921 and the Kronstadt uprising. It found expression in the increasing resistance of the workers to Bolshevik industrial policy (and in particular to Trotsky's attempts to militarize the trade unions). It also found expression in proletarian opposition to Bolshevik attempts to evict all other tendencies from the soviets, thus effectively gagging all those seeking to re-orient socialist construction along entirely different lines.

At an early stage several tendencies had struggled against the bureaucratic degeneration of the Revolution. By posthumously excluding them from the ranks of the revolutionary, Trotskyists, Leninists and others commit a double injustice. Firstly they excommunicate all those who foresaw and struggled against the nascent bureaucracy *prior to 1923*, thereby turning a deaf ear to some of the most pertinent and valid criticisms ever voiced against the bureaucracy. Secondly they weaken their own case, for if the demands for freely elected soviets, for freedom of expression (proletarian democracy) and for workers' management of production were wrong in 1921, why did they become partially correct in 1923? Why are they correct now? If in 1921 Lenin and Trotsky represented the "real interests" of the workers (against the actual workers), why couldn't Stalin? Why couldn't Kadar in Hungary in 1956? The Trotskyist school of hagiography has helped to obscure the real lessons of the struggle against the bureaucracy.

***

When one seriously studies the crucial years after 1917, when the fate of the Russian Revolution was still in the melting pot, one is driven again and again to the tragic events of the Kronstadt uprising of March 1921. These events epitomize, in a bloody and dramatic manner, the struggle between two concepts of the Revolution, two revolutionary methods, two types of revolutionary ethos. Who decides what is or is not in the long term interests of the working class? What methods are permis-

---

69   For information concerning their programme see *The Workers' Opposition* by Alexandra Kollontai. This was first published in English in Sylvia Pankhurst's *Workers' Deadnought* in 1921 and republished in 1961 as Solidarity Pamphlet 8.

70   The history of such groups as the *Workers' Truth* group or the *Workers' Struggle* group still remains to be written.

sible in settling differences between revolutionaries? And what methods are double-edged and only capable in the long run of harming the Revolution itself?

There is remarkably little of a detailed nature available in English about the Kronstadt events. The Stalininst histories, revisited and re-edited according to the fluctuating fortunes of Party functionaries, are not worth the paper they are written on. They are an insult to the intelligence of their readers, deemed incapable of comparing the same facts described in earlier and later editions of the same book.

Trotsky's writings about Kronstadt are few and more concerned at retrospective justification and at scoring debating points against the Anarchists[71] than at seriously analyzing this particular episode of the Russian Revolution. Trotsky and the Trotskyists are particularly keen to perpetuate the myth that they were the first and only coherent anti-bureaucratic tendency. All their writings seek to hide how far the bureaucratization of both Party and soviets had already gone by 1921 - i.e. how far it had gone during the period when Lenin and Trotsky were in full and undisputed control. The task for serious revolutionaries today is to see the link between Trotsky's attitudes and pronouncements during and before the "great trade union debate" of 1920–21 and the healthy hostility to Trotskyism of the most advanced and revolutionary layers of the industrial working class. This hostility was to manifest itself - arms in hand - during the Kronstadt uprising. It was to manifest itself again two or three years later - this time by folded arms - when these advanced layers failed to rally to Trotsky's support, when he at last chose to challenge Stalin, within the limited confines of a Party machine, towards whose bureaucratization he had signally contributed.[72]

Deutscher in *The Prophet Armed* vividly depicts the background of Russia during the years of Civil War, the suffering, the economic dislocation, the sheer physical exhaustion of the population. But the picture is one-sided, its purpose to stress that the "iron will of the Bolsheviks" was the only element of order, stability and continuity in a society that was hovering on the brink of total collapse. He pays scant attention to the attempts made by groups of workers and revolutionaries - both within the Party and outside its ranks - to attempt social reconstruction on an entirely dif-

---

71   An easy enough task after 1936, when some well-known anarchist "leaders" (*sic!*) entered the Popular Front government in Catalonia at the beginning of the Spanish Civil War — and were allowed to remain there by the anarchist rank and file. This action — in an area where the anarchists had a mass basis in the labour movement — irrevocably damned them, just as the development of the Russian Revolution had irrevocably damned the Mensheviks, as incapable of standing up to the test of events.

72   Three statements from Trotsky's *Terrorism and Communism* (Ann Arbor: University of Michigan Press, 1961), first published in June 1920, will illustrate the point:

"The creation of a socialist society means the organization of the workers on new foundations, their adaptation to those foundations and their labour re-education, with the one *unchanging* end of the increase in the productivity of labour..." (p.146).

"I consider that if the Civil War had not plundered our economic organs of all that was strongest, most independent, most endowed with initiative, we should undoubtedly have *entered the path of one-man management* in the sphere of economic administration much sooner and much less painfully" (pp. 162—163).

"We have been more than once accused of having substituted for the dictatorship of the soviets the dictatorship of our own Party... In the substitution of the power of the Party for the power of the working class there is nothing accidental, and in reality there is no substitution at all. The Communists express the fundamental interests of the working class..." (p. 109).

So much for the "anti-bureaucratic" antecedents of Trotskyism. It is interesting that the book was highly praised by Lenin. Lenin only took issue with Trotsky on the trade union question at the Central Committee meeting of November 8 and 9, 1920. Throughout most of 1920 Lenin had endorsed all Trotsky's bureaucratic decrees in relation to the unions.

ferent basis, from below.[73] He does not discuss the sustained opposition and hostility of the Bolsheviks to workers' management of production[74] or in fact to any large-scale endeavour which escaped their domination or control. Of the Kronstadt events themselves, of the Bolshevik calumnies against Kronstadt and of the frenzied repression that followed the events of March 1921, Deutscher says next to nothing, except that the Bolshevik accusations against the Kronstadt rebels were "groundless". Deutscher totally fails to see the direct relation between the methods used by Lenin and Trotsky in 1921 and those other methods, perfected by Stalin and later used against the Old Bolsheviks themselves during the notorious Moscow trials of 1936, 1937 and 1938.

In Victor Serge's *Memoirs of a Revolutionary* there is a chapter devoted to Kronstadt.[75] Serge's writings are particularly interesting in that he was in Leningrad in 1921 and supported what the Bolsheviks were doing, albeit reluctantly. He did not however resort to the slanders and misrepresentations of other leading Party members. His comments throw light on the almost schizophrenic frame of mind of the rank and file of the Party at that time. For different reasons neither the Trotskyists nor the anarchists have forgiven Serge his attempts to reconcile what was best in their respective doctrines: the concern with reality and the concern with principle.

Easily available and worthwhile *anarchist* writings on the subject (in English) are virtually non-existent, despite the fact that many anarchists consider this area relevant to their ideas. Emma Goldman's *Living My Life* and Berkman's *The Bolshevik Myth* contain some vivid but highly subjective pages about the Kronstadt rebellion. *The Kronstadt Revolt* by Anton Ciliga (produced as a pamphlet in 1942) is an excellent short account which squarely faces up to some of the fundamental issues. It has been unavailable for years. Voline's account, on the other hand, is too simplistic. Complex phenomena like the Kronstadt revolt cannot be meaningfully interpreted by loaded generalizations like "as Marxists, authoritarians and statists, the Bolsheviks could not permit any freedom or independent action of the masses". (Many have argued that there are strong Blanquist and even Bakuninist strands in Bolshevism, and that it is precisely these departures from Marxism that are at the root of Bolshevism's "elitist" ideology and practice.) Voline even reproaches the Kronstadt rebels with "speaking of power (the power of the soviets) instead of getting rid of the word and of the idea altogether..." The practical struggle however was not against "words" or even "ideas". It was a physical struggle against their concrete incarnation in history (in the form of bourgeois institutions). It is a symptom of anarchist muddleheadedness on this score that they can both reproach the Bolsheviks with dissolving the Constituent Assembly[76]...and the Kronstadt rebels for proclaiming that they stood for soviet power! The "Soviet anarchists" clearly perceived what was at stake - even if many of their successors fail to. They fought to defend the deepest

---

73   For an interesting account of the growth of the Factory Committees Movement − and of the opposition to them of the Bolsheviks at the First All-Russian Trade Union Convention (January 1918), see Maximov's *The Guillotine at Work* (Chicago, 1940).

74   At the Ninth Party Congress (March 1920) Lenin introduced a resolution to the effect that the task of the unions was to explain the need for a "maximum curtailment of administrative collegia and the gradual introduction of individual management in units directly engaged in production" (Robert V. Daniels, *The Conscience of the Revolution* (Cambridge, Mass., 1960), p.124).

75   Serge's writings on this matter were first brought to the attention of readers in the UK in 1961 (*Solidarity*, I, 7). This text was later reprinted as a pamphlet.

76   See Nicolas Walter's article in *Freedom* (October 28, 1967) entitled "October 1917: No Revolution at All".

conquest of October - soviet power - against *all* its usurpers, including the Bolsheviks.

***

Our own contribution to the fiftieth anniversary celebrations will not consist in the usual panegyrics to the achievements of Russian rocketry. Nor will we chant paeans to Russian pig-iron statistics. Industrial expansion may be the prerequisite for a fuller, better life for all but is in no way synonymous with such a life, unless *all* social relations have been revolutionized. We are more concerned at the social costs of Russian achievements.

Some perceived what these costs would be at a very early stage. We are interested in bringing their prophetic warnings to a far wider audience. The final massacre at Kronstadt took place on March 18, 1921, exactly fifty years after the slaughter of the Communards by Thiers and Galliffet. The facts about the Commune are well known. But fifty years after the Russian Revolution we still have to seek basic information about Kronstadt. The facts are not easy to obtain. They lie buried under the mountains of calumny and distortion heaped on them by Stalinists and Trotskyists alike.

The publication of this pamphlet in English, at this particular time, is part of this endeavour. Ida Mett's book *La Commune de Cronstadt* was first published in 1938. It was republished in France ten years later but has been unobtainable for several years. In 1962 and 1963 certain parts of it were translated into English and appeared in *Solidarity* (II, 6 to 11). We now have pleasure in bringing to English-speaking readers a slightly abridged version of the book as a whole, which contains material hitherto unavailable in Britain.

Apart from various texts published in Kronstadt itself in March 1921, Ida Mett's book contains Petrichenko's open letter of 1926, addressed to the British Communist Party. Petrichenko was the President of the Kronstadt Provisional Revolutionary Committee. His letter refers to discussions in the Political Bureau of the CPGB on the subject of Kronstadt, discussions which seem to have accepted that there was no extraneous intervention during the uprising. (Members of the CP and others might seek further enlightenment on the matter from King Street, whose archives on the matter should make interesting reading.)

Ida Mett writes from an anarchist viewpoint. Her writings however represent what is best in the revolutionary tradition of "class struggle" anarchism. She thinks in terms of a collective, proletarian solution to the problems of capitalism. The rejection of the class struggle, the anti-intellectualism, the preoccupation with transcendental morality and with personal salvation that characterize so many of the anarchists of today should not for a minute detract "Marxists" from paying serious attention to what she writes. We do not necessarily endorse all her judgments and have- in footnotes - corrected one or two minor factual inaccuracies in her text. Some of her generalizations seem to us too sweeping and some of her analyses of the bureaucratic phenomenon too simple to be of real use. But as a chronicle of what took place before, during and after Kronstadt, her account remains unsurpassed.

Her text throws interesting light on the attitude to the Kronstadt uprising shown at the time by various Russian political tendencies (anarchists, Mensheviks, Left and Right S.R.s, Bolsheviks, etc.). Some whose approach to politics is superficial in the extreme (and for whom a smear or a slogan is a substitute for real understanding) will point accusingly to some of this testimony, to some of these resolutions and manifestos as evidence irrevocably damning the Kronstadt rebels. "Look", they will say, "what the Mensheviks and Right SRs were saying. Look at how they were calling for a return to the Constituent Assembly, and at the same time proclaiming their solidarity with Kronstadt. Isn't this proof positive that Kronstadt was a counter-revolutionary upheaval? You yourselves admit that rogues like Victor Chernov, President elect of the Constituent Assembly, offered to help the Kronstadters? What further evidence is needed?"

We are not afraid of presenting *all* the facts to our readers. Let them judge for themselves. It is our firm conviction that most Trotskyists and Leninists are - and are kept - as ignorant of this period of Russian history as Stalinists are of the period of the Moscow Trials. At best they vaguely sense the presence of skeletons in the cupboard. At worst they vaguely parrot what their leaders tell them, intellectually too lazy or politically too well-conditioned to probe for themselves. Real revolutions are never "pure". They unleash the deepest passions of men. People actively participate or are dragged into the vortex of such movements for a variety of often contradictory reasons. Consciousness and false consciousness are inextricably mixed. A river in full flood inevitably carries a certain amount of rubbish. A revolution in full flood carries a number of political corpses - and may even momentarily give them a semblance of life.

During the Hungarian Revolution of 1956 many were the messages of verbal or moral support for the rebels, emanating from the West, piously preaching the virtues of bourgeois democracy or of free enterprise. The objective of those who spoke in these terms were anything but the institution of a classless society. But their support for the rebels remained purely verbal, particularly when it became clear to them what the real objectives of the revolution were: a fundamental democratization of Hungarian institutions *without* a reversion to private ownership of the means of production.

The backbone of the Hungarian revolution was the network of workers' councils. Their main demands were for workers' management of production and for a government based on the councils. These facts justified the support of revolutionaries throughout the world. Despite the Mindszentys. Despite the Smallholders and Social-Democrats - or their shadows - now trying to jump on to the revolutionary bandwagon. The class critierion is the decisive one.

Similar considerations apply to the Kronstadt rebellion. Its core was the revolutionary sailors. Its main objectives were ones with which no real revolutionary could disagree. That others sought to take advantage of the situation is inevitable - and irrelevant. It is a question of who is calling the tune.

***

Attitudes to the Kronstadt events, expressed nearly fifty years after the event often provide deep insight into the political thinking of contemporary revolutionaries. They may in fact provide a deeper insight into their conscious or unconscious aims than many a learned discussion about economics, or philosophy, or about other episodes of revolutionary history.

It is a question of one's basic attitude as to what socialism is all about. What are epitomized in the Kronstadt events are some of the most difficult problems of revolutionary strategy and revolutionary ethics: the problems of ends and means, of the relations between Party and masses, in fact of whether a Party is necessary at all.

Can the working class by itself only develop a trade union consciousness".[77] Should it even be allowed, at all times, to go that far?[78]

Or can the working class develop a deeper consciousness and understanding of its interests than can any organization allegedly acting on its behalf? When the Stalinists or Trotskyists speak of Kronstadt as "an essential action against the class enemy", when more "sophisticated" revolutionaries refer to it as a "tragic necessity", one is entitled to pause for a moment. One is entitled to ask how seriously they accept Marx's dictum that "the emancipation of the working class is the task of the working class itself". Do they take this seriously or do they pay mere lip-service to the words? Do they identify socialism with the autonomy (organizational and ideological) of the working class? Or do they see themselves, with their wisdom as to the "historical interests" of others, and with their judgments as to what should be "permitted", as the leadership around which the future elite will crystallize and develop? One is entitled not only to ask...but also to suggest the answer!

SOLIDARITY PAMPHLET 27 (NOVEMBER 1967)

---

77   Lenin proclaimed so explicitly in his *What Is To Be Done?* (1902).

78   In a statement to the tenth Party Congress (1921) Lenin refers to a mere *discussion* on the trade unions as an "absolutely impermissible luxury" which "we" should not have permitted. These remarks speak unwitting volumes on the subject (and incidentally deal decisively with those who seek desperately for an "evolution" in their Lenin).

11. THE RUSSIAN ANARCHISTS – AND KROPOTKIN

This book was to be expected.[79] What was not expected is that it should turn out quite readable. It is a serious attempt to rescue the Russian anarchists from the realms of demonology and myth to which they have been relegated for several decades by the combined malevolence of bourgeois and Bolshevik historians - and by the uninformed panegyrics of their own supporters.

Traditional historians - whether of the "right" or "left" - tend to view all history through the eyes of the victors. They worship the established fact. For them only the real is rational. Defeated dissidents, dynamiters, dreamers and demagogues are wrong, almost by definition.

The trouble starts when one looks at the fruits of the "rationality" that triumphed. Bolshevism emerged victorious from the great battlefield of conflicting interests, from the great cauldron of hopes and aspirations that was the Russia of 1917. But today, fifty years later, what do we see? "Marxism" being used to justify some of the worst tyrannies in history. "Socialist" states which resemble their bourgeois counterparts not only in their deepest essence (the hierarchical relationship of rulers to ruled, the authoritarian pattern of industrial management, etc.) but also in many of their superficial trappings. It is hardly surprising that there should be a resurgence of interest in other, more libertarian, strands of revolutionary thought and action.

A factual framework is needed for this alternative vision of ends and means. It is here that Avrich's book proves useful. The author does not attempt a serious sociological analysis of the various strands of Russian anarchism. What he does is to survey the field as a whole, without digging too deep in any particular area. The author is not a revolutionary. He patronizingly dismisses the deepest of working class aspirations - that for freedom in production - as a quest for an obviously unattainable Golden Age. He does however provide enough factual material to justify a reappraisal of many current views as to what happened in 1917 and immediately after.

For far too long most revolutionaries have had an extremely one-sided view of the history of the Russian Revolution. Events have all been perceived and assessed through the deforming prism of Bolshevism. Those educated in this school really know very little about some of the cardinal issues. All they know for instance about Russian "economism" and about "its lack of a programme and perspective" is through Lenin's scathing strictures in *What Is To Be Done?* Avrich will broaden their outlook. If they have ever heard of Machajski and of his forebodings that Marxism would turn out to be the ideology of a new aristocracy based on nationalized property (an aristocracy of managers, administrators, technical experts and professional politicians which would rule while manual workers remained enslaved by those whose "capital" was the specialized knowledge needed to operate a complex industrial economy) it would only have been through references in Trotsky's autobiography or through Trotsky's polemical writings of 1939 and 1940, claiming that Russia was still a "workers' state". Again, Avrich will tell them more.

---

79   Paul Avrich, *The Russian Anarchists* (Princeton University Press, 1967).

Traditional Marxists will doubtless have heard of the polemics waged by both Bolsheviks and Mensheviks against the terrorist anarchists of *Chernoe Znamia* and *Beznachalie*. They may have heard of the retorts that Marx's disciples included hordes of intellectuals "bent on drowning the will to act in a mighty torrent of words" or "spending their time in libraries, studying and writing about predetermined revolutions". But few will know that some of the most telling arguments against the flamboyantly heroic but incorrigibly romantic terrorists (to whom Avrich devotes excessive attention) came from such early Russian anarcho-syndicalists as Daniel Novomirsky and the group around him in Odessa.

The average Communist or Trotskyist is understandably allergic to Kropotkin and to his notions that "co-operation rather than conflict is at the root of the historical process…" (a co-operation that clearly transcended the barriers of class). But is he aware of the hostility engendered, within *anarchist* ranks, against this "genteel anarchism" whose "nostalgic yearning for a simpler but fuller life" led Kropotkin to idealize the autonomous social units of a bygone age? Maximov, the most sane and serious of the anarcho-syndicalists, might have had Kropotkin in view when in 1918 he scorned the Manilovs[80] in the anarchist-communist camp as "romantic visionaries who pined for pastoral utopias, oblivious of the complex forces at work in the modern world".

Avrich provides interesting information on the role of the anarchists in the Russian Revolution itself, but in rather a haphazard and anecdotal manner, as the author does not himself seem to appreciate the cardinal significance of some of the things he is talking about. He discusses - almost in passing - the phenomenal growth of the factory committees during 1917 and early 1918 and the sustained and concerted drive of the Bolsheviks to incorporate them in the structure of the unions, the better eventually to emasculate them altogether. He tells of Lenin's creation, as early as December 1917, of the *Vesenka* (Supreme Economic Council), one of whose main functions was to absorb the All-Russian Council for Workers' Control, thereby seeking to stem the syndicalist tide. Few traditional Marxists will have heard of the great debates that took place, in January 1918, at the First All-Russian Congress of Trade Unions, on the question of the control of industry (workers' control versus State control) or of the even more fundamental debate on workers' control versus workers' management.[81] Many will be surprised to learn that at this Congress the Bolsheviks were supported by the SRs and by Martov and the Menshevik delegates, one of whom deplored that "an anarchist wave in the shape of factory committees and workers' control was sweeping over our Russian labour movement". At this Congress the Marxist scholar Ryazanov (a recent convert to Bolshevism if not to the realities of industrial labour) advised the factory committees to "commit suicide" by becoming an "integral element" of the official trade union structures.

Most Communists or Trotskyists will be amazed to learn (as was the present reviewer) that by the beginning of 1921 Lenin had become so alarmed at the revival of syndicalist tendencies among the factory workers and intellectuals of his own party that he placed on the Index the works of Fernand Pelloutier, an important figure of the French syndicalist movement. On all these matters Avrich's book brings a mass of well-documented, if only half-digested, material of exceptional interest and relevance, most of it culled from original Russian sources.

---

80   Manilov was a day-dreaming landowner in Gogol's *Dead Souls*.

81   Unfortunately few modern syndicalists seem to have heard of it either.

Finally the book does not degenerate into an uncritical apologia of "anarchism" of the kind that does such harm to the libertarian cause. It is not in the tradition of so much anarchist writing which is more concerned in commemorating than in understanding. Throughout, the Russian anarchists are discussed in a ruthlessly demystified manner.

We are told of the muddleheaded Bakunin, correctly denouncing the idea that a tiny band of conspirators could carry out a *coup d'état* in the interests of the people as "a heresy against common sense and historical experience", yet determined to create his own "secret society" of conspirators, whose members would be subject to the "strictest discipline" and subordinated to a "small revolutionary directorate" - a directorate which was to remain intact even after the revolution, in order to forestall the establishment of an "official dictatorship". We are reminded of the "anarcho-patriots" - who as late as 1916 - were still supporting the first imperialist war in the name of anarchist "principles" (the famous "Manifesto of the Sixteen" was signed by "some of the most eminent anarchists in Europe", men like Kropotkin, Varlaam Cherkezov, Jean Grave, Charles Malato, Christian Cornelissen, James Guillaume and others).

Avrich also tells us how many prominent anarchists became supporters of the Bolshevik regime. Some (like Alexander Ge) became high officials in the Cheka (anarcho-coppers?). Others (like Iuda Roschin, formerly prominent in the *Chernoe Znamia* terrorist movement) decided that theory was important after all… and evolved "an anarchist theory of the dictatorship of the proletariat". Yet others, like the Gordin brothers, erstwhile contributors to the virulently anti-Bolshevik paper *Burevestnik* (The Stormy Petrel) came to support the Bolsheviks, seeing in them apostates from the Marxist creed because of their voluntarism and constant emphasis on the role of revolutionary will, which was taken to imply a break with the categories and theories of economic determinism. (One of the Gordin brothers eventually became a Protestant missionary, the other the founder of the Jewish Ethical Society.)

Throughout, Avrich emphasizes the "congenital inability" of the anarchists to subordinate personal differences to the good of the movement. He stresses their tendency to personalize their ideological quarrels, many of which were centred on essentially abstract matters. Then, as now, they produced few ideas but many words. Then, as now, the words meant all things to all men. Then, as now, "anarchism" could accommodate people on both sides of the barricades. Only some of the syndicalists emerge as capable of discussing ideas coherently and of intervening meaningfully in real areas of struggle. They, of course, were not paralyzed by the organization phobia that afflicted all other libertarian tendencies.

In the next issue of Solidarity *L.S. (of Aberdeen) objected:*

Although I have no particular wish to defend an "apostolic succession" of anarchist thought, I feel I must question the side-comment on Kropotkin in Maurice Brinton's review. The reference is to Kropotkin's "notions that 'co-operation rather than conflict is at the root of the historical process…' (a co-operation that clearly transcended the barriers of class)". The parenthetical assumption is inaccurate, and does no justice to Kropotkin's thought. His theory of mutual aid applied to evolution rather than to the stages of historical development, and is opposed to the idea of "survival of the fittest" (an aspect of Darwinism that has proved its usefulness to fascist theoreticians) rather than to Marxist concepts of class struggle. Kropotkin believed that groups co-operating successfully, not the strong preying on the weak, tended to survive. In primitive societies there would be no question of cutting across class barriers; and when class conflicts arose at a later stage, few socialists could dispute that organization in a co-operative manner becomes essential for the insurgent classes if they are to overthrow their oppressors and survive.

The extent to which Kropotkin was aware of the nature and potency of class conflict in history is manifest in his volume on The Great French Revolution (London, 1909). A massive work, in which a Solidarist could certainly pick out evidence of "muddleheadedness", it nevertheless gives a comprehensive and supremely class-conscious account of events from the first stirrings of the revolution in the 1780s to the "triumph of reaction" in Thermidor 1794. The description of bourgeois methods, using workers and peasants against king and nobles, then turning to repression if popular movements threatened to get out of their control, is probably unequalled in the historiography of the French Revolution; and Kropotkin's constant, unequivoval sympathy with the betrayed, defeated and still oppressed people is anything but 'genteel'!

Maurice Brinton replied:

Kropotkin's theory of "mutual aid" may or may not be a more plausible interpretation of the facts of *biological* evolution than Darwin's theory of "natural selection through the survival of the fittest". This has little to do, however, with the main issue, namely whether Kropotkin's theory has any relevance to the understanding of the *historical* process, i.e. to *human* history.

Kropotkin himself certainly believed his concepts of "mutual aid" were relevant to sociology as well as to biology. (L.S. seems in two minds on this point: she first states that Kropotkin's theory of mutual aid applies "to evolution rather than to the stages of historical development" - but then proceeds to give examples clearly drawn from the realm of sociology.)

In my opinion the sociological relevance of Kropotkin's theory is limited to relations *within a class* (he vividly describes the sense of solidarity within certain social groups). The concept clearly does *not* apply to the struggle between classes. And since the days of slavery class struggle has been a constant feature of human history. Unlike most animal species the genus *Homo Sapiens* has from an early stage been divided into classes, these being determined by the relations men come into with other men in the course of economic life. The class struggle (and not "mutual aid" between classes) has moulded the face of history.

Did Kropotkin's ideas of "co-operation" transcend the class barriers? In the ultimate test of Kropotkin's own political life they clearly did. But they did so in his earlier writings too. These are full of "sweet reason" rather than anger. His aim is to convince and reason with (rather than to overthrow) those who oppress the masses. He does not really understand the class struggle. In *Mutual Aid* (Pelican edition (1939), p.229) he could decry "the teachings of mutual hatred and pitiless struggle which came, adorned with the attributes of science, from obliging philosophers and sociologists". The book received rave notices in the journals of the Victorian Establishment. It is no accident that so many of Kropotkin's supporters today are either pacifists or anarchists of the "back-to-the-simple-country-life" type. There is, in all this, an internal coherence.

It is true, as L.S. says, that Kropotkin's book (*The Great French Revolution, 1789-1793*) reveals the "extent to which Kropotkin was aware of the nature and potency of class conflict in history". But this assertion is double-edged. The major work analysing this tremendous upheaval *from a class point of view* remains Daniel Guérin's *La Lutte de classes sous la Première République* (Paris, 1946). This outstanding work contains a brilliant analysis of the historiographers of the French Revolution, from conservatives such as Thiers, via liberals such as Michelet (incidentally much admired by Kropotkin) down to Stalinists like Mathiez. Of Kropotkin, Guérin (now an anarchist) says: "Just like Jaurès the social-democrat, Kropotkin the libertarian has not entirely freed himself from modes of thought inherited from bourgeois democracy". Kropotkin's failing is hardly surprising. At a time when the understanding of history was being revolutionized, he could make the inane statement that "modern socialism has added absolutely nothing to the ideas that were circulating among the French people between 1789 and 1794" (*loc. cit.*, p.580).

There is nothing as painful as getting to grips with new ideas - or as supplementing emotion with understanding. Anarchist abstentionism in both these areas seems, alas, to be as old as the hills.

SOLIDARITY, IV, 11 AND 12 (JANUARY AND MARCH 1968)

12. FRANCE: REFORM OR REVOLUTION

French bourgeois society is today being rocked to its foundations. Ten million workers are on strike. Factories, building sites, shipyards, shops, schools and universities have been taken over by those who work there. The whole transport system is at a standstill. The red flag has been hoisted over railway stations and state theatres, pitheads and sedate educational establishments. Tens of thousands of people of all ages are discussing every aspect of life in packed-out, non-stop meetings in every available schoolroom and lecture hall. Even the peasants are moving, driving their tractors into the market places of country towns and challenging the authorities. The police force is vacillating. Even the "elite" paramilitary formations of the bourgeois state – the CRS – are being subjected to repeated drubbings in the streets.

No one "called" for this general strike. No one foresaw this tremendous upsurge of the masses, which caught all the traditional organizations of the "left" with their pants down. The pent-up criticism, anger, resentment and frustration of millions of young people against a society which treated them as objects is exploding in the greatest challenge to established French society since the days of the Paris Commune.

In the circumstances, the demands put forward by different sections of the French "left" are most revealing. The bourgeois politicians can see no further than a ministerial reshuffle. They are prepared to sacrifice a few big names in order to canalize the movement back into safe, parliamentary channels. Their game is so obvious that no one is likely to be fooled by it. As for the Socialist Party (SFIO), it is utterly discredited by years of opportunist and class-collaborationist policies. After all, it was a "socialist" Minister of the Interior, Jules Moch, who created the hated CRS. When the million-strong demonstration marched past the SFIO headquarters on the Boulevard de Magenta, on May 13, they shouted "Guy Mollet, to the museum".

The Communist Party and the CGT have been dragged into a tornado which they had not foreseen, do not understand, and whose development has constantly escaped their control. From the outset they have been more concerned about being outflanked on the left than in developing this tremendous mass movement. During the last three weeks every issue of *L'Humanité* has contained denunciations of the students and warnings against "provocateurs", "irresponsible elements", "anarchists" and "Trotskyists". (The bourgeois press speaks much the same language.) The Communists refer to Cohn-Bendit, one of the student leaders, as an agent of the CIA (while Prime Minister Pompidou hints that he is an agent of the Chinese). It seems beyond their combined comprehension that he might be what he claims to be: an "agent" of the Nanterre students.

The demands put forward by the CGT are very limited ones: a wage increase, a shortening of the working week, a lowering of the retiring age, the abolition of charges recently imposed on social security benefits, and the recognition of trade union organization in the factories. These demands are perfectly legitimate and justified, but also perfectly compatible with the continued rule of the bourgeoisie. Yet it is precisely this rule which the advanced sections of the workers and students are prepared to challenge. None of the industrial demands put forward by the CGT is in any way revolutionary. Even if granted, the ruling class could take everything back tomorrow through inflation or devaluation.

At the political level, the Communist Party sees no further than the replacement of the Gaullist regime by a "popular front" led by Mitterand, in which the CP would be "adequately" represented. At a time when every social institution (from the *lycées* to the Football Federation, from managerial authority in the factories to Parliament itself) is being questioned and challenged, the Communist Party can see no further than a reshuffle of seats in the Palais Bourbon.

The present movement started earlier this year at Nanterre, near Paris, when groups of students decided to challenge the central assumptions of bourgeois education by direct action methods (interruption of lectures, holding political meetings on the campus, etc.). They proclaimed that they rejected the whole hierarchical structure of the university, its selection and examination procedures, its administrative methods and more especially its function as a provider of industrial sociologists and psychologists whose purpose in life would be to help control and manipulate the working class. Confronted with this quite deliberate and openly admitted "provocation", the state authorities committed one bureaucratic blunder after another, each of which was to permit the student movement to take another leap forward. The police were eventually called into the faculties, thus provoking the total and irrevocable disaffection of the whole student community.

None of the traditional parties has really grasped what the students were after… or rather they grasp it only too well. None are prepared to face the implications of the student challenge - namely that to explode the class basis of the university is to present established society with an intolerable threat. That is why the Communist Party still talks about the "student agitation" in terms of "bigger educational budgets", "more teachers", "better facilities", etc, instead of describing its real and profoundly revolutionary content.

This also explains why every attempt by the revolutionary students to link up with rank-and-file workers now occupying the factories is being strenuously and often physically opposed by the CGT apparatus. The students are talking about workers' power, about a free society, things which the bureaucrats do not want the workers to think too much about. At Nantes, a student delegation from Paris, sent to establish contact with an occupied factory, was handed over to the police by a group of CGT pickets who happened to be Stalinist hacks. These attempts at dividing the movement, successful at first, are beginning to break down as the students show, in action, their militancy and their readiness to pursue the struggle to the bitter end.

It is this student militancy which terrifies every conservative layer of French society, from the readers of the *Figaro* to the elderly functionaries of the CGT. The students have shown that Gaullism is not omnipotent, that it is possible to fight back against the oppressive apparatus of the bourgeois state, and that it is possible to pass from a critique of bourgeois education to a total critique, in action, of the capitalist state.

Alone, of course, the students cannot change society. But student militancy has triggered off a massive working class response, compounded of sympathy, hatred of the police, and the advocacy of their own specific demands. The fate of the revolution now hinges on an unanswerable, yet all important question. Will the workers' objectives remain confined to improvements *within* the system? Or will they, like the students, take up the struggle on a much broader front? Will they eventually struggle against modern bureaucratic capitalist society, in all its multiple manifestations? Only if the workers undertake this far more difficult fight, a fight which no one can wage for them, a fight which implies a ruthless struggle against "their own" organizations, will the revolution be successful in any real sense. Only on the basis of such a struggle will it become impossible for various bureaucratic leaderships to take the movement in hand again, and lead it up a blind alley.

What of the other groups, to the left of the Communist Party? At a time when everything is still possible, when more and more people are realizing that the future will only contain what people put into it now, the imagination of many self-styled "revolutionaries" remains caught up in the bureaucratic thinking of a previous epoch.

The various Trotskyist groups fail to see the tremendous potentialities of the situation. Their main preoccupation is to establish *their* leadership over the mass movement. They all say that what is missing is the Party (which they all interpret as their particular party). None of them have confidence in the ability of the workers or students to solve their problems without this kind of tutelage. Some call for the Communists to take power (just as in this country they asked you to vote Labour at the last election) in order to "take the masses through the experience". Their economic demands only differ quantitatively from the Stalinist ones. They all engage in a kind of revolutionary auction. For instance, *Voix Ouvrière* advocates a minimum monthly wage of 1000 new francs, instead of the 600 new francs advocated by the CGT.

Trotskyist groups such as the FER (Fédération des Etudiants Révolutionnaires) are calling for organizational measures such as the setting up of a hierarchy of strike committees (with a national strike committee at the top) representing the various strike-bound factories and enterprises. Given the present relationship of forces, the Stalinists would be in an overwhelming majority on such bodies. The idea is to "expose" the Stalinists, should they seek to liquidate the strike in exchange for financial concessions from the employers or parliamentary concessions from the bourgeois state. From this "exposure", the Trotskyists hope to benefit. The incalculable damage done to the working class in the process is dismissed as an inevitable overhead.

The practical acts of the Trotskyists have proved equally nefarious. On the "night of the barricades" (May 10, 1968), despite repeated appeals for help, the FER refused to cancel its mass meeting at the Mutualité and to send reinforcements to assist the students and workers who were already engaged in a bitter fight with the CRS, on the barricades of the Rue Gay-Lussac, hardly a mile away. When several hundred FER members and sympathisers eventually turned up at 1.00 am, it was only to advise students to disperse. In the words of Chisseray, one of the Trotskyist "leaders", it was "necessary above all to preserve the revolutionary vanguard from an unnecessary massacre". The fact has been widely discussed in the mass assemblies, held night after night in the packed amphitheatres of Censier and La Sorbonne. Thousands are undergoing an extremely rapid education, through practice, as to the nature of Stalinism and Trotskyism and how they both seek to manipulate the mass movement in their own respective interests.

At first only a handful of revolutionary socialists and anarchists appreciated the tremendous opportunities now opening up. These groups, which are tending more and more to get together, are talking in terms of a *total* social revolution, of workers' management of production (*autogestion*) and of the need for workers' councils. In fact this radical viewpoint now presents the traditional left with the most widely-based challenge it has ever had to face. On the initiative of the revolutionaries, hundreds of *Comités d'action* have been set up in various factories and districts of Paris and other large towns. These committees consist of workers and students, agreed upon a programme of direct action in a given locality or enterprise and who also see the need to develop the mass movement as quickly, widely and radically as possible. Their activities are already getting an enthusiastic response, not only among wide layers of the student population but among smaller layers of young workers. If and when the working class as a whole itself takes up these demands (and gives them flesh and blood) the door will at least be open for a total, final challenge to French capitalist society, a challenge it will no longer be able to contain.

SOLIDARITY LEAFLET (MAY 1968).

13. FRANCE: THE THEORETICAL IMPLICATIONS

This pamphlet[82] produced five months after the events it describes is not really an attempt to analyze the French events of May and June 1968. At this level - as we shall show - it epitomizes the theoretical incapacity of even the more sophisticated representatives of the contemporary Marxist Left. The Cliff-Birchall text is something quite different. It is a factional document, aimed primarily at influencing the discussion on the "organizational question" now taking place within International Socialism between Leninists and libertarian revolutionaries.

After a major earthquake, everyone longs for a return to order. The French events are no exception. Today the Préfecture de Police wants order in the streets. The Minister of Education wants order in the universities. The CGT and Communist Party want order in the factories. And the traditional revolutionaries want order... in the realm of ideas.

But it is the hallmark of all truly revolutionary events that they show no more respect for established ideas than they do for established institutions. All major social upheavals in history have gone far beyond the anticipations of even the most radical revolutionaries of the previous period. Whether immediately recognized or not, they have raised *new* issues, thrown up *new* social forms and created *new* problems of theory and practice. The French Revolution of 1968 was no exception.

During the Commune of 1871 the Paris workers put forward the demands for a ceiling on wages and for the eligibility and revocability of all officials. These demands had not been - and could not have been - anticipated in Marx's writings. When the first soviets appeared in Russia in 1905 their significance was not apparent to Lenin or to the Bolsheviks. They had not been anticipated in any Party programme. But both Marx and Lenin were to incorporate the autonomous creations of the French and Russian workers into their own theoretical frameworks. It is a symptom of the degeneration of the contemporary Left that nothing similar has happened - or been felt necessary - in relation to recent events in France.

The pamphlet under review is like a piece of Gruyère cheese, full of holes and with a thick and rather mouldy rind. It fails to recognize any of the *new phenomena* (new in themselves or new to traditional theory) witnessed earlier this year in France. It fails to grasp the tremendous implications of the new type of issue ("self-management") around which the struggle was initially fought. The question of nationalization, plugged by revolutionaries for decades, just did not enter anyone's mind. Isn't this worthy of comment?

The traditional organizations, confronted with a human flood tide of this size, were initially swept aside. The massive influx into them, prophesied by sundry revolutionaries for years just did not materialize. In fact these hollow shells only retained any residual influence to the extent that people had reservations as to their own capacity to manage things for themselves. This isn't even sensed. Instead the pamphlet learnedly dissects the minor fluctuations of the CGT and CFDT votes, without stressing that less than 20% of French workers belong to a union *of any kind* - and without seeking to assess the deep significance of *that* phenomenon, at a time when

---

82   Tony Cliff and Ian Birchall, *France: The Struggle Goes On* (London: Socialist Review Publishing Co.).

ten million workers are prepared to occupy their factories in the biggest general strike in history.

The pamphlet does not sense the *new specific weight* now to be allocated in the revolutionary process to previously marginal layers of society, to new strata of the working class or even to new age groups. For instance, never before in history has one seen massive and militant political demonstrations of schoolboys aged fifteen or sixteen.

Nor does the pamphlet recognize the *new dynamic* through which the struggle unfurled, a dynamic which is itself a product of the increasing bureaucratization of all social institutions under modern capitalism. In a society where everything is planned and anticipated (except that the manipulated should erupt against their manipulation) deliberate and systematic "provocation" - like that indulged in by the March 22 Movement - can, and did, have profound repercussions. The *new revolutionaries* (whose ideas and style of action aren't even suspected as a *new* element in the situation) clearly anticipated the bureaucratic responses to their new pinpricks, each of which succeeded in escalating the conflict in the desired direction.

In its conclusions, the Cliff-Birchall pamphlet goes no further than to echo what Trotsky wrote about the French events... of June 1936. (Trotsky's views were probably already out of date at that time.) In discussing, finally, what is now needed in Britain, the authors come down - yes, wait for it - for a Revolutionary Party built on the principles of "democratic centralism", the latter defined straight out of L.D.B.'s writings of... 1924. *Parturiunt montes; nascetur ridiculus mus.*[83]

The French events of May and June 1968 have sounded the death knell of Western bureaucratic capitalist society. But they also herald the end of all those "revolutionary" groups whose basic concepts of "hierarchically structured leadership" so integrally reflect the society around them that they fail to recognize that the masses themselves have already gone beyond these conceptions. The decomposition of "vanguardist" politics will be an integral part of the decomposition of bourgeois-bureaucratic authoritarianism in general. When this dog dies its fleas will die with it.

For revolutionaries who want to understand events (and not just tail-end them or live them as visitations from outer space) the upheaval in France has profound theoretical implications. In this article we can only formulate some of the more urgent questions which no one seems to be asking, let alone seeking to answer.

1. The most clear and obvious thing about the French events is that, a month before they took place, their imminence and quality was clear and obvious to no one. Why didn't either the French Establishment - or the French revolutionaries - anticipate what was about to happen?

Gaullism was about to enter its tenth year. It basked in complacent self-confidence. It had "modernized" the French economy, extricated France from the Algerian imbroglio, broken free of the American embrace, developed a French Hydrogen Bomb, even cleaned up the facades of the Louvre and of the Opéra. Over this period the gross national product had been increasing at an average rate of 5% per annum (in volume terms, i.e. at constant prices) and real wages by about the same amount. True, over the last eighteen months, unemployment had been rising slightly,[84] but by and large the economic basis of the regime seemed fairly stable. Not even

---

83　"The mountains are in labour; an absurd mouse will be born".

84　From 240,000 to 280,000 according to official statistics. These may be unreliable for a number of reasons but even if the figures are increased by 50% this still represents only some 2% of the labour force. This increase in unemployment, which affects mainly young people, is neither "cyclical" nor "technological" but "demographic".

the most percipient of Gaullists could have sensed the social cataclysm that lay immediately ahead.

But neither had this been sensed by the revolutionaries. A perusal of *Voix Ouvrière*, *Révoltes*, or *Avant-Garde* for the early months of 1968 gives no inkling of awareness that France was on the threshold of a major convulsion. The content of these papers could have been written at any time during the last ten (or twenty, or thirty) years. They contained the usual denunciations of the economic policy of the government, the usual "exposures" of the "betrayals" of the CGT and of the Communist Party (combined with descriptions of perennially unsuccessful attempts to capture positions within these outfits), the usual prognostications as to the likelihood of slump in the more or less distant future (on account of the "insurmountable economic contradictions of capitalism"), the customary denunciation of the latest crime of the Stalinist bureaucracy, and the ritual epilogue: the need to build the revolutionary party of Leninist type (of which each tendency saw itself as the sole, historically-predetermined nucleus). Early in 1968, all this was being recited as usual, but without any *special* sense of urgency.

This convergence of outlooks between Establishment and established revolutionaries is really most interesting. Its deep roots lie in the fact that both used the same kind of yardstick. They looked at production, consumption, wages and employment. They used the same kind of thermometer to assess the clinical condition of the body politic. They both looked for the same kind of symptoms of possible disease. Neither seemed aware that new diseases might develop, with symptoms of an entirely new kind, or that the thermometer itself might now be quite the wrong kind of instrument with which to diagnose them. From opposite sides of the (then largely metaphorical) barricades they shared a common outlook on life. When Marx said that the dominant ideas of each epoch were the ideas of its ruling class, little did he foresee how deeply true this statement would one day become.

It is of little concern to revolutionaries that the bourgeoisie should have been incapable of foreseeing the crisis towards which it was heading. What should concern them, however, are the shortcomings of their own philosophy, with its bold claim to be the means "not only of interpreting the world, but of changing it".

We don't want to be misunderstood. Our critique is not that traditional theory failed to predict the precise moment when the upheaval would take place. It's not a question of faulty revolutionary chronometry. (Only the crudest determinists have ever attempted to use Marxism in this way.) It is a question of whether established Marxist categories can now provide even an elementary insight into the kind of upheaval that is on the historical agenda. In relation to France, they clearly failed. Why? And what are the implications of this failure? What would aircraft pilots say of a brand of radar that didn't even suspect, in the immediate vicinity, the presence of a mountain 20,000 feet high?

2. The second lot of questions flow automatically from the first. Are the traditional criteria (level of employment, level of consumption, etc.) still adequate in assessing the social tensions within a given society and hence the proximity or otherwise of a revolutionary upheaval? Or do they need to be replaced or amplified by other criteria, more difficult to quantify (sense of alienation, sense of dissatisfaction with the nature of work or the quality of life, rejection of established

---

It is related to the sudden increase in births in the years which immediately followed the war (1945–1950). The "overcrowding" in the universities is partly due to the same cause. That the authorities should have chosen to ride "the bulge" rather than to expand production or increase the number of lecture halls is another question.

values, gap between expectations and reality, desire to break out of the proletarian condition, whatever the level of wages, etc.). The main danger here is to avoid a lapse into mysticism. But even Marxists must admit that "man does not live by bread alone"...

Both bourgeois and revolutionary historians have until now seen the preconditions of social revolution in mainly economic terms. Men have revolted because the social system has been incapable of providing them with the basic economic necessities of life. Past revolutionary upheavals have tended to occur in condition of economic duress, or in the wake of wars, or both (Paris, 1871; Russia, 1905 and 1917; Germany, 1918; Hungary, 1919; the British General Strike, 1926; the Belgian General Strike, 1960–61). This has never been a thoroughly satisfactory explanation of revolutionary upheavals (Spain 1936 and Hungary 1956 have always been notoriously difficult to interpret on this basis). We believe this kind of interpretation is likely to be less and less satisfactory in the future.

The French Thunderbolt fell out of a fairly clear economic sky. The students whose struggle played so important a role were not starving. Over 90% of them were of bourgeois or petty bourgeois origin. The workers at Sud-Aviation and Renault, who initiated the factory occupations, were among the best paid in the country. The "traditional" criteria do not help one understand the real nature of such events.

We don't doubt that those who are unable to develop a new idea of their own will now devote their energy and time to skillful use of the "retrospectoscope". They will belatedly discern in the pattern of industrial struggle in France, during the early months of 1968, the obvious harbingers of what in fact followed. The pamphlet under review does this at some length. The endeavour is rather pointless however. The man-hours lost through strikes during 1967 or during the first three months of 1968 have certainly been exceeded on many occasions during other arbitrary three or twelve month periods of the Gaullist reign. The fairly recent police violence against workers at Rhodiaceta (Lyon), Caen and Redon had had its bloody antecedents during the great miners' strike of 1949 and in the Charonne massacre of 1962. The level of unemployment may have risen from 1.5% to 2% of the labour force during the last few months but this in itself hardly represents the transgression of some critical point below which nothing happens and above which everything suddenly becomes possible (unemployment levels incidentally have been consistently higher in Britain).

One has to look elsewhere for the beginnings of an interpretation. The "old mole of history" had been burrowing deep. The bureaucratic society had generated new tensions of its own – some of which are clearly anticipated in Cardan's *Modern Capitalism and Revolution*[85]. The gulf between expectations and reality had been steadily widening and this not only in relation to consumption. So had the gulf between order-givers and order-takers, at all levels of society. Attitudes had been changing – even attitudes to the presence of 400,000 unemployed. Traditional values had been disintegrating. Whole new layers of society had been proletarianized, *not* according to the Marxist model of absolute or relative pauperization, but in the sense of a profound transformation of the nature of their world. The increasing bureaucratization of society at all levels had not only rendered the traditional organization meaningless for hundreds of thousands of young people, but had also ensured that those in authority were less and less capable of understanding and controlling a reality whose real nature constantly eluded them.

---

85   This book is essential to an understanding of our epoch.

It is on the basis of considerations such as these – however tenuous and inadequately defined at the moment – that one should attempt a reconstruction of revolutionary theory. Ideas cannot remain static while reality changes – nor can a new reality be grasped without a revolution in ideas. Religion may reflect a neurotic insecurity when confronted with the unknown. It is a form of false consciousness. Traditional theory is now in danger of playing exactly the same role.

But there is nothing as painful as a new idea. Some will deny the need for any kind of theoretical framework or – at most – will cling to a few primitive slogans (state: bad; self-activity: good). Others will prefer to hang on to a schema which they sense to be inadequate rather than embark on the difficult yet imperative task now confronting serious revolutionaries – that of the collective elaboration of a new revolutionary theory.

3. Why did the revolutionary upheaval start among the students? Why did they struggle with such militancy and courage? Was their revolt just a "spark" or "fuse" which "detonated" the working class? Or has it a deeper significance at its own level?

Two attitudes seem to be emerging on this subject. Both are inadequate.

One attitude, epitomized in the *Black Dwarf* (and also put forward in some of the writings of the German SDS), sees the students as the "new revolutionary vanguard". It assigns to them the role assigned to the proletariat in classical revolutionary theory. It more or less explicitly puts forward the view that the working class is becoming or had become integrated into the "affluent society" and that it has lost all revolutionary potential.

Cliff and Birchall correctly take Wright Mills and Marcuse to task for "denying the revolutionary potentiality of the working class" and for "describing students and intellectuals as the main vehicle for revolutionary action now and in the future". But it is interesting – although hardly surprising – that they fail to identify the real fount of this pernicious doctrine. In 1901 Kautsky (in his draft programme for the Austrian Social-Democratic Party) wrote that it was "absolutely untrue" that socialist consciousness was a "necessary and direct result of the proletarian class struggle". "Modern socialist consciousness could arise only on the basis of profound scientific knowledge". "The vehicle of science was not the proletariat but the bourgeois intelligentsia". "Socialist consciousness is something introduced into the proletarian struggle from without".[86] Lenin, in his *What Is To Be Done?*, endorsed Kautsky's views on this matter describing them as a "profoundly true and important utterance".[87] The ideological premise for this conclusion was Lenin's belief that "the working class, by its own efforts, is able only to develop trade union consciousness".[88] It requires no great effort to understand all the substitutionist practices that must inevitably flow – and have inevitably flowed – from such a conception. In their absolute rejection of the notion that the working class, through its own experiences in modern industrial society, can, does and must autonomously accede to a socialist consciousness, Marcuse and Lenin have more in common than the followers of either would like to believe.

The fallacy of this first attitude should be obvious. If the working class cannot come to understand socialism – and want it – there can be no socialist perspective.

---

86   *Neue Zeit*, XX (1901–'02), I, No.3, p.79.

87   Lenin, *Selected Works*, II, p.61

88   *Ibid.*, p.33.

There can only be the replacement of one ruling elite by another. However "enlightened" and "revolutionary" the new elite may be, it will sooner or later come to express its own interests, rather than those of the working class.

The second attitude to students (shared by most "orthodox" Marxists) is less naive but just as short-sighted. It correctly sees the students as a minority in modern industrial society, the need for the majority to move if anything fundamental is to happen and the fact that this majority, in advanced industrial countries, is the working class. Its inadequacy is that it cannot transcend the conception of student action as just a "catalyst", "fuse" or "spark", capable of igniting the powder kegs of industrial discontent but devoid of any deeper significance at its own level.

This is to underestimate the increasing importance (and increasing vulnerability) today of both the university and of education generally. Both help maintain the social cohesion of class society. Reinforcing patriarchal authority, both help perpetuate (at the ideological level) the prevailing relations of hierarchy and domination. In the long run both prove more effective mechanisms for helping the slaves accept their slavery than either police or prison. In the realm of ideas they provide the basic mechanism for the replication of bourgeois-bureaucratic society, of its values and assumptions, generation after generation. But the *lycées* and universities of France are now full of students, with heads full of "subversive" thoughts. The night-long discussions of last May, in occupied schools and faculties, among young people, will leave indelible marks.

The university churns out the technologists, sociologists, industrial psychologists, computer programmers, managers, time-and-motion experts, in short the whole administrative personnel of the modern industrial machine. In France substantial numbers of students began to refuse the future role assigned to them as "watchdogs of capital". If this mood lasts (and particularly if it spreads beyond the faculties of sociology, philosophy or psychology), the effects could be profound. In May even such traditional disciplines as medicine and law were not immune from the general ferment. Closing particular faculties or even whole universities would be a double-edged weapon for the authorities, an open admission of failure, a permanent mutilation of the liberal image they have been at such pains to protect.

Workers on strike can stop assembly lines. But a deep implantation of "subversives" in universities could disrupt the mass production of conformist cadres, and prove an additional spoke in the wheels of bourgeois society. The Establishment can tolerate students demanding bigger credits for higher education. It cannot tolerate demands that the universities "be converted into Red bases", or that they "provide facilities for continuous political forums, open to all", etc. Revolutionaries in France now see the universities as permanent foci of contestation of bourgeois ideology, permanent running sores on the body of bourgeois society. The current backwardness of the student movement in Britain makes it difficult for us soberly to conceive of this here, but last year few in France would have thought it possible either. The theory of French "exceptionalism" - based on such undoubted realities as the rigidity of official French institutions, the widespread hatred of the *flics* (cops) in France, and the undoubted French aptitude for critical revolutionary thought - should not be taken too far.

These aspects of what the students did in May 1968 differ from what "intellectuals" have done in previous revolutions (1871, 1917, or even in Hungary in 1956). Then, they helped articulate popular demands. Now, by making radical demands of their own, demands which cannot be encompassed by the system, they are opening a second front in the onslaught against bourgeois society. Fully aware of the dangers of being trapped in a "ghetto" of university politics, the modern French revolutionaries also reject the false alternative of struggling for purely student demands or total and exclusive immersion in the working class fight. This new type of consciousness isn't even hinted at in the Cliff-Birchall pamphlet.

The totality of the student rejection of bourgeois society explains the totality of their dedication to the revolutionary cause and the totality of their involvement in the struggle on the streets. It was not the product of economic misery. It reflected something more fundamental. The students were being denied the right to be themselves – and had become aware of the fact. They were not risking loss of sight and limb (amid the gas grenades and batons of the CRS) for a 3% annual increase in the size of the educational budget. They were fighting for the right to reappropriate what bourgeois society was taking from them. When this dormant consciousness is aroused in other layers of the population, the effect will be irresistible. *This* is the real lesson and hope of the French events of May 1968.

SOLIDARITY, V, 8 (MARCH 1969)

14. THE EVENTS IN FRANCE

This book,[89] although hastily compiled to meet the mass demand for such works which followed the events of May 1968, is nevertheless essential reading. It is an exciting piece of living history, written by articulate and active participants, one of whom became the spokesman for a wide layer of student revolutionaries. The original French version was called *Le Gauchisme - remède à la maladie sénile du communisme* - a witty and meaningful rejoinder to Lenin's denunciation of left-wing communism as an "infantile disorder". The English title is unfortunately quite meaningless.

Starting with the student revolt in modern industrial societies, the authors analyze the background to the March 22 Movement, the spread of the ideas of May to sections of the working class, the strategy of the bourgeois state, the Gaullist phenomenon and - in considerable detail - the role of the Communist Party and its historical roots in ideology and previous practice.

The authors' thinking is throughout clearly influenced by material published in *Socialisme ou Barbarie, Internationale Situationniste, Informations et Correspondance Ouvrières, Noir et Rouge*, and *Recherches Libertaires*, an ideological debt freely, but rather erratically, acknowledged. The "plagiarism" is extensive, intelligently selective and thoroughly commendable, ensuring a wide audience for views as yet insufficiently known. Great chunks, for instance, of the Solidarity Pamphlet on *The Workers' Opposition* are to be found in the authors' discussion of the nature of Bolshevism. As the authors nicely put it: "Cohn-Bendit is simply the anonymous author of all these reviews".

I have but one criticism and it has been voiced before. It is a note of scepticism concerning the implied proximity of total revolution. It is hard to accept that, last May, it was touch and go whether everything would be swept aside. Or to believe that if, on the morning of May 25, Paris had awoken with several ministries occupied, Gaullism would have collapsed... and self-management become an objective immediately to be fulfilled.

The grip of class society unfortunately exerts itself at a much deeper level than the authors appear to suspect. Even the decomposition of bourgeois state power - and one could argue whether it was as profound as they believe - is no guarantee that bourgeois institutions will be replaced by consciously created socialist ones. The essential precondition for a radical and total social transformation is the change, brought about through the class struggle itself, in the attitudes of the mass of the population, i.e. the working class. These attitudes today are not only coloured by the traditional organizations but are constantly reinforced by the very conditions of capitalist production and of life in capitalist society (passivity of workers subjected to domination by machines, pressure of financial insecurity, preoccupation with only immediate things, etc.). These attitudes (which add up to the more or less widespread acceptance of slavery by the majority of the slaves) are one of the main causes for the perpetuation of bourgeois or bureaucratic rule. (Other factors act in an opposite direction, constantly compelling people to question the methods, priorities and rela-

---

89   Gabriel Cohn–Bendit and Daniel Cohn–Bendit, *Obsolete Communism: The Left-Wing Alternative* (London: André Deutsch, 1968) also: (Oakland: AK Press, 2000).

tions of capitalist production.) The ideological superstructure of capitalist society isn't as "fragile" as many revolutionaries seem to think. It has enormous resilience and to shatter it a whole epoch of sustained and conscious struggle will be necessary. The French events undoubtedly initiated such a period. But by ignoring this facet, the Cohn-Bendit book at times unconsciously lapses into a system of ideas in which the role of active minorities would seem to be paramount. Paradoxically, it is a system of ideas which thus explicitly formulated the authors would be the first to reject.

SOLIDARITY, V, 9 (APRIL 1969)

15. CAPITALISM AND SOCIALISM

What is basically wrong with capitalism? Ask a number of socialists and you will get a number of different answers. These will depend on their vision of what socialism might be like and on their ideas as to what political action is all about. Revolutionary libertarian socialists see these things very differently from the trad "left". This article is not an attempt to counterpoise two conceptions of socialism and political action. It is an attempt to stress a facet of socialist thought that is in danger of being forgotten.

When one scratches beneath the surface, "progressive" capitalists, liberals, Labour reformists, "communist" macro-bureaucrats and Trotskyist mini-bureaucrats all see the evils of capitalism in much the same way. They all see them as primarily economic ills, flowing from a particular pattern of ownership of the means of production. When Khrushchev equated socialism with "more goulash for everyone" he was voicing a widespread view. Innumerable quotations could be found to substantiate this assertion.

If you don't believe that traditional socialists think in this way, try suggesting to one of them that modern capitalism is beginning to solve some economic problems. He will immediately denounce you as having "given up the struggle for socialism". He cannot grasp that slumps were a feature of societies that state capitalism had not sufficiently permeated and that they are not intrinsic features of capitalist society. "No economic crisis" is, for the traditional socialist, tantamount to "no crisis". It is synonymous with "capitalism has solved its problems". The traditional socialist feels insecure, as a socialist, if told that capitalism can solve this kind of problem, because for him this is *the* problem, par excellence, affecting capitalist society.

The traditional "left" today has a crude vision of man, of his aspirations and his needs, a vision moulded by the rotten society in which we live. It has a narrow concept of class consciousness. For them class consciousness is primarily an awareness of "non-ownership". They see the "social problem" being solved as the majority of the population gain access to material wealth. All would be well, they say or imply, if as a result of their capture of state power (and of their particular brand of planning) the masses could only be ensured a higher level of consumption. "Socialism" is equated with full bellies. The filling of these bellies is seen as the fundamental task of the socialist revolution.

Intimately related to this concept of man as essentially a producing and consuming machine is the whole traditional "left" critique of laissez-faire capitalism. Many on the "left" continue to think we live under this kind of capitalism and continue to criticize it because it is inefficient (in the domain of production). The whole of John Strachey's writings prior to World War II were dominated by these conceptions. His *Why You Should Be a Socialist* sold nearly a million copies – and yet the ideas of freedom or self-management do not appear in it, as part of the socialist objective. Many of the leaders of today's "left" graduated at his school, including the so-called revolutionaries. Even the usual vision of communism, "from each according to his ability, to each according to his needs", usually relates, in the minds of

"Marxists", to the division of the cake and not at all to the relations of man with man and between man and his environment.

For the traditional socialist "raising the standard of living" is the main purpose of social change. Capitalism allegedly cannot any longer develop production. (Anyone ever caught in a traffic jam, or in a working class shopping area on a Saturday afternoon, will find this a strange proposition.) It seems to be of secondary importance to this kind of socialist that under modern capitalism people are brutalized at work, manipulated in consumption and in leisure, their intellectual capacity stunted or their taste corrupted by a commercial culture. One must be "soft", it is implied, if one considers the systematic destruction of human beings to be worth a big song and dance. Those who talk of socialist objectives as being *freedom in production* (as well as out of it) are dismissed as "Utopians".

Were it not that misrepresentation is now an established way of life on the "left", it would seem unnecessary to stress that as long as millions of the world's population have insufficient food and clothing, the satisfaction of basic material needs must be an essential part of the socialist programme (and in fact of *any* social programme whatsoever, which does not extol the virtues of poverty.) The point is that by concentrating entirely on this aspect of the critique of capitalism the propaganda of the traditional "left" deprives itself of one of the most telling weapons of socialist criticism, namely an exposure of what capitalism does to people, particularly in countries where basic needs have by and large been met. And whether Guevarist or Maoist friends like it or not, it *is* in these countries, where there is a proletariat, that the socialist future of mankind will be decided.

This particular emphasis in the propaganda of the traditional organizations is not accidental. When they talk of increasing production in order to increase consumption, reformists and bureaucrats of one kind or another feel on fairly safe ground. Despite the nonsense talked by many "Marxists" about "stagnation of the productive forces", bureaucratic capitalism (of both the Eastern and Western types) *can* develop the means of production, has done so and is still doing so on a gigantic scale. It can provide (and historically has provided) a gradual increase in the standard of living – at the cost of intensified exploitation during the working day. It can provide a fairly steady level of employment. So can a well-run gaol. But on the ground of the subjection of man to institutions which are not of his choice, the socialist critiques of capitalism and bureaucratic society retain all their validity. In fact, their validity increases as modern society simultaneously solves the problem of mass poverty *and* becomes increasingly bureaucratic and totalitarian.

It will probably be objected that some offbeat trends in the "Marxist" movement do indulge in this wider kind of critique and in a sense this is true. Yet whatever the institutions criticized, their critique usually hinges, ultimately, on the notion of the unequal distribution of wealth. It consists in variations on the theme of the corrupting influence of money. When they talk for instance of the sexual problem or of the family, they talk of the economic barriers to sexual emancipation, of hunger pushing women to prostitution, of the poor young girl sold to the wealthy man, of the domestic tragedies resulting from poverty. When they denounce what capitalism does to culture they will do so in terms of the obstacles that economic needs puts in the way of talent, or they will talk of the venality of artists. All this is undoubtedly of great importance. But it is only the surface of the problem. Those socialists who can only speak in these terms see man in much less than his full stature. They see him as the bourgeoisie does, as a consumer (of food, of wealth, of culture, etc.). The essential, however, for man is to fulfil *himself*. Socialism must give man an opportunity to create, not only in the economic field but in all fields of human endeavour. Let the cynics smile and pretend that all this is petty-bourgeois utopianism. "The problem", Marx said, "is to organize the world in such a manner that man experiences in it the truly human, becomes accustomed to experience himself as a man, to assert his true individuality".

Conflicts in class society do not simply result from inequalities of distribution, or flow from a given division of the surplus value, itself the result of a given pattern of ownership of the means of production. Exploitation does not *only* result in a limitation of consumption for the many and financial enrichment for the few. This is but one aspect of the problem. Equally important are the attempts by both private and bureaucratic capitalism to limit – and finally to suppress altogether – the *human* role of man in the productive process. Man is increasingly expropriated from the very management of his own acts. He is increasingly alienated during all his activities, whether individual or collective. By subjecting man to the machine – and through the machine to an abstract and hostile will – class society deprives man of the real purpose of human endeavour, which is the constant, conscious transformation of the world around him. That men resist this process (and that their resistance implicitly raises the question of self-management) is as much a driving force in the class struggle as the conflict over the distribution of the surplus. Marx doubtless had these ideas in mind when he wrote that the proletariat "regards its independence and sense of personal dignity as more essential than its daily bread".

Class society profoundly inhibits the natural tendency of man to fulfil himself in the objects of his activity. In every country of the world this state of affairs is experienced day after day by the working class as an absolute misfortune, as a permanent mutilation. It results in a constant struggle at the most fundamental level of production: that of conscious, willing participation. The producers utterly reject (and quite rightly so) a system of production which is imposed upon them from above and in which they are mere cogs. Their inventiveness, their creative ability, their ingenuity, their initiative may be shown in their own lives, but are certainly not shown in production. In the factory these aptitudes may be used, but to quite different and "non-productive" ends! They manifest themselves in a resistance to production. This results in a constant and fantastic waste compared with which the wastage resulting from capitalist crises or capitalist wars is really quite trivial!

Alienation in capitalist society is not simply economic. It manifests itself in many other ways. The conflict in production does not "create" or "determine" secondary conflicts in other fields. Class domination manifests itself in all fields, at one and the same time. Its effects could not otherwise be understood. Exploitation, for instance, can only occur if the producers are expropriated from the management of production. But this presupposes that they are partly expropriated at least from the capacities of management – in other words from culture. And this cultural expropriation in turn reinforces those in command of the productive machine. Similarly a society in which relations between people are based on domination will maintain authoritarian attitudes in relation to sex and to education, attitudes creating deep inhibitions, frustrations and much unhappiness. The conflicts engendered by class society take place in every one of us. A social structure containing deep antagonisms reproduces these antagonisms in variable degrees in each of the individuals comprising it.

There is a profound dialectical inter-relationship between the social structure of a society and the attitudes and behaviour of its members. "The dominant ideas of each epoch are the ideas of its ruling class", whatever modern sociologists may think. Class society can only exist to the extent that it succeeds in imposing a widespread acceptance of its norms. From his earliest days man is subjected to constant pressures designed to mould his views in relation to work, to culture, to leisure, to thought itself. These pressures tend to deprive him of the natural enjoyment of his activity and even to make him accept this deprivation as something intrinsically good. In the past this job was assisted by religion. Today the same role is played by "socialist" and "communist" ideologies. But man is not infinitely malleable. This is why the bureaucratic project will come unstuck. Its objectives are in conflict with fundamental human aspirations.

We mention all this only to underline the essential identity of relations of domination - whether they manifest themselves in the capitalist factory, in the patriarchal family, in the authoritarian upbringing of children or in "aristocratic" cultural traditions. We also mention these facts to show that *the socialist revolution will have to take all these fields within its compass, and immediately, not in some far distant future.* The revolution must of course start with the overthrow of the exploiting class and with the institution of workers' management of production. But it will immediately have to tackle the reconstruction of social life in *all* its aspects. If it does not, it will surely die.

SOLIDARITY, V, 6 (DECEMBER 1968)

16. CAPITALISM AND SOCIALISM: A REJOINDER

"I never read a book before reviewing it. It prejudices one so" (Sydney Smith).

"They were standing under a tree, each with an arm round the other's neck, and Alice knew which was which in a moment, because one of them had 'DUM' embroidered on his collar, and the other 'DEE'. 'I suppose they've each got 'TWEE-DLE' round at the back of the collar', she said to herself..." (Lewis Carroll, Through the Looking Glass).

"Capitalism and Socialism" tried to break new ground. It sought to differentiate the kind of critique libertarian socialists should be making of capitalism from the purely economic (and therefore restrictive) critique made by the "traditional left". The article also sought to link this more total critique with a complementary (more total) vision of a free society, a society in which man would not only be free at the level of production but also free in all other areas where he is at present oppressed or alienated.

Under the title "Bread or Freedom" the following issue of *Solidarity* carried an attack on this article by J.S., roundly denouncing it as "rancid puritanism", "monasticism", "soggy humanitarianism" and "an argument against socialism".

Arguments are about ideas, and ideas cannot be wished away by appending labels to them, however derogatory. They have to be discussed on their own merit. This, J.S.'s article fails to do. Instead, like a man stung in a sensitive spot, he flings himself upon his horse and rides off madly in all directions. Two main ingredients of my original article seem to stick in J.S.'s throat. One is what he calls my "method", the basic weapon of which is "the amalgam". The other is my attack on the notion that "the conflicts and evils of society flow from a particular pattern of *ownership* of the means of production". According to J.S. "those who hold this view are correct in doing so". In my view this assessment of the roots of the conflict in modern society is both inadequate and incomplete.

***

The word "amalgam" implies the "lumping together" for the purposes of denunciation (or administrative action, such as liquidation) of people holding fundamentally dissimilar political viewpoints, but whose conjunctural objectives may superficially appear to coincide. J.S. points out that "Stalin could show that fascists, Trotskyists and anarchists were opposed to his regime. Fascists planned to invade the Soviet Union. Therefore Trotskyists were part of a fascist-Trotskyist conspiracy to carry out this invasion".[90]

This kind of smearing by "amalgam" is widely practiced in all parts of the political spectrum. It assumes a low level of political sophistication among those at whom it is addressed. Fascist politicians - or the more reactionary employers - denounce all their opponents as "reds" (without worrying unduly as to their doctrinal differences).

---

90   The example chosen is (significantly?) rather a late variant of the technique. For Solidarists, more interesting historical antecedents would be *Pravda's* denunciation (March 3, 1921) of the Kronstadt insurrection as "a White Guard plot ... expected and undoubtedly prepared by the French counter-revolution", or Lenin's assertion (*Selected Works*, vol. IX, p.98) that "White Guard generals...played a great role in this (the Kronstadt uprising). This is fully proved". Khrushchev later "proved" that the Hungarian Revolution of 1956 was an American plot.

Establishment Liberals call the Young Liberals "anarcho-syndicalists". Labour leaders appeal to the loyalty of their supporters, denouncing dissidence as "Tory-inspired". Trade union leaders, threatened with a rank-and-file challenge to their authority, can only think in terms of "anarchist conspiracy". "Left" critiques of the Communist Party are all, of course, initiated by the Economic League, and opposition to the General Secretary in Clapham High Street must of necessity originate in Scotland Yard.

But is the conceptual category of a "trad left" an "amalgam"? In politics one should not accept people at their own self-assessment, but seek objectively to evaluate their ideas and actions. Has the "trad left" - despite its squabbles - more in common than it realizes? Has it a common denominator of values, ideas, priorities, methods of action and methods of argument? Do its component parts share (whether explicitly or not) certain basic assumptions? Is the very heat engendered by its internal disputations the living proof that its publicists share common premises? "Capitalism and Socialism" asserted that there were such common premises and that this explained both the nature and limitations of the trad left's critique of capitalism and the narrowness of its vision of socialism might be like. There is nothing accidental in this phenomenon. The poisoned ideological fount is none other than the persistence of class society, of its values and of its ideology. The longer bourgeois or bureaucratic societies survive, the more deeply will bourgeois (or bureaucratic) ideology permeate the thinking of those who originally set out to destroy these societies. That "the dominant ideas of each epoch are the ideas of its ruling class" has now become true in a much deeper sense than Marx could have ever foreseen.

At this stage it is worth disposing of one objection voiced in "Bread or Freedom", namely that one cannot jointly label as trad socialists "those who wish to establish a society modelled on Soviet Russia *and* those who believe Russia is State Capitalist;[91] bureaucrats like Kosygin and Gomulka *and* revolutionary socialists like Kuron and Modzelewsi;[92] our present government *and* those who are trying to fight back against its anti-working class policies".[93]

Leaving aside the fanciful examples chosen, the implication of this kind of argument is that political controversy - in particular *heated* controversy - necessarily implies a difference over fundamentals. This just isn't true. When the Stalinists in Russia eliminated their Trotskyist opponents by methods of physical terror it was no proof that they stood for anything basically different. Both accepted the inability of the working class to transcend a trade union consciousness. Both endorsed the primacy of the party. Both participated in the slander and suppression of their "left" opponents, both outside the Party (Kronstadt) and within it (the Workers' Opposition and other groups).[94] The argument that because people fight against one another they cannot share wide common premises is too simple by half. Torquemada had

---

91   I carefully refrained from mentioning this political species. I am nevertheless accused of attacking them. Mark Twain once said: "Get your facts first, then you can distort them as much as you like".

92   I didn't mention these comrades either, most of whose criticism of the Polish bureaucracy I would accept. Their critique, incidentally, closely parallels the arguments developed in issues 19, 20 and 21 of *Socialisme ou Barbarie*, all of which were widely distributed in Poland in 1956 and early 1957. We were in fact the first to publish sections of the Polish text in English (*Solidarity*, IV, 2, 3 and 4). J.S. isn't just apathetic to facts, but actively hostile to them!

93   Here the imputation is partly correct. Only I would word it rather differently: "our present government *and* those (Communist Party, Trotskyist 'entrists' of every kind) who helped put it there".

94   When, in 1927, Stalin arrested those responsible for the Trotskyist underground printing press (headed by Mrachkovsky) he was able to refute their objections without much difficulty, remarking: "They say such things are unknown in the history of the Party. This is not true. What about the Myasnikov group? And the Workers'

various Catholic theologians burned at the stake. Is one resorting to an "amalgam" if one proclaims the *common* mystification of both executioner and victim, manifested in their *common* belief in God, the Catholic Church, and the necessity for a "correct" interpretation of Papal writ? Has J.S. never heard of "false consciousness"? Is the Left by some miracle, immune from it? At a cruder level, is a violent settlement of scores between gangsters necessarily an affirmation of deep ideological differentiation?

***

One of the charges in J.S.'s article is that I "refuse to specify the characteristics of the traditional left". If by "refuse" he means "omit", his claim is true. The article, however, was about something specific: the attitude of the trad left to what was wrong with capitalism. If J.S. seeks to widen the terms of the debate, I am quite willing. Here goes (briefly for shortage of space prevents full treatment of each proposition):

a) Among the identifying features of the trad left (whether Fabian or Bolshevik) are an ingrained belief in man's incapacity to manage his own affairs without an elite or leadership of some kind (themselves!). In this, both reflect the typically bourgeois concept of "masters and men".

b) The trad left places the question of formal ownership (as distinct from control)[95] at the centre of its preoccupations. It believes that solving society's economic problems by planning and the increase in the productivity of labour will necessarily result in society's other problems being solved.

c) Wilson, Gollan, Healy (and both Stalin and Trotsky in their lifetime) would all assert that Russia (economically speaking) was a "fundamentally different" kind of society from that existing in the West. Libertarian Socialists would not. It all depends on what one considers "fundamental". The yardstick of the former ("amalgam" again?) would be the presence or degree of "competition", "planning", "nationalization", etc. The yardstick of the latter: human freedom as expressed in workers' self-management.

d) Many in the "Marxist" section of the trad left believe in a revolutionary theory based on allegedly objective laws. But they also hold that they alone can "correctly" interpret this theory (hence the multiplicity of the mutually hostile "Marxist" organizations). Under appropriate conditions these beliefs lead them to assume what Trotsky called the Party's "historical birthright". In defence of this birthright the Party is prepared to manipulate (and if necessary shoot) workers in the interest of a higher, "historically determined" purpose, which *it* has grasped, even if the masses haven't.

At the more mundane level the trad left can be recognized by its deeply ingrained conservatism and its ideological sterility. It is the living embodiment of Bagehot's aphorism that "one of the greatest pains to human nature is the pain of a new idea". At a time when everything is being revolutionized more deeply and rapidly than in any other period of history, only their "revolutionary" ideology seems to remain static. A "frantic search for novelty" (to use J.S.'s phrase) should be the prime

---

Truth group? Does not everyone know that Comrades Trotsky, Zinoviev and Kamenev themselves supported the arrest of the members of these groups?" (Robert Conquest, *The Great Terror* (London: Macmillan, 1968), p.130).

95   As will be shown, J.S. shares this confusion between "property relations" (ownership) and "relations of production" (which are essentially authority relations).

preoccupation of those slowly sinking in an antediluvian morass of half-truths and outmoded concepts. But for them, as for all conservatives, "novelty" is a term of opprobrium.

Those who seem frightened of new ideas might at least rearrange their prejudices once in a while. But even this seems to be asking too much. In argument, they defend their errors as if they were defending their inheritance. All buttoned up by impeccable little coats of complacency, they are like a man who will not look at the new moon out of deference for the old one. They react to the ideological stimuli like Pavlovian dogs in an early stage of conditioning with a non-discriminatory and purely salivatory response. When for instance I claim that those who only see man as a consumer see him in "much less than his full stature", I am accused of drawing "a sharp distinction between man as a consumer and man's urge to fulfil himself". When I claim the "essential *identity* of relations of domination, whether they manifest themselves in the capitalist factory, in the patriarchal family or in the authoritarian upbringing of children" and suggest that the "socialist revolution will have to take all these fields within its compass, and immediately", I am arraigned for describing fields "neatly fenced of from each other" and "not organically connected". The mind boggles at such feats of logic! J.S. even ends up by stating that "Capitalism and Socialism" "insinuates that society's ills are not due to the existence of the capitalist system". How much further can polemical creativity go? In more senses than one J.S.'s article epitomizes the response of a traditional Marxist when confronted with a new idea: noise, fog, distortion, invention, childish imputation of reactionary motives, etc, etc.

***

J.S. defines the nature of the capitalist system as "a particular pattern of *ownership* of the means of production" (my emphasis). To avoid being misunderstood, he defends the trad socialists in their vision of the evil of society as "flowing from a particular pattern of *ownership* of the means of production".

This is putting the clock back nearly a decade. It is tragedy that after eight years of the existence of *Solidarity* and after the publication of such sophisticated texts as *The Meaning of Socialism*, *Socialism or Barbarism* and *Modern Capitalism and Revolution* there should persist such confusion between "property relations" and the much more fundamental "relations of production". This confusion can even lead J.S. to assert that "Capitalism and Socialism" is in "complete contradiction with *Solidarity* practice". The contrary is in fact the case.

Since the first issues of *Solidarity* we have stressed that the crisis of contemporary society is a manifold one which cannot be fully understood solely in terms of the "private ownership of the means of production". This wider awareness has helped comrades who accept *Solidarity* ideas to intervene meaningfully in disputes such as King Hill, the anti-bomb movement, the student upsurge and in industrial disputes in which questions of job control were paramount. It enabled us to be the first to respond to events like the revolt at Berkeley (in 1964) and to recent developments in France (which had very little to do with "property relations" but a great deal to do with relations of another kind). It is a deep awareness of the totality of the crisis of all capitalist values and all capitalist institutions that explains our own survival in an initially hostile political environment and the recent wide response evoked by ideas similar to our own. If we had spoken exclusively of "property relations" or of "contradictions within the economy", we would have been condemned to the role of a sect, because we would only have been dealing with *one* aspect of social reality, blowing it up to the exclusion of all others.

But "double think" can go still further. J.S. proves that it is possible both to believe that the crisis stems from the pattern of ownership and to claim that for trad socialists "the relations of production determine the other social relationships". Confusion not only reigns…it pours! The trad socialists (Labour Party lefts, Communists, orthodox Trotskyists, Maoists, etc.) believe that "property relations" are paramount. The more sophisticated among them will claim that the juridical super-structure ("property relations") necessarily corresponds with the "relations of pro-duction". In fact as Marx (and later many others) have shown[96] the "property rela-tions" may serve to mask the reality of the relations of production. If trad socialists ever came to acknowledge that the "relations of production" were fundamental, they would have to accept the relevance of our deepest critique of Leninism and Trotskyism, with their imposition of authoritarian relations in production from the earliest weeks in 1918. Sooner or later they would have to envisage the logical link between Leninism and Stalinism. This they are clearly not yet prepared to do. Neither, apparently, is J.S.

---

96   See, for instance, Tony Cliff, *Russia: A Marxist Analysis,* or earlier texts in *Socialsme ou Barbarie.*

17. A QUESTION OF POWER

Few of us run our own lives. This is because we have no control over the main decisions that affect us. These decisions are made by small self-perpetuating minorities. This situation cannot be "democratically" changed. What our rulers call "democracy" is a system which operates for their own protection. As long as their "democracy" is not seriously challenged, their dominating position in society is secure.

Their threatened use of violence is intended to frustrate any challenge. It is implicit in the large police force, the courts, and the armed forces which they control. The limited freedom that their "democracy" allows us is further restricted or curtailed altogether whenever they think their power is seriously threatened.

They hold the power to maintain their power. This is key to their security. They determine the kind of education provided, and the ways and means of providing it. By controlling what and how people are taught, those who rule us seek to preserve the structure of existing society. Children are educated first through the family - i.e. through the already-conditioned parents. Then the education factories (schools and universities) take over. Their aim is to produce people conditioned to fit into this rat-race society.

Workers created trade unions and political parties to change all this. But gradually adopting similar patterns of organization to those of their oppressors, and by concentrating the struggle almost solely on improving working conditions and living standards, the original revolutionary intentions have been bypassed. Working people have gained considerable material advantages but they have lost control of their own organizations. Today the hierarchies are in control. They can neither be removed nor brought back to the initial aim of freeing people.

Those who dominate production dominate society. So long as they have their kind of industrial stability, control will remain in their hands. This control enables them to continue deciding what is to be produced, who is to produce it, where, when, how, and in what quantities. All this conflicts with the interests of the real producers - the workers. Those who run our lives continually seek ways of blurring the conflict and of manipulating workers into accepting that management alone is capable of making these decisions.

The union hierarchy assists them in this fraud. While acting as middlemen in the labour market, the union bosses do all they can to frustrate any awareness in workers of their own ability to run industry. In fact, so-called working class organizations are today an essential part of the set up. The formation of new unions or parties would not solve the problem. In today's conditions, they would suffer the same fate as the old ones.

But the system is contested. There is a constant struggle in which the objective is self-management. In a large majority of disputes, workers have taken real democratic decisions to act without the consent of the union bureaucrats (so-called unofficial strikes). This is one of the signs that our rulers' "industrial stability" is under strain. The strain is also visible in the education factories, where students are increasingly demanding the right to take decisions on fundamental issues. There are many other signs of the crisis that is affecting every aspect of this society.

Solidarity participates in the struggle wherever possible. We try to expose the true situation. We seek to strengthen the confidence of working people in their *own* ability to manage their *own* lives - at work and outside of it. People's reliance on others to do things for them has led to defeat after defeat. It is time for victories! Victories depend on people consciously taking action themselves. To help in the development of this consciousness is the only reason for the existence of *Solidarity*.

SOLIDARITY LEAFLET, JULY 1969

18. SOLIDARITY AND THE NEO-NARODNIKS

Big Flame (henceforth abbreviated *B.F.)* is a Merseyside group which publishes occasional broadsheets relating to working class struggles. Some of their publications have been excellent – we have even used some of their material – but others are pretty confused. They have never made any clear statements about their political beliefs, largely because *as a group* they do not appear to have any. In private conversations some call themselves anarchists, some Maoists, and some "third worldists". Still others boast about being non-political. What unites them is a certain concept of industrial work, which they believe can transcend politics.

A few weeks ago Solidarity (London) and other Solidarity groups received a couple of undated photostated sheets from the publishers of *B.F.* In these they severely criticise our most recent pamphlet *Under New Management? The Fisher-Bendix Occupation.* They even describe some of the views put forward in this pamphlet as "criminal". The subject matter they object to had not previously been discussed between us.

We feel that the matters raised – and the method in which they were raised – deserve wider discussion. They are examples of much that is wrong with the movement. We have therefore decided to publish the *B.F.* letter in full, together with a reply. In the course of this reply we hope to initiate a wider *political* discussion of the differences between "militants" and "revolutionaries" – and of the differences between the concept of "autonomy" and the concept of "spontaneity". We hope that this discussion will transcend our particular differences with *Big Flame.*

To give readers a better insight into the way *B.F.* viewed the recent struggle at Fisher-Bendix we are also publishing excerpts from their Broadsheet about the dispute. Having read these documents carefully we suggest that readers look again at our pamphlet – and draw their own conclusions.

The Big Flame letter

This is a letter of criticism addressed to Solidarity (London) about their recent pamphlet, Under New Management? The Fisher Bendix Occupation. We think that the pamphlet itself is a product of the way in which Solidarity works, and that it shows a large gap between your theory and practice. Despite your theory of self-activity and self-management, you are mainly a pamphlet-producing group. Therefore your response to any important issue is to write a pamphlet or an article about it. But because as a group you are divorced from working class struggles you are unable to write about the situation with any real understanding.

A clear example of this is the way Solidarity acted about Fisher-Bendix. Three of your members came up to Kirkby to visit the factory. But what can you understand from a visit? The draft for the pamphlet was written on the basis of a discussion with members of the Occupation Committee. Coming in from the outside, not knowing anyone in the factory, you could only speak to the Committee, but remember, you get their view, which is not necessarily that of all the workers.

Throughout the pamphlet there is a constant confusion between workers and shop stewards. You say: "The stewards remaining in the factory had given the signal for workers to join in a march to the Admin Block as previously arranged with the stewards who were 'negotiating'". In fact, this march on the Admin Block was not organized or led by the stewards, but by a group of young workers. Effectively you have denied the autonomy and self-activity of these workers - something which Solidarity has spent much time denouncing other groups for doing. But, as we said, this kind of thing is inevitable from the whole way in which you write about struggles, whilst being divorced from them. At least, when groups like I.S. [International Socialism] do this, they know they're doing it - though this is also the logic of their posititition, which says that they must recruit shop stewards as being the vanguard of the working class. Obviously they cannot criticize them too much if they want to recruit them. And they were trying very hard to recruit Jack Spriggs, the convenor.

Although you say "the stewards then started to plan a course of action", and that "the stewards were now negotiating with their own objectives in mind", and again, "It was agreed that the workers would respond to a call from the stewards...", yet you are also able to say "the workers set about organizing committees to take charge of various aspects of the occupation". This is not so, the stewards did it.

Towards the end of the pamphlet we have some euphoria about how the occupation was run. We quote: "The workers are developing their own self-confidence to act for themselves. They are showing in practice how to solve problems on the basis of real democratic decision-making. I learned something very new at Fisher-Bendix. We asked about how decisions were made. How did the committees function?" "The Occupation Committee was based on the original Shop Stewards Committee covering the workers as members of different unions. But it was now an autonomous committee with many additions designed to run the occupation in daily contact with all the workers. This is the great advantage of an occupation. There are always rank and file workers on hand to see what is going on. They can constantly be consulted, or for that matter intervene if they feel it is necessary".

The reality was very different. All the decisions and all the interesting activity was done by the committee. Relationships did not basically change during the occupation. There was still a passive majority and an active minority, who ran the show. The mass meetings did not "send a thrill right through" anyone. They were passive events. The only speakers were those from the platform, sometimes only the convenor would speak. The speeches were followed by applause and a ritual show of hands for the TV cameras. There were no important questions asked or any general discussion. Everything was left to the committee and merely ratified by the mass meetings. Even at the last mass meeting, there was no discussion about the details or the implications of the agreement, which had been mediated by Harold Wilson.

When you say that the committee "was now an autonomous committee" that was truer than you think. It was autonomous unto itself and not really accountable to the workers because, with so little real involvement or information themselves, they were in no position to question the committee. There were several workers who were very critical of the way the committee was set up and the way it operated. But there were not enough of them, so they did not feel confident or strong enough to voice their criticisms.

Whilst saying all this, we don't really blame the people on the committee. They acted in the way that good trade unionists always do and within the structures that they have always known. Because of this it is all the more criminal for revolutionary groups like Solidarity to bolster up these attitudes and these structures, which help to maintain the passivity of masses of working class people.

Excerpts from the B.F. Broadsheet ("Bendix: How the Workers Took Over (A Group of Workers Say How It Happened"))

After the Xmas holiday the factory grew tense. Thorn's said the run down would begin on January 3rd, a Monday. Everybody felt things were coming to a head. Sit-ins were being discussed.

There was a false start on the 4th, Tuesday, when the stewards issued a half hour ultimatum to the bosses. But it was soon extended for 24 hours. It was obvious Thorn's didn't really take our threats seriously. They weren't taking any precautions against a sit-in. Over the last few weeks some of us had got together because we felt something had to be done about the close down. There were about eighteen of us. Our idea was to stage a demonstration that would prove to management that we were dead serious, the stewards were not alone in the struggle. On Wednesday the ultimatum ran out and the stewards were meeting the management in the boardroom. We were only certain about five minutes before it happened that we wanted a demo. And we had to keep quiet because of security.

So when we started the march to the Adminstration, it wasn't really spontaneous for us. About 150 workers filed up the stairs shouting "Industrial Assassin", but as we got nearer to the boardroom it turned into a softer chant of "Out, out, out!"

This was it. We'd forced the issue, and shown how militant we were, but outside the boardroom door we suddenly felt childish. Nobody wanted to go in. It was like a barrier at the door that we hadn't the nerve to cross, after we'd spent months and years taking orders from the managers. Outside there was this terrible feeling of frustration because nobody would walk in. Suddenly, Tom, probably knowing there was no choice, stepped in and the rest followed. Once you're in, there's no problem - they're only men.

Within a few minutes the boardroom was packed tight with over fifty of us. The atmosphere was so tense that one wrong word would have turned it into a barney. Then Jack Spriggs, the convenor, got up and told the management they had fifteen minutes to make up their minds or we would have to ask them to leave the premises. If they were scared - and they must have been, seeing the looks on our faces - they didn't show it. Of course they left. You see, there comes a point when demos have to stop and action begins. We'd no idea until it happened that there would be an occupation that morning. It just happened spontaneously, it came out of the situation, and suddenly everybody knew what we had to do without anyone saying "right, lad, we're going to have a sit-in!"

During the nine week strike, only about fifty of us were involved, it was difficult to find pickets and some workers were out there fourteen hours a day. I also think we're doing Thorn's more damage this way. Of course a sit-in would be useless if Thorn's were skint, but we don't believe they are. They've got orders for £1m worth of radiators for the next few years. I think this has shown the utter folly of strikes. Women we couldn't get out with us on the nine week strike are now involved as anyone else in the occupation.

And there's another thing about sit-ins. He (pointing to a worker across the table) works nine feet away from me but this is the first time I ever talked to him. This has brought us all closer together and everybody's talking about things. In a way, we're not so inhibited now! These sit-ins should be the start of our industrial revolution. The workers should be left to run the factories providing they do it efficiently. We can't leave it to anybody else anymore. There's no choice between the governments.

The problem here is that we're not all involved in what's going on. Twenty stewards are doing nearly everything. I'm just a glorified telephone arranging pickets, so that a few people can go to meetings to make decisions I'll follow. There weren't enough stewards - one department has two for 240 men. It's a big problem we're going to have a sort out together if we're going to stick together.

Our reply

Leaving aside for the moment the abuse ("criminal" bolstering up of reactionary attitudes and structures), the snide allegations ("mainly a pamphlet producing group…divorced from working class struggles"), and the factual inaccuracies ("coming from the outside…you could only speak to the Committee") - all of which we will deal with later - the *B.F.* letter contains two main criticisms of the Solidarity pamphlet.

The first is that the Solidarity pamphlet understressed the action of the rank and file and overstressed the role of the shop stewards. Solidarity, it is alleged, constantly failed to differentiate between workers and stewards. Underlying this criticism is, of course, the assumption that the stewards at Fisher-Bendix were totally integrated into the trade union bureaucracy. According to *B.F.* the march on the Admin Block and the occupation of the Boardroom were "not organized or led by the stewards". The march and occupation are described as "spontaneous" events, led by a group of young workers. "We'd no idea, until it happened, that there would be an occupation that morning. It just happened spontaneously. It came out of the situation". According to *B.F.*, the Solidarity pamphlet "effectively denied the autonomy and self-activity of these workers, something which Solidarity has spent much time denouncing other groups for doing".

The second criticism is that the Solidarity pamphlet did the very opposite. It was "euphoric". It overstressed rank and file participation during the occupation and understressed the bureaucratic manoeuvres of the union machine. To our version of what happened at Fisher-Bendix, *B.F.* counterposes another reality. "All the decisions and all the interesting activity was done by the Committee. Relationships did not basically change during the occupation. There was still a passive majority and an active minority, who ran the show". Solidarity is no longer accused of denying anyone's autonomy. We are now accused of alleging autonomy where in fact there is none.

According to *B.F.* both defects in our pamphlet stem from a common source: the fact that we "are divorced from working class struggle".

Let us deal with these criticisms one by one, bringing them down from the realm of fantasy and submitting them to a confrontation with a few hard facts.

Firstly to dispose of some red herrings. We reject the allegation that Solidarity is "mainly a pamphlet producing group", divorced from working class struggle. We certainly produce pamphlets (which is presumably better than *not* producing pamphlets, and probably marginally better, i.e. of more lasting value, than producing broadsheets). But we also try to produce and propagate *ideas*, not just about working class struggle, but about all areas where the system is being challenged, about *politics* in fact. We also feel that these ideas should be *coherent*. In our opinion an informed and conscious working class, *understanding* what it wants, *knowing how* it will have to struggle to achieve it and *aware* of the obstacles (internal and external) it will have to overthrow, is an essential pre-condition for any significant social change. We hold this belief most deeply, as it is for us the basis both of meaningful struggle today and of non-manipulated, self-managed society tomorrow. And because of this we are as much concerned with the direction in which we are moving as with the movement itself. "All movement and no direction" is certainly not our motto. We are concerned with the lasting effects of what we do or say, rather than with demagogic declarations or mindless buzzing around from one dispute to another.

Secondly, did we get an accurate idea of what was going on at Fisher-Bendix? Seven comrades visited the place, two of them twice. They were experienced comrades with long records of struggle as militants, stewards and convenors. We don't like to engage in such "prolier than thou" declamations and are only prompted to do so to refute the innacurate allegations of the *B.F.* letter.

Who did our comrades speak to in their search for information? It is quite untrue that they "only spoke to the Committee". They spoke to many rank-and-file workers, in addition to stewards and to those active on some of the Committees. They spoke to workers just sitting around, and to others playing cards or bingo. It is true – and here *B.F.* may have a point – that had we spoken to more workers, on more occasions, other facts may have emerged. But we preferred urgently to disseminate those facts we did get hold of (in the hope that they would further the development of the struggle itself) than to stay at home and get none of the facts (for which we would doubtless also have been criticized by *B.F.*).

Let us now turn to the two specific areas of *B.F.*'s criticism of the Solidarity pamphlet. We can imagine no better way of vindicating our view of what happened than by taking up some of the statements made by...*B.F.* itself. When one is as politically confused as *B.F.* one doesn't worry unduly about holding and disseminating mutually contradictory views. Unfortunately they can't all be simultaneously true and some of the chickens will inevitably come home to roost.

First, was the occupation "spontaneous"? Was it decided on the spur of the moment by people who "had no idea, until it happened, that there would be an occupation that morning"? This is what *B.F.* alleges.

Let the *B.F. Broadsheet* refute the *B.F.* letter. In their article, "Bendix: How the Workers Took Over (A Group of Workers Say How It Happened)", we are told that after the Christmas holiday "sit-ins were being discussed". So the idea of a sit-in was around. The day before the sit-in started a group of workers were discussing a demonstration to show that "the stewards were not alone in the struggle". If this revealing sentence means anything at all, it means that the stewards were contemplating action and that the groups of workers were also feeling the need for it and were planning for it.

Let us now turn to the central event: the famous march onto the Admin Block. Was it really decided only five minutes before it happened? If the march was as "spontaneous" as *B.F.* alleges, can they explain why, during the march, the master keys to all parts of the plant were taken from the place where they were usually kept (as we reported in our pamphlet)? Was this some kind of "spontaneous", divine foresight? Did those who "spontaneously" started the demo think of the keys…before they even knew there was going to be an occupation of the Boardroom? Or does *B.F.* deny the whole episode of the keys?

We now reach the door of the Boardroom. According to the *B.F.* Broadsheet there was "a terrible feeling of frustration – because nobody would walk in. Suddenly Tom, probably knowing there was no choice, stepped in and the rest followed". But who was this mysterious Tom, whose hand was being thus guided by an inexorable destiny? Why has Tom got no surname? Could he possibly be one of those reactionary stewards, whom Solidarity is constantly mixing up with workers? To be more specific, could he be one Tom Staples, Treasurer of the Occupation Committee, Secretary of the Kirkby, Huyton and Prescott Trades Council, and a member of a political party for which neither *B.F.* nor Solidarity have much time?

Let us continue our "spontaneous" excursion with *B.F.* Jack Spriggs, the Works Convenor, gets up in the Boardroom. He tells the management "they had fifteen minutes to make up their minds". Was Jack really saying the first thing that passed through his head? Was he really acting on the spur of the moment? Was his statement really an impromptu utterance, *not previously discussed with other stewards*? Are we really to believe that Jack Spriggs had been inadvertently sucked into a demonstration led by eighteen young workers, not quite knowing what was happening to him and what it might all lead to?[97] *B.F.* should really not project its own naivety onto others.

In our pamphlet we mention the *systematic preparation* for the sit-in. We describe how workers from Fisher-Bendix had, over a period of weeks, visited U.C.S. and Plessey's – and more recently Allis-Chalmers. We report how they had studied various types of occupation, to see what would best suit their own particular circumstances and needs. Is this true or isn't it? Would *B.F.* like to face our informants and tell them they were inventing all this? Had there or had there not been extensive discussions about appropriate modes of action? Are we really to believe that nobody knew the occupation was going to take place on that particular day? Anyone saying this at Bendix would be laughed out of court.

There are other strange omissions in the *B.F.* account of events. There is no mention of the fact that there had been a joint meeting of staff and manual workers (the first for many a month) on the day before the occupation. Or of the fact that the workers and some of the staff in the Admin Block immediately joined the shopfloor workers, as part of a concerted plan of action. Why are these crucial facts omitted? Could it be because they clash with *B.F.*'s account of how the occupation developed?

To ignore some facts and to distort others – in order to show that the Fisher-Bendix occupation was the outcome of a purely "spontaneous" action by a group of young workers – and to assert that the stewards had nothing at all to do with it – is rather pointless. It is not going to kid any of those who took part. Are the "facts" being presented in this way in order to encourage others to act in a similar way? Is the purpose to create a myth? Such cynical manipulation of the facts reveals a basically contemptuous attitude, unfortunately quite widespread among certain sections of the "revolutionary" movement today. What is implied is that workers are too stu-

---

97   As far back as December 11, 1971, *Socialist Worker* carried an interview with Jack Spriggs in which he explained how "inside the Fisher-Bendix factory a 50p levy is being built up as a fighting fund…ultimately, our main weapon will be the sit-in strike… A sit-in here will provide a focal point for a fightback against unemployment throughout Merseyside".

pid to accept reality as it is and therefore have to be jogged along with injections, at the appropriate time, of doses of revolutionary mythology.

Let us now turn to B.F.'s second point. Was the occupation as bureaucratically run as B.F. implies? Didn't the relationship change, just a little, during the sit-in? Didn't *anything* new emerge? Is the balance sheet totally negative? Was it a dispute "just like any other"?

To ask these questions is to answer them. We presume (although we would like reassurance on this point) that B.F. would not have been interested in this dispute if it had been "just like any other". Again their own account (in their Broadsheet) refutes what they say (in their letter). We are told (in the Broadsheet) that "these workers no longer leave everything to their shop stewards and the negotiators" and that they now "have a new attitude to politics". Either this is true (in which case the criticism they make of Solidarity's decription of the occupation collapses). Or it is untrue (in which case they are again engaging in their little game of revolutionary myth-making). The Broadsheet claims that "women we couldn't get out with us on the nine week strike are now as involved as anyone else in the occupation…this has brought us closer together and *everybody is talking about things*". (Hardly a picture of "a passive majority and an active minority".)

We are finally told (again in the Broadsheet) that "in the last few days, at Bendix, workers have got to know for the first time people who often worked right next to them. *For the first time they are all working together themselves.*" How do B.F. square up all this with their statement that "relationships did not basically change during the occupation". How basic is basic? If they mean that there was no revolution they are right. If they mean that hundreds of people didn't find themselves doing things or thinking things they had neither done nor thought before, they are wrong. Is B.F. allergic to such facts? Or is it just that they are not too concerned about such trifles as reality, coherence and consistency?

But B.F.'s muddleheadedness doesn't end there. Their Broadsheet tells us that "twenty stewards are doing nearly everything". Their letter implies that these twenty-odd characters were dominating every one of the very numerous Committees, taking every decision, miraculously getting everything endorsed, systematically denying a voice to the rank and file. If B.F. believe all this, the first prize for Utter Confusion must surely go to their statement that "there weren't enough stewards". B.F. must think their readers are utter morons!

We don't dispute that there were, in all probability, bureaucratic and manipulatory aspects to the behaviour of certain shop stewards at Fisher-Bendix. We are not claiming that from one day to the next people nurtured in the tradition of bureaucratic maneuvering changed their spots. In our pamphlet, *written at the height of the occupation*, we warned that "if occupation is pushed and manipulated by such people (i.e. by trade union officials or members of 'vanguard' type parties) the very form it takes may result in workers being denied the right themselves to manage their own struggles. Under such circumstances occupation would not automatically result in a more advanced type of struggle". But at Fisher-Bendix this was not, at that stage, the main point. We were interested in what was new in Fisher-Bendix, not in what is the common denominator of so many industrial disputes today.

The point of a pamphlet like ours was to bring to other workers information denied them by the mass media and by the traditional revolutionary press. This information to be helpful must, of necessity, hinge on the new developments thrown up in the course of the struggle itself. If nothing more important emerges from the reading of our pamphlet than that some workers in struggle grasp the need to concentrate in their own hands as many as possible of the *physical* resources of the firm (i.e. the full implications of the "raid " on the Moorgate Road stores), as well as the need to involve *their relatives* in collective decision-taking, then our pamphlet, in our opinion, will have been well worth producing. If *B.F.* believe that *all* stewards, in *all* circumstances, are irreversibly integrated into the trade union bureaucracy, they should say so openly in their publications. They don't. One can only conclude that they speak with one voice in their public utterances – and with another when they throw shit on other groups.

All this flows, of course, from an inability to think dialectically, to see contradictory aspects of reality at any given time, to recognize what is a developing tendency (to be encouraged, assisted and publicized) and what is a declining one (to be helped to the grave or just ignored).

In the simplistic world of *B.F.* everything is seen in black and white. The workers are seen as the embodiment of good (even when they talk of running the factories "efficiently", which in the context of their present consciousness means according to the norms of bourgeois cost-effectiveness). The shop stewards, on the other hand, are seen as *totally* integrated into the trade union bureaucracy. The fact that stewards are usually elected regularly and are revocable (whereas the trade union officials are often neither) just doesn't come into the picture. Things can't be described as they are; they must conform to models. "My mind is made up, don't confuse me with facts". For instance *B.F.*'s letter claims that the members of the Occupation Committee "acted in the way that good trade unionists always do and within the structures they have always known". This is both inaccurate and leads *B.F.* to turn a blind eye to what was really new and immensely encouraging in the Fisher-Bendix occupation, namely *the notion of mass meetings attended by wives and relatives, who in this way would be less liable to the pernicious pressures of the mass media*.

Did the stewards in fact "act in the way that good trade unionists always do"? Sit-ins bring workers from different unions together *as workers*. Is this really one of the traditional concerns of the trade union bureaucracy? Why does *B.F.* regard the stewards, also faced with the sack, as the *inevitable* enemies of the workers, under *all* circumstances? Are they not workers too, also liable to be affected by the redundancies, and also interested in struggling against them in the most efficient way possible? We have repeatedly denounced the usurpation of the function of shop steward by members of various vanguard sects. We saw no reason however to drive a wedge between stewards and men in a situation like Fisher-Bendix, where there was not much conflict of interests.

Blindness to what was new also led *B.F.* to underestimate the signficance of the seizure of the stores from the Moorgate Road Depot, at a very early stage of the dispute. Are raids of this kind now to be regarded as routine operations, run by trade union officials? We felt such events were important and we stressed them because they show that workers are beginning to think with their heads (instead of with their balls), to plan their actions (instead of just reacting to events). Some revolutionaries could well follow the example being set.

In our pamphlet we welcomed the development of sit-ins, for which we have been systematically campaigning for many years. We also warned of their limitations.

We tried to place this tactic in the context of a number of possible methods of struggle. All this is too complicated for B.F., who in their new found enthusiasm for the sit-in denounce "the utter folly of strikes". We would have enjoyed watching them expound this doctrine to the miners' pickets, outside any large power station. This nonsense again flows from B.F.'s "all-or-none", "one-or-the-other", totally undifferentiated approach to real problems. We don't consider this particularly helpful. Sure, the B.F. Broadsheet makes no great demands on those who read it. But this is for the simple reason that it makes no such demands on those who write it.

Where the confusion of B.F.'s "politics" (or rather "non-politics") reached its zenith was in their publication - in the Broadsheet - of a "Statement from the Workpeople". This wasn't a statement from the workpeople at all, as anyone with an ounce of political savvy would immediately have recognized . It was a Stalinist-inspired *political* document, signed by a number of the *real* local trade union bureaucrats. B.F. published it without comment. They therefore appeared to endorse what the document said. The document supports the actions of Merseyside Labour M.P.s in the House of Commons. These fakers want to call for an "enquiry" - in political terms an investigation sponsored by a government representing the interests of Capital. The "statement" then proceeded to denounce the Tories for their attitude to closures and unemployment. But it didn't utter a squeak about massive closures and sackings under a Labour government, *which also represented the interests of Capital.* If all this isn't mystification with a vengeance, what the hell is it? Solidarity is accused of not being able to distinguish between workers and shop stewards. We deny this charge, but it is certainly a less serious one than confusing the voice of the "workpeople" with the farts of the local Stalinist apparatus.

There is no vacuum in politics. The "non-politics" of B.F. leads directly to the uncritical dissemination, by an allegedly revolutionary paper, of the politics of our opponents.

***

This leads us to discuss, in conclusion, two important areas which differentiate us from groups such as B.F.. One concerns "autonomy" and "spontaneity". The other the difference between being a "militant" and being a "revolutionary".

There seems to be a great deal of confusion, in the revolutionary movement, about such concepts as "autonomy" and "spontaneity". The words are *not* synonymous, as is so often assumed.

Autonomous, strictly speaking, means that "which makes its own laws" and therefore, by implication, "which acts in its own interests". An autonomous working class action is one in which workers have acted with their own, independent, class objective in mind. These objectives are *totally different* from the objective of "their" employers, of "their" firm, of "their" country, or of "their" union leaders. Autonomous class action becomes possible when the working class see itself as "a class for itself" (to use Marx's phrase) - i.e. as a class consciously, explicitly and collectively concerned with its own fate in society.

Full autonomy has both *ideological* and *organizational* components. Ideological autonomy denotes that one has gained as much understanding and insight as possible into the influences that mould one's thinking. It means that one's thinking has been freed, as much as possible, of alien class influences, of alien class values, of alien class "rationality". To gain ideological autonomy is a difficult process. It requires that one identify the numerous residues of bourgeois thinking we all carry with us, because of the society in which we live. These are often much more powerful and deeply implanted than people imagine. The working class struggle for autonomy is the struggle to free itself of all that lingers on, in its thinking, in its habits and in its own patterns of organization, of the society it is fighting against.

For revolutionaries, to assist working class autonomy means to denounce the various mystifications that prevent the working class form achieving this kind of insight. Among such mystifications are the Leninist myth that "the working class can only achieve a trade union consciousness", the myth that socialist consciousness has to be injected into the working class movement by middle class professional revolutionaries, the myth that Russia and China are some kind of "workers' state", the myth that the Labour Party is a working class party, etc., etc. To assist the development of genuine autonomy means a conscious refusal to pander to working class backwardness, to working class confusion or to working class illusions, for the sake of immediate popularity. It means consciously vaccinating oneself against the disease of "workeritis", a condition in which everything the working class says or does, however reactionary, is miraculously endowed with transcendentally positive qualities.

Organizational autonomy means the creation or development of organizations totally controlled by the workers themselves and with which they can totally identify. No such organizations exist today. At certain times and in certain places workers' councils have approximated to this type of organization.

Revolutionaries should constantly be advocating the organizational autonomy of the working class, the breaking of all bonds which tie the working class to bodies controlled by the employers or by their state. They should denounce the stranglehold of the trade union bureaucracy on working class organization. But if such organizations are to be genuinely autonomous, revolutionaries will also have to denounce their usurpation or their manipulation by Stalinists, Trotskyist or Maoist micro-bureaucrats. In practice this would mean explaining the real nature of the Stalinist-controlled Liaison Committee for the Defence of Trade Unions, of the SLL-controlled[98] All Trades Unions Alliance and of similar bodies. Patiently explaining the real nature of these bureaucracies is a *political* task. It cannot be done by simply piling invective on particular opponents because of their ethnic background or sexual habits. These methods do not contribute to *autonomous* politics. On the contrary they pander to the most backward tendencies among workers.

It will be seen that *autonomous* action requires a high level of working class consciousness. It can take place suddenly - or on the contrary be spread out over a considerable period. It is not in the least "spontaneous".

"Spontaneity", on the other hand, denotes something which seems to happen without apparent cause, without obviously being the result of previous preparation. In the sense of an "effect without a cause" there is probably no such thing as "spontaneity" in politics (or in life). Human reactions are always largely determined by previous experiences.

If the person who reacts "spontaneously" is not *consciously* aware of why he is acting in a given way, this does not at all mean that there are no causes for his actions. It only means that the causes elude him because they are subconscious. Such subconscious drives reflect previous conditioning. From a class point of view "spontaneous" actions may be positive or negative. They may reflect tendencies to genuine autonomy or they may reflect all the prejudices of established society.

---

98   Socialist Labour League.

"Spontaneous" action is usually taken to mean action which breaks out without having been planned beforehand. It does not in the least follow that such an action will be in the long-term interests of workers. It could be "spontaneously" reactionary.

Of course, when there are positive "spontaneous" actions (i.e. "spontaneous" actions which assist or reflect the development of class autonomy) these should be reported fully. *Of course* groups of *conscious* militants can play an important role in triggering off crucial events. We have described this process repeatedly in our publications, whether dealing with particular industrial disputes or with larger events like the Hungarian Revolution or May 1968 in France. But one shouldn't invent "spontaneous" actions, out of deference to some nebulous concept of "spontaneity". And it is even less permissible to ignore *real* actions, because you have disagreements with those who initiated them. This history "à la carte" helps no one: tidying up reality is a fruitless pastime. Only the truth is revolutionary.

Because of our opposition to traditional (Bolshevik) types of revolutionary organisation, *Solidarity* is often accused by the trad revs of being advocates of "spontaneity".[99] With a blissful disregard for evidence they do this, despite our constant endeavour to avoid using politically meaningless terms like "spontaneity". B.F. reflects another kind of confusion. We are accused of denying "autonomy" to a group of workers because, in our pamphlet, we did not mention one of their allegedly "spontaneous" actions. We have argued earlier about the facts themselves. It is difficult to argue here about the ideas, because words are used without any real thought as to their meaning.

There is also much confusion in the political scene today, as to the differences between "militants" and "revolutionaries". The main difference between them is a question of *politics* (we don't mean party or institutionalized politics, but politics in the full sense of the term, namely concern about everything that goes on around us and in particular about the relations of people to the society they wish to overthrow).

A *militant* is someone who sees only a part of social reality. His or her struggle is confined to a limited area (industry, education, the tenants' movement, women's liberation, etc.).

A *revolutionary*, on the other hand, seeks to develop an overall understanding (and hence an overall theory) concerning the structure of class society. He is interested in the various mechanisms which hold it together and whereby it perpetuates itself. This should lead him to examine a wide range of phenomena, including the internalization of the values of class society into his own thinking and behaviour.

A militant may be involved in a very radical struggle, say at work, and then come home and wallop his kid (or his wife) who want to play or talk, whereas he wants to watch the telly. He will not realize that his actions at home are in complete contradiction with his struggle at work, because he does not relate them. He does not realize the relevance of his personal attitudes to a generalization and a better understanding of the meaning of his struggle. He is not aware of the necessity to place his struggle at work into the wider context of the struggle for the liberation of people in *all* aspects of their lives and at *all* levels.

Similarly many women may achieve deep insight into their centuries-old exploitation (by both men and class society) and yet fail to perceive the significance

---

99   The latest example of this nonsense is to be found in Tariq Ali's *The Coming British Revolution* (Jonathan Cape, 1972), p.143. Apparently *"Solidarity's* belief in spontaneously–generated political consciousness" leads us to "deny the need for any organization". Both the premise and the conclusion are false. The "argument", moreover, is a *non sequitur*.

of authoritarian relations to other areas of life. Some of the most vociferous militants of women's liberation can, for instance, consider themselves "Maoists". They can boast of the "equality of women in China" and ignore the fact that, until recently, of over a hundred members of the Central Committee of the Chinese Communist Party there were only two women: Lin Piao's wife and Mao's. And we don't know what's happened to the former!

A revolutionary, aware of the need of this wider outlook and of integrating his experiences (and those of others) into a coherent pattern, will therefore make a more total criticism of the social and economic order. He or she will consider any form of human self-activity in struggle - be it economic, political, sexual, social or cultural - as *relevant* to the general struggle towards a self-managed society.

It does not follow that a revolutionary holds any truth or blueprint, nor that he or she has solved all the contradictions of his or her life, or of his or her relationships with other people. These contradictions being *social* cannot be solved on an individual level.

But the fundamental difference between revolutionaries and militants is that the latter will rarely be even aware that they (and everybody else) have such problems. They will often dismiss any attempt at discussing them as irrelevant to - or a "diversion" from - their particular struggles, precisely because they haven't yet (for various reasons) generalized the meaning of these struggles into a total critique of society at all levels.

We have been told that the production of historical pamphlets - or of such pamphlets as *The Crisis of Modern Society* and *The Irrational in Politics* - are "a waste of time" because they are not "activity". We have been told that work among scientists or heated arguments about ideas are a "diversion from the class struggle". We shudder to think of the type of "socialism" that would be introduced by those who feel that the subjects dealt with in these publications are "marginal" and "can be left to look after themselves". It is because of our belief that they can be rationally discussed - with industrial workers as with any other group of people, and that this is important - that Solidarity is a *political organization* and not just a journal of industrial agitation. We feel that lasting effects on people's thinking is more likely to flow from involvement in *all* that affects them in their everyday life, and not just from involvement in their struggles at work.

But our concept of being "revolutionaries" (as distinct from just militants) is very different from what is generally understood by the term. By "being revolutionaries" we don't mean - as the Leninists do - belonging to some Vanguard Party, destined to lead the masses into the promised land. The Leninists consider themselves as embodying some kind of absolute, "revealed" truth, and as being the incarnation of the "historical interests of the working class". For us, being revolutionaries only means seeing a little further than others. What we see should change, as does society itself. For us there is no such thing as an absolute truth, whether in politics or elsewhere, and the idea of a complete and final theory - embodied in the practice of some Party - is, in the modern era, nothing but a bureaucrat's dream and, moreover, a tool helping him manipulate the oppressed. For us, revolutionaries are not an isolated elite, destined to any vanguard role. They are a product (albeit the most lucid one) of the disintegration of existing society and of the growing awareness of what it will have to be replaced by.

***

Heated political arguments are useful among revolutionary groups, provided they share a certain measure of understanding. Argument is difficult if one group consistently refuses to spell out its views, an attitude which itself reveals much more than it conceals.

B.F.'s sudden outburst against our coverage of the Fisher-Bendix occupation highlights this problem. We have attempted to answer their misrepresentation, point by point. But that is not enough. What prompted B.F. to launch such a caricature of a critique? Was it a difference in political outlook? To grant this would imply that B.F. had previously expressed its *own* political conceptions, its own "world-view". But this is precisely what B.F. has failed to do. Nowhere, to our knowledge, has B.F. explained its reason for existing as a tendency separate from the rest of the left.

This would involve answering certain questions. For instance what does B.F. think of the shop stewards movement, of the different trade union bureaucracies, of the very concept of trade unionism, of the Labour Party, of the Communist Party and its industrial base, of the traditional groups of the Leninist left? What do they think of the various "national liberation struggles', of Premier Castro, Che Guevara, Chairman Mao, Uncle Ho, peasant struggles, urban guerillaism, the IRA? And what about all the other areas of everyday life which express clearly the decay and instability of this system, outside of the mere economistic emphasis of B.F.?

Is this not politics? If not, why not? A philistine disregard for substance is seen in this pearl, culled from their *Bulletin* (October 1971): "We want to help establish a network. But we want it to be a network of activists, who attempt to link and show the relevance of different struggles. We don't want to send (our *Bulletin*) to people who aren't prepared to do anything". The criteria for earning B.F.'s approval is then doing… "anything". But what? Populist activism is based on myth, the myth which claims that working class origins themselves constitute a guarantee for being revolutionary. Such an attitude is found mainly among impatient middle class radicals, who have half-digested socialism and are ashamed of their background. Since the trade union bureaucracy is mostly composed of people coming from the working class, some of the intellectuals infected with this kind of populism tend to confuse the bureaucracy with the class itself. Thus an informal fusion, usually ideological, occurs between the "worker-populist" and various currents which seek to reform the unions. Such a trend has already emerged, for example, in B.F.'s uncritical publication of *Lessons of the Postal Strike* by the Merseyside Postal Alliance. The pamphlet has good material in it, but is marred by mystifying conclusions such as "our union needs to be democratized".

B.F.'s lack of coherence is understandable. The "worker-populist" considers that "support" for "masses in struggle" is enough. Criticism of the *political content* of these struggles is considered divisive, sectarian or coming from "academic quarters". The attempt is thus made to *consciously* castrate any revolutionary critique, based on clear theoretical concepts. B.F. attempts to drive a reactionary wedge between revolutionary workers and other revolutionaries. It does so by pandering to the worst anti-intellectual prejudices of many workers. Historically these prejudices have been whipped up by the trade union bureaucracy (the nauseating recent example of Ray Gunter is there to emphasize the point). Prejudices have also been whipped up by various political parties that have acquired a working class electorate, often with disastrous results for working people. B.F.'s anti-intellectualism isolates those numerous worker-intellectuals, within any working class, who by their own sustained efforts and persistent devotion to the liberation of their class, have long since abandoned prejudices which still haunt *B.F.*

If all that *B.F.* can offer as a political explanation of itself is recipes for collective "involvement", certain questions still remain. On what basis will decisions be taken? What are the group's politics? The last ten years have seen dozens of groups appear which have sought to avoid "politics" (some within the Solidarity movement itself). They have all either disappeared without leaving a trace or - more particularly in the United States - they have degenerated, and in their decrepitude become either liberal or Stalinoid "third-worldist". "Going to the working class" is not a political programme or a critique of society. It is not even the basis for a viable group, as our "neo-Narodniks" will sooner or later discover.

B.F.'s practical activities (or those of any group) implicitly define a world-view. It is high time the supporters of *B.F.* sought explicitly to ascertain the views of those who founded their group. The fact that *B.F.*'s politics haven't been made clear up till now leads one to suspect that a deeply manipulative game is being played, a game in the tradition of the Leninist left. The example of certain Italian groups is there for all to see.

The libertarian left in Britain has been weak in showing that conscious intervention can help make an "uncritical" mass action a more coherent and lasting one. The difference is enormous. Working people don't live in a vacuum and part of their age-long problem is the deep cleavage between what they *do* and what they *say* they are doing. The question is not to clap from the sidelines and enter into raptures about "self-management" whenever one sees a group of workers attempting to control their own lives in living struggle. Varying degrees of "self-management" are implicit in the daily existence of working people, and become deeper and explicit in struggle, simply because no struggle can be won, even in trade union terms, without a measure of self-activity. The *revolutionary* dimension appears and develops when the conscious and deliberate critique of society by the working class fuses with its practical "self-activity", reinforcing it, and in turn being nourished by the elemental drive of a class striving for full self-consciousness. It is here that groups of "pamphleteers" - yes, "pamphleteers" like Solidarity - can and must intervene and fuse their *politics* with the revolutionary action of masses of people. People who just do "anything" will probably end up doing the donkey work for the reactionary tendencies in any such mass activity.

B.F. has no consistent politics, on *any* issue. On any particular issue, it must therefore have a whole series of formulas, copied from the whole range of left organizations in Britain and elsewhere. Thus at times it might appear to uphold the strivings of the rank and file; at others it will confuse these strivings with the actions of the trade union bureaucracy (thus consciously adopting a semi-Trotskyist stance). This "attitude" must of course extend to *all* areas of the group's involvement: student milieu, "youth culture", women's liberation, Claimants' Unions, community politics, etc. And, if its roots were Leninist yesterday, they might become Leninist again tomorrow. After all, if politics is just a question of "doing something" then the rest can all be bought - at bargain prices - in any revolutionary supermarket.

We have no monopoly of the truth and do not for a minute deny *B.F.*'s - or anyone else's - right to be as critical as they like of Solidarity's ideas or methods of action. We do however demand that criticisms be honest and informed - aimed at helping the movement forward - and not just ignorant gossip. We are, we confess, surprised at *B.F.*'s method. To disseminate "information" about the allegedly "criminal" attitude of another tendency in the movement (without having first attempted to ascertain the facts by approaching that organization directly - and while maintaining a facade of comrade relations) is not in keeping with expected norms of behaviour between libertarians. It smacks of a very different tradition. We can see no rational reason for the malevolence behind *B.F.*'s letter, which we can only construe as a hostile act. We will not be mealy-mouthed or pull our punches in answering back. Our reply however, unlike their attack, will be both political and principled. Nothing but good can come from such a confrontation of views and methods.

SOLIDARITY *DISCUSSION BULLETIN*, FEBRUARY 1972.

19. INTRODUCTION TO MURRAY BOOKCHIN, *ON SPONTANEITY AND ORGANIZATION*

There can be few words more misused in politics than the word "spontaneity". It is often used to denote something which seems to happen without obvious cause, without apparently being the result of previous preparation. In the sense of "an effect without a cause" there is probably no such thing as "spontaneity" - either in politics or life. Human behaviour is always influenced by previous experience. If a person is not *consciously* aware of *why* he is acting in a particular way, this does not all mean that there are no causes for what he is doing. It only means that causes elude him.

Murray Bookchin does not use the word "spontaneity" in this crude and unreflecting way. It is important to stress this semantic point in this short introduction to his essay (first published in *Liberation* early in 1972). In Bookchin's own words: "Spontaneity is not mere impulse... " It does not imply "undeliberated behaviour and feeling". "Spontaneity is behaviour, feeling and *thought* that is free of *external* constraint, of *imposed* restriction". It is "not an uncontrolled effluvium of passion and action". "Insofar as the individual removes the fetters of domination that have stifled her or his self-activity, she or he is acting, feeling and thinking spontaneously".

Bookchin here uses the word "spontaneity" as we would use the word "autonomy". Literally speaking autonomous means "which makes its own laws" and therefore, by implication "which acts in its own interests". With the advocacy of spontaneity, understood in this sense, we have no significant disagreement with Bookchin. Our own views on this matter are outlined in greater detail in *Solidarity and the Neo-Narodniks*.

Full autonomy has both organizational and ideological implications. Bookchin deals with both in some depth. He points out that "spontaneity does not preclude organization and structure", thereby nailing a very widespread Leninist distortion of the libertarian case. Bookchin stresses that spontaneity, in the sense in which he uses the term "ordinarily yields non-hierarchical forms of organization".

We would go perhaps further, and stress that no collective autonomy is meaningful which does not have organizational repercussions. Autonomous activity and life - whether in the realm of practice or in the realm of ideas - is impossible in hierarchically-structured organizations. As Bookchin points out "the tragedy of the socialist movement is that it opposes organization to spontaneity and tries to assimilate the social process to political and organizational instrumentalism".

The main impact of Bookchin's essay is however on the need for ideological autonomy, for breaking all the intellectual fetters of the past, for sweeping the cobwebs away that still clutter so much of the thinking of the left. His greatest insight is his statement of the need to eliminate domination in *all* its forms, not merely material exploitation.

He stresses "the widespread erosion of authority as such - in the family, in the schools, in vocational and professional areas, in the Church, in the Army, indeed in virtually every institution that supports hierarchical power and every relationship that is marked by domination". He takes the whole discussion into areas largely avoided by the left, and is not scared of challenging many of their most fundamental assumptions. In this his own writing is a vindication of his belief in a creative, conscious and coherent spontaneity. "Consciousness", he tells us, "has its own history within the material world, and increasingly gains sway over the course of material reality. Humanity is capable of transcending the realm of blind necessity, it is capable of giving nature and society rational direction and purpose".

If the mass of the population is to become the creative subject of history – and not just an inert object compelled to do certain things because of the conditions of its existence – this kind of message must be taken seriously and its implications thought out. For all those who, whatever their age, are not suffering from a hardening of the categories, Bookchin's views are an important contribution to an ongoing debate.

SOLIDARITY PAMPHLET 49, DECEMBER 1975

20. PREFACE TO PIERRE CHAULIEU, *WORKERS' COUNCILS AND THE ECONOMICS OF A SELF-MANAGED SOCIETY*

To the best of our knowledge there have been no serious attempts by modern libertarian revolutionaries to grapple with the economic and political problems of a totally self-managed society.

What might the structure, social relations and decision-making institutions of such a society look like, in an advanced industrial country, in the second half of the twentieth century? Is the technological basis of modern life so complex that all talk of workers' management of production can be dismissed as pure "utopia" (as both the beneficiaries – and most of the victims – of the present social order would have us believe)?

Or, on the contrary, isn't this allegation itself the real mystification? Doesn't historical experience, and in particular the working class experience of recent decades, prove the very opposite? Don't the very advances of science enhance the feasibility of a rational form of social organization, where real power would lie in the hands of the producers themselves?

This pamphlet seeks to deal with some of these questions. The events of the last few years show quite clearly that this is no longer a "theoretical" preoccupation, relating to some remote and problematic future. On the contrary it is a real, immediate and down-to-earth concern. At any time between now and the end of the century, hundreds of thousands – nay, millions – of men and women may well be confronted with problems of the kind here discussed. And the solutions ordinary people may collectively provide to these problems will depend whether humanity really moves to something new, or whether we just exchange one servitude for another.

Let us immediately circumscribe the relevant area. We are *not* concerned with the recipes and double-talk of various "reformed" or "partially reformed" bureaucracies. We are not concerned with "workers' control" seen as an adjunct or decoration to nationalization and the political power of some vanguard party. We are not discussing how to run, from above, a system of workers'-management-from-below (as in Yugoslavia). We want to go a little deeper than those Polish bureaucrats, the only recent addition to whose wisdom seems to be that one shouldn't increase prices, without warning, the week before Christmas. We won't be examining what happened in Spain in 1936, firstly because this has been done before and better than we could, and secondly because it only has limited relevance to the problems of an advanced industrial country, in the last third of the twentieth century.

Nor, for much the same reasons, will we examine the withered remains of what may briefly have flowered in the Algerian countryside, before being swept away in 1965 by Boumedienne's theocratic putsch (to the plaudits, be it remembered, of the rulers of "Communist" China). Nor will we echo Castro's paeans to the "socialist" work ethic, his exhortations to his followers to "cut yet more sugar cane", or his fulminations against sundry slackers, uttered without ever seeking to discover the real source of their "slackness": their lack of involvement in the fundamental decisions and their refusal to participate in their own exploitation.

At the other end of the political spectrum, we will only deal in passing with those who believe that *all* work and *all* sorrow, *all* limitations on human freedom and *all* compulsion, could immediately be swept away, and that socialism implies the immediate transcending of the human condition. With the decay of every social order, various millennial doctrines tend to flourish. We endorse the vision but are concerned with the steps for making it reality.

Those whom we might call "cornucopian socialists"[100] will probably denounce us for discussing the organization and transformation of work (instead of its abolition). But such is the capacity of our minds for mutually incompatible ideas that the very comrades who talk of abolishing all work will take it for granted that, under socialism, lights will go on when they press switches, and water flow when they turn taps. We would gently ask them how the light or water will get there, who will lay the cables or pipes – and who, before that, will make them. We are not of those who believe that reservoirs and power stations are divine dispensations to socialist humanity – or that there is no human or social cost involved in their creation. We are intensely concerned, on the other hand, about how *collectively* to determine whether the cost is acceptable, and how it should be shared.

In considering various aspects of a self-managed society we will not be discussing the insights, however shrewd, of various writers of science fiction. Their undoubted merit is that they, at least, have perceived the fantastic scope of what could be possible, even today. Unlike Jules Verne, we aren't planning to proceed *20,000 Leagues Under the Sea* or even to undertake a *Journey to the Centre of the Earth*. We just want to walk widely and freely on its surface, in the here and now. In this, we will immediately differentiate ourselves from most modern revolutionaries, who under pretext of "keeping their feet on earth" remain waist-deep in concrete.

This pamphlet is based on a text by P. Chaulieu, "Sur le Contenu du Socialisme", which first appeared in the summer of 1957 in *Socialisme ou Barbarie*). It is important to keep the date in mind. The text was written just *after* the Hungarian Workers' Councils had been ruthlessly suppressed, following a prolonged and heroic struggle in which hundreds of thousands of workers had put forward demands for the abolition of norms, for the equalization of wages, for workers' management of production, for a Federation of Workers' Councils, and for control from below of all institutions exercising any kind of decisional authority.

The text was written *before* the momentous developments of the sixties, before the massive growth of "do-it-yourself" politics, and before the Berkeley events of 1964 (which showed the explosive new tensions modern capitalist society was busily producing). It was written before the vast spread – at least in Europe – of the "youth revolt" (with its deep questioning of the "work ethic" as such – and of so many other aspects of bourgeois culture) and before the development of the women's liberation movement (with its widespread critique not only of the economic exploitation of women but of the more subtle forms of exploitation inherent in the attribution of fixed polarities and roles to the two sexes). Finally it was written more than a decade before the great events of May 1968 (despite the fact that the movement's demands

---

100   The Cornucopia or horn of plenty was a horn overflowing with fruit and flowers which, for the Romans, symbolized abundance.

for *autogestion* (self-management) at times sound like the reverberating echoes of what the text is talking about).

Way ahead of its time in 1957, the text seems dated, in some respects, in 1972 – no so much in what is says, which retains great freshness and originality, but in what it does not and could not say. Why, in view of all this, is Solidarity publishing this document at this particular time? The answer is twofold. Firstly because the text remains, in our opinion, the most cogent, lucid and comprehensive vision of the *economic* structure of a modern self-managed society ever to have been published. Secondly, because we feel that a discussion on this theme is now fairly urgent.

The text does not evade difficulties but faces them honestly and openly. Its scope is wide. How could institutions be made comprehensible? How could they be effectively controlled from below? How could relevant information be made available to all, so that meaningful decisions might be taken collectively? How could genuinely democratic planning function, in an advanced industrial society? But the text deals with much more: with the essential changes a socialist society would have to introduce in the very structure of work, with how a genuine consumer "market" might function, with problems of agriculture, with the political representation of those who do not work in large enterprises, and with the meaning of politics in a society based on Workers' Councils.

Revolutionaries usually react to all this in one of three ways.

For the Leninists of all ilk there is no problem. They may pay lip-service to "proletarian democracy", "Workers' Councils" and "workers' control", but know in their bones that, wherever necessary, their Party (which has as great a role to play after the revolution as before) will take the appropriate decisions. They dismiss workers' self-management with derogatory comments about "socialism in one factory" or with profundities like "you can't have groups of workers doing whatever they like, without taking into account the requirements of the economy as a whole". In this they are tilting at men of straw, for libertarian revolutionaries have never claimed any such thing. Moreover the Leninists utterly fail to understand what is here being proposed: we are not discussing "workers' control" (seen as some adjunct or decoration to a hierarchy of political organs, which would genuinely embody decisional authority, and which would not be directly based on the producers themselves). What we are proposing and discussing is something much more fundamental, a total reorganization of society, a reorganization involving every one of its social relations and basic institutions.

Non-Leninist revolutionaries will react to what we say in two different ways. Either: "Why worry about such things? Blueprints are a waste of time. The workers themselves will decide when the time comes". Or more simplistically: "Under socialism there just won't be any problems of this kind. All present problems stem from the material scarcity of capitalism which a 'free society' will immediately abolish". The text argues most cogently why these are shortsighted answers and describes what will probably happen if libertarian revolutionaries refrain from discussing these matters *as from now*.

One may accept or reject what the author proposes (we aren't ourselves all agreed on his various views). But it cannot be claimed that he fails to tackle a whole range of new problems. We are here firmly in the era of the computer, of the knowledge explosion, of wireless and television, of input–output matrices, and of the problems of today's society. We have left the quieter waters of Owen's *New View of Society*

(1813), or Morris's *News from Nowhere* (1891), of Blatchford's *Merrie England* (1894), or of sundry other socialist or anarchist utopias of earlier years.

Let us not be misunderstood. We are not passing value judgements. We are not decrying the sensitivity and deep humanity that permeated the vision of many earlier revolutionaries. We are merely claiming that the technological infrastructures of their societies and of ours are so immeasurably different as to make comparisons rather meaningless. Although we hate much that we see around us – and in particular many of the products of misapplied science – we don't want to move the clock back (incidentally, a remarkably fruitless occupation). We see no advantage in candles or coke over electricity, or in carrying water from the well when it can be got from tap. We want to control and humanize *this* society (by means commensurate with its vastness), not to seek refuge in some mythical golden past. Nor do we use the word "utopia" in any derogatory sense, as contemporary Marxists so often do. We are using it in a purely etymological sense. Strictly speaking "utopian" means that "which exists nowhere". When we say that the author's proposals are *not* utopian we are saying no more than that his mental constructs are but extrapolations from what *already* exists here and now, from experiences the working class has *already* been through and from institutions it has *already* created.

We would like to contribute this pamphlet to the serious and sustained discussion now taking place among libertarian revolutionaries about *all* aspects of a self-managed society. This discussion is already ranging widely and fruitfully over such fields as education, conditioning by the family, internalized repression, urbanism, town planning, ecology, new forms of art and communication, new relations between people, and between people and the essential content of their lives. In this surge of questioning one dimension is, however, missing. The dimension is that of *economic organization*. The silence here is quite deafening. Sure, there are occasional distant echoes of what de Leon said before the First World War about "socialist industrial unions" – or about what the various syndicalists have proclaimed, with diminishing credibility, about the need for "one big union". For modern revolutionaries, however, this is totally inadequate. Perhaps what we propose isn't good enough either, but at least it tries to grapple with the problems of *our* epoch.

Although economic organization isn't the be-all and end-all of life, it is the precondition of a great deal else. And it is high time revolutionary libertarians started discussing this subject rationally. They must realize that if they have no views on these matters, others (the trad revs) do. Politics, like nature, abhors a vacuum. If we don't want the economic tyranny of Party-dominated structures – masquerading as "socialism" or "workers' control" – it is high time we explained, and in some detail, what *we* mean by workers' management of production and a society genuinely based on Workers' Councils.

***

Conservatives will say that what is here outlined threatens the rights of management. They are dead right. The non-political will proclaim what many left politicos believe (but are reluctant to articulate), namely that all this is "pie in the sky" because in industry as elsewhere there must always be leaders, and the hierarchical organization is both inevitable and intrinsically rational. The liberals and Labour lefts – aware of the increasing cynicism with which people now regard them – will proclaim that what we say is "what they meant all along", when they were talking about "workers' participation". Having failed to grasp the essence of what we are talking about, they will then doubtless start arguing how it could all be introduced by parliamentary legislation!

There will be more subtle criticisms too. Those alarmed at the monstrosities of modern science – or those naturally suspicious of what they do not fully understand – will shy away from the text's bold advocacy of subjugating the most modern techniques to the needs of democracy. They will remember the "plan factory", the matrices and the coefficients, forget who will be determining them, and denounce the text as a "technocratic" view of socialism. The text will be criticized by many anarchists as containing Marxist residues (for instance it still attributes an enormous specific weight, in the process of social change, to the industrial proletariat, a weight which the author himself would probably gauge differently today). Moreover the document still envisages a "transitional" society between capitalism and communism, as Marx did in his *Critique of the Gotha Programme*. We will be told that the technical capacity of industry has increased so vastly in the last decades as to invalidate the need for such a phase of history. We hope to initiate a wide discussion on this issue.

Many Marxists will denounce the text as an anarchist dream (anarchist dreams are better than Marxist nightmares – but we would prefer, if possible, to remain awake!). Some will see the text as a major contribution to the perpetuation of wage slavery – because it still talks of "wages" and doesn't call for the immediate abolition of "money" (although clearly defining the radically different meanings these terms will acquire in the early stages of a self-managed society).

The text will also be dismissed by many in the underground. They will consider it irrelevant because it does not call for the immediate "abolition" of work. A more sophisticated criticism – but along the same lines – will be directed at us by the Situationists who constantly talk of "Workers' Councils"…while demanding the abolition of work! Unfortunately they seem to confuse attacks on the *work ethic* and on alienated labour, both of which are justified and necessary, with attacks on work itself. Such an approach fails to relate to the problems of transforming what exists here and now into what could open the way to a new society, for the construction of which, whether we like it or not, many million man-hours of labour will probably have to be expended.

Finally the more percipient supporters of women's liberation will correctly point out that as long as millions of women have to stay at home they will be grossly under-represented in the various schemes the pamphlet envisages. The answer here is neither to consider housework as an "industry" and encourage housewives to organize industrially (which would perpetuate the present state of affairs), nor for all authority to be vested in locality-based units. The position of women will change radically and new forms of representation will undoubtedly be created. All these are areas deserving the widest possible attention.

We hope that what is best in the text will survive the crossfire. We are frequently told: "your critique of modern society is telling enough. But it is negative. These are enormous problems. How would *you* like to see things organized?" Well, here at least is the draft of an answer, based on a coherent system of ideas. We will tell our questioner that a society, economically organized along the lines here described, would be infinitely preferable to what modern capitalist society has to offer us. And to those on the "far left" we would say that such a society would also be preferable to what they and their "vanguard parties" are concocting "on our behalf". The ball would then clearly be in their court. They would have to relate to what the libertarians were saying, about economics as well as about other things. That alone in our opinion is reason enough for putting forward our views.

SOLIDARITY PAMPHLET 40, MARCH 1972.

21. WILHELM REICH 1

This pamphlet[101] consists of a translation of Reich's famous essay, "What is Class Consciousness?", first published in 1934 (under the pseudonym of Ernst Parell). It includes an introduction, some well-chosen illustrations, an excerpt from the Preface to the third (1945) edition of Reich's *Mass Psychology of Fascism* and the full text of the *Sexpol Manifesto* of 1936.

The subject is topical in view of the resurgence of interest in Reich's writings and of the new awareness, at least among some revolutionaries, of the many factors influencing class consciousness, delaying its appearance or distorting its features. The essay is essential reading for anyone interested in looking a little deeper than the surface of things, or dissatisfied with the facile political "explanations" which are the stock-in-trade of so many on the Left.

Unfortunately Reich's text, while containing many insights of deep significance, is vitiated by a number of Leninist residues. Throughout Reich endorses the belief that "the leadership must bring revolutionary consciousness to the masses". He claims that "awareness of the social situation, of the means of its mastery and of the correct path to socialism must be concentrated in the revolutionary vanguard". Party members are described as the "engineers…bricklayers and carpenters" of the building of socialism. Lenin is described as "the greatest mass psychologist of all time". All this moreover is not merely a verbal tribute: it permeates much of the practical approach. It is always the Party which is failing to understand the real nature of class consciousness, failing to stress this or that in its propaganda, and thereby failing to evoke the appropriate echoes.

It would be a tragedy, however, if modern revolutionaries saw no further than these hang-ups and, in their revulsion, failed to get to grips with Reich's main message, namely that "one of the reasons for the failure of the revolutionary movement is that the real life of individuals is played out on a different level than the instigators of social revolution believe". "While we were presenting the masses with grandiose historical analyses and economic arguments about the contradictions of imperialism, their innermost feelings were being kindled for Hitler". Still shocked at the "total failure" of the German Left, in the early 1930s "to seize the imagination and enthusiasm of the masses", Reich is making a plea for a revolutionary political psychology. This is a useful approach, provided it is seen as a means of gaining a new awareness into the springs of human behaviour, rather than as a means of developing a new manipulative technique.

Despite its title, Reich's essay is not really about the nature of class consciousness. It is about all that prevents the growth of such consciousness. Although constantly stressing the need for revolutionary leadership, Reich is realist enough to perceive that even the best of leadership cannot *create* class consciousness. It could not even contribute to the growth of such consciousness if it were not "inherent in the daily experience of the working class". The main problem for Reich is to seek what it is, in society at large (and in the practice of revolutionaries, in particular), which inhibits the growth of that consciousness.

---

101   Wilhelm Reich, *What is Class Consciousness?* (London: Socialist Reproduction, 1971).

"If you want to develop class consciousness", Reich writes, "you must at least know what you want to develop, why it does not spontaneously develop under the pressure of deprivations of every sort and hence what stops it doing so". Queries of this type, Reich reminds us, would always cause intense annoyance among party functionaries or activists of all kinds, a clear indication that the Left were not even aware of the importance of these questions, let alone capable of providing an answer. In this respect the "scene" doesn't seem to have changed much.

Reich starts by contrasting the "consciousness" of the leaders and the consciousness of the masses. The leaders know "about the contradictions of the capitalist economic system, the terrific possibilities of socialist planning, the necessity of social revolution in order to accommodate the form of appropriation to the form of production". They know all about the "progressive and reactionary forces in history". The consciousness of the masses "is remote from such knowledge and from wide perspective. It is concerned with petty, banal, everyday questions". The leaders "grasp the objective socio-economic process, those external conditions of an economic and social nature to which the individuals constituting society are subjected". The masses, on the other hand, are "completely unconcerned by the quarrels of Russia and Japan, or England and America – or in the development of the productive forces". Mass consciousness is "made up of concern about food, clothing, family relationships, the possibilities of sexual satisfaction in the narrowest sense, sexual pleasure and amusements in a broader sense, such as the cinema, theatre, fairground entertainments and dancing". It is concerned "with the difficulties of bringing up children, with furnishing the house, with the length and utilization of free time, etc. If politics are to bring about international socialism, they "must find the connection with the petty, banal, primitive, simple everyday life and wishes of the broadest mass of the people, in all the specificity of their situation in society".

Reich then turns to the "traditional allegiances" and to the "wishes, anxieties, ideas and thoughts" which inhibit the development of class consciousness. He points out that "political reaction, with Fascism and the Church at its head, demands of the working masses the renunciation of earthly happiness, obedience, propriety, abjuration and self-sacrifice". Reaction "grows politically fat from the fulfilment of these demands by the masses themselves". It bases itself "on the guilt feelings of every member of the proletariat, upon their usual unassuming moderation, upon their tendency to undergo privation with dumb willingness and sometimes even with joy". Reaction and the Church exploit the identification of the masses with the glorious Führer whose "love for the nation" is substituted for real satisfaction of popular needs.

Reich then comes to the kernel of his analysis. Revolutionaries must recognize that "the principle of renunciation is harmful, stupid and reactionary". "The principle of full earthly pleasure by which Reich does not mean "beer and skittles" must be set against the political reactionaries' principle of renunciation". "The moderation of the "simple man", the prime virtue as far as Church and Fascism are concerned, is from the standpoint of socialism his greatest fault, one of the many elements which militate against his class consciousness." *"We are heading up a dead-end"*, Reich writes, *"if we consider class consciousness an ethical quality"* and hence compete with the bourgeoisie and its agents on grounds of their choosing. It would not only be futile but harmful to condemn, for instance, "adolescent sexuality, the character of prostitutes, the depravity of the criminal and immorality of the thief". (Reich clearly differentiates this attitude from any "romantic admiration for the world of crime".) He points out that "everything which goes by the name of morality and ethics today stands unequivocally in the service of the oppression of working humanity". "Everything that supports and strengthens the bourgeois order and attaches people to it is an impediment to class consciousness". On the other hand "everything that is in contradiction with the bourgeois order, that contains the seeds of revolt, may be regarded as an element of class consciousness".

Reich warns that the right will exploit these "amoral" conceptions in its propaganda. This doesn't matter he says, for the right has anyway always considered the left as thieves (who want to expropriate the means of production). Failure to deal with these matters, or "holier than thou" attitudes on the part of the left will only drive the frustrated and misunderstood masses into the arms of reaction.

We have touched on this subject in previous issues of *Solidarity*, perhaps without appreciating its full significance. In industrial struggles, for instance, there is nearly always a very strong urge among workers, to "make the dispute official", to project an image of being moderate, sensible people, acting constitutionally and within the framework of a procedure "agreed" by both sides. Instead of defending a sacked steward, as being a good militant, doing things that the trade union bureaucracy will not and cannot do, he is defended as "only implementing official union policy", etc.

From where do these conformist attitudes stem? Dealing with inhibiting influences, Reich stresses the importance of the early rebellion against the parents. "Sexual inhibition, the fear of sexual activity and the corresponding feelings of guilt are always either reactionary or at least inhibit revolutionary thinking. Sexual oppression is so immediately perceptible for the child - and class problems for the most part so alien to its thinking - that there is no question of a choice in this matter. Early, correct sexual knowledge does not merely create a lively attachment to the person giving it, does not merely destroy all the child's usual mistrust of adults, but constitutes in itself the best foundation for irreligious thinking and hence for class feeling". The ideological struggle against "being good" is seen by Reich as "one of the most important tasks on the ideological front". Attachment to the parents, on the other hand, is "a powerful, inhibiting element, which can never be exploited by revolutionaries in the interests of social revolution". Reich points out that these are class questions, not personal matters. The Church was well aware of all this, even if the revolutionaries, permeated by bourgeois inhibitions, were not. The Church was not afraid to discuss "these so-called taboo subjects. As far as *it* was concerned, children masturbating *was* a political matter". It required care and sensitivity to discuss these subjects with children. "Revolutionaries should at least not get in the way, by chiming in with the Church".

Reich then discusses such things as "parades, uniforms and military music", all seen as factors damaging the development of a critical consciousness. The Right would always be better than the Left at the game of pageantry, at creating myths and in mobilizing people around them. The task of the Left was to blend natural emotion with real understanding. This required patience and some insight into what went on in people's minds. It required understanding their unarticulated fears and doubts, the pressure to which they were submitted in the home or more generally outside of the work situation. "A worker can never be brought to *class* feeling by simply being called on to strike, as those obtuse individuals demand who do not know what goes on in a worker's mind." The message, here, is as relevant today as when first uttered nearly forty years ago. Honest discussion about *all* aspects of life will, on the other hand, gain workers to the revolutionary cause, "if not immediately for a strike, certainly for later, when such islands of comprehension of the psychology of the masses come together in suburbs, towns and provinces, and the feeling that there are people who know exactly what is preoccupying one, arousing one's indignation, holding one back, driving one on and at the same time restricting one begins to gather people like an avalanche".

In a passage of deep relevance to what might happen tomorrow Reich writes "that in the course of the last ten years adolescents, adults, men and women, people from every walk of life have passed through the revolutionary organizations without becoming attached or committed to the revolutionary cause". What drove them in, in the first place? "Not uniforms, not material advantage, merely vague socialist conviction, revolutionary feeling". Why did they not stay in? "Because the organizations failed to develop this revolutionary feeling". Why did people lapse into indifference, or go over to the Right? "Because there were bourgeois structures in them that were not destroyed". Why were they not destroyed? "Because nobody knew what to promote and what to destroy". The desired objective could not be achieved by appeals to discipline not even "by music and marching, for the others the Right could do that a lot better". Nor could it be done with slogans "for the political clamour of the others was better and more powerful". "The only thing which the revolutionary organizations could, *without competition,* have offered the masses and which in reality they did not offer…would have been the *knowledge* of what the uneducated, oppressed children of capitalism, hankering both after freedom and after authoritarian protection really wanted, without themselves being clearly aware of it". The revolutionaries should have put all this into words, and said it for the masses, in their own language, "but organizations which dismissed all psychology as counter-revolutionary were not up to such tasks". Underlying these formulations of Reich's are a number of very important matters (the role of intellectuals in the revolutionary movement, the importance of knowledge as a basis of self-activity, the growth of "consciousness", etc.) which we cannot here go into.

Among other interesting insights of Reich's one might mention his observations that organizations which saw themselves "the preordained leaders of the coming revolution" repelled people and would be swamped in the revolution itself. Reich also repeatedly stressed that revolutionary propaganda should be positive. It should not be frightened of discussing the future, as concretely as possible. Fear of revolution was partly the product of ignorance. The broad "apolitical" masses would have a decisive effect upon the fate of the revolution. Revolutionaries should therefore find them where they were. They should "politicize private life, fairs, dance halls, cinemas, markets, bedrooms, hostels and betting shops". Long before the Situationists (or *Solidarity)* came on the scene Reich had proclaimed that "revolutionary energy lies in everyday life".

This synopsis can only give a partial insight into the sort of problems Reich is dealing with. It should be enough, however, to cause serious revolutionaries to ask themselves a few questions about what they are *really* doing, about the emphases and priorities of their work, about the "triumphalist" myths some are so busy concocting and about the *lasting* content of their "interventions".

22. WILHELM REICH 2

Socialist Reproduction are to be congratulated for popularizing this little-known text of Wilhelm Reich's which appeared simultaneously, in 1929, in *Unter dem Banner des Marxismus* (the theoretical journal of the German Communist Party) and in its Russian equivalent *Pod Znameniem Marxisma*.[102] It is a symptom of the void in both psychoanalytic and meaningful radical literature today that we have to thread our way back for more than four decades to find a sensible discussion of these interesting matters.

Unlike previous texts of Reich's to which we have referred in either the review of *What is Class Consciousness?* or the pamphlet *The Irrational in Politics*, "Dialectical Materialism and Psychoanalysis" is of no immediate relevance to an understanding of human needs or of the founts of human action. It is something very different: an attempt by Reich to reply to some of his critics (in both the psychoanalytic and Marxist movements).

It is important to situate the text in the Germany of the late twenties. In 1929 Reich's break with Freud was on the horizon, its roots clearly understood. Personal relations with Freud, however were not as yet embittered. The break with the Stalinists was also in the offing. Relations were bitter but had not as yet been traced back to their ideological source. In 1929 Reich is walking two tightropes. He uses Freud to argue against Freud and the Freudians - and Marx to argue against the Marxists. It is a difficult endeavour, as we have learned from our own experience.

Reich starts by pointing out (rightly in my opinion) that most of those on the left who were criticizing Freudian psychoanalysis or Marxism were doing so on the basis of an inadequate knowledge of either - or both. He sought to define the proper object of psychoanalysis as "the study of the psychological life of man in society", an "auxiliary to sociology", "a form of social psychology". He defined limits for the discipline. He freely admits that the Marxists are right when they reproach certain representatives of the psychoanalytic school with attempting to explain what cannot be explained by that method. But, he points out "they are wrong when they identity the method with those who apply it… and blame the method for their mistakes".

Both psychoanalysis and Marxism are seen by Reich as "science" (psychoanalysis as the science of psychological phenomena and Marxism of social phenomena) and by implication as unarguably valid. That the categories and values of science might themselves be products of historical evolution is barely envisaged. In this whole approach Reich is echoing the "scientific" ethos of the epoch, which had its roots in the rise of the bourgeoisie and its drive to control and dominate nature, rather than to live in harmony with it.

Reich vigorously defends psychoanalysis against the charge of being idealist. To the indictment that it arose "during the decadence of a decaying bourgeoisie" he retorts that Marxism did too. "So what?", he rightly asks. He dismisses those who crudely attack all knowledge as "bourgeois knowledge". "A culture", he points out, "is not uniform like a bushel of peas…the beginnings of a new social order germinate in the womb of the old…by no means everything that has been created by bourgeois hands in the bourgeois period is of inferior value and useless to the society of

---

102   Wilhelm Reich, *Dialectical Materialism and Psychoanalysis* (London: Socialist Reproduction, 1972).

the future". Reich attacks the simplistic mechanical materialism of those who would claim that psychological phenomena as such do not exist, that "only objective facts which can be measured and weighed are true, not the subjective ones". He sees this as an understandable but nevertheless misguided reaction against the Platonic idealism still dominating bourgeois philosophy. He demolishes Vogt's once popular thesis that "thought is a secretion of the brain, in the same way that urine is a secretion of the kidney". To dispose of this nonsense Reich calls Marx to his rescue, the Marx of the *Theses on Feuerbach*, the Marx who wrote that it was not good enough to say that "changed men were the products of…changed upbringing" because this forgot "that it is men that change circumstances". Psychological activity, Reich correctly insists, has a material reality and is a force in history that only the most shortsighted would deny.

There is no reason, Reich argues, why psychoanalysis should not have a materialist basis. He boldly plunges the Freudian categories and concepts into the reality of the class society around them. "The reality principle as it exists today", he writes, "is a principle of *our* society". Adaptation to *this* reality is a conservative demand. "The reality principle of the capitalist era imposes upon the proletarian a maximum limitation of his needs, while appealing to religious values such as modesty and humility…the ruling class has a reality principle which serves the perpetuation of its power. If the proletarian is brought up to accept *this* reality principle - if it is presented to him as absolutely valid, e.g. in the name of culture, this means an affirmation of the proletarian's exploitation and of capitalist society as a whole". Reich submits other Freudian categories to the same kind of historical and sociological critique, while seeking to retain their essence. The "unconscious" too, he points out, may acquire new symbols in an era of technological change. Zeppelins, in dreams, could assume the same sexual significance as snakes.

Having argued, more or less convincingly, that there can be - and in fact that there is - a materialist basis to psychoanalysis and that the subject requires no roots in metaphysical morality, Reich goes on to try and show that psychoanalysis is also dialectical. And here he comes unstuck. Like Lysenko and his genetics, Reich has to "tidy up" the rich reality of his insights (not to mention Freud's) to make them fit into a ludicrous mould of "unity of opposites", "transformations of quantity into quality" and "negations of the negation", all drawn straight from the simplistic pages of old pop Engels's *Dialectics of Nature*. Paul Mattick laid this particular ghost a number of years ago and it is sad to see Socialist Reproduction resurrect it without comment. Those pages are certainly the Achilles' heel of the whole essay. For all his protestations that psychoanalysis is an empirically verifiable set of propositions, Reich shows that he is nevertheless caught in a methodological trap of his own making…and that he is not really an unhappy prisoner. Someday, someone should write about the anal–eroticism of the system–makers, from Marx and Darwin, via Trotsky, to Reich. Why did they *all* suffer badly from piles?

Reich finally discusses the sociological position of psychoanalysis. He is here on firmer soil. Like Marxism, psychoanalysis is a product of the capitalist era. It is a reaction to that era's ideological superstructure, the cultural and moral conditions of modern man in society. Reich brilliantly analyses the ambivalent relations to sexuality of the nascent bourgeoisie and the role of the Church during the bourgeois revolutions. The bourgeoisie now had to barricade itself against "the people" by moral laws of its own. Double standards of sexual morality emerged, well analyzed in other of Reich's writings. "Just as Marxism", Reich concludes, "was sociologically the expression of man becoming conscious of the laws of economics and of the exploitation of a majority by a minority, so psychoanalysis is the expression of man becoming conscious of the social repression of sex".

In lines of great lucidity, but already seeded with that bitterness that was later to consume him, Reich even foresees the frenetic commercial exploitation of a debased psychoanalysis. Capitalism rots everything. "The capitalist mode of existence was strangling psychoanalysis, both from the outside and the inside". "In bourgeois society psychoanalysis was condemned to sterility, if to nothing worse, as an auxiliary science to the science of education in general". Psychoanalytic education would only come to fruition with the social revolution. Psychoanalytic educators who believed otherwise were living in a fool's paradise. "Society is stronger than the endeavours of its individual members". They would "suffer the same fate as the priest who visited an unbelieving insurance agent on his death bed, hoping to convert him, but in the end went home with an insurance policy".

The pamphlet is well produced. There is a good introduction, marred only by the fatuous statement that "through the twenties...Leninism in the hands of Stalin was rapidly becoming transformed into the ideological litany of the new managerial class that was being established throughout Russia". Alas, Leninism was not "becoming" anything. It had been just that for many a year - certainly since October and probably from much earlier. Whether we discuss Lenin's views on sex (see *The Irrational in Politics*) or his views on the virtues of "one man management" (see *The Bolsheviks and Workers' Control*) the clues are there for those who can read them.

SOLIDARITY, VII, 3 (1972)

23. THE SEXUAL REVOLUTION

This is an important and yet a disappointing book.[103] Written by a psychotherapist deeply versed in Marx and Reich, its main theme is that to be effective "the sexual revolution must be aware of its radicalism" and that "we must differentiate between permissiveness and a revolution in fundamental sexual attitudes". According to these yardsticks the current sexual revolution is diagnosed as having failed. "Sexual liberation was intended to be a catalyst for social change that would go to the roots of authoritarian society and transform it. But the sexual revolution has got stuck in an advocacy of permissiveness and has not touched the deep structure of society; it has only produced attitudes of defiance and rebelliousness which emphasize a negative dependence upon the superego establishment. Liberation from pleasure-anxiety has been transformed into a worship of alienated sexuality in the form of a commodity. The superego is managing quite nicely to use the superficial aspirations of permissiveness for its own purpose by making a business of it, and our 'revolutionaries' are falling for the deception".

The author starts with a devastating critique of "the scene" today. "The uncompromising and critical evaluation of all that exists, the urge to understand reality in order to change it according to consciously-held values is being replaced by petty rebellions and revolutionary posturings". What we have is a worship of naked slogans, raw emotionalism, "the illusion in the omnipotence of impulses, the belief that through acts of violence the establishment will disappear or that by negating it in fantasy it will crumple up and vanish". Today "the search for a revolutionary alternative takes the form of a flight from reason, a regression to the irrational, while rationalism has degenerated into expertise in the service of the technological establishment". "In their retreat from reason and in their search for surreal experience the pseudo-revolutionaries weaken human autonomy and leave real decision-making to others". In all this there is little I would disagree with, although I don't necessarily endorse the author's attempt, in later chapters, to provide a psychoanalytical interpretation of these phenomena.

The book contains important sections on the sadism that pervades so much "liberated" literature (interpreted in terms of people living out "their perverse secondary drives"), striking examples being drawn from the now defunct journal *OZ*. The pages dealing with women's liberation are all well worth reading. Discussing "sex as a commodity" the author claims that "now that the sexual revolution has released us from the compulsions of secrecy, sexual commodities are flooding the market and are becoming the most profitable area of capitalism next to the market of aggression". Perhaps the theoreticians of *International Socialism* should now start talking about "the permanent sex economy"?

Of particular interest to the reviewer was the author's attempt at psychoanalytic analysis of the phenomenon of alienation. Social authority is seen as the "institutionalization of the superego". "Alienation is only possible if economic forces can utilize a psychic readiness in men to be estranged from themselves and from the products of their labour". It is argued that "the conversion of man's creative ability into a commodity is based upon compulsion of making a gift-offering of himself and his

---

103   George Frankl, *The Failure of the Sexual Revolution* (London: Kahn and Averill,1974).

149

product to his superego, to God and the social authority". The whole attempt at a synthesis of Marx and Freud is taken further than has been attempted hitherto.

Scattered among heavier stuff are a number of interesting and amusing insights, often described in telling phrases. I particularly enjoyed the author's account of man as a "purpose-following animal", of the twentieth century as the "graveyard of revolutionary hopes", of the contemporary trend towards mysticism as "a great rummaging in the historical lumber-room of dead cultures", of the supermarket as the modern temple: "...where cathedrals once stood and men gathered to worship the visible or invisible God, now the shops are places of worship and the commodities displayed take the place of the Altar and the Cross. Communion is now through the cash nexus and buying and selling the ritual of salvation". There are also intellectually stimulating explorations of "patriarchal paranoia", of the significance of drama and ritual in various cultures, of the significance of circumcision, of romanticism in literature and of the growth of Madonna worship in the twelth century. Few would disagree with conclusions to the effect that "commercial and pseudo-revolutionary sexual liberation promotes a depersonalized and regressive sexuality, leaving the fundamental unconscious repressions intact".

Yet despite these insights the author seems trapped, in my opinion, in Marxist and Reichian ideas and formulations which repeatedly strike a jarring note. His political outlook is at times quite naive. He speaks of the Popular Front regime in Spain as the "Spanish Socialist Republic" and of the emergence of Stalinism in Russia as "a betrayal of communism" (rather than as the perfectly legitimate and totally coherent ideology of a new ruling class). The alienation of modern workers in production is described as "not confined to capitalism" – thereby implying that there exist in the world of today societies that are other than capitalist ones. Lenin is stated to have advocated a "semi-authoritarian centralism". We are told that there is nothing to indicate that Marx predicted the future world revolution "on the ground of its presumed inevitability". (Has the author never heard of the famous passage in *Capital* where we are informed that "with the inevitability of a law of nature, capitalist production begets its own negation"?)

The author's uncritical endorsement of Reich also strikes a jarring note. We are told that "Reich drew attention to the sympathetoconic [*sic*, twice] processes of the musculature" but not that (as was well known even in Reich's day) the sympathetic nervous system exerts no influence on striated muscle. We are told (and it is true) that sexual disturbances can create somatic disturbances – but also (and it is meaningless) that the "respiratory, gastric and urethral organs – including the kidney and gall bladder – can become sick if the libido connected with them is disturbed". Some of the author's other ventures into the medical field are equally bizarre. We are informed that Byron, who "had had to key up his life to a high state of tension," was found at post-mortem (at the age of 36) to have had "sutures of the brain" that were "entirely obliterated". Now there are no sutures in the brain (only in the skull) and if skull sutures are not fused by the age of 36 there is something profoundly the matter with the person concerned (probably hydrocephalus). We are also told that, before Freud, "neurotic symptoms" were considered "as neurological pathologies, to be treated electrically or chemically". Chronologically, this is nonsense. ECT was only popularized by Cerletti and Bini in Rome in 1938. It was first used in the USA in 1940.

Two final criticisms are of a more substantial nature. When it comes down to practical prescriptions the author calls for the "abolition of the Oedipus complex" and the "creation of a new culture". This is to be done through education, through the inculcation in parents of healthier attitudes to child upbringing (in particular towards the manifestations of the infant's "polymorphous erotic sensations" and the later more explicit demands of the child's genital sexuality). Fair enough. But surely this is not sufficient. To confine oneself to such an attitude would be to restrict oneself to the role of a sort of SPGBer of the sexual revolution. The sexual revolution is not just a question of education. It is also a question of struggle, of the struggle to transform *all* aspects of social reality.

Finally, and this to my mind is its most serious defect, the book as a whole seems to lack balance in its assessment of contemporary changes in sexual mores. Only the negative aspects of the current state of play are dealt with in any detail. On this score there are few grounds to dispute the author's conclusions. But the author fails to stress many of the positive aspects of the breaking up of the old taboos. He lacks patience and empathy with the young, while correctly taking issue with many exaggerated claims. His somewhat strident condemnation of certain aspects of today's sexual practices sounds, at times, almost puritanical. Is he echoing here some of the later writings of Reich who towards the end of his life, not only repudiated (as is well known) his earlier political writings but also (which is less well known, even to "Reichians") some of his earlier sexological writings, fearing they would be invoked to unleash, in Reich's own words, "a free-for-all fucking epidemic". Frankl is also deafeningly silent on the whole issue of homosexuality and of "gay liberation". Is he here too being a faithful disciple of Reich at the expense of neglecting an important dimension of the current sexual revolution?[104]

SOLIDARITY, VII, 12 (NOVEMBER 1974)

---

104   According to Charles Rycroft, *Reich* (Glasgow: Fontana/Collins, 1971), Wilhelm Reich, when asked to accept a homosexual for treatment, stated: *"Ich will mit solchen Schweinereien nichts zu tun haben"* ("I don't want to have anything to do with such disgusting matters").

24. AS WE SEE IT

1. Throughout the world the vast majority of people have no control whatsoever over the decisions that most deeply and directly affect their lives. They sell their labour power while others who own or control the means of production accumulate wealth, make the laws and use the whole machinery of the State to perpetuate and reinforce their privileged positions.

2. During the past century the living standards of working people have improved. But neither these improved living standards, nor the nationalization of the means of production, nor the coming to power of parties claiming to represent the working class have basically altered the status of the worker. Nor have they given the bulk of mankind much freedom outside of production. East and West, capitalism remains an inhuman type of society where the vast majority are bossed at work and manipulated in consumption and leisure. Propaganda and policemen, prisons and schools, traditional values and traditional morality all serve to reinforce the power of the few and to convince or coerce the many into acceptance of a brutal, degrading and irrational system. The "Communist" world is not communist and the "Free" world is not free.

3. The trade unions and the traditional parties of the left started in business to change all this. But they have come to terms with the existing patterns of exploitation. In fact they are now essential if exploiting society is to continue working smoothly. The unions act as middlemen in the labour market. The political parties use the struggles and aspirations of the working class for their own ends. The degeneration of working class organizations, itself the result of the failure of the revolutionary movement, has been a major factor in creating working class apathy, which in turn has led to further degeneration of both parties and unions.

4. The trade unions and political parties cannot be reformed, "captured", or converted into instruments of working class emancipation. We don't call however for the proclamation of new unions, which in the conditions of today would suffer a similar fate to the old ones. Nor do we call for militants to tear up their union cards. Our aims are simply that the workers themselves should decide on the objectives of their struggles and that the control and organization of these struggles should remain firmly in their own hands. The *forms* which this self-activity of the working class may take will vary considerably from country to country and from industry to industry. Its basic *content* will not.

5. Socialism is not just the common ownership and control of the means of production and distribution. It means equality, real freedom, reciprocal recognition and a radical transformation in all human relations. It is man's understanding of his environment and of himself, his domination over his work and over such social institutions as he may need to create. These are not secondary aspects, which will automatically follow the expropriation of the ruling class. On the contrary they are essential parts of the whole process of social transformation, for without them no genuine social transformation will have taken place.

6. A socialist society can therefore only be built from below. Decisions concerning production and work will be taken by Workers' Councils composed of elected and revocable delegates. Decisions in other areas will be taken on the basis of the widest possible discussion and consultation among the people as a whole. This democratization of society down to its very roots is what we mean by "workers' power".

7. *Meaningful action*, for revolutionaries, is whatever increases the confidence, the autonomy, the initiative, the participation, the solidarity, the equalitarian tendencies and the self-activity of the masses and whatever assists in their demystification. *Sterile and harmful action* is whatever reinforces the passivity of the masses, their apathy, their cynicism, their differentiation through hierarchy, their alienation, their reliance on others to do things for them and the degree to which they can therefore be manipulated by others – even by those allegedly acting on their behalf.

8. No ruling class in history has ever relinquished its power without a struggle and our present rulers are unlikely to be an exception. Power will only be taken from them through the conscious, autonomous action of the vast majority of the people themselves. The building of socialism will require mass understanding and mass participation. By their rigid hierarchical structure, by their ideas and by their activities, both social-democratic and Bolshevik types of organizations discourage this kind of understanding and prevent this kind of participation. The idea that socialism can somehow be achieved by an elite party (however "revolutionary") acting "on behalf of" the working class is both absurd and reactionary.

9. We do not accept the view that by itself the working class can only achieve a trade union consciousness. On the contrary we believe that its conditions of life and its experiences in production constantly drive the working class to adopt priorities and values and to find methods of organization which challenge the established social order and established pattern of thought. These responses are implicitly socialist. On the other hand, the working class is fragmented, dispossessed of the means of communication, and its various sections are at different levels of awareness and consciousness. The task of the revolutionary organization is to help give proletarian consciousness an explicitly socialist content, to give practical assistance to workers in struggle, and to help those in different areas to exchange experiences and link up with one another.

10. We do not see ourselves as yet another leadership, but merely as an instrument of working class action. The function of *Solidarity* is to help all those who are in conflict with the present authoritarian social structure, both in industry and in society at large, to generalize their experience, to make a total critique of their condition and of its causes, and to develop the mass revolutionary consciousness necessary if society is to be totally transformed.

SOLIDARITY, IV, 6 (APRIL 1967)

25. AS WE DON'T SEE IT

When, in 1967, we first published *As We See It* we felt it would be both accurate and a fairly concise summary of our views. Alternatives had been discussed and every possible effort had been made to avoid ambiguities. We thought we had produced a fairly explicit text, acceptance of which should be the basis of adherence to a *Solidarity* group.

Over the years we have come to realize that we were wrong. There was either something the matter with the document - or with some of those who read it. Or perhaps there was something the matter with us - for having thought the text was self-explanatory. Radicals repeatedly told us that they agreed with every word of the statement…and in the next breath asked us why we were not doing faction work in the Labour Party, or living in communes, or campaigning for the trade union "lefts", or eulogizing the Black Panthers or Karume's anti-imperialist regime in Zanzibar, or participating in the anti-Common-Market agitation. Some even asked why we were not advocating the launching of a "real revolutionary, Leninist party".

We now feel it necessary to dot some i's and cross some t's. What follows is an attempt to state explicitly thoughts that were only hinted at, and to formulate in writing propositions that were only implied. *As We Don't See It* would convey the general tenor of what follows. In an attempt to avoid further ambiguity we will also discuss some matters that were not dealt with in the original text.

***

1. "Throughout the world" means exactly what it says. It does not mean everywhere except Social-Democratic Sweden, Castro's Cuba, Tito's Yugoslavia, Israel's kibbutzim or Sékou Touré's Guinea. "Throughout the world" includes pre-Stalinist, Stalinist and post-Stalinist Russia, Ben Bella's and Boumedienne's Algeria and the People's Republics of Uzbekistan and North Vietnam. Everywhere also includes Albania (and China).

Our comments about contemporary society apply to all these countries just as much as to the USA or to Britain (under either Labour or Conservative governments). When we talk of privileged minorities who "control the means of production" and who "use the whole machinery of the state" to maintain themselves in power we are making a universal critique to which, at the moment, we can see no exceptions.

It *follows* that we don't regard any of these countries as socialist and that we don't act as if we had lurking suspicions that they might be something other than what they are: hierarchically-structured class societies based on wage slavery and exploitation. Their identification with socialism - even as deformed variants - is a slander against the very concept of socialism (abortions, after all, share some of the attributes of their parents). It is moreover a source of endless mystification and confusion. It also follows from this basic assessment that we do not support China against Russia, or Russia against China (or alternatively the one and then other), that we do not carry NLF flags on demonstrations (the enemies of our enemies are not necessarily our friends), and that we refrain from joining sundry choruses demand-

155

ing more East-West trade, more Summit Conferences or more ping-pong diploma-cy.

In every country of the world the rulers oppress the ruled and persecute gen-uine revolutionaries. In every country the main enemy of the people is their own rul-ing class. This alone can provide the basis of genuine internationalism of the oppressed.

2. Socialism cannot be equated with the "coming of power of parties claiming to represent the working class". Political power is a fraud if working people do not take over and retain power *in production*. If they achieve such power, the organs exerting it (Workers' Councils) will take and implement all the necessary political deci-sions. *It follows* that we don't advocate the formation of "better" or "more revolu-tionary" political parties whose objective would remain the "capture of state power". The *Party*'s power may grow out of the barrel of a gun. The power of the *working class* grows out of its management of the economy and of society as a whole.

Socialism cannot be equated with such measures as the "nationalization of the means of production". These may help the rulers of various class societies to ration-alize *their* system of exploitation and solve *their own* problems. We refuse to choose between options defined by our class enemies. *It follows* that we don't urge nation-alization (or anything else for that matter) on governments of either "right" or "left".

Section 2 implies that modern capitalism *can* further develop the means of pro-duction. At a cost, it can improve living standards. But neither of these has any social-ist content. Anyone who wants three square meals a day and the prospect of end-less employment can find them in any well-run gaol. *It follows* that we don't denounce capitalism primarily on the basis of its inadequacies in these fields. Socialism, for us, is not about transistors for the prisoners. It is about the destruction of the industrial prison itself. It is not only about more bread, but about who runs the bakery.

The section finally emphasizes the multiple methods whereby the system per-petuates itself. By mentioning *propaganda* as well as policemen, *schools* as well as prisons, *traditional values* and *traditional morality* as well as traditional methods of physical coercion, the section stresses an important obstacle to the achievement of a free society, namely the fact that the vast majority of the exploited and the manip-ulated have internalized and largely accepted the system's norms and values (for example such concepts as hierarchy, the division of society into order-givers and order-takers, wage labour, and the polarity of sexual roles) and consider them intrin-sically rational. Because of all this *it follows* that we reject as incomplete (and hence inadequate) notions which attribute the perpetuation of the system solely to police repression or to the "betrayals" of various political or trade union leaders.

A crisis of values and an increased questioning of authority relations are, how-ever, developing features of contemporary society. The growth of these crises is one of the preconditions for socialist revolution. Socialism will only be possible when the majority of people understand the need for social change, become aware of their ability to transform society, decide to exert their collective power to this end, and know with what they want to replace the present system. *It follows* that we reject analyses (such as those of every variety of Leninist or Trotskyist) who define the main crisis of modern society as "a crisis of leadership". They are all generals in search of an army, for whom recruitment figures are the main yardstick of success. For us revolutionary change is a question of consciousness: the consciousness that would make generals redundant.

3. When we refer to the "traditional parties of the left" we don't only have in mind the social-democratic and "communist" parties. Parties of this type have administered, administer and will continue to administer exploitative class societies. Under the title of "traditional parties of the left" we also include the trad revs (traditional revolutionaries), i.e. the various Leninist, Trotskyist and Maoid sects who are the carriers of state capitalist ideology and the embryonic nuclei of repressive, state-capitalist power.

These groups are prefigurations of alternative types of exploitation. Their critiques of the social-democratic and "Stalinist" or "revisionist" left appear virulent enough, but they never deal with fundamentals (such as the structure of decision-making, the locus of power, the primacy of the Party, the existence of hierarchy, the maximization of surplus value, the perpetuation of wage labour, and inequality). This is no accident and flows from the fact that they themselves accept these fundamentals. Bourgeois ideology is far more widespread than many revolutionaries believe and has in fact deeply permeated their thinking. In this sense Marx's statement about "the dominant ideas of each epoch being the ideas of its ruling class" is far more true than Marx could ever have anticipated.

As far as authoritarian class society (and the libertarian-socialist alternative) is concerned *the trad revs are part of the problem, not part of the solution*. Those who subscribe to social-democratic or Bolshevik ideology are themselves either victims of the prevailing mystification (and attempts should be made to demystify them), or they are the conscious exponents and future beneficiaries of a new form of class rule (and should be ruthlessly exposed). In either case *it follows* that there is nothing "sectarian" in systematically proclaiming opposition to what they stand for. Not to do so would be tantamount to suppressing our critique of half of the prevailing social order. It would mean to participate in the general mystification of traditional politics (where one thinks one thing and says another) and to deny the very basis of our *independent* political existence.

4. Because the traditional parties cannot be "reformed", "captured", or converted into instruments of working class emancipation - and because we are reluctant to indulge in double-talk and double-think - *it follows* that we do not indulge in such activities as "critically supporting" the Labour Party at election time, calling for "Labour to Power" between elections, and generally participating in sowing illusions, the better at a later date to "take people through the experience" of seeing through them. The Labour and Communist Parties may be marginally superior to the Conservative Party in driving private capitalism along the road to state capitalism. The trad revs would certainly prove superior to them both. But we are not called upon to make any choice of the kind: it is not the role of revolutionaries to be the midwives of new forms of exploitation. *It follows* that we would rather fight for what we want (even if we don't immediately get it) than fight for what we don't want...and get it.

The trade union bureaucracy is an essential component of developing state capitalist societies. The trade union leaders neither "betray" nor "sell out" when they manipulate working class struggles and seek to use them for their own ends. They are not "traitors" when they seek to increase their material rewards or to lessen the frequency with which they have to submit to election - they are acting logically and according to their own interests, which just happen to be different from those of working people. *It follows* that we do not urge people to elect "better" leaders, to "democratize" the unions or to create new ones, which under the circumstances of today would suffer exactly the same fate as the old ones. All these are "non-issues" about which only those who have failed to grasp the real root of the problem can get worked up.

The real need is to concentrate on the *positive* task of building the alternative (both in people's minds and in reality), namely *autonomous job organizations*, linked to others in the same industry and elsewhere, and controlled from below. Sooner or later such organizations will either enter into conflict with the existing outfits claiming to "represent" the working class (and it would be premature at this stage to define the possible forms of this conflict), or they will bypass the old organizations altogether.

5. This section differentiates our concept of socialism from most of those prevailing today. Socialism, for us, is not just a question of economic reorganization from which other benefits will "inevitably" follow, without *consciously* being fought for. It is a *total* vision of a *completely* different society. Such a vision is linked to the *total critique* of capitalism we have previously referred to.

Social-democrats and Bolsheviks denounce equality as "utopian", "petty-bourgeois", or "anarchist". They dismiss the advocacy of freedom as "abstract", and reciprocal recognition as "liberal humanism". They will concede that the radical transformation of all social relations is a valid ultimate objective, but cannot see it as an essential, immediate ingredient of the very process of meaningful change.

When we talk of "man's positive self-consciousness" and of "his understanding of his environment and of himself" we mean the gradual discarding of myths and of all types of false consciousness (religion, nationalism, patriarchal attitudes, the belief in the rationality of hierarchy, etc.). The precondition of human freedom is the understanding of all that limits it. Positive self-consciousness implies the gradual breakdown of that state of chronic schizophrenia in which - through conditioning and other mechanisms - most people succeed in carrying mutually incompatible ideas in their heads. It means accepting coherence, and perceiving the relation of means and ends. It means exposing those who organize conferences about "workers' control"…addressed by union officials elected for life. It means patiently explaining the incompatibilities of "people's capitalism", "parliamentary socialism", "Christian communism", "anarcho-Zionism", "Party-led 'workers' councils'", and other such rubbish. It means understanding that a non-manipulative society cannot be achieved by manipulative means or a classless society through hierarchical structures. This attempt at both gaining insight and at imparting it will be difficult and prolonged. It will doubtless be dismissed as "intellectual theorizing" by every "voluntarist" or "activist" tendency, eager for short cuts to the promised land and more concern with movement than with direction.

Because we think people can and should understand what they are doing, *it follows* that we reject many of the approaches so common in the movement today. In practice this means avoiding the use of revolutionary myths and the resort to manipulated confrontations, intended to raise consciousness. Underlying both of these is the usually unformulated assumption that people cannot understand social reality and act rationally on their own.

Linked to our rejection of revolutionary myths is our rejection of ready-made political labels. We want no gods, not even those of the Marxist or anarchist pantheons. We live in neither the Petrograd of 1917 nor the Barcelona of 1936. We are *ourselves*: the product of the disintegration of traditional politics, in an advanced industrial country, in the second half of the twentieth century. It is to the problems and conflicts of *that* society that we must apply ourselves.

Although we consider ourselves part of the "libertarian left" we differ from most strands of the "cultural" or "political" underground. We have nothing in common, for instance, with those petty entrepreneurs, now thriving on the general confusion, who simultaneously promote such commodities as oriental mysticism, black magic, the drug cult, sexual exploitation (masquerading as sexual liberation) - seasoning it all with big chunks of populist mythology. Their dissemination of myths and their advocacy of "non-sectarian politics" do not prevent them from taking up, in practice, many reactionary stances. In fact, they ensure it. Under the mindless slogan of "Support for people in struggle", these tendencies advocate support for various nationalisms (today always reactionary) such as those of both IRAs and of all the NLFs.

Other strands, calling themselves "libertarian Marxist", suffer from middle class feelings of guilt which make them prone to workeritis. Despite this, their practice is both reformist and substitutionalist. For instance, when they (correctly) support struggles for limited objectives, such as those of squatters or Claimants' Unions, they often fail to stress the revolutionary implications of such collective direct action. Historically, direct action has often clashed with the reformist nature of the objectives pursued. Again, such tendencies support the IRAs and NLFs and refrain from criticizing the Cuban, North Vietnamese or Chinese regimes. Having rejected the Party, they nevertheless share with Leninism a bourgeois concept of consciousness.

Because we think our politics should be coherent we also reject the approach of others in the libertarian movement who place their whole emphasis on personal liberation or who seek individual solutions to what are social problems. We dissociate ourselves from those who equate the violence of the oppressor with the violence of the oppressed (in condemnation of "all violence"), and from those who place the rights of strikers on the picket line on the same footing as the right of scabs to blackleg (in an abstract defence of "freedom as such"). Similarly, anarcho-Catholicism and anarcho-Maoism are internally incoherent outlooks, incompatible with revolutionary self-activity.

We feel that there should be some relation between our vision of socialism and what we do here and now. *It follows* that we seek as from now, and starting with those closest to us, to puncture some of the more widely held political myths. These are not confined to the "right" - with its belief that hierarchy and inequality are of the essence of the human condition. We consider irrational (and/or dishonest) that those who talk most of the masses (and of the capacity of the working class to create a new society) should have the least confidence in people's ability to dispense with leaders. We also consider it irrational that most radical advocates of "genuine social change" should incorporate in their own ideas, programmes and organizational prescriptions so many of the values, priorities and models they claim to oppose.

6. When we say that socialist society will be "built from below", we mean just that. We do *not* mean "initiated from above and then endorsed from below". Nor do we mean "planned from above and later checked from below". We mean there should be no separation between organs of decision and organs of execution. This

is why we advocate workers' "management" of production, and avoid the ambiguous demand for workers' "control". (The differences - both theoretical and historical - between the two are outlined in the introduction to our book on *The Bolsheviks and Workers' Control, 1917–1921.*)

We deny the revolutionary organization any specific prerogative in the post-revolutionary period, or in the building of the new society. Its main function in this period will be to stress the primacy of the Workers' Councils (and of bodies based on them) as instruments of decisional authority, and to struggle against all those who would seek to lessen or to bypass this authority - or to vest power elsewhere. Unlike others on the left who dismiss thinking about the new society as "preoccupation with the cookshops of the future" we have outlined our ideas about a possible structure of such a society in some detail in our pamphlet on *Workers' Councils and the Economics of a Self-Managed Society.*

7. This section is perhaps the most important and least understood of the whole statement. It is the key to how we view our *practical work*. It defines yardsticks with which we can approach everyday political life and rationally use our mental and physical resources. It explains why we consider certain questions significant while others are dismissed as non-issues. Within the limits of our own coherence, it explains the content of our paper.

Because we do not consider them of particular relevance to the attitudes and aptitudes we seek to develop, we do not get worked up about such matters as parliamentary or trade union elections (getting others to do things for one), the Common Market or the convertibility crisis (partisan involvement in the problems of the rulers is of no help to the ruled), or about the struggle in Ireland or various putsches in Africa ("taking sides" in struggles waged under the domination of a totally reactionary false consciousness). We cannot ignore these events without ignoring a portion of reality but we can at least avoid endowing them with a relevance to socialism they do not possess. Conversely we think the Hungarian Revolution of 1956 and the French events of May 1968 *were* deeply significant (for they were struggles against bureaucracy, and attempts at self-management in both Eastern and Western contexts).

These yardsticks also help clarify our attitude to various industrial disputes. While most are a challenge to the employer, some have a deeper socialist content than others. Why for instance are "unofficial" actions on conditions of work, waged under the close control of the rank and file, usually of deeper significance than "official" actions on questions of wages, run from afar by the union bureaucrats? In terms of the development of socialist consciousness *how* a struggle is waged and what it is *about* are of fundamental importance. *Socialism*, after all, *is about who takes the decisions*. We believe this needs stressing, *in practice, from now*.

In our accounts of disputes our guide line is that one cannot tidy up reality, and that more is gained by honestly analyzing real difficulties than by living in a mythical world, where one takes one's wishes for reality. *It follows* that we seek to avoid the "triumphalist" (in reality manipulatory) tone that mars so much of the "interventions" of the trad revs.

Finally the emphasis on self-activity, and its warning about the harmful effects of manipulation, substitutionism or reliance on others to do things for one have deeper implications, or relevance to our own organization.

8. We are not pacifists. We have no illusions about what we are up against. In all class societies, institutional violence weighs heavily and constantly on the oppressed. Moreover the rulers of such societies have always resorted to more explicit physical repression when their power and privileges were really threatened. Against repression by the ruling class we endorse the people's right to self-defence, by whatever means be appropriate.

The power of the rulers feeds on the indecision and confusion of the ruled. Their power will only be overcome if confronted with ours: the power of a conscious and self-reliant majority, knowing what it wants and determined to get it. In modern industrial societies the power of such a majority will lie where thousands congregate daily, to sell their labour power in the production of goods and services.

Socialism cannot be the result of a putsch, of the capture of some Palace, or of the blowing up of some Party or Police Headquarters, carried out "on behalf of the people" or "to galvanize the masses". If unsuccessful, all that such actions do is to create martyrs and myths – and to provoke intensified repression. If "successful", they would only substitute one ruling minority for another, i.e. bring about a new form of exploitative society. Nor can socialism be introduced by organizations themselves structured according to authoritarian, hierarchical, bureaucratic or semi-military patterns. All that such organizations have instituted (and, if "successful", are likely to continue instituting) are societies in their own image.

The social revolution is no Party matter. It will be the action of the immense majority, acting in the interests of the immense majority. The failures of social-democracy and of Bolshevism are the failure of a whole concept of politics, a concept according to which the oppressed could entrust their liberation to others than themselves. This lesson is gradually entering mass consciousness and preparing the ground for a genuinely libertarian revolution.

9. Because we reject Lenin's concept that the working class can only develop a trade union (or reformist) consciousness *it follows* that we reject the Leninist prescription that socialist consciousness has to be brought to the people from outside, or injected into the movement by political specialists: the professional revolutionaries. It further follows that we cannot behave as if we held such beliefs.

Mass consciousness, however, is never a theoretical consciousness, derived individually through the study of books. In modern industrial societies socialist consciousness springs from the real conditions of social life. These societies generate the conditions for an adequate consciousness. On the other hand, because they are class societies, they usually inhibit accession to that consciousness. Here lies both the dilemma and the challenge confronting modern revolutionaries.

There *is* a role for conscious revolutionaries. *Firstly*, through personal involvement, in one's own life and where possible at one's own place of work. (Here the main danger lies in "prolier than thou" attitudes, which lead people either to believe that there is little they can do if they are not industrial workers, or to pretend to be what they are not, in the false belief that the only relevant areas of struggle are in relation to industry.) *Secondly*, by assisting others in struggle, by providing them with help or information they are denied. (Here the main danger lies in the offering of "interested help", where recruitment of the militant to the "revolutionary" organization is as much an objective of the "help" as is his victory in the struggle in which he is involved.) *Finally*, by pointing out and explaining the deep (but often hidden) relations between the socialist objective and what people are driven to do, through their own experiences and needs. (This is what we mean when we say revolutionaries should help make "explicit" the "implicitly" socialist content of many modern struggles.)

10. This section should differentiate *Solidarity* from the traditional type of political organization. We are not a leadership and do not aspire to be one. Because we do not want to lead or manipulate others, we have no use for hierarchy or for manipulatory mechanisms within our own ranks. Because we believe in the autonomy - ideological and organizational - of the working class, we cannot deny groups such autonomy within the Solidarity movement itself. On the contrary, we should seek to encourage it.

On the other hand we certainly wish to influence others and to disseminate Solidarity ideas (not just any ideas) as widely as possible. This requires the co-ordinated activity of people or groups, individually capable of self-activity and of finding their own level of involvement and their own areas of work. The instruments of such co-ordination should be flexible and vary according to the purpose for which co-ordination is required.

We do not reject organizations as necessarily implying bureaucracy. If we held such views there would be no socialist perspective whatsoever. On the contrary, we hold that organizations whose mechanisms (and their implications) are understood by all can alone provide the framework for democratic decision-making. There are no institutional guarantees against the bureaucratization of revolutionary groups. The only guarantee is the perpetual awareness and self-mobilization of their members. We are aware, however, of the danger of revolutionary groups becoming "ends in themselves". In the past, loyalties to groups have often superseded loyalties to ideas. Our prime commitment is to the social revolution - not to any particular political group, not even to Solidarity. Our organizational structure should certainly reflect the need for mutual assistance and support. But we have *no* other ulterior objectives, aspirations or ambitions. We therefore do not structure ourselves as if we had.

SOLIDARITY PAMPHLET, 1972

26. THE MALAISE ON THE LEFT

Forget for a moment the scare campaigns of the recent elections: Scanlon and Jones presented by the yellow press as proselytizers of red revolution, Mr. Wilson in the garb of a latter-day Kerensky opening the gates to Bolshevism or worse, bank clerks freezing (*à la portugaise*) the funds of fleeting fascists, the great fear of the bourgeoisie about a "mafia of fanatical socialists" in control of the commanding heights...of the National Executive of the Labour Party!

The reality is less lurid – and less encouraging. What we see around us is a confident and aggressive movement, increasingly aware of the fact that real power does not lie in Parliament, but profoundly divided as to objectives, strategy and tactics – and completely at sea as to values and priorities. So divergent are its component strands that one has to ask, quite bluntly, whether one can legitimately speak of a movement. Among thinking socialists there is a deep malaise.

The purpose of this article is to explore the roots of this malaise, and to show that they lie in the transformations of class society itself. Over the last few decades – and in many different areas – established society has itself brought about the number of the things that the revolutionaries of yesterday were demanding. This has happened in relation to economic attitudes, in relation to certain forms of social organization, and in relation to various aspects of the personal and sexual revolutions. When this adaptation in fact *benefits* established society, it is legitimate to refer to it as "recuperation". This article seeks to start a discussion on the limits of recuperation.[105]

Recuperation, of course, is nothing new. What is perhaps new is the extent to which most "revolutionaries" (whether they be demanding "more nationalization", more "self-management" or "more personal freedom") are unaware of the system's ability to absorb – and in the long run benefit from – these forms of "dissent". Class society has a tremendous resilience, a great capacity to cope with "subversion", to make icons of its iconoclasts, to draw sustenance from those who would throttle it. Revolutionaries must constantly be aware of this strength, otherwise they will fail to see what is happening around them. If certain sacred cows (or certain previous formulations, now found to be inadequate) have to be sacrificed, we'd rather do the job ourselves.

Recuperation of economic demands

Keynesian economic policies, once considered radical threats to bourgeois society, are today widely accepted as essential to the functioning of modern capitalism. The demands for nationalization of the mines or railways, for national health insurance, for unemployment benefit and for state pensions have been totally recuperated. Despite occasional nostalgic (and largely irrelevant) glances into the past, no Conservative politician, seeking to retain a shred of credibility, would today advocate the return of the mines or of the railways to private ownership – or the dismantling of the essential structure of the "welfare" state. All socialists would agree, thus far.

---

105 The discussion as to whether "self-management" can be equated with "socialism" has already begun among libertarians on the continent.

But there is then a parting of the ways. We would claim that the centralization of all the means of production in the hands of the state – the most "radical" demand of the *Communist Manifesto* – has been achieved in many parts of the world without any corresponding enhancement in the areas of human freedom. In fact an exploiting society, divided into order-givers and order-takers, functions far better on this type of economic base, which eliminates many of the irrationalities of laissez-faire capitalism. Whatever the human aspirations of their rank and file, the ideologies and programmes of Social Democratic, Communist, Trotskyist or Maoist groups in the West provide the most articulate demands for this kind of social organization. These groups are the midwives of State Capitalism. They may differ as to tempo and as to tactics. They may argue about what they consider to be (for others) the acceptable or unacceptable costs. But their fundamental objective is the same – and is moreover in keeping with the deepest requirements of Capital itself. *Pace* the ghosts of Hayek and of Schumpeter, *pace* Enoch Powell and Keith Joseph, the division of society into rulers and ruled will not be abolished by the abolition of the "free market" or, for that matter, by anything that Messrs. Wilson or Gollan (or the "theoreticians" of any of the Marxist sects) may have in mind.

Moreover all over the Third World (from Sékou Touré's Guinea to North Vietnam, from Iraq to Zanzibar) "Marxist-Leninist" ideas are today influencing the birth and moulding the economic life of many developing countries. All are ruthlessly exploitative societies, geared to the rapid development of the productive forces. Today this is only possible on the basis of intense primary accumulation, carried out on the backs of the peasantry. Here again erstwhile revolutionary ideas are becoming vehicles for new forms of enslavement.

To paraphrase Marx, it is not what men think they are doing that matters. What matters is the objective result of their beliefs and actions. Class society can well recuperate the economic demands of the traditional left. It is not of fundamental importance, in this respect, whether various ruling classes are fully aware of what is happening to them. They clearly differ from one another in the degree of insight they have achieved into their own long-term, historical interests. The more far-sighted among them now accept the centralization of the means of production in the hands of the State as the essential precondition for the growth of the productive forces. For most Marxist socialists (and for the bourgeoisie) this growth is *the* fundamental issue. This is what unites them. This is were the bourgeois vision and the Marxist vision coalesce. For both of them economic growth is what politics (and ultimately what life itself) is all about. There are few other dimensions to their thinking. For both of them the future is mainly about "more of the same". And the rest? The rest is for "after the revolution". At best, it will look after itself. At worst, if one speaks to a traditional Marxist about such issues as women's liberation, ecology, the "counter-culture", etc. one is denounced as a "diversionist" in tones showing how deeply the work ethic, patriarchal attitudes and value system of the existing society have permeated their thinking.

Recuperation of institutional forms

Sections of the left have fortunately gone far beyond the demands for nationalization, planning, etc. In the wake of the Russian Revolution small groups of "left" communists clearly foresaw the course of events which this type of "socialism" would lead to. Slandered by Lenin, denounced by the "orthodox" communists, they warned of what lay ahead: the rule of the party would soon result in the emergence of a new ruling class, based not on the private ownership of the means of production but on a monopoly of decisional authority in all areas of economic, political and social life. To the hegemony of the Party and to the omniscience of its Central Committee the left communist counter-poised the knowledge and power of an enlightened and autonomous working class. They posited the institutional form this power would take: the Workers' Councils. This was no genial blueprint for a new society sucked out of the thumb of a Gorter or a Pannekoek. From the Paris Commune to the Russian Revolution of 1917 the "council" form of organization had been the living historical product of the class struggle itself. The warnings of these earlier revolutionaries have been fully justified.

But their vision remains limited. Despite Pannekoek's interests in science and philosophy, Ruhle's interest in pedagogy, and Korsch's stress on the need for a deep-going cultural critique, most of the writings of the left communists centred on problems of work and of production and distribution. They lived in a very different era from our own, and had little of significance to say about what have become very important areas of social life: bureaucratization, alienation in consumption and leisure, authoritarian conditioning, the "youth revolt", women's liberation, etc. Even some of their institutional proposals have been partly overtaken by events.

The recuperation of the demand for working class power at the point of production and for a society based on Workers' Councils has, for instance, taken on a particularly sinister form. Confronted with the bureaucratic monstrosity of Stalinist and post-Stalinist Russia, yet wishing to retain some credibility among their working class supporters, various strands of Bolshevism have sought posthumously to rehabilitate the concept of "workers' control". Although "workers' control" was only referred to once in the documents of the first four congresses of the Communist International it has recently become one of the Top Ten Slogans. Between 1917 and 1921 all attempts by the working class to assert real power over production - or to transcend the narrow role allocated to it by the Party - were smashed by the Bolsheviks, after first having been denounced as anarchist or anarcho-syndicalist deviations. Today workers' control is presented as a sort of sugar coating to the pill of nationalization of every Trotskyist or Leninist micro-bureaucrat on the make. Those who strangled the viable infant are now hawking the corpse around. The Institute for Workers' Control even runs annual conferences, addressed and dominated by trade union officials appointed for life. Those who are not prepared to allow workers to control their own organizations here and now serenade sundry simpletons with fanciful tunes as to their fate in the future. Recuperation here is taking place amid incredible confusion.

For a long time the advocacy of genuine workers' control (or, as we prefer to call it, workers' self management)[106] remained confined to small groups of revolutionaries swimming against the great bureaucratic tide. Following the French events of May 1968 the demand took on a new reality and a new coherence. People began to see self-management as the dominant theme (and Workers' Councils as the institutional form) of a new society in which bureaucracy would be eliminated, and in which ordinary people would at last achieve genuine power over many aspects of

---

106   For a discussion about the differences between the two concepts, see the Introduction to *The Bolsheviks and Workers' Control, 1917–1921*.

their everyday life. But this again was to ignore the system's capacity for integrating dissent and harnessing it to its own advantage.

Can the demand for self-management be geared to the requirements of class society itself? An honest answer would be "yes, in some respects". Yes, providing those operating the self-management still accepted the values of the system. Yes, if it remained strictly localized. Yes, provided it was eviscerated of all political content. Car assembly plants seeking to obtain the participation of the workers have been operating for some time in the Volvo and Saab factories in Sweden. Under the "with it" guise of enriching the workers' job, employers have continued to enrich themselves. Groups of workers are allowed to manage their own alienation. The powers-that-be seek to resuscitate the anaemic institutions of existing society (increasingly abandoned by those expected to make them function) with transfusions of "participation". No wonder the slogan has been taken up by everyone from Gaullist deputies to our own Liberals.

Revolutionaries are in some measures to blame for this confusion of form and content. They have insufficiently warned against the dangers inherent in any attempts at self-management with capitalism. And, in relation to the future, they have insufficiently stressed the limitations of the demand. Self-management and Workers' Councils are means to liberation. They are not liberation itself. Many revolutionaries have, moreover, tended to underestimate the complex problems of society as a whole. These have to be considered in addition to the problems of particular groups of workers. Our vision has never been "the railways to the railwaymen, the dust to the dustmen". We are not for self-managed insurance empires, for self-managed advertising companies, for the self-managed production of nuclear weapons.

This is not to say that self-management will not be the dominant theme, and the council probably the institutional form of any kind of socialist society. But they are no more than that. Into those particular bottles many wines can be poured. In contemporary society self-management could very well develop on a reformist, racist, nationalistic or militaristic basis. The historical precedents are here. Many Workers' Councils in Germany - in December 1918, and again later on - voted to surrender power to parliamentary institutions. Between 1930 and 1945 the vast majority of the British and German people identified with their respective rulers and mobilized themselves (or allowed themselves to be mobilized) in the defence of interests that were not their own. Israeli self-managed kibbutzim are vehicles for the dissemination of Zionist ideology and for implementing (anti-Arab) discrimination, i.e. anti-socialist policies. In Northern Ireland, amid an "unparalleled explosion of self-management", the self-activity of a civilian population recently brought down a government…in the name of sectarian and mystified objectives. The lessons are clear. *Self-management, divorced from socialist politics, is meaningless.*

Recuperation of "proto-Marxist" demands

Confronted with the fact that established society has successfully co-opted both the economic objectives and some of the institutional prescriptions of those who wanted to challenge it, radicals have responded in a numbers of ways.

One response has been to delve deeper into Marx. The 'communist project' is redefined in proto-Marxist terms. We now have Marx *à la carte*. What is stressed is not what was the historical reality of Marxism (even in Marx's day) but a vision which, although valid, seldom went beyond the realm of rhetoric. The Marx of "the proletarians have no Fatherland" replaces the Marx of the Franco-Prussian war of 1870-71 who supported first Bismarck's armies, then - after Sedan - the forces of the Second Empire. The Marx who denounced the slogan "a fair day's wage for a fair day's work" (arguing instead for "the abolition of the wages system") replaces the more prosaic Marx, manoeuvring among the Lucrafts and the Maltman Barrys in the counsels of the First International. The Marx who thundered that "the emancipation of the working class is the task of the working class itself" erases the pathetic figure of the Marx of 1872, cooking the last congress of the International (the only one he attended in person), inventing non-existing delegations, shifting the venues of future meetings to harass the supporters of the equally authoritarian Bakunin.

But are even these proto-Marxist prescriptions adequate? Is the "abolition of frontiers" any kind of guarantee as to the type of regime that will hold sway over the new, frontierless expanse? Is the vision of an exploitative society, fusing the techniques of domination of both East and West, just a nightmare dreamed up by the writers of science fiction? Is the abolition of the wage labour any guarantee against exploitation and alienation? Were there not exploitative societies long before wage labour appeared on the historical scene? Wage labour underpins and reinforces hierarchies of power. Its abolition does not necessarily abolish such hierarchies. Class society might even recuperate demands of this kind.

Recuperation of the "personal revolution"

Another response of those confronted with the tremendous recuperative powers of established society has been a tendency to seek individual emancipation, to create in the "here and now" microcosms of the alternative society. Some advocates of this viewpoint see the growth of social freedom as the by-product of the addition of one "free" individual to another, rather like workers going to Ruskin College to become "emancipated one by one". This type of revolt, as long as it is conceived in purely individual terms, can readily be recuperated by established society. Individual revolt, whether in clothing or in hair styles, whether in food preferences or in musical tastes, whether in sexual mores or in philosophical attitudes, readily becomes a commodity to be frenetically exploited in the interests of Capital itself. (The important book, *The Failure of the Sexual Revolution'* by George Frankl, deals with this theme.)

The limits of recuperation

In *The Irrational in Politics* we wrote that exploiting society would not be able to tolerate "the mass development of critical, demystified, self-reliant, sexually emancipated, autonomous, non-alienated persons, conscious of what they want *and prepared to struggle for it*". We still hold this idea to be basically correct. Its core - that one cannot conceive of any genuinely liberatory movement without genuinely liberated individuals - seems irrefutable. But our formulation was inadequate. We should have spoken of individuals prepared *collectively* to struggle for what they wanted. And we should have spoken more about the *objectives* of the struggle. We should have described more clearly what the vision was, in our eyes at least. The *socialist* transformation of society is not an automatic process, or a reflex activity. It requires a sense of direction. There may be many roads to the promised land but it can surely only help if people know where they are going.

Let us take it for granted that meaningful activity needs to be collective, that social transformation needs emancipated individuals, and that the institutional framework of any new society will probably be based, in part at least, on those forms which the struggle itself has repeatedly thrown up at its moments of deepest insight and creativity. What we now need to think about – and to discuss widely throughout the libertarian left – is the *political content* of an activity that *consciously* seeks both to avoid recuperation and to be relevant to the conditions of today.

Are certain yardsticks necessary to define such an activity? I personally think the answer is "yes" – with the proviso that the definition must be seen as an ongoing process. Should revolutionaries who share common objectives group together, first to discuss their objectives and then to fight for them? Again I think the answer is "yes". "Political inexistentialism" is only relevant if one thinks there is some divine guidance ensuring that every struggle helps move society in a socialist direction.

It is only if libertarians speak openly about these questions that they will be able to present a credible alternative to the authoritarian left. If socialism is the creation of forms of living that will enable all – free from external constraints or internalized inhibitions – to rise to their full stature, to fulfil themselves as human beings, to enjoy themselves, to relate to one another without treading on anybody (and this is as good a definition of socialism as any other) – we should say so loud and clear. And we should not be afraid of criticizing any activities – however "self-managed" – that lead in an opposite direction. Socialism, after all, is about a specific way of socializing. In this discussion we must not forget the economic prerequisites of what we seek. Nor must we confuse them with the objective itself. Finally we must not underestimate the forces we are up against, including the recuperative powers of established society. An ongoing reassessment of the degree to which one's former goals have been recuperated is the most effective antidote to the malaise on the left, and the only possible prescription for remaining a revolutionary.

SOLIDARITY, VII, 12 (NOVEMBER 1974)

27. FACTORY COMMITTEES AND THE DICTATORSHIP OF THE PROLETARIAT

It is a welcome sign of the times that a serious exchange of radical opinion is now under way concerning the formative period of the Russian state, and *Critique* is to be congratulated on having played a part in the initiation of this discussion. How deep the confrontation goes will, of course, depend on how open the journal remains to those in the revolutionary movement who do not accept the label of "Marxist", but who feel they may nevertheless have something of relevance to contribute.

In your last issue, Chris Goodey claims that "it is only the current practice and experience of the world movement for socialist revolution that is beginning to allow us an overall view of the battle-stations which we have unthinkingly maintained for a long time". In a very general sense that is, of course, true. But elements of a serious critique antedated - and by a considerable period - "May 1968 in France, the Prague events and the Chilean Revolution". Some of those who initiated this critique would moreover shudder to find themselves subsumed under the "we" that Goodey refers to. They did not wait until the late sixties to express their views. As early as 1918 they had clearly seen the direction in which Russian society was moving and proclaimed a principled opposition, often at the cost of their lives. It is a tragic fact, for which Leninists of all kinds (Stalinists, Trotskyists, Maoists, and the advocates of various theories of "state capitalism", i.e. International Socialists, Bordigists, "Marxist Humanists", etc.) must carry their full share of responsibility, that we know less today about the early weeks of Russian Revolution than we do, for instance, about the history of the Paris Commune.

"Unfortunately it is not the workers who write history. It is always 'the others.'"[107] "Official" historians seldom have eyes to see or ears to hear the acts and words which express the autonomous activity of the working class. They think in terms of institutions, congresses, leaders. In the best instances they will vaunt rank-and-file activity as long as it coincides with their own conceptions. But they "will radically condemn it or impute the basest of motives to it as soon as it deviates from that line".[108] They seem to lack the categories of thought necessary to perceive life as it really is. To them an activity which has no leader or programme, no institutions and no statutes, can only be conceptualized as "troubles", "disorder", "anarchy". In the words of Cardan "the spontaneous activity of the masses belongs, by definition, to what history suppresses".[109]

Goodey is correct when he claims it is "part of the revolutionary process to demystify our own history" and when he points out that the struggle for "direct forms of working people's power at the point of production" has been "hidden and ignored". (The formulation in the passive is, however, disingenuous. By whom was it

---

107 Paul Cardan, "Le Rôle de l'idéologie bolchevique dans la naissance de la bureaucratie", *Socialisme ou Barbarie*, no. 35 (January–March 1964). This text was subsequently published in English as Solidarity Pamphlet 24, *From Bolshevism to the Bureaucracy* (1967).

108 *Ibid.*

109 *Ibid.*

hidden? And why was it ignored?) But he is profoundly wrong when he attributes this silence of the "Marxist left" to such ideological shortcomings as lack of "temerity" or insufficient "capacity for self-criticism". A proper evaluation of these matters cannot but lead, for anyone with even moderate pretensions to intellectual honesty, to a complete break with Leninism in all its aspects and to a re-examination of certain basic Marxist beliefs.

A steady trickle of documentation is now coming to light concerning the role of the Factory Committees in the Russian Revolution.[110] Goodey sees these Committees as "the most powerful institution in Russia by the end of 1917" and in this he is certainly right. He is also correct in claiming that "this power later submerged". What is lacking in his article, however, is the serious attempt to explain what happened in between, when it happened, why it happened, and to whom it happened. The "submergence" of which Goodey speaks was well advanced, if not virtually completed, by May 1918, i.e. *before* the Civil War and the "Allied" intervention really got under way. The traditional explanations of the degeneration of the Russian revolution are just not good enough.

In my view, Goodey's silence on these essential questions is unavoidable. It flows directly from his honestly declared political position. He sees Party and State as "indirect forms of workers' power", and explicitly absolves the Leninist Party from any blame in the degeneration. He claims that "even in our present world, in spite of the fact that bureaucratic degeneration is inherent in the 'workers' state' and the 'workers' party', these are still the necessary complement to forms of direct workers' power". He only conceives these forms of direct workers' power as "effective antibodies against that degeneration". He nowhere posits them as the necessarily dominant units in the initiation of policy, in other words as the basic nuclei of the new society. With this kind of overall outlook a serious analysis of the smashing of the Factory Committees is virtually impossible, for the Bolshevik Party was to play a dominant role in this tragedy. There is nothing more utopian than the belief that the Russian working class could have maintained its power through a "workers' party" or a "workers' state" when it had already lost that power at the point of production.

I have elsewhere[111] sought to bring together material from disparate sources and to document as concisely and yet as fully as possible the various stages of a process which led, within the short period of four years, from the tremendous upsurge of the Factory Committee movement (a movement which both implicitly and explicitly sought to alter the relations of production) to the establishment of unquestioned domination by a monolithic and bureaucratic agency (the Party) over all aspects of economical and political life. I argued that as this agency was not itself based on production, its rule could only epitomize the continued limitation of the authority of the workers in the productive process. This necessarily implied the perpetuation within society at large.

It is impossible, within the space available, to recapitulate all the evidence here. The first stage of the process under discussion was the subordination of the Factory Committees to the All-Russian Council for Workers' Control in which the unions (themselves already strongly under Party influence) were heavily represented. This

---

110   Carr's *The Bolshevik Revolution, 1917–1923* (Macmillan, 1952), Daniels's *The Conscience of the Revolution* (Harvard University Press, 1960), Avrich's *The Russian Anarchists* (Princeton University Press, 1967) and Kaplan's *Bolshevik Ideology* (Owen, 1969) provide an excellent starting point for anyone interested in the discussion.

111   *The Bolsheviks and Workers' Control, 1917–1921* (Solidarity, 1970).

took place very shortly after the coming to power of the Soviet Government. The second phase - which almost immediately followed the first - was the incorporation of this All-Russian Council for Workers' Control into the Vesenka (Supreme Economic Council), even more heavily weighted in favour of the unions, but also comprising direct nominees of the state (i.e. of the Party). By early 1918 the Bolsheviks were actively seeking to merge the Committees into the trade union structures. The issue provoked heated discussions at the First All-Russian Congress of Trade Unions (January 7–14, 1918) which saw desperate attempts, led mainly by anarcho-syndicalists, to maintain the autonomy of the Committees, against the advice Ryazanov who urged the Committees "to commit suicide by becoming an integral element of the trade union structure".[112] During the next two years a sustained campaign was waged to curb the power of the unions themselves, for the unions, albeit in a very indirect and distorted way, could still be influenced by the working class. It was particularly important for the new bureaucracy to replace this power by the authority of direct party nominees. These managers and administrators, nearly all appointed from above, gradually came to form the basis of a new ruling class. The important point, as far as the re-evaluation of history is concerned, is that each of these steps was to be resisted, but each fight was to be lost. Each time, the "adversary" appeared in the garb of the new "proletarian" power. And each defeat was to make it more difficult for the working class itself directly to manage production, i.e. fundamentally to alter its status as a subordinate class.

Goodey claims that the "essence of the libertarian argument is that the level of the productive forces plays a less determining role in the development of history than the existence of hierarchy: in the revolutionary process that hierarchy takes the form of 'authoritarianism' among the leaders (in this case the Bolshevik Party) and 'false consciousness' among the masses in submitting to what they consider their natural leaders". It is difficult to know from where he can derive such a crudely psychological formulation of the libertarian case. As far as I know, no libertarian has argued that the level of the productive forces is either "more" or "less" important than the role of ideas and attitudes in influencing historical development. Both are important. What libertarians have stressed (and most Marxists have signally refused to recognize) is that the conceptions and attitudes of the dominant Party were as much an objective fact of history - influencing the evolution of events at critical moments - as were production statistics for electricity or steel.

Goodey claims that the libertarian argument "can be nailed quite easily" and I find it a compliment that he should choose my essay on which to practice his skills as a carpenter. He focuses attention on one particular episode I describe in the hope that by challenging its factual accuracy he can somehow impugn the credibility of the rest. He correctly defines the area of the discussion. "The argument is that Lenin and Bolshevik leaders suppressed the factory committees immediately on the seizure of power, because they held too much real power". Right on! Goodey is also correct in attributing to me the view "the legislation on workers' control immediately after October was elaborated in totally different ways by Lenin and by the committees' leaders". Again, right on! There is abundant evidence (summarized in my text) to substantiate this view. The Achilles' heel of my thesis is allegedly my reference to a document drawn up by certain members of the Central Council of Petrograd Factory

---

112   D.B. Ryazanov in *Pervy vserossiiskii s'yezd professionalnykh soyuzov*, *7–14 yanvarya 1918 g.* (First All-Russian Congress of Trade Unions, January 7 to 14, 1918) (Moscow, 1918), p.235.

Committees on how the economy should have been run immediately after the October events. I am quite prepared to take up the challenge on this rather narrow basis.

According to Goodey (and he devotes three pages to the matter) my knowledge of the document in question was "fifth hand". I had inherited from one Didier Limon[113] "an amputated quotation, bearing the wrong date, the wrong title, and the wrong authors". I had then "rewritten the text". Strong stuff. Unfortunately, on every single point Goodey is wrong.

According to Goodey the fateful history of this document was as follows. It was originally published in part in *Izvestia* (December 7, 1917) and fully in *Narodnoe Khozyaistvo* (no. 1, 1918). Lozovsky, a Bolshevik trade unionist, allegedly altered its title from "Draft Instructions on Workers' Control" to "Practical Manual for the Execution of Workers' Control". This was done in his book, *Rabochii Kontrol*, which according to Goodey was written "in November of 1917". (Goodey does not explain how Lozovsky could, in November 1917, have been distorting the title of a text that had not yet been published, but this is a minor point.) Then, still according to Goodey's chronology, Pankratova took up the text in her writings of 1923.[114] For reasons of her own she dated it February 6, 1918 (i.e. after the First Trade Union Congress, which sought to "fuse from above" the Factory Committees and the Unions). Goodey is to be congratulated in detecting this early piece of falsification by one of Stalin's pet historians. But the relevance of this to what either Limon or I wrote totally escapes me: neither of us gave the wrong date for the text under discussion.

According to Goodey, Limon takes over from Pankratova "the wrong title and the wrong date and adds his own embellishments". He truncates a quotation in the text and changes the authorship of the original document, attributing it to the "non-Bolshevik leaders of the All-Russian Council of the Factory Committees". On all these scores, Goodey is wrong. Limon did *not* get his facts[115] via Pankratova. The "secret" can now be let out of the bag. Limon got his facts from someone who had seen the documentation at the first hand, and before Pankratova had even thought of writing about it. I have also seen this original source. Even Goodey could have had access to it, had he been less concerned in proving the bad faith of those he disagrees with politically, and had he chosen to check with Limon. (Limon is, after all, on the Editorial Board of *Autogestion*, for which Goodey is the "correspondent for Great Britain".)

The "original" source is Chapter 8 ("Les Soviets d'usine à l'oeuvre') of Max Hoschiller's book *Le Mirage Sovietique* (Paris: Payot, 1921). Hoschiller was a French revolutionary who spoke Russian well. The authenticity of his account is vouched for by no less a figure than André Merrheim who wrote the Preface to Hoschiller's book.[116] It was in fact at Merrheim's suggestion that Hoschiller went to Russia.

Now what does Hoschiller say as to the authorship, the title, and the content of the controversial document?

---

113   Didier Limon, "Lenine et le contrôle ouvrier" (*Autogestion* (Paris), no. 4 (1967)).

114   Pankratova's article on "The Factory Committees in Russia at the Time of the Revolution (1917–1918)" was published in the previously mentioned issue of *Autogestion*.

115   Personal communication from Didier Limon.

116   Merrheim, one-time secretary of the French Metalworkers' Federation and co-author of the Charter of Amiens, was one of the important figures of the anti–war movement in France during the First World War. He was an active participant in the Zimmerwald Conference of anti-war socialists.

Hoschiller makes it clear that in the weeks preceding the revolution it was the anarchists who were striking the tune (*"donnaient le la"*) in the Factory Committees and that the Bolsheviks could only trail along after them (*"étaient bien obligés de marcher à leur remorque"*). On December 7, 1917, the decree setting up the Vesenkha (Supreme Economic Council) was promulgated.[117] The Vesenkha comprised some members of the All-Russian Council of Workers' Control (a very indirect sop to the Factory Committees), massive representation of all the new Commissariats and a number of experts, nominated from above, in a consultative capacity. According to Hoschiller the leaders of the Factory Committees, dissatisfied with Lenin's concessions (*"mécontents en dépit de toutes les concessions du chef du gouvernement"*), did not implement the decisions but elaborated their own decree in the form of a "Practical Manual for the Implementation of Workers' Control" (*"élaborerent leur propre décret sous forme d'un 'Manuel Pratique pour l'Execution du Contrôle Ouvrier'"*). Hoschiller describes how jealously he had kept the eight great in-folio sheets, printed in double columns, that had been widely distributed in the streets of Petrograd. He has clearly seen the original, which is more than can be said with any confidence of Lozovski, Pankratova...or even of Goodey.

Goodey then takes issue with Limon's attribution of this text to the "non-Bolshevik leaders of the All-Russian Council of Factory Committees". Is he really suggesting that the "Manual" was a Party document? Reference to the Hoschiller text shows that it was no such thing. One particular prescription of the "Manual" epitomizes this point. The "Manual" spoke of "Regional Federations of Factory Committees" and of the need for a "National Union of Factory Committees". But even Deutscher is forced to point out that such demands were diametrically opposed to Party policy at the time. "A few weeks after the upheaval the Factory Committees attempted to form their own national organization....The Bolsheviks now called upon the trade unions to render a special service to the nascent Soviet State and to discipline the Factory Committees. The unions came out firmly against the attempt of the Factory Committees to form a national organization of their own. They prevented the convocation of a planned All-Russian Congress of Factory Committees".[118] It ill behoves various Bolsheviks, after all this, to denounce the Factory Committees as only having had parochial preoccupations.

Two other facts stress the wide divergence of approach already obvious at this stage between the Leninists and the leaders of the Factory Committees. First the very real difficulties Lenin experienced in getting wide support for his "Draft Decrees on Workers' Control". These were originally published in *Pravda* (on November 3, 1917) but only ratified by the V.Ts.I.K. (All-Russian Central Executive Committee of the Soviets) eleven days later, after heated opposition from the rank and file of the Factory Committees.[119] Secondly the fact that *Izvestiya* (December 13, 1917) found it necessary to publish a text ("General Instructions on Workers' Control in Conformity

---

117   Sobraniye uzakonenii 1917–1918, no. 4, art. 58.

118   Isaac Deutscher, *Soviet Trade Unions* (London: Royal Institute for International Affairs, 1950), p. 17.

119   According to Carr (*The Bolshevik Revolution*, Vol. 2 (Pelican edition, 1966), p.73) "in the controversy behind the scenes which followed the publication of Lenin's draft, the trade unions became the unexpected champions of order, discipline and centralized direction of production; and the revised draft decree finally presented to V.Ts.I.K. on 14–27 November 1917 was the result of a struggle between the trade unions and the Factory Committees which repeated the struggle at the October Conference". (The First All–Russian Conference of Factory Committees had been held on October 17–22, 1917.)

with the Decree of November 14") which became widely known as the "Counter-Manual".

Concerning the substance of the passage under dispute Hoschiller's text makes it crystal clear that Limon has "amputated" nothing. Quoting from the introduction to the "Manual", Hoschiller (p.167) writes that workers' control *"ne doit pas être considéré dans le sens étroit d'une révision mais dans le sens plus large de 'l'ingérance'"*. Full stop. (A full stop put by Hoschiller, not by Limon. And a reasonable place, I would have thought, at which to end a quotation.) That my own reference to this document included, through the carelessness of a misplaced unquote, a few words that were Limon's hardly constitutes "rewriting the text" and alters precisely nothing to the substance of the matter.[120]

So there you have it. No plot. No "fifth hand knowledge" of a "shop-soiled" quotation. No Lozovsky as the "evident" original secondary source of all the rest. No wrong dates inherited from Pankratova. No Limon changing the authorship of the document. No truncating of quotations. All these are figments of Goodey's imagination and he should clearly stop prattling about "attitudes to verifiable facts". If this is really the best your contributor can do to "nail" the libertarian argument those who manufacture bandages for sore thumbs are in for a boom.

But let us return to the main argument. Goodey claims that "if…there was a nascent bureaucracy in 1917, then the Factory Committees were part of it". This is totally to misunderstand the concept of bureaucracy. It attributes to the word a restricted meaning, of little value to those who seek radically to change society. The classical Marxist conceptions are here totally inadequate. A bureaucracy is not just "officialdom" or a "social stratum enjoying certain material privileges" or a "gendarme, ensuring a certain pattern of distribution under conditions of want". If the concept of self-management is to have any meaning a bureaucracy must be seen as a group seeking to manage *from the outside* the activities of others. If that group has a monopoly of decisional authority, its bureaucratic potential will be vastly enhanced. In this sense if there was a nascent bureaucracy by the end of 1917 in Russia it was certainly not to be found in the Factory Committees. It was to be found in the Party itself. Certain Party attitudes here played a very important role. Trotsky himself (if we must refer to him) perceptively described all this. Referring to the Third Party Congress (April 25–May 10, 1905) he spoke of "the young revolutionary bureaucrat already emerging as a type. They were far more intransigent and severe with the revolutionary working men than with themselves, preferring to domineer".[121] No less a man than Lenin had written that "a worker-agitator who shows any talent should not work in the factory".[122] Is it any wonder that with these conceptions the Party soon lost all contact with the class?

Goodey seeks to prove his point that the Factory Committees belong to the nascent bureaucracy by looking at the later careers of certain Factory Committees' leaders: men such as Chubar, Matvei, Zhivotov and Skrypnik. That non-Bolshevik leaders of the Factory Committees later supported the Bolsheviks is indisputable. But so what? It is not unknown for individual shop stewards to end up as foremen. Does this really prove anything beyond the capacity of established power, in its various garbs, to recuperate dissent? Does the fact that Alexandra Kollontai later became a

---

120   Brinton, *op. cit.*, p. 62.

121   Leon Trotsky. *Stalin* (London: Hollis and Carter, 1947), p.61.

122   Lenin, *Sochineniya*, IV, p. 44.

Stalinist ambassador invalidate her earlier writings on the emancipation of women? Does Trotsky's later Bolshevism invalidate his prophetic warnings of 1904 on the subject of the Party substituting itself for the working class?[123]

If Goodey is really interested in the history of what happened to the personnel of the Factory Committees (and not to just a few of their leaders) a fruitful area might be the history of the various syndicalist groups, and in particular of the "Revolutionary Centre of Factory Committees", a body of anarchist inspiration which competed for a while with the All-Russian Council of Factory Committees, without ever succeeding in supplanting it, so many were the obstacles put in its path. The search will, I suspect, prove disappointing. Systematic persecution of "left" dissidents soon became a way of life. Proletarian partisans of the individual Factory Committees tried to resist and to regroup but their resistance was easily overcome.[124] The search also might encompass the fate of groupings of Bolshevik origin, such as Masnikov's *Workers' Group* (an offspring from the Workers' Opposition) and of Bogdanov's *Workers' Truth*. One fact such a search will reveal - and of this there can be little doubt - is that this group had perceived (as early as 1921, without the privilege of hindsight, and far more clearly than does Chris Goodey) that the "dictatorship of the proletariat" had been liquidated *pari passu* with the liquidation of the Factory Committees.

CRITIQUE, NO. 4 (SPRING 1975)

---

123   See *Our Political Tasks*.

124   Maurice Dobb. *Soviet Economic Development since 1917* (New York, 1948), pp. 89–90.

28. THE ULSTER WORKERS' COUNCIL GENERAL STRIKE

The general strike which completely paralyzed Northern Ireland from the 14th to the 28th May was one of the most complete and total strikes the British Isles has ever seen. What happened showed the power of a mass workers' movement to bring the authorities to their knees. The inability of the government to deal with the threat only emphasizes the increasing vulnerability of the system to such challenges: as the technology and complexity of production develop, military intervention appears ham-handed and becomes increasingly ineffective.

In spite of all its limitations and the reactionary character of some its components, the struggle in Ulster also emphasized the creative potential of the working class, its ability to ensure the distribution of essential food, the organization of mass pickets, the ability to control the movement and the allocation of fuel and other supplies to essential users. Significantly enough, joint supply arrangements for both Protestant and Catholic areas began to emerge.

There can be little doubt that the strike, after a patchy start, gained widespread support from the Protestant working class. Intimidation there was: most notoriously at Larne, where the Ulster Defence Association (UDA) left no one with much choice in the matter. But, as Brendon Clifford of the Workers' Association pointed out, "Wouldn't it be remarkable if some groups of white-collar workers were defying a campaign of intimidation that was paralyzing tens of thousands of hardened engineering workers?"[125]

Support for the strike came from housewives, old-age pensioners, whole working–class families, in fact - from the whole spectrum of the Protestant working class. The "return to work" on 26th May organized by local trade-union officials, some of them Communist Party members, and led by Len Murray, General Secretary of the TUC, was a complete flop. But perhaps it gave a useful foretaste of the role of the TUC in the event of a major class confrontation in Britain.

A similar mobilization for different political objectives, or even for similar objectives but by different participants, would probably have received the enthusiastic support of the traditional left - with marches, demonstrations, resolutions and petitions. But in this case we got the Social Democratic and Labour Party (SDLP) and some other "lefties" calling on the Labour government to act sternly and use troops on a wide scale against the strikers.

On the 27th May, at the behest of the "socialist" SDLP, troops were moved into seventeen petrol stations "to ensure petrol supplies". The response was a complete ban by the Ulster Workers' Council (UWC) on all work on electricity generation, gas, water supplies and sewerage disposal. The next day the Northern Ireland Executive collapsed. The strike had been "successful".

Now that workers in the north have discovered their own power they will also discover that their conditions remain completely unchanged - "victory" notwithstanding. We hope that they will begin to act increasingly in their own interests rather than for "loyalism".

---

125   Letter to *Guardian*, May 28, 1974.

The general strike in Ulster will provides us with no blueprints for taking power or redirecting society towards socialist objectives. It got nowhere near the point of running society which would include actually producing the necessities of life. It only scratched the surface of distributing available supplies according to the immediate needs of the working-class community.

How different would the situation be in Ireland today if there had been a socialist movement committed to working-class unity, rather than the slavish and uncritical support given to Catholic nationalism by the traditional left which over the years has actually contributed to worsening sectarian divisions?

There is clear evidence that the working class in the north of Ireland, whether Catholic or Protestant, is beginning to act as force independent of either the British or Irish ruling class. It is beginning to show its hostility to the nationalist politicians whom for so long they have been content to follow. Even Glen Barr, a leader of the UWC, showed some awareness of this when he gave an interview to the Irish Radio on 23rd June.[126] He said, "The Protestant community have shown their willingness to cast off the old-style politicians who waved the Union Jack every five years. We hope that the Roman Catholic community would now do the same and reject the Tricolour waving politicians from their side so that we can get down to proper clean politics – class politics".The final outcome of the struggle is still anyone's guess. But the importance of the strike cannot be ignored by any of the analysts, soothsayers, manipulators and would-be political leaders of right or left.

All those who have for so long been shouting "Victory to the IRA" now find themselves in a difficult position. Their mindless generalizations about British Imperialism in Ulster and support for Irish Catholic nationalism have placed them where they belong: among all the other self-appointed leaderships, miles away from where the new movement is emerging, miles away from anywhere workers struggle for their own interests refusing to heed the "saviours from on high"!

The positive aspects of the strike should not be exaggerated. The authoritarian and paramilitary UDA with its strong right-wing connections was a still a dominant force. The Craigs, Wests and Paisleys were reluctantly allowed to climb aboard the bandwagon. But the experience of active involvement in organizing the practicalities of daily life, and the demonstration of working-class strength and solidarity – however limited – may not be so easily erased from people's memories. This does not mean that we should "support" the UWC or blind ourselves to its character. We should not kid ourselves that sectarianism is still not a dominating factor in the working class on both sides of the religious divide. But it is also too easy (and is far more common) to overstress the reactionary character of the May mobilization. Certainly some reactionary features emerged but, as usual, reality is rather more complicated than slogans.

For us, workers' self-management is the necessary institutional form for a free society, but it must have a socialist content. It is therefore important to make a clear distinction between self-activity, even on a mass scale, and socialist self-management: i.e. self-management geared to the objective of creating a non-alienated, non-exploitative, non-authoritarian society in which wage labour has been abolished.

SOLIDARITY, VII, 11 (JULY 1974)

---

126 *Sunday Times*, June 30, 1974.

29. PORTUGUESE DIARY 1[127]

Evora is at the heart of the Alentejo, and the Alentejo is the heartland of the agrarian revolution. The latifundia are vast and for decades have been neglected. The soil is dry and hard, and upon it grow olives and cork. Wheat and maize would also grow readily if it were ploughed and watered. But this would interfere with the joys of hunting.

It is here that the class struggle has erupted in one of its most advanced forms. The agricultural labourers have seized many of the large estates. In some the former owners have fled, occasionally leaving "managers" to defend their interests. In others they have remained, seeking to repossess their property through the courts or through direct action. The balance of power varies from village to village, estate to estate.

We sleep on the floor of a large isolated farmhouse about three miles from town. Some fifteen Portuguese comrades have been lodging there every night for several months. The farm has been expropriated by the local Institute for Agricultural Reorganization (IRA) in which libertarian revolutionaries work in uneasy alliance with the representative of the Ministry of Agriculture and members of the local MFA (Movement of the Armed Forces). Their aim is to help the farm workers to solve some of their practical problems which immediately and inevitably crop up in the wake of occupations. The libertarians want to assist, without substituting themselves for those they are seeking to help. It is an almost impossible task.

The farm comprises a large communal living room in which meals are taken at daybreak or sundown. From it passages lead to a number of communicating rooms, stripped of all furniture and fittings, except for mattresses strewn on the floor. There is running water and electricity. There is beer in the fridge and bread and cheese are brought back from the town each day. There are also sten guns amid the guitars. Dispossessed landlords have threatened to string the young revolutionaries up from the nearest lamp-post at the opportune time, "when we return to power". Under such a threat the wine tastes sweeter and life is lived to the full.

On our first evening we drive out in a jeep some thirty miles to Santana do Campo. The villagers have a problem. They want representatives of the IRA there, "to help them bring pressure on the government". Several farms were occupied in the morning. The owners have paid no wages for several weeks. Two managers were locked up that very afternoon "to help the absentee landlord face up to his responsibilities".

The people are gathered in the local school – 130 agricultural workers with their wives and kids, and quite a number of the old folk. As so often in the countryside, the school is the only public hall. The lights can be seen from a long way off. They illuminate rugged faces, as varied as their owners, and quite unlike the crude stereotyped models of the Maoist posters. The whole village has turned up to elect the Council and to decide what to do with the two men incarcerated in the stable. Everyone knows everyone. Anyone over sixteen can be nominated and can cast a vote. Little tickets are handed out. Some of the older women decline to take one. Anyone can write anyone else's name on the slip. The eight people securing the

127   This diary describes some experiences during August 1975.

179

highest number of votes will constitute the Council. Speeches are unnecessary. It is in struggle, over the last few months, that credentials were earned. The selected names are read out by four "tellers", the tickets sorted into little piles. The new Council has been elected.

The main problem is then outlined to the visitors from the Evora IRA. Two opinions emerge: a union representative urges caution. (The Agricultural Workers' Union is affiliated to Intersindical, the trade union federation dominated by the PCP (Portuguese Communist Party). The Minister of Agriculture, who is sympathetic to the Party, must not be embarrassed.) Others suggest a different course of action. "Give them no food or drink. Let the news out. The Bank will cough up soon enough". No one discusses the PCP or its politics as such. The two alternatives are mutually exclusive. The radical proposal secures a majority. The cheque materializes within 24 hours.

***

The following day we set out in the jeep, in the full heat of the early afternoon, to visit a big farm where the workers are reluctant to impose any kind of control on the owner. The farm, built in 1945, is beautifully laid out. The main buildings and barns are painted blue and white. Cows are grazing in the fields and watch us pass impassively. Only the turkeys noisily announce our arrival as the jeep edges its way between them, raising a great cloud of dust.

The farm workers are gathered in a large barn, eight or ten of them, sitting on sacks of grain, talking heatedly. Our party enters: three young agronomists from the Evora Institute for Agricultural Reorganization (with long hair and determined expressions), a young officer in uniform (with even longer hair) and us two political tourists. An excited argument gets under way and lasts about an hour. The local MFA is keen to ensure that the workers elect a committee which would exercise some "control" on the owner and prevent him from doing "economic sabotage" - such as slaughtering cattle, disposing of his tractors or selling the grain (instead of keeping it for sowing). The workers are not convinced. The farm is a "model farm". The boss has maintained reasonable relations with his men, often working among them. The paternalism has had its effects. The men lack confidence. An old, edentulous worker fiercely articulates their innermost fears. "If we elect a committee, the boss will sack some of us. Work is hard to come by these days. If we make things difficult for him, will he continue to pay our wages? Come on, young man, yes, you with the gun, answer us. Look at all the problems in the other farms in the area!" It is strange to see his innate conservatism clash with the vision of the young revolutionaries. The visitors depart: mission unfulfilled.

Later that afternoon we go to another big farm, 35 miles away in the opposite direction. On the way we pass through whitewashed Alentejo villages, bespattered with red slogans. These villages are strongholds of the PCP. The agricultural workers are natural, genuine, down-to-earth communists. They want to share and share alike. No one seeks individually to appropriate anything. The Party calls itself communist. The workers vote for it. It's as simple (and as complicated) as that. The inability to read fosters and sustains a fierce radicalism. The workers are not confused by the tortuous ambiguities of the politicians.

The farm, near Oriola, is owned by an absentee Spanish landlord. The last two miles have been very rough track, which only the jeep can cover. The workers have taken the farm over, despite the government's half-hearted undertakings not to allow the expropriation of foreign-owned properties. The men have had no pay for ten weeks. There are big stocks of cork, neatly piled up, to be sold. But the lorry has been stolen. There are problems too with the vegetable produce. To be sold in the cities, refrigeration is needed. People are fed up with eating tomatoes.

The Communist Party's solution to all these problems is simple, eminently "practicable". All occupied farms should become state farms. The Ministry of Agriculture will eventually pay the wages. A state trust will be set up to buy the produce, provide the lorries, look after problems of distribution. The workers are tempted, but instinctively suspicious. They want to get together with other workers on other farms to discuss things with them, to create co-operatives, to deal directly with the population in the towns. They distrust the parasitic officials, sitting in their offices in far away Lisbon. But they are desperately in need of money to buy shoes, shirts, soap, string, nails and agricultural implements. The men who work the farm over the hill have a tractor which isn't being used full-time. Will the Army please instruct them to release it for a while? A joint meeting is arranged to thrash things out. The Institute will try to arrange a bridging loan from the local bank. A lorry will be provided to take the cork into the town. Ad hoc solutions are improvised. The wolf is kept from the door for a short while. The Institute has done a job of first aid. Hope will survive a little longer.

Amid the wasps, an old woman is washing her linen at the fountain. The crickets are chirping. The sky is unbelievably blue.

***

The Second Congress of Revolutionary Councils of Workers, Soldiers and Sailors (CRTSM) was held on August 2 and 3, 1975, in Lisbon's Technological Institute, a vast concrete building at the top of a hill. Posters announcing it (in the best "socialist-realist" style) had broken out like a rash on the city's walls several days beforehand. Once the paste had dried they ripped off easily, to the delight of large contingents of revolutionary tourists in search of souvenirs.

We attended the afternoon session on the second day. At the entrance, a vast display of duplicated literature, distributed free. Posters are on sale, their price escalating rapidly as it becomes obvious that demand will exceed supply.

The foyer is packed with young people. Most look like students and a substantial proportion are not from Portugal - one hears almost as much French and German as Portuguese. Young PRP (Revolutionary Proletarian Party) supporters answer questions. Few relate to work, its problems, its tyranny, its organization, its transcendence. Most are about Cuba, or Chile, or the political allegiances of this or that Army commander. The answers stress Portuguese particularism. The Army will be with the people. Otelo (Saraiva de Carvalho) has made friendly noises about the PRP.

We go up a flight of wide stone steps, with impressive columns on either side. The meeting is due to start in a vast hall which has doubtless harboured many a degree-giving ceremony or governmental function. Row upon row of wooden chairs. About 600 people are present. The same mixture as before. Very few workers (quite a number had apparently been there the previous day but had not attended for a second dose). No readily identifiable sailors. Banners on the walls seek nostalgically to recapture the atmosphere - and even the vocabulary - of the Petrograd of 1917: "*Fora com a canalha! Poder a quem trabalha!* - Out with the scum! Power to the workers! Long live the Socialist Revolution!" In the haze of cigarette smoke, the leftists dream on: the Technological Institute is Smolny; the Lisnave shipyards, the Putilov plant.

At the far end of the hall is an elevated platform, on which a long table has been erected. Seated behind it, perhaps a dozen comrades, most of them bearded, two of them women. In front of the leaders are neat stacks of cyclostyled notes. Slightly to one side of the High Table the television crews with their wires, floodlights and other paraphernalia, are busy creating images. The 1970s are here, regardless.

The afternoon session starts about an hour late. Several speeches from the platform, most of them lasting a half an hour or more. "Various analyses", we are told, "of the current situation". No interruptions. No laughter. No protests. No cheers. As platform speaker succeeds platform speaker the texts of their "contributions", already duplicated, are handed out by stewards. Only one speaker elicits any enthusiasm - a soldier in civvies. It transpires he is making a "critical analysis" of a text recently issued by COPCON (the section of MFA devoted to Internal Security!). Some of the formulations are being challenged in the best tradition of dialectical nit-picking. The legitimacy of that particular fount of revolutionary wisdom is not, however, being questioned.

People quietly drift in and out throughout the proceedings. It is formal, well-behaved, self-disciplined and incredibly dull - an exercise in "revolutionary" masochism. It has upon it the hallmark of death - or rather of a verbose stillbirth. The corridors outside are plastered with slogans. The revolution is suffocating under the written word. In the gents' toilets, amid the usual graffiti, a wit has scrawled "PC = *Joaquim Agostinho (Primeiro Ciclista Português)*".

After three hours we drift out. Near the exit we pass a large notice board. On it are listed the workplaces "represented" at the Congress. It looks impressive: factories of all kinds, transport depots, shipyards, telephone exchanges, hospitals, banks, shops, offices, all the areas in modern society where people are exploited and oppressed. On direct enquiry however - and after our refusal to accept evasive answers - it was admitted that although members or supporters of the PRP worked in these various places, very few were attending in a delegate capacity. The whole episode left an unpleasant flavour of manipulation.

I doubt we will hear much more of the CRTSM. When the next upsurge develops, it will find different forms and a different content.

***

Guimaraes is a small industrial town, some forty miles north of Porto. The Sousabreu textile factory there is typical of many in the region, reflecting many of the problems of Portuguese capitalism.

The factory, which makes towels, was occupied on September 14, 1974, after it had been abandoned by its owner. Earlier in the year the boss, who owned another factory in the town, had begun to move out the more modern dying equipment under pretext of repairs. He had also removed the lorry.

33 workers (22 women and 11 men) had taken over the factory to preserve their livelihood, and decided to continue production. They had had to learn everything from scratch. They bought the cotton at local wholesale rates and sold directly to shopkeepers, to visitors, to political sympathizers, and even at the gates of local factories. To start with they had sold part of the stocks to pay their own wages. They had received little help from the local textile and metalworkers' sections of Intersindical, which were dominated by the PCP. The Party's support for self-man-

aged units was highly selective. And Sousabreu was not a unit of which the Party approved.

The workers had elected a Committee of seven which met almost daily. There were also fairly frequent assemblies grouping everyone in the factory. They all worked 48 hours a week. There had been a sustained attempt at equalizing earnings. The average wage was 127 escudos (just over £2) a day. The machine minders earned 190 escudos, the newly taken-on apprentice 70 escudos. The main theme discussed at recent general assemblies had been whether to take on more labour.

The factory consisted of a number of large, fairly dilapidated hangars adjoining one another, in one of which the looms were situated. The machines looked at least thirty years old and were noisy and dusty. There were cobwebs everywhere and little light filtered in. The first task of the socialist revolution would be a sustained attack on capitalist technology. But here there were scarcely funds enough for wages, let alone for modernizing the plant.

In the adjoining rooms women were checking the towels, folding them, packing them in plastic cases. The room was brighter and they spoke to one another. I approached a woman in her forties who had worked there for fifteen years. What was now different? "For one", she said, "there are no longer foremen breathing down your neck. There used to be three foremen in this room alone. We now decide the pace of our own work, and no longer live in fear of displeasing someone. We run the place ourselves. If I want to go shopping one afternoon, or if one of the children is ill, we can consult together and have a little time off, without loss of earnings. No one takes advantage. We know that our collective livelihood depends on producing a certain number of towels each month".

Adversity had bred a firm solidarity. When earnings were low, the most needy had been provided for first. Everyone seemed aware of the others' problems. Recently things had not been too bad. This year, for the first time ever, they had enjoyed a fortnight's holiday with pay.

Their main complaints were about the way people deformed the meaning of what they were doing. Their wall posters showed an intense awareness of their own condition. There can be few factories in the world plastered with excerpts from Marx's *Economic and Philosophic Manuscripts*. They knew well enough that they were still wage slaves, and that what was being self-managed was their own alienation. They worked harder now than they did before. But they had gained a confidence in themselves that they had not felt previously. They had held "round table" discussions with representatives of other self-managed factories to establish links and to exchange both experiences and products. They had even bartered shirts for towels, one of them told us with a twinkle in his eye. They had discovered a great deal about the functioning of capitalist society which would be of use to them "when the real time came". They had also learned very quickly about the trade unions, which had refused to help them or had only damned them with faint praise. Above all, they had learned a lot about themselves.

***

The PCP headquarters in Famalicao, north of Porto, lie shattered. Before April 1974 it was widely believed by those in power that literacy bred subversion. There was only one place in the town where the wealthy could obtain secondary education: an expensive private school, solidly built and set behind a row of tall trees.

With the collapse of the Caetano regime the building had been taken over by the local PCP cell. I couldn't help thinking what an ideal Stalinist redoubt it made, separated by its high walls from the bustle of the multitude, set on higher ground, its impressive drive redolent with respectability. From here the Party had carried out its manipulations of local government, of trade union branches, of co-operatives, of the granting of agricultural credit. The reaction had been handed things on a plate.[128]

After an open air meeting, early in August, a crowd protesting against the unrepresentative nature of several local bodies had set siege to the school and tried to burn it down. Party militants had fired from the upper windows, injuring two demonstrators. The MFA had arrived on the scene to "restore order" (their fire had killed two more demonstrators).

MFA interventions in such episodes had, we were told, been interesting to watch. At times the soldiers would threaten the crowd with their weapons, turning their backs on the besieged Stalinists. On other occasions they would turn their backs to the crowd, confronting the Party members with their guns. Attitudes had varied from locality to locality, regiment to regiment, moment to moment. At Famalicao the soldiers had faced the crowd, seeking to restrain it. After a siege of 48 hours the local Party stalwarts had been ordered by Party Headquarters in Lisbon to evacuate the premises. The Army had then left almost immediately. During the whole siege there had been no sign of working class support in the town, not even a token strike. The institutions controlled by the Party apparatus were empty shells. The Party had no roots in real life.

Popular anger had then erupted. The place looked as if it had been hit by a tornado. An overturned car, burnt out, lay grotesquely in the road outside. The drive was littered with charred papers, posters, Party cards. A disconsolate leaflet announced a meeting that was never to take place.

The MRPP (Maoists) issued a statement welcoming "the people's retribution against the social-fascists". It wasn't however as simple as that. The red flag had been burned. A Portuguese flag now stuck out provocatively from an attic window. Beneath it, a large inscription proclaimed, "Building to be taken over for refugees from Angola".

SOLIDARITY, VIII, 3 (DECEMBER 1975)

---

128   The reaction already had an economic and ideological base in the North, based on the structure of land tenure, on the fears of impoverished small farmers of being rendered poorer still, and on systematic propaganda by the Church.

30. PORTUGUESE DIARY 2

April 19, 1976, a Rádio Televisão Português crew, in a van, is doing a programme on "the vision of socialism". It is stopping in the street, at factory gates, in markets, talking to people and recording their replies. It's a tight fit inside: seven people and lots of equipment.

We make for Barreiro, an industrial town across the river from Lisbon. Once there, there is no problem getting to the giant CUF chemical works. The sky is grey, part cloud, part smoke. The walls are grey too, but bespattered with the red of posters. The plant, the stacks, the water towers hovering above us look as if built in the last century. Long streets of hangers, stores, sheds, many with broken windows. There is noise, and rust and the plaster is peeling off the front of many buildings. Heavy smells hang in the air. The road is in poor repair. An old-fashioned capitalism clearly cohabits with the new.

We pace through mean little streets of minute, decrepit terraced housing. "Sulphuric Acid Street". "Candle Grease Street". Capitalism even murders the imagination. The houses were built six, seven decades ago, possibly more. People still live there - sort of.

This is the heartland of the PCP, its ideological and physical domain. Its posters are everywhere. A gigantic PCP balloon is tied to a rope between two rooftops. "Unity with the MFA". "Vote PCP". The van stops and the crew take up their positions near to a group of women of indeterminate age, going in. They are not in the least shy and talk readily. "Socialism?" - "A steady job!" - "Like this?" - No answer. A steady drizzle is falling. "Like this?", the producer repeats. The women, sensing something strange, turn on him, abuse the television, and march off, their fists raised, shouting "PCP! PCP!"

**

There are joyful moments, too. Walking along the Tagus waterfront, between the Station and the Praça do Comércio we stop in front of a particularly fine example of mural art. Enormous. Unforgettable. "Socialist realism" at its hideous best.

The reds and yellows are gaudy as usual - caricatures of real colour. The oppressed have very square jaws, very short hair, enormous arms, a very determined look. The proletariat, as seen by the Maoists is clearly more brawn than brain: the sort of animal any skilful Leninist could easily ride to the revolution! But the "anarcho-cynicalists" have been at work. Modern capitalism requires modern transport. The MRPP leader is calling for a cab.

**

Another story about taxis. In Elvas, in the East, some of the estates belonging to big landlords have been taken over by those who work them. The usual pattern is for the agricultural workers to occupy first and seek authority later - from the local centre of the IRA.

One recently expropriated *latifundiário* (*latifundista* in Spanish) also happened to own the biggest taxi business in town. His drivers disliked him heartily and were much impressed with the new goings on in the co-operative. So they took over the taxis.

But the cult of authority dies hard. The act had to be "legitimized", entered "into the books". So the cab drivers all turn up one morning at the IRA Headquarters for an "official" sanction. The Ministry of Agriculture has files on tenants, trees, *touros*...and technical aid – but nothing on how legally to appropriate a fleet of taxis. The Revolution creates its own surrealist precedents.

***

May Day, 1976. Top of the Avenida Almirante Reis in Lisbon. The demonstration called by Intersindical is marching past. Municipal workers in their Sunday best. Railway workers in serried ranks, decorated lorries packed with agricultural workers carrying pitchforks. Occasional singing. Very occasional laughter. Sellers do a roaring trade in political stickers, selling to those watching the procession: stickers for the Association of Collectivized Farms, for the Housing Fund, for student or women's groups. Schoolteachers, building workers, hospital workers chant "Intersindical, Intersindical" as they pass, ten or twelve abreast. Twenty thousand people march by – apparently far fewer than last year. The traffic has prudently been stopped, although Portuguese motorists have learnt patience – the hard way.

It is a fine warm day. Banners, unbelievably, still demand "Unity with the MFA" – the very MFA which is now the main brake on the revolution. They also demand the right to full employment and vigilance against fascists.

Do I sense a certain weariness? There is none of the exaltation, of the euphoria of even a few months ago – as if people realized that it would take more than mural graffiti to bring down the walls of capital. The Party is everywhere, though nowhere in its true garb. In the Association of University Professors. In the Association of Municipal Associations. The bank employees march by shouting "No to Reaction!" One or two Tenants' Committees carry colourful banners...demanding government loans. The two groups march next to each other. Someone should introduce them to one another!

At the end of the procession a mass of red flags and a few hundred very young people shouting raucously: *"Unidad sindical, unidad sindical"*. One might be dreaming. They want the PCP and PS (Socialist Party) to take power, in order to expose them. And Intersindical too. To form a government "without generals or capitalists". Yes, the Trots. In their rightful place. At the tailend of a Stalinist demonstration.

SOLIDARITY, VIII, 4 (JULY 1976)

31. INTRODUCTION TO PHIL MAILER, *PORTUGAL: THE IMPOSSIBLE REVOLUTION?*

This is an uncooked slice of history. It is the story of what happened in Portugal between April 25, 1974, and November 25, 1975 - as seen and felt by a deeply committed participant. It depicts the hopes, the tremendous enthusiasm, the boundless energy, the total commitment, the released power, even the revolutionary innocence of thousands of ordinary people taking a hand in the remoulding of their lives. And it does so against the background of an economic and social reality which placed limits on what could be done. This tension dominates the whole narrative.

Phil's book is not only a perspective account of real events. It is an attempt at a new type of historiography. The official statements of the MFA and of the political parties, and the pronouncements of politicians, are relegated to appendices. The text proper explodes with life, the life of people seeking - in many contradictory ways - to write a chapter of their own history.

Characters and events literally hustle one another off these pages. Images remain, pell-mell, like an afterglow. The intoxication and euphoria of the first few weeks. Politics in the first person. The crowds in the streets. Civilians clambering over tanks and armoured cars. The atmosphere of the great days: May Day and September 28, 1974; March 11, 1975. Strikes and occupations. The declarations of people in bitter struggle which, in their concern for fundamentals, seemed to echo the thunder of the *Communist Manifesto*. Lisbon dockers, talking of a "total remodelling of society", of a struggle which would have to be waged "outside the unions", given the total involvement of such bodies in the iniquities of the previous regime. The sheer poetry of some landworkers' documents, asking what will happen "now the sowing time is over and the olives have been picked". The tenants' committees. The non-manipulable struggle of those at the very bottom of the social ladder, the shanty town dwellers, for whom nobody had the audacity to claim he was speaking. Taxi drivers wanting the Institute for the Reorganization of Agriculture to take over…their taxis. The Revolution creating its own surrealist precedents. The Second Congress of Councils, in the Technological Institute in Lisbon, complete with latter-day Leninists dreaming of Smolny and Putilov, amid the paraphernalia of modern television. Revolutionary tourists and their hang-ups. Soldiers inviting civilians into the RASP[129] barracks for a weeklong festival, sing-song and orgy…of political discussion. The seemingly endless birthpangs which only produced a still-born infant. The surfeit of revolutionary rhetoric and the return to reality. The problems and anxieties, the achievements and the failures. The joy and the sadness. The longings and the frustrations. And, throughout, the concern (in the words of Spinoza) "neither to laugh nor to weep, but to understand".

***

Why did the revolutionary process not develop further in Portugal? A meaningful social revolution comes about when a large number of people seek a total change in the conditions of their existence. Massive pressures had certainly built up within Salazarist Portugal. But the aims of those opposed to the old society were dis-

---

129   Artillery Regiment of Serra do Pilar (near Porto).

parate. For varying reasons different groups wanted an end to the colonial wars, to the futility and frustrations of a long period of compulsory military service, to the censorship, and to the ubiquity of the hated PIDE (International Police for the Defence of the State). The consensus, however, hardly went any further. Beyond this the paths diverged. The forward-looking section of the Portuguese bourgeoisie had one objective – a liberal capitalist society, in which they would accumulate wealth in a "civilized" manner. "Anti-fascism" was the ideal cover for a crying need to modernize the bourgeois state. A liberal capitalist society provided a freer framework for the important business of making money. The "trouble" was that the working class too had aims of its own, less explicitly formulated perhaps, but in conflict with the above. Its very conditions of existence compelled it to struggle. The objectives of the PCP and of the various left groups amounted to various forms of state capitalism. At every stage their actions sought to canalize popular discontent into channels which enhanced either the power of the state, or the power of the political parties themselves. They manipulated the social disaffection to achieve a society in which they themselves would wield political power as the "legitimate representatives of the illiterate masses". This was the reality, perceived or not, behind all their rhetoric.

The working class concentrated in the great conurbations of Lisbon, Setúbal and Porto, of Braga and Aveiro – but numerically weak and scattered elsewhere – met both successes and reverses in gaining specific objectives of its own. Initially, in the strike movement that preceded April 25 (and was to gain such impetus after that date) the working class succeeded for a while in imposing a certain redistribution in its own favour of the total social product. It created autonomous organizations, the Workers' Committees (CTs) and Federations of CTs (like Inter-Empresas). But no amount of wishful thinking – or of Bolshevik bravado – could circumvent the hard facts of social geography. There were vast areas of the country where a smallholding peasantry, intensely property conscious, exerted an enormous weight. There was the legacy of intimidation, temporal and spiritual, by policemen and priests. And there were other facts of equal relevance. A social revolution is not just a reflex response to the iniquities and oppressions of an existing order. Such responses may bring a society crashing to its knees. They do not ensure that it is replaced by one that is qualitatively different. Such an outcome requires a vision, shared by a substantial number of people, of a totally different way of life.

Did the working class of Portugal – or any substantial part of it – have such a vision? Who knows? There were certainly attempts to reduce wage differentials, to elaborate a pattern of distribution that would bypass traditional market mechanisms, to break down the barriers between intellectual and manual labour, to produce and live together according to different norms. But these were, more often than not, empirical adaptations to specific circumstances: the need to raise the miserable living standards of Cabo Verdian building workers, to dispose of the products of some self-managed factory, to solve practical problems in some shanty town, or to administer some seized *latifundio*. More fundamental social objectives, such as the abolition of hierarchy, of wage labour and of commodity production, were never really on the historical agenda.

The proletariat, both urban and rural, was one of the driving forces of the Portuguese upheaval. Of this, there can be no doubt. But its forward surge, in the months after April 1974, was eventually broken. Piecemeal the ruling class succeeded in re-establishing their order, their discipline, their ownership of land, houses and plant, and – through a fine admixture of coercion and co-optation – the productivity of "their" workers. The working class advance was broken by a combination of factors of significance to all concerned in the dynamics of revolution.

Firstly, the upsurge did not take place in an economic or geographical vacuum. Portugal could not be isolated from the world market. It is a "poor" country. Large areas of its production are geared to world demand and it has to import many of its finished goods. None of the fundamental problems could be solved on the Portuguese arena alone. Portuguese capitalism was but a link in a vast international network: the onslaught against it was doomed to failure if confined to Portugal. The workers of Portugal remained isolated, deprived of their natural allies. During the crucial months the Spanish tinder failed to ignite.

Within this general context of economic dependence and revolutionary isolation there were many specific difficulties. There was fear, induced by the harsh realities of unemployment (some of it deliberately engineered by Portuguese capitalists). During 1974–5 some 10% of the working population was constantly out of work. Life was hard. After some initial gains wages were more or less frozen – throughout a period of intense inflation (up to 18% per annum). The gross national product fell by some 24%. There was then the painful awakening from certain illusions, the illusion for instance that the working class had "allies", as distinct from people who were prepared to ride it (as one would a horse) to "the revolution". The relevant implications began to dawn, namely that the workers could not leave it to others (such as "progressive" officers or student radicals) to solve their problems for them. They began taking the appropriate measure: the creation of autonomous organizations controlled from below. But then the old enemy reappeared in a new garb. Those who used words with the same ease as the peasant his scythe or the bricklayer his trowel began to organize, to dominate, to manipulate the *plenários*. There was a massive retreat from political activity, in disgust at the behaviour of the leftist sects. There was the feeling of despair and impotence in relation to the enormity of the tasks to be solved.

The Portuguese working class proved unable – at this moment in time – of further developing the autonomous forms of organization needed, were they even to hold what had been gained. The Leninist groups here bear a tremendous, almost a historic, responsibility. Instead of helping to develop and consolidate the new creations of the class, they did all in their power to make the movement conform to textbook models. They talked learnedly of Kerensky and Kornilov when people needed confidence in their own ability to organize textile production, to distribute and process the season's cork, to find storage facilities for rural produce being sent directly to towns. Their concerns were not felt to be genuine, and their relationship to the real movement was never sensed to be an honest one. For example those who spoke loudest about "arming the people" in fact ensured that available weapons went to their own particular groups. They identified themselves with the proletariat, but the proletariat refused to return the compliment.

Yet, when all is said and done, one further fact remains, enormous in its implications. In April 1975 the Portuguese people voted for the Constituent Assembly. A year later they elected an Assembly of the Republic. Even the smallest political groups participated, their message stridently proclaimed from every wall and rooftop. As far as political propaganda and access to the media are concerned these were the two "freest" years in Portuguese history. The apparatus of repression was largely in disarray. The electoral campaigns were possibly more vigorous and more sustained, more varied and more vitriolic than at any other time, in any other bourgeois democracy. Parties legally put up posters advocating armed insurrection. In June 1976 a President was elected: Eanes, the law-and-order candidate, campaigning against "states within the state", polled over 60% of the vote.

It is too easy to attribute this event solely to the factors we have mentioned, important though they be. The vote also represented a yearning for stability, for a breathing space, for a predictable pattern to everyday life, for the easier option of delegated authority. It was a repudiation, hopefully temporary, of the din of discussion, of the pressure to participate, of the stress of responsibility, of the fatigue and frustration of an involvement that seemed to lead nowhere. It was the personal price one paid to escape the demand for permanent stalemate in the political and social arena outside. It is a new pattern of bourgeois recuperation. Realists will recognize it as a hallmark of the vastness of the task ahead.

***

Several lessons can be drawn from the Portuguese experience, lessons which transcend the frontiers of Portugal. The foremost, I think, is that in future upheavals the traditional revolutionaries will prove "part of the problem, not part of the solution". The Portuguese events bring irrefutable testimony to this assertion. Past revolutions faced two main dangers. They could be annihilated by those whose privileges they threatened (Paris, 1871; Germany, 1918–19; Spain, 1936; Hungary 1956). Or they could be destroyed from within, through bureaucratic degeneration (as happened to the Russian Revolution of 1917). A third alarming risk now looms on the horizon. It is the risk of genuinely radical upheavals being deviated into state capitalist channels. It is the danger that any new creation (in the realm of ideas, relationships or institutions) will immediately be pounced upon, penetrated, colonized, manipulated - and ultimately deformed - by hordes of power-hungry "professional revolutionaries", midwives of state capitalism, and all the more dangerous because draped in the red flag.

These people bring with them attitudes and patterns of behaviour deeply (if not always consciously) moulded by Lenin's notion that the workers, left to themselves, "can only develop a trade union consciousness". Their current organizational practices and their prescriptions for the future are bureaucratic to the core. Because of all the extraneous matter they drag in their historical wake and seek to inject into live situations (like some flies their larvae into living flesh) these "professional revolutionaries" (Stalinists, Maoists, Trotskyists and Leninists of various kinds) succeed, between them, in polluting the very concept of independent political action. Their preoccupation with leadership destroys initiative. Their concern for the correct line discourages experiment. Their obsession with the past is a blight on the future. They create around themselves a wasteland of cynicism and disgust, of smashed hopes and disillusion, that buttresses the deepest dogma of bourgeois society, namely that ordinary people are incapable of solving their own problems, by themselves and for themselves. Otelo Saraiva de Carvalho was wrong when he endorsed the anarchist jest that *cozido* (a local dish of boiled meats and potatoes) was the only specifically Portuguese thing to be had. There was more. The Portuguese upheaval of 1974–5 coined a new word for the political lexicon, an adjective that demoted an aspiration: the word "*apartidário*". The literal translation is "non-party". But the term reflects the longing for genuine autonomy in struggle, for an activity that is not manipulated by some *cúpula* (political clique) or other.

Another lesson, intimately linked to the first, concerns the role of the MFA, illusions which were to be rudely shattered on November 25, 1975. The left not only did nothing to dispel these illusions, it in fact constantly reinforced them. The army is a fundamental pillar of class rule and it is dangerous nonsense to believe that it can somehow be transformed into something else, into an instrument of social change for instance. To believe that this can be brought about through gaining the leadership of certain regiments, or through the creation of rank and-and-file committees in certain battalions is positively suicidal. In Portugal, the "putschist and militarist conception of the social revolution"[130] was to have dire consequences for the working class.

Leninist groups are permeated through and through with Jacobin (i.e. bourgeois) notions concerning the conquest of power.[131] The citizen armies of the French Revolution may have toppled the old feudal structures, enabling the bourgeoisie to assume political power and the bourgeois mode of production (which existed before the revolution and was capable of autonomous development) to gain unfettered ascendancy. But the socialist revolution is something very different. The working class does not already have its own mode of production operating within bourgeois society. The revolution will be a protracted process of conscious social creation. Its concerns are as much the capture of the hearts and minds of ordinary people and the discarding of outmoded beliefs as the capture of some Winter Palace or the deposition of some feudal monarch. It neither begins nor ends with the military question. This is not to say that the ruling classes will peacefully surrender what they have. But this is another question.

The Leninist groups in Portugal, given their views, failed to conduct any systematic propaganda against the MFA *as such*.[132] They failed to denounce the totally mystifying concept of the "alliance" between the MFA and "the people". They equated political power with military power in the crudest possible way. Elements of the Portuguese experience fed this disastrous identification. After April 25 there was certainly an overlap between military and political apparatuses. Moreover the lessening of autonomous working class action – an ebb-tide to which the Leninists had signally contributed – created an atmosphere in which their substitutionist attitudes could further flourish. The "revolutionaries" placed their faith – and even what cadres they could – in COPCON. They boasted, with a wink, of their contacts in the upper echelons of this body. In their hands the social struggle became reduced to a question of intrigues, of tactical alliances and manoeuvres, of giving critical support to one lot of officers against another, to one military clique against another. Groups on

---

130   C. Reeve, *L'Expérience portugaise: la conception putschiste de la révolucion sociale* (Paris: Spartacus, May–April 1976), p.25. This short text is by far the best thing to have been written on this subject. I have borrowed from it freely.

131   Such conceptions had a certain validity during the bourgeois revolution. They might even be relevant, in a completely different context, to situations such as Vietnam or China, where weak bureaucratic regimes could not of themselves assume the ascendancy (through the new modes of production they embodied) but needed the help of a military apparatus to break down the old barriers.

132   The Maoist MRPP (Movement for the Reorganization of the Party of the Proletariat) was an exception, but its later attitudes to the coup of November 25 and to Eanes in the presidential elections of June 1976 finally deprived it of all credibility.

the "extreme left" described the MFA as guarantor the of the Revolution". In the words of Cohn-Bendit:

> they spoke of power just like everyone else does. There was nothing emptier than their description of it…They don't ask what does the conquest of social power mean? No, they don't go beyond the question of centralized, politico-military power.[133]

Social power was something more difficult to grasp, and far more difficult to achieve. "It was the reality of work relations, with hierarchy, in people's heads".

The debacle of November 25 (described with feeling and wit in Phil's narrative) left a trial of confusion and disarray. If anything is to be learned from it we must speak bluntly. To accept the primacy of the Army (i.e. of an institution moulded by capitalism and permeated by capitalist values) in the Portuguese situation was doubly nefarious. It fostered reliance on others, which was bad enough. But more specifically it fostered reliance on a body which, when the crunch came, would turn out to be *on the other side*. Constantly to emphasize the preponderant role of the Army was tantamount to injecting deeply bourgeois ideas (submission to leaders, the centralization of power into very few hands, the abdication of the right to determine objectives or to participate in decision-making) into what was undoubtedly a movement for social change. The damage proved incalculable. Strange partners peddled this mystification. The PCP did all in its power to boost the MFA as a "guarantor of democracy". It proclaimed that "no country, not even the oldest democratic countries, allows open calls to desertion and agitation in the armed forces". It exerted pressure on deserters and those avoiding call-up "to do their military service, like all other young Portuguese".[134] Meanwhile the leftist groups, with their "contracts" and "areas of influence" in the middle echelons of the MFA, covered up for the early strike-breaking role of the Army.

Some people still talk about "Portuguese particularism", about the "specificity of the Portuguese situation", about Portugal being "different". They still describe the MFA as having been "the motor of the revolution". To do this they have to stress the role of the Unit Assemblies (ADUs) and of rank-and-file organizations such as SUV (Soldiers United Will Win). This mythology must be exploded before it gains a foothold.

The ADUs were created from above, in 1974, as "structures for rank-and-file participation". They were to be based on a new "revolutionary" discipline, "agreed and not imposed", and on a "hierarchy of aptitudes".[135] Their concerns, however, never extended beyond the walls of the barracks. Their real implantation varied from region to region. The role of the MFA officers remained preponderant within them. Communication between ADUs remained in the hands of such officers. Even at a General Assembly of one of the "red" regiments of the Lisbon area, in December 1974, it was stressed that the function of the assembly was "consultative, a function of education and information". The Fifth Division, in which there was deep PCP penetration, did all it could to promote the ADUs. Its influence within the MFA reached its peak at the time of the Fifth Provisional Government of Vasco Gonçalves. But this influence (which sought to make of the Fifth Division a political education centre for the Armed Forces as a whole) was not associated with any real shift of power

---

133   *Libération* (Paris), December 12, 1975.

134   Alvaro Cunhal, at a meeting of the Communist Youth.

135   *Jornal do MFA*, October 25, 1974.

towards the base. Attempts to increase the area of authority of the ADUs provoked an indignant statement by the Cabinet for the Dynamization of the Army (linked to the Fifth Division). "The ADUs", it was stressed, "are organs for advising and supporting the Command…In no way do they question the authority and the responsibility of the Command in the realm of decisions".[136]

At this point a "left" critique of the military politics of the PCP had gained a certain hearing. It originated around officers close to the PRP (and to COPCON) who saw in the way the PCP was alienating support an opening for their own implantation into the military apparatus, and hence into the apparatus of the state. This tendency sought a base in the social movement outside the army. The COPCON documents of early summer 1975 reflect these aspirations.

But the virtual eviction of the PCP from the government a few weeks later (and the victory of "the Nine" over the Gonçalvists in the military apparatus) were to lead to a PCP volte-face. It began endorsing the "radical" COPCON proposals it had previously denounced. At last, some of leftists saw a chance to consummate the lust of a lifetime, to have a united front with the PCP. It was against this background that the semi-clandestine SUV groups began to emerge, "real" rank-and-file groups, "committed to the class struggle", highly critical of the "anti-democratic structures of the ADUs". But the SUV were themselves being manipulated by leftist groups in search of new tactics for the capture of state power. Their call was "Reactionaries, out of the barracks!". This could only imply one thing: "Barracks, yes, but commanded by leftist officers".[137]

The moment of truth arrived. On November 25 fewer than 200 commandos "overcame" several "red" regiments armed to the teeth. Among the regiments that "surrendered" were those that had been most loudly proclaiming that "their leaders were not only behind them but in front of them, that they were revolutionaries". The whole elaborate and mystifying set-up collapsed: ADUs, Soldiers' Commissions, Vigilance Committees, SUV. All this showed itself for what it was: precisely nothing. "Isolated, divided, without links with one another, without information, and above all without initiative, the rank-and-file soldiers were in a state of total dependence upon the military hierarchy, upon the 'progressive' officers".[138] They followed orders, faithfully and confidently: orders to arm, orders to disarm, orders to defend themselves, orders to stop defending themselves, orders to remain within the barracks, orders to move out of them. Meanwhile the "progressive" officers, caught up in political manoeuvres, tempted by political deals, one eye on possible "compromises" cooked up in the Presidential Palace, either abandoned the barracks or got themselves arrested…"to avoid bloodshed". The rank-and-file soldiers were handed over in a triple shackle, political, ideological and organizational. The veil was ripped asunder. The "military policy" of all the leftist groups was revealed for what it was: a pathetic faith in what the attitude of the "progressive officers" would be when confronted with a choice.

One of the RAL-1 (First Light Infantry Regiment) soldiers put it very simply: "On November 25 we suddenly had the impression that there was no command, nothing! Progressively we felt we were entirely alone".[139] After months on a Leninist diet, to be suddenly without "left" leaders spelled starvation:

---

136 *Expresso*, July 26, 1975.

137 Reeve, *op.cit.*, p.11.

138 *Ibid.*, pp.15–16.

After a year of agitation in the army, the rank-and-file groups never played any important role. They never achieved the least control over the functioning of the military machine. On the contrary, they ended up reinforcing the lack of initiative of the soldiers, their belief in the "good army", the army of "progressive officers".[140]

It takes no great effort to see the similarity between the military "policies" of the left in Portugal and their attitudes to such matters as Parliament and the trade unions elsewhere. In each instance they propose to the revolutionary movement to fight on the territory - and with the weapons - of the class enemy. And then they seem surprised that they are defeated - or that, if "victorious", the fruits of their victory prove rather different from what they had expected.

A final by-product of the Portuguese events - bizarre this time, rather than sinister - was the appearance of a new political hybrid: the social-democratic Maoist. Throughout the Portuguese upheaval their hatred of the "social-fascists" of the PCP drove the MRPP into some very strange political alliances. They welcomed the bombings of the PCP headquarters in the summer of 1975 as evidence of "popular justice against the revisionists". In the trade union field they concluded a whole series of electoral alliances with the PS and PPD[141] - and even with CDS[142] - aimed at diminishing the influence of the PCP. They responded the victorious officers of November 25 with being too indulgent in relation to "the principal enemy: social-fascism". In fact they welcomed the coup. "The situation is excellent", they claimed in December 1975. "Revisionism is being increasingly unmasked".[143] In the presidential elections of June 1976 the MRPP even urged their supporters to vote for Eanes, the PS–backed law-and-order candidate. The telling critiques which the MRPP made of the PRP-BR (Revolutionary Proletarian Party - Revolutionary Brigades), whose setting up of "workers' councils" the MRPP accurately described as "providing a mass basis for COPCON" - will soon be forgotten when the MRPP itself is seen to have provided a similar basis for the PS or for "the Nine". But then, for all its verbal leftism and denunciations of the MFA, does not the MRPP itself propose "a democratic and popular revolution, made not only by workers and peasants but by other revolutionary sectors of society, such as small and medium shopkeepers, small and medium farmers, small and medium industrialists, etc."[144]

***

The book deals clearly, concretely and honestly with the problems and limitations of self-management, attempted in a capitalist context. To take over a factory or farm abandoned by their owners is a natural enough reaction of workers seeking to maintain a living in an environment they know. But the capitalist market immediately obtrudes. Outlets have to be found for the goods produced. The relation of the "self-managed" enterprise to the outside world remains all-pervading. Disposing of stocks - or even of capital equipment - to pay oneself wages is no lasting solution. The "need" to sell one's labour power - with all that this entails - persists, unrelenting. In Portugal the price paid for the enhanced internal democracy of certain work-

---

139   Interview of a RAL-1 soldier, in *Portugal, Espoir du Socialisme*

140   Reeve, *op.cit.*, p.27.

141   Popular Democratic Party (capitalist party of the centre).

142   Social and Democratic Centre (in fact a right–wing party which regrouped many of the fascists after April 25).

143   *O tempo e o modo* (theoretical journal of the MRPP), December 1975.

144   *Ibid.*

shops or farms was often a lengthening of the working day, or an intensification of the labour process to "allow" the self-managed unit to remain economically "viable". In this sense islands of self-management became islands of capitalist recuperation. In Guimaraes I saw a self-managed textile factory, its walls plastered with extracts from Marx's *Economic and Philosophic Manuscripts*. The workers don't need to be told that this is self-managed alienation. They live it daily, in their flesh. But what is the real, practical, immediate alternative? Is it communist production? Is it the scrapheap of capitalist unemployment? Or is it something else, something variable, something created anew, every day, in a thousand different workplaces, moulded by the differing relation of forces there? No generalization can cover all that was created, the full variety of the experience or the bitterness engendered by failure. Whatever the concrete forms evolved the essential, as always, is to avoid telling lies, to avoid mystifying both oneself and others.

All this of course had little to do with the cardinal relationship of self-management to socialism. Some speak today as if the Portuguese experience in some sense invalidated this relationship, as if it proved that self-management had nothing to do with socialism, as if all talk of self-management was the ultimate recuperative plot of Machiavellian capitalism. The confusion - where it is not deliberate, and therefore dishonest - shows a pathetic conceptual poverty. That, under capitalism, self-management may become a potent means of capitalist recuperation is undoubted. But what has this to do with the question of whether self-management is the essential institutional (not economic, but institutional) framework of socialist society?

One can certainly conceive of self-management without socialism. But can one imagine any socialism worth living under without self-managed individuals, collectivities and institutions? Those who can visualize such a society should let us share their vision. But they should seek to make it as explicit as possible. *Who*, if not those directly involved, would have the greatest say in the fundamental decisions? And *how* would such a non–self-managed "socialist" society differ from all the monstrous societies we see around us today, societies in which minorities take all the fundamental decisions and - through their access to information and power - perpetuate their own privileges?

***

To an outsider there was much that was very specifically Portuguese in the Portuguese upsurge. The will to dare the unknown, to disregard the advice of "experts", to take history and reality by the scruff of the neck - all that is summed up in the term *sebastianismo*[145] - was very evident in the early months. Without batting an eyelid at the enormity of what they were attempting, young revolutionaries (and older ones) talked seriously of a direct transition from fascism to libertarian communism. They acted as if a belief in miracles could drive people to attempt - and, who knows, perhaps even to achieve - the "impossible".

Like all radical endeavours in history the upsurge was a joyful affair, at least to start with. An immensely popular song, after April 25, was entitled *"Gaivota"* (The Seagull). Poster wit, although perhaps never achieving the insights of May 1968 in

---

145   In June 1578 Dom Sebastião, a 24-year-old monarch, sailed out of the Tagus to conquer Morocco from Moulay Abdel Malik. It was an insane enterprise, carried out against the advice of all his counsellors. Dom Sebastião's forces were annihilated in the battle of Alcácer-Quibir, in North Africa. The young king's body was never recovered and this gave rise to the belief that he would return someday to save Portugal. Throughout the Spanish occupation that followed one false Dom Sebastião after another kept appearing, rekindling hopes of an eventual, messianic liberation.

France, nevertheless developed into a telling instrument of social critique. The anarchists insured that it was used as often against the "left" as against more obvious targets. With the joy went a very Portuguese toughness.

The *fado* persisted, not as an embodiment of despair and resignation (as claimed by the superficial sociologists of song) but as a down–to–earth and uncompromising statement of the life of the poor. I recall a letter Phil once wrote me. He was entering the Alentejo:

> The tiny hills begin to roll across the flat countryside. Crouched eucalyptus trees hide in the barren dales. Here is a land of tradition, of rich struggles against elements and landowners alike, a land of wine, olives and music, of everyday survival, difficult to penetrate except by those who care for it. It is as if the stunted growth of the trees said all that needed to be said about hardship, abandonment, work - about the constant fight against a poor and unyielding soil on which lived giant women and monstrous men. But however ungrateful the land, the spirit was never crippled…

Although not songs of revolt the *fados* testify to this indestructibility of those oppressed, to this deep unity of man and nature. Romany roots endow some songs with a fierce pride, with a scorn for what "the bourgeois" will think or say, enabling them boldly to deal with such themes as women's right to sexual pleasure. No sentimentality, no soothing syrup. Love may mean pain, but is worth it. No neurotic trendiness. Just things as they are. Is not this the raw material of which revolution will be made?

Other features too had their roots in history. As their documents show the MFA was probably one of the most articulate and prolific group of soldiers the world has ever produced. In this they reflected the *intellectualismo* of the Portuguese elite. "Intellectuality" would be an inadequate translation. The term - as I was repeatedly told in Portugal - really denotes something else, a concern with speaking rather than with the core of things. Its loci are the cafés, not the cloisters of Coimbra. Eça de Queirós, the Aveiro novelist of the end of the nineteenth century, grasped this and made of it the kernel of some of his most scathing satires. His second *Farpa*, published in 1871, could have been written in the summer of 1975, a lampoon of later Leninist sects rather than of the bourgeois parties of his day:

> There are four political parties in Portugal: the Historical Party, the Regenerating Party, the Reformist Party and the Constitutional Party. There are, of course, others, more anonymous, only known to a few families. The four official parties, with newspapers and headquarters, are in perpetual and irreconcilable antagonism, always fighting amongst themselves in their leading articles. They have tried to restore peace, to unify. Impossible! The only thing they have in common is the ground of the Chiado, on which they all tread, and the Arcade which shelters them…
>
> All four are Catholic. All four are centralizing. All four have the same yearning for order. All four want progress and cite the case of Belgium …
>
> The conflagration is immense.

Forty years before the French Revolution, Sebastião José de Carvalho e Melo, First Marquis of Pombal, had declared war on clerical reaction and obscurantism, disbanded monasteries and convents and expelled the Jesuits from Portugal. The revolution of 1910 gave a new impetus to his ideas. But the Salazar regime made peace with the church and the Jesuits crept back. One morning, not long after Salazar had effected this reconciliation, people passing Pombal's huge statue at the top of Lisbon's Avenida da Liberdade, were delighted to read, in enormous letters of black pitch - all shiny on the white marble - the following inscription:

Vem cá baixo, marquês

Porque eles estão cá outra vez!

(Come down, Marquis

Because they're back again!)[146]

Today the old faces are creeping out once more. The gains of the early months are being whittled away piecemeal. The owners are reappearing - sometimes as managers. One would like to urge the spirit of 1974-5 to descend from its reified pedestal and help sweep the rubbish away. Who knows when it will move again? For the moment things are fairly quiet. But even the widespread disillusion has a certain Portuguese tinge to it. The early "revolutionary innocence" may have been lost. But the faintly amused nostalgia the Portuguese call *saudade* prevents sad sophistication degenerating into pure cynicism.

***

An impossible revolution? Yes, some will argue. Impossible within the confines of Portugal. Impossible because no island of libertarian communism can exist in a sea of capitalist production and of capitalist consciousness. Impossible because the upsurge was rooted - as in concrete - in the underdevelopment of Portuguese society as a whole. Impossible, given the social composition of modern Portugal, the weight of the northern, smallholding peasantry, the influence of the Church, the erosive and demobilizing effects of chronic poverty and unemployment. Impossible, finally, it is claimed, because state capitalism, not socialism, was "objectively" on the historical agenda, and because of the state-capitalist mentality of the "socialist" revolutionaries.

But men and women have always dreamed "impossible" dreams. They have repeatedly sought to "storm heaven" in the search for what they felt to be right. Again and again they have struggled for objectives difficult to attain, but which they sensed to embody their needs and desires. It is this capacity which makes of human beings the potential subjects of history, instead of its perpetual objects. This is why a study of the Portuguese events of 1974-5 is relevant to modern revolutionaries.

How should revolutionary libertarians have reacted to the Portuguese events? To have sat at home, dismissing the revolution as "impossible", was out of question. Should they, to paraphrase Lenin, have started struggling before anyone else, and not ceased struggling until after everyone else had?[147] "Struggling" can be as meaningful - or meaningless - as any other activity. It depends on the ends being fought for, and on the means being used. The revolutionary libertarian seeks to convince working people of their ability to organize and manage their own affairs, to foster a critical spirit towards external groups claiming to be on their side (including his or her own) and to expose the illusions spread by such (mainly Leninist) groups. This is a constant, everyday task which the libertarian revolutionary sees as his or her main concern. Perhaps in Portugal the opportunity for revolution has receded for the time being, but this role of the revolutionary never ceases (and has certainly not ceased in Portugal). Soon, in Spain, the Stalinists will be dusting down the living

---

146   Quoted by Peter Fryer and McGowan Pinheiro, *Oldest Ally* (London: Dobson, 1961).

147   Lenin, 'The Crisis of Menshevism', *Collected Works*, vol.2, p.351.

corpse of La Passionaria - a far more potent symbol of "resistance" than Alvaro Cunhal. The Illusionists will be at work again, having learned nothing from the experience of Portugal, and living on the battle cries of 1936.

Words such as "possible" and "impossible" have an historical dimension as well as an immediate one. What is impossible today may become feasible tomorrow. Moreover it may become feasible *because* of today's unsuccessful endeavours. To declare a revolution "impossible" is to pass a verdict on a process, as if it were an isolated event. It is to deny to those indicted the right to be judged by posterity. There are fruitful defeats in history as well as sterile victories. The Paris Commune defeat of 1871 was in the minds of the Russian revolutionaries of 1917. The events of Kronstadt (1921) or of Hungary (1956) still evoke echoes. They helped mould revolutionary libertarian attitudes that are very much part of current thinking.

But there is more. Preconceived ideas are not just *ideological* straitjackets. To declare a revolution "impossible" may, under certain circumstances, contribute to obstructing it. The masses in action are always more revolutionary than the most revolutionary of the revolutionary organizations. The reasons are obvious. The revolutionary organizations are wedded to past models (usually 1917). The masses want to create the future.

Some people see history as a railway line, leading to a predetermined goal. They see the action of classes as just generating the steam which will enable great men, or great parties ("the drivers of the locomotives of history", to use Stalin's monstrous phrase) to take charge of events. This is a prescription for bourgeois practices, for it legitimizes the power (both today and tomorrow) of those who think they know the track - and of those who think they can handle the engine.

No goal (certainly no political goal) can be defined as clearly as this. Material conditions (including cultural conditions) influence what is feasible and what is not. But they do not *determine* it, in any univocal sense. There is seldom, if ever, only one way of solving the problems created by a given pattern of economical or social organization. History shows how quite different forms of living, and quite different constellations of belief, proved possible on the basis of fairly similar technological infrastructures.

"Be realistic, demand the impossible", the walls of Paris proclaimed in May 1968. The words had a significance that went far deeper than their ability to startle. The first echoes were heard in Portugal. Where life pulsates, there is expectation. Sooner or later struggle breaks down the obstacles to the fulfilment of one's needs. Who knows where and in what form, the subterranean stream of human hope will next surge to the surface?

SOLIDARITY BOOK, 1977

32. INTRODUCTION TO PAUL CARDAN, *REDEFINING REVOLUTION*

"If, contrary to all probabilities, the October Revolution fails during the course of the present war, or immediately thereafter, to find its continuation in any of the advanced countries; and if, on the contrary, the proletariat is thrown back everywhere and on all fronts - then we should doubtless have to pose the question of revising our conception of the present epoch and its driving forces. In that case it would be a question not of slapping a copybook label on the USSR or the Stalinist gang but of re-evaluating the world historical perspective for the next decades if not centuries..."148

The October Revolution did not "find its continuation in any of the advanced countries" in the aftermath of World War II. Yet nowhere was the necessary re-evaluation of Marxism attempted, least of all by the Trotskyists. This re-evaluation is today imperative, for a number of reasons.

Marxist ideas have influenced the birth and moulded the shape of new societies all over the world. All have been ruthlessly exploitative societies, geared to the development of the productive forces, on the basis of intensive primitive accumulation and of the centralization of the means of production in the hands of state bureaucracies. What needs to be challenged are the very roots of the ideology and of the philosophy which inspired their creation.

We consider Marxism inadequate, not only as a system of ideas capable of leading to libertarian revolutionary action, but also as a method. A method deals with a number of categories, seeking to relate them in a specified way to one another. But if these categories are themselves the products of historical development it is obvious that at some stage revolutionaries will have to go beyond them, if only to grasp the new reality, the better to change it. At some stage we will have to choose between developing further as revolutionaries...and remaining Marxists.

The very concept of "scientific socialism" must be challenged if one is to understand human relationships. It is not true that "active social forces work exactly like natural forces".[149] Social development cannot be brought down to the level of a chemical reaction. In a chemical reaction there is no element of choice. *There is a choice* wherever people are concerned. The water in a kettle cannot choose not to boil when the kettle is placed on the fire. Workers can choose not to strike, even when under pressure. And socialism is about people.

A sophisticated Marxist, Anton Pannekoek, was led very far by this idea of "scientific socialism".[150] He believed that one could determine laws of human evolution, in the same way that one could study the laws of gravitation (Pannekoek was himself an astronomer). He arrived at the conclusion that man was the summit of the evolution of animal species, the "chosen" animal so to speak, gifted with ideal abilities. Human evolution was inevitable. Man himself was no accident. Man was bound

---

148   L. Trotsky, *In Defence of Marxism* (New York: Pioneer Publishers, 1942), pp. 14–15.

149   F. Engels, *Socialism: Utopian or Scientific* (Moscow, 1955), p. 108.

150   A. Pannekoek, *Anthropogenesis* (North Holland, 1953).

to be the perfect animal, destined to dominate the world. He could develop no ethic other than one of domination.

With the rise of capitalism natural and social science became a new type of religion (scientism). Two of scientism's greatest proponents were Darwin and Marx.[151] Pannekoek was one of the latter-day priests. It does not follow that one must reject everything that Darwin or Marx said. On the contrary, we would not think and act the way we do if they had not made important contributions to the development of human thought. But we must now try and go beyond them. There is no such thing as a "system of laws" that will always explain all we know of natural history and of the physical world. Even less is there a "system" that can explain all of social history. Many people however - on the left and elsewhere - are still addicted to this idea of a complete system, containing all the answers. It is part of a character structure, itself manifested in the particular ideas taken up.

Modern society is geared towards crushing any attempt at self-activity and at autonomous thinking. We are always encouraged to rely on others to choose and decide for us, and to provide the answers to all our problems. Many people, especially among the young, are deeply disillusioned with the values of this society. Yet a number of them join Marxist organizations or become Jesus freaks or adepts of some guru. This is not so surprising, considering the fact that in all of these outfits all the answers are provided. The disciples are relieved of the need to decide or choose for themselves. The Party line - or the word of the Master - does it for them. They are no longer burdened by the responsibilities of decisions to be made. A deep feeling of insecurity attracts people like a magnet towards any closed system of ideas which will relieve from anxiety in the face of the unknown. For may people the most frightful and distressing thing is not knowing the future.

The following essay, first published in *Socialisme ou Barbarie*, no. 34, in 1964, does not provide yet another blueprint for ideological or "emotional" security. Quite the opposite. Nor is it intended to be the theoretical bible of *Solidarity*. Many will find differences - even contradictions - with some of the author's earlier writings. They will be right. The author himself was at one time a Trotskyist. People evolve, change, develop new ideas. Only fossilized dogmatists can pride themselves on not having changed their ideas for the last thirty or forty years.

We publish this pamphlet not because we agree with every word in it but because we think it a stimulating and fruitful contribution to the development of revolutionary theory. The text aims to uncover new problems. It asks many new questions and is not concerned with salvaging old answers.

SOLIDARITY PAMPHLET 44 [1974]

---

151   That Marx wanted to dedicate *Capital* to Darwin was no accident. Darwin refused, feeling he had a "bad" enough reputation already.

33. INTRODUCTION TO CORNELIUS CASTORIADIS, HISTORY AS CREATION

"All fixed, fast-frozen relations, with their train of ancient and venerable prejudices and opinions are swept away, all new formed ones become antiquated before they can ossify. All that is solid melts into air, and all that is holy is profaned..."

(Karl Marx and Friedrich Engels, *Manifesto of the Communist Party*, 1848)

These words are even truer today than when they were written 130 years ago. In the nineteenth century the idea of progress was self-evident: the body of scientific knowledge grew and grew and rapidly became incorporated into the fabric of expanding capitalism. In the 1890s some physicists even predicted that all there was to know about the universe would soon be within their grasp. The figure of twenty years was bandied about. Great "unifying" theories were being thrown up: Clerk Maxwell's electromagnetic theory, the Universal Theory of Gravitation, Mendeleyev's Periodic Table of Elements, Darwin's theory of the Origin of Species through Natural Selection. The great intellectual edifice of nineteenth century science was an imposing counterpoint to the remorseless surge of the industrial revolution, which during this period was changing the face of Europe. Technology seemed omnipotent. The bourgeoisie had dethroned God and instituted the realm of Reason. It believed that everything was inherently rational, determinable, quantifiable. (It had to be, in order to be bought and sold.)

This was the science that the founders of "scientific socialism" had sucked into their bones: the science of elegant universalism, of cosmological laws to which there were no exceptions, of systems that would encompass the whole of reality in their net. The very structure of this kind of thinking reflected the confident ambitions of a capitalism in full development. In the air was the promise that life itself would soon be amenable to the same mathematical manipulations that had successfully predicted the motions of the stars, the combination of atoms and the propagation of light.

It is scarcely surprising that, as an offshoot or extension of bourgeois objectivist rationalism, a grand theory of history and social change (namely Marxism) was also to emerge, based on the methodological premises and impregnated with the scientific euphoria of the nineteenth century. This particular setting "provided both the bricks and mortar for such a theory...largely predetermining even what were to be its dominant categories". The economy seemed the obvious basis of all social relations, and was solemnly theorized as such. The techniques of capitalist production were consecrated as scientifically inevitable although criticism was levied at how the product was distributed. Capitalist models of organization and efficiency were imported into the radical movement. Under the guise of revolutionary theory, an ideology was born and was to develop, the ideology of a bureaucracy whose ascendancy was still in the future.

Bourgeois historians were by no means immune from this movement. They started asserting that their subject was "a science, no less and no more"[152] and as

---

152 J.B. Bury (1861–1927) in 'The Science of History' (a lecture delivered in Cambridge, in 1902). See F. Stern (ed.), *The Varieties of History: From Voltaire to the Present* (London: Macmillan, 1970), p.210.

such they were necessarily obliged to meet the "scientific demand for completeness and certainty".[153] As E.P. Cheyney succinctly put it: "History, the great course of human affairs, has been the result not of voluntary action on the part of individuals or groups of individuals, much less of chance, but has been subject to law".[154] The task of the historian was no longer even to attempt to discover "what actually happened"[155] but rather to discover those laws.

Science, however, did not stop in the nineteenth century. Since the turn of the century it has undergone a series of major revolutions. Its texture and content are radically different today from what they were a few decades ago. The uncertainty principle seems here to stay. The effects of the observer on the "thing" observed are noted in field after field. The inter-reactions of systems are now a topic for study, rather than predictions concerning the position or behaviour of the individual components. The non-hierarchical units of ecological systems are more relevant to us today than studies of linear progressions leading from simple to more complex unicellular organisms, from these to multicellular forms of life and from the latter right "up" to the summits of biological evolution inhabited by human kind.

Scientific insights today both reflect deep changes in prevailing philosophy and help further to deepen them. Apart, it would appear from revolutionary theory, everything today is up for re-examination. Additional knowledge is no longer automatically equated with progress.[156] Scientists are increasingly questioning the methods and structure of science, its rigid separation of the subjective from the objective, its equation of technology with advance (not to mention the way it misuses knowledge). But the advocates of "scientific" socialism spare themselves these doubts. They ignore this process of self-questioning. The "science" of their "scientific socialism" seems immune from the crisis of science as a whole. Many such people start striving to change the course of history only after becoming convinced that the direction of history is independent of their will! They see history as a train running along a track, an analogy drawn - oh, so tellingly and revealingly - from the Industrial Revolution. Some would prefer a "freer" metaphor, perhaps that of a torrent (at times a flood, at times a trickle), earthbound certainly by the laws of gravity, but within those limits able to circumvent or remove obstacles, and certainly capable, when necessary, of shaping its own bed and even changing it. But this metaphor too, basing itself as it does on the phenomena of natural science, bears the imprint - and has all the limitations - of a period.

Objections to Marxism, at a coherently argued level, usually come from two main sources: from downright reactionaries defending the existing order, or from the methodological nit-pickers of the academic establishment, more concerned with point-scoring (or with public display of their erudition) than with a genuine understanding of the world around them. It is rare today to find a philosophical critique of Marx coming from those who, like him, seek radically to transform society. A thought-out critique that is both libertarian and revolutionary, and that moreover

---

153   Lord Acton (1834–1902) in "Letter to the Contributors to the *Cambridge Modern History*" (*loc. cit.*, p.247).

154   *American Historical Review*, 1924.

155   Leopold von Ranke (1795–1886) in "Preface to *Histories of the Latin and German Nations from 1494–1514*" (*loc. cit.*, p.57).

156   The debate about genetic engineering is a case in point. Some scientists talk of voluntary self-censorship by the scientific community. A Nobel Prize winner can now write: "I fear for the future of science as we have known it, for human kind, for life on Earth. The new technology excites me...yet the price is high, perhaps too high" (George Wald, *The Sciences* (New York: Academy of Sciences, September-October 1976)).

identifies Marxism as a useful philosophy for the bureaucracy, is rarer still. The need for such an approach is now obvious.

Revolutionaries must challenge the dominant ideology, in whatever guise it may present itself. If Marxism now provides the philosophical cornerstone of new hierarchical and exploitative regimes, it is a relevant target for us. Philosophical ideas and assumptions are as much part of what holds these new societies together as are institutional violence, policemen and - ultimately - the armed forces of the state. A challenge of this kind is a legitimate endeavour. The seeds of new social orders always sprout, as philosophical assumptions, long before the revolution. (The revolutionary bureaucrat, incidentally, also appears before the revolution!) Philosophically ideas contribute to the intellectual climate which helps shape societies. The Enlightenment preceded the French Revolution: the bourgeoisie won its philosophical battles against the aristocracy and the clergy long before it secured its own political ascendency. Bourgeois society is today in crisis. In the wings are the Marxists: the ideologues of the bureaucracy.

Marxist assumptions today permeate the thinking of those who see themselves as the midwives of new societies. There are plenty of examples of what these assumptions are tending to produce, and have in fact already produced. We refuse to believe that these creations are all "historical accidents" (no society can be that accident-prone). Our century is littered with "revolutions" which gave birth to authoritarian and repressive regimes, officially upholding Marx's ideas, even teaching them in schools and universities. These regimes are obsessed with such notions as "scientific socialism" and the "unfettered development of the productive forces". Many have by and large achieved such demands of the *Communist Manifesto* (1848) as " the centralization of credit" or "the means of communication and transport in the hands of the state". "The extension of factories and instruments of production", owned by the same state, is nowadays taken for granted by all "progressive" regimes.

But the future is not settled. The libertarian revolution is not a utopian project. In this perspective the unseating of authority, especially of so-called "revolutionary" authority, is an act of liberation. For objectivist rationalism applied to history is tantamount to purging history of all that is creative and alive (and therefore unpredictable) within it. Genuine creation is the act of producing that which is *not* totally implicit in the previous state of affairs. Such creation plays a major role in history. By its very nature it defies the dictates of predetermination. For those who see history as the unfurling of a dialectical process which leads inevitably "forward" towards a particular brand of "socialism" (or which grants history - as sole alternative - the right to stagnate in capitalist barbarism) there is no *real* history. There are just mechanisms. There is no more history in such an outlook than there is in a chemical reaction (however explosive) produced by mixing ingredients of known composition, with known properties, in the appropriate proportions, and in the right sequence.

What areas of choice does history offer us? If there are none, are we merely acting out a drama scripted by Him, Her, It or They? Whether the agency be the bearded God of the Christians, the imageless God of the Judaeo-Muslims, the Mother-Goddess of early civlizations,[157] Hegel's Logos, or the Unfurling of the Materialist Dialectic (leading to the inevitable emergence of the communist humanity) matters little in this respect. Can rationalism ("the ratio of all we have already known", as Blake once put it) fully forecast the creations we have yet to make? If it can, there is noth-

---

157   Isis in Egypt, Danu in India, Ishtar in Babylon, Nana in Sumer, Ashtoreth in the "Bible Lands".

ing original in anything we do. If it cannot, then the power of rationalism has certain inherent limitations. If a "scientific" theory of history can predict history, there is no such thing as genuine choice. If it cannot, then "scientific" interpretations of the past are subject to the same limitations as similar prediction of the future.

Castoriadis's critique of "rationalism" does not throw reason out of the window. It merely challenges its omnipotence and seeks to define its limits. Nor does his critique of objectivism deny that phenomena exist independently of the human mind. It merely stresses that the human mind moulds what it perceives, endowing it with signification. At the level of natural phenomena, new interpretations lead to new exploration. At the level of social phenomena, the human mind shapes new attitudes, new roles and eventually new institutions. The critique of what Marx himself (in *The German Ideology*) was to call "the tyranny of concepts" is deeply subversive. The struggle against "all that is" now forces revolutionaries to rethink issues long considered "settled", rescuing in the process the term "praxis" (creative and self-transforming activity) from its widespread confusion with "practice" (the application of rationality to concrete tasks). Against this background it is not really surprising that the philosophical ideas of Karl Marx should be deemed ripe for re-examination. This critique of fixed, fast-frozen relations is, after all, only an aspect of the intellectual climate of our time.

SOLIDARITY PAMPHLET 54, JULY 1978

34. SUDDENLY THIS SUMMER

For those who see themselves as revolutionaries, two attitudes are possible to the events of the Polish summer. The first seeks to minimize their significance. It points out that there is nothing very radical in the demand for 'free trade unions',[158] particularly when voiced by nationalist reformists, and religious ones to boot. The demand is dismissed as a gigantic diversion, fraught with all the dangers inherent in illusory projects.

Rooted knee-deep in their analysis of the past, people who hold such views will argue that the trade unions are no solution to the problems of the working class. The unions, by their very essence (i.e. independently of time and place) are "organs of class collaboration" and "prisons for the proletariat". "Free trade unions", such people would stress, will readily be recuperated by the Polish state. Such an attitude (for it is attitude as much as a reasoning) reminds one of Marx's initial timidity in relation to the Paris Commune – and of Lenin's initial myopia in relation to the Soviets of 1905.

Such an approach contains some seeds of abstract truth (a union is indeed just a broker of labour power, under any circumstances). But it also shows great poverty of imagination and a total absence of feeling for living reality. It fails to grasp all that is *new* in the Polish experience. It seeks, instead, to interpret this experience in the categories of the past. It doesn't feel revolution as a creative act, as "a conclusion that exceeds the premises", as the entry of thousands of people on to territory uncharted on *anyone's* political atlas. Not to sense all this shows the chasm between old-time revolutionaries (whose thinking is always rooted in past revolutions) and people in action (who are always seeking to make the next one).

The second attitude to the Polish events would say: "forget the words (trade unions) and look at the content" (autonomous self-managed organizations, controlled from below, and involving all areas of social life). It would stress the specific geographical, historical and cultural contexts in which these demands were now being voiced: societies in which every area of autonomy had been ruthlessly colonized, societies in which the Party leaderships believed they had already achieved their objective – the social atomization of the population.

The Polish summer, in *this* perspective, would be seen as the first mass movement of a self-conscious working class against the institutional legacies of Leninism (i.e. against societies in which unions were conceived of as "transmission belts between the Party and the masses"). The Gdansk strike would be an example of a

---

158 It is worth pointing out that this label was devised by sections of the media in the West. The demand of the Gdansk MKS (Inter-Factory Strike Committee) was for "independent, self–managed unions". The term "free" trade unions is a crude attempt at pre-emptive recuperation. It quite strongly conveys associations – if only of the verbal kind – with the "free" world, the "free" enterprise system, Radio "Free" Europe, etc. The MKS – and the Polish Solidarnosc movement which has grown out of it – has repeatedly stated that it is not seeking the restoration of the means of production to private ownership.

Of all the papers in the West only *Le Monde* has correctly conveyed the full nuances of what the Polish workers are trying to create: "des syndicats indépendants et autogérés". To translate this as "self–governing" unions, as *The Times* and *The Guardian* have intermittently done, is also misleading. Countries (or institutions) may be "self–governing", jealous of their frontiers, extremely autocratic. (It all depends on who the "governors" are.) "Self–managed" on the other hand implies that the locus of power is at the base. And it doesn't preclude even very close association with similarly structured bodies.

tremendous upsurge of the "class for itself" (as Marx would have said) – and the action in question would be the repudiation of Marxist-Leninist objectives, even by the generations which the "Marxist Party" had itself brought up!

In this approach the whole focus shifts away from weeping about the crucifixes or sniggering about the carnations.[159] Central to it would be Walesa's statements that, in the new organizations, delegates would not be separated from those they represented (and would in fact remain at work, at least part of the time); that the organizations would seek to break down the barriers between intellectual and manual labour; that representatives would receive working men's wages "or even less" (*Libération*, September 13, 1980); that "the journals of the new unions would publish whatever they wanted, whether anyone liked it or not" (*Guardian*, September 1).

A sympathetic (not sentimental) approach would emphasize the almost unbelievable capacity for organization and coordination shown by the strikers, which rendered the task of the state power infinitely more difficult. It would admire their practical skill, rather than denounce them for some of the things they have been compelled – tongue in cheek – to say.

The Polish summer is a challenge, at all levels, to the dominant ideology in Eastern Europe. As such it is sure to have enormous repercussions. It questions the basic doctrinal postulates which underpin these societies. These are seldom honestly stated. They are that the main demands outlined in the *Communist Manifesto* ("to wrest, by degrees, all capital from the bourgeoisie, to centralize all instruments of production in the hands of the State") somehow ensure the "socialist" nature of the regimes that follow. They ensure no such thing – even when dished up with a *sauce tartare*: the rule of the vanguard party.

If revolutionaries are unaware of the challenge posed by any autonomous organization (trade union or flying university or what-have-you), Russia's rulers certainly aren't. Islands of autonomy, in societies such as theirs, are potential bases of dual power. The dyke of the official lie once breached, a whole ocean of people just seeking the truth could come pouring through. How else can we explain Russia's desperate attempt to circumscribe the focus of infection, the omission of all serious reference to the Polish events in their own press, the sudden disappearance of even "Eurocommunist" journals from their libraries and reading rooms, their talk of "dividing socialism from within" (*The Times*, September 29) and their constant calls for "the restoration of a democracy which conforms to Leninist norms".

For Poland's rulers things are even more bleak. We note the frightened statement of a leading Polish Party member (*Observer*, August 24) that "the opposition is now *inside* the working class". Comrade, it is even worse than that! After the events of 1970 the workers can no longer be conned by reshuffling your Party leadership. They have understood that confidence – like matches – can only be used once! The main opposition to Leninism, in Poland, is not just "inside the working class". It *is* the working class…and what spells your doom is that the workers know it.

The situation is fraught with danger and ambiguities. Our admiration is not an admiration of voyeurs – and our support is not uncritical. But the things that worry

---

159   And, even here, the new approach would be both more charitable and more open. It would remember that Anna Walentynowicz who had worked all her life in the shipyard (initially as a welder, later as a crane driver) first got into trouble with the authorities when she organized, not a strike over wages, but a collection among her workmates to put flowers on the graves of her fellow workers shot down ten years earlier. Such apparently "trifling" episodes should teach us more modesty in seeking to understand what drives human beings to action, and to unravel the strange matrices of identity in which such autonomous action is now embedded.

us are not those that worry the crypto-Stalinists - or those who like their revolutions "pure". Jan Litinski, the editor of *Robotnik*, describes (*Libération*, September 9) a visit to the miners of Wazbrzych. "The men would come to the founding committee of the union as to a new power, of which they expected both instructions and protection. Having lived for 35 years in a totalitarian state it was hard to learn that one could defend oneself without seeking refuge behind authority". Here lies the main danger. Here, and in an excessive reliance on their new charismatic leaders who may turn out to have feet of clay. "To be radical", according to Litinski, "is to work to change all that".

Polish workers are already deserting the official unions in their hundreds of thousands. They are joining the Solidarity network. The old unions were indeed "transmission belts"...to the comfortable corridors of power. To join the new organizations, on the other hand, is to be catapulted in the opposite direction, to the very front line of contestation and political strife. It is quite naïve to believe that the new unions will somehow be able to avoid finding *political* answers to the political onslaught that is sure to be launched against them.

How seriously, in the last analysis, do we take the prescription that "the emancipation of the working class is the task of the workers themselves"? Is it just rhetoric? Or do we really mean it? And if we mean it, why can't the class be granted the autonomy to choose its *means* - as well as its *ends* - and to label them as it wishes?

SOLIDARITY SUPPLEMENT ON 'SUMMER IN GDANSK', IN *SOLIDARITY: FOR SOCIAL REVOLUTION*, 14 (OCTOBER-NOVEMBER 1980)

35. MAKING A FRESH START

"Without the development of revolutionary theory there can be no development of revolutionary practice" (Cornelius Castoriadis, 1949).

Solidarity was formed in 1959 and the group developed its perspectives for the most part during the 1960s. Probably the greatest single influence on this development was the work of the French theorist Cornelius Castoriadis (also know as Paul Cardan) which appeared in the journal *Socialisme ou Barbarie* between 1949 and 1965. Over the years Solidarity published a significant selection of Castoriadis's texts in a series of pamphlets, and these, far more than the programmatic statements *As We See It* and *As We Don't See It*, came to characterize the group's orientation towards the world.

In many respects Castoriadis's *Socialisme ou Barbarie* writings have stood the test of time very well: they certainly demand the continued attention of all those concerned with socialist theory and practice. Much has changed since the *Socialisme ou Barbarie* period, however, both in society at large and in the realm of ideas, and, unsurprisingly, certain aspects of Castoriadis's theories are beginning to show their age.

This is perhaps most notable if we take a look at the economic analysis put forward in the essay, *Modern Capitalism and Revolution*. Written in 1959, at the height of the unprecedentedly sustained economic boom which followed the Second World War, it presents us with both a continuingly relevant critique of the scientistic categories of classical Marxist political economy, and a projection of certain trends within modern capitalism which has been somewhat overtaken by events. Specifically it seems from the vantage point of 1982 that *Modern Capitalism and Revolution* overestimates the stability of the Western ruling classes' success in "controlling" and "preventing major crises of the classical type". Today almost every national economy of the industrialized West is gripped by a profound and prolonged recession. Unemployment has risen to levels inconceivable twenty, fifteen, or even ten years ago, the level of industrial output is stagnating and the Keynesian consensus which lay behind governmental policies in the boom years appears to be in tatters. Quite obviously these changed conditions demand that Castoriadis's account in *Modern Capitalism and Revolution* be brought up to date and significantly revised.

Castoriadis's economic projections are not the only parts of his theory which have become problematic with the passing of time: there are also difficulties to be faced in his rejection of Marxism as a whole and in his espousal of a councilist paradigm of revolutionary practice. When Castoriadis asked in 1964, "Where since 1923 [when Lukács's *History and Class Consciousness* was published] has anything been produced which has advanced Marxism?", he was taking a stance which, though provocative (since it effectively dismissed the work of such theorists as Gramsci, Korsch, Pannekoek, Marcuse and Sartre), was certainly defensible (since whatever advances *had* come from Reich, Gramsci *et al* had been almost totally submerged in the appalling idiocies of Marxist orthodoxy). In other words, it was possible in 1964 to take "Marxism" to mean "vulgar Marxism" - it could be identified with "Marx-Engels-Kautsky-Lenin-Trotsky-Stalin thought".

Today such an identification is less easy. The submerged unofficial Marxist tradition had been rediscovered, and there has been a dramatic growth of new Marxist theory, at least some of which cannot be dismissed with a casual gesture. Of course, the rediscovery of the unorthodox Marxists of the past has lead to much sterile fetishization of "sacred texts", and most new Marxist theory has been execrable - particularly in Britain, where the Althusserian poison administered in massive doses by *New Left Review* paralyzed the minds (though not unfortunately the writing hands) of a large section of the left intelligentsia for more than a decade. What is more, any advances within Marxist theory have been effectively ignored by the vast majority of the activist Marxist left, who remain imprisoned by a conceptual framework which is beneath contempt. Nevertheless, there can be little doubt that it is now far more difficult to argue an informed rejection of the content of Marxism than it was twenty years ago. For such a critique to be rigorous, it would have to contend not only with the dire orthodoxy Castoriadis so efficiently laid to waste, but also with the far more sophisticated work of both the unorthodox Marxists of old and such contemporary theorists as Habermas, Lefebvre, Gorz, Thompson, the Italian autonomists and the many Marxist feminists.

This is not to claim that a critique of Marxism which goes beyond an assault on vulgar Marxism is *impossible*. Nor is it to deny the contributions made by Castoriadis to such a project, particularly in his post-*Socialisme-ou-Barbarie* writings. Neither is it to argue that a rejection of the Marxist label on grounds other than a critique of the content of all self-professed Marxist theories cannot be justified: a strong case can be made for refusing the mantle of Marxism because its assumption by even the most relevant of theorists serves to reinforce the faith of the crudest Leninist in the fundamental correctness of his or her idiotic and dangerous beliefs. All the same, the fact remains that many of the developments in Marxist theory over the last two decades deserve our critical attention: one of the tasks of this new series of *Solidarity* magazine will be to attempt to assess their worth.

If developments in the theoretical sphere have been massive since Castoriadis wrote in *Socialisme ou Barbarie*, so too have changes in oppositional social practice. The developing general tendencies of the latter - towards the adoption of new forms of workplace struggle in the face of the changing character of work and the continued degeneration of traditional working class organizations, and towards the opening up of new areas of contestation outside the conventional limits of the class struggle - were grasped by Castoriadis with a remarkable prescience.[160] Perhaps unsurprisingly he had, however, little to say on the possibility of this "new movement" being integrated and effectively neutralized by adapting capitalism. And today, when "workers' self-management" (albeit in a hideously distorted form) is advocated by every established political party, the "youth revolt" has become the passive consumption of the products of the entertainment industry, and "feminism" is as much the ideology of the upwardly mobile career woman as it is the basis for a genuinely oppositional movement, this silence is clearly inadequate.

What is more, Castoriadis retained a vision of a post-revolutionary society run by Workers' Councils,[161] the usefulness of which has been seriously brought into

---

160   See *The Crisis of Modern Society* (*Solidarity* Pamphlet 23).

161   See *Workers' Councils and the Economics of a Self-Managed Society* (*Solidarity* Pamphlet 40).

question by precisely the growth of contestation outside the sphere of production which he predicted. Workers' Councils are perhaps a crucially necessary part of any self-managed socialist society: but to consider them as the organizational basis of such a society - as Castoriadis and with him *Solidarity* have tended to suggest - it is to fall prey to the productivist illusion which characterizes so much crude Marxist theory and practice.

Now the increasingly apparent outdatedness of certain parts of our theory does not in itself justify our beginning a new series of *Solidarity* magazine. Indeed it could be - and has been - used as an argument for disbanding Solidarity. Quite obviously we believe the obsolescence of certain elements of our theory is less a cause for despair than an invigorating challenge. But why is this?

Well, firstly and most importantly, we do not think that those of our ideas made questionable by the passage of time are anything like the totality of our perspective, nor do we see them as the foundations of our politics. Although our critique of existing society and of traditional programmes for changing it needs to be further developed, it remains essentially sound enough to act as a springboard for such development. There is not the space here to elaborate upon this assertion. We can only state our convictions that the current world recession does not invalidate our critique of classical Marxist crisis theory; that the sophistication of some modern Marxism cannot relegitimate the tired old platitudes of Marxist orthodoxy; that the fate of the new social movements does not necessitate a retreat from our emphasis on contestation outside the traditional politico-economic sphere; that the inappropriateness of councilism to modern conditions does not undermine either our critique of the tendencies towards bureaucratization deeply imbedded in the theory and practice of traditional working class organizations and parties of the left, or our emphasis of self-activity in struggle.

Secondly, we believe that whatever development is required is well within our capacity. This is not to pre-empt the necessary process of discussion: we have no magic formulae up our sleeves, nor would we wish to have. It is, however, to state that, unlike too many on the British libertarian left, we are not afraid of critical thinking.

This said, theory is by no means all we plan to publish. At present there is no British periodical that habitually carries detailed and accurate critical reports of actual struggles - a situation which stems largely from the left's quite innocent (though harmful) preoccupation with forcing the complexities of real life into simplistic and outmoded interpretative frameworks, but which is also the product of a predilection for "tactical" distortions of reality. We aim to do all we can to rectify this state of affairs, by publishing in-depth secondhand accounts and firsthand testimonies of contemporary social conflicts, in industry and elsewhere.

Our older readers will recognize our twin priorities of interrogating radical social theory and investigating the practice of oppositional social movements as being very much those of the old *Solidarity: For Workers' Power* journal published by London Solidarity from 1959 to 1977, when *Solidarity* fused with the group *Social Revolution*. It must be emphasized that the similarity of objectives does not mean that we are motivated by some escapist nostalgia for the "good old days". Even though *Solidarity: For Workers' Power* was a more incisive and valuable publication than its successor *Solidarity: For Social Revolution*, it was hardly perfect even in its time and its time has now passed. We are prepared to learn from our history, but we have no desire to use it as an emotional crutch.

SOLIDARITY, N.S., I, 1 (1982)

36. ABOUT OURSELVES 1

Are you dissatisfied with your present existence? Certainly important decisions about your life are out of your control and in the hands of managers and officials of one kind or another. It's likely that you don't know your workmates and neighbours very well, and often feel lonely or anxious for no obvious reason. The pressure to consume and to obtain the necessary cash means that daily life remains a soul-destroying struggle.

Of course, socialists and social reformers were offering answers to these problems before Marx was a twinkle in his father's eye, but despite bloody revolutions, struggles for trade union rights and the election of reformers to government, there has been no fundamental change. The "Communist" world is not free. Genuine freedom means the end of wage labour and economic inequality, the liberation of personal and social relations among human beings - a transformation of society which would be totally revolutionary in scope.

But when we come to examine most radical or revolutionary movements we find that in practice they have little to do with freedom. Hierarchical organization and veneration of gurus go hand in hand with a willingness to manipulate and sacrifice campaigns and issues in order to "build the revolutionary party". The real movement for freedom is not to be found in formal organizations, but rather in the responses of ordinary people who feel downtrodden and cheated. Solidarity is not the "leadership" of this movement but merely a small part within it. In our pamphlets and magazine we attempt to broaden and deepen the growing criticism of modern society in theory and in practice.

We try to learn from the history of ordinary people which lies hidden beneath the history of the leaders and generals. For us, as revolutionaries, meaningful action is whatever increases the confidence, autonomy, initiative, participation, solidarity, egalitarian tendencies and self-activity of the masses, and whatever assists in their demystification. Sterile and harmful action is whatever reinforces the passivity of the masses, their apathy, cynicism, differentiation through hierarchy, alienation, reliance on others to do things for them, and the degree to which they can therefore be manipulated by others, even those acting on their behalf.

SOLIDARITY, N.S, I, 2 (1983?)

37. ABOUT OURSELVES 2

Solidarity is presently published by a small group of libertarian socialists in London. Its primary aim is to encourage discussion and intelligent analysis of the world in which we live - from a libertarian socialist perspective.

We believe that this is an important aim for a number of reasons. First of all, we feel it is necessary to break decisively with the anti-modernism of the traditional anarchist milieu. It is no longer relevant to rely on the experience of the Spanish Revolution as the paradigm of revolutionary practice; and it is pointless today to centre our theoretical discussions on the debates of the anarchist movement of the late nineteenth and early twentieth centuries. The world has changed since then.

Second, we feel that it is necessary to counter the blind actionism found in many anarchists. To change the world it is necessary to interpret it: the "refusal of thought" so prevalent in the anarchist milieu - which is closely related to its predilection for outdated models of revolution - has done untold harm to the cause of libertarian social revolution.

This does not mean that we are unaware of the dangers of isolation in the ivory towers of theoretical discussion; still less does it mean that we are uncritical of the role "revolutionary intellectuals" have played in usurping self-managed struggles. Neither does it mean that we have any time for the rigid "lineism" and sectarian rituals of denunciation typical of many other small groups on the revolutionary scene. Rather, we are committed to an open process of clarifying ideas as part of a more general development of practice. We do not consider this activity as having a particularly privileged place in the revolutionary project. We are one group of people among many engaged in the process of debate and we have neither the resources nor the arrogance to attempt to cover "everything worth covering".

SOLIDARITY, N.S., I, 3 (1983?)

38. CASTORIADIS'S ECONOMICS REVISITED

Modern Capitalism and Revolution by Cornelius Castoriadis (Paul Cardan) was drafted in 1959, published by Solidarity in 1965 and issued in a second edition in 1974, bearing a new introduction by the author in which he declined to make any significant alterations to his original conclusions.

In that introduction, Castoriadis listed six assertions from the original text as having been central to the analysis presented, and which he considered remained totally vindicated by events up to 1974. These were:

1. That the standard of living of the working class would rise and continue to rise.
2. That permanent unemployment did not any more, and would not in the future, have the numerical significance it had previously had in the history of capitalism.
3. That the capitalist state had become able to control the level of overall economic activity and to prevent major crises of over-production.
4. That the absence of political activity by the masses (privatization) would form the central problem confronting the action of revolutionaries during the coming period.
5. That new attitudes on the part of youth expressed a total rejection of the system by the young and that this signified that established society was becoming unable to breed a new generation which would reproduce the existing state affairs.
6. That the revolutionary movement could no longer treat as relevant the narrow "economic" and "political" issues and ought to be concerned first of all with the questions men and women face in their real everyday life (i.e. there existed a crisis of the whole social fabric).

Of these assertions numbers 1, 2, and 3 appear to have been proven wrong. There is most definitely an economic crisis of global proportions, the consequences of which include the driving down of working class living standards both in the "Third World", and a similar pattern of rising unemployment which in global terms probably greatly exceeds the experience of previous world crises. The ruling classes do not appear to be in control, and the signs are of a turn to the classical solution: world war.

What remains astonishing, however, is the extent to which assertion 4 continues to hold true. While Marxists point to the economic crises and chant "I told you so", they can take little comfort from the continuing refusal of the working class to show serious evidence of the classical predicted response. For the present period the fundamental problem is the absence of generalized working class political activity. On the obverse side, it is also evident that there is a marked lack of enthusiasm for ruling class propaganda - the Falklands spirit failed to catch fire despite a barrage of continuing media coverage, and the sight of Reagan lighting candles for the Poles evinces disgust. The tragedy of all this, from which no one can derive any comfort, is that it evidences the extent to which bureaucratic capitalism has demoralized and desensitized the mass of the people into a state of apathetic negativity.

There are exceptions, which relate to assertions 5 and 6 above. It is still true that the young have presented a permanent problem of socialization to their parent societies in ways not previously experienced, and the youth unemployment has done nothing to help. But it is equally true that this has not assumed anything like revolutionary consciousness. For the most part it remains alienated, isolated, sporadic, easily recuperated and contained into environments where it can be exploited and policed. The problem has been put into the ghetto where it assumes the character of an eyesore – and no more.

It is equally true that questions have been asked by a wide range of people on a wide range of issues cutting into the most intimate corners of everyday life. It is also evident, however, that this has posed absolutely no threat to the status quo, no fundamental challenge to any institution or part of the capitalist social fabric, beyond what could be absorbed through reform and a moderate cultural shift. What did filter through has taken a back seat to personal economic survival.

Beyond these examples – unless one pins widely optimistic hopes on a movement isolated in Poland and swamped by nationalist and religious ideology, or on isolated resistance by steel workers in France, Belgium and England bent on stealing each other's jobs, or as some do on the re-emergence of a mass peace movement in Western Europe – there is not much sign of life. On balance, what is left of Castoriadis's six assertions?

When a theory is disproved by the facts, or has to face facts which it did not and could not predict – or which it cannot interpret – it is well-known that it can always be rescued, through resort to additional hypotheses, provided the sum total of the hypotheses remains logically consistent. This might work up to a point. But beyond that the heaping of hypotheses upon hypotheses is nearly always the sign that a theory is dead.[162]

In fact, even using this hard test set by Castoriadis for Marxism to his own work, the core of his theory remains intact. The fundamental contradiction of capitalism still remains in the necessity for capitalism on the one hand to reduce workers to simple executors of tasks, and on the other, in the impossibility for it to continue to function if it succeeds in so doing. Capitalism needs to achieve mutually incompatible objectives: the participation and the exclusion of the worker in production – as of all citizens in relation to politics. This is the real contradiction of contemporary society and the ultimate source of its crises. The present world economic crisis, in its origins, its development and its consequences, is a continuation of that struggle. Far from being a refutation of Castoriadis's theories it is their complete vindication, since in his theories economic crisis does not fuel class struggle but rather it is class struggle which fuels the economic crisis. We are not witnessing a mystical conjuncture in an uncomputable combination of falling rates of profit, long waves, short waves and medium waves, etc.; we are witnessing the failure of the ruling class to attain its prime social objectives. The only mystery is what happens next.

SOLIDARITY, N.S., I, 3 (1983?)

---

162   Introduction to *Modern Capitalism and Revolution* (1974 edition), p.2.

39. ABOUT OURSELVES 3

Solidarity is a small group which tries to show that being a revolutionary socialist does not mean accepting the "merits" of party discipline and the "correct line". Unlike many groups on the left, we do not have to check our views against a series of sacred texts before deciding that they are ideologically acceptable. This means, for instance, that while we believe the women's liberation movement to be an integral part of any movement for the general liberation of humanity, we regard it as a matter of course that we should be free to challenge any idea or part of that movement which we think does not advance that goal. It means that because we oppose imperialism we oppose all imperialisms, including that of the USSR, and we do not assume that people involved in "national liberation struggles" are therefore exempt from criticism. Too often have we seen self-styled socialists in the West support and indeed idolize the leaders of such movements, only to have their blindness cruelly exposed when these leaders seize power and create their dictatorships "in the name of the people". Such muting of criticism has, we believe, done greater harm to the cause of socialism throughout the world than almost any repression could have. Again, because we disagree with Tory policies we see no reason why we should disqualify ourselves from criticizing those of Labour; those who make mouthings about peace and equality while supporting the rule of bureaucrats are no better than those who speak freedom and the need for lower taxation while boosting the armed forces and cutting public services. We do not assume that nothing has changed since Marx wrote, and we are equally happy to criticize the ideas of Friedman and Sherman, Marx and Lenin, Keynes, Trotsky, or Castoriadis.

When it comes to our editorial policy in this magazine, the absence of party discipline seems to have confused readers not accustomed to the idea. None of the articles in this paper reflect any party line. Each is a statement of the author's own views. We are not afraid to disagree in public or to publish material whose ideas we reject if we think that it raised important issues; we are not happy that it should be assumed that we all think the same, and that because we have published something we necessarily agree with all or indeed any of the points it makes. We have published a brief statement of our general views under the title *As We See It* but this is not intended to be our final word on the subject; rather, it is a means of clarifying our thought.

Finally, Solidarity is not just a magazine; it is also a grouping of activists. As such, we welcome co-operation with others and information about struggles with a positive socialist content.

SOLIDARITY, N.S., I, 4 (1984?)

40. ABOUT OURSELVES 4

Throughout the world, the vast majority of people have no control whatsoever over the decisions that most deeply and directly affect their lives. During the last century the living standards of working people have improved. But improved living standards, nationalization of the means of production, "national liberation", and the coming to power of parties claiming to represent the working class, have not basically altered the status of the worker as worker. East and West, capitalism remains an inhuman type of society where the vast majority are bossed at work and manipulated in consumption and leisure.

The trade unions and political parties cannot be reformed or converted into instruments of working class emancipation. The workers themselves should decide on the objectives of their struggles, and the control and organization of these struggles should remain firmly in their hands. The *forms* which this self-activity of the working class will take may vary considerably from country to country and from industry to industry; its basic *content* will not. Socialism is not just common ownership and distribution: it means equality, real freedom, the end of oppression based on restrictive male-female social roles, reciprocal recognition and a radical transformation of all human relationships. It is people's understanding of their environment and themselves, their domination over their work and such social institutions as they may need to create. These are not secondary aspects, which will automatically follow the expropriation of the old ruling class. On the contrary, they are essential parts of the whole process of social transformation, for without them no genuine social transformation will have taken place. A socialist society can therefore only be built from below. Genuine freedom will only be possible when our lives are no longer the object of economic, cultural and political forces which we experience as external to ourselves, and which constantly tend to regenerate capitalist or authoritarian social relations. A socialist society would therefore abolish not only social classes, hierarchies and other structures of domination, but also wage labour and production for the purpose of sale or exchange on the market.

SOLIDARITY, N.S., 1, 6-7 (SPRING 1985)

PARIS: MAY 1968

INTRODUCTION

This is an eyewitness account of two weeks spent in Paris during May 1968. It is what one person saw, heard or discovered during that short period. The account has no pretence at comprehensiveness. It has been written and produced in haste, its purpose being to inform rather than to analyze - and to inform quickly.

The French events have a significance that extends far beyond the frontiers of modern France. They will leave their mark on the history of the second half of the twentieth century. French bourgeois society has just been shaken to its foundations. Whatever the outcome of the present struggle, we must calmly take note of the fact that the political map of Western capitalist society will never be the same again. A whole epoch has just come to an end: the epoch during which people could say, with a semblance of verisimilitude, that "it couldn't happen here". Another epoch is starting: that in which people *know* that revolution is possible under the conditions of modern bureaucratic capitalism.

For Stalinism too, a whole period is ending: the period during which Communist Parties in Western Europe could claim (admittedly with dwindling credibility) that they remained revolutionary organizations, but that revolutionary opportunities had never really presented themselves. This notion has now irrevocably been swept into the proverbial "dustbin of history". When the chips were down, the French Communist Party and those workers under its influence proved to be the final and most effective "brake" on the development of the revolutionary self-activity of the working class.

A full analysis of the French events will eventually have to be attempted for, without an understanding of modern society, it will never be possible consciously to change it. But this analysis will have to wait for a while until some of the dust has settled. What can be said now is that, if honestly carried out, such an analysis will compel many "orthodox" revolutionaries to discard a mass of outdated slogans and myths and to reassess contemporary reality, particularly the reality of modern bureaucratic capitalism, its dynamic, its methods of control and manipulation, the reasons for both its resilience and its brittleness and - most important of all - the nature of its crises. Concepts and organizations that have been found wanting will have to be discarded. The new phenomena (new in themselves or new to traditional revolutionary theory) will have to be recognized for what they are and interpreted in all their implications. The *real* events of 1968 will then have to be integrated into a new framework of ideas, for without this *development* of revolutionary theory, there can be no *development* of revolutionary practice - and in the long run no transformation of society through the *conscious* actions of men.

RUE GAY-LUSSAC

Sunday, May 12.

The Rue Gay-Lussac still carries the scars of the "night of the barricades". Burnt-out cars line the pavement, their carcasses a dirty grey under the missing paint. The

223

cobbles, cleared from the middle of the road, lie in huge mounds on either side. A vague smell of tear gas still lingers in the air.

At the junction with the Rue des Ursulines lies a building site, its wire-mesh fence breached in several places. From here came material for at least a dozen barricades: planks, wheelbarrows, metal drums, steel girders, cement mixers, blocks of stone. The site also yielded a pneumatic drill. The students couldn't use it, of course - not until a passing building worker showed them how, perhaps the first worker actively to support the student revolt. Once broken, the road surface provided cobbles, soon put to a variety of uses.

All that is already history.

People are walking up and down the street, as if trying to convince themselves that it really happened. They aren't students. The students themselves know what happened and why it happened. They aren't local inhabitants either. The local inhabitants saw what happened, the viciousness of the CRS[163] charges, the assaults on the wounded, the attacks on innocent bystanders, the unleashed fury of the state machine against those who had challenged it. The people in the streets are the ordinary people of Paris, people from neighbouring districts, horrified at what they have heard over the radio or read in their papers and who have come for a walk on a fine Sunday morning to see for themselves. They are talking in small clusters with the inhabitants of the Rue Gay-Lussac. The Revolution, having for a week held the university and the streets of the Latin Quarter, is beginning to take hold of the minds of men.

On Friday, May 3rd, the CRS had paid their historic visit to the Sorbonne. They had been invited in by Paul Roche, Rector of Paris University. The Rector had almost certainly acted in connivance with Alain Peyrefitte, Minister of Education, if not with the Elysée itself. Many students had been arrested, beaten up, and several were summarily convicted.

The unbelievable - yet thoroughly predictable - ineptitude of this bureaucratic "solution" to the "problem" of student discontent triggered off a chain reaction. It provided the pent-up anger, resentment and frustration of tens of thousands of young people with both a reason for further action and with an attainable objective. The students, evicted from the university, took to the street, demanding the liberation of their comrades, the reopening of their faculties, the withdrawal of the cops.

Layer upon layer of new people were soon drawn into the struggle. The student union (UNEF) and the union representing university teaching staff (SNESup) called for an unlimited strike. For a week the students held their ground, in ever bigger and more militant street demonstrations. On Tuesday, May 7, 50,000 students and teachers marched through the streets behind a single banner, *"Vive La Commune"*, and sang the *Internationale* at the Tomb of the Unknown Soldier, at the Arc de Triomphe. On Friday, May 10, students and teachers decided to occupy the Latin Quarter en masse. They felt they had more right to be there than the police, for whom barracks were provided elsewhere. The cohesion and sense of purpose of the demonstrators terrified the Establishment. Power couldn't be allowed to lie with this rabble, who had even had the audacity to erect barricades.

Another inept gesture was needed. Another administrative reflex duly materialized. Fouchet (Minister of the Interior) and Joxe (Deputy Prime Minister) ordered Grimaud (Superintendent of the Paris police) to clear the streets. The order was con-

---

163   Compagnie Républicaine de Sécurité - the riot police.

firmed in writing, doubtless to be preserved for posterity as an example of what not to do in certain situations. The CRS charged...clearing the Rue Gay-Lussac and opening the doors to the second phase of the Revolution.

***

In the Rue Gay-Lussac and in adjoining streets, the battle-scarred walls carry a dual message. They bear testimony to the incredible courage of those who held the area for several hours against a deluge of tear gas, phosphorous grenades and repeated charges of club-swinging CRS. But they also show something of what the defenders were striving for...

Mural propaganda is an integral part of the revolutionary Paris of May 1968. It has become a mass activity, part and parcel of the Revolution's method of self-expression. The walls of the Latin Quarter are the depository of a new rationality, no longer confined to books, but democratically displayed at street level and made available to all. The trivial and the profound, the traditional and the esoteric, rub shoulders in this new fraternity, rapidly breaking down the rigid barriers and compartments in people's minds. *"Désobéir d'abord: alors écris sur les murs (Loi du 10 Mai 1968)"* reads an obviously recent inscription, clearly setting the tone. *"Si tout le peuple faisait comme nous"* (If everybody acted like us...) wistfully dreams another in joyful anticipation, I think, rather than in any spirit of self-satisfied substitutionism. Most of the slogans are straightforward, correct and fairly orthodox: *"Libérez nos camarades"*; *"Fouchet, Grimaud, démission"*; *"A bas l'Etat policier"*; *"Grève Générale Lundi"*; *"Travailleurs, Etudiants, solidaires"*; *"Vive les Conseils Ouvriers"*. Other slogans reflect the new concerns: *"La Publicité te manipule"*; *"Examens = Hiérarchie"*; *"L'art est mort, ne consommez pas son cadaver"*; *"A bas la société de consommation"*; *"Debout les damnés de Nanterre"*. The slogan, *"Baisses-toi et broute"* (Bend your head and chew the cud), was obviously aimed at those whose minds are still full of traditional preoccupations.

"Contre la fermentation groupusculaire" moans a large scarlet inscription. This one is really out of touch. For everywhere there is a profusion of pasted-up posters and journals: *Voix Ouvrière*, *Avant-Garde* and *Révoltes* (for the Trotskyists), *Servir le Peuple* and *Humanité Nouvelle* (for the devotees of Chairman Mao), *Le Libertaire* (for the Anarchists), *Tribune Socialiste* (for the PSU).[164] Even odd copies of *L'Humanité* are pasted up. It is difficult to read them, so covered are they with critical comments.

On a hoarding, I see a large advertisement for a new brand of cheese: a child biting into an enormous sandwich. *"C'est bon le fromage* So-and-So" runs the patter. Someone has covered the last few words with red paint. The poster reads *"C'est bon la Révolution"*. People pass by, look, and smile.

***

I talk to my companion, a man of about 45, an "old" revolutionary. We discuss the tremendous possibilities now opening up. He suddenly turns towards me and comes out with a memorable phrase: "To think one had to have kids and wait twenty years to see all this..." We talk to others in the street, to young and old, to the "political" and the "unpolitical", to people at all levels of understanding and commitment. Everyone is prepared to talk - in fact everyone wants to. They all seem remarkably articulate. We find no one prepared to defend the actions of the administration. The "critics" fall into two main groups.

---

164   Parti Socialiste Unifié – left–wing socialist party.

The "progressive" university teachers, the Communists, and a number of students see the main root of the student "crisis" in the backwardness of the university in relation to society's current needs, in the quantitative inadequacy of the tuition provided, in the semi-feudal attitudes of some professors, and in the general insufficiency of job opportunities. They see the university as unadapted to the modern world. The remedy for them is adaptation: a modernizing reform which would sweep away the cobwebs, provide more teachers, better lecture theatres, a bigger educational budget, perhaps a more liberal attitude on the campus and, at the end of it all, an assured job.

The rebels (which include some but by no means all of the "old" revolutionaries) see this concern with adapting the university to modern society as something of a diversion. For it is modern society itself which they reject. They consider bourgeois life trivial and mediocre, repressive and repressed. They have no yearning (but only contempt) for the administrative and managerial careers it holds out for them. They are not seeking integration into adult society. On the contrary, they are seeking a chance radically to contest its adulteration. The driving force of their revolt is their own alienation, the meaninglessness of life under modern bureaucratic capitalism. It is certainly not a purely economic deterioration in their standard of living.

It is no accident that the "revolution" started in the Nanterre faculties of Sociology and Psychology. The students saw that the sociology they were being taught was a means of controlling and manipulating society, not a means of understanding it in order to change it. In the process they discovered revolutionary sociology. They rejected the niche allocated to them in the great bureaucratic pyramid, that of "experts" in the service of a technocratic Establishment, specialists of the "human factor" in the modern industrial equation. In the process they discovered the importance of the working class. The amazing thing is that, at least among the active layers of the students, these "sectarians" suddenly seem to have become the majority: surely the best definition of any revolution.

The two types of "criticism" of the modern French educational system do not neutralize one another. On the contrary, each creates its own kind of problems for the university authorities and for the officials at the Ministry of Education. The real point is that one kind of criticism - what one might call the quantitative one - could in time be coped with by modern bourgeois society. The other - the qualitative one - never. This is what gives it its revolutionary potential. The "trouble with the university", for the powers that be, isn't that money can't be found for more teachers. It can. The "trouble" is that the university is full of students - and that the heads of the students are full of revolutionary ideas.

Among those we speak to there is a deep awareness that the problem cannot be solved in the Latin Quarter, that isolation of the revolt in a student "ghetto" (even an "autonomous" one) would spell defeat. They realize that the salvation of the movement lies in its extension to other sectors of the population. But here wide differences appear. When some talk of the importance of the working class it is as a substitute for getting on with any kind of struggle themselves, an excuse for denigrating the students' struggle as "adventurist". Yet it is precisely because of its unparalleled militancy that the students' action has established that direct action works, has begun to influence the younger workers and to rattle the established organizations. Other students realize the relationship of these struggles more clearly. We will find them later at Censier, animating the "worker-student" Action Committees. But enough, for the time being, about the Latin Quarter. The movement has already spread beyond its narrow confines.

MAY 13: FROM RENAULT TO THE STREETS OF PARIS

Monday, May 13. 6.15 am, Avenue Yves Kermen.
A clear, cloudless day. Crowds begin to gather outside the gates of the giant Renault works at Boulogne-Billancourt. The main trade union *centrales* (CGT, CFDT and FO) have called a one-day general strike. They are protesting against police violence in the Latin Quarter and in support of long-neglected claims concerning wages, hours, the age of retirement and trade-union rights in the plants.

The factory gates are wide open. Not a cop or supervisor in sight. The workers stream in. A loud-hailer tells them to proceed to their respective shops, to refuse to start work and to proceed, at 8.00 am, to their traditional meeting place, an enormous shed-like structure in the middle of the Ile Seguin (an island in the Seine entirely covered by parts of the Renault plant).

As each worker goes through the gates, the pickets give him a leaflet, jointly produced by the three unions. Leaflets in Spanish are also distributed (over 2,000 Spanish workers are employed at Renault). French and Spanish orators succeed one another, in short spells, at the microphone. Although all the unions are supporting the one-day strike, all the orators seem to belong to the CGT.[165] It's their loudspeaker…

6.45 am.
Hundreds of workers are now streaming in. Many look as if they had come to work rather than to participate in mass meetings at the plant. The decision to call the strike was only taken on the Saturday afternoon, after many of the men had already dispersed for the weekend. Many seem unaware of what it's all about. I am struck by the number of Algerian and black workers. There are only a few posters at the gate, again mainly those of the CGT. Some pickets carry CFDT[166] posters. There isn't an FO[167] poster in sight. The road and walls outside the factory have been well covered with slogans: "One-day strike on Monday"; "Unity in defence of our claims"; "No to the monopolies".

The little café near the gates is packed. People seem unusually wide-awake and communicative for so early an hour. A newspaper kiosk is selling about three copies of *L'Humanité* for every copy of anything else. The local branch of the Communist Party is distributing a leaflet calling for "resolution, calm, vigilance and unity" and warning against "provocateurs".

The pickets make no attempt to argue with those pouring in. No one seems to know whether they will obey the strike call or not. Less than 25 per cent of Renault workers belong to any union at all. This is the biggest car factory in Europe.

The loudhailer hammers home its message: "The CRS have recently assaulted peasants at Quimper, and workers at Caen, Rhodiaceta (Lyon) and Dassault. Now they are turning on the students. The regime will not tolerate opposition. It will not modernize the country. It will not grant us our basic wage demands. Our one-day

165 Confédération Générale du Travail – the Communist trade-union federation.

166 Confédération Française Démocratique du Travail – the Socialist trade-union federation.

167 Force Ouvrière – 'non-political' trade-union organization.

strike will show both Government and employers our determination. We must compel them to retreat." The message is repeated again and again, like a gramophone record. I wonder whether the speaker believes what he says, whether he even senses what lies ahead.

Text of CGT Poster, Placarded All over Boulogne-Billancourt

WORKERS BEWARE!

For some months the most diverse publications have been distributed by elements recruited in a milieu foreign to the working class.

The authors of these articles remain anonymous most of the time, a fact which fully illustrates their dishonesty. They give the most weird and tempting titles to their papers, the better to mislead: *Luttes Ouvrières*; *Servir le Peuple*; *Unité et Travail**; *Lutte Communiste*; *Révoltes*; *Voix Ouvrière*; *Un Group d'Ouvriers*.

The titles may vary but the content has a common objective: to lead the workers away from the CGT and to provoke divisions in their ranks, in order to weaken them.

At night, their commandos tear up our posters. Every time they distribute something at the gates, the police is not far off, ready to protect their distribution, as was the case recently at LMT. Recently they attempted to invade the offices of the Labour Exchange at Boulogne. Their activities are given an exaggerated publicity on the Gaullist radio and in the columns of the bourgeois press.

This warning is no doubt superfluous for the majority of Renault workers, who, in the past, have got to know about this kind of agitation. On the other hand the younger workers must be told that these elements are in the service of the bourgeoisie, who has always made use of these pseudo-revolutionaries whenever the rise of united left forces has presented a threat to its privileges.

It is therefore important not to allow these people to come to the gates of our factory, to sully our tradeunion organization and our CGT militants, who are tirelessly exerting themselves in defence of our demands and to bring about unity. These elements always reap a fat reward at the end of the day for their dirty work, and for the loyal services given to the bosses (some now occupy high positions in the mangagement of the factory).

This having been said, the CGT (Renault) Committee calls on the workers to continue the fight for their demands, to intensify their efforts to ensure greater unity of the trade union and democratic forces, and to strengthen the ranks of the CGT struggling for these noble objectives.

The Trade Union Bureau, CGT, Renault.

---
* This is a fascist publication. All the others are "left" publications. A typical amalgam technique.

At 7.00 am a dozen Trotskyists of the FER (Fédération des Etudiants Révolutionaires) turn up to sell their paper *Révoltes*. They wear large red and white buttons proclaiming their identity. A little later another group arrives to sell *Voix Ouvrière*. The loudspeaker immediately switches from an attack on the Gaullist government and its CRS to an attack on "provocateurs" and "disruptive elements, alien to the working class". The Stalinist speaker hints that the sellers are in the pay of the government. As they are here, "the police must be lurking in the neighbourhood". Heated arguments break out between sellers and CGT officials. The CFDT pickets are refused the use of the loudhailer. They shout *"démocratie ouvrière"* and defend the right of the "disruptive elements" to sell their stuff. A rather abstract right, as not a sheet is sold. The front page of *Revoltés* carries an esoteric article on Eastern Europe.

Much invective (but no blows) is exchanged. In the course of an argument I hear Bro. Trigon (delegate to the second electoral "college" at Renault) describe Danny Cohn-Bendit as *"un agent du pouvoir "* (an agent of the authorities). A student takes him up on this point. The Trots don't. Shortly before 8.00 am they walk off, their "act of presence" accomplished and duly recorded for history.

At about the same time, hundreds of workers who had entered the factory leave their shops and assemble in the sunshine in an open space a few hundred yards inside the main gate. From there they amble towards Ile Seguin, crossing one arm of the River Seine on the way. Other processions leave other points of the factory and converge on the same area. The metallic ceiling is nearly 200 feet above our heads. Enormous stocks of components are piled up right and left. Far away to the right an assembly line is still working, lifting what looks like rear car seats, complete with attached springs, from the ground to first floor level.

Some 10,000 workers are soon assembled in the shed. The orators address them through a loudspeaker from a narrow platform some forty feet up. The platform runs in front of what looks like an elevated inspection post but which I am told is a union office inside the factory.

The CGT speaker deals with various sectional wage claims. He denounces the resistance of the government "in the hands of the monopolies". He produces facts and figures dealing with the wage structure. Many highly skilled men are not getting enough. A CFDT speaker follows him. He deals with the steady speed-up, with the worsening of working conditions, with accidents and with the fate of man in production. "What kind of life is this? Are we always to remain puppets, carrying out every whim of the management?" He advocates uniform wage increases for all (*augmentations non-hiérarchisées*). An FO speaker follows. He is technically the most competent, but says the least. In flowery rhetoric he talks of 1936, but omits all reference to Léon Blum. The record of FO is bad in the factory and the speaker is heckled from time to time. The CGT speakers then ask the workers to participate en masse in the big rally planned for that afternoon. As the last speaker finishes, the crowd spontaneously breaks out into a rousing *Internationale*. The older men seem to know most of the words. The younger workers only know the chorus. A friend nearby assures me that in twenty years this is the first time he has heard the song sung inside Renault (he has attended dozens of mass meetings in the Ile Seguin). There is an atmosphere of excitement, particularly among the younger workers.

The crowd then breaks up into several sections. Some walk back over the bridge and out of the factory. Others proceed systematically through the shops where a few hundred blokes are still at work. Some of these men argue but most seem only too glad for an excuse to stop and join in the procession. Gangs weave their way, joking and singing, amid the giant presses and tanks. Those remaining at work are ironically cheered, clapped or exhaled to "step on it" or "work harder". Occasional foremen look on helplessly, as one assembly line after another is brought to a halt.

Many of the lathes have coloured pictures plastered over them: pin-ups and green fields, sex and sunshine. Anyone still working is exhorted to get out into the daylight, not just to dream about it. In the main plant, over half a mile long, hardly twelve men remain in their overalls. Not an angry voice can be heard. There is much good-humoured banter. By 11.00 am thousands of workers have poured out into the warmth of a morning in May. An open-air beer and sandwich stall, outside the gate, is doing a roaring trade.

Monday, May 13, 1.15 pm.
The streets are crowded. The response to the call for a 24-hour general strike has exceeded the wildest hopes of the trade unions. Despite the short notice Paris is paralyzed. The strike was only decided 48 hours ago, after the "night of the barricades". It is moreover "illegal". The law of the land demands a five-day notice before an "official" strike can be called. Too bad for legality. A solid phalanx of young people is walking up the Boulevard de Sébastopol, towards the Gare de l'Est. They are proceeding to the student rallying point for the giant demonstration called jointly by the unions, the students' organization (UNEF) and the teachers' associations (FEN and SNESup).

There is not a bus or car in sight. The streets of Paris today belong to the demonstrators. Thousands of them are already in the square in front of the station. Thousands more are moving in from every direction. The plan agreed by the sponsoring organizations is for the different categories to assemble separately and then to converge on the Place de la République, from where the march will proceed across Paris, via the Latin Quarter: to the Place Denfert-Rochereau. We are already packed like sardines for as far as the eye can see, yet there is more than an hour to go before we are due to proceed. The sun has been shining all day. The girls are in summer dresses, the young men in shirtsleeves. A red flag is flying over the railway station. There are many red flags in the crowd and several black ones too.

A man suddenly appears carrying a suitcase full of duplicated leaflets. He belongs to some left *groupuscule* or other. He opens his suitcase and distributes perhaps a dozen leaflets. But he doesn't have to continue alone. There is an unquenchable thirst for information, ideas, literature, argument, polemic. The man just stands there as people surround him and press forward to get the leaflets. Dozens of demonstrators, without even reading the leaflet, help him distribute them. Some 6,000 copies get out in a few minutes. All seem to be assiduously read. People argue, laugh, joke. I witnessed such scenes again and again.

Sellers of revolutionary literature are doing well. An edict, signed by the organizers of the demonstration, that "the only literature allowed would be that of the organizations sponsoring the demonstration" (*L'Humanité*, 13 May 1968) is being enthusiastically flouted. This bureaucratic restriction (much criticized the previous evening when announced at Censier by the student delegates to the Coordinating Committee) obviously cannot be enforced in a crowd of this size. The Revolution is bigger than any organization, more tolerant than any institution "representing" the masses, more realistic than any edict of any Central Committee.

Demonstrators have climbed on to walls, on to the roofs of bus stops, on to the railings in front of the station. Some have loudhailers and make short speeches. All the "politicos" seem to be in one part or other of this crowd. I can see the banner of the Jeunesse Communiste Révolutionnaire, portraits of Castro and Che Guevara, the banner of the FER, several banners of Servir le Peuple (a Maoist group) and the banner of the UJCML (Union de la Jeunesse Communiste Marxiste-Léniniste), another Maoist tendency. There are also banners from many educational establishments now occupied by those who work there. Large groups of *lycéens* (high school kids) mingle with the students as do many thousands of teachers.

At about 2.00 pm the student section sets off, singing the *Internationale*. We march twenty to thirty abreast, arms linked. There is a row of red flags in front of us, then a banner fifty feet wide carrying four simple words: *"Etudiants, Enseignants, Travailleurs, Solidaires"*. It is an impressive sight.

The whole Boulevard de Magenta is a solid seething mass of humanity. We can't enter the Place de la République, already packed full of demonstrators. One can't even move along the pavements or through adjacent streets. Nothing but people, as far as the eye can see.

As we proceed slowly down the Boulevard de Magenta, we notice on a third-floor balcony, high on our right, an SFIO (Socialist Party) headquarters. The balcony is bedecked with a few decrepit-looking red flags and a banner proclaiming "Solidarity with the Students". A few elderly characters wave at us, somewhat self-consciously. Someone in the crowd starts chanting *"O-por-tu-nistes"*. The slogan is taken up, rhythmically roared by thousands, to the discomfiture of those on the balcony who beat a hasty retreat. The people have not forgotten the use of the CRS against the striking miners in 1958 by "socialist" Minister of the Interior Jules Moch. They remember the "socialist" Prime Minister Guy Mollet and his role during the Algerian War. Mercilessly, the crowd shows its contempt for the discredited politicians now seeking to jump on the bandwagon. *"Guy Mollet, au musée"*, they shout, amid laughter. It is truly the end of an epoch.

At about 3.00 pm we at last reach the Place de la République, our point of departure. The crowd here is so dense that several people faint and have to be carried into neighbouring cafés. Here people are packed almost as tight as in the street, but can at least avoid being injured. The window of one café gives way under the pressure of the crowd outside. There is a genuine fear, in several parts of the crowd, of being crushed to death. The first union contingents fortunately begin to leave the square. There isn't a policeman in sight.

Although the demonstration has been announced as a joint one, the CGT leaders are still striving desperately to avoid a mixing-up, on the streets, of students and workers. In this they are moderately successful. By about 4.30 pm the students' and teachers' contingent, perhaps 80,000 strong, finally leaves the Place de la République. Hundreds of thousands of demonstrators have preceded it, hundreds of thousands follow it, but the "left" contingent has been well and truly "bottled-in". Several groups, understanding at last the CGT's manoeuvre, break loose once we are out of the square. They take short cuts via various side streets, at the double, and succeed in infiltrating groups of a hundred or so into parts of the march ahead of them or behind them. The Stalinist stewards walking hand in hand and hemming the march in on either side are powerless to prevent these sudden influxes. The student demonstrators scatter like fish in water as soon as they have entered a given contingent. The CGT marchers themselves are quite friendly and readily assimilate the newcomers, not quite sure what it's all about. The students' appearance, dress and speech do not enable them to be identified as readily as they would be in Britain.

The main student contingent proceeds as a compact body. Now that we are past the bottleneck of the Place de la République the pace is quite rapid. The student group nevertheless takes at least half an hour to pass a given point. The slogans of the students contrast strikingly with those of the CGT. The students shout *"Le Pouvoir aux Ouvriers"* (All Power to the Workers); *"Le Pouvoir est dans la rue"* (Power lies in the street); *"Libérez nos camarades"*. CGT members shout *"Pompidou, démission"* (Pompidou, resign). The students chant *"De Gaulle, assassin"*, or *"CRS-SS"*. The CGT: *"Des sous, pas de matraques"* (Money, not police clubs) or *"Défense du pouvoir d'achat"* (Defend our purchasing power). The students say *"Non à l'Université de classe"*. The CGT and the Stalinist students, grouped around the banner of their paper *Clarté* reply *"Université Démocratique"*. Deep political differences lie behind the differences of emphasis. Some slogans are taken up by everyone, slogans such as *"Dix ans, c'est assez"*, *"A bas l'Etat policier"*, or *"Bon anniversaire, mon Général"*. Whole groups mournfully intone a well-known refrain: *"Adieu, de Gaulle"*. They wave their handkerchiefs, to the great merriment of the bystanders.

As the main student contingent crosses the Pont St.-Michel to enter the Latin Quarter it suddenly stops, in silent tribute to its wounded. All thoughts are for a moment switched to those lying in hospital, their sight in danger through too much tear gas or their skulls or ribs fractured by the truncheons of the CRS. The sudden, angry silence of this noisiest part of the demonstration conveys a deep impression of strength and resolution. One senses massive accounts yet to be settled.

At the top of the Boulevard St.-Michel I drop out of the march, climb on to a parapet lining the Luxembourg Gardens, and just watch. I remain there for two hours as row after row of demonstrators marches past, thirty or more abreast, a human tidal wave of fantastic, inconceivable size. How many are they? 600,000? 800,000? A million? 1,500,000? No one can really number them. The first of the demonstrators reached the final dispersal point hours before the last ranks had left the Place de la République, at 7.00 pm.

There were banners of every kind: union banners, student banners, political banners, non-political banners, reformist banners, revolutionary banners, banners of the Mouvement contre Armement Atomique, banners of various Conseils de Parents d'Elèves, banners of every conceivable size and shape, proclaiming a common abhorrence at what had happened and a common will to struggle on. Some banners were notedly applauded, such as the one saying *"Libérons l'information"* (Let's have a free news service) carried by a group of employees from the ORTF. Some banners indulged in vivid symbolism, such as the gruesome one carried by a group of artists, depicting human hands, heads and eyes, each with its price tag, on display on the hooks and trays of a butcher's shop.

Endlessly they filed past. There were whole sections of hospital personnel, in white coats, some carrying posters saying *"Où sont les disparus des hopitaux?"* (Where are the missing injured?). Every factory, every major workplace seemed to be represented. There were numerous groups of railwaymen, postmen, printers, Metro personnel, metal workers, airport workers, market men, electricians, lawyers, sewermen, bank employees, building workers, glass and chemical workers, waiters, municipal employees, painters and decorators, gas workers, shop girls, insurance clerks, road sweepers, film studio operators, busmen, teachers, workers from the new plastic industries, row upon row upon row of them, the flesh and blood of modern capitalist society, an unending mass, a power that could sweep *everything* before it, if it but decided to do so.

My thoughts went to those who say that the workers are only interested in football, in the *tiercé* (horse-betting), in watching the telly, in their annual *congés* (holidays), and that the working class cannot see beyond the problems of its everyday life. It was so palpably untrue. I also thought of those who say that only a narrow and rotten leadership lies between the masses and the total transformation of society. It was equally untrue. Today the working class is becoming conscious of its strength. Will it decide, tomorrow, to use it?

I rejoin the march and we proceed towards Denfert-Rochereau. We pass several statues, sedate gentlemen now bedecked with red flags or carrying slogans such as *"Libérez nos camarades"*. As we pass a hospital silence again descends on the endless crowd. Someone starts whistling the *Internationale*. Others take it up. Like a breeze rustling over an enormous field of corn, the whistled tune ripples out in all directions. From the windows of the hospital some nurses wave at us.

At various intersections we pass traffic lights which by some strange inertia still seem to be working. Red and green alternate, at fixed intervals, meaning as little as bourgeois education, as work in modern society, as the lives of those walking past. The reality of today, for a few hours, has submerged all of yesterday's patterns.

The part of the march in which I find myself is now rapidly approaching what the organizers have decided should be the dispersal point. The CGT is desperately keen that its hundreds of thousands of supporters should disperse quietly. It fears them, when they are together. It wants them nameless atoms again, scattered to the four corners of Paris, powerless in the context of their individual preoccupations. The CGT sees itself as the only possible link between them, as the divinely ordained vehicle for the expression of their collective will. The Mouvement du 22 Mars, on the other hand, had issued a call to the students and workers, asking them to stick together and to proceed to the lawns of the Champ de Mars (at the foot of the Eiffel Tower) for a massive collective discussion on the experiences of the day and on the problems that lie ahead.

At this stage I sample for the first time what a *service d'ordre* composed of Stalinist stewards really means. All day, the stewards have obviously been anticipating this particular moment. They are very tense, clearly expecting "trouble". Above all else they fear what they call *débordement*, i.e. being outflanked on the left. For the last half-mile of the march five or six solid rows of them line up on either side of the demonstrators. Arms linked, they form a massive sheath around the marchers. CGT officials address the bottled-up demonstrators through two powerful loudspeakers mounted on vans, instructing them to disperse quietly via the Boulevard Arago, i.e. to proceed in precisely the opposite direction to the one leading to the Champ de Mars. Other exits from the Place Denfert-Rochereau are blocked by lines of stewards linking arms.

On occasions like this, I am told, the Communist Party calls up thousands of its members from the Paris area. It also summons members from miles around, bringing them up by the coachload from places as far away as Rennes, Orléans, Sens, Lille and Limoges. The municipalities under Communist Party control provide further hundreds of these "stewards", not necessarily Party members but people dependent on the goodwill of the Party for their jobs and future. Ever since its heyday of participation in the government (1945-47) the Party has had this kind of mass base in the Paris suburbs. It has invariably used it in circumstances like today. On this demonstration there must be at least 10,000 such stewards, possibly twice that number.

The exhortations of the stewards meet with a variable response. Whether they are successful in getting particular groups to disperse via the Boulevard Arago depends of course on the composition of the groups. Most of those which the students have not succeeded in infiltrating obey, although even here some of the younger militants protest: "We are a million in the streets. Why should we go home?" Other groups hesitate, vacillate, start arguing. Student speakers climb on walls and shout: "All those who want to return to the telly, turn down the Boulevard Arago. Those who are for joint worker-student discussions and for developing the struggle, turn down the Boulevard Raspail and proceed to the Champ de Mars".

Those protesting against the dispersion orders are immediately jumped on by the stewards, denounced as "provocateurs" and often manhandled. I saw several comrades of the Mouvement du 22 Mars physically assaulted, their portable loud-hailers snatched from their hands and their leaflets torn from them and thrown to the ground. In some sections there seemed to be dozens, in others hundreds, in others thousands of "provocateurs". A number of minor punch-ups take place as the stewards are swept aside by these particular contingents. Heated arguments break out, the demonstrators denouncing the Stalinists as "cops" and as "the last rampart of the bourgeoisie".

A respect for facts compels me to admit that most contingents followed the orders of the trade-union bureaucrats. The repeated slanders by the CGT and Communist Party leaders had had their effect. The students were "trouble-makers", "adventurers", "dubious elements". Their proposed action would only lead to a massive intervention by the CRS (who had kept well out of sight throughout the whole of the afternoon). "This was just a demonstration, not a prelude to Revolution". Playing ruthlessly on the most backward sections of the crowd, and physically assaulting the more advanced sections, the apparatchiks of the CGT succeeded in getting the bulk of the demonstrators to disperse, often under protest. Thousands went to the Champ de Mars. But hundreds of thousands went home. The Stalinists won the day, but the arguments started will surely reverberate down the months to come.

At about 8.00 pm an episode took place which changed the temper of the last sections of the march, now approaching the dispersal point. A police van suddenly came up one of the streets leading into the Place Denfert-Rochereau. It must have strayed from its intended route, or perhaps its driver had assumed that the demonstrators had already dispersed. Seeing the crowd ahead the two uniformed gendarmes in the front seat panicked. Unable to reverse in time in order to retreat, the driver decided that his life hinged on forcing a passage through the thinnest section of the crowd. The vehicle accelerated, hurling itself into the demonstrators at about fifty miles an hour. People scattered wildly in all directions. Several people were knocked down and two were seriously injured. Many more narrowly escaped. The van was finally surrounded. One of the policemen in the front seat was dragged out and repeatedly punched by the infuriated crowd, determined to lynch him. He was finally rescued in the nick of time, by the stewards. They more or less carried him, semi-conscious, down a side street where he was passed horizontally, like a battered blood sausage, through an open ground-floor window.

To do this, the stewards had had to engage in a running fight with several hundred very angry marchers. The crowd then started rocking the stranded police van. The remaining policeman drew his revolver and fired. People ducked. By a miracle no one was hit. A hundred yards away the bullet made a hole, about three feet above ground level, in a window of Le Belfort, a big café at 297 Boulevard Raspail. The stewards again rushed to the rescue, forming a barrier between the crowd and the police van, which was allowed to escape down a side street, driven by the policeman who had fired at the crowd.

Hundreds of demonstrators then thronged round the hole in the window of the café. Press photographers were summoned, arrived, duly took their close-ups - none of which, of course, were ever published. (Two days later *L'Humanité* carried a few lines about the episode, at the bottom of a column on page 5.) One effect of the episode is that several thousand more demonstrators decided not to disperse. They turned and marched down towards the Champ de Mars, shouting *"Ils ont tiré à Denfert"* (They've shot at us at Denfert). If the incident had taken place an hour earlier, the evening of 13 May might have had a very different complexion.

THE SORBONNE "SOVIET"

On Saturday, May 11, shortly before midnight, M. Pompidou, Prime Minister of France, overruled his Minister of the Interior, his Minister of Education, and issued orders to his "independent" judiciary. He announced that the police would be withdrawn from the Latin Quarter, that the faculties would reopen on Monday, May 13, and that the law would "reconsider" the question of the students arrested the previous week. It was the biggest political climb-down of his career. For the students, and for many others, it was the living proof that direct action worked. Concessions had been won through struggle which had been unobtainable by other means.

Early on the Monday morning the CRS platoons guarding the entrance to the Sorbonne were discreetly withdrawn. The students moved in, first in small groups, then in hundreds, later in thousands. By midday the occupation was complete. Every *tricolore* was promptly hauled down, every lecture theatre occupied. Red flags were hoisted from the official flagpoles and from improvised ones at many windows, some overlooking the streets, others the big internal courtyard. Hundreds of feet above the milling students, enormous red and black flags fluttered side by side from the chapel dome.

What happened over the next few days will leave a permanent mark on the French educational system, on the structure of French society and - most important of all - on the minds of those who lived and made history during that hectic first fortnight. The Sorbonne was suddenly transformed from the fusty precinct where French capitalism selected and moulded its hierarchs, its technocrats and its administrative bureaucracy into a revolutionary volcano in full eruption whose lava was to spread far and wide, searing the social structure of modern France.

The physical occupation of the Sorbonne was followed by an intellectual explosion of unprecedented violence. Everything, literally everything, was suddenly and simultaneously up for discussion, for question, for challenge. There were no taboos. It is easy to criticize the chaotic upsurge of thoughts, ideas and proposals unleashed in such circumstances. "Professional revolutionaries" and petty bourgeois philistines criticized to their heart's content. But in so doing they only revealed how they themselves were trapped in the ideology of a previous epoch and were incapable of transcending it. They failed to recognize the tremendous significance of the new, of all that could not be apprehended within their own pre-established intellectual categories. The phenomenon was witnessed again and again, as it doubtless has been in every really great upheaval in history.

Day and night, every lecture theatre was packed out, the seat of continuous, passionate debate on every subject that ever preoccupied thinking humanity. No formal lecturer ever enjoyed so massive an audience, was ever listened to with such rapt attention - or given such short shrift if he talked nonsense.

A kind of order rapidly prevailed. By the second day a noticeboard had appeared near the front entrance announcing what was being talked about, and where. I noted: "Organization of the struggle"; "Political and trade union rights in the University"; "University crisis or social crisis?"; "Dossier of police repression"; "Self-management"; "Non-selection" (or how to open the doors of the University to everyone); "Methods of teaching"; "Exams"; etc. Other lecture theatres were given over to the Students-Workers Liaison Committees, soon to assume great importance. In yet other halls, discussions were under way on "sexual repression", on "the colonial question", on "ideology and mystification". Any group of people wishing to discuss anything under the sun would just take over one of the lecture theatres or smaller rooms. Fortunately there were dozens of these.

The first impression was of a gigantic lid suddenly lifted, of pent-up thoughts and aspirations suddenly exploding, on being released from the realm of dreams into the realm of the real and the possible. In changing their environment people themselves were changed. Those who had never dared say anything suddenly felt their thoughts to be the most important thing in the world and said so. The shy became communicative. The helpless and isolated suddenly discovered that collective power lay in their hands. The traditionally apathetic suddenly realized the intensity of their involvement. A tremendous surge of community and cohesion gripped those who had previously seen themselves as isolated and impotent puppets, dominated by institutions that they could neither control nor understand. People just went up and talked to one another without a trace of self-consciousness. This state of euphoria lasted throughout the whole fortnight I was there. An inscription scrawled on a wall sums it up perfectly: *"Déjà dix jours de bonheur"* (Ten days of happiness already).

In the yard of the Sorbonne, politics (frowned on for a generation) took over with a vengeance. Literature stalls sprouted up along the whole inner perimeter. Enormous portraits appeared on the internal walls: Marx, Lenin, Trotsky, Mao, Castro, Guevara, a revolutionary resurrection breaking the bounds of time and place. Even Stalin put in a transient appearance (above a Maoist stall) until it was tactfully suggested to the comrades that he wasn't really at home in such company.

On the stalls themselves every kind of literature suddenly blossomed forth in the summer sunshine: leaflets and pamphlets by anarchists, Stalinists, Maoists, Trotskyists (three varieties), the PSU and the non-committed. The yard of the Sorbonne had become a gigantic revolutionary drug-store, in which the most esoteric products no longer had to be kept beneath the counter but could now be prominently displayed. Old issues of journals, yellowed by the years, were unearthed and often sold as well as more recent material. Everywhere there were groups of ten or twenty people, in heated discussion, people talking about the barricades, about the CRS, about their own experiences, but also about the Commune of 1871, about 1905 and 1917, about the Italian left in 1921 and about France in 1936. A fusion was taking place between the consciousness of the revolutionary minorities and the consciousness of whole new layers of people, dragged day by day into the maelstrom of political controversy. The students were learning within days what it had taken others a lifetime to learn. Many *lycéens* came to see what it was all about. They too got sucked into the vortex. I remember a boy of fourteen explaining to an incredulous man of sixty why students should have the right to depose professors.

Other things also happened. A large piano suddenly appeared in the great central yard and remained there for several days. People would come and play on it, surrounded by enthusiastic supporters. As people talked in the lecture theatres of neo-capitalism and of its techniques of manipulation, strands of Chopin and bars of jazz, bits of *La Carmagnole* and atonal compositions wafted through the air. One evening there was a drum recital, then some clarinet players took over. These "diversions" may have infuriated some of the more single-minded revolutionaries, but they were as much part and parcel of the total transformation of the Sorbonne as were the revolutionary doctrines being proclaimed in the lecture halls.

An exhibition of huge photographs of the "night of the barricades" (in beautiful half-tones) appeared one morning, mounted on stands. No one knew who had put it up. Everyone agreed that it succinctly summarized the horror and glamour, the anger and promise of that fateful night. Even the doors of the chapel giving on to the yard were soon covered with inscriptions. "Open this door - *Finis, le tabernacles*". "Religion is the last mystification". Or more prosaically: "We want somewhere to piss, not somewhere to pray".

The massive outer walls of the Sorbonne were likewise soon plastered with posters - posters announcing the first sit-in strikes, posters describing the wage rates of whole sections of Paris workers, posters announcing the next demonstrations, posters describing the solidarity marches in Peking, posters denouncing the police repression and the use of CS gas (as well as of ordinary tear-gas) against the demonstrators. There were posters, dozens of them, warning students against the Communist Party's bandwagon jumping tactics, telling them how it had attacked their movement and how it was now seeking to assume its leadership. Political posters in plenty. But also others, proclaiming the new ethos. A big one for instance near the main entrance, boldly proclaimed *"Défense d'interdire"* (Forbidding forbidden). And others, equally to the point: "Only the truth is revolutionary"; "Our revolution is greater than ourselves"; "We refuse the role assigned to us, we will not be trained as police dogs". People's concerns varied but converged. The posters reflected the deeply libertarian prevailing philosophy. "Humanity will only be happy when the last capitalist has been strangled with the guts of the last bureaucrat". "Culture is disintegrating. Create!" "I take my wishes for reality for I believe in the reality of my wishes". Or more simply: "Creativity, spontaneity, life".

In the street outside, hundreds of passers-by would stop to read these improvised wall-newspapers. Some gaped. Some sniggered. Some nodded assent. Some argued. Some, summoning their courage, actually entered the erstwhile sacrosanct premises, as they were being exhorted to by numerous posters proclaiming that the Sorbonne was now open to all. Young workers who "wouldn't have been seen in that place" a month ago now walked in groups, at first rather self-consciously, later as if they owned the place, which of course they did.

As the days went by, another kind of invasion took place: the invasion by the cynical and the unbelieving, or - more charitably - by those who "had only come to see". It gradually gained momentum. At certain stages it threatened to paralyze the serious work being done, part of which had to be hived off to the Faculty of Letters, at Censier, also occupied by the students. It was felt necessary, however, for the doors to be kept open, 24 hours a day. The message certainly spread. Deputations came first from other universities, then from high schools, later from factories and offices, to look, to question, to argue, to study.

The most telling sign, however, of the new and heady climate was to be found on the walls of the Sorbonne corridors. Around the main lecture theatres there is a maze of such corridors: dark, dusty, depressing, and hitherto unnoticed passage-ways leading from nowhere in particular to nowhere else. Suddenly these corridors sprang to life in a firework of luminous mural wisdom – much of it of Situationist inspiration. Hundreds of people suddenly stopped to read such pearls as: "Do not consume Marx. Live it". "The future will only contain what we put into it now". "When examined, we will answer with questions". "Professors, you make us feel old". "One doesn't compose with a society in decomposition". "We must remain the maladjust-ed ones". "Workers of all lands, enjoy yourselves". "Those who carry out a revolution only halfway through merely dig themselves a tomb (St. Just)". "Please leave the PC (Communist Party) as clean on leaving as you would like to find it on entering ". "The tears of the philistines are the nectar of the gods". "Go and die in Naples, with the Club Mediterranée". "Long live communication, down with telecommunication". "Masochism today dresses up as reformism". "We will claim nothing. We will ask for nothing. We will take. We will occupy". "The only outrage to the Tomb of the Unknown Soldier was the outrage that put him there". "No, we won't be picked up by the Great Party of the Working Class". And a big inscription, well displayed: "Since 1936 I have fought for wage increases. My father, before me, also fought for wage increases. Now I have a telly, a fridge, a Volkswagen. Yet all in all, my life has always been a cunt's life. Don't discuss with the bosses. Eliminate them".

Day after day the courtyard and corridors are crammed, the scene of an inces-sant bi-directional flow to every conceivable part of the enormous building. It may look like chaos, but it is the chaos of a beehive or of an anthill. A new structure is gradually being evolved. A canteen has been organized in one big hall, people pay what they can afford for glasses of orange juice, *menthe*, or *grenadine* – and for ham or sausage rolls. I inquire whether costs are covered and am told they more or less break even. In another part of the building a children's crèche has been set up, else-where a first-aid station, elsewhere a dormitory. Regular sweeping-up rotas are organized. Rooms are allocated to the Occupation Committee, to the Press Committee, to the Propaganda Committee, to the Student-Worker Liaison Committees, to the committees dealing with foreign students, to the Action Committees of *Lycéens*, to the committees dealing with the allocation of premises, and to the numerous commissions undertaking special projects such as the compil-ing of a dossier on police atrocities, the study of the implications of autonomy, of the examination system, etc. Anyone seeking work can readily find it.

The composition of the committees was very variable. It often changed from day to day, as the committees gradually found their feet. To those who pressed for instant solutions to every problem it would be answered: "Patience, comrade. Give us a chance to evolve an alternative. The bourgeoisie has controlled this university for nearly two centuries. It has solved nothing. We are building from rock bottom. We need a month or two…"

Confronted with this tremendous explosion which it had neither foreseen nor been able to control the Communist Party tried desperately to salvage what it could of its shattered reputation. Between May 3rd and May 13th every issue of *L'Humanité* had carried paragraphs either attacking the students or making slimy innuendoes about them. Now the line suddenly changed.

The Party sent dozens of its best agitators into the Sorbonne to "explain" its case. The case was a simple one. The Party "supported the students" – even if there were a few "dubious elements" in their leadership. It "always had". It always would.

Amazing scenes followed. Every Stalinist "agitator" would immediately be surrounded by a large group of well-informed young people, denouncing the Party's counter-revolutionary role. A wall paper had been put up by the comrades of *Voix Ouvrière* on which had been posted, day by day, every statement attacking the students to have appeared in *L'Humanité* or in any of a dozen Party leaflets. The "agitators" couldn't get a word in edgeways. They would be jumped on (non-violently). "The evidence was over there, comrade. Would the Party comrades like to come and read just exactly what the Party had been saying not a week ago? Perhaps *L'Humanité* would like to grant the students space to reply to some of the accusations made against them?" Others in the audience would then bring up the Party's role during the Algerian War, during the miners' strike of 1958, during the years of *tripartisme* (1945–1947). Wriggle as they tried, the "agitators" just could not escape this kind of "instant education". It was interesting to note that the Party could not entrust this "salvaging" operation to its younger, student members. Only the "older comrades" could safely venture into this hornets' nest. So much so that people would say that anyone in the Sorbonne over the age of forty was either a copper's nark or a Stalinist stooge.

The most dramatic periods of the occupation were undoubtedly the *Assemblées Générales*, or plenary sessions, held every night in the giant amphitheatre. This was the soviet, the ultimate source of all decisions, the fount and origin of direct democracy. The amphitheatre could seat up to 5,000 people in its enormous hemicycle, surmounted by three balcony tiers. As often as not every seat was taken and the crowd would flow up the aisles and on to the podium. A black flag and a red one hung over the simple wooden table at which the chairman sat. Having seen meetings of fifty break up in chaos it is an amazing experience to see a meeting of 5,000 get down to business. Real events determined the themes and ensured that most of the talk was down to earth.

The topic having been decided, everyone was allowed to speak. Most speeches were made from the podium but some from the body of the hall or from the balconies. The loudspeaker equipment usually worked but sometimes didn't. Some speakers could command immediate attention, without even raising their voice. Others would instantly provoke a hostile response by the stridency of their tone, their insincerity or their more or less obvious attempts at manoeuvring the assembly. Anyone who waffled, or reminisced, or came to recite a set-piece, or talked in terms of slogans, was given short shrift by the audience, politically the most sophisticated I have ever seen. Anyone making practical suggestions was listened to attentively. So were those who sought to interpret the movement in terms of its own experience or to point the way ahead.

Most speakers were granted three minutes. Some were allowed much more by popular acclaim. The crowd itself exerted a tremendous control on the platform and on the speakers. A two-way relationship emerged very quickly. The political maturity of the Assembly was shown most strikingly in its rapid realization that booing or cheering during speeches slowed down the Assembly's own deliberations. Positive speeches were loudly cheered – at the end. Demagogic or useless ones were impatiently swept aside. Conscious revolutionary minorities played an important catalytic role in these deliberations, but never sought – at least the more intelligent ones – to impose their will on the mass body. Although in the early stages the Assembly had its fair share of exhibitionists, provocateurs and nuts, the overhead costs of direct democracy were not as heavy as one might have expected.

There were moments of excitement and moments of exhortation. On the night of May 13th, after the massive march through the streets of Paris, Daniel Cohn-Bendit confronted J. M. Catala, general secretary of the Union of Communist Students, in front of the packed auditorium. The scene remains printed in my mind.

"Explain to us", Cohn-Bendit said, "why the Communist Party and the CGT told their militants to disperse at Denfert-Rochereau, why it prevented them joining up with us for a discussion at the Champ de Mars?"

"Simple, really", sneered Catala. "The agreement concluded between the CGT, the CFDT, the UNEF and the other sponsoring organizations stipulated that dispersal would take place at a predetermined place. The Joint Sponsoring Committee had not sanctioned any further developments…"

"A revealing answer", replied Cohn-Bendit, "the organizations hadn't foreseen that we would be a million in the streets. But life is bigger than the organizations. With a million people almost anything is possible. You say the Committee hadn't sanctioned anything further. On the day of the Revolution, comrade, you will doubtless tell us to forego it 'because it hasn't been sanctioned by the appropriate sponsoring committee'…"

This brought the house down. The only ones who didn't rise to cheer were a few dozen Stalinists. Also, revealingly, those Trotskyists who tacitly accepted the Stalinist conceptions – and whose only quarrel with the CP is that it had excluded them from being one of the "sponsoring organizations".

That same night the Assembly took three important decisions. From now on the Sorbonne would constitute itself as a revolutionary headquarters ("Smolny", someone shouted). Those who worked there would devote their main efforts not to a mere reorganization of the educational system, but to a total subversion of bourgeois society. From now on the University would be open to all those who subscribed to these aims. The proposals having been accepted the audience rose to a man and sang the loudest, most impassioned *Internationale* I have ever heard. The echoes must have reverberated as far as the Elysée Palace on the other side of the River Seine…

THE CENSIER REVOLUTIONARIES

At the same time as the students occupied the Sorbonne, they also took over the Centre Censier (the new Paris University Faculty of Letters).

Censier is an enormous, ultra-modern, steel-concrete-and-glass affair situated at the south-east corner of the Latin Quarter. Its occupation attracted less attention than did that of the Sorbonne. It was to prove, however, just as significant an event. For while the Sorbonne was the shop window of revolutionary Paris – with all that that implies in terms of garish display – Censier was its dynamo, the place where things really got done.

To many, the Paris May Days must have been an essentially nocturnal affair: nocturnal battles with the CRS, nocturnal barricades, nocturnal debates in the great amphitheatres. But this was but one side of the coin. While some argued late into the Sorbonne night, others went to bed early for in the mornings they would be hand-ing out leaflets at factory gates or in the suburbs, leaflets that had to be drafted, typed, duplicated, and the distribution of which had to be carefully organized. This patient, systematic work was done at Censier. It contributed in no small measure to giving the new revolutionary consciousness articulate expression.

Soon after Censier had been occupied a group of activists commandeered a large part of the third floor. This space was to be the headquarters of their proposed "worker–student action committees". The general idea was to establish links with groups of workers, however small, who shared the general libertarian-revolutionary outlook of this group of students. Contact having been made, workers and students would cooperate in the joint drafting of leaflets. The leaflets would discuss the immediate problems of particular groups of workers, but in the light of what the students had shown to be possible. A given leaflet would then be jointly distributed by workers and students, outside the particular factory or office to which it referred. In some instances the distribution would have to be undertaken by students alone, in others hardly a single student would be needed.

What brought the Censier comrades together was a deeply felt sense of the revolutionary potentialities of the situation and the knowledge that they had no time to waste. They all felt the pressing need for direct action propaganda, and that the urgency of the situation required of them that they transcend any doctrinal differences they might have with one another. They were all intensely political people. By and large, their politics were those of that new and increasingly important historical species: the ex-members of one or other revolutionary organization.

What were their views? Basically they boiled down to a few simple propositions. What was needed just now was a rapid, autonomous development of the working-class struggle, the setting up of elected strike committees which would link union and non-union members in all strike-bound plants and enterprises, regular meetings of the strikers so that the fundamental decisions remained in the hands of the rank and file, workers' defence committees to defend pickets from police intimidation, a constant dialogue with the revolutionary students aimed at restoring to the working class its own tradition of direct democracy and its own aspiration to self-management (*autogestion*), usurped by the bureaucracies of the trade unions and the political parties.

For a whole week the various Trotskyist and Maoist factions didn't even notice what was going on at Censier. They spent their time in public and often acrimonious debates at the Sorbonne as to who could provide the best leadership. Meanwhile, the comrades at Censier were steadily getting on with the work. The majority of them had "been through" either Stalinist or Trotskyist organizations. They had left behind them all ideas to the effect that "intervention" was meaningful only in terms of potential recruitment to their own particular group. All recognized the need for a widely-based and moderately structured revolutionary movement, but none of them saw the building of such a movement as an immediate, all important task, on which propaganda should immediately be centred.

Duplicators belonging to "subversive elements" were brought in. University duplicators were commandeered. Stocks of paper and ink were obtained from various sources and by various means. Leaflets began to pour out, first in hundreds, then in thousands, then in tens of thousands as links were established with one group of rank-and-file workers after another. On the first day alone, Renault, Citroën,

Air France, Boussac, the Nouvelles Messageries de Presse, Rhône-Poulenc and the RATP (Métro) were contacted. The movement then snowballed.

Every evening at Censier, the action committees reported back to an *Assemblée Générale* devoted exclusively to this kind of work. The reactions to the distribution were assessed, the content of future leaflets discussed. These discussions would usually be led off by the worker contact who would describe the impact of the leaflet on his workmates. The most heated discussion centred on whether direct attacks should be made on the leaders of the CGT or whether mere suggestions as to what was needed to win would be sufficient to expose everything the union leaders had (or hadn't) done and everything they stood for. The second viewpoint prevailed.

The leaflets were usually very short, never more than 200 or 300 words. They nearly all started by listing the workers' grievances - or just by describing their conditions of work. They would end by inviting workers to call at Censier or at the Sorbonne. "These places are now yours. Come there to discuss your problems with others. Take a hand yourselves in making known your problems and demands to those around you." Between this kind of opening and this kind of conclusion, most leaflets contained one or two key political points.

The response was instantaneous. More and more workers dropped in to draft joint leaflets with the students. Soon there was no lecture room big enough for the daily *Assemblée Générale*. The students learned a great deal from the workers' self-discipline and from the systematic way in which they presented their reports. It was all so different from the "in-fighting" of the political sects. There was agreement that these were the finest lectures ever held at Censier!

Among the more telling lines of these leaflets, I noted the following:

Air France leaflet: "We refuse to accept a degrading 'modernization' which means we are constantly watched and have to submit to conditions which are harmful to our health, to our nervous systems and an insult to our status of human beings…We refuse to entrust our demands any longer to professional trade union leaders. Like the students, we must take the control of our affairs into our own hands."

Renault leaflet: "If we want our wage increases and our claims concerning conditions of work to be secure, if we don't want them constantly threatened, we must now struggle for a fundamental change in society…As workers we should ourselves seek to control the operation of our enterprises. Our objectives are similar to those of the students. The management (*gestion*) of industry and the management of the university should be democratically ensured by those who work there…"

Rhône-Poulenc leaflet: "Up till now we tried to solve our problems through petitions, partial struggles, the election of better leaders. This has led us nowhere. The action of the students has shown us that only rank-and-file action could compel the authorities to retreat…the students are challenging the whole purpose of bourgeois education. They want to take the fundamental decisions themselves. So should we. *We* should decide the purpose of production, and at whose cost production will be carried out."

District leaflet (distributed in the streets at Boulogne-Billancourt): "The government fears the extension of the movement. It fears the developing unity between workers and students. Pompidou has announced that 'the government will defend the Republic'. The Army and police are being prepared. De Gaulle will speak on the

24th. Will he send the CRS to clear pickets out of strikebound plants? Be prepared. In workshops and faculties, think in terms of self-defence…"

Every day dozens of such leaflets were discussed, typed, duplicated, distributed. Every evening we heard of the response: "The blokes think it's tremendous. It's just what they are thinking. The union officials never talk like this". "The blokes liked the leaflet. They are sceptical about the 12 per cent. They say prices will go up and that we'll lose it all in a few months. Some say let's push all together now and take on the lot." "The leaflet certainly started the lads talking. They've never had so much to say. The officials had to wait their turn to speak…"

I vividly remember a young printing worker who said one night that these meetings were the most exciting thing that had ever happened to him. All his life he had dreamed of meeting people who thought and spoke like this. But every time he thought he had met one all they were interested in was what they could get out of him. This was the first time he had been offered disinterested help. I don't know what has happened at Censier since the end of May. When I left, sundry Trots were beginning to move in, "to politicize the leaflets" (by which I presume they meant that the leaflets should now talk about "the need to build the revolutionary Party"). If they succeed - which I doubt, knowing the calibre of the Censier comrades - it will be a tragedy.

The leaflets *were* in fact political. During the whole of my short stay in France I saw nothing more intensely and relevantly political (in the best sense of the term) than the sustained campaign emanating from Censier, a campaign for constant control of the struggle from below, for self-defence, for workers' management of production, for popularizing the concept of Workers' Councils, for explaining to one and all the tremendous relevance, in a revolutionary situation, of revolutionary demands, of organized self-activity, of collective self-reliance.

As I left Censier I could not help thinking how the place epitomized the crisis of modern bureaucratic capitalism. Censier is no educational slum. It is an ultra-modern building, one of the showpieces of Gaullist *grandeur*. It has closed-circuit television in the lecture theatres, modern plumbing, and slot machines distributing 24 different kinds of food - in sterilized containers - and ten different kinds of drink. Over 90 per cent of the students there are of petty bourgeois or bourgeois backgrounds. Yet such is their rejection of the society that nurtured them that they were working duplicators 24 hours a day, turning out a flood of revolutionary literature of a kind no modern city has ever had pushed into it before. This kind of activity had transformed these students and had contributed to transforming the environment around them. They were simultaneously disrupting the social structure and having the time of their lives. In the words of a slogan scrawled on the wall: *"On n'est pas là pour s'emmerder"* (you'll have to look this one up in the dictionary).

GETTING TOGETHER

When the news of the first factory occupation (that of the Sud Aviation plant at Nantes) reached the Sorbonne - late during the night of Tuesday, May 14th - there were scenes of indescribable enthusiasm. Sessions were interrupted for the announcement. Everyone seemed to sense the significance of what had just happened. After a full minute of continuous, delirious cheering, the audience broke into a synchronous, rhythmical clapping, apparently reserved for great occasions.

On Thursday, May 16, the Renault factories at Cléon (near Rouen) and at Flins (north-west of Paris) were occupied. Excited groups in the Sorbonne yard remained glued to their transistors as hour by hour news came over of further occupations. Enormous posters were put up, both inside and outside the Sorbonne, with the most up-to-date information of which factories had been occupied: the Nouvelles Messageries de Presse in Paris, Kléber-Colombes at Caudebec, Dresser-Dujardin at Le Havre, the naval shipyard at Le Trait…and finally the Renault works at Boulogne-Billancourt. Within 48 hours the task had to be abandoned. No noticeboard - or panel of noticeboards - was large enough. At last the students felt that the battle had really been joined.

Early on the Friday afternoon an emergency *Assemblée Générale* was held. The meeting decided to send a big student deputation to the occupied Renault works. Its aim was to establish contact, express student solidarity and, if possible, discuss common problems. The march was scheduled to leave the Place de la Sorbonne at 6.00 pm.

At about 5.00 pm thousands of leaflets were suddenly distributed in the amphitheatre, in the Sorbonne yard and in the streets around. They were signed by the Renault Bureau of the CGT. The Communist Party had been working…fast. The leaflets read:

> We have just heard that students and teachers are proposing to set out this afternoon in the direction of Renault. This decision was taken without consulting the appropriate trade union sections of the CGT, CFDT and FO.

> We greatly appreciate the solidarity of the students and teachers in the common struggle against the *pouvoir personnel* (i.e. de Gaulle) and the employers but are opposed to any ill-judged initiative which might threaten our developing movement and facilitate a provocation which would lead to a diversion by the government.

> We strongly advise the organizers of this demonstration against preceding with their plans.

> We intend, together with the workers now struggling for their claims, to lead our own strike. We refuse any external intervention, in conformity with the declaration jointly signed by the CGT, CFDT and FO unions, and approved this morning by 23,000 workers belonging to the factory.

The distortion and dishonesty of this leaflet defy description. No one intended to instruct the workers how to run the strike and no student would have the presumption to seek to assume its leadership. All that the students wanted was to express solidarity with the workers in what was now a common struggle against the state and the employing class.

The CGT leaflet came like an icy shower to the less political students and to all those who still had illusions about Stalinism. "They won't let us get through". "The workers don't want to talk with us". The identification of workers with "their" organizations is very hard to break down. Several hundred who had intended to march to Billancourt were probably put off. The UNEF vacillated, reluctant to lead the march in direct violation of the wishes of the CGT.

Finally some 1,500 people set out, under a single banner, hastily prepared by some Maoist students. The banner proclaimed: "The strong hands of the working class must now take over the torch from the fragile hands of the students". Many joined the march who were not Maoists and who didn't necessarily agree with this particular formulation of its objectives.

Although small when compared to other marches, this was certainly a most political one. Practically everyone on it belonged to one or other of the *groupuscules*: a spontaneous united front of Maoists, Trotskyists, anarchists, the comrades of the Mouvement du 22 Mars and various others. Everyone knew exactly what he was doing. It was this that was so to infuriate the Communist Party.

The march sets off noisily, crosses the Boulevard St.-Michel, and passes in front of the occupied Odéon Theatre (where several hundred more joyfully join it). It then proceeds at a very brisk pace down the Rue de Vaugirard, the longest street in Paris, towards the working-class districts to the south-west of the city, growing steadily in size and militancy as it advances. It is important we reach the factory before the Stalinists have time to mobilize their big battalions…

Slogans such as *"Avec nous, chez Renault"* (Come with us to Renault), *"Le pouvoir est dans la rue"* (Power lies in the street), *"Le pouvoir aux ouvriers"* (Power to the workers), are shouted lustily, again and again. The Maoists shout *"A bas le gouvernement gaulliste anti-populaire de chomage et de misère"* – a long and politically equivocal slogan, but one eminently suited to collective shouting. The *Internationale* bursts out repeatedly, sung this time by people who seem to know the words – even the second verse!

By the time we have marched the five miles to Issy-les-Moulineaux it is already dark. Way behind us now are the bright lights of the Latin Quarter and of the fashionable Paris known to tourists. We go through small, poorly lit streets, the uncollected rubbish piled high in places. Dozens of young people join us en route, attracted by the noise and the singing of revolutionary songs such as *La Jeune Garde*, *Zimmerwald*, and the song of the Partisans. *"Chez Renault, chez Renault"*, the marchers shout. People congregate in the doors of the bistros, or peer out of the windows of crowded flats to watch us pass. Some look on in amazement but many – possibly a majority – now clap or wave encouragement. In some streets many Algerians line the pavement. Some join in the shouting of *"CRS - SS"*, *"Charonne"*, *"A bas l'Etat policier"*. They have not forgotten. Most look on shyly or smile in an embarrassed way. Very few join the march.

On we go, a few miles more. There isn't a gendarme in sight. We cross the Seine and eventually slow down as we approach a square beyond which lie the Renault works. The streets here are very badly lit. There is a sense of intense excitement in the air.

We suddenly come up against a lorry, parked across most of the road, and fitted with loudspeaker equipment. The march stops. On the lorry stands a CGT official. He speaks for five minutes. In somewhat chilly tones he says how pleased he is to see us. "Thank you for coming, comrades. We appreciate your solidarity. But please no provocations. Don't go too near the gates as the management would use it as an excuse to call the police. And go home soon. It's cold and you'll need all your strength in the days to come".

The students have brought their own loudhailers. One or two speak, briefly. They take note of the comments of the comrade from the CGT. They have no intention of provoking anyone, no wish to usurp anyone's functions. We then slowly but quite deliberately move forwards into the square, on each side of the lorry, drowning the protests of about a hundred Stalinists in a powerful *Internationale*. Workers in neighbouring cafés come out and join us. This time the Party had not had time to mobilize its militants. It could not physically isolate us.

Part of the factory now looms up right ahead of us, three storeys high on our left, two storeys high on our right. In front of us, there is a giant metal gate, closed and bolted. A large first floor window to our right is crowded with workers. The front row sit with their legs dangling over the sill. Several seem in their teens; one of them waves a big red flag. There are no *tricolores* in sight – no "dual allegiance" as in other occupied places I had seen. Several dozen more workers are on the roofs of the two buildings.

We wave. They wave back. We sing the *Internationale*. They join in. We give the clenched fist salute. They do likewise. Everybody cheers. Contact has been made.

An interesting exchange takes place. A group of demonstrators starts shouting "*Les usines aux ouvriers*" (The factories to the workers). The slogan spreads like wildfire through the crowd. The Maoists, now in a definite minority, are rather annoyed. (According to Chairman Mao, workers' control is a petty bourgeois, anarcho-syndicalist deviation.) "*Les usines aux ouvriers*"…ten, twenty times the slogan reverberates round the Place Nationale, taken up by a crowd now some 3,000 strong.

As the shouting subsides, a lone voice from one of the Renault roofs shouts back: "*La Sorbonne aux Etudiants*". Other workers on the same roof take it up. Then those on the other roof. By the volume of their voices they must be at least a hundred of them, on top of each building. There is then a moment of silence. Everyone thinks the exchange has come to an end. But one of the demonstrators starts chanting: "*La Sorbonne aux ouvriers*". Amid general laughter, everyone joins in.

We start talking. A rope is quickly passed down from the window, a bucket at the end of it. Bottles of beer and packets of fags are passed up. Also revolutionary leaflets. Also bundles of papers (mainly copies of *Server le Peuple* – a Maoist journal carrying a big title, *Vive la CGT*). At street level there are a number of gaps in the metal facade of the building. Groups of students cluster at these half-dozen openings and talk to groups of workers on the other side. They discuss wages, conditions, the CRS, what the lads inside need most, how the students can help. The men talk freely. They are not Party members. They think the constant talk of provocateurs a bit far-fetched. But the machines must be protected. We point out that two or three students inside the factory, escorted by the strike committee, couldn't possibly damage the machines. They agree. We contrast the widely open doors of the Sorbonne with the heavy locks and bolts on the Renault gates – closed by the CGT officials to prevent the ideological contamination of "their" militants. How silly, we say, to have to talk through these stupid little slits in the wall. Again they agree. They will put it to their *dirigeants* (leaders). No one seems, as yet, to think beyond this.

There is then a diversion. A hundred yards away a member of the FER gets up on a parked car and starts making a speech through a loudhailer. The intervention is completely out of tune with the dialogue that is just starting. It's the same gramophone record we have been hearing all week at the Sorbonne. "Call on the union leaders to organize the election of strike committees in every factory. Force the union leaders to federate the strike committees. Force the union leaders to set up a national strike committee. Force them to call a general strike throughout the whole of the country". (This at a time when millions of workers are already on strike without any call whatsoever.) The tone is strident, almost hysterical, the misjudging of the mood monumental. The demonstrators themselves drown the speaker in a loud *Internationale*. As the last bar fades the Trotskyist tries again. Again the demonstrators drown him.

Groups stroll up the Avenue Yves Kermen, to the other entrances to the factory. Real contact is here more difficult to establish. There is a crowd outside the gate, but most of them are Party members. Some won't talk at all. Others just talk slogans.

We walk back to the square. It is now well past midnight. The crowd thins. Groups drop into a couple of cafés which are still open. Here we meet a whole group of young workers, aged about eighteen. They had been in the factory earlier in the day.

They tell us that at any given time, just over 1,000 workers are engaged in the occupation. The strike started on the Thursday afternoon, at about 2.00 pm, when the group of youngsters from shop 70 decided to down tools and to spread into all parts of the factory asking their mates to do likewise. That same morning they had heard of the occupation of Cléon and that the red flag was floating over the factory at Flins. There had been a hint of talk about what to do. At a midday meeting tile CGT had spoken vaguely of a series of rotating strikes, shop by shop, to be initiated the following day.

The movement spread at an incredible pace. The youngsters went round shouting *"Occupation! Occupation!"* Half the factory had stopped working before the union officials realized what was happening. At about 4.00 pm Sylvain, a CGT secretary, had arrived with loudspeaker equipment to tell them, "they weren't numerous enough, to start work again, that they would see tomorrow about a one–day strike". He is absolutely by-passed. At 5.00 pm Halbeher, general secretary of the Renault CGT, announces, pale as a sheet, that "the CGT has called for the occupation of the factory". "Tell your friends", the lads say. *"We started it.* But will we be able to keep it in our hands? *Cà, c'est un autre problème…"*

Students? Well, hats off to anyone who can thump the cops that hard! The lads tell us of two of their mates who disappeared from the factory altogether ten days ago "to help the Revolution". Left family, jobs, everything. And good luck to them. "A chance like this comes once in a lifetime". We discuss plans, how to develop the movement. The occupied factory could be a ghetto, *"isolant les durs"* (isolating the most militant). We talk about camping, the cinema, the Sorbonne, the future. Almost until sunrise…

"Attention aux Provocateurs"

Social upheavals, such as the one France has just been through, leave behind them a trail of shattered reputations. The image of Gaullism as a meaningful way of life, "accepted" by the French people, has taken a tremendous knock. But so has the image of the Communist Party as a viable challenge to the French Establishment.

As far as the students are concerned the recent actions of the PCF (Parti Communiste Français) are such that the Party has probably sealed its fate in this milieu for a generation to come. Among the workers the effects are more difficult to assess and it would be premature to attempt this assessment. All that can be said is that the effects are sure to be profound although they will probably take some time to express themselves. The proletarian condition itself was for a moment questioned. Prisoners who have had a glimpse of freedom do not readily resume a life sentence.

The full implications of the role of the PCF and of the CGT have yet to be appreciated by British revolutionaries. They need above all else to be informed. In this section we will document the role of the PCF to the best of our ability. It is important to realize that for every ounce of shit thrown at the students in its official publications, the Party poured tons more over them at meetings or in private conversations. In the nature of things it is more difficult to document this kind of slander.

Friday, May 3

A meeting was called in the yard of the Sorbonne by UNEF, JCR, MAU and FER to protest at the closure of the Nanterre faculty. It was attended by militants of the Mouvement du 22 Mars. The police were called in by Rector Roche and activists from all these groups were arrested.

The UEC (Union des Etudiants Communistes) didn't participate in this campaign. But it distributed a leaflet in the Sorbonne denouncing the activity of the *groupuscules* (abbreviation for *groupes miniscules*, tiny groups):

> The leaders of the leftist groups are taking advantage of the shortcomings of the government. They are exploiting student discontent and trying to stop the functioning of the faculties. They are seeking to prevent the mass of students from working and from passing their exams. These false revolutionaries are acting objectively as allies of the Gaullist power. They are acting as supporters of its policies, which are harmful to the mass of the students and in particular to those of modest origin.

On the same day *L'Humanité* had written: "Certain small groups (anarchists, Trotskyists, Maoists) composed mainly of the sons of the big bourgeoisie and led by the German anarchist Cohn-Bendit, are taking advantage of the shortcomings of the government…etc…" (see above). The same issue of *L'Humanité* had published an article by Marchais, a member of the Party's Central Committee. This article was to be widely distributed, as a leaflet, in factories and offices:

> Not satisfied with the agitation they are conducting in the student milieu – an agitation which is against the interests of the mass of the students and favours fascist provocateurs – these pseudo-revolutionaries now have the nerve to seek to give lessons to the working-class movement. We find them in increasing numbers at the gates of factories and in places where immigrant workers live, distributing leaflets and other propaganda. These false revolutionaries must be unmasked, for objectively they are serving the interests of the Gaullist power and of the big capitalist monopolies.

Monday, May 6

The police have been occupying the Latin Quarter over the weekend. There have been big student street demonstrations. At the call of UNEF and SNESup 20,000 students marched from Denfert-Rochereau to St.-Germain-des-Prés calling for the liberation of the arrested workers and students. Repeated police assaults on the demonstrators: 422 arrests, 800 wounded.

L'Humanité states:

> One can clearly see today the outcome of the adventurous actions of the leftist, anarchist, Trotskyist and other groups. Objectively they are playing into the hands of the government…The discredit into which they are bringing the student movement is helping feed the violent campaigns of the reactionary press and of the ORTF, who by identifying the actions of these groups with those of the mass of the students are seeking to isolate the students from the mass of the population…

Tuesday, May 7

UNEF and SNESup call on their supporters to start an unlimited strike. Before discussions with the authorities begin they insist on:

> (a) a stop to all legal action against the students and workers who have been questioned, arrested or convicted in the course of the demonstrations of the last few days;
>
> (b)the withdrawal of the police from the Latin Quarter and from all University premises;
>
> (c)a reopening of the closed faculties.

In a statement showing how completely out of touch they were with the deep motives of the student revolt, the "Elected Communist Representatives of the Paris Region" declared in *L'Humanité*:

> The shortage of credits, of premises, of equipment, of teachers...prevent three students out of four from completing their studies, without mentioning all those who never have access to higher education...This situation has caused profound and legitimate discontent among both students and teachers. It has also favoured the activity of irresponsible groups whose conceptions can offer no solution to the students' problems. It is intolerable that the government should take advantage of the behaviour of an infinitesimal minority to stop the studies of tens of thousands of students a few days from the exams...

The same issue of *L'Humanité* carried a statement from the Sorbonne-Lettres (teachers) branch of the Communist Party:

> The Communist teachers demand the liberation of the arrested students and the reopening of the Sorbonne. Conscious of our responsibilities, we specify that this solidarity does not mean that we agree with or support the slogans emanating from certain student organizations. We disapprove of unrealistic, demagogic and anti-Communist slogans and of the unwarranted methods of action advocated by various leftist groups.

On the same day Georges Séguy, general secretary of the CGT, spoke to the press about the programme of the Festival of Working Class Youth (scheduled for May 17–19, but subsequently cancelled): "The solidarity between students, teachers and the working class is a familiar notion to the militants of the CGT...It is precisely this tradition that compels us not to tolerate any dubious or provocative elements, elements which criticize the working class organizations..."

Wednesday, May 8

A big students' demonstration called by UNEF has taken place in the streets of Paris the previous evening. The front page of *L'Humanité* carries a statement from the Party Secretariat: "The discontent of the students is legitimate. But the situation favours adventurist activities, whose conception offers no perspective to the students and has nothing in common with a really progressive and forward-looking policy".

In the same issue, J. M. Catala, general secretary of the UEC (Union des Etudiants Communistes) writes that "the actions of irresponsible groups are assisting the Establishment in its aims...What we must do is ask for a bigger educational budget which would ensure bigger student grants, the appointment of more and better qualified teachers, the building of new faculties..."

The UJCF (Union des Jeunesses Communistes de France) and the UJFF (Union des Jeunes Filles Françaises) distribute a leaflet in a number of *lycées*. *L'Humanité* quotes it approvingly:

> We protest against the police violence unleashed against the students. We demand the reopening of Nanterre and of the Sorbonne and the liberation of all those arrested. We denounce the Gaullist power as being mainly [!] responsible for this situation. We also denounce the adventurism of certain irresponsible groups and call on the *lycéens* to fight side by side with the working class and its Communist Party...

Monday, May 13

Over the weekend Pompidou has climbed down. But the unions, the UNEF and the teachers have decided to maintain their call for a one-day, general strike. On its front page *L'Humanité* publishes, in enormous headlines, a call for the 24-hour strike followed by a statement from the Political Bureau:

> The unity of the working class and of the students threatens the regime...This creates an enormous problem. It is essential that no provocation, no diversion should be allowed to divert any of the forces struggling against the regime or should give the government the flimsiest pretext to distort the meaning of this great fight. The Communist Party associates itself without reservation with the just struggle of the students...

Wednesday, May 15

The enormous Monday demonstrations in Paris and other towns - which incidentally prevented *L'Humanité* as well as other papers from appearing on the Tuesday - were a tremendous success. In a sense they triggered off the "spontaneous" wave of strikes which followed within a day or two. *L'Humanité* publishes, on its front pages a statement issued the day before by the Party's Political Bureau. After taking all the credit for May 13th, the statement continues:

> The People of Paris marched for hours in the streets of the capital showing a power which made any provocation impossible. The Party organizations worked day and night to ensure that this great demonstration of workers, teachers and students should take place in maximum unity, strength and discipline...It is now clear that the Establishment confronted with the protests and collective action of all the main sections of the population, will seek to divide us in the hope of beating us. It will resort to all methods, including provocation. The Political Bureau warns workers and students against any adventurist endeavours which might, in the present circumstances, dislocate the broad front of the struggle which is in the process of developing, and provide the Gaullist power with an unexpected weapon with which to consolidate its shaky rule...

Saturday, May 18

Over the past 48 hours strikes with factory occupations have spread like a trail of gunpowder, from one corner of the country to the other. The railways are paralyzed, civil airports fly the red flag. ("Provocateurs" have obviously been at work!) *L'Humanité* publishes on its front page a declaration from the National Committee of the CGT:

From hour to hour strikes and factory occupations are spreading. This action, started on the initiative of the CGT and of other trade-union organizations [sic!], creates a new situation of exceptional importance…Long accumulated popular discontent is now finding expression. The questions being asked must be answered seriously and full notice taken of their importance. The evolution of the situation is giving a new dimension to the struggle…While multiplying its efforts to raise the struggle to the needed level, the National Committee warns all CGT militants and local groups against any attempts by outside groups to meddle in the conduct of the struggle, and against all acts of provocation which might assist the forces of repression in their attempts to thwart the development of the movement…

The same issue of the paper devoted a whole page to warning students of the fallacy of any notions of "student power" - en passant attributing to the Mouvement du 22 Mars a whole series of political positions they had never held.

Monday, May 20

The whole country is totally paralyzed. The Communist Party is still warning about "provocations". The top right hand corner of L'Humanité contains a box labelled "WARNING":

Leaflets have been distributed in the Paris area calling for an insurrectionary general strike. It goes without saying that such appeals have not been issued by our democratic trade union organizations [it does indeed - MB]. They are the work of provocateurs seeking to provide the government with a pretext for intervention…The workers must be vigilant to defeat all such manoeuvres…

In the same issue, Etienne Fajon, of the Central Committee, continues the warnings:

The Establishment's main preoccupation at the moment is to divide the ranks of the working class and to divide it from other sections of the population…Our Political Bureau has warned workers and students, from the very beginning, against venturing slogans capable of dislocating the broad front of the struggle. Several provocations have thus been prevented. Our political vigilance must clearly be maintained…

The same issue devoted its central pages to an interview of M. Georges Séguy, general secretary of the CGT, conducted over the Europe No 1 radio network. In these live interviews, various listeners phoned questions in directly. The following exchanges are worth recording:

Question. M. Séguy, the workers on strike are everywhere saying that they will go the whole hog. What do you mean by this? What are your objectives?

Answer. The strike is so powerful that the workers obviously mean to obtain the maximum concessions at the end of such a movement. The whole hog for us, trade unionists, means winning the demands that we have always fought for, but which the government and the employers have always refused to consider. They have opposed an obtuse intransigence to the proposals for negotiations which we have repeatedly made.

The whole hog means a general rise in wages (no wages less than 600 francs per month), guaranteed employment, an earlier retirement age, reduction of working hours without loss of wages, and the defence and extension of trade-union rights within the factory. I am not putting these demands in any particular order because we attach the same importance to all of them.

Question. If I am not mistaken the statutes of the CGT declare its aims to be the overthrow of capitalism and its replacement by socialism. In the present circumstances, that you have yourself referred to as "exceptional" and "important", why doesn't the CGT seize this unique chance of calling for its fundamental objectives?

Answer. This is a very interesting question. I like it very much. It is true that the CGT offers the workers a concept of trade unionism that we consider the most revolutionary insofar as its final objective is the end of the employing class and of wage labour. It is true that this is the first of our statutes. It remains fundamentally the CGT'S objective. But can the present movement reach this objective? If it became obvious that it could, we would be ready to assume our responsibilities. It remains to be seen whether all the social strata involved in the present movement are ready to go that far.

Question. Since last week's events I have gone everywhere where people are arguing. I went this afternoon to the Odéon Theatre. Masses of people were discussing there. I can assure you that all the classes who suffer from the present regime were represented there. When I asked whether people thought that the movement should go further than the small demands put forward by the trade unions for the last ten or twenty years, I brought the house down. I therefore think that it would be criminal to miss the present opportunity. It would be criminal because sooner or later this will have to be done. The conditions of today might allow us to do it peacefully and calmly and will perhaps never come back. I think this call must be made by you and the other political organizations. These political organizations are not your business, of course, but the CGT is a revolutionary organization. You must bring out your revolutionary flag. The workers are astounded to see you so timid.

Answer. While you were bathing in the Odéon fever, I was in the factories. Amongst workers. I assure you that the answer I am giving you is the answer of a leader of a great trade union, which claims to have assumed all its responsibilities, but which does not confuse its wishes with reality.

A caller. I would like to speak to M. Séguy. My name is Duvauchel. I am the director of the Sud Aviation factory at Nantes.

Séguy. Good morning, sir.

Duvauchel. Good morning, Mr General Secretary. I would like to know what you think of the fact that for the last four days I have been sequestrated, together with about twenty other managerial staff, inside the Sud Aviation factory at Nantes.

Séguy. Has anyone raised a hand against you?

Duvauchel. No. But I am prevented from leaving, despite the fact that the general manager of the firm has intimated that the firm was prepared to make positive proposals as soon as free access to its factory could be resumed, and first of all to its managerial staff.

Séguy. Have you asked to leave the factory?

Duvauchel. Yes!

Séguy. Was permission refused?

Duvauchel. Yes!

Séguy. Then I must refer you to the declaration I made yesterday at the CGT'S press conference. I stated that I disapproved of such activities. We are taking the necessary steps to see they are not repeated.

But enough is enough. The Revolution itself will doubtless be denounced by the Stalinists as a provocation! By way of an epilogue it is worth recording that at a packed meeting of revolutionary students, held at the Mutualité on Thursday, May 9th, a spokesman of the (Trotskyist) Organisation Communiste Internationaliste could think of nothing better to do than call on the meeting to pass a resolution calling on Séguy to call a general strike!!!

FRANCE, 1968

This has undoubtedly been the greatest revolutionary upheaval in Western Europe since the days of the Paris Commune. Hundreds of thousands of students have fought pitched battles with the police. Nine million workers have been on strike. The red flag of revolt has flown over occupied factories, universities, building sites, shipyards, primary and secondary schools, pitheads, railway stations, department stores, docked transatlantic liners, theatres, hotels. The Paris Opéra, the Folies Bergères and the building of the National Council for Scientific Research were taken over, as were the headquarters of the French Football Federation – whose aim was clearly perceived as being "to prevent ordinary footballers enjoying football".

Virtually every layer of French society has been involved to some extent or other. Hundreds of thousands of people of all ages have discussed every aspect of life in packed-out, non-stop meetings in every available schoolroom and lecture hall. Boys of fourteen have invaded a primary school for girls shouting *"Liberté pour les filles"*. Even such traditionally reactionary enclaves as the Faculties of Medicine and Law have been shaken from top to bottom, their hallowed procedures and institutions challenged and found wanting. Millions have taken a hand in making history. This is the stuff of revolution.

Under the influence of the revolutionary students, thousands began to query the whole principle of hierarchy. The students had questioned it where it seemed the most "natural": in the realms of teaching and knowledge. They proclaimed that democratic self-management was possible – and to prove it began to practice it themselves. They denounced the monopoly of information and produced millions of leaflets to break it. They attacked some of the main pillars of contemporary "civilization": the barriers between manual workers and intellectuals, the consumer society, the "sanctity" of the university and of other founts of capitalist culture and wisdom.

Within a matter of days the tremendous creative potentialities of the people suddenly erupted. The boldest and most realistic ideas – and they are usually the same – were advocated, argued, applied. Language, rendered stale by decades of bureaucratic mumbo-jumbo, eviscerated by those who manipulate it for advertizing purposes, suddenly reappeared as something new and fresh. People re-appropriated it in all its fullness. Magnificently apposite and poetic slogans emerged from the anonymous crowd. Children explained to their elders what the function of education should be. The educators were educated. Within a few days, young people of twenty attained a level of understanding and a political and tactical sense which many who had been in the revolutionary movement for thirty years or more were still sadly lacking.

The tumultuous development of the students struggle triggered off the first factory occupations. It transformed both the relation of forces in society and the image, in people's minds, of established institutions and of established leaders. It compelled the State to reveal both its oppressive nature and its fundamental incoherence. It exposed the utter emptiness of Government, Parliament, Administration - and of *all* the political parties. Unarmed students had forced the Establishment to drop its mask, to sweat with fear, to resort to the police club and to the gas grenade. Students finally compelled the bureaucratic leaderships of the "working-class organizations" to reveal themselves as the ultimate custodians of the established order.

But the revolutionary movement did still more. It fought its battles in Paris, not in some underdeveloped country, exploited by imperialism. In a glorious few weeks the actions of students and young workers dispelled the myth of the well-organized, well-oiled modern capitalist society, from which radical conflict had been eliminated and in which only marginal problems remained to be solved. Administrators who had been administering everything were suddenly shown to have had a grasp of nothing. Planners who had planned everything showed themselves incapable of ensuring the endorsement of their plans by those to whom they applied. This most modern movement should allow real revolutionaries to shed a number of the ideological encumbrances which in the past had hampered revolutionary activity. It wasn't hunger which drove the students to revolt. There wasn't an "economic crisis" even in the loosest sense of the term. The revolt had nothing to do with "under-consumption" or with "over-production". The "falling rate of profit" just didn't come into the picture. Moreover, the student movement wasn't based on economic demands. On the contrary, the movement only found its real stature, and only evoked its tremendous response, when it went beyond the economic demands within which official student unionism had for so long sought to contain it (incidentally with the blessing of all the political parties and "revolutionary" groups of the "Left"). And conversely it was by confining the workers' struggle to purely economic objectives that the trade union bureaucrats have so far succeeded in coming to the assistance of the regime.

The present movement has shown that the fundamental contradiction of modern bureaucratic capitalism isn't the "anarchy of the market". It isn't the "contradiction between the forces of production and the property relations". The central conflict to which all others are related is the conflict between order-givers (*dirigeants*) and order-takers (*éxécutants*). The insoluble contradiction which tears the guts out of modern capitalist society is the one which compels it to exclude people from the management of their own activities and which at the same time compels it to solicit their participation, without which it would collapse. These tendencies find expression on the one hand in the attempt of the bureaucrats to convert men into objects (by violence, mystification, new manipulation techniques - or "economic" carrots) and, on the other hand, in mankind's refusal to allow itself to be treated in this way.

The French events show clearly something that all revolutions have shown, but which apparently has again and again to be learned anew. There is no "inbuilt revolutionary perspective", no "gradual increase of contradictions", no "progressive development of a revolutionary mass consciousness". What are given are the contradictions and the conflicts we have described and the fact that modern bureaucratic society more or less inevitably produces periodic "accidents" which disrupt its functioning. These both provoke popular intervention and provide the people with opportunities for asserting themselves and for changing the social order. The functioning of bureaucratic capitalism creates the conditions within which revolutionary consciousness may appear. These conditions are an integral part of the whole alienating hierarchical and oppressive social structure. Whenever people struggle, sooner or later they are compelled to question the whole of that social structure.

These are ideas which many of us in Solidarity have long subscribed to. They were developed at length in some of Paul Cardan's pamphlets. Writing in *Le Monde* (May 20, 1968) E. Morin admits that what is happening today in France is "a blinding resurrection: the resurrection of that libertarian strand which seeks concilation with Marxism, in a formula of which *Socialisme ou Barbarie* had provided a first synthesis a few years ago..." As after every verification of basic concepts in the crucible of real events, many will proclaim that these had always been their views. This, of course isn't true.[168] The point however isn't to lay claims to a kind of copyright in the realm of correct revolutionary ideas. We welcome converts, from whatever sources and however belated.

We can't deal here at length with what is now an important problem in France, namely the creation of a new kind of revolutionary movement. Things would indeed have been different if such a movement had existed, strong enough to outwit the bureaucratic manoeuvres, alert enough day by day to expose the duplicity of the "left" leaderships, deeply enough implanted to explain to the workers the real meaning of the students' struggle, to propagate the idea of autonomous strike committees (linking up union and non-union members), of workers' management of production and of Workers' Councils. Many things which could have been done weren't done because there wasn't such a movement. The way the students' own struggle was unleashed shows that such an organization could have played a most important catalytic role without automatically becoming a bureaucratic "leadership". But such regrets are futile. The non-existence of such a movement is no accident. If it *had* been formed during the previous period it certainly wouldn't have been the kind of movement of which we are speaking. Even taking the "best" of the small organizations – and multiplying its numbers a hundredfold – wouldn't have met the requirements of the current situation. When confronted with the test of events all the "'left'" groups just continued playing their old gramophone records. Whatever their merits as depositories of the cold ashes of the revolution – a task they have now carried out for several decades – they proved incapable of snapping out of their old ideas and routines, incapable of learning or of forgetting anything.[169]

The new revolutionary movement will have to be built from the new elements (students and workers) who have understood the real significance of current events. The revolution must step into the great political void revealed by the crisis of the old society. It must develop a voice, a face, a paper – and it must do it soon.

---

168   We recall for instance a long review of *Modern Capitalism and Revolution* in *International Socialism* (no. 22) where, under the heading "Return to Utopia", Cardan was deemed to have "nothing to say in relation to theory". His prediction that people would eventually reject the emptiness of the consumer society were described as "mere moralizing" and as "doing credit to a Christian ascetic". The authors should perhaps visit the new monastery at the Sorbonne.

169   We are not primarily referring to Trotskyist groups such as the FER, which on the night of the barricades, despite repeated appeals for help, refused to cancel their mass meeting at the Mutualité or to send reinforcements to assist students and workers already engaged in a bitter fight with the CRS on the barricades of the Rue Gay-Lussac. We are not referring to their leader Chisseray who claimed it was "necessary above all to preserve the revolutionary vanguard from an unnecessary massacre". Nor are we referring to the repeated Maoist criticisms of the students' struggle, uttered as late as May 7th. What we are referring to is the inability of any Trotskyist or Maoist group to raise the real issues demanded in a revolutionary situation, i.e. to call for workers' management of production and the formation of Workers' Councils. None of these groups even touched on the

We can understand the reluctance of some students to form such an organiza-tion. They feel there is a contradiction between action and thought, between spon-taneity and organization. Their hesitation is fed by the whole of their previous expe-rience. They have seen how thought could become sterilizing dogma, organization become bureaucracy or lifeless ritual, speech become a means of mystification, a rev-olutionary idea become a rigid and stereotyped programme. Through their actions, their boldness, their reluctance to consider long-term aims, they had broken out of this straightjacket. But this isn't enough.

Moreover many of them had sampled the traditional "left" groups. In all their fundamental aspects these groups remain trapped within the ideological and orga-nizational frameworks of bureaucratic capitalism. They have programmes fixed once and for all, leaders who utter fixed speeches, whatever the changing reality around them, organizational forms which mirror those of existing society. Such groups reproduce within their own ranks the division between order-takers and order-givers, between those who "know" and those who don't, the separation between scholastic pseudo-theory and real life. They would even like to impose this division into the working class, whom they all aspire to lead, because (and I was told this again and again) "the workers are only capable of developing a trade-union con-sciousness".

But these students are wrong. One doesn't get beyond bureaucratic organiza-tion by denying all organization. One doesn't challenge the sterile rigidity of finished programmes by refusing to define oneself in terms of aims and methods. One does-n't refute dead dogma by the condemnation of all theoretical reflection. The students and young workers can't just stay where they are. To accept these "contradictions" as valid and as something which cannot be transcended is to accept the essence of bureaucratic capitalist ideology. It is to accept the prevailing philosophy and the pre-vailing reality. It is to integrate the revolution into an established historical order.

If the revolution is only an explosion lasting a few days (or weeks), the estab-lished order - whether it knows it or not - will be able to cope. What is more - at a deep level - class society even needs such jolts. This kind of "revolution" permits class society to survive by compelling it to transform and adapt itself. This is the real dan-ger today. Explosions which disrupt the imaginary world in which alienated societies tend to live - and bring them momentarily down to earth - help them eliminate out-moded methods of domination and evolve new and more flexible ones.

Action or thought? For revolutionary socialists the problem is not to make a synthesis of these two preoccupations of the revolutionary students. It is to destroy the social context in which such false alternatives find root.

SOLIDARITY PAMPHLET 30 [JUNE 1968]

---

sort of questions the revolutionary students were touching on day and night: the relations of production in the capitalist factory, alienation at work whatever the level of wages, the division between leaders and led within the factory hierarchy or within the "working–class" organizations themselves. All that *Humanité Nouvelle* could coun-terpoise to the constantly demobilizing activities of the CGT was the immensely demystifying slogan, *"Vive la CGT"* ('The CGT isn't *really* what it appears to be, comrade".) All that *Voix Ouvrière* could counterpoise to the CGT's demand for a minimum wage of 600 francs was… a minimum wage of 1,000 francs. This kind of revolu-tionary auction (in purely economic demands), after the workers had been occupying the factories for a number of weeks, shows the utter bankruptcy of revolutionaries who fail to recognize a revolution. *Avant-Garde* correctly attacked some of the ambiguities of *autogestion* (self-management) as advocated by the CFDT, but failed to point out the deeply revolutionary implications of the slogan.

THE IRRATIONAL IN POLITICS

INTRODUCTION

Propaganda and policemen, prisons and schools, traditional values and tra-ditional morality all serve to reinforce the power of the few and to convince or coerce the many into acceptance of a brutal, degrading and irrational system. (from As We See It - Solidarity's statement of purpose)

This pamphlet is an attempt to analyze the various mechanisms whereby mod-ern society manipulates its wage (and house) slaves into accepting their slavery and – at least in the short term – seems to succeed. It does not deal with "police" and "jails" as ordinarily conceived but with those internalized patterns of repression and coer-cion, and with those intellectual prisons in which the "mass individual" is today entrapped.

The pamphlet starts by giving a few examples of the irrational behaviour - at the level of politics - of classes, groups and individuals. It proceeds to reject certain facile "interpretations" put forward to explain these phenomena. It probes the vari-ous ways in which the soil (the individual psyche of modern man) has been rendered fertile (receptive) for an authoritarian, hierarchical and class-dominated culture. It looks at the family as the locus of reproduction of the dominant ideology, and at sexual repression as an important determinant of social conditioning, resulting in the mass production of individuals perpetually craving authority and leadership and for-ever afraid of walking on their own or of thinking for themselves. Some of the prob-lems of the developing sexual revolution are then discussed. The pamphlet con-cludes by exploring a new dimension in the failure of the Russian Revolution. Throughout the aim is to help people acquire additional insight into their own psy-chic structure. The fundamental desires and aspirations of the ordinary individual, so long distorted and repressed, are in deep harmony with an objective such as the lib-ertarian reconstruction of society. The revolutionary "ideal" must therefore be made less remote and abstract. It must be shown to be the fulfilment - starting here and now - of peoples' own independent lives.

The pamphlet consists of two main essays: 'The Irrational In Politics' and 'The Russian Experience'. These can be read independently. The subject matter does not overlap although the main arguments interlock at several levels. The essays are fol-lowed by an appendix: an excerpt from Clara Zetkin's *Reminiscences of Lenin*, which illustrates an aspect of Lenin's thinking little known - or desirably forgotten - by all those Leninists now jumping on the bandwagon of women's liberation.

Frequent references will be found to the works of Wilhelm Reich. This should not be taken to imply that we subscribe to all that Reich wrote - a point spelt out in fuller and more specific detail later on. In the area that concerns us Reich's most rel-evant works were written in the early 1930s. At that time, although critical of devel-opments in Russia (and more critical still of the policy of the German Communist Party) Reich still subscribed to many of their common fundamental assumptions. Even later he still spoke of the "basic socialism of the Soviet Union"[170] and muted his criticisms of the Bolshevik leaders to an extent that is no longer possible for us, writ-

---

170   Wilhelm Reich, *The Sexual Revolution* (New York: The Noonday Press, 1962), p.204.

ing four decades later. Moreover such is the influence of authoritarian conditioning that even those who have achieved the deepest insight into its mechanisms cannot fully escape its effects. There is an undoubted authoritarian strand in Reich.[171]

A final point concerns the section on the historical roots of sexual repression. The author (who is neither a historian nor an anthropologist) found this difficult to write. There seems little doubt, on the evidence available, that sexual repression arose at a specific point in time and fulfilled a specific social function – although experts differ as to many of the details. The difficulty here has been to steer a middle course between the great system builders of the nineteenth century – who tended to "tidy up reality" in order to make it conform to their grandiose generalizations – and the theoretical nihilism of many contemporary social scientists who refuse to see the forest for the trees. For instance the reluctance of Establishment anthropologists to envisage their subject from a cultural-evolutionary viewpoint often stems, one suspects, from fear of the revolutionary implications of such an approach and of its implicit threat to contemporary institutions. We share none of these fears and can therefore look into this area without anxiety.

THE IRRATIONAL IN POLITICS

1. Some Examples

For anyone interested in politics the "irrational" behaviour of individuals, groups or large sections of the population looms as an unpleasant, frightening, but incontrovertible fact. Here are a few examples.

Between 1914 and 1918 millions of working people slaughtered one another in the "war to end wars". They died for ends which were not theirs, defending the interests of their respective rulers. Those who had nothing rallied to their respective flags and butchered one another in the name of "Kaiser" or "King and Country". Twenty years later the process was repeated, on an even vaster scale.

In the early 1930s the economic crisis hit Germany. Hundreds of thousands were out of work and many were hungry. Bourgeois society revealed its utter incapacity even to provide the elementary material needs of men. The time was ripe for radical change. Yet at this critical juncture millions of men and women (including very substantial sections of the German working class) preferred to follow the crudely nationalistic, self-contradictory (anti-capitalist and anti-communist) exhortations of a reactionary demagogue, preaching a mixture of racial hatred, puritanism and ethnological nonsense, rather than embark on the unknown road of social revolution.[172]

In New Delhi in 1966 hundreds of thousands of half-starving Indian peasants and urban poor actively participated in the biggest and most militant demonstration the town had ever known. Whole sections of the city were occupied, policemen attacked, cars and buses burnt. The object of this massive action was not, however, to protest against the social system which maintained the vast mass of the people in a state of permanent poverty and made a mockery of their lives. It was to denounce some contemplated legislation permitting cow slaughter under specific circumstances. Indian "revolutionaries" meanwhile were in no position to make meaningful

---

171   See for instance the recent biography by his third wife, Ilse Ollendorf Reich, *Wilhelm Reich* (London: Elek, 1969).

172   The popular vote for Nazi candidates in the last stages of the Weimar Republic increased from 800,000 to 6.5 millions in September 1930. See A. Rosenberg, *A History of the German Republic* (London: Methuen, 1936), pp. 275, 304.

comment. Did they not still allow their parents to fix their marriages for them and considerations of caste repeatedly to colour their politics?

In Britain several million working people, disappointed with the record of the present Labour Government, with its wage freeze and attempted assault on the unions, will vote Conservative within the next few weeks. As they did in 1930. And in 1950–51. Or, to the unheard tune of encouragement from self-styled revolutionaries, they will vote Labour, expecting (or not) that things will be "different next time".

At a more mundane level the behaviour of consumers today is no more "rational" than that of voters or of the oppressed classes in history. Those who understand the roots of popular preference know how easily demand can be manipulated. Advertizing experts are fully aware that rational choice has little to do with consumer preferences. When a housewife is asked why she prefers one product to another the reasons she gives are seldom the real ones (even if she is answering in total good faith).

Largely unconscious motives even influence the ideas of revolutionaries and the type of organization in which they choose to be active. At first sight it might appear paradoxical that those aspiring to a non-alienated and creative society based on equality and freedom should "break" with bourgeois conceptions...only to espouse the hierarchical, dogmatic, manipulatory and puritanical ideas of Leninism. It might appear odd that their "rejection" of the irrational and arbitrarily imposed behaviour patterns of bourgeois society, with its demands for uncritical obedience and acceptance of authority, should take the form of that epitome of alienated activity: following the tortuous "line" of a vanguard Party. It might seem strange that those who urge people to think for themselves and to resist the brainwashing of the mass media should be filled with anxiety whenever new ideas raise their troublesome heads within their own ranks.[173] Or that revolutionaries today should still seek to settle personal scores through resort to the methods prevailing in the bourgeois jungle outside. But, as we shall show, there is an internal coherence in all this apparent irrationality.

2. Some Inadequate Explanations

Confronted with disturbing facts like mass popular support for imperialist wars or the rise of fascism a certain type of traditional revolutionary can be guaranteed to provide a stereotyped answer. He will automatically stress the "betrayal" or "inadequacy" of the Second or Third Internationals, or of the German Communist Party...or of this or that leadership which, for some reason or another, failed to rise to the historical occasion. (People who argue this way don't even seem to appreciate that the repeated *tolerance* by the masses of such "betrayals" or "inadequacies" itself warrants a serious explanation.)

Most sophisticated revolutionaries will lay the blame elsewhere. The means of moulding public opinion (press, radio, TV, churches, schools and universities) are in the hands of the ruling class. These media consequently disseminate ruling-class ideas, values and priorities - day in, day out. What is disseminated affects all layers

---

173   We have recently heard it quite seriously proposed in an allegedly libertarian organization – our own – that no one should speak on behalf of the organization before submitting the substance of his proposed comments to a "meetings committee", lest anything new be suddenly sprung on the unsuspecting and presumably defenceless ranks of the ideologically emancipated.

174   To accept this as an "explanation" would be to vest in ideas a power they cannot have, namely the power

of the population, contaminating everyone. Is it surprising, these revolutionaries will ask with a withering smile, that under such circumstances the mass of people still retain reactionary ideas?[174]

This explanation, although partially correct, is insufficient. In the long run it will not explain the continued acceptance by the working class of bourgeois rule - or that such rule has only been overthrown to be replaced by institutions of state capitalist type, embodying fundamentally similar hierarchical relationships (cult of leader, total delegation of authority to an "elite" Party, worship of revealed truth to be found in sacred texts or in the edicts of the Central Committee). If - both East and West - millions of people cannot face up to implications of their exploitation, if they cannot perceive their enforced intellectual and personal underdevelopment, if they are unaware of the intrinsically repressive character of so much that they consider "rational", "commonsense", "obvious", or "natural" (hierarchy, inequality and the puritan ethos, for instance), if they are afraid of initiative and of self-activity, afraid of thinking new thoughts and of treading new paths, and if they are ever ready to follow this leader or that (promising them the moon), or this Party or that (undertaking to change the world "on their behalf"), it is because there are powerful factors conditioning their behaviour *from a very early age* and inhibiting their accession to a different kind of consciousness.

Let us consider for a moment - and not through rose-tinted spectacles - the average middle-aged working-class voter today (it matters little in this respect whether he votes "Conservative" or "Labour"). He is probably hierarchy-conscious, xenophobic, racially-prejudiced, pro-monarchy, pro-capital-punishment, pro-law-and-order, anti-demonstrator, anti-longhaired students and anti-dropout. He is almost certainly sexually repressed (and hence an avid, if vicarious, consumer of the distorted sexuality endlessly depicted in the pages of the *News of the World*). No "practical" Party (aiming at power through the ballot-box) would ever dream of appealing to him through the advocacy of wage equality, workers' management of production, racial integration, penal reform, abolition of the monarchy, dissolution of the police, sexual freedom for adolescents or the legalization of pot. Anyone proclaiming this kind of "transitional programme" would not only fail to get support but would probably be considered some kind of a nut.

But there is an even more important fact. Anyone trying to discuss matters of this kind will almost certainly meet not only with disbelief but also that positive hostility that often denotes latent anxiety.[175] One doesn't meet this kind of response if one argues various meaningless or downright ludicrous propositions. Certain subjects are clearly emotionally loaded. Discussing them generates peculiar resistances that are hardly amenable to rational argument.

It is the purpose of this pamphlet to explore the nature and cause of these resistances and to point out that they are not innate but socially determined. (If they were innate, there would be no rational or socialist perspective whatsoever.) We will be led to conclude that these resistances are the result of a long-standing conditioning, going back to earliest childhood, and that this conditioning is mediated through the whole institution of the patriarchal family. The net result is a powerful

---

totally to dominate material conditions, neutralizing the influence of the economic facts of life. It is surprising that this should never have occurred to our "Marxists".

175   In the words of Thomas Mann in *Buddenbrooks*: "We are most likely to get angry and excited in our opposition to some idea when we ourselves are not quite certain of our position, and are inwardly tempted to take the other side".

reinforcement and perpetuation of the dominant ideology and the mass production of individuals with slavery built into them, individuals ready at a later stage to accept the authority of schoolteacher, priest, employer and politician (and to endorse the prevailing pattern of "rationality"). Understanding this collective character structure gives one new insight into the frequently "irrational" behaviour of individuals or social groups and into the "irrational in politics". It might also provide mankind with new means of transcending these obstacles.

3. The Ignored Area and the Traditional Left

This whole area has been largely ignored by Marxist revolutionaries. The appropriate tool for understanding this aspect of human behaviour – namely psychoanalysis – was only developed in the first two decades of this century. Freud's major contribution to knowledge (the investigation of causality in psychological life, the description of infantile and juvenile sexuality, the honest statement of fact that there was more to sex than procreation, the recognition of the influence of unconscious instinctual drives – and of their repression – in determining behaviour patterns, the description of how such drives are repressed in accordance with the prevailing social dictates, the analysis of the consequences of this repression in terms of symptoms, and in general "the consideration of the unofficial and unacknowledged sides of human life")[176] only became part of our social heritage several decades after Marx's death. Certain reactionary aspects of classical psychoanalysis (the "necessary" adaptation of the instinctual life to the requirements of a society whose class nature was never explicitly proclaimed, the "necessary" sublimation of "undisciplined" sexuality in order to maintain "social stability", "civilization" and the cultural life of society,[177] the theory of the death instinct, etc.) were only to be transcended later still by the revolutionary psychoanalysis of Wilhelm Reich[178] and others.

Reich set out to elaborate a social psychology based on both Marxism and psychoanalysis. His aim was to explain how ideas arose in men's minds, in relation to the real condition of their lives, and how in turn such ideas influenced human behaviour. There was clearly a discrepancy between the material conditions of the masses and their conservative outlook. No appeal to psychology was necessary to understand why a hungry man stole bread or why workers, fed up with being pushed around, decided to down tools. What social psychology had to explain however "is not why the starving individual steals or why the exploited individual strikes, but why the majority of starving individuals do *not* steal, and the majority of exploited individuals do *not* strike". Classical sociology could "satisfactorily explain a social phenomenon when human thinking and acting serve a rational purpose, when they serve the satisfaction of needs and directly express the economic situation. It fails,

---

176   B. Malinowski, *Sex and Repression in Savage Society* (Cleveland : Meridian Books, 1966), p.6.

177   An example (among many) of Freud's reactionary pronouncements is to be found in his essay, *The Future of an Illusion*, published in 1927, in which he wrote: "It is just as impossible to do without control of the mass by a minority as it is to dispense with coercion in the work of civilization. The masses are lazy and unintelligent: they have no love for instinctual renunciation, and they are not convinced by argument of its inevitability; and the individuals composing them support one another in giving free rein to their indiscipline".

178   An excellent study dealing with both Reich, the psychoanalyst, and Reich, the revolutionary, has recently been published in Switzerland (Michel Cattier, *La Vie et l'Oeuvre du Docteur Wilhelm Reich* (Lausanne: La Cité, 1969)). It is essential reading for anyone seriously concerned at understanding the tragic life of this remarkable man. The author of this pamphlet has borrowed deeply from this source.

however, when human thinking and acting *contradict* the economic situation, when, in other words, they are irrational".[179]

What was new, at the level of revolutionary theory, in this kind of concern? Traditional Marxists had always underestimated – and still underestimate – the effect of ideas on the material structure of society. Like parrots, they repeat that economic infrastructure and ideological superstructures mutually interact. But then they proceed to look upon what is essentially a dialectical, two-way relationship as an almost exclusively one-sided process (economic "base" determining what goes on in the realm of ideas). They have never sought concretely to explain how a reactionary political doctrine could gain a mass foothold and later set a whole nation in motion (how, for instance, in the early 1930s, Nazi ideology rapidly spread throughout all layers of German society, the process including the now well documented massive desertion of thousands of Communist militants to the ranks of the Nazis).[180] In the words of a "heretical" Marxist, Daniel Guérin, author of one of the most sophisticated social, economic and psychological interpretations of the fascist phenomenon:

> Some people believe themselves very "Marxist" and very "materialist" when they neglect human factors and only concern themselves with material and economic facts. They accumulate figures, statistics, percentages. They study with extreme precision the deep causes of social phenomena. But because they don't follow with similar precision how these causes are reflected in human consciousness, living reality eludes them. Because they are only interested in material factors, they understand absolutely nothing about how the deprivations endured by the masses are converted into aspirations of a religious type.[181]

Neglecting this subjective factor in history, such "Marxists" – and they constitute today the overwhelming majority of the species – cannot explain the lack of correlation between the economic frustrations of the working class and its lack of will to put an end to the system which engenders them. They do not grasp the fact that when certain beliefs become anchored in the thinking (and influence the behaviour) of the masses, they become themselves material facts of history.

What was it therefore, Reich asked, which in the real life of the oppressed limited their will to revolution? His answer was that the working class was readily influenced by reactionary and irrational ideas because such ideas fell on fertile soil.[182] For the average Marxist, workers were adults who hired their labour power to capitalists and were exploited by them. This was correct as far as it went. But one had to take into account all aspects of working class life if one wanted to understand the political attitudes of the working class. This meant one had to recognize some obvious facts, namely that the worker had a childhood, that he was brought up by parents themselves conditioned by the society in which they lived, that he had a wife and

---

179   W. Reich, *The Mass Psychology of Fascism* (New York: Orgone Institute Press, 1946), p. 15.

180   No, we are not "slandering" those courageous German anti-fascists who were the first to die in Hitler's concentration camps. We are only saying that for every Communist of this kind, at least two others joined the Nazis, while dozens of others said nothing and did nothing.

181   D. Guérin, *Fascisme et Grande Capital* (Paris: Gallimard, 1945), p.88. Also available as *Fascism and Big Business* (New York: Pathfinder Press, 1973).

182   In the next section we will describe how the "soil" is rendered "fertile" for the acceptance of such ideas. At this stage we would only like to point out that other sections of the population are also affected. Ruling classes, for instance, are often mystified by their own ideology. But politically this is a phenomenon of lesser significance (ruling elites in fact benefit by the maintenance of ideological mystification and of irrational social systems which proclaim the "need" for such elites!).

children, sexual needs, frustrations, and family conflicts. Overcrowding, physical fatigue, financial insecurity, and back-street abortions rendered these problems particularly acute in working-class circles. Why should such factors be neglected in seeking to explain working-class behaviour? Reich sought to develop a total analysis which would incorporate such facts and attach the appropriate importance to them.

4. The Process of Conditioning

In learning to obey their parents, children learn obedience in general. This deference learned in the family setting will manifest itself whenever the child faces a "superior" in later life. Sexual repression - by the already sexually repressed parents[183] - is an integral part of the conditioning process.

Rigid and obsessional parents start by imposing rigid feeding times on the newborn. They then seek to impose regular potting habits on infants scarcely capable of maintaining the sitting posture. They are obsessed by food, bowels, and the "inculcating of good eating habits". A little later they will start scolding and punishing their masturbating five-year-old. At times they will even threaten their male children with physical mutilation.[184] (They cannot accept that children at that - or any other age for that matter - should derive pleasure from sex.) They are horrified at their discovery of sexual exhibitionism between consenting juniors in private. Later still, they will warn their twelve-year-old boys of the dire dangers of "real masturbation". They will watch the clock to see what time their fifteen-year-old daughters get home, or search their son's pockets for contraceptives. For most parents, the child-rearing years are one long, anti-sexual saga.

How does the child react to this? He adapts by trial and error. He is scolded when he masturbates. He adapts by repressing his sexuality. Attempted affirmation of sexual needs then takes the form of revolt against parental authority. But this revolt is again punished. Obedience is achieved through punishment. Punishment also ensures that forbidden activities are invested with feelings of guilt[185] which may be (but more often aren't) sufficient to inhibit them.[186]

The anxiety associated with the fulfilment of sexual needs becomes part of the anxiety associated with all rebellious thoughts or actions (sexuality and all manifestations of rebelliousness are both indiscriminately curbed by the "educators"). The child gradually comes to suppress needs whose acting out would incur parental displeasure or result in punishment, and ends up afraid of his sexual drives and of his tendencies to revolt. At a later stage another kind of equilibrium is achieved which has been described as "being torn between desires that are repugnant to my conscience and a conscience repugnant to my desires".[187] The individual is "marked like a road map from head to toes by his repressions".[188]

---

183   For a discussion of the historical roots of the whole process of sexual repression, see section 6.

184   For an extremely amusing account of this kind of conditioning in a New York Jewish family – and of its consequences – see *Portnoy's Complaint* by Philip Roth (London: Cape, 1968)…also referred to as *The Gripes of Roth*.

185   Parents are "the outstanding producers and packagers of guilt in our time" (Roth, *op. cit.*, p. 36).

186   The unstable equilibrium is known as "publicly pleasing my parents, while privately pulling my putz" (*ibid.*, p. 37).

187   *Ibid.*, p. 32.

188   *Ibid.*, p. 124.

In the little boy, early repression is associated with an identification with the paternal image. In a sense, this is a prefiguration of the later "country or party". The father, in this sense, is the representative of the state and of authority in the family nucleus.

To neutralize his sexual needs and his rebellion against his parents, the child develops "overcompensations". The unconscious revolt against the father engenders servility. The fear of sexuality engenders prudery. We all know those old maids of both sexes, ever on the alert against any hint of sexuality among children. Their pre-occupations are obviously determined by deep fears of their own sexuality. The reluctance of most revolutionaries to discuss these topics is similarly motivated.

Another frequent by-product of sexual repression is to split sexuality into its component parts. Tenderness is given a positive value, whereas sensuality is condemned. A dissociation between affection and sexual pleasure is seen in many male adolescents and leads them to adopt double sexual standards. They idealize some girl on a pedestal while seeking to satisfy their sexual needs with other girls whom they openly or subconsciously despise.

The road to a healthy sex life for adolescents is blocked by both external and internal obstacles. The external obstacles (difficulty in finding an undisturbed place, difficulty in escaping from family surveillance, etc.) are obvious enough. The internal (psychological) obstacles may, at times, be severe enough to influence the perception of the sexual need. The two kinds of obstacles (internal and external) mutually reinforce one another. External factors consolidate sexual repression and the sexual repression predisposes to the influence of the external factors. The family is the hub of this vicious circle.

However apparently successful the repression, the repressed material is, of course, still there. But it is now running in subterranean channels. Having accepted a given set of "cultural'" values, the individual must now defend himself against anything that might disrupt the painfully established equilibrium. He has constantly to mobilize part of his psychological potentialities against the "disturbing" influences. In addition to neuroses and psychoses the "energy" expended in this constant repression results in difficulties in thought and concentration, in a diminution of awareness and probably in some impairment of mental capacity. "Inability to concentrate" is perhaps the most common of neurotic symptoms.

According to Reich, the

> suppression of the natural sexuality in the child, particularly of its genital sexuality, makes the child apprehensive, shy, obedient, afraid of authority, "good" and "adjusted" in the authoritarian sense; it paralyzes the rebellious forces because any rebellion is laden with anxiety; it produces, by inhibiting sexual curiosity and sexual thinking in the child, a general inhibition of thinking and of critical faculties. In brief, the goal of sexual repression is that of producing an individual who is adjusted to the authoritarian order and who will submit to it in spite of all misery and degradation....The result is fear of freedom, and a conservative, reactionary mentality. *Sexual repression aids political reaction, not only through this process which makes the mass individual passive and unpolitical, but also by creating in his structure an interest in actively supporting the authoritarian order.*[189]

When a child's upbringing has been completed the individual has acquired something more complex and harmful than a simple obedience response to those in

---

189 Reich, *The Mass Psychology of Fascism, op. cit.* pp. 25–26. (My emphasis – M.B.)

authority. He has developed a whole system of reactions, regressions, thoughts, rationalizations, which form a character structure adapted to the authoritarian social system. The purpose of education – both East and West – is the mass production of robots of this kind who have so internalized social constraints that they submit to them automatically.

Psychologists and psychiatrists have written pages about the *medical* effects of sexual repression.[190] Reich however constantly reiterated its *social* function, exercised through the family. The purpose of sexual repression was to anchor submission to authority and the fear of freedom into people's "character armour". The net result was the reproduction, generation after generation, of the basic conditions necessary for the manipulation and enslavement of the masses.

5. The Function of the Family

In his classical study on *The Origin of the Family, Private Property and the State*, Engels attributes three main functions to the family in capitalist society:

(a) It was a *mechanism for the transmission of wealth through inheritance*, a process which permitted the dominant social groups to perpetuate their economic power. This has undoubtedly been an important function of the bourgeois family. However Engels's hope that "with the disappearance of private property the family would lose its last reason to exist" has not materialized. The private ownership of the means of production has been abolished in Russia for over fifty years and yet the family (in the compulsive, bourgeois sense) still seems deeply embedded both in Russian consciousness and in Russian reality. By a strange paradox, it is in the capitalist West that the bourgeois family is being submitted to the most radical critique – in both theory and practice.

(b) The family was also a *unit of economic production*, particularly in the countryside and in petty trade. Large-scale industry and the general drift to the towns character-istic of the twentieth century have markedly reduced the significance of this function.

(c) The family was finally *a mechanism for the propagation of the human species*. This statement is also correct, in relation to a whole period of human history. It should not, of course, be taken to imply that, were it not for the civil or religious marriages of the bourgeois type (what Engels called "those permits to practise sex") the propa-gation of the human species would abruptly cease! Other types of relationships (more or less lasting, monogamous – or otherwise – while they last) are certainly conceivable. In a communist society technological changes and new living patterns would largely do away with household chores. The bringing up of children would probably not be the exclusive function of one pair of individuals for more than a short time. What are usually given as psychological reasons for the perpetuation of the compulsive marriage are often just rationalizations.

Engels's comments about the family, partly valid as they still are (and valid as they may have been) don't really allow one to grasp the full significance of this insti-

---

190   This factual approach is a relatively recent development. As Kinsey, Pomeroy and Martin point out in their famous study on the *Sexual Behaviour of the Human Male* (Philadelphia: Saunders,1948), pp. 21–22: "From the dawn of human history, from the drawings left by primitive peoples, on through the developments of all civiliza-tions (ancient, classic, oriental, medieval and modern), men have recorded their sexual activities and their thinking about sex. The printed literature is enormous and the other material is inexhaustible...[This literature] is at once an interesting reflection on man's absorbing interest in sex and his astounding ignorance of it; his desire to know and his unwillingness to face the facts; his respect for an objective scientific approach to the problems involved and his overwhelming urge to be poetic, pornographic, literary, philosophical, traditional and moral...in short, to do anything except ascertain the basic facts about himself".

tution. They ignore a whole dimension of life. Classical psychoanalysis hinted at a further function: the transmission of the dominant cultural pattern. Revolutionary psychoanalysis was to take this concept much further.

Freud himself had pointed out that the parents brought up their children according to the dictates of their own (the parents') superegos:[191]

> In general parents and similar authorities follow the dictates of their own super-egos in the upbringing of children....In the education of the child they are severe and exacting. They have forgotten the difficulties of their own childhood, and are glad to be able to identify themselves fully at last with their own parents, who in their day subjected them to such severe restraints. The result is that the superego of the child is not really built upon the model of the parents but on that of the parents' superego. It takes over the same content, it becomes the vehicle of tra-dition and of all the age-long values which have been handed down in this way from generation to generation...Mankind never lives completely in the present; the ideologies of the superego perpetuate the past, the traditions of the race and the people, which yield but slowly to the influence of the present and to new developments. So long as they work through the superego, they play an impor-tant part in man's life, quite independently of economic conditions.[192]

Reich was to develop these ideas to explain the lag between class conscious-ness and economic reality, and the tremendous social inertia represented by habits of deference and submission among the oppressed. In order to do this he had to launch a frontal attack on the institution of the bourgeois family, an assault which was to provoke heated attacks on him. These were to be launched not only by reac-tionaries and religious bigots of all kinds, but also by orthodox psychoanalysts[193] and by orthodox Marxists.[194]

"As the economic basis (of the family) became less significant", Reich wrote, "its place was taken by the political function which the family now began to assume. Its cardinal function, that for which it is mostly supported and defended by conserva-tive science and law, is that of serving as a *factory for authoritarian ideologies and conservative structures*. It forms the educational apparatus through which practically every individual of our society, from the moment of drawing his first breath, has to pass...*it is the conveyor belt between the economic structure of conservative society and its ideological* superstructure".[195]

Reich probed ruthlessly into familial behaviour. The predominating type (the "lower-middle-class" family) extended high up the social scale, but even further down into the class of industrial workers. Its basis was "the relation of the patriarchal father to his wife and children...because of the contradiction between his position in the

---

191   According to the Freudian model, the personality consists of the id, the ego and the superego. The first and last are unconscious. The id is the sum total of the instinctual drives of the individual. The superego is a kind of internal policeman, originating in the constraints exercised on the individual 'on behalf of society' by parents and other educators. The ego is man's conscious self.

192   S. Freud, *New Introductory Lectures on Psychoanalysis* (London: The Hogarth Press, 1933), pp. 90–91.

193   In 1927 Freud himself warned Reich, his former pupil, that in attacking the family he was "walking into a hornet's nest". In August 1934, Reich was to be expelled from the German Association of Psychoanalysts.

194   Reich was expelled from the German Communist Party in 1933. In December 1932 the Party had forbidden the circulation of his works in the Communist Youth Movement, among whom they had evoked a considerable echo. Marxist and psychoanalyst, Reich saw his work condemned by those who claimed to be the standard bearers of Marxism and psychoanalysis. A little later, the Nazis were also to forbid the circulation of his works in Germany.

195   Reich, *The Sexual Revolution, op.cit.,* p. 72.

productive process (subordinate) and his family function (boss) he is a sergeant-major type. He kowtows to those above, absorbs the prevailing attitudes (hence his tendency to imitation) and dominates those below. He transmits the governmental and social concepts and enforces them".[196] The process is "mitigated in the industrial workers' milieu by the fact that the children are much less supervised".[197]

Nearly all reactionaries clearly perceive that sexual freedom would subvert the compulsive marriage and with it the authoritarian structure of which the family is a part. (The attitude of the Greek colonels towards miniskirts, co-education and "permissive" literature would be a textbook example of what we are talking about.) Sexual inhibitions must therefore be anchored in the young.

> Authoritarian society is not concerned about '"morality per se". Rather, the anchoring of sexual morality and the changes it brings about in the organism create that specific psychic structure which forms the mass-psychological basis of any authoritarian social order. The vassal-structure is a mixture of sexual impotence, helplessness, longing for a Führer, fear of authority, fear of life, and mysticism. It is characterized by devout loyalty and simultaneous rebellion...People with such a structure are incapable of democratic living. Their structure nullifies all attempts at establishing or maintaining organizations run along truly democratic principles.[198] They form the mass-psychological soil on which the dictatorial or bureaucratic tendencies of their democratically elected leaders can develop.[199]

A class society can only function as long as those it exploits accept their exploitation. The statement would seem so obvious as hardly to need elaboration. Yet there are, on the political scene today, groups who maintain that the conditions are "rotten ripe for revolution" and that only the lack of an appropriate leadership prevents the revolutionary masses, yearning for a total transformation of their conditions of life, from carrying out such a revolution. Unfortunately, this is very far from being the case. In an empirical way even Lenin perceived this. In April 1917 he wrote: "The bourgeoisie maintains itself not only by force, but also by the lack of consciousness, by the force of custom and habit among the masses".[200]

It is obvious that if large sections of the population were constantly questioning the principles of hierarchy, the authoritarian organization of production, the wages system, or other fundamental aspects of the social structure, no ruling class could maintain itself in power for long. For rulers to continue ruling it is necessary that those at the bottom of the social ladder not only accept their condition, but eventually lose even the sense of being exploited. Once this psychological process has been achieved the division of society becomes legitimized in peoples' minds. The exploited cease to perceive it as something imposed on them from without. The oppressed have internalized their own oppression. They tend to behave like robots, programmed not to rebel against the established order. The robots may even seek

---

196   *Ibid.,* p. 73.

197   *Ibid.,* p. 75.

198   The relevance of this to most "left" organizations hardly needs stressing. The revolutionaries themselves – in this as in so many other respects – are among the worst enemies of the revolution.

199   *Ibid.,* p. 79.

200   V. I. Lenin, *Selected Works,* vol. VI, p. 36. Lenin wrote this despite a complete lack of understanding or awareness of the mechanisms whereby "the force of custom and habit among the masses" were mediated and perpetuated. This lack of understanding was to lead to his open hostility to the sexual revolution which swept Russia in the wake of the Civil War and to contribute yet another element to the bureaucratic degeneration.

to defend their subordinate position, to rationalize it and will often reject as "pie-in-the-sky" any talk of emancipation. They are often impermeable to progressive ideas. Only at times of occasional insurrectionary outbursts do the rulers have to resort to force, as a kind of reinforcement of a conditioning stimulus.

Reich describes this process as follows:

> It is not merely a matter of imposing ideologies, attitudes and concepts on the members of society. It is a matter of a deep-reaching process in each new generation of the formation of a psychic structure which corresponds to the existing social order, in all strata of the population...Because this order moulds the psychic structure of all members of society it reproduces itself in people...*the first and most important place of reproduction of the social order is the patriarchal family* which creates in children a character which makes them amenable to the later influence of an authoritarian order...this characteriological anchoring of the social order explains the tolerance of the suppressed toward the rule of the upper class, a tolerance which sometimes goes as far as the affirmation of their own subjugation...The investigation of character structure, therefore, is of more than clinical interest. It leads to the question why it is that ideologies change so much more slowly than the socio-economic base, why man as a rule lags so far behind what he creates and which should and could change him. The reason is that the character structure is acquired in early childhood and undergoes little change.[201]

To return to the title of this pamphlet, it is this collective character structure, this "protective" armour of rigid and stereotyped reactions and thoughts, which determines the irrational behaviour of individuals, groups or large masses of people. In the words of Spinoza our job is "neither to laugh nor to weep, but to understand". It is in this collective character structure of the masses that one might find explanations for the proletariat's lack of class consciousness, for its acceptance of the established order, for its ready endorsement of reactionary ideas, for its participation in imperialist wars. It is also here that one should seek the cause of dogmatism, of religious attitudes in politics, of conservatism among "revolutionaries" and of the anxieties generated by the new. It is here that one should seek the roots of "the irrational in politics".

6. The Historical Roots

Not all human societies are - or have been - sexually repressed. There is considerable evidence that the sexual ethos and mores of certain early societies - and of certain "primitive" societies today - are very different from those of "modern, western man".

It is impossible to understand how or why sexual repression originated - and what influences maintain, enhance or weaken it - without seeing the problem in a much wider context, namely that of the historical evolution of relations between the sexes, in particular of the evolution of such human relationships as kinship and marriage. These are the central concerns of modern social anthropology.

The whole subject is like a minefield, littered with methodological and terminological trip wires. About a hundred years ago a number of important books were published which shook established thinking to the roots in that they questioned the

---

201   Preface to first edition of W. Reich, *Character Analysis* (London: Vision Press Ltd., 1958), pp. xxii, xxiii, xxiv.

202   Among such books one should mention J.J. Bachofen's *Das Mutterrecht* (Stuttgart, 1861), J.F. McLennan's *Primitive Marriage* (London: Black, 1865), and *Studies in Ancient History* (London: Macmillan, 1876), L.H. Morgan's *Ancient Society* (New York: Holt, 1870), and *Systems of Consanguinity and Affinity of the Human*

immutability of human institutions and behaviour.[202] The authors of these books played an important role in the history of anthropology. They sought to put the subject on a firm historical basis. They pointed out important connections between forms of marriage and sexual customs on the one hand and - on the other hand - such factors as the level of technology, the inheritance of property, and the authority relations prevailing within various social groups, etc. They founded the whole study of kinship and gave it its terminology. But carried away in the great scientific and rationalist euphoria of the late nineteenth century these authors generalized far beyond what was permissible on the basis of the available data. They constructed great schemes and drew conclusions about the history of mankind which some modern experts have politely described as "famous pseudo-historical speculations"[203] and others as "quite staggeringly without foundation".[204]

We will now briefly summarize these "classical" conceptions (in relation to the areas which concern us) with a view to commenting on what is still valid within them, what is dubious and what can no longer be accepted in the light of modern knowledge.

In primitive societies the level of technology was very low and there was no surplus product to be appropriated by non-productive sections of the community. There was an elementary, "biological" division of labour: the men, who were stronger, went out hunting or sowed the fields; the women prepared the meals and looked after the children. It was held that in these societies "group marriages" were common. As a result it was difficult or impossible to know the father of any particular child. The mother, of course, was always known and descent was therefore acknowledged in matrilinear terms. Such societies were described as "matriarchal". With improvements in technology (the discovery of bronze and copper, the smelting of iron ore, the manufacture of implements, the development of new methods of soil cultivation and of rearing cattle) it soon became possible for "two arms to produce more than one mouth could consume". War and the capture of slaves became a meaningful proposition. The economic role of the men in the tribe soon assumed a preponderance which was no longer in keeping with their equivocal social status. In Engels's words:

> as wealth increased, it on the one hand gave the man a more important status in the family than the woman, and on the other hand it created a stimulus to utilize this strengthened position to overthrow the traditional order of inheritance in favour of his children. But this was impossible as long as descent according to mother-right prevailed.[205]

According to the "classical" theory a profound change then took place, probably spread over many centuries, which Engels described as "the world historic defeat of the female sex".[206] The males gradually became the dominant sex, both economically and socially. Women became a commodity to be exchanged against cattle or weapons. With further changes in the productivity of labour, a definite social surplus was now being produced. Those who had access to this surplus sought to institu-

---

Family (Washington: Smithsonian Institute, 1877), Engels's The Origin of the Family, Private Property and the State (Zurich, 1884), and E. Westermarck's The History of Human Marriage (London: Macmillan, 1889).

203 See A. R. Radcliffe-Brown and D. Forde's African Systems of Kinship and Marriage (Oxford University Press, 1950), p. 72.

204 R. Fox, Kinship and Marriage (Harmondsworth: Penguin Books, 1967), p. 18.

205 F. Engels, The Origin of the Family, Private Property and the State (Moscow: F.L.P.H., 1954), p. 92.

206 Ibid., p. 94.

tionalize their right to it as "private property" and to leave part of it to their descendants. But to do this they had to know who their descendants were. Hence the appearance of the patriarchal family, of monogamous marriage, and of a sexual morality which stressed female chastity and which demanded of women virginity before marriage and faithfulness during it. Female unfaithfulness becomes a crime punishable by death for it allows doubts to arise as to the legitimacy of the descendants.

What is false in this schema is the notion – often explicitly stated – that the whole of mankind went through a series of states characterized by specific forms of social organization and specific patterns of inheritance.

There is little evidence that societies based on "matriarchy"[207] or even on "mother-right" were universally dominant forms. It is wrong to regard any contemporary tribe in which matrilinear descent still pertains as some kind of fossil, arrested at an earlier stage of evolutionary development.[208] It is also wrong to associate specific marriage forms with specific levels of technological development ("group marriage" for "savage society", "the syndiasmic family" for "barbarism", "the monogamous marriage" for "civilization", etc.). This is not to say that kinship systems are arbitrary. They are adaptable and have certainly been adapted to fulfil varying human needs. These "needs" have differed widely according to population density, climatic conditions, land fertility, and numerous other variables, known and unknown. The alternatives "patriarchal"–"matriarchal" are moreover extremely naive.[209] We now know that we must distinguish between matrilinear, patrilinear or "cognatic" (kinship through both lines) patterns of inheritance and between matrilocal and patrilocal (who lives where?) patterns of abode, and that these in turn exercise considerable influence on social and sexual mores. There are also differences between person-to-person relationships and obligations (inheritance, etc.) and group obligations (in relation to common or impartible land, to ancestor worship, to "duties" to avenge death, etc.) and these may conflict. Reality is extremely complex in its manifestations and these cannot today be as readily "tidied up" as they were in the past. Moreover the "very rigidity of the [classical] theories makes them difficult to use and is in stark contrast to the malleability of human beings".[210]

What remains therefore of the classical schema? Firstly, the intellectual courage and ambition of seeking to grasp reality in its totality and of not seeking refuge behind the complexity of facts to proclaim the incoherence of nature. When one hears that "modern anthropology" has "invalidated Morgan" one is reminded of oft-heard verdicts that "modern sociology" has "invalidated Marx". At one level this is true but there is also a deliberately entertained confusion between perspective and detail, between method and content, between intention and fulfilment.

---

207 There has probably never been a truly "matriarchal" society in the sense of a mirror image of patriarchal society. The notion of such a society where wives hold the purse strings, order their husbands about, beat them up from time to time and take all the important decisions concerning both individuals and the tribe as a whole is at best a retrospective projection or nightmare of guilt–laden males.

208 It is interesting that the best known modern matrilinear societies (the Nayars of Kerala and the Menangkabau Malays) far from being "primitive" are advanced, literate and cultured people, who have produced an extensive literature. The Khasi of Assam are less advanced but are far from being savages. As Radcliffe–Brown and Forde point out (*African Systems of Kinship and Marriage*) "the typical instances of mother–right are found not amongst the most primitive people but in advanced or relatively advanced societies".

209 In this they resemble many of the "alternatives" propounded today by many so-called revolutionaries (for instance "monogamous marriage" or "communes" for life "after the Revolution").

210 Fox, *op. cit.*, p. 63.

At the more specific level it remains true that the appearance of a social surplus led to a struggle for its appropriation and to attempts to restrict its dispersal by institutionalized means. It is also true that by and large this process was associated with a progressive restriction of female sexual rights and with the appearance of an increasingly authoritarian morality. Although some matrilinear societies may have been sexually inhibited, and although not all patriarchal societies are necessarily repressive, it remains true that by and large the more widespread the "patriarchal" functions the more repressive the societies have been. Modern psychoanalysis may throw further light on the mechanisms whereby this came about. At this point we can only pinpoint an area that badly needs to be studied.

The "inferior" status of women soon came to be widely accepted. Over the centuries, throughout slave society, feudal society and capitalist society - but also in the many parts of the world which have not gone through this sequence - a whole ethos, a whole philosophy and a whole set of social customs were to emerge which consecrated this subordinate relationship, both in real life and in the minds of both men and women.

The sacred texts of the Hindus limit women's access to freedom and to material belongings. The Ancient Greeks were profoundly misogynist and relegated their women to the gynecaeum. Pythagoras speaks of "a good principle which created order, light and man - and a bad principle which created chaos, darkness and woman". Demosthenes proclaimed that "one took a wife to have legitimate children, concubines to be well looked after and courtesans for the pleasures of physical love". Plato in his *Republic* declares that "the most holy marriages are those which are of most benefit to the State". The fathers of the Christian Church soon succeeded in destroying the early hopes of freedom and emancipation which had led many women to martyrdom. Women became synonymous with eternal temptation. They are seen as a constant "invitation to fornication, a trap for the unwary". St. Paul states that "man was not created for woman, but woman for man". St. John Chrysostome proclaims that "among all wild beasts, none are as dangerous as women". According to St. Thomas Aquinas "woman is destined to live under man's domination and has no authority of her own right".

These attitudes are perpetuated in the dominant ideology of the Middle Ages and even into more recent times. Milton, in *Paradise Lost,* proclaims that "man was made for God and woman was made for man". Schopenhauer defines woman as "an animal with long hair and short ideas", and Nietzsche calls her "the warrior's pastime". Even the muddleheaded Proudhon sees her as "housewife or courtesan" and proclaims that "neither by nature or destiny can woman be an associate, a citizen or a holder of public office". Kaiser Wilhelm the Second defined a role for women (later echoed by the Third Reich) as being *"Kirche, Küche, Kinder"* (Church, Kitchen and Kids).

In 1935 Wilhelm Reich wrote a major work, *Der Einbruch der sexual-moral,* which discussed how an authoritarian sexual morality developed. In it Reich discusses some interesting observations of Malinowski's concerning the inhabitants of the Trobriand Islands (off Eastern New Guinea), where matrilinear forms of kinship prevailed. (Reich had met Malinowski in London in 1934.) Among the Trobrianders there was free sexual play during childhood and considerable sexual freedom during adolescence. Tics and neuroses were virtually unknown and the general attitude to life was easy and relaxed. Reich discusses however the practice whereby, among the ruling groups, certain girls were encouraged to marry their first cousins (the sons of their mother's brother), thereby enabling marriage settlements to be recuperated and remain within the family. Whereas sexual freedom was widespread among all other young Trobrianders, those destined for a marriage of this kind were submitted from an early age to all sorts of sexual taboos. Economic interests – the accumulation of wealth within the ruling group – determined restrictions of sexual freedom within this group.

Reich vividly contrasts the Trobrianders and other sexually uninhibited societies with classical patriarchal societies which produce mass neurosis and mass misery through sexual repression. With the strengthening of patriarchy:

> the family acquires, in addition to its economic function, the far more significant function of changing the human structure from that of the free clan member to that of the suppressed family member...the relationship between clan members, which was free and voluntary, based only on common vital interests, is replaced by a conflict between economic and sexual interests. Voluntary achievement in work is replaced by compulsive work and rebellion against it. Natural sexual sociality is replaced by the demands of morality; voluntary, happy love relationship is replaced by genital repression, neurotic disturbances and sexual perversions; the naturally strong, self-reliant biological organism becomes weak, helpless, dependent, fearful of God; the orgiastic experiencing of nature is replaced by mystical ecstasy, "religious experience" and unfulfilled vegetative longing; the weakened ego of the individual seeks strength in the identification with the tribe, later the "nation", and with the chief of the tribe, later the patriarch of the tribe and the king of the nation.[211] With that the birth of the vassal structure has taken place; the structural anchoring of human subjugation is secured.[212]

7. Wilhelm Reich and the Sexual Revolution

Those who want to change society must seek to understand how people act and think in society. This is not a field in which traditional revolutionaries are at home. For reasons we have shown they feel distinctly uncomfortable in it. Reich's views on sexual conditioning are certainly of relevance here, whatever one may think of other aspects of his work.[213]

Some possible misunderstandings should be cleared up immediately. We are not saying that the sexual revolution is *the* revolution. We have not abandoned the fight for the Revolution to become "prophets of the better orgasm". We are not in transit from collective revolutionary politics to individual sexual emancipation. We are not saying that sexual factors are to be *substituted* for economic ones in the understanding of social reality or that understanding sexual repression will automatically generate an insight into the mechanisms of exploitation and alienation which are at the root of class society. Nor are we endorsing Reich's later writings, whether in the field of biology or in the field of politics.

---

211   Or with the Party — or the General Secretary of the Party.

212   Reich, *The Sexual Revolution, op. cit.,* pp. 161–2.

213   In the last years of his life Reich developed paranoid symptoms and quarrelled with nearly all his erstwhile supporters. He was driven mad, at least in part, by the apparently insoluble contradiction "no social revolution without sexual revolution — no sexual revolution without social revolution". Ilse Ollendorf Reich, *Wilhelm Reich, op. cit.,* gives a fairly objective account of the last phase of the life of this remarkable man.

What we *are* saying is that revolution is a total phenomenon or it is nothing,[214] that a social revolution which is not *also* a sexual revolution is unlikely to have gone much below the surface of things and that sexual emancipation is not something that will "come later", "automatically" or as a "by-product" of a revolution in other aspects of peoples' lives. We are stressing that no "understanding" of social reality can be total which neglects the sexual factors and that sexual repression itself has both economic origins and social effects. We are trying to explain some of the difficulties confronting revolutionaries and some of the real problems they are up against – here and now. We are finally trying to explain why the task of the purely "industrial" militant or of the purely "political" revolutionary is so difficult, unrewarding and in the long run sterile.

Unless revolutionaries are clearly aware of *all* the resistances they are up against, how can they hope to break them down? Unless revolutionaries are clearly aware of the resistances (i.e. the unsuspected influences of the dominant ideology) within themselves, how can they hope to come to grips with the problems of others?

How much of the life of the ordinary person is devoted to "politics" (even in basic terms of organized economic struggle) and how much to problems of inter-personal relationships? To ask the question is already to provide an answer. Yet just look at the average Left political literature today. Reading the columns of the *Morning Star*, *Workers' Press* or *Socialist Standard* one doesn't get a hint that the problems discussed in this pamphlet even exist. Man is seen as a ridiculous fragment of his full stature. One seldom gets the impression that the traditional revolutionaries are talking about real people, whose problems in relation to wives, parents, companions or children occupy at least as much of their lives as their struggle against economic exploitation. Marxists sometimes state (but more often just imply) that a change in the property relations (or in the relations of production) will initiate a process which will eventually solve the emotional problems of mankind (an end to sexual misery through a change in the leadership?). This does not follow in the least. If Marx is right, that "socialism is man's positive self-consciousness", the struggle at the level of sexual emancipation must be waged in explicit terms and victory not just left to happen (or not happen) in the wake of economic change. It is difficult, however, to convince the average revolutionary of this. Their own "character armour" renders them impervious to the basic needs of many of those on whose behalf they believe they are acting. They are afraid to politicize the sexual question because they are afraid of what is in themselves.

What are the practical implications of the ideas we have here outlined? Can the sexual revolution take place within a capitalist context? Can a total revolution take place while people are still sexually repressed? We hope, in this section, to show that even posing the question in these terms is wrong and that there is a profound dialectical relation between the two which should never be lost sight of.

Reich originally hoped it might be possible to eliminate people's neuroses by education, explanation and a change in their sexual habits. But he soon came to realize that it was a waste of time to line patients up for the analyst's couch if society was producing neuroses faster than analysts were capable of coping with them. Capitalist society was a mass-production industry as far as neuroses were concerned. And where it did not produce well-defined clinically recognizable neuroses, it often produced "adaptations" that crippled the individual by compelling him to submit. (In

---

214   As St. Just once emphasized, "those who will only carry out half a revolution dig their own graves".

modern society submission and adaptation are often the price paid for avoiding an individual neurosis.) Growing awareness of this fact led Reich increasingly to question the whole pattern of social organization and to draw revolutionary conclusions. He came to see that "the sexual problem" was deeply related to authoritarian social structures and could not be solved short of overthrowing the established order.

At this point many would have abandoned psychoanalysis for radical politics of the classical type. What makes Reich such an interesting and original thinker is that he also perceived the converse, namely that it would be impossible fundamentally to alter the existing social order as long as people were conditioned (through sexual repression and an authoritarian upbringing) into accepting the fundamental norms of the society around them. Reich joined the Austrian Communist Party in July 1927 following the shootings in Schattendorf and Vienna.[215] He participated in meetings, leafletting, demonstrations, etc. But he simultaneously continued to develop revolutionary psychoanalysis, guiding it into biologically uncharted territory. He took it from where it ceased to be a comfortable profession into areas where it began to be a dangerous occupation. He set up free sexual hygiene clinics in the working-class districts of Vienna. These proved extremely popular. They gave Reich a very deep insight not only into the sexual and economic misery of the population, but also into "the acquired irrational structure of the masses" which made "dictatorship through utilization of the irrational possible".[216] In Reich's writings "man" as patient and "man" as social being merged more and more into one. Reich's very experiences in politics (the endorsement and "justification" of police brutality by large sections of the Austrian population, the acceptance of authority even by the starving, the relatively easy accession to power by the Nazis in Germany, the triumph of the "political pirates" over the "repressed and hungry masses") led him to question ever more deeply the mechanisms whereby the dominant ideology permeated the ranks of the oppressed, to search ever more thoroughly for the roots of the "irrational in politics".

Reich's conclusions have already been indicated: people's character structure prevents them from becoming aware of their real interests. The fear of freedom, the longing for order (of any kind), the panic at the thought of being deprived of a leader, the anxiety with which they confront pleasure or new ideas, the distress caused by having to think for oneself, all act against any wish at social emancipation. "Now we understand", Reich wrote, "a basic element in the 'retroaction of ideology on the economic base'. Sexual inhibition alters the structure of the economically suppressed individual in such a manner that he thinks, feels and acts against his own material interests".

It might be thought that only pessimistic conclusions could flow from such an analysis. If a rational attitude to sexuality is impossible under capitalism (because the continuation of capitalism precludes the development of rationality in general), and if no real social change is possible as long as people are sexually repressed (because

---

215   Early in 1927, in the little Austrian town of Schattendorf, some members of the Heimwehr (a paramilitary, right-wing formation, part of which later defected to the Nazis) had opened fire from a barricaded inn on a peaceful procession of Socialist workers, killing two and wounding many. On July 14 the assassins were acquitted by a judge faithful to the Old Regime. The following day there was a mass strike and street demonstrations in Vienna, in the course of which the crowd set fire to the Palace of "Justice". The police opened fire at short range. 85 civilians, all workers, were killed, some of them by police whom they were actually trying to rescue from the burning building. Most of the dead were buried in a mass "Grave of Honour" provided by the Vienna Council, then under Socialist control. The events proved a turning-point in Austrian history. For further details see *Fallen Bastions*, by G.E.R. Geyde.

216   Reich, *The Mass Psychology of Fascism, op. cit.*, p. 212.

this conditions their acceptance of authority) the outlook would seem bleak indeed, in relation to both sexual and social revolutions.

Cattier's biography of Reich contains a passage which brilliantly illustrates this dilemma:

> When Reich was with his patients he had noticed that they would mobilize all their defence reactions against him. They would hang on to their neurotic equilibrium and experience fear as the analyst got near the repressed material. In the same way revolutionary ideas slither off the character armour of the masses because such ideas are appealing to everything that people had had to smother within themselves in order to put up with their own brutalization.
>
> It would be wrong to believe that working people fail to revolt because they lack information about the mechanisms of economic exploitation. In fact revolutionary propaganda which seeks to explain to the masses the social injustice and irrationality of the economic system falls on deaf ears. Those who get up at five in the morning to work in a factory, and have on top of it spend two hours of every day on underground or suburban trains, have to adapt to these conditions by eliminating from their minds anything that might put such conditions in question again. If they realized that they were wasting their lives in the service of an absurd system they would either go mad or commit suicide. To avoid achieving such anxiety-laden insight they justify their existence by rationalizing it.[217] They repress everything that might disturb them and acquire a character structure adapted to the conditions under which they must live. Hence it follows that the idealistic tactic consisting of explaining to people that they were oppressed is useless, as people have had to suppress the perception of oppression in order to live with it. Revolutionary propagandists often claim they are trying to raise people's level of consciousness. Experience shows that their endeavours are seldom successful. Why? Because such endeavours come up against all the unconscious defence mechanisms and against all the various rationalizations that people have built up in order not to become aware of the exploitation and of the void in their lives.

This sombre image has far more truth in it than most revolutionaries can comfortably admit. But in the last analysis it is inadequate. It is inadequate because it implies totally malleable individuals, in whom total sexual repression has produced the prerequisites for total conditioning and therefore for total acceptance of the dominant ideology. The image is inadequate because it is undialectical. It does not encompass the possibility that attitudes might change, that the "laws" governing psychological mechanisms might alter, that a fight against sexual repression (dictated by sexual needs themselves) might loosen the "character armour" of individuals and render them more capable of rational thought and action. In a sense the model described implies a vision of psychological reactions as something unalterable and fixed, governed by objective laws which operate independently of the actions or wishes of men. In this sense it bears a strange similarity to the image of capitalism present in the mind of so many revolutionaries.[218] But neither the external nor the internal world of man in fact exist in this form. The working class does not submit to its history, until one day it makes it explode. Its continuous struggle in production

---

217   This is absolutely correct. It is often the most oppressed economically and the most culturally deprived who will argue most strenuously about the need for leaders and hierarchy and about the impossibility of equality or workers' management, all of which are vehemently described as contrary to "human nature" (MB).

218   See Paul Cardan, *Modern Capitalism and Revolution* (in particular Chapter 9, "Capitalist Ideology Yesterday and Today").

constantly modifies the area in which the next phase of the struggle will have to be fought. Much the same applies to man's struggle for sexual freedom.

Reich himself was aware of this possibility. In the preface to the first edition of *Character Analysis* (1933) he wrote: "Gradually, with the development of the social process, there develops an increasing discrepancy between enforced renunciation and increased libidinal tension: *this discrepancy undermines 'tradition' and forms the psychological core attitudes which threaten the anchoring*".

8. Limits and Perspectives

The "undermining of tradition" to which Reich referred has certainly progressed within recent years. The change in traditional attitudes is both gaining momentum and becoming more explicit in a manner which would have surprised and delighted Reich. Seeing the havoc around him in the working-class districts of Vienna and Berlin (in the late 1920s and early 1930s) Reich wrote brilliant and bitter pages about the sexual misery of adolescence, about the damage done to the personality by guilt about masturbation, about ignorance and misinformation concerning birth control, about the high cost of contraceptives, about back-street abortions (so often the fate of the working-class girl or the housewife) and about the hypocrisy of the "compulsive" bourgeois marriage with its inevitable concomitant of jealousy, adultery and prostitution. Real sexual freedom for the young, Reich wrote, would mean the end of this type of marriage. Bourgeois society needed bourgeois marriage for one of the cornerstones of its edifice. For Reich any large-scale sexual freedom was inconceivable within the framework of capitalism.

What has happened has been rather different from anything Reich could have foreseen. In advanced industrial societies the persistent struggle of the young for what is one of their fundamental rights - the right to a normal sex life from the age at which they are capable of it - has succeeded in denting the repressive ideology, in bringing about changes and in modifying the ground on which the next stage of the struggle will have to be fought. Adolescents are breaking out of the stifling atmosphere of the traditional family, an act which could be of considerable significance. Information and practical help about birth control is now available, even to the non-married. The increasing financial independence of young people and the discovery of oral contraception provide a solid material foundation for the whole process. The attitude to "illegitimacy" is gradually changing. The upbringing of children is more enlightened. Abortion is now more widely available, divorce much easier and the economic rights of women more widely recognized. Understanding is increasing. People are beginning to grasp that society itself engenders the antisocial behaviour which it condemns. It is true that all this has only been achieved on a small scale, only in some countries[219] and only in the face of tremendous opposition. It is also true that, as in Reich's day, every concession is "too late and too little", belatedly recognizing established facts rather than blazing a new trail. Moreover none of the "reformers" are as yet demystified or unrepressed enough to boldly trumpet the message that sex is a natural and pleasurable activity - or that the right to sexual happiness is a basic human right. It is rarely proclaimed that throughout history the prac-

---

219   In Catholic or Muslim countries, sexual repression remains a pillar of the social order, but even the Catholic Church is having trouble (both with its clergy and with its youth). Among the Palestinian guerillas women are fighting alongside men. This fight cannot be waged wearing a yashmak or accepting traditional Arab values as to the role and function of women in society.

tice of sex has never had procreation as its main end, whatever the preachings of moralists, priests, philosophers or politicians. But despite these limitations the fact of a developing sexual revolution is undeniable, irreversible and of deep significance.

As in other areas, the attempt at sexual emancipation encounters two kinds of response from established society: frontal opposition - from those who still live in the Victorian era - and an attempt at recuperation. Modern society seeks first to neutralize any threat presented to it, and ultimately to convert such challenges into something useful to its own ends. It seeks to regain with one hand what it has been compelled to yield with the other: parts of its control of the total situation.

In relation to sex, the phenomenon of recuperation takes the form of first alienating and reifying sexuality, and then of frenetically exploiting this empty shell for commercial ends. As modern youth breaks out of the dual stranglehold of repressive traditional morality and of the authoritarian patriarchal family it encounters a projected image of free sexuality which is in fact a manipulatory distortion of it. The image is often little more than a means of selling products. Today sex is used to sell everything from cigarettes to real estate, from bottles of perfume to pay-as-you-earn holidays; from hair lotions to models of next year's car. The potential market is systematically surveyed, quantified, exploited. The "pornographic" explosion on Broadway (New York) now caters for a previously repressed clientele of massive proportions and varied tastes. Here as elsewhere it is often a question of consumer research. Separate booths and displays are arranged for homosexuals (active and passive), for fetishists, for sadists, for masochists, for voyeurs, etc. Fashion advertizing, striptease shows and certain magazines and movies all highlight the successful development of sex into a major consumer industry.

In all this sex is presented as something to be consumed. But the sexual instinct differs from certain other instincts. Hunger can be satisfied by food. The "food" of the sexual instinct is, however, another human being, capable of thinking, acting, suffering. The alienation of sexuality under the conditions of modern capitalism is very much part of the general alienating process, in which people are converted into objects (in this case, objects of sexual consumption) and relations are drained of human content. Undiscriminating, compulsive sexual activity is not sexual freedom - although it may sometimes be a preparation for it (which repressive morality can never be). The illusion that alienated sex is sexual freedom constitutes yet another obstacle in the road to total emancipation. Sexual freedom implies a realization and understanding of the autonomy of others. Unfortunately, most people don't yet think in this way.

The recuperation by society of the sexual revolution is therefore partly successful. But it creates the basis for a deeper and more fundamental challenge. Modern society can tolerate alienated sexuality, just as it tolerates alienated consumption, wage increases which do not exceed increases in the productivity of labour, or colonial "freedom" in which the "facts of economic life" still perpetuate the division of the world into "haves" and "have nots". Modern capitalism not only tolerates these "challenges" but converts them into essential cogs of its own expansion and perpetuation. It seeks to harness the sexual demands of youth by first distorting them and then by integrating them into the present system, in much the same way as working class demands are integrated into the economy of the consumer society. From a potential liberating force these demands tend thereby to be converted into a further mechanism of repression. What exploiting society will not long be able to tolerate, however, is the mass development of critical, demystified, self-reliant, sexually emancipated, autonomous, non-alienated persons, conscious of what they want and prepared to struggle for it.

The assertion of the right to manage one's own life, in the realm of sex as in the realm of work, is helping to disintegrate the dominant ideology. It is producing less compulsive and obsessional individuals, and in this respect preparing the ground for libertarian revolution. (In the long run even the traditional revolutionaries, that repository of repressed puritanism, will be affected.)

The incessant questioning and challenge to authority on the subject of sex and of the compulsive family can only complement the questioning and challenge to authority in other areas (for instance on the subject of who is to dominate the work process – or of the purpose of work itself). Both challenges stress the autonomy of individuals and their domination over important aspects of their lives. Both expose the alienated concepts which pass for rationality and which govern so much of our thinking and behaviour. The task of the conscious revolutionary is to make both challenges explicit, to point out their deeply subversive content, and to explain their inter-relation. To understand revolutionary psychoanalysis is to add a new dimension to the Marxist critique of ideologies and to the Marxist understanding of false consciousness. Only then will we have the tools to master our own history, will socialism ("man's positive self-consciousness") be a real possibility, and will man be able to break once and for all with the "irrational in politics" and with the irrational in life.

THE RUSSIAN EXPERIENCE

In the years following the Russian Revolution, "official" thought and action concerning sexual matters were coloured by four main facts:

(a) The novelty, depth and vast scale of the problems which the Bolsheviks had inherited. The new tasks had to be tackled at a time when innumerable other problems claimed urgent attention. In the struggle for sexual freedom classical Marxist teaching provided no blueprint as to "what was to be done". Despite the vast social intellectual and cultural turmoil, despite the widespread breaking up of families and despite the disintegration of many traditional values, there was no clear or coherent vision as to what ought eventually to follow.

(b) This lack of conscious purpose was associated with a widespread, false, and rather naive belief that the abolition of economic exploitation and the promulgation of new, progressive legislation were sufficient to ensure the liberation of women. It was thought that this liberation (often conceived of in the restrictive sense of "equal rights") would automatically follow the changes in the ownership of property and it was assumed that its growth would be guaranteed by the new laws and institutions of the "workers' state".

(c) There was massive unawareness of the significance of sexual repression – and of the traditional morality based upon it – as a central factor in social conditioning. Only a small minority of revolutionaries saw a *conscious* sexual revolution as the indispensable means of deepening and completing the proposed social transformation, through changing the mental structure of the mass individual.

(d) Among many of the Bolshevik leaders there was a gross lack of insight as to their own repressive conditioning in matters of sex and as to the impact this could be having on their thoughts and actions. Many had had a fairly typical authoritarian upbringing. Later, deportation, imprisonment and struggle under conditions of persecution and illegality had prevented most of the Old Guard from enjoying a normal sex life. After the Revolution a retrospective virtue was made out of what had been a historical necessity, and this "dedication" was made an ideal not only for "the vanguard" but for the masses themselves. Many leading Bolsheviks considered propaganda for sexual freedom as a "diversion from the real struggle". (So do many would-be Bolsheviks today!) Some of them were actively to oppose all attempts at such propaganda. These various factors were to play their part in the series of internal defeats that followed the great events of 1917. They were to undermine important areas of human freedom, conquered in the first few months of the Revolution. The inhibition of the sexual revolution in Russia was to combine with other defeats (discussed at length elsewhere)[220] to reinforce the whole process of bureaucratic degeneration.

Classical Marxism contained little from which the Bolsheviks could have sought practical guidance. True, Engels had written passages with which no libertarian could quarrel.[221] But there were other passages, more doctrinaire in nature.[222] Moreover, Engels's historical analyses had constantly emphasized the social background against which the sexual revolution was to take place but had rarely dealt with the content of the process. As for Marx he had certainly stigmatized bourgeois marriage and the bourgeois family. He had mercilessly flayed the whole hypocrisy of bourgeois morality. But he had also denounced the "movement counterpoising universal private property to private property", a movement which "finds expression in the bestial form of counterpoising to marriage (certainly a form of exclusive private property) the community of women, in which a woman becomes a piece of communal and common property…" If such a movement triumphed, the woman would pass "from marriage to general prostitution…from the relationship of exclusive marriage with the owner of private property to a state of universal prostitution with the community".[223] The terms are emotionally loaded and the antithesis suggested is a false one. (Marx still formulates the alternative to individual property in terms of property - and not in terms of the free self-determination of both men and women. It is in much the same vein that Engels still speaks of "surrender").

However ambiguous or indistinct the "guidelines" may have been in 1917 the problems requiring solution were real and practical enough. The cultural heritage of Tsarism had to be uprooted. This was an enormous task. Tsarist laws had certainly "protected" the family. They decreed that the husband "had to love his wife like his

---

220 See *The Bolsheviks and Workers' Control, 1917–1921*.

221 "What we can conjecture at present about the regulation of sex relationships after the impending effacement of capitalist production is, in the main, of a negative character, limited mostly to what will vanish. But what will be added? That will be settled after the new generation has grown up: a generation of men who will never in all their lives have had occasion to purchase a woman's surrender either with money or with any other means of social power, and of women who have never been obliged to surrender to any man out of any other consideration other than that of real love, or to refrain from giving themselves to their beloved for fear of the economic consequences. Once such people appear, they won't care a rap about what we today think they should do. They will establish their own practice and their own public opinion…and that's the end of it!" (Engels, *The Origin of the Family, Private Property and the State, op. cit.*, pp. 137–8).

222 Describing for instance the effects of the Industrial Revolution which uprooted women from the home and drove them into factories, Engels says (in *The Condition of the Working Class in England in 1844*) that at times women even became the breadwinners while the husbands stayed at home as housekeepers. According to Engels this was "an insane state of things" which "unsexes the man and takes from the woman all womanliness". The notion that woman's place is in the home has some strange advocates!

223 K. Marx, *Economic and Philosophic Manuscripts of 1844* (Moscow: Foreign Languages Publishing House, 1961), pp. 99–100.

own body". The wife "owed unlimited obedience to the husband". Men could call on the police to compel women to return to the happy home. Parents could have their children of either sex confined to prison "for wilfully disobeying parental power". Young people contracting marriage without parental consent were also liable to imprisonment. Only religious marriages were deemed legal. Divorces, which only the Church could grant, were costly and only available to the rich.

All this reactionary legislation was swept aside by the new marriage decrees of December 19 and 20, 1917. These proclaimed the total equality of the contracting parties, an end to the legal incapacity of women, and the end of "indissoluble" marriage through the ready availability of divorce. The husband was deprived of his prerogative of domination over the family. Women were given the right freely to determine their name, domicile and citizenship. Any man over the age of eighteen (and any woman over the age of sixteen) could contract a marriage. As far as the offspring were concerned, no difference was recognized between "natural parentage" and "legal parentage".

Divorce was made very easy. The only criterion was mutual agreement between the parties. When a partner wanted to relinquish a sexual companionship he did not have to "give reasons". Marriage and divorce became purely private matters. The registration of a relationship was not mandatory. Even when a relationship was registered sexual relationships with others were not "prosecuted". (Not telling the partner about another relationship was, however, considered "fraud".) The obligation to pay alimony persisted for six months only after a separation, and only came into force if the partner was unemployed or otherwise incapable of earning a living. A law of 1919 legalized abortion during the first three months of pregnancy. All the old legislation directed against homosexuality amongst adults was repealed. Aspirations in this whole area of personal freedom are summarized by the jurist Hoichbarg, who wrote in the *Preface to the Bolshevik Marriage Code of 1919* that "the institution of marriage carried within itself the seeds of its own destruction" and that "the family still persisted only because we are dealing with socialism in a nascent state".

The newly proclaimed laws were radical indeed. Writing in *Pravda* on September 15, 1919, Lenin could truthfully state that "in the Soviet Republic not a stone remains of the laws that confined women to an inferior status". Particularly degrading had been the laws "which had deprived her of her rights and which have often humiliated her - that is to say the laws on divorce, the laws distinguishing natural from legitimate children, the laws demanding the determination of fatherhood before the upkeep of the child could be considered". Lenin also seems to have been aware of the fact that "laws were not enough" and that "even when a full equality of rights has been achieved the oppression of women would continue". But he saw this persisting oppression solely in terms of the domestic chores which for a while would still be her lot.:

> In most cases such chores were the least productive, the most barbarous and the heaviest to fall on women's shoulders. For women to be totally free and the real equal of man household chores must be made a public responsibility and the women must participate in general production.[224]

Communal kitchens, creches and kindergartens - combined with access to all kinds of labour - were seen as the essential ingredients of woman's emancipation.

---

224 In 1916 Lenin had denounced a capitalism which maintained woman as "the slave of the household, imprisoned in the bedroom, the kitchen and the nursery" (*Sochineniya*, XIX, pp. 232–3).

"The abolition of private property on the land and in the factories *alone* opens the road", wrote Lenin, "to the total and emancipation of women". Along this road there would be a "transition from the small individual household to the big socialist household".[225] This vision was undoubtedly shared by most of the leading Bolsheviks, who saw "women's liberation" as the summated freedoms from economic exploitation and from domestic slavery. The repressive mechanisms whereby female subjugation had become internalized in the minds of millions of women were not even suspected.

The new laws, it is true, provided a framework within which future attempts might be made, free from external constraints, at constructing human relationships of a new type. It is also true that the Bolsheviks wished to break patriarchal power. But they were only dimly aware of the role of the patriarchal family as the "structure-forming cell of class society"[226] – as "the structural and ideological place of reproduction of every social order based on authoritarian principles".[227] Still less did they realize the role of sexual repression in perpetuating such important aspects of the dominant ideology as the compliance with authority and the fear of freedom. Had they been more conscious of these facts many practical problems would have been differently managed, many fruitless discussions by-passed, many retrogressive statements or acts avoided. The revolutionaries would have shown less tolerance with the spokesmen of the old ideology and morality, many of whom had been left in high positions, from where they were inflicting untold damage upon the developing cultural revolution. The Bolsheviks repeatedly stressed that the new laws were "only the beginning". But a beginning of what? Wilhelm Reich points out that in the heated discussions of that period the conservatives seemed always to have the edge in all the arguments and the most ready access to all the "proofs". The revolutionaries "were prepared neither theoretically nor practically for the difficulties which the cultural revolution brought with it".[228] They knew little about the psychic structure of the generation they were seeking to win over from ideological allegiance to the Tsarist patriarchate. They were certainly trying to do something new, but they

> felt very clearly that they were not able to put the "new" thing into words. They fought valiantly, but finally tired and failed in the discussion, partly because they themselves were caught in old concepts, from which they were unable to shake loose.[229]

The Revolution encountered tremendous problems. The compulsive family had only been legally abolished. The attitudes on which it was based persisted. Economic difficulties persisted too. And "as long as society could not guarantee security to all adults and adolescents this guarantee remained the function of the family".[230]. The family therefore continued to exist. Its demands conflicted more and more with the new social obligations and aspirations of the group. The "life-affirmative sexual relationships in the collectives" struggled against the old family ties which "pervaded every corner of everyday life and the psychic structure".[231] For instance:

---

225   Pravda, March 8, 1921.

226   Reich, *The Sexual Revolution, op. cit.*, p. 166.

227   *Ibid.*, p. 157.

228   *Ibid.*, pp. 169–70.

229   *Ibid.*, p. 168.

230   *Ibid.*, p. 167.

231   *Ibid.*, p. 160.

parents, proletarians included, did not like to see their adolescent daughters go to meetings. They feared that the girls would "go wrong" – that is start a sexual life. Though the children ought to go to the collective, the parents still made their old possessive demands on them. They were horrified when the children began to look at them with a critical eye".[232]

Even in the most radical circles girls could still be denounced as "promiscuous", thereby revealing the deep-seated residual moral condemnation of female sexuality underlying all the "revolutionary" rhetoric.

The economic whip hand of the patriarchal father over wife and children was certainly loosened. But the increased opportunities for sexual happiness did not as yet mean the psychic capacity to enjoy such happiness. The internalized constraints had barely been dented. Everything was still distorted by the legacy of the past. "Infantile attitudes and pathological sexual habits" persisted. Family members would drown out unconscious antagonisms to one another with a forced affection and sticky dependence. "One of the main difficulties was the inability of the women – genitally crippled and unprepared for economic independence as they were – to give up their slave-like protection of the family"[233] and the substitute gratification which they derived from their domination over the children. Those whose whole lives were sexually empty and economically dependent had made of the upbringing of children the be-all and end-all of their existence. It was difficult to combat these possessive tendencies and this misuse of power on the part of the mothers without real insight to their origin. The mothers fought bitterly against any restriction of these powers.

Everyday life proved much more conservative than economy mainly because it was a much less conscious process. The revolutionaries were not equipped either ideologically or in terms of their own upbringing to intervene effectively in the heated discussions that raged up and down the country on the "sexual question". There was no theory of the sexual revolution. Trotsky's pamphlet *Problems of Life,*[234] written in 1923, does not even mention the sexual question. Many Bolshevik leaders took refuge in the formula that "sexuality was a private matter". This was unfortunate and "essentially an expression of the inability of the members of the Communist Party to manage the revolution in their own personal lives".[235]

There was undoubtedly considerable malaise, at least to begin with. Many young people felt that these were important questions which should be honestly and openly talked about. Kollontai gives some idea of what was being discussed.[236] A functionary, Koltsov, points out that the key questions

> are never discussed. It is as if for some reason they were being avoided. I myself have never given them serious thought. They are new to me.

Another, Finkovsky, pinpoints the reasons for this avoidance:

> The subject is rarely talked about because it hits home too closely with everybody... The Communists usually point to the golden future and thus avoid getting into acute problems...the workers know that in Communist families things are even worse than in their own.

---

232 *Ibid.*, p. 182.

233 *Ibid.*, p. 160.

234 *Voprosy byta*, Moscow, 1923 (translated by Z. Vengerova (London: Methuen, 1924)).

235 Reich, *The Sexual Revolution, op. cit.*, p. 172.

236 A. Kollontai, *Novaya moral i rabochi klass* (The new morality and the working class) (Moscow, 1919), pp. 65 ff.

Yet another official, Tseitlin, stressed that these were "exactly the questions which interest the workers, male and female alike". When such questions were the topic of Party meetings people would hear about it and flock to attend them. "They keep asking these questions and find no answers". Reich points out that ordinary people, without sexological training or knowledge, were describing exactly what is contended by sex-economy, namely that "the interest of the mass-individual is not political but sexual".[237]

Answers were in fact being provided. They were inadequate, incomplete, and sometimes positively harmful. Sex "education" was slipping into the hands of public hygienists, biologists, urologists and professors of philosophy, ethics and sociology. The repercussions soon began to be felt - the cultural revolution began to wither at the roots. The "heated discussions" eventually died down. The impetus provided by the new legislation petered out - clearly revealing the obvious fact that a sexual revolution could not, like an economic revolution, be expressed through plans and laws. To be successful it had to manifest itself in all the details of everyday personal life. But here it encountered major obstacles. The revolution in the ideological superstructure had not yet taken place. The "bearer of this revolution, the psychic structure of human beings" was not yet changed.[238]

Apart from the internalized inhibitions of the mass individual - a legacy of the past - change was also being inhibited from without (i.e. as a result of the internalized inhibitions of those now in authority). Lenin denounced the youth movement as being "exaggeratedly interested in sex".[239] The youth had been "attacked by the disease of modernity in its attitude towards sexual questions". All this was "particularly harmful, particularly dangerous". The new "flourishing sexual theories" arose out of the personal need of people "to justify personal abnormality in sexual life before bourgeois morality". They were being peddled by "little yellow-beaked birds who had just broken from the egg of bourgeois ideas". Psychoanalysis was to be mistrusted for it "grew on the dirty soil of bourgeois society". All that was relevant in this new concern with sexual matters "the workers had already read in Bebel, long ago". The new sexual life young people were trying to create was "an extension of bourgeois brothels". Within a short while every timid official, every repressed reactionary was to be found echoing Lenin's famous phrase: "Thirst must be satisfied - but will the normal man in normal circumstances lie down in the gutter and drink out of a puddle, or out of a glass with a rim greasy from many lips?"[240]

The more farsighted among the revolutionaries sensed the backsliding, but their prescription was an intensification of the calls for industrialization. The lack of purely economic prerequisites for radical social change was stressed again and again. But as Reich points out:

---

237   Reich, *The Sexual Revolution, op. cit.*, p. 174.

238   *Ibid.*, p. 159.

239   See Appendix to this pamphlet for the source of various quotes from Lenin on the question of sex. The authenticity of Clara Zetkin's account has never been questioned. Her *Reminiscences of Lenin* have been produced many times by official Communist publishing houses, both in Russia and elsewhere.

240   Lenin's metaphors concerning "the gutter" and "puddles" are revealing on two grounds. Implicit in them are (a) the conception that sex is intrinsically dirty, and (b) the conception that sex is a relation with an object — water — rather than a relationship with another human being. The second point, it is true, is mitigated by Lenin's later statement that "two lives are concerned..." But the overall image was to be remembered long after the qualifying statement had been forgotten.

the attitude "first the economic questions, *then* those of everyday life" was wrong and only the expression of the unpreparedness for the seemingly chaotic forms of the cultural revolution…true, a society which is exhausted by civil war, which is unable immediately to establish public kitchens, laundries and kindergartens must first of all think of the economic prerequisites… But it was not just a matter of lifting the masses to the level of the capitalist countries… It was also necessary to be clear as to the nature of the new culture…the cultural revolution posed infinitely more difficult problems than the political revolution. This is easy to understand. The political revolution requires essentially nothing but a strong trained leadership and the confidence of the masses in it. The cultural revolution, however, requires an alteration in the psychic structure of the mass individual. About this there was hardly any scientific, let alone practical, concept at that time.[241]

It might perhaps be added that the dissemination of what little knowledge there was, instead of being actively encouraged, was being actively opposed by most of the Russian leaders. Attempts at establishing various kinds of "counter-milieu" – such as youth communes – were now also being actively discouraged by the authorities.

It was naive indeed to expect "progressive" legislation plus new property relations to solve these fundamental problems. The change in property relations may have prepared the ground for a new society but men alone were going to build it. For such a task a different kind of vision was necessary and it was precisely such a vision that was lacking.

Too many factors were combining to prevent the formal, legal changes that had been proclaimed from really influencing the course of events. As Reich was later to point out "an ideology or programme can only become a revolutionary power of historical dimensions if it achieves a deep-reaching change in the emotions and instinctual life of the masses". It influenced the development of society either "by passively tolerating despotism and suppression" or "by adjustment to the technical process of development instituted by the powers that be", or finally "by actively taking part in social development, as for example in a revolution". No concept of historical development could be called revolutionary "if it considers the psychic structure of the masses as nothing but the result of economic processes and not *also* as their motive power".[242] In the Russian Revolution the psychic structure of the masses never became – and was never allowed to become – a "revolutionary power of historical dimensions".

Between 1920 and about 1933 the situation gradually regressed to the point where the sexual ideology of the leading groups in the USSR could no longer be distinguished from that of the leading groups in any conservative country. Summing up the whole process Reich wrote that the leaders of the new Russian state could not be blamed for not knowing the solution to these problems,

> but they must be blamed for avoiding the difficulties, for taking the line of least resistance, for not asking themselves what it all meant, for talking about the revolution of life without looking for it in real life itself, for misinterpreting the existing chaos as a "moral chaos" (using the terms in the same sense as the political reaction) instead of comprehending it as chaotic conditions which were inherent in the transition to new forms, and last but not least for repudiating the contri-

---

241   Reich, *The Sexual Revolution, op. cit.*, pp. 175–6.
242   *Ibid.*, p. 169.

butions to an understanding of the problem which the German sex-political movement had to offer.[243]

In March 1934 the law punishing homosexuality was reintroduced into the Soviet Union. In June 1935 an editorial in *Pravda* wrote that "only a good family man could be a good Soviet citizen". By early 1936 a Russian trade union paper (*Trud*, April 27, 1936) could write:

> abortion, which destroys life, is inadmissible in any country. Soviet woman has the same rights as Soviet man, but that does not absolve her from the great and honourable duty [*sic*!] imposed on her by nature: she is to be a mother. She is to bear life.[244] And this is certainly not a private matter, but a matter of great social significance.[245]

A decree of June 27, 1936, was to prohibit abortion. A further decree of July 8, 1944, established that "only a legally recognized marriage entails rights and duties for both husband and wife". In other words "illegitimate" children - or the offspring of non-registered relationships - reverted to their earlier inferior status. Unmarried couples living together were urged to "regularize" their relationship. Divorce would only be allowed "in important cases" and after "full consideration of all the relevant facts by a special tribunal". The cult of motherhood was given official blessing. An official Stalinist publication[246] could boast that "on June 1, 1949, in Soviet Russia, there were over two million mothers with families of five or six children who hold the 'maternity medal'; 700,000 with families of seven, eight or nine children holding the 'Glory to Motherhood' medal; and 30,000 mothers of ten or more children entitled to the medal of 'Heroine Mother'". (Enough to warm the heart of the most reactionary of Popes!) The author proclaims that "Soviet legislation on the question of the family

---

243   *Ibid.*, p. 190.

244   The myth that childbearing and rearing are the fulfilment of a woman's destiny is among the most pernicious and damaging myths that imprison her. It has harmful effects on the children themselves. The situation is well described in the following passage taken from an article by Laurel Limpus, *Liberation of Women, Sexual Repression, and the Family* (recently reprinted by Agit Prop, London): 'Having children is no substitute for creating one's own life, for producing. And since so many women in this culture devote themselves to nothing else, they end up by becoming intolerable burdens upon their children because in fact these children are their whole lives'. Juliet Mitchell, *Women: The Longest Revolution*, has caught the situation exactly: 'At present, reproduction in our society is often a kind of sad mimicry of reproduction. Work in a capitalist society is an alienation of labour in the making of a social product which is confiscated by capital. But it can still sometimes be a real act of creation, purposive and responsible, even in conditions of the worst exploitation. Maternity is often a caricature of this. The biological product – the child – is treated as if it were a solid product. Parenthood becomes a kind of substitute for work, an activity in which the child is seen as an object created by the mother, in the same way that a commodity is created by a worker. Naturally, the child does not literally escape, but the mother's alienation can be much worse than that of the worker whose product is appropriated by the boss. No human being can create another human being. A person's biological origin is an abstraction. The child as an autonomous person inevitably threatens the activity which claims to create it continually merely as a possession of the parent. Possessions are felt as extensions of the self. The child as a possession is supremely this. Anything the child does is therefore a threat to the mother herself who has renounced her autonomy through this misconception of her reproductive role. There are few more precarious ventures on which to base a life.'

"So we have the forty or fifty-year-old woman complaining to her grown child: 'But I gave you everything'. This is quite true: this is the tragedy. It is a gift the child hardly wanted, and indeed, many children are daily mutilated by it. And it leaves women at the waning of their years with the feeling that they have been deceived, that their children are ungrateful, that no one appreciates them because they have come to the realization that they have done nothing".

245   In his *Principles of Communism*, Engels had written that the socialist revolution "would transform the relations between the sexes into purely private relations, only concerning the people participating in them and in which society had not to intervene".

has always been inspired by Marxism–Leninism" and that "its evolution, over a thirty-year period, had always had as its constant concern the wish to defend woman and to free her. This preoccupation had led the Soviet legislator from free divorce to regulated divorce and from legal abortion to the prohibition of abortion"!

From the middle thirties on, various critics of the bureaucracy became increasingly vocal. Trotsky's book *The Revolution Betrayed*, first published in 1936, contains an interesting chapter on "Family, Youth and Culture". In it Trotsky stigmatized those who proclaimed that woman had to accept "the joys of motherhood". This was "the philosophy of the priest endowed also with the powers of a gendarme". Trotsky correctly points out that the "'problem of problems' had not been solved: the forty million Soviet families remained in their overwhelming majority nests of medievalism, female slavery and hysteria, daily humiliation of children, feminine and childish superstition".

> The most compelling motive of the present cult of the family [was] undoubtedly the need of the bureaucracy for a stable hierarchy of relations and for the disciplining of youth by means of forty million points of support for authority and power.

The description is excellent. What is lacking is any real understanding of how it all came about. Economic and cultural backwardness are still seen as the sole ingredients of the failure. A whole dimension is missing. The role of Bolshevik obscurantism in relation to sex is not even suspected. One would search in vain among Trotsky's voluminous writings for any criticism, however muted, of what Lenin had said on the subject.

In the last twenty years - despite a steady "development of the productive forces" - the sexual counter-revolution has gained even further momentum. The distance travelled is perhaps best epitomized in a book by T.S. Atarov, "Physician Emeritus of the Russian Soviet Socialist Republic". The book, published in Moscow in 1959, is called *Problems of Sexual Education*,[247] and reveals the full extent of the sexual Thermidor. The author proclaims that "Soviet marriage is not only a private matter. It is a question involving society and the State". Young people are denounced who have pre-marital intercourse "without even experiencing guilt". "Unadapted elements" in Russian society are denounced, who had even sought to give "philosophical expression" to their attitude - in other words who had sought to argue a coherent case against the sexually repressive ideology of the Party leaders. Atarov bemoans the fact that young people "don't seem to realize the difference between puberty and sexual maturity" and that they seem to believe "that the mere existence of sexual desire is a justification for its satisfaction". But there were also encouraging signs. "Under Soviet conditions masturbation is no longer the mass phenomenon it was in the past". But "unfortunately" it still persisted. According to Atarov, various factors tended to perpetuate this alarming state of affairs, factors such as "tight fitting clothing in the nether parts, the bad habits of boys who keep their hands in their pockets or under their blankets or who lie on their stomachs, constipation and full bladders, the reading of erotic books and the contemplation of the sexual activities of animals".

---

246   *La Femme et le Communisme* (Paris: Editions Sociales ,1951).

247   For a detailed review, see "Sexual Thermidor", *Solidarity*, IV, 8 (July 1967).

How was one to fight this menace to the stability of Russian society? Yes! How did you guess? "Regular meals, hard beds, exercise, walking, sport and gymnastics, in fact anything that deflect the child's attention from sexual preoccupations".[248] Discussing menstruation, Atarov is even more with it! "Under no circumstances should any cotton or gauze appliance be inserted into the vagina as so many women do". The "outer parts" should be washed twice a day with warm boiled water. Our political spinster advises that "young people should be forbidden from serving in cafés, restaurants or bars for the atmosphere in these places encourages them to indulge in pre-marital relations". "No illness", he stresses, "was ever caused through abstinence, which is quite harmless for young and less young alike". In a frightening phrase Atarov sums up the spirit of his book. "The law cannot concern itself with every case of immoral conduct. The pressure of public concern must continue to play the leading role against all forms of immorality". The vice squad and public opinion were again to be the pillars of the sexual Establishment.

Readers will grasp the deeply reactionary significance of Atarov's pronouncements, particularly when endorsed by the full might of the Russian Educational Establishment (over 100,000 copies of Atarov's book were sold within a few days of the publication of the first edition). The "public opinion" which Atarov refers to is the one which had sought emancipation for a short while in 1917, but had soon been dragged back into the old rut of bigotry and repression. It could now be used again for censorious ends - as it had been for generations in the past.

Official Russian sexual morality - as seen through other official works - today resembles the kind of "advice to parents" dished out about 1890 by the bourgeois do-gooders of that time.[249] One finds in it all the fetishes of bourgeois sexual morality - or more generally of all systems of morality characterizing class societies of patriarchal type. Everything is there: all the reactionary anti-life ideas pompously disguised as "science", every backward prejudice, all the hypocritical bad faith of screwed-up and repressed puritans. But these "irrational" ideas not only have definite social roots (which we have sought to expose). They also have a precise significance and a specific function. In this they closely resemble the repressive morality which still prevails (although on a diminishing scale) in some Church-dominated Western countries.

Both East and West these ideologies aim at denying to individuals the autonomous (i.e. the conscious and self-managing) exercise of their own activities. They aim at depriving people of freedom and responsibility in a fundamental realm and at obliging them to conform to externally imposed norms and to the pressures of "public opinion" rather than to criteria determined by each person according to his own needs and experience. The objective of these repressive and alienating moralities is the mass creation of individuals whose character structure complements and reinforces the hierarchical structure of society. Such individuals will revert to infantile attitudes when confronted with those who symbolize authority, with those who incarnate - at the scale of society - the image of their parents (i.e. rulers of the state,

248   Lenin had also spoken (see Appendix) of "healthy sport, swimming, racing, walking, bodily exercises of every kind" as giving young people more than "eternal theories and discussions about sexual problems". "Healthy bodies, healthy minds", he said, echoing the words of Juvenal ("mens sana in corpore sano", Satires, 10, 356), the Stoic moralist and misogynist who had "exposed the vices" of ancient Rome.

249   Much contemporary sexological Russian literature reads like the works of Scout founder Baden–Powell, but with the word "socialism" occasionally scattered among the references to "duty", "loyalty", "discipline", "service", and "patriotism".

managers of industry, priests, political pundits, etc.). In the Russian context they will comply with the edicts of the Central Committee, obediently follow the zigzags of the Party line, develop religious attitudes to the Holy Writings, etc. Such individuals will also react in an anxiety-laden manner when confronted with deviants of all kinds (perceptive writers, poets, cosmopolitans, the apostles of "modernity", those with long hair and those with long ideas). Is it really surprising that the most sexually repressed segment of the Russian population (obese, middle-aged women) still seem to be the main vehicle for the dissemination of "public opinion" and of the prevailing *kulturnost*[250] despite the crèches, despite the kitchens, despite the kindergartens – and despite the nationalization, nearly two generations ago, of the vast majority of the means of production?

APPENDIX: CLARA ZETKIN, *REMINISCENCES OF LENIN*

Lenin seldom talked about sex. Stripped of their "revolutionary" rhetoric, his occasional pronouncements on the subject were those of a puritan bigot.

Because of Lenin's eminence and authority in other fields his views on sex exerted considerable influence. They were seized upon and repeated ad nauseam by all those opposed to any radical change in the field of sex relations. In this sense they played a significant role in the sexual counter-revolution which we have sought to outline in the previous essay.

We here publish an excerpt from the chapter "Women, Marriage and Sex" of Clara Zetkin's book Reminiscences of Lenin (New York: International Publishers, 1934). This book was written in 1924, shortly after Lenin's death. Zetkin, a founding member of the German Communist Party, is speaking to Lenin in the Kremlin, in the summer of 1920.

Lenin continued: "Your list of sins, Clara, is still longer. I was told that questions of sex and marriage are the main subjects dealt with in the reading and discussion evenings of women comrades. They are the chief subject of interest, of political instruction and education. I could scarcely believe my ears when I heard it. The first country of proletarian dictatorship surrounded by the counter-revolutionaries of the whole world, the situation in Germany itself requires the greatest possible concentration of all proletarian, revolutionary forces to defeat the ever-growing and ever-increasing counter-revolution. But working women comrades discuss sexual problems and the question of forms of marriage in the past, present and future. They think it their most important duty to enlighten proletarian women on these subjects. The most widely read brochure is, I believe, the pamphlet of a young Viennese woman comrade on the sexual problem. What a waste! What truth there is in it the workers have already read in Bebel, long ago. Only not so boringly, not so heavily written as in the pamphlet, but written strongly, bitterly, aggressively, against bourgeois society.

"The extension of Freudian hypotheses seems 'educated', even scientific, but it is ignorant bungling. Freudian theory is the modern fashion. I mistrust the sexual theories of the articles, dissertations, pamphlets, etc., in short, of that particular kind of literature which flourishes luxuriantly in the dirty soil of bourgeois society. I mistrust those who are always contemplating the several questions, like the Indian saint his navel. It seems to me that these flourishing sexual theories which are mainly hypothetical, and often quite arbitrary hypotheses, arise from the personal need to

---

250   See "Letter from a Friend in Russia", *Solidarity*, VI, 3 (19 January 1970), for a description of these attempts to enforce this "behaviour expected of cultured people".

justify personal abnormality or hypertrophy in sexual life before bourgeois morality, and to entreat its patience. This masked respect for bourgeois morality seems to me just as repulsive as poking about in sexual matters. However wild and revolutionary the behaviour may be, it is still really quite bourgeois. It is, mainly, a hobby of the intellectuals and of the sections nearest them. There is no place for it in the Party, in the class conscious, fighting proletariat".

I interrupted here, saying that the questions of sex and marriage, in a bourgeois society of private property, involve many problems, conflicts and much suffering for women of all social classes and ranks. The war and its consequences had greatly accentuated the conflicts and sufferings of women in sexual matters, had brought to light problems which were formerly hidden from them. To that were added the effects of the revolution. The old world of feeling and thought had begun to totter. Old social ties are entangling and breaking, there are tendencies towards new ideological relationships between man and woman. The interest shown in these questions is an expression of the need for enlightenment and reorientation. It also indicates a reaction against the falseness and hypocrisy of bourgeois society. Forms of marriage and of the family, in their historical development and dependence upon economic life, are calculated to destroy the superstition existing in the minds of working women concerning the external character of bourgeois society. A critical, historical attitude to those problems must lead to a ruthless examination of bourgeois society, to a disclosure of its real nature and effects, including condemnation of its sexual morality and falseness. All roads lead to Rome. And every real Marxist analysis of any important section of the ideological superstructure of society, of a predominating social phenomenon, must lead to an analysis of bourgeois society and of its property basis, must lead to the realization, "this must be destroyed".

Lenin nodded laughingly: "There we have it! You are defending counsel for your women comrades and your Party. Of course what you say is right. But it only excuses the mistakes made in Germany; it does not justify them. They are, and remain, mistakes. Can you really seriously assure me that the questions of sex and marriage were discussed from the standpoint of a mature, living, historical materialism? Deep and many-sided knowledge is necessary for that, the clearest Marxist mastery of a great amount of material. Where can you get the forces for that now? If they existed, then pamphlets like the one I mentioned would not be used as material for study in the reading and discussion circles. They are distributed and recommended, instead of being criticized. And what is the result of this futile, un-Marxist dealing with the question? That questions of sex and marriage are understood not as part of the large social question? No, worse! The great social question appears as an adjunct, a part, of sexual problems. The main thing becomes a subsidiary matter. That does not only endanger clarity on that question itself, it muddles the thoughts, the class consciousness of proletarian women generally.

"Last and not least. Even the wise Solomon said that everything has its time. I ask you: Is now the time to amuse proletarian women with discussions on how one loves and is loved, how one marries and is married?... Now all the thoughts of women comrades, of the women of the working people, must be directed towards the proletarian revolution. It creates the basis for a real renovation in marriage and sexual relations. At the moment other problems are more urgent than the marriage forms of Maoris or incest in olden times. The question of Soviets is still on the agenda for the German proletariat. The Versailles Treaty and its effect on the life of the working woman - unemployment, falling wages, taxes, and a great deal more. In short, I maintain that this kind of political, social education for proletarian women is false, quite, quite false. How could you be silent about it? You must use your authority against it".

I have not failed to criticize and remonstrate with leading women comrades in the separate districts, I told my angry friend. He himself knew that a prophet is never recognized in his own country or family. By my criticism I had laid myself open to the charge of "strong survivals of social-democratic ideology and old-fashioned Philistinism". But at last my criticism had begun to take effect. Questions of sex and marriage were no longer the central feature of discussion. But Lenin continued the thread of thought further.

"I know, I know", he said. "I have also been accused by many people of Philistinism in this matter, although that is repulsive to me. There is much hypocrisy and narrow-mindedness in it. Well, I'm bearing it calmly! The little yellow-beaked birds who have just broken from the egg of bourgeois ideas are always frightfully clever. We shall have to let that go. The youth movement too is attacked with the disease of modernity in its attitude towards sexual questions and in being exaggeratedly concerned with them". Lenin gave an ironic emphasis to the word modernity and grimaced as he did so. "I have been told that sexual questions are the favourite study of your youth organizations, too. There is supposed to be a lack of sufficient orators on the subject. Such misconceptions are particularly harmful, particularly dangerous in the youth movement. They can very easily contribute towards over-excitement and exaggeration in the sexual life of some of them, to a waste of youthful health and strength. You must fight against that, too. There are not a few points of contact between the women's and youth movements. Our women comrades must work together systematically with the youth. That is a continuation, an extension and exaltation of motherliness from the individual to the social sphere. And all the awakening social life and activity of women must be encouraged, so that they can discard the limitations of their Philistine individualist home and family psychology. But we'll come to that later.

"With us, too, a large part of the youth is keen on 'revising bourgeois conceptions and morality' concerning sexual questions. And, I must add, a large part of our best, our most promising young people. What you said before is true. In the conditions created by the war and the revolution the old ideological values disappeared or lost their binding force. The new values are crystallizing slowly, in struggle. In the relations between man and man, between man and woman, feelings and thoughts are becoming revolutionized. New boundaries are being set up between the rights of the individual and the rights of the whole in the duties of individuals. The matter is still in a completely chaotic ferment. The direction, the forces of development in the various contradictory tendencies are not yet clearly defined. It is a slow and often a very painful process of decay and growth. And particularly in the sphere of sexual relationships, of marriage and the family. The decay, the corruption, the filth of bourgeois marriage, with its difficult divorce, its freedom for the man, its enslavement for the woman, the repulsive hypocrisy of sexual morality and relations fill the most active minded and best people with deep disgust...

"The changed attitude of the young people to questions of sexual life is of course based on a 'principle' and a theory. Many of them call their attitude 'revolutionary' and 'Communistic'. And they honestly believe that it is so. That does not impress us old people. Although I am nothing but a gloomy ascetic, the so-called 'new sexual life' of the youth – and sometimes of the old – often seems to me to be purely bourgeois, an extension of bourgeois brothels. That has nothing whatever in common with freedom of love as we Communists understand it. You must be aware of the famous theory that in Communist society the satisfaction of sexual desires, of love, will be as simple and unimportant as drinking a glass of water. This glass of water theory has made our young people mad, quite mad. It has proved fatal to many young boys and girls. Its adherents claim that it is Marxist. But thanks for such Marxism which directly and immediately attributes all phenomena and changes in the ideological superstructure of society to its economic basis! Matters aren't quite as simple as that. A certain Frederick Engels pointed that out a long time ago with regard to historical materialism.

"I think this glass of water theory is completely un-Marxist, and moreover, anti-social… Of course, thirst must be satisfied. But will the normal man in normal circumstances lie down in the gutter and drink out of a puddle, or out of a glass with a rim greasy from many lips? But the social aspect is most important of all. Drinking water is of course an individual affair. But in love two lives are concerned, and a third, a new life, arises. It is that which gives it its social interest, which gives rise to a duty towards the community.

"As a Communist I have not the least sympathy for the glass of water theory, although it bears the fine title 'satisfaction of love'. In any case, this liberation of love is neither new nor Communist. You will remember that about the middle of the last century it was preached as the 'emancipation of the heart' in romantic literature. In bourgeois practice it became the emancipation of the flesh. At that time the preaching was more talented than it is today, and as for the practice, I cannot judge. I don't mean to preach asceticism by my criticism. Not in the least. Communism will not bring asceticism, but joy of life, power of life, and a satisfied love life will help to do that. But in my opinion the present widespread hypertrophy in sexual matters does not give joy and force to life, but takes it away. In the age of revolution that is bad, very bad.

"Young people, particularly, need the joy and force of life. Healthy sport, swimming, racing, walking, bodily exercises of every kind, and many-sided intellectual interests. Learning, studying, inquiry, as far as possible in common. That will give young people more than eternal theories and discussions about sexual problems and the so-called 'living to the full'. Healthy bodies, healthy minds! Neither monk nor Don Juan, nor the intermediate attitude of the German Philistines. You know young comrade ——? A splendid boy, and highly talented. And yet I fear that nothing good will come out of him. He reels and staggers from one love affair to the next. That won't do for the political struggle, for the revolution. And I wouldn't bet on the reliability, the endurance in struggle of those women who confuse their personal romances with politics. Nor of the men who run after every petticoat and get entrapped by every young woman. No, no! that does not square with the revolution".

Lenin sprang up, banged his hand on the table, and paced the room for a while.

"The revolution demands concentration, increase of forces. From the masses, from individuals. It cannot tolerate orgiastic conditions, such as are normal for the decadent heroes and heroines of D'Annunzio. Dissoluteness in sexual life is bourgeois, is a phenomenon of decay. The proletariat is a rising class. It doesn't need intoxication as a narcotic or a stimulus. Intoxication as little by sexual exaggeration as by alcohol. It must not and shall not forget, forget the shame, the filth, the savagery of capitalism. It receives the strongest to fight from a class situation, from the Communist ideal. It needs clarity, clarity, and again clarity. And so I repeat, no weakening, no waste, no destruction of forces. Self-control, self-discipline is not slavery, not even in love. But forgive me, Clara, I have wandered far from the starting-point of our conversation. Why didn't you call me to order? My tongue has run away with me. I am deeply concerned about the future of our youth. It is a part of the revolution. And if harmful tendencies are appearing, creeping over from bourgeois society into the world of revolution – as the roots of many weeds spread – it is better to combat them early. Such questions are part of the women question".

Introduction to the 1975 Edition

We first published this text in June 1970. A great deal has happened since then. The works of Wilhelm Reich have become available in many cheap editions and his ideas are widely known among revolutionaries.[251] The rise of the Women's Liberation Movement has ensured that many of the notions rather tentatively put forward in this pamphlet are now widely accepted. The debate about "sexual liberation" and about "sexual politics" in general has in fact gone a lot further than was envisaged in these pages.

What is striking, however, is the disparity between radical attitudes in this area (now shared by many) and the continued acceptance by most so-called revolutionaries (Stalinists, Trotskyists, Maoists, etc.) of authoritarian practices and institutions. Whether we like it or not these groups and the ideas they peddle still dominate the political scene. We hope our pamphlet may contribute to subverting their orthodoxies and incidentally help some of them come to libertarian politics.

The author has two main criticisms of the original text. The first is that it was insufficiently critical of Reich's concept of the centrality of sexual repression in the genesis of authoritarian conditioning. Reich undoubtedly achieved many valid insights in this field, but other factors are also clearly involved and an overwhelmingly unidimensional approach (such as Reich's) in the long run creates more problems (both practical and theoretical) than it solves.

Secondly, the original text, while correctly stressing the social dimension of the problem of sexual liberation, was probably too optimistic in its hopes that it would prove easy for individuals to break with a process of conditioning as old as class society itself, and to live as rational, emancipated human beings, free of sexual inhibitions, yet considerate of the feelings of others.[252]

These two considerations do not detract, however, from the relevance of this area. They should, on the contrary, be seen as a spur to further investigation into the roots of human belief and behaviour. If socialism is, in the phrase of the young Marx, "man's positive self-consciousness", then all endeavours to deepen our understanding of *how* people think, and *why* they think and feel certain things, seem both worthwhile and necessary.

SOLIDARITY PAMPHLET 33, JUNE 1970; 2ND EDN., AUGUST 1975.

---

251   See our reviews of Reich's *What is Class Consciousness?* and his *Dialectical Materialism and Psychoanalysis* [reprinted above as "Wilhelm Reich 1" and "Wilhelm Reich 2"].

252   See our review of George Frankl's *The Failure of the Sexual Revolution* [reprinted above as "The Sexual Revolution"].

THE BOLSHEVIKS AND WORKERS' CONTROL, 1917–1921: THE STATE AND COUNTER-REVOLUTION

INTRODUCTION

This pamphlet has two aims. It seeks to contribute new factual material to the current discussion on "workers' control". And it attempts a new kind of analysis of the fate of the Russian Revolution. The two objectives, as will be shown, are inter-related.

Workers' Control

"Workers' control" is again being talked about. Nationalization (whether of the Western or Eastern variety) and the rule of the "Party of the working class" (whether of the Eastern or Western variety) have manifestly failed. They have not satisfied the hopes and expectations of ordinary people – or given them any real say in deter-mining the conditions under which they live. This has created new interest in the subject of "workers' control" and in ideas which, in a different context, were common currency at the beginning of the century.

Today people as different as Young Liberals and Labour "lefts", tired trade union officials and "Trotskyists" of one kind or another – not to mention anarcho-syndical-ists and "libertarian Marxists" – all talk about "workers' control". This suggests one of two things. Either these people have common objectives – which seems unlikely – or the words serve to mask as much as they convey. We hope to dispel some of the confusion by recalling how, at a critical stage of history, the advocates of different conceptions of "workers' control" confronted one another and by showing who won, why they won, and what the consequences were to be.

This return to the historical roots of the controversy is not motivated by an addiction to archivism or by a partiality for the esoteric. The revolutionary movement in Britain – unlike that in several European countries – has never been much con-cerned with theory, preferring on the whole an empirical, "suck-it-and-see" kind of approach. This may at times have helped it avoid becoming bogged down in the swamps of metaphysical speculation but the overhead costs – in terms of clarity and consistency – have been heavy. Without a clear understanding of objectives and of the forces (including ideological forces) impeding advance – in short without a sense of history – the revolutionary struggle tends to become "all movement and no direc-tion". Without clear perspectives, revolutionaries tend to fall into traps – or be divert-ed into blind alleys – which, with a little knowledge of their own past, they could eas-ily have avoided.

The confusion about workers' control (at least in Britain) is partly terminologi-cal. In the British movement (and to a lesser extent in the English language) a clear-cut distinction is seldom made between "control" and "management", functions which may occasionally overlap but are usually quite distinct. In French, Spanish or Russian political literature two separate terms (*contrôle* and *gestion*, *control* and *gerencia*, *kontrolia* and *upravleniye*) refer respectively to partial or total domination of the producers over the productive process. A moment's reflection will make it obvious why one must make this distinction.

Two possible situations come to mind. In one the working class (the collective producer) takes all the fundamental decisions. It does so directly, through organisms of its own choice with which it identifies itself completely or which it feels it can totally dominate (Factory Committees, Workers' Councils, etc.). These bodies, composed of elected and revocable delegates probably federate on a regional and national basis. They decide (allowing the maximum possible autonomy for local units) what to produce, how to produce it, at what cost to produce it, at whose cost to produce it. The other possible situation is one in which these fundamental decisions are taken "elsewhere", "from the outside", i.e. by the State, by the Party, or by some other organism without deep and direct roots in the productive process itself. The "separation of the producers from the means of production" (the basis of all class society) is maintained. The oppressive effects of this type of arrangement soon manifest themselves. This happens whatever the revolutionary good intentions of the agency in question, and whatever provisions it may (or may not) make for policy decisions to be submitted from time to time for ratification or amendment.

There are words to describe these two states of affairs. *To manage* is to initiate the decisions oneself, as a sovereign person or collectivity, in full knowledge of all the relevant facts. *To control* is to supervise, inspect or check decisions initiated by others. "Control" implies a limitation of sovereignty or, at best, a state of duality of power, wherein some people determine the objectives while others see that the appropriate means are used to achieve them. Historically, controversies about workers' control have tended to break out precisely in such conditions of economic dual power.

Like all forms of dual power, economic dual power is essentially unstable. It will evolve into a consolidation of bureaucratic power (with the working class exerting less and less of the control). Or it will evolve into *workers' management*, with the working class taking over all managerial functions. Since 1961, when *Solidarity* started advocating "workers' management of production", others have begun to call for "workers' *direct* control", "workers' *full* control", etc. - so many tacit admissions of the inadequacy (or at least ambiguity) of previous formulations.

It would be a shortsighted view to see in all this a question of linguistic purism, a terminological or doctrinal quibble. We have to pay a ransom to both the past and the present. We have not appeared on the political scene from nowhere. We are part of a revolutionary libertarian tradition for whom these concepts had deep significance. And we are not living in a political vacuum. We are living in a specific historical context, in which a constant struggle is taking place. In this struggle the conflicting interests of different social strata (bourgeoisie, bureaucracy and proletariat) are expressed in different types of demands, more or less clearly formulated. Different ideas about control and management figure prominently in these controversies. Unlike Humpty Dumpty we cannot make words mean exactly what we choose.

The revolutionary movement itself moreover is one of the forces on this social arena. Whether we like it or not - and whether it fully appreciates it or not - most of the revolutionary movement is impregnated with the ethos, traditions and organizational conceptions of Bolshevism. And in the history of the Russian Revolution - particularly between 1917 and 1921 - the issue of "workers' control" versus "workers' management" loomed large. "From 1917 to 1921 the issue of industrial administration was the most sensitive indicator of the clash of principles about the shaping of the new social order... It was the most continuous and provocative focus of actual conflict between the communist factions".[253] And, it should be stressed, between the Bolsheviks and other tendencies in the revolutionary movement. Thousands of revolutionaries were to be killed and hundreds of thousands incarcerated, fighting it out.

Most of those now entering the revolutionary movement will be unfamiliar with these controversies. A virtue should not however be made of this state of affairs. Clarification is essential, but here new problems arise. The methodological poverty, ahistoricism (at times even anti-intellectualism) among so many of those revolutionaries who *do* have some knowledge as to what actually happened is a first tragic obstacle. And it is one of the ironies of the present situation that those others (the residual legatees of Bolshevism) who talk loudest about the "need for theory" and the "need to study history" should be those with the most to hide (should their own historical antecedents really be unearthed) and with the most to lose (should a coherent alternative emerge to challenge their ossified beliefs).

Some of the confusion about "workers' control" is neither terminological nor due to ignorance concerning past controversies. It is deliberate. Today, for instance, one finds some hardened, old-time Leninists or Trotskyists (in the Socialist Labour League, International Marxist Group or in the "leadership" of International Socialism for instance) advocating "workers' control" without batting an eyelid. Seeking to capitalize on the confusion now rampant in the movement, these people talk of "workers' control" as if (a) they meant by these words what the politically unsophisticated might think they mean (i.e. that working people should themselves decide about the fundamental matters relating to production) and (b) as if they - and the Leninist doctrine to which they claim to adhere - had always supported demands of this kind, or as if Leninism had always seen in workers' control the universally valid foundation of a new social order, rather than just a *slogan* to be used for manipulatory purposes in specific and very limited historical contexts.[254]

The question of self-management is not esoteric. Its discussion - in the sharpest possible terms - is not sectarian. Self-management is what the revolution of our time is all about. This in itself would justify a pamphlet such as the present one. A study of this period (Russia, 1917–1921) has, however, deeper implications. It could provide

---

253 R. V. Daniels, *The Conscience of the Revolution* (Harvard University Press, 1960), p. 81.

254 Not all Trotskyist tendencies practice this kind of deception. Some are unambiguously reactionary. For instance K. Coates and A. Topham state "it seems sensible for us to speak of 'workers' control' to indicate the aggressive encroachment of Trade Unions [*sic!*] on management powers, in a capitalist framework, and of 'workers' self-management' to indicate attempts to administer a socialized economy democratically" (*Industrial Democracy in Great Britain* (London: MacGibbon & Kee, 1968, p. 363). Trotsky himself was just as straightforward. Although not making of workers' control a function to be exercised by the unions he distinguished clearly enough between "control" and "management". "For us the slogan of control is tied up with the period of dual power in production which corresponds to the transition from the bourgeois regime to the proletarian.... In the language of all mankind by control is understood surveillance and checking by one institution over the work of another. Control may be very active, authoritative and all embracing. But it still remains control. The very idea of this slogan is an outgrowth of the transitional regime in industry, when the capitalist and his administrators can no longer take a step without the consent of the workers, but on the other hand, when the workers have not as yet...acquired the technique of management, nor yet created the organs essential for this" (L. Trotsky, *What Next? Vital Questions for the German Proletariat*, 1932).

the basis for a new kind of analysis of the fate of the Russian Revolution, a task to which we will now briefly turn.

The Russian Revolution

To propose a new way of looking at what happened in Russia in 1917 (and after) is synonymous with an invitation to be misunderstood. If moreover the questions asked and the methodology suggested happen to differ from those in current use the proposal almost becomes a guarantee. As we have had occasion to mention before misrepresentation is a way of life on the traditional left, for whom nothing is quite as painful as a new idea.

Over the last fifty years all the existing organizations of the left have elaborated a whole mythology (and even a whole anti-mythology) about the Russian Revolution. The parliamentary fetishists of Social Democracy see "the failure of Bolshevism" in its "anti-democratic practices". The original sin, for them, was the dissolution of the Constituent Assembly. The self-styled "Communist" movement (Stalinists, Trotskyists, Maoists, etc.) talks with filial pride of the "glorious, socialist, October Revolution". They seek to vaunt and popularize its original achievements while differing in their appreciations of what happened subsequently, when it happened, why it happened and to whom it happened. For various anarchists the fact that the State or "political power" was not immediately "abolished" is the ultimate proof and yardstick that nothing of fundamental significance really occurred.[255] The SPGB (Socialist Party of Great Britain) draw much the same conclusion, although they attribute it to the fact that the wages system was not abolished, the majority of the Russian population not having had the benefit of hearing the SPGB viewpoint (as put by spokesmen duly sanctioned by their Executive Committee) and not having then sought to win a Parliamentary majority in the existing Russian institutions.

On all sides people seek to use the Russian Revolution with a view to integrating it into their own propaganda - only retaining of it those aspects which happen to conform with their own particular analysis of history, or their own particular prescriptions for the present. Whatever was new, whatever seemed to contradict established theories or break out of established categories, has been systematically "forgotten", minimized, distorted, denied.

Any attempt to re-evaluate the crucial experience of 1917-1921 is bound to evoke opposition. The first to react will be the "apparatchiks" who for years have been protecting "revolutionary" organizations (and "revolutionary" ideology) from the dual threats of subversion and renewal. Opposition will also be found however in the minds of many honest militants, seeking the road to genuinely revolutionary politics. One isn't dealing here with a simple psychological resistance but with a much deeper phenomenon which cannot be explained away by reference to the reactionary role and influence of various "leaderships". If the average militant has difficulty in understanding the full significance of some of the problems raised in the early stages of the Russian Revolution, it is because these problems are amongst the most important and difficult (if not *the* most important and difficult) ever to have confronted the working class. The working class made a revolution that went beyond

---

255   An example of such an over simplified analysis of the fate of the revolution can be found in Voline, *Nineteen-Seventeen* (London: Freedom Press, 1954). "The Bolshevik Party, once in control, installed itself as absolute master. It was quickly corrupted. It organized itself as a privileged caste. And later it flattened and subjected the working class in order to exploit it, under new forms, in its own interests".

a mere change in the political personnel at the top. It was able to expropriate the former owners of the means of production (thereby profoundly altering the existing property relations). But to what extent was it able to go beyond even this? To what extent was it able - or prepared - to revolutionize the relations of production? Was it willing to destroy the authority structure which the relations of production embody and perpetuate in all class societies? To what extent was it prepared itself to manage production (and thereby the whole of society), or to what extent was it inclined to delegate this task to others? And to what extent was the dominant ideology to triumph, compelling the working class to substitute for its avowed enemies a Party that claimed to speak "on its behalf"?

To answer these questions is a major task beset with pitfalls. One of the dangers confronting anyone seeking dispassionately to analyze the "heroic period of the Russian Revolution" is the danger of "retrospective identification" with this or that tendency or individual then active on the political scene (Osinsky, Kollontai, Maximov, Makhno or Myasnikov, for instance). This is a pointless political pastime. It leads rapidly to a state of mind where instead of seeking to understand the broad course of events (which is a relevant preoccupation) revolutionaries find themselves asking such questions as "what should have been done at this or that moment?"; "was this or that action premature?"; "who was right at this or that Congress?"; etc. We hope to have avoided this snare. When, for instance, we study the struggle of the Workers' Opposition against the leadership of the Party (in 1920 and 1921) it is not for us a question of "taking sides". It is a question of *understanding* what the forces in conflict really represented. What, for instance, were the motives (and the ideological and other limitations) of those who appeared to be challenging the drift to bureaucratization in every aspect of social life?

Another danger (or another form of the same danger) threatens those venturing into this field for the first time, while still befuddled by the official mythology. It is the danger of becoming entangled in the very legend one is seeking to destroy. Those, for instance, seeking to "demolish" Stalin (or Trotsky, or Lenin) may successfully achieve their immediate objective. But they may "succeed" at the expense of not seeing, sensing or recording the most fundamental new features of this period: the autonomous action of the working class seeking totally to alter the conditions of its existence. We hope to have avoided this trap. If we have quoted at some length the statements of prominent individuals it is only insofar as they epitomize the ideologies which, at a given point in history, guided the actions and thoughts of men. Throughout the account, moreover, we have felt that the only way seriously to deal with what the Bolsheviks said or did was to explain the social role of their utterances and actions.

We must now state our own methodological premises. We hold that the "relations of production" - the relations which individuals or groups enter into with one another in the process of producing wealth - are the essential foundations of any society. A certain pattern of relations of production is the common denominator of all class societies. This pattern is one in which the producer does not dominate the means of production but on the contrary both is "separated from them" and from the products of his own labour. In all class societies the producer is in a position of subordination to those who manage the productive process. Workers' management of production - implying as it does the total domination of the producer over the productive process - is not for us a marginal matter. It is the core of our politics. It is the only means whereby authoritarian (order-giving, order-taking) relations in production can be transcended and a free, communist or anarchist, society introduced.

We also hold that the means of production may change hands (passing for instance from private hands into those of a bureaucracy, collectively owning them) *without this revolutionizing the relations of production*. Under such circumstances – and whatever the formal status of property – the society is still a class society for production is still managed by an agency other than the producers themselves. Property relations, in other words, do not necessarily reflect the relations of production. They may serve to mask them – and in fact they often have.[256]

This much of the analysis is fairly widely accepted. What has not been hitherto attempted is to relate the history of the Russian Revolution to this overall conceptual framework. Here we can only indicate the broad lines of such an approach.[257] Seen in this light the Russian Revolution represents an unsuccessful attempt by the Russian working class to break out of relations of production that were proving increasingly oppressive. The massive upsurge of 1917 proved strong enough to smash the political supremacy of the bourgeoisie (by shattering the economic base on which it was founded: the private ownership of the means of production). It altered the existing system of property relations. But it did not prove strong enough (despite heroic attempts in this direction) to alter the authoritarian relations of production characteristic of all class societies. Sections of the working class (those most active in the Factory Committee Movement) certainly attempted to influence the Revolution in this direction. But their attempt failed. It is worth analyzing the causes of this failure – and seeing how new masters came to replace the old ones.

What were the forces pitted against those seeking a total transformation of the conditions of industrial life? First, of course, there was the bourgeoisie. The bourgeoisie had *everything* to lose in such a total social upheaval. Confronted with workers' management, it stood to lose not only its *ownership* of the means of production but also the possibility of *privileged positions* vested in expertise and in the exercise of decisional authority. No wonder the bourgeois breathed a sigh of relief when they saw that the leaders of the Revolution would "go no further than nationalization" and were keen to leave intact the order-giver/order-taker relationship in industry and elsewhere. True, large sections of the bourgeoisie fought desperately to regain their lost property. The Civil War was a protracted and bloody affair. But thousands of those who, through custom and culture, were more or less closely attached to the expropriated bourgeoisie were very soon offered the opportunity to re-enter the "revolutionary stronghold" – by the back door as it were – and to resume their role as managers of the labour process in the "Workers' State". They seized this unexpected opportunity eagerly. In droves they either joined the Party – or decided to co-operate with it, cynically welcoming every utterance by Lenin or Trotsky in favour of "labour discipline" or "one-man management". Many were soon to be appointed

---

256   For a full discussion of this concept – and of all its implications – see P. Chaulieu, "Les rapports de production en Russie", *Socialisme ou Barbarie*, no. 2 (May–June 1949). Although the concept may surprise many "Marxists" it is of interest that Engels had clearly perceived it. In his letter to Schmidt (October 27, 1890) he wrote: "In a modern state, law must not only correspond to the general economic condition and be its expression, but must also be an *internally coherent* expression which does not, owing to inner contradictions, reduce itself to nought. And in order to achieve this, the faithful reflection of economic conditions suffers increasingly… The reflection of economic relations as legal principles is necessarily…a topsy-turvy one…" (Marx-Engels, *Selected Correspondence* (Moscow: Foreign Languages Publishing House, n.d.) pp. 504–5).

257   That such an analysis might be possible was suggested in an excellent short pamphlet: J. Barrot, *Notes pour une analyse de la Révolution Russe* (Paris: Librairie "La Vieille Taupe", n.d.).

(from above) to leading positions in the economy. Merging with the new political-administrative "elite", of which the Party itself formed the nucleus, the more "enlightened" and technologically skilled sections of the "expropriated class" soon resumed dominant positions in the relations of production.

Secondly, the Factory Committee Movement had to cope with openly hostile tendencies on the "left", such as the Mensheviks. The Mensheviks repeatedly stressed that as the Revolution could only be of bourgeois-democratic type there could be no future in attempts by the workers to manage production. All such endeavours were denounced as "anarchist" and "utopian". In places the Mensheviks proved a serious obstacle to the Factory Committee Movement, but the opposition was anticipated, principled and consistent.

Thirdly – and far more difficult to see through – was the attitude of the Bolsheviks. Between March and October the Bolsheviks supported the growth of the Factory Committees, only to turn viciously against them in the last few weeks of 1917, seeking to incorporate them into the new union structure, the better to emasculate them. This process, which is fully described in the pamphlet, was to play an important role in preventing the rapidly growing challenge to capitalist relations of production from coming to a head. Instead the Bolsheviks canalized the energies released between March and October into a successful onslaught against the political power of the bourgeoisie (and against the property relations on which that power was based). At this level the Revolution was "successful". But the Bolsheviks were also "successful" in restoring "law and order" in industry – a law and order that reconsolidated the authoritarian relations in production, which for a brief period had been seriously shaken.

Why did the Party act in this manner? To answer this question would require a much fuller analysis of the Bolshevik Party and of its relation to the Russian working class than we can here attempt. Again one would have to steer clear both of mythology ("the great Bolshevik Party", "the weapon forged by Lenin", "the spearhead of the Revolution", etc.) and of anti-mythology ("the Party as the embodiment of totalitarianism, militarism, bureaucracy", etc.), seeking constantly to understand rather than to rant or rave. At the superficial level both the Party's ideology and its practice were firmly rooted in the specific historical circumstances of Tsarist Russia, in the first decade of this century. Illegality and persecution partly explain (although they do not justify) the Party's organizational structure and its conception of its relationship to the class.[258] What is more difficult to understand is the naivety of the Bolshevik leaders who don't seem to have appreciated the effects that this type of organization and this type of relationship to the class would inevitably have on the subsequent history of the Party.

Writing of the early history of the Party no lesser an exponent of Bolshevik orthodoxy than Trotsky was to state:

> The habits peculiar…to a political machine were already forming in the underground. The young revolutionary bureaucrat was already emerging as a type. The conditions of conspiracy, true enough, offered rather meagre scope for such formalities of democracy as elections, accountability and control. Yet undoubtedly the Committee men narrowed these limitations considerably more than necessity demanded. They were far more intransigent and severe with the revolutionary working men than with themselves, preferring to domineer even on occasions

---

258 Both explicitly outlined in the theory (cf. Lenin, *What Is To Be Done?* and *One Step Forwards, Two Steps Back*) and in the *practice* of Bolshevism, between 1901 and 1917.

that called imperatively for lending an attentive ear to the voice of the masses. Krupskaya notes that, just as in the Bolshevik committees, so at the Congress itself, there were almost no working men. The intellectuals predominated. "The Committee man", writes Krupskaya, "was usually quite a self-confident person...as a rule he did not recognize any internal party democracy...did not want any innovations...did not desire and did not know how to adapt himself to rapidly changing conditions".[259]

What all this was to lead to was first hinted at in 1905. Soviets had appeared in many places.

The Petersburgh Committee of the Bolsheviks was frightened at first by such an innovation as a non-partisan representation of the embattled masses. It could find nothing better to do than to present the Soviet with an ultimatum: immediately adopt a Social-Democratic programme or disband. The Petersburgh Soviet as a whole, including the contingent of Bolshevik working men as well, ignored this ultimatum without batting an eyelid.[260]

Broué, one of the more sophisticated apologists of Bolshevism, was to write that "those in the Bolshevik Party who were the most favourable to the Soviets only saw in them, in the best of cases, auxiliaries for the Party...only belatedly did the Party discover the role it could play in the Soviets, and the interest that the Soviets presented for increasing the Party's influence with a view to leading the masses".[261] The problem is put here in a nutshell. The Bolshevik cadres saw their role as the leadership of the revolution. Any movement not initiated by them or independent of their control could only evoke their suspicion.[262] It has often been said that the Bolsheviks were "surprised" by the creation of the Soviets: this euphemism should not mislead us. The reaction of the Bolsheviks was of far deeper significance than mere "surprise" - it reflected a whole concept of revolutionary struggle, a whole concept of the relationship between workers and revolutionaries. The *action* of the Russian masses themselves, as far back as 1905, was already to condemn these attitudes as outdated.

This separation between the Bolsheviks and the masses was to be revealed repeatedly during 1917. It was first witnessed during the February Revolution, again at the time of the *April Theses*, and later still at the time of the July days.[263] It has repeatedly been admitted that the Party made "mistakes" both in 1905 and in 1917. But this "explanation" explains nothing. What one should be asking is what made these mistakes possible? And one can answer only if one understands the *type of work* undertaken by the Party cadres, from the creation of the Party right up to the time of the Revolution. The Party leaders (from those on the Central Committee down to those in charge of local groups) had been placed, through the combined effects of the conditions of the struggle against Tsarism and of their own organizational conceptions,

259   L. Trotsky, *Stalin* (London, 1947), p. 61. The Congress referred to is the Third Party Congress (April 25 – May 10, 1905).

260   *Ibid*, pp. 64–65.

261   P. Broué, *Histoire du Parti Bolshevik* (Paris: Editions de Minuit, 1963), p. 35.

262   The same attitude was to be found within the Party itself. As Trotsky himself was to say, this time approvingly: "The statutes should express the leadership's organized distrust of the members, a distrust manifesting itself in vigilant control from above over the Party" (I. Deutscher, *The Prophet Armed* (Oxford University Press, 1954), p. 76.

263   No, we are not saying that the military overthrow of the Provisional Government was possible in July. We are merely stressing how out of touch the Party was with what the masses really wanted.

in a situation which allowed them only tenuous links with the real workers' movement. "A worker-agitator", wrote Lenin,

> who shows any talent and is at all promising *should not work in the factory*. We must see to it that he lives on Party support...and goes over to an underground status.[264]

No wonder the few Bolshevik cadres of working-class origin soon lost real contacts with the class.

The Bolshevik Party was torn by a contradiction which helps explain its attitude before and after 1917. Its strength lay in the advanced workers who supported it. There is no doubt that this support was at times widespread and genuine. But these workers could not control the Party. The leadership was firmly in the hands of professional revolutionaries. In a sense this was inevitable. A clandestine press and the dissemination of propaganda could only be kept going regularly by militants constantly on the move and at times compelled to seek refuge overseas. A worker could only become a Bolshevik cadre on condition he ceased work and placed himself at the disposal of the Party, which would then send him on special missions, to this or that town. The apparatus of the Party was in the hands of revolutionary specialists. The contradiction was that the real living forces that provided the strength of the Party could not control it. As an institution, the Party totally eluded control by the Russian working class. The problems encountered by the Russian Revolution after 1917 did not bring about this contradiction, they only served to exacerbate it. The attitude of the Party in 1917 and after are products of its history. This is what rendered so futile most of the attempts made within the Party by various oppositions between 1918 and 1921. They failed to perceive that a given ideological premise (the preordained hegemony of the Party) led necessarily to certain conclusions in practice.

But even this is probably not taking the analysis far enough. At an even deeper level the very conception of this kind of organization and this kind of relationship to the mass movement reflect the unrecognized influence of bourgeois ideology, even on the minds of those who were relentlessly seeking to overthrow bourgeois society. The concept that society must necessarily be divided into "leaders" and "led", the notion that there are some born to rule while others cannot really develop beyond a certain stage have from time immemorial been the tacit assumptions of every ruling class in history. For even the Bolsheviks to accept them shows how correct Marx was when he proclaimed that "the ruling ideas of each epoch are the ideas of its ruling class". Confronted with an "efficient", tightly-knit organization of this kind, built on ideas of this kind, it is scarcely surprising that the emerging Factory Committees were unable to carry the Revolution to completion.

The final difficulty confronting the Committees was inherent in the Committee Movement itself. Although certain individuals showed extraordinary lucidity, and although the Committee Movement represents the highest manifestation of the class struggle achieved in 1917, the movement as a whole was unable to understand what was happening to it and to offer any serious resistance. It did not succeed in generalizing its experience and the record it left is, unfortunately, very fragmentary. Unable to proclaim its own objectives (workers' self-management) in clear and positive terms, it was inevitable that others would step into the vacuum. With the bourgeoisie in full disintegration, and the working class as yet insufficiently strong or conscious

---

264   Lenin, *Sochineniya* (Works), IV, p. 441.

to impose *its own* solutions to the problems tearing society apart, the triumphs of Bolshevism and of the bureaucracy were both inevitable.

An analysis of the Russian Revolution shows that in allowing a specific group, separate from the workers themselves, to take over the function of managing production, the working class loses all possibility of even controlling the means of producing wealth. The separation of productive labour from the means of production results in an exploiting society. Moreover, when institutions such as the Soviets could no longer be influenced by ordinary workers, the regime could no longer be called a soviet regime. By no stretch of the imagination could it still be taken to reflect the interests of the working class. *The basic question: who manages production after the overthrow of the bourgeoisie? should therefore now become the centre of any serious discussion about socialism.* Today the old equation (liquidation of the bourgeoisie = workers' state) popularized by countless Leninists, Stalinists and Trotskyists is just not good enough.

In 1917 the Russian workers created organs (Factory Committees and Soviets) that might have ensured the management of society by the workers themselves. But the Soviets passed into the hands of Bolshevik functionaries. A state apparatus, separate from the masses, was rapidly reconstituted. The Russian workers did not succeed in creating new institutions through which they would have managed both industry and social life. This task was therefore taken over by someone else, by a group whose specific task it became. The bureaucracy organized the work process in a country of whose political institutions it was also master.

All this necessitates a serious re-evaluation of several basic concepts. "Workers' power" cannot be identified or equated with the power of the Party – as it repeatedly was by the Bolsheviks. In the words of Rosa Luxemburg, workers' power must be implemented

> by the class, not by a minority, managing things in the name of the class. It must emanate from the active involvement of the masses, remain under their direct influence, be submitted to control by the entire population, result from the increasing political awareness of the people.

As for the concept of "taking power" it cannot mean a semi-military putsch, carried out by a minority, as it obviously does for so many who still seem to be living in the Petrograd of 1917. Nor can it only mean the defence – however necessary – of what the working class has won against attempts by the bourgeoisie to win it back. What "taking power" really implies is that the vast majority of the working class at last realizes its ability to manage both production and society – and organizes to this end.

This text is in no sense an economic history of Russia between 1917 and 1921. It is, at best, a selective industrial chronology. In most instances the facts speak for themselves. In a few places, we have taken the opportunity of describing our own views, particularly when we felt that all the protagonists in the great historical debates were wrong, or trapped in a system of ideas that prevented them from appreciating the real significance of what was happening. Events such as the stages of the Civil War are only mentioned in order to place various controversies in context – and to nail once and for all the allegation that many of the measures described were taken "as a result of the Civil War".

It will probably be objected that, throughout the narrative, greater stress has been placed on various struggles within the Party than on the actions of the millions who, for one reason or another, never joined the Party or who, from the beginning, saw through what it was endeavouring to do. The "charge" is true but the short-coming almost unavoidable. The aspirations of thousands of people, their doubts, their hesitations, their hopes, their sacrifices, their desire to transform the conditions of their daily life and their struggles to do so are undoubtedly as much a moulding force of history as the resolutions of Party Congresses or the speeches of Party leaders. Yet an activity that has neither rules nor statutes, neither tribunes nor troubadours, belongs almost by definition to what history suppresses. An awareness of the problem, however acute, will not generate the missing material. And an essay such as this is largely a question of documentation. The masses make history, they do not write it. And those who do write it are nearly always more concerned with ancestor worship and retrospective justification that with a balanced presentation of the facts.

Other charges will also be made. The quotations from Lenin and Trotsky will not be denied but it will be stated that they are "selective" and that "other things, too" were said. Again, we plead "guilty". But we would stress that there are hagiographers enough in the trade whose "objectivity" (like Deutscher's for instance) is but a cloak for sophisticated apologetics. There is moreover another reason for unearthing this material. Fifty years after the Revolution - and long after its "isolation" has been broken - the bureaucratic system in Russia clearly bears little resemblance to the model of the Paris Commune (elected and revocable delegates, none receiving more than a working man's wage, etc., etc.). In fact Russia's social structure has scarcely any anticipation in the whole corpus of Marxist theory. It therefore seems more relevant to quote those statements of the Bolshevik leaders of 1917 which helped determine Russia's evolution rather than those other statements which, like the May Day speeches of Labour leaders, were forever to remain in the realm of rhetoric.

Note on Dates
On February 14, 1918, Russia abandoned the old Julian calendar and adopted the Gregorian one in use in Western Europe. February 1 became February 14. Old style dates have been observed up to this point. New style dates thereafter.

1917

FEBRUARY
Strikes and bread riots in Petrograd. Angry street demonstrations against the Government. Troops, sent to restore order, fraternize with demonstrators. Soviets reappear in several cities, for the first time since 1905.

February 27
Abdication of Nicholas II. Formation of Provisional Government (Prince Lvov as Prime Minister).

MARCH
Factory and Shop Committees,[265] Workers' Councils and Councils of Elders

---
265 *Fabzavkomy*: short for *fabrichno–zavodnye komitety*.

appear in every major industrial centre of European Russia. From the onset, their demands are not limited to wages or hours but challenge many managerial prerogatives.

In several instances Factory Committees were set up because the previous owners or managers had disappeared during the February turmoil. Most of those who later drifted back were allowed to resume their positions – but had to accept the Factory Committees. "The proletariat", wrote Pankratova,[266] "without legislative sanction, started simultaneously to create all its organizations: Soviets of Workers' Deputies, trade unions and Factory Committees".[267] A tremendous working-class pressure was developing all over Russia.

March 10

First formal capitulation by a significant body of employers. Agreement signed between Executive Committee of the Petrograd Soviet and Petrograd Manufacturers' Association, granting the eight-hour day in some enterprises and "recognizing" some of the Committees. Most other employers refused to follow suit. For instance on March 14 the Committee for Commerce and Industry declared that "the question of the eight-hour day cannot be resolved by reciprocal agreement between workers and employers, because it is a matter of state importance." The first major fight of the Factory Committees took place on this issue.

The eight-hour day was soon imposed in Petrograd, either with the reluctant consent of the employers or unilaterally by the workers. The "recognition" of the Factory Committees proved much more difficult to impose, both employers and State recognizing the threat to them inherent in this form of organization.

April 2

Exploratory Conference of Factory Committees of Petrograd War Industries, convened on the initiative of the workers of the Artillery Department. This Conference was to proclaim what were, at that time, the most advanced "terms of reference" for any Factory Committee. Paragraphs 5 to 7 of the proclamation stipulated:

> From the Factory Committee should emanate all instructions concerning internal factory organization (i.e. instructions concerning such matters as hours of work, wages, hiring and firing, holidays, etc.). The factory manager to be kept notified…

---

266   Anna Mikhailovna Pankratova joined the Bolshevik Party in 1919 as an Odessa University student. She wrote a number of books on the history of the Russian labour movement and later became a professor at Moscow University and at the Academy of Social Sciences. In 1952 she was elected to the Central Committee of the Party and the following year became editor-in-chief of the Party journal, *Voprosii Istorii* (Questions of History). She died in 1957.

Published before the era of systematic historical distortion, her pamphlet on the Factory Committees contains interesting material. Her scope and vision are however seriously limited because of her endorsement of two fundamental Bolshevik assumptions: (a) "that the role of the Factory Committees ends either with the ebb of the revolutionary tide or with the victory of the Revolution" and (b) that the "demands and aspirations arising from the depths of the working class are given formulation, and provided with ideological content and organizational cement through the Party...The struggle for workers' control took place under the leadership of the Party, which had allowed [*sic!*] the proletariat to take political and economic power".

267   A.M. Pankratova, *Fabzavkomy Rossii v borbe za sotsialisticheskuyu fabriku* (Russian Factory Committees in the Struggle for the Socialist Factory) (Moscow, 1923), p.9. Parts of this important document were published in the French journal, *Autogestion*, no. 34 (December 1967) and the page numbers refer to the French version.

The whole administrative personnel (management at all levels and technicians) is taken on with the consent of the Factory Committee which has to notify the workers of its decisions at mass meetings of the whole factory or through shop committees...

The Factory Committee controls managerial activity in the administrative, economic and technical fields...representatives of the Factory Committee must be provided, for information, with all official documents of the management, production budgets and details of all items entering or leaving the factory...[268]

April 7

Publication of *April Theses*, shortly after Lenin had returned to Petrograd from abroad. Only reference to workers' control is in Thesis 8: "Our immediate task shall not be the 'introduction of socialism' but to bring social production and distribution of products...under the control of the Soviet of Workers' Deputies".

April 23

The new government had to make some verbal concessions. It passed a law partially "recognizing" the Committees but carefully restricting their influence. All the key issues were left to the "mutual agreement of the parties concerned" - in other words there was no *statutory* obligation on the employers to deal directly with the Committees.

The workers however showed little concern about the provisions of the law. "They commented, in their own fashion, on the law of April 23...They determined their own terms of reference, in each factory, steadily expanding their prerogatives and decided on what their representatives might do, according to the relation of forces in each particular instance".[269]

Lenin writes: "Such measures as the nationalization of the land and of the banks and syndicates of capitalists, or at least the immediate establishment of the *control* of the Soviets of Workers' Deputies over them (measures which do not in any way imply the 'introduction of socialism') must be absolutely insisted on and whenever possible introduced by revolutionary means". Such measures were "entirely feasible economically" and without them it would be "impossible to heal the wounds of the war and prevent the impending collapse".[270]

To Lenin's basic ideas of workers' control as a "curb on the capitalists" and "a means of preventing collapse", a third was soon to be added with recurs in much of Lenin's writing of this period. It is the concept of workers' control as a "prelude to nationalization". For instance: "We must at once prepare the Soviets of Workers' Deputies, the Soviet of Deputies of Bank Employees, etc., to proceed to the adoption of feasible and practicable measures for the merging of all the banks into one single national bank, to be followed by the establishment of the control of the Soviets of Workers' Deputies over the banks and syndicates and then by their nationalization".[271]

---

268   *Ibid.*, pp. 12–13.

269   *Ibid.*, p. 12.

270   V.I. Lenin, "Tasks of the Proletariat in Our Revolution", *Selected Works*, VI, p. 62.

271   V.I. Lenin, "Political Parties and Tasks of the Proletariat", *ibid.*, pp. 85–6.

MAY

More and more employers were "having to cope" with Factory Committees. The bourgeois press launched a massive campaign against the eight-hour day and the Committees, trying to smear the workers in the eyes of the soldiers as lazy, greedy good-for-nothings, leading the country to ruin through their "excessive" demands. The workers' press patiently explains the real causes of industrial stagnation and the real conditions of working-class life. At the invitation of various Factory Committees, Army delegates were sent to "verify" conditions at the rear. Then they publicly testified as to the truth of what the workers were saying...

May 17

In *Pravda* Lenin explicitly endorses the slogan of workers' control, declaring that "the workers must demand the *immediate* realization of control, *in fact* and without fail, by the workers themselves".[272]

May 20

Lenin produces draft for a new Party programme:

> The Party fights for a more democratic workers' and peasants' republic, in which the police and standing army will be completely abolished and replaced by the universally armed people, by a universal militia. All official persons will not only be elected but also subject to recall at any time upon the demand of a majority of the electors. All official persons, without exception, will be paid at a rate not exceeding the average wage of a competent worker.

At the same time Lenin calls for the "unconditional *participation* [my emphasis] of the workers in the control of the affairs of the trusts" – which could be brought about "by a decree requiring but a single day to draft".[273] The concept that "workers' participation should be introduced by legislative means (i.e. from above) clearly has an illustrious ancestry.

May 29

Kharkov Conference of Factory Committees. In certain respects the provinces were in advance of Petrograd and Moscow. The Kharkov Conference demanded that the Factory Committees become "organs of the Revolution...aiming at consolidating its victories". "The Factory Committees must take over production, protect it, develop it". "They must fix wages, look after hygiene, control the technical quality of products, decree all internal factory regulations and determine solutions to all conflicts".[274] Some non-Bolshevik delegates even proposed that the Committees should take over the factories directly and exercise all managerial functions.

May 30–June 5

First full Conference of Petrograd Factory Committees. The Conference met in the Tauride Palace, in the same hall where three months earlier the State Duma (Parliament) had assembled. At least half the Committee represented were from the

272   V.I. Lenin, "Materials on Revision of Party Programme", *ibid.*, pp. 116–117.

273   V.I. Lenin, "Ruin is Threatening", *ibid.*, p. 142.

274   I. Kreizel, *Iz istorii profdvizheniya g. Kharkova v 1917 godu* (On the History of the Trade Union Movement in Kharkov in 1917) (Kharkov, 1921). Referred to by Pankratova, *op. cit.*, p. 15.

engineering industry. "The long and flowery speeches of the bourgeois parliamentarians had given way to the sincere, simple and usually concise contributions of 'deputies' who had just left their tools or their machines, to express for the first time in public their humiliations, their class needs and their needs as human beings".[275]

Bolshevik delegates were in a majority. Although most of their contributions centred on the need to introduce workers' control as a means of "restoring order" and "maintaining production", other viewpoints were also voiced. Nemtsov, a Bolshevik metal worker, proclaimed that the

> working of the factories is now in the exclusive hands of higher management. We must introduce the principle of election. To assess work…we don't need the individual decisions of foremen. By introducing the elective principle we can control production.

Naumov, another delegate, claimed that "by taking into our own hands the control of production we will learn about its practical aspects and raise it to the level of future socialist production".[276] We are a long way here from the later Bolshevik advocacy of the "efficiency" of one-man management and from their later practice of appointments from above.

The Conference was widely attended. Even M.I. Skobelev, Menshevik Minister of Labour in the Provisional Government, was to address it. His contribution was of interest as a sort of anticipation of what the Bolsheviks would be saying before the year was up. Skobelev asserted that:

> the regulation and control of industry was a task for the State. Upon the individual class, especially the working class, lies the responsibility for helping the state in its organizational work.

He also stated that "the transfer of enterprises into the hands of the people at the present time would not assist the Revolution". The regulation of industry was the function of Government, not of autonomous Factory Committees. "The Committees would best serve the workers' cause by becoming subordinate units in a state-wide network of trade unions".[277]

A similar viewpoint was put by Rozanov, one of the founders of the Professional Workers' Union. His assertions that the "functions of the Factory Committees were ephemeral" and that "Factory Committees should constitute the basic elements of the unions" were sharply criticized. Yet this is exactly the role to which - within a few months - the Factory Committees were to be relegated by Bolshevik practice. At this stage, however, the Bolsheviks were critical of the idea (the unions were still largely under Menshevik influence).

Lenin's address to the Conference contained a hint of things to come. He explained that workers' control meant "that the majority of workers should enter all responsible institutions and that the administration should render an account of its actions to the most authoritative workers' organizations".[278] Under "workers' control" Lenin clearly envisaged an "administration" other than the workers themselves.

The final resolution, supported by 336 of the 421 delegates, proclaimed the Factory Committees "fighting organizations, elected on the basis of the widest

---

275 Pankratova, *op. cit.*, p. 19.

276 *Ibid.*, p. 19.

277 *Pervaya rabochaya konferentsiya fabrichno–zavodskikh komitetov* (First Workers' Conference of Factory Committees) (Petrograd, 1917).

278 V.I. Lenin, *Sochineniya*, XX, p. 459.

democracy and with a collective leadership". Their objectives were the "creation of new conditions of work". The resolution called for "the organization of thorough control by labour over production and distribution" and for "a proletarian majority in all institutions having executive power".[279]

The next few weeks witnessed a considerable growth of the Factory Committees. Wherever they were strong enough (both before but especially after the October Revolution, when they were abetted by local Soviets) the Committees "boldly ousted the management and assumed direct control of their respective plants".[280]

June 16
First All-Russian Congress of Soviets.

June 20–28
A trade union conference held in Petrograd passed a resolution which stipulated that "the trade unions, defending the rights and interests of hired labour...cannot take upon themselves administrative-economic functions in production".[281] The Factory Committees were relegated to the role of seeing to it "that laws for the defence of labour were observed and that collective agreements concluded by the unions were also observed". The Factory Committees were to agitate for the entrance of all workers of the enterprise into the union. They should "work to strengthen and extend the trade unions, contribute to the unity of their fighting action" and "increase the authority of the unions in the eyes of unorganized workers".[282]

This conference, dominated by Mensheviks and Social Revolutionaries, had considerable misgivings concerning the Factory Committees. It expressed these by advocating that the Committees should be elected *on the basis of lists drawn up by the trade unions.*

The Bolshevik theses, presented to the conference by Glebov-Avilov, suggested that for the conduct of workers' control "economic control commissions" should be attached to the central administration of the unions. These commissions were to be made up of members of the Factory Committees and were to co-operate with the latter in each individual enterprise. The Factory Committees were not only to perform "control functions" for the trade unions but were also to be financially dependent upon the union.[283]

The conference set up an All-Russian Central Council of Trade Unions, to which representatives were elected in proportion to the numerical strength of the various political tendencies present at the conference.

At this stage the Bolsheviks were riding two horses, seeking to gain the ascendancy in both the unions and the Committees. They were not averse to a considerable amount of double talk in the pursuit of this double objective. In unions under strong Menshevik control, the Bolsheviks would press for considerable autonomy

279 S. O. Zagorsky, *State Control of Industry in Russia during the War* (New Haven, 1928), pp. 174–5.

280 Daniels,*op. cit.,* 1960), p. 83.

281 *Tretya vserossiiskaya konferentsiya professionalnykh soyuzov: Rezolyutsii prinyatiya na zasedaniakh konferentsii 20–28 Iyunya / 3–11 Iyulya 1917 g* (Third All–Russian Conference of Trade Unions: Resolutions Adopted at the Sessions of the Conference of June 20–28 / July 3–11, 1917) (Petrograd, n.d.), p. 18.

282 *Ibid.,* para 6.

283 *Ibid.,* p. 323.

for the Factory Committees. In unions under their own control, they would be far less enthusiastic about the matter.

It is necessary at this stage to say a few words about the role of the unions before and immediately after the February Revolution.

Before 1917 the unions had been relatively unimportant in Russian labour history. Russian industry was still very young. Under Tsardom (at least until the turn of the century) trade-union organization had been illegal and persecuted.

> In suppressing trade unionism Tsardom unwittingly put a premium upon revolutionary political organization…Only the most politically-minded workers, those prepared to pay for their conviction with prison and exile, could be willing to join trade unions in these circumstances…whereas in Britain the Labour Party was created by the trade unions, the Russian trade unions from their beginning led their existence in the shadow of the political movement.[284]

The analysis is correct – and moreover of much deeper significance than Deutscher probably realized. The Russian trade unions of 1917 reflected this peculiar development of the Russian working-class movement. On the one hand the unions were the auxiliaries of the political parties, which utilized them for recruiting purposes and as a mass to be manoeuvred.[285] On the other hand the union movement, reborn in a sense after February 1917, was pushed forward by the more educated workers: the leadership of the various unions reflected the predominance of a sort of intellectual elite, favourable at first to the Mensheviks and Social Revolutionaries, but later won over, in varying proportions, to the Bolsheviks.

It is important to realize that from the beginning of the Revolution the unions were tightly controlled by political organizations, which used them to solicit support for their various actions. This explains the ease with which the Party was able – at a later date – to manipulate the unions. It also helps one understand the fact that the unions (and their problems) were often to prove the battleground on which political differences between the Party leaders were again and again to be fought out. Taken in conjunction with the fact that the Party's whole previous development (including its tightly centralized structure and hierarchical organizational conceptions) had tended to separate it from the working class, one can understand how heavily the cards were stacked against any autonomous expression or even voicing of working-class aspirations. In a sense these found a freer expression in the Soviets than in either the Party or the trade unions.

Be that as it may trade union membership increased rapidly after February, workers taking advantage of their newly won freedom.

> During the first months of 1917 [union] membership rose from a few scores of thousands to 1.5 million…But the practical role of the trade unions did not correspond to their numerical strength… In 1917 strikes never assumed the scale and power they had in 1905… The economic ruin of Russia, the galloping inflation, the scarcity of consumers' goods, and so on, made normal "bread and butter" struggle look unreal. In addition the threat of mobilization hung over would-

---

284 I. Deutscher, *Soviet Trade Unions* (London: Royal Institute of International Affairs, 1950), pp. 1–2.

285 We are not here "denouncing" the fact that the unions were being influenced by political parties. Nor are we advocating anything as simplistic as "keeping politics out of the unions". We are simply describing the real state of affairs in Russia in 1917, with a view to assessing its significance in the subsequent development of the Russian Revolution.

be strikers. The working class was in no mood to strive for limited economic advantage and partial reforms. The entire social order of Russia was at stake.[286]

June–July

Persistent efforts of Mensheviks fully to subordinate the Factory and Plant Committees to the trade unions. These were successfully resisted by a temporary alliance of anarchists - objecting on grounds of principle - and of Bolsheviks acting on the basis of tactical considerations.

The autonomous Factory Committee Movement found its highest development and most militant expression in the engineering industry.[287] This is of particular relevance as it explains the drastic measures the Bolsheviks had to resort to, in 1922, to break the independent organizations of the engineering workers.

July 26–August 3

Sixth Party Congress. Milyutin declares: "We will ride on the crest of the economic wave of the movement of the workers and we will turn this spontaneous movement into a conscious political movement against the existing state power".[288]

August 7–12

Second Conference of Factory Committees of Petrograd, its Environs, and Neighbouring Provinces, held at the Smolny Institute.

The Conference resolved that ¼% of the wages of all workers represented should go to support a "Central Soviet of Factory Committees", thus made financially independent of the unions.[289] Rank-and-file supporters of the Factory Committees viewed the setting up of this "Central Soviet" with mixed feelings. On the one hand they sensed the need for co-ordination. On the other hand they wanted this co-ordination to be carried out from below, by themselves. Many were suspicious of the motives of the Bolsheviks, on whose initiative the "Central Soviet" had been bureaucratically set up. The Bolshevik Skrypnik spoke of the difficulties of the Central Soviet of Factory Committees, attributing them "in part to the workers themselves". Factory Committees had been reluctant to free their members for work in the Centre. Some of the Committees "refrained from participation in the Central Soviet because of Bolshevik predominance in it".[290] V. M. Levin, another Bolshevik, was to complain that the workers "didn't distinguish between the conception of control and the conception of taking possession".[291]

The Second Conference adopted a whole number of statutes, regulating the work of the Committees, the duties of the management (*sic!*), procedures for electing

---

286   Deutscher, *Soviet Trade Unions, op. cit.,* p.13.

287   See statistics on political strikes in V. L. Meller and A. M. Pankratova, *Rabocheye dvizheniye v 1917 godu* (The Workers' Movement in 1917), pp. 16, 20. Also M. G. Fleer, *Rabocheye dvizheniye v godu voiny* (The Workers' Movement in the War Years) (Moscow, 1925), pp. 4–7.

288   *Shestoi s'yezd RSDRP (b): Protokoly* (The Sixth Congress of the RSDWP (b): Protocols) [1917]; (Moscow: IMEL, 1934), p. 134.

289   *Oktyabrskaya revolutsiya i fabzavkomy: materiali po istorii fabrichno–zavidskikh komitetov* (The October Revolution and the Factory Committees: Materials for a History of the Factory Commitees) (Moscow, 3 vols., 1927–1929), I, pp. 229, 259. These volumes (henceforth referred to as *Okt. Rev. i Fabzavkomy*) are the most useful source on the Factory Committees.

290   *Ibid.,* p. 190.

291   *Ibid.,* p. 171.

the Committees, etc.[292] "All decrees of Factory Committees" were declared compulso-ry "for the factory administration as well as for the workers and employees - until such time as those decrees were abolished by the Committee itself, or by the Central Soviet of Factory Committees". The Committees were to meet regularly *during work-ing hours*. Meetings were to be held on days designated by the Committees them-selves. Members of the Committees were to receive full pay - from the employers - while on Committee business. Notice to the appropriate administrative personnel was to be deemed sufficient to free a member of the Factory Committee from work so that he might fulfill his obligations to the Committee. In the periods between meetings, selected members of the Factory Committees were to occupy premises, within the factory, at which they could receive information from the workers and employees. Factory administrations were to provide funds "for the maintenance of the Committees and the conduct of their affairs". Factory Committees were to have "control over the composition of the administration and the right to dismiss all those who could not guarantee normal relations with the workers or who were incompe-tent for other reasons".

> All administrative factory personnel can only enter into service with the consent
> of the Factory Committee, which must declare its [sic!] hirings at a General
> Meeting of all the factory or through departmental or workshop committees.

The "internal organization" of the factory (working time, wages, holidays, etc.) was also to be determined by the Factory Committees. Factory Committees were to have their own press and were "to inform the workers and employees of the enterprise concerning their resolutions by posting an announcement in a conspicuous place". But as the Bolshevik Skrypnik realistically reminded the Conference, "we must not forget that these are not normal statutes confirmed by the Government. They are our platform, on the basis of which we will fight". The basis of the demands was "cus-tomary revolutionary right".

August

Campaign launched by Provisional Government against "Factory Committees" in the Railways. Kukel, Vice-Minister for the Navy, proposes proclamation of martial law on the Railways and the creation of commissions entitled to "dissolve the Committees". (This is the voice of the bourgeoisie in August 1917 - not of Trotsky, in August 1920! See *August 1920*.)

At a Government-sponsored "consultation with the rank-and-file" held in Moscow on August 10 the catastrophic condition of the Railways was to be attrib-uted to the existence of the Railway Committees:

> According to an enquiry conducted at a meeting of Railway Managers, 5,531
> workers had been nominated to participate in these Committees on the 37 main
> lines. These people were absolved of all commitments to work. On the basis of
> an average minimum of 2,000 rubles, this little business was costing the
> Government 11 million rubles. And this only concerned 37 of the 60 main
> lines...[293]

At about the same time Struve, a well-known bourgeois ideologist and econo-mist, was writing that "just as in the military field the elimination of officers by sol-diers leads to the destruction of the Army (because it implies a legalization of revolt

---

292 These are described in great detail in *Okt. Rev. i Fabzavkomy*.

293 Pankratova, *op. cit.*, p. 25.

incompatible with the very existence of the Army), so in the economic field: the substitution of managerial power by workers' management implies the destruction of normal economic order and life in the enterprises".[294]

A little later in the month a Conference of Employers was held in Petrograd. It set up a Union of Employers' Associations. The main function of the new organization was described by its president Bymanov as "the elimination of interference by the Factory Committees in what are managerial functions".

August 11

First issue of *Golos Truda*, published in Russia under banner of the Union of Anarcho-Syndicalist Propaganda.

August 25

Golos Truda, in a famous article headed "Questions of the Hour", wrote:

> We say to the Russian workers, peasants, soldiers, revolutionists: above all, continue the revolution. Continue to organize yourselves solidly and to unite your new organizations: your communes, your unions, your committees, your soviets. Continue, with firmness and perseverance, always and everywhere to participate more and more extensively and more and more effectively in the economic life of the country, continue to take into your hands, that is into the hands of your organizations, all the raw materials and all the instruments indispensable to your labour. Continue the Revolution. Do not hesitate to face the solution of the burning questions of the present. Create everywhere the necessary organizations to achieve these solutions. Peasants, take the land and put it at the disposal of your committees. Workers, proceed to put in the hands of and at the disposal of your own social organizations - everywhere on the spot - the mines and the subsoil, the enterprises and the establishments of all sorts, the works and factories, the workshops and the machines.

A little later, issue No. 15 of the same paper urged its readers to

> begin immediately to organize the social and economic life of the country on new bases. Then a sort of "dictatorship of labour" will begin to be achieved, easily and in a natural manner. And the people would learn, little by little, to do it.

During this period there were a number of important strikes (tannery and textile workers in Moscow, engineering workers in Petrograd, petrol workers in Baku, miners in the Donbas).

> There was a common feature to these struggles: the employers were prepared to make concessions through increased wages but categorically refused to recognize any rights to the Factory Committees. The workers in struggle...were prepared to fight to the bitter end not so much on the question of wage increases as on the question of the recognition of their factory organizations.[295]

One of the main demands was the transfer to the Committees of the rights of hiring and firing. The inadequacies of the "law" of April 23 were by now widely realized. Demands for the Soviets to take the power were beginning to evoke an echo. "During

---

294   *Ibid.*, p. 25.
295   *Ibid.*, p. 29. So much for the workers 'only being capable of trade-union consciousness'.

its struggle for a 'factory constitution' the working class had become aware of the need itself to manage production".[296]

August 28

In response to an increasing campaign in the bourgeois journals against the Factory Committees and "working class anarchism", the Menshevik Minister of Labour Skobelev issued his famous "Circular No. 421" forbidding meetings of the Factory Committees during working hours ("because of the need to devote every energy and every second to intensive work"). The circular authorized management to deduct from wages time lost by workers in attending Committee meetings. This was at a time when Kornilov was marching on Petrograd, and "when the workers were rising, threatening, to the defence of the Revolution without considering whether they were doing so during working hours or not".[297]

SEPTEMBER

Bolshevik Party wins majorities in both Petrograd and Moscow Soviets.

September 10

Third Conference of Factory Committees. On September 4, another circular from the Ministry of Labour had stated that the right of hiring and firing of workers belonged to the owners of the enterprise. The Provisional Government, by now very alarmed at the growth of the Factory Committees, was striving desperately to curtail their power.

The Menshevik Kolokolnikov attended the Conference as the representative of the Ministry of Labour. He defended the circulars. He "explained" that the circulars did not deprive the workers of the right of *control over* hiring and firing…but only of the right to hire and fire. "As the Bolsheviks were themselves to do later Kolokolnikov defined control as supervision over policy, as opposed to the right of making policy."[298]

At the conference a worker called Afinogenev asserted that "all parties, not excluding the Bolsheviks, entice the workers with the promise of the Kingdom of God on earth a hundred years from now…We don't need improvement in a hundred years time, but now, immediately."[299] The Conference, which only lasted two sessions, decreed that it would seek the immediate abolition of the circulars.

September 14

Meeting of the Government-sponsored **Democratic Conference**. Emphasizing that the tasks of the Factory Committees were "essentially different" from those of the trade unions, the Bolsheviks requested 25 seats for the Factory Committees. (The same number had been allocated by the Government to the unions.)

---

296   *Ibid.,* p. 36.

297   *Novy Put* (New Path), October 15, 1917, nos. 1–2. *Novy Put* was the organ of the Central Soviet of Factory Committees.

298   F.I. Kaplan, *Bolshevik Ideology* (London: Peter Owen, 1969), p. 83.

299   *Okt. Rev. i Fabzavkomy,* II, p. 23.

September 26

Lenin writes: "The Soviet Government must immediately introduce throughout the state workers' control over production and distribution". "Failing such control...famine and catastrophe of unprecedented dimensions threaten the country from week to week".[300]

For several weeks the employers had been resorting to lockouts on an increasing scale in an attempt to break the power of the Committees. Between March and August 1917, 586 enterprises employing over 100,000 workers had been closed down,[301] sometimes because of the lack of fuel or raw materials but often as a deliberate attempt by the employers to evade the increasing power of the Committees. One of the functions of workers' control was seen as putting an end to such practices.

October 1

Publication of Lenin's *Can the Bolsheviks Retain State Power?* This text contains certain passages which help one understand many subsequent events:

> When we say workers' control, always associating that slogan with the dictatorship of the proletariat, and always putting it after the latter, we thereby make plain what state we have in mind... If it is a proletarian state we are referring to (i.e. the dictatorship of the proletariat) then workers' control can become a national, all-embracing, omnipresent, extremely precise and extremely scrupulous *accounting* [emphasis in original] of the production and distribution of goods.

In the same pamphlet Lenin defines the type of "socialist apparatus"(or framework) within which the function of accountancy (workers' control) will be exercised:

> *Without big banks socialism would be impossible of realization.* The big banks are a "stable apparatus" we need for the realization of socialism and which we shall *take from capitalism ready made.* Our problem here is only to lop away that *which capitalistically disfigures* this otherwise excellent apparatus and to make it still *bigger,* still more democratic, still more comprehensive...

> A single huge state bank, with branches in every rural district and in every factory - that will already be *nine-tenths of a socialist apparatus.*

According to Lenin this type of apparatus would allow "general state *book-keeping,* general state accounting of the production and distribution of goods", and would be "something in the nature, so to speak, of the *skeleton* of a socialist society".[302]

No one disputes the importance of keeping reliable records, but Lenin's identification of workers' control in a "workers' state" with the function of accountancy (i.e. checking the implementation of decisions taken by others) is extremely revealing. Nowhere in Lenin's writings is workers' control ever equated with fundamental decision-taking (i.e. with the initiation of decisions) relating to production (how much to produce, how to produce it, at what cost, at whose cost, etc.).

Other writings by Lenin in this period reiterate that one of the functions of workers' control is to prevent sabotage by the higher bureaucrats and functionaries:

300   V.I. Lenin, "The Aims of the Revolution", *Selected Works*, VI, pp. 245–6.

301   V. P. Milyutin, *Istoriya ekonomicheskogo razvitiya SSSR, 1917–1927* (History of the Economic Development of the USSR) (Moscow and Leningrad, 1927), p. 45.

302   Lenin's emphasis throughout.

As for the higher employees…we shall have to treat them as we treat the capitalists - roughly. They, like the capitalists, will offer resistance…we may succeed with the help of workers' control in rendering such resistance impossible.[303]

Lenin's notions of workers' control (as a means of preventing lockouts) and his repeated demands for the "opening of the books" (as a means of preventing economic sabotage) referred both to the immediate situation, *and to the months which were to follow the Revolution*. He envisaged a period during which, in a workers' state, the bourgeoisie would still retain the formal ownership and effective management of most of the productive apparatus. The new state, in Lenin's estimation, would not be able immediately to take over the running of industry. There would be a transitional period during which the capitalists would be coerced into co-operation. "Workers' control" was seen as the instrument of this coercion.

October 10

Fourth Conference of Factory Committees of Petrograd and its Environs. The main business on the agenda was the convocation of the first All-Russian Conference of Factory Committees.

October 13

Golos Truda calls for "total workers' control, embracing all plant operations, real and not fictitious control, control over work rules, hiring and firing, hours and wages and the procedures of manufacture".

Soviets and Factory Committees were appearing everywhere at a phenomenal rate. Their growth can be explained by the extremely radical nature of the tasks confronting the working class. Soviets and Committees were far more closely associated with the realities of everyday life than were the unions. They therefore proved far more effective mouthpieces of fundamental popular aspirations.

During this period intensive propaganda was conducted for libertarian ideas:

> Not a single newspaper was closed, not a single leaflet, pamphlet or book confiscated, not a single rally or mass meeting forbidden… True the Government at that period was not averse to dealing severely with both Anarchists and Bolsheviks. Kerensky threatened many times to "burn them out with red hot irons". But the Government was powerless, because the Revolution was in full swing.[304]

As already pointed out, the Bolsheviks *at this stage* still supported the Factory Committees. They saw them as "the battering ram that would deal blows to capitalism, organs of class struggle created by the working class on its own ground".[305] They also saw in the *slogan* of "workers' control" a means of undermining Menshevik influence in the unions. But the Bolsheviks were being "carried along by a movement which was in many respects embarrassing to them but which, as a main driving force of the revolution, they could not fail to endorse"[306]. During the middle of 1917 Bolshevik support for the Factory Committees was such that the Mensheviks were to accuse them of "abandoning" Marxism in favour of anarchism.

---

303   Lenin, *Selected Works*, VI, pp. 265–7.

304   G. P. Maximov, *Syndicalists in the Russian Revolution* (London: Direct Action pamphlet, no. 11), p. 6.

305   Pankratova, *op. cit.*, p. 5.

306   E. H. Carr, *The Bolshevik Revolution* (Penguin edn.), II, p. 80.

Actually Lenin and his followers remained firm upholders of the Marxist conception of the centralized state. Their immediate objective, however, was not yet to set up the centralized proletarian dictatorship, but to decentralize as much as possible the bourgeois state and the bourgeois economy. This was a necessary condition for the success of the revolution. In the economic field therefore, the Factory Committee, the organ on the spot, rather than the trade union was the most potent and deadly instrument of upheaval. Thus the trade unions were relegated to the background...[307]

This is perhaps the most explicit statement of why the Bolsheviks at this stage supported workers' control and its organizational vehicle, the Factory Committees. Today only the ignorant or those willing to be deceived can still kid themselves into believing that proletarian power, *at the point of production* was ever a fundamental tenet or objective of Bolshevism.

October 17–22

First All-Russian Conference of Factory Committees, convened by *Novy Put* (New Path) a paper "strongly coloured with a new kind of anarcho-syndicalism, though no anarcho-syndicalists were on its staff".[308]

According to later Bolshevik sources, of the 137 delegates attending the Conference there were 86 Bolsheviks, 22 Social Revolutionaries, 11 anarcho-syndicalists, 8 Mensheviks, 6 "maximalists" and 4 "non-party".[309] The Bolsheviks were on the verge of seizing power, and their attitude to the Factory Committees was already beginning to change. Shmidt, future Commissar for Labour in Lenin's government, described what had happened in many areas:

At the moment when the Factory Committees were formed, the trade unions actually did not yet exist. The Factory Committees filled the vacuum.[310]

Another Bolshevik speaker stated:

the growth of the influence of the Factory Committees has naturally occurred at the expense of centralized economic organizations of the working class such as the trade unions. This of course is a highly abnormal development which has in practice led to very undesirable results.[311]

A different viewpoint was stressed by a delegate from Odessa. He declared that "the Control Commissions must not be mere checking commissions but must be the cells of the future, which even now are preparing for the transfer of production into the hands of the workers".[312] An anarchist speaker argued:

the trade unions wish to devour the Factory Committees. There is no popular discontent with the Factory Committees, but there is discontent with the trade unions. To the worker the trade union is a form of organization imposed from without. The Factory Committee is closer to them.

---

307   Deutscher, *Soviet Trade Unions, op. cit.*, pp. 15–16.

308   Maximov, *op. cit.*, pp. 11–12..

309   *Okt. Rev. i Fabzavkomy*, II, p. 114.

310   *Ibid.*, II, p. 188.

311   *Ibid.*, II, p. 190.

312   *Ibid.*, II, p. 180.

Returning to a theme that was to recur repeatedly he also emphasized that "the Factory Committees were cells of the future... They, not the State, should now administer".[313]

Lenin at this stage saw the tremendous importance of the Factory Committees...as a means of helping the Bolshevik Party to seize power. According to Ordzhonikidze he asserted:

> we must shift the centre of gravity to the Factory Committees. The Factory Committees must become the organs of insurrection. We must change our slogan and instead of saying "All Power to the Soviets" we must say "All Power to the Factory Committees".[314]

A resolution was passed at the Conference proclaiming that "workers' control – *within the limits assigned to it by the Conference* – was only possible under the political and economic rule of the working class". It warned against "isolated" and "disorganized" activities and pointed out that "the seizure of factories by the workers and their operation for personal profit was incompatible with the aims of the proletariat".[315]

October 25

Overthrow of Kerensky's Provisional Government. Proclamation of Council of People's Commissars (*Sovnarkom*) during opening session of **Second All-Russian Congress of Soviets**.

October 26

At Second All-Russian Congress of Soviets, Bolshevik spokesmen proclaimed:

> The Revolution has been victorious. All power has passed to the Soviets... New laws will he proclaimed within a few days dealing with workers' problems. One of the most important will deal with workers' control of production and with the return of industry to normal conditions. Strikes and demonstrations are harmful in Petrograd. We ask you to put an end to all strikes on economic and political issues, to resume work and to carry it out in a perfectly orderly manner... Every man to his place. The best way to support the Soviet Government these days is to carry on with one's job.[316]

Without apparently batting an eyelid Pankratova could write that "the first day of workers' power was ushered in by this call to work and to the edification of the new kind of factory".[317]

Publication of **Decree on the Land**. Lands of nobility, church and crown transferred to custody of peasants.

November 3

Publication in *Pravda* of Lenin's "Draft Decree on Workers' Control".[318] This pro-

---

313   *Ibid.*, II, p. 191.

314   G.K. Ordzhonikidze, *Izbrannye statii i rechi 1911–1937* (Selected Articles and Speeches) (Moscow, 1939), p. 124.

315   Pankratova, *op. cit.*, pp. 48–9.

316   *Ibid.*, p. 50.

317   *Ibid.*, p. 51.

318   V. I. Lenin, *Selected Works*, VI, pp. 410–11.

vided for the "introduction of workers' control of the production, warehousing, purchase and sale of all products and raw materials in all industrial, commercial, banking, agricultural and other enterprises employing a total of not less than five workers and employees – or with a turnover of not less than 10,000 rubles per annum".

Workers' control was to be "carried out by all the workers and employees in a given enterprise, either directly if the enterprise is small enough to permit it, or through delegates to be immediately elected at mass meetings". Elected delegates were to "have access to all books and documents and to all warehouses and stocks of material, instruments and products, without exception".

These excellent, and often quoted, provisions in fact only listed and legalized what had already been achieved and implemented in many places by the working class in the course of the struggles of the previous months. They were to be followed by three further provisions, of ominous import. It is amazing that these are not better known. In practice they were soon to nullify the positive features of the previous provisions. They stipulated (point 5) that "the decisions of the elected delegates of the workers and employees were legally binding upon the owners of enterprises" but that they could be *"annulled by trade unions and congresses"* (our emphasis). This was exactly the fate that was to befall the decisions of the elected delegates of the workers and employees: the trade unions proved to be the main medium through which the Bolsheviks sought to break the autonomous power of the Factory Committees.

The Draft Decree also stressed (point 6) that "in all enterprises of state importance" all delegates elected to exercise workers' control were to be "answerable to the State for the maintenance of the strictest order and discipline and for the protection of property". Enterprises "of importance to the State" were defined (point 7) – and this has a familiar tone for all revolutionaries – as *"all enterprises working for defence purposes, or in any way connected with the production of articles necessary for the existence of the masses of the population"* (our emphasis). In other words practically any enterprise could be declared by the new Russian State as "of importance to the State". The delegates from such an enterprise (elected to exercise workers' control) were now made answerable to a higher authority. Moreover if the trade unions (already fairly bureaucratized) could "annul" the decisions of rank-and-file delegates, what real power in production had the rank and file? The Decree on Workers' Control was soon proved, in practice, not to be worth the paper it was written on.[319]

November 9

Decree dissolving Soviet in the People's Commissariat of Posts and Telegraphs.[320]

The concept of workers' control had spread even to the Civil Service. A Soviet of Employees had taken control of the People's Commissariat of Posts and Telegraphs and another had established itself in the Admiralty. On November 9 an appeal was issued by the People's Commissar for the Ministry (*sic*) of Posts and Telegraphs which concluded: "I declare that no so-called initiatory groups or com-

---

319 It is quite dishonest for those who should know better (see article by T. Cliff in *Labour Worker* of November 1967) to trumpet these decrees on workers' control as something they never were – and were never intended to become.

320 *Sobraniye Uzakonenii 1917–18* (Collection of Statutes 1917–18), no. 3, art. 30.

mittees for the administration of the department of Posts and Telegraphs can usurp the functions belonging to the central power and to me as People's Commissar".[321]

November 14

Lenin expected his "draft statutes on Workers' Control" to be ratified, with only minor modifications, by the All-Russian Central Executive Committee of the Soviets (V.Ts.I.K.) and by the Council of People's Commissars (*Sovnarkom*). In fact his proposals were to give rise to heated discussion and to be criticized from both right and left. Lozovsky, a Bolshevik trade unionist, was to write:

> To us, it seemed that the basic control units should only act within limits rigorously determined by higher organs of control. But the comrades who were for the decentralization of workers control were pressing for the independence and autonomy of these lower organs, because they felt that the masses themselves would incarnate the principle of control.[322]

Lozovsky believed that

> the lower organs of control must confine their activities within the limits set by the instructions of the proposed All-Russian Council of Workers' Control. We must say it quite clearly and categorically, so that workers in various enterprises don't go away with the idea that the factories belong to them.

Despite heated protests from the rank and file - and after nearly two weeks of controversy - a "compromise" was adopted in which the trade unions - now the "unexpected champions of order, discipline and centralized direction of production"[323] - had clearly won the upper hand. The new text was adopted by the All-Russian Central Executive Committee of the Soviets (V.Ts.I.K.) on November 14 (by 24 votes to 10), ratified by the Council of People's Commissars on November 15 and released the following day. Milyutin, who presented the revised decree to the V.Ts.I.K., explained somewhat apologetically that "life overtook us" and that it had become urgently necessary to "unite into one solid state apparatus the workers' control which was being operated on the spot". "Legislation on workers' control which should logically have fitted into the framework of an economic plan had had to precede legislation on the plan itself".[324] There could be no clearer recognition of the tremendous pressures from below and of the difficulties the Bolsheviks were experiencing in their attempts to canalize them.

In the revised decree Lenin's eight original points had now increased to fourteen.[325] The new decree started with the ingenious statement that: "In the interests of a planned regulation of the national economy" the new Government "recognized the authority of workers' control throughout the economy". But there had to be a firm hierarchy of control organs. Factory Committees would be "allowed" to remain the control organ of each individual enterprise. But each Committee was to be responsible to a "Regional Council of Workers' Control", subordinated in turn to an "All-

---

321   Carr, *op. cit.*, II, p. 77, n. 1.

322   A. Lozovsky, *Rabochii Kontrol* (Workers' Control) (Petrograd: Socialist Publishing House, 1918), p. 10.

323   Carr, *op. cit.*, II p. 73.

324   *Protokoly zasedanii VTsIK 2 sozyva* (1918), p. 60.

325   See Appendices to Lenin, *Sochineniya*, XXII. Also D. L. Limon , "Lenine et le contrôle ouvrier", *Autogestion*, December 1967.

Russian Council of Workers' Control".[326] The composition of these higher organs was decided by the Party.

The trade unions were massively represented in the middle and higher strata of this new pyramid of "institutionalized workers' control". For instance the All-Russian Council of Workers' Control was to consist of 21 "representatives": five from the All-Russian Central Executive Committee of the Soviets, five from the Executive of the All-Russian Council of Trade Unions, five from the Association of Engineers and Technicians, two from the Association of Agronomists, two from the Petrograd Trade Union Council, one from each All-Russian Trade Union Federation numbering fewer than 100,000 members (two for Federations of over this number)…and five from the All-Russian Council of Factory Committees! The Factory Committees often under anarcho–syndicalist influence had been well and truly "cut down to size".

Long gone were the days when Lenin had asserted "the source of power is not a law previously discussed and passed by parliament, but the direct initiative of the masses from below, in their localities - outright 'seizure', to use a popular expression".[327]

The very mention however in the decree of an "All-Russian Council of Factory Committees" meant that side by side with the "official" structure of organs of "workers' control" another structure was still present, almost inevitably antagonistic: the pyramid of organs representing the Factory Committees. It also shows that the Factory Committee Movement was still seeking to co-ordinate its activities on a nationwide basis. Even this minor representation for the Factory Committees had been a tactical concession on Lenin's part and events were soon to show that the leaders of the Russian government had no intention of accepting for long this potential threat to the hegemony of the Party and of its supporters within the unions. The Party got to work. "Those who had paid most lip-service to workers' control and purported to 'expand' it were in fact engaged in a skilful attempt to make it orderly and innocuous by turning it into a large scale, centralized, public institution".[328]

Bolshevik propaganda, in later years, was constantly to reiterate the theme that the Factory Committees were not a suitable instrument for organizing production on a national scale. Deutscher for instance claims that, almost from their creation, the "anarchic characteristics of the Committees made themselves felt: every Factory Committee aspired to have the last and final say on all matters affecting the factory, its output, its stocks of raw material, its conditions of work, etc., and paid little or no attention to the needs of industry as a whole".[329] Yet in the very next sentence Deutscher points out that

> a few weeks after the upheaval [the October Revolution] the Factory Committees attempted to form *their own* national organization, which was to secure their virtual economic dictatorship. The Bolsheviks now called upon the trade unions to render a special service to the nascent Soviet State and to discipline the Factory Committees. The unions came out firmly against the attempt of the Factory Committees to form a national organization of their own. They prevented the convocation of a planned All-Russian Congress of Factory Committees and demanded total subordination on the part of the Committees.

---

326 *Sbornik dekretov i postanovlenii po narodnomu khozyaistvu (25 oktyabrya 1917 g–25 oktyabrya 1918 g)* (Moscow, 1918, pp. 171–72)

327 Lenin, *Selected Works*, VI, pp. 27–8.

328 Carr, *op. cit.*, II, p.75.

329 Deutscher, *Soviet Trade Unions, op. cit.*, p.17.

The essential precondition for the Committees to have started tackling region-al and national tasks was their federation on a regional and national basis. It is the height of hypocrisy for latter-day Bolsheviks to blame the Committees of 1917-18 for showing only parochial preoccupations when the Party itself was to do all in its power to prevent the Committees from federating from below, in an autonomous manner. The Bolshevik-sponsored "Central Soviet of Factory Committees" was wound up, after the overthrow of the Provisional Government, as quickly as it had been set up. The Revolutionary Centre of Factory Committees, a body of anarchist inspiration which had been going for several months, never succeeded in supplant-ing it, so many were the obstacles put in its path.

Some comments are called for in relation to these developments. The disor-ganization created by the war and by the resistance of the employing class (mani-fested as sabotage or desertion of their enterprises) clearly made it imperative to minimize and if possible eliminate unnecessary struggles, *between Factory Committees*, such as struggles for scanty fuel or raw materials. There was clearly a need to co-ordinate the activity of the Committees on a vast scale, a need of which many who had been most active in the Committee Movement were well aware. The point at issue is not that a functional differentiation was found necessary between the various organs of working-class power (Soviets, Factory Committees, etc.) or that a definition was sought as to what were local tasks and what were regional or national tasks. The modalities of such a differentiation could have been - and prob-ably would have been - determined by the proposed Congress of Factory Committees. The important thing is that a *hierarchical* pattern of differentiation was *externally* elaborated and imposed, by an agency *other than* the producers them-selves.

A Bolshevik spokesman described the situation, as seen through the eyes of those now in power: "Instead of a rapid normalization of production and distribu-tion, instead of measures which would have led towards a socialist organization of society, we found a practice which recalled the anarchist dreams of autonomous productive communes".[330] Pankratova puts the matter even more bluntly:

> During the transitional period one had to accept the negative aspects of workers' control, which was just a method of struggle between capital and labour. But once power had passed into the hands of the proletariat [i.e. into the hands of the Party] the practice of the Factory Committees of acting as if they owned the fac-tories became anti-proletarian.[331]

These subtleties were however above the heads of most workers. They took Bolshevik propaganda about workers' control at face value. They didn't see it as "something transitional" or as "just a stage towards other methods of normalization of economic life".[332] For them it was not just a means of combating the economic sabotage of the ruling class or a correct tactical slogan, decided in committee as "appropriate" to a given stage of the "developing revolution". For the masses "work-ers' control" was the expression of their deepest aspirations. Who would be boss in the factory? Instinctively they sensed that who managed production would manage all aspects of social life. The subtle difference between "control" and "management"

---

330   I.I. Stepanov–Skvortsov, *Ot rabochego kontrolya k rabochemu upravleniyu* (From Workers' Control to Workers' Management) (Moscow, 1918).

331   Pankratova, *op. cit.*, p. 54.

332   *Ibid.*, p. 54.

of which most Bolsheviks were deeply aware[333] eluded the masses. The misunderstanding was to have bloody repercussions.

The November 1917 Decree on Workers' Control appeared to give official sanction to the drive of the working class towards total domination of the conditions of its life. A metalworkers' paper wrote that "the working class by its nature...should occupy the central place both in production and especially in its organization...All production in the future will...represent a reflection of the proletarian will and mind".[334] Whereas before October workers' control had usually taken a passive, observational form, workers' committees now took on an increasingly important role in the overall management of various enterprises. "For several months following the Revolution the Russian working class enjoyed a degree of freedom and a sense of power probably unique in its history".[335]

There is unfortunately little detailed information available concerning this most interesting period. The data available usually comes from sources (either bourgeois or bureaucratic) fundamentally hostile to the very idea of workers' management and solely concerned in proving its "inefficiency" and "impracticability". An interesting account of what happened at the Nobel Oil refinery has been published.[336] This illustrates the fundamental tendency of the working class towards self-management and the hostility it encountered in Party circles. Other examples will doubtless come to light.

November 28

Meeting of the newly decreed All-Russian Council of Workers' Control.

The previous disagreements reappeared.[337] Larin, representative of the Bolshevik fraction in the unions, declared that

the trade unions represent the interests of the class as a whole whereas the Factory Committees only represent particular interests. The Factory Committees should be subordinated to the trade unions.

Zhivotov, spokesman of the Factory Committee movement, declared:

In the Factory Committees we elaborate instructions which come from below, with a view to seeing how they can be applied to industry as a whole. These are the instructions of the workshop, of life itself. They are the only instructions that can have real meaning. They show what the Factory Committees are capable of, and should therefore come to the forefront in discussions of workers' control.

The Factory Committees felt that

control was the task of the committee in each establishment. The committees of each town should then meet...and later establish co-ordination on a regional basis.

---

333   Unlike so many anarchists of today, most anarchists at the time were also well aware of the difference. Voline (*op. cit.*, p. 77) says: "the anarchists rejected the vague, nebulous slogan of 'control of production'. They advocated expropriation — progressive but immediate — of private industry by the organizations of collective production".

334   N. Filippov, *Ob organizatsii proizvodstva* (On the Organization of Production), *Vestnik metallista* (The Metalworker's Herald), January 1918, pp. 40, 43.

335   P. Avrich, *The Russian Anarchists* (Princeton University Press, 1967), p.162.

336   Voline, *op. cit.*, pp. 139–145. Voline's section of "personal experiences" is well worth reading.

337   See Limon, *op. cit.*, p. 74.

The setting up of the All-Russian Council of Workers' Control by the Bolsheviks was clearly an attempt to bypass the Committee movement. The attempt proved partly successful. The Factory Committees continued their agitation. But their voice, silenced by administrative means, only evoked a feeble echo within the All-Russian Council itself dominated as it was by Party nominees.

In January 1918 Ryazanov was to declare that the body had only met once (and in May 1918 that it had never really met at all). According to another source it "tried to meet" but couldn't gather a quorum.[338]

What is certain is that it never really functioned at all. It is difficult to say whether this was due to systematic Bolshevik boycott and obstruction, to lack of understanding on the part of non-Bolshevik revolutionaries as to what was actually happening, or whether it was due to the genuine weakness of the movement, unable to burst through the bureaucratic straitjacket in which it was being progressively incarcerated. All three factors probably played a part.

November 28
Decree dissolving Soviet in the Admiralty.[339]

December 5
Decree issued[340] setting up a **Supreme Economic Council** (Vesenka) to which were assigned the tasks of working out "a plan for the organization of the economic life of the country and the financial resources of the government". The Vesenka was to "direct to a uniform end" the activities of all existing economic authorities, central and local, including the All-Russian Council of Workers' Control.[341] The Vesenka was to be "attached to the Council of People's Commissars" (itself made up entirely of members of the Bolshevik Party).

The composition of the Vesenka was instructive. It comprised a few members of the All-Russian Council of Workers' Control (a very indirect sop to the Factory Committees), massive representation from all the new Commissariats and a number of experts, nominated from above in a "consultative capacity". The Vesenka was to have a double structure: (a) the "centres" (Glavki), designed to deal with different sectors of industry, and (b) the regional organs: the "local Council of National Economy" (Sovnarkhozy).

At first the "left" Bolsheviks held a majority of the leading positions on the Vesenka. The first Chairman was Osinsky and the governing bureau included Bukharin, Sakolnikov, Milyutin, Lomov and Schmidt. Despite its "left" leadership the new body "absorbed" the All-Russian Council of Workers' Control before the latter had even got going. This step was openly acknowledged by the Bolsheviks as a move towards "statization" (ogosudarstvleniye) of economic authority. The net effect of the setting up of Vesenka was to silence still further the voice of the Factory Committees. As Lenin put it a few weeks later, "we passed from workers' control to the creation

---

338   Carr, *op. cit.*, II, p. 75, n. 3.

339   *Sobraniye Uzakonenii 1917–1918*, no. 4, art. 58.

340   *Ibid.*, no. 5, art. 83.

341   *Natsionalizatsiya promyshlennosti v SSSR: sbornik dokumentov i materialov, 1917–1920 gg* (The Nationalization of Industry in the USSR: Collected Documents and Source Material) (Moscow, 1954), p. 499.

342   Lenin, *Sochineniya*, XXII, p. 215.

of the Supreme Council of National Economy".[342] The function of this Council was clearly to "replace, absorb and supersede the machinery of workers' control."[343]

A process can now be discerned, of which the rest of this pamphlet will seek to unravel the unfolding. It is a process which leads, within a short period of four years, from the tremendous upsurge of the Factory Committee Movement (a movement which both implicitly and explicitly sought to alter the relations of production) to the establishment of unquestioned domination by a monolithic and bureaucratic agency (the Party) over all aspects of economic and political life. This agency not being based on production, its rule could only epitomize the continued limitation of the authority of the workers in the productive process. This necessarily implied the perpetuation of hierarchical relations within production itself, and therefore the perpetuation of class society.

The first stage of this process was the subordination of the Factory Committees to the All-Russian Council for Workers' Control in which the unions (themselves already strongly under Party influence) were heavily represented. The second phase – which almost immediately followed the first – was the incorporation of this All-Russian Council for Workers' Control into the Vesenka, even more heavily weighted in favour of the unions, but also comprising direct nominees of the State (i.e. of the Party). The Vesenka was momentarily allowed to retain a "left" Communist leadership. A little later these "lefts" were to be removed. A sustained campaign was then launched to curb the power of the unions which, albeit in a very indirect and distorted way, could still be influenced by the working class. It was particularly important to curb such power as the unions still held in relation to production – and to replace it by the authority of direct Party nominees. These managers and administrators, nearly all appointed from above, gradually came to form the basis of the new bureaucracy.

Each of these steps was to be resisted, but each fight was to be lost. Each time the adversary appeared in the garb of the new "proletarian" power. And each defeat was to make it more difficult for the working class itself directly to manage production, i.e. fundamentally to alter the relations of production. Until these relations of production had been altered the revolution could not really be considered to have achieved its socialist objective, whatever the pronouncements of its leaders. This is the real lesson of the Russian Revolution.

The problem can be envisaged in yet another way. The setting up of the Vesenka represents a partial fusion – in a position of economic authority – of trade-union officials, Party stalwarts and "experts" nominated by the "workers' state". But these are not three social categories "representing the workers". They were three social categories which were already assuming managerial functions – i.e. were already dominating the workers in production. Because of *their own* antecedent history each of these groups was, for different reasons, already somewhat remote from the working class. Their fusion was to enhance this separation. The result is that from 1918 on, the new State (although officially described as a "workers' state" or a "soviet republic" – and although by and large supported by the mass of the working class during the Civil War) was not in fact an institution managed by the working class.[344]

---

343 Carr, *op. cit.*, II, p. 80.

344 It is not a question of counterpoising, as various anarchists do, "the movement of the masses" to "dictatorship by the state" but of understanding the specific form of the new authority relations which arose at that particular point of history.

If one can read between the lines (and not be blinded by terms such as "workers' state" and "socialist perspective", which only reflect the false consciousness so prevalent at the time), the following account by Pankratova as to what was at stake in the formation of the Vesenka is most informative. "We needed", she said

> a more efficient form of organization than the Factory Committees and a more flexible tool than workers' control. We had to link the management of the new factories to the principle of a single economic plan and we had to do it in relation to the socialist perspectives of the young workers' state…the Factory Committees lacked practice and technical know-how…The enormous economic tasks of the transition period towards socialism necessitated the creation of a single organism to normalize the national economy on a statewide basis. The proletariat understood this. [This was wishful thinking, if ever there was (MB).] Freeing the Factory Committees of their mandates, which no longer corresponded to the new economic needs, the workers delegated authority to the newly created organs, the Council of National Economy.

She concludes with a telling sentence: "The Petrograd Factory Committees, which in May 1917 had proclaimed the need for workers' control, unanimously buried the idea at the time of the Sixth Conference".[345]

Subsequent events were to show that although these were the aims and perspectives of the Party leadership, they were far from being accepted by the Party rank and file, let alone by the masses, "on whose behalf" the Party was already assuming the right to speak.

December (early)

Publication of Lenin's *State and Revolution* (which had been written a few months earlier). In this major theoretical work there is little discussion of workers' control and certainly no identification of socialism with "workers' management of production". Lenin speaks in rather abstract terms of "immediate change such that all fulfil the functions of control and supervision, that all become 'bureaucrats' for a time, and that no one therefore can become a 'bureaucrat'".

This was part of the libertarian rhetoric of the Bolshevism of 1917. But Lenin, as usual, had his feet firmly on the ground. He spelled out what this would mean in practice. The development of capitalism created the "economic prerequisites" which made it "quite possible, immediately, overnight after the overthrow of the capitalists and the bureaucrats, to supersede them in the control of production and distribution, in the work of keeping account of labour and its products by the armed workers, by the whole of the armed population":

> The accountancy and control necessary for this have been so utterly simplified by capitalism that they have become the extraordinarily simple operations of checking, recording and issuing receipts, which anyone who can read and write and who knows the first four rules of arithmetic can perform.[346]

There is no mention of who will initiate the decisions which the masses will then "check" and "record". *State and Revolution* includes the interesting phrase: "We want the socialist revolution with human nature as it is now, with human nature that cannot dispense with subordination, control and managers".[347]

---

345   Pankratova, *op. cit.*, p. 59.
346   Lenin, *Selected Works*, VII, pp. 92–3.
347   *Ibid.*, p. 47

The year 1917 certainly saw a tremendous social upheaval. But it was a utopian dream to assume that socialism could be achieved without a large proportion of the population both understanding and wanting it. The building of socialism (unlike the development of capitalism, which can safely be left to market forces) can only be the *self-conscious and collective act of the immense majority*.

DECEMBER

Publication, by the Central Council of the Petrograd Factory Committees, of the famous **Practical Manual for the Implementation of Workers' Control of Industry**. To the intense annoyance of Party members this was widely distributed in the suburbs of Petrograd.

The main value of this pamphlet is that it deals with how "workers' control" could rapidly be extended into "workers' management". Neither in Lenin's view - nor in that of the authors (despite the title) - was there any confusion between "control" and "management". Lenin was advocating "workers' control" and his whole practice, after the revolution, was to denounce attempts at workers' management as "premature", "utopian", "anarchist", "harmful", "intolerable", etc. It would be tragic if the ahistoricism and anti-theoretical bias of much of the libertarian movement today allowed new militants to fall into old traps or compelled them again to take turnings that at best lead nowhere - or at worst on to the grounds of previous defeats.

The *Manual* made a number of concrete suggestions to the Factory Committees. Each Committee should set up four control commissions, "entitled to invite the attendance of technicians and others in a consultative capacity" (so much for the widely peddled lie that the Factory Committees were not prepared to associate the technicians or specialists in their work).

The functions of the four commissions were to be: (a) the organization of production; (b) the reconversion from war production; (c) the supply of raw materials; and (d) the supply of fuel. The proposals are developed in considerable detail. It is stressed throughout that "workers' control" is *not* just a question of taking stock of the supplies of raw materials and fuel (cf. Lenin's "Socialism is stocktaking; every time you take stock of iron bars or of pieces of cloth, that is socialism"),[348] but that it is intimately related to the transformation of these raw materials within the factory - in other words with the totality of the work processes culminating in a finished product.

The "production commission" should be entrusted with the task of establishing the necessary links between the different sections of the factory, of supervising the state of the machinery, of advising on and overcoming various deficiencies in the arrangement of the factory or plant, *of determining the coefficients of exploitation* in each section, of deciding on the optimum number of shops, and of workers in each shop, of investigating the depreciation of machines and of buildings, of determining job allocations (from the post of administrator down) and of taking charge of the financial relations of the factory.

The authors of the *Manual* announce that they intend to group the Factory Committees into Regional Federations and these in turn into an All-Russian Federation. And to be sure there was no misunderstanding they stressed that:

> workers' control of industry, as a part of workers' control of the totality of economic life, must not be seen in the narrow sense of a reform of institutions but

---

348   Speech of November 4, 1917, to the Petrograd Workers' and Soldiers' Soviet.

in the widest possible sense: that of moving into fields previously dominated by others. Control should merge into management.

In practice the implementation of workers' control took on a variety of forms, in different parts of Russia. These were partly determined by local conditions but primarily by the degree of resistance shown by different sections of the employing class. In some places the employers were expropriated forthwith, "from below". In other instances they were merely submitted to a supervisory type of "control", exercised by the Factory Committees. There was no predetermined model to follow. The various practices and experiments were at first the subject of heated discussions. These were not a waste of time, as was later to be alleged. They should be seen as essential by all who accepted that the advance towards socialism can only come about through the *self-emancipation* of the working class. The discussions unfortunately were soon to be drawn to a close.

December 13

Isvestiya publishes the ***General Instructions on Workers' Control in Conformity with the Decree of November 14***. These became known as the ***Counter-Manual*** and represent the finished expression of the Leninist point of view.[349]

The first four sections deal with the organization of workers' control in the factories and with the election of control commissions. The next five sections decree the duties and rights of these commissions, stressing which functions they should undertake and which should remain the prerogative of the owner-managers. *Section 5* stresses that insofar as the commissions play any real role in the management of enterprises, this role should be confined to supervising the carrying out of directives issued by those Central Government agencies "specifically entrusted with the regulation of economic activity on a national scale". *Section 7* states that:

> the right to issue orders relating to the management, running and functioning of enterprises remains in the hands of the owner. The control commissions must *not* participate in the management of enterprises and have no responsibilities in relation to their functioning. This responsibility also remains vested in the hands of the owner.

Section 8 specifies that the commissions should not concern themselves with matters relating to finance, all such matters being the prerogative of the Central Governmental Institutions. *Section 9* specifically forbids the commissions from expropriating and managing enterprises. They are however entitled to "raise the question of taking over enterprises with the Government, through the medium of the higher organs of workers' control". *Section 14* finally puts down on paper what had been in the minds of the Bolshevik leaders for several weeks. Even at a local level the Factory Committees were to be made to merge with the union apparatus:

> The control commissions in each factory were to constitute the executive organs of the "control of distribution section" of the local trade-union federation. The activities of the control commissions should be made to conform with the decisions of the latter.

The fact that these "general instructions" were issued within a fortnight of the setting up of the Vesenka clearly shows the systematic lines along which Lenin and

---

349   Both the *Manual* and the *Counter-Manual* should be translated into English. An idea of their contents can be obtained from Limon, *op. cit.*, although the article degenerates in places into sophisticated Leninist apologetics.

his collaborators were thinking. They may have been "right" or they may have been "wrong". (This depends on one's ideas of the kind of society they were trying to bring about.) But it is ridiculous to claim - as so many do today - that in 1917 the Bolsheviks really stood for the full, total and direct control by working people of the factories, mines, building sites or other enterprises in which they worked, i.e. that they stood for workers' self-management.

December 20

The official trade-union journal *Professional'ny Vestnik* (Trade-Union Herald) published a "Resolution Concerning the Trade Unions and the Political Parties". "Without turning into independent organs of political struggle, into independent political parties or appendages to them, the trade unions cannot remain indifferent to the problems advanced by the political struggle of the proletariat". After these banal generalities the resolution came down to earth. "Joining their destiny organizationally with some political party, the trade unions, as fighting class organizations of the proletariat, must support the political slogans and tactics of that proletarian party, which at the given moment approaches more closely than others the solution of the historical tasks, etc. etc…"

The same issue of the paper carried an article by the Bolshevik Lozovsky protesting against the Bolshevik policy of suppressing by violence workers' strikes against the new government. "The tasks of the trade unions and of the Soviet power is the isolation of the bourgeois elements who lead strikes and sabotage, but this isolation should not be achieved merely by mechanical means, by arrests, by shipping to the front or by deprivation of bread cards":

> Preliminary censorship, the destruction of newspapers, the annihilation of freedom of agitation for the socialist and democratic parties is for us absolutely inadmissible. The closing of the newspapers, violence against strikers, etc., irritated open wounds. There has been too much of this type of "action" recently in the memory of the Russian toiling masses and this can lead to an analogy deadly to the Soviet power.

That a leading Party member should have to speak in this manner is a telling indictment of how widespread these practices must have been. This was increasingly the method by which the Party was seeking to settle its differences not only with its bourgeois opponents but with its more articulate opponents within the working-class movement itself. Withdrawal of bread cards deprived those subject to it of the legal right to rations, i.e. of the right to eat. Individuals deprived of their cards would be forced to obtain food on the black market or by other illegal means. Their "crimes against the State" would then be used as legal means of "neutralizing" them.

It was in this atmosphere concerning Party, unions and non-Party masses (euphemistically described as "bourgeois elements") that the big debate of January 1918 was to take place.

December 23

Decree setting up a network of Regional Councils of National Economy (Sovnarkhozy) under the supervision of the Vesenka:

> Each regional Sovnarkhoz was [to be] a replica in miniature of Vesenka at the Centre. It was to be divided into fourteen sections for different branches of pro-

duction and was to contain representatives of local institutions and organizations…

Each Sovnarkhoz could set up "smaller units incorporating the corresponding organs of workers control where the latter had come into being". "What had been created was a central economic department with local offices".[350]

1918

January 6

Dissolution of Constituent Assembly. The detachment which dispersed the Assembly was led by an anarchist Kronstadt sailor, Zheleznyakov, now commandant of the Tauride Palace Guard. He unseated the Chairman of the Assembly, Victor Chernov, with the blunt announcement: "The guard is tired".[351]

January 7–14

First All-Russian Congress of Trade Unions held in Petrograd.

Two main themes were to dominate the Congress. What were to be the relations between the Factory Committees and the unions? And what were to be the relations between the trade unions and the new Russian state? Few delegates, at this stage, sensed the close relationship between these two questions. Still fewer perceived how a simultaneous resolution of the first question in favour of the unions and of the second in favour of the new "workers' state" would soon emasculate the Committees and in fact irrevocably undermine the proletarian nature of the regime.

The arguments at this Congress reflected matters of deep significance and will be referred to in some detail. In the balance lay the future of the Russian working class for many decades to come.

According to Lozovsky (a Bolshevik trade unionist), "the Factory Committees were so much the owners and masters that three months after the Revolution they were to a significant degree independent of the general controlling organs".[352] Maisky, then still a Menshevik, said that in his experience "it was not just some of the proletariat but most of the proletariat, especially in Petrograd, who looked upon workers' control as if it were actually the emergence of the kingdom (*tsarstvo*) of socialism". He lamented that among the workers "the very idea of socialism is embodied in the concept of workers' control".[353] Another Menshevik delegate deplored the fact that "an anarchist wave in the shape of Factory Committees and workers' control was sweeping over our Russian labour movement".[354] D.B. Ryazanov,[355] a recent convert to Bolshevism, agreed with the Mensheviks on this

350 Carr, *op. cit.*, II, pp. 82–3.

351 Avrich, *op. cit.*, p. 156. (Several secondary references given.)

352 *Pervy vserossiiski s'yezd professionalnykh soyuzov, 7–14 yanvarya 1918 g* (First All-Russian Congress of Trade Unions, 7–14 January, 1918) (Moscow, 1918), p. 193. (Henceforth referred to as the First Trade Union Congress.)

353 *Ibid.*, p. 212.

354 *Ibid*, p. 48.

355 D. B. Ryazanov, a Marxist scholar best known as the historiographer of the International Workingmen's Association (the First International), later became the founder of the Marx-Engels Institute in Moscow and published a biography of Marx and Engels.

point and urged the Factory Committees "to commit suicide by becoming an integral element of the trade-union structure".[356]

The few anarcho-syndicalist delegates to the Congress "fought a desperate battle to preserve the autonomy of the Committees...Maximov[357] claimed that he and his fellow anarcho-syndicalists were 'better Marxists' than either the Mensheviks or the Bolsheviks – a declaration which caused a great stir in the hall".[358] He was alluding no doubt to Marx's statement that the liberation of the working class had to be brought about by the workers themselves.[359]

Maximov urged the delegates to remember "that the Factory Committees, organizations introduced directly by life itself in the course of the Revolution, were the closest of all to the working class, much closer than the trade unions".[360] The function of the Committees was no longer to protect and improve the conditions of the workers. They had to seek a predominant position in industry and in the economy. "As the offspring of the Revolution the Committees would create a new production on a new basis".[361] The unions "which corresponded to the old economic relations of Tsarist times had lived out their time and couldn't take on this task".[362] Maximov anticipated "a great conflict between state power in the centre and the organizations composed exclusively of workers which are found in the localities".[363]

> The aim of the proletariat was to co-ordinate all activity, all local interest, to create a centre but not a centre of decrees and ordinances but a centre of regulation, of guidance – and only through such a centre to organize the industrial life of the country.[364]

Speaking on behalf of the Factory Committees a rank-and-file worker, Belusov, made a scathing attack on the Party leaders. They continually criticized the Committees "for not acting according to rules and regulations" but then failed to produce any coherent plan of their own. They just talked:

---

356 First Trade Union Congress, p. 235.

357 Gregori Petrovich Maximov, born in 1893. Graduated as an agronomist in Petrograd in 1915. Joined the revolutionary movement while still a student. In 1918 joined the Red Army. When the Bolsheviks used the Army for police work and for disarming the workers he refused to obey orders and was sentenced to death. The solidarity of the steelworkers' union saved his life.

Edited anarcho-syndicalist papers *Golos Truda* (Voice of Labour) and *Novy Golos Truda* (New Voice of Labour). Arrested March 8, 1921, during the Kronstadt uprising. Released later that year following a hunger strike, but only after the intervention of European delegates attending Congress of Red Trade Union International. Sought exile abroad.

In Berlin edited *Rabotchi Put* (Labour's Path), paper of Russian syndicalists in exile. Later went to Paris and finally settled in Chicago. Died 1950. Author of various works on anarchism and on the Bolshevik terror (*The Guillotine at Work*, 1940).

358 Avrich, *op. cit.*, p.168.

359 It is interesting that as great a "Marxist" as Rosa Luxemburg was to proclaim at the founding Congress of the German Communist Party (January 1919) that the trade unions were destined to disappear, being replaced by Councils of Workers' and Soldiers' Deputies and by Factory Committees (*Bericht über die Verhandlung des Gründungparteitages der KPD* (1919), pp. 16, 80).

360 First Trade Union Congress, p. 85.

361 *Ibid.*, p. 239.

362 *Ibid.*, p. 215.

363 *Ibid.*, p. 85.

364 *Ibid.*, p. 85.

All this will freeze local work. Are we to stand still locally, wait and do nothing? Only then will we make no mistakes. Only those who do nothing make no mistakes.

Real workers' control was the solution to Russia's economic disintegration. "The only way out remaining to the workers is to take the factories into their own hands and manage them".[365]

Excitement in the Congress reached a climax when Bill Shatov[366] characterized the trade unions as "living corpses" and urged the working class "to organize in the localities and create a free, new Russia, without a God, without a Tsar, and without a boss in the trade union". When Ryazanov protested Shatov's vilification of the unions, Maximov rose to his comrade's defence, dismissing Ryazanov's objections as those of a white-handed intellectual who had never worked, never sweated, never felt life. Another anarcho-syndicalist delegate, Laptev by name, reminded the gathering that the revolution had been made "not only by the intellectuals, but by the masses"; therefore it was imperative for Russia to "listen to the voice of the working masses, the voice from below".[367]

The anarcho-syndicalist resolution calling for "real workers' control, not state workers' control", and urging "that the organization of production, transport and distribution be immediately transferred to the hands of the toiling people themselves and not to the state or some civil service machine made up of one kind or other of class enemy" was defeated. (The main strength of the anarcho-syndicalists was among the miners of the Debaltzev district in the Don Basin, among the portworkers and cement workers of Ekaterinodar and Novorossiysk and among the Moscow railway workers. At the Congress they had 25 delegates (on the basis of one delegate per 3,000–3,500 members).[368]

The new government would have none of all this talk about extending the power of the Committees. It clearly recognized in the unions a "more stable" and "less anarchic" force (i.e. a force more amenable to control from above) in which it could provisionally vest administrative functions in industry. The Bolsheviks therefore urged "the trade-union organizations, as class organizations of the proletariat constructed according to the industrial principle, to take upon themselves the main task of organizing production and of restoring the weakened productive forces of the country".[369] (At a later stage the Bolsheviks were to fight tooth and nail to divest the unions of these very functions and place them firmly in the hands of Party nominees. In fact the Party demands of January 1918 were again and again to be thrown back in the face of the Bolshevik leaders during the next three years. This will be dealt with further on.)

---

365 *Ibid.*, p. 221.

366 Vladimir Shatov, born in Russia, emigrated to Canada and USA. In 1914 secretly reprinted 100,000 copies of Margaret Sanger's notorious birth-control pamphlet, *Family Limitation*. Worked as machinist, longshoreman and printer. Joined IWW. Later helped produce *Golos Truda*, weekly anarcho-syndicalist organ of the Union of Russian Workers of the United States and Canada. Returned to Petrograd in July 1917 and "replanted *Golos Truda* in the Russian capital". Later became member of Petrograd Military Revolutionary Committee and an officer of the 10th Red Army. In 1919 he played important role in defence of Petrograd against Yudenich. In 1920 became Minister of Transport in the Far Eastern Soviet Republic. Disappeared during the 1936–38 purges.

367 Avrich, *op. cit.*, pp. 168–9.

368 Maximov, *op. cit.*, pp. 12 – 13.

369 Quoted (in German) by A. S. Shlyapnikov, *Die Russischen Gewerkshaften* (The Russian Trade Unions) (Leipzig, 1920).

The Congress, with its overwhelming Bolshevik majority, voted to transform the Factory Committees into union organs.[370] The Menshevik and Social Revolutionary delegates voted *with* the Bolsheviks for a resolution proclaiming that "the centralization of workers' control was the task of the trade unions".[371] "Workers' control" was defined as "the instrument by which the universal economic plan must be put into effect locally".[372] "It implied the definite idea of standardization in the sphere of production".[373] It was too bad if the workers read more into the term than this. "Just because the workers misunderstand and falsely interpret workers' control is no reason to repudiate it".[374] What the Party meant by workers' control was spelt out in some detail. It meant, *inter alia*, that

> it was not within the competence of the lower organs of workers' control to be entrusted with financial control function…this should rest with the highest organs of control, with the general apparatus of management, with the Supreme Council of National Economy. In the sphere of finance everything must be left to the higher organs of workers' control.[375]

> For workers' control to be of maximum use to the proletariat it was absolutely necessary to refrain from atomizing it. Workers of individual enterprises should not be left the right to make final decisions on questions touching upon the existence of the enterprise.[376]

A lot of re-education was needed and this was to be entrusted to the "economic control commissions" of the unions. They were to inculcate into the ranks of the workers the Bolshevik conception of workers' control:

> The trade unions must go over each decree of the Factory Committees in the sphere of control, explain through their delegates at the factories and shops that control over production does not mean the transfer of the enterprise into the hands of the workers of a given enterprise, that it does not equal the socialization of production and exchange.[377]

Once the Committees had been "devoured" the unions were to be the intermediate agency through which workers' control was gradually to be converted into state control.

These were not abstract discussions. Underlying the controversies, what was at stake was the whole concept of socialism: workers' power or the power of the Party acting on behalf of the working class. "If workers succeeded in maintaining their ownership of the factories they had seized, if they ran these factories for themselves, if they considered the revolution to be at an end, if they considered socialism to have been established - then there would have been no need for the revolutionary leadership of the Bolsheviks."[378]

The bitterness with which the issue of the Factory Committees was discussed highlights another point:

---

370 First Trade Union Congress, p. 374.

371 *Ibid.*, pp. 369–70.

372 *Ibid.*, p. 369.

373 *Ibid.*, p. 192.

374 *Ibid.*, p. 230.

375 *Ibid.*, p. 195.

376 *Ibid.*, p. 369.

377 Adopted Resolution (*ibid*, p. 370).

378 Kaplan, *op. cit.*, p. 128.

> Although the Bolsheviks were in a majority at the first All-Russian Conference of
> Factory Committees – and although as representatives of the Factory Committees
> they could force resolutions through this Conference they could not enforce res-
> olutions against the opposition of the Factory Committees themselves… The
> Factory Committees accepted Bolshevik leadership only so long as divergences in
> goals were not brought to the test.[379]

The First Trade Union Congress also witnessed a heated controversy on the
question of the relation of the trade unions to the state. The Mensheviks claiming
that the Revolution could only usher in a bourgeois-democratic republic, insisted on
the autonomy of the unions in relation to the new Russian state. As Maisky put it: "If
capitalism remains intact, the tasks with which trade unions are confronted under
capitalism remain unaltered".[380] Others too felt that capitalism would reassert itself
and that the unions should do nothing that would impair their power. Martov put a
more sophisticated viewpoint. "In this historic situation", he said

> this government cannot represent the working class alone. It cannot but be a *de
> facto* administration connected with a heterogeneous mass of toiling people, with
> proletarian and non-proletarian elements alike. It cannot therefore conduct its
> *economic* policy along the lines of consistently and clearly expressed working
> class interests.[381]

The trade unions could. Therefore the trade unions should retain a certain independence in relation to the new state. It is interesting that in his 1921 controversy
with Trotsky – when incidentally it was far too late – Lenin was to use much the same
kind of argument. He was to stress the need for the workers to defend themselves
against "their own" state, defined as not just a "workers' state, but a workers' and
peasants' state" and more over one with "bureaucratic deformations".

The Bolshevik viewpoint, supported by Lenin and Trotsky and voiced by
Zinoviev, was that the trade unions should be subordinated to the government,
although not assimilated with it. Trade-union neutrality was officially labelled a
"bourgeois" idea, an anomaly in a workers' state.[382] The resolution adopted by the
Congress clearly expressed these dominant ideas:

> The trade unions ought to shoulder the main burden of organizing production
> and of rehabilitating the country's shattered economic forces. Their most urgent
> tasks consist in their energetic participation in all central bodies called upon to
> regulate output, in the organization of workers' control [sic!], in the registration
> and distribution of the labour force, in the organization of exchange between
> town and countryside…in the struggle against sabotage and in enforcing the
> general obligation to work…
>
> As they develop the trade unions should, in the process of the present socialist
> revolution, become organs of socialist power, and as such they should work in
> co-ordination with and *subordination* to other bodies in order to carry into effect
> the new principles…The Congress is convinced that in consequence of the fore-
> shadowed process, *the trade unions will inevitably become transformed into
> organs of the socialist state*. Participation in the trade unions will for all people
> employed in any industry be their duty *vis-à-vis* the State".

---

379   *Ibid.*, p. 181.
380   First Trade Union Congress, p.11.
381   *Ibid.*, p. 80.
382   *Ibid.*, p. 364.

The Bolsheviks did not unanimously accept Lenin's views on these questions. While Tomsky, their main spokesman on trade-union affairs, pointed out that "sectional interests of groups of workers had to be subordinated to the interests of the entire class"[383] – which like so many Bolsheviks he wrongly identified with the hegemony of the Bolshevik Party – Ryazanov argued that

> as long as the social revolution begun here has not merged with the social revolution of Europe and of the whole world…the Russian proletariat….must be on its guard and must not renounce a single one of its weapons…it must maintain its trade union organization.[384]

According to Zinoviev, the "independence' of the trade unions under a workers' government could mean nothing except the right to support 'saboteurs'". Despite this Tsyperovich, a prominent Bolshevik trade unionist, proposed that the Congress ratify the right of unions to continue to resort to strike action in defence of their members. A resolution to this effect was however defeated.[385]

As might be expected the dominant attitude of the dominant Party (both in relation to the Factory Committees and in relation to the unions) was to play an important role in the subsequent development of events. It was to prove as much an "objective fact of history" as the "devastation" and the "atomization of the working class" caused by the (subsequent) Civil War. It could, in fact, be argued that Bolshevik attitudes to the Factory Committees (and the dashing of the great hopes that these Committees represented for hundreds of thousands of workers) were to engender or reinforce working-class apathy and cynicism, and contribute to absenteeism and to the seeking of private solutions to what were social problems, all of which the Bolsheviks were so loudly to decry. It is above all essential to stress that the Bolshevik policy in relation to the Committees and to the unions which we have documented in some detail was being put forward twelve months *before* the murder of Karl Liebknecht and of Rosa Luxemburg – i.e. before the irrevocable failure of the German Revolution, an event usually taken as "justifying" many of the measures taken by the Russian rulers.

January 15–21

First All-Russian Congress of Textile Workers held in Moscow. Bolsheviks in a majority. The Congress declared that "workers' control is only a transitional step to the planned organization of production and distribution".[386] The union adopted new statutes proclaiming that "the lowest cell of the union is the Factory Committee whose obligation consists of putting into effect, in a given enterprise, all the decrees of the union".[387] Even the big stick was waved. Addressing the Congress, Lozovsky stated that "if the local patriotism of individual factories conflicts with the interests of the whole proletariat, we unconditionally state that we will not hesitate before *any measures* [my emphasis, MB] for the suppression of tendencies harmful to the toilers".[388] The Party, in other words, can impose its concept of the interests of the working class, even against the workers themselves.

---

383   *Ibid.,* preface.

384   *Ibid.,* p. 27.

385   *Ibid.,* p. 367.

386   *Vsesoyuzny s'yezd professionalnykh soyuzov tekstilshchikov i fabrichnykh komitetov* (Moscow, 1918), p. 8.

387   *Ibid.,* p. 5.

388   *Ibid.,* p. 30.

January 23–31
Third All-Russian Congress of Soviets.

FEBRUARY
Bolshevik decree nationalizing the land.

March 3
Signature of **Brest-Litovsk Peace Treaty**.

Decree issued by Vesenka defining the functions of technical management in industry. Each administrative centre was to appoint to every enterprise under its care a *commissioner* (who would be the government representative and supervisor) and *two directors* (one technical and the other administrative). The technical director could only be overruled by the government commissioner or by the "Central Direction" of the industry. (In other words only the "administrative director" was under some kind of control from below.)

The decree laid down the principle that "in nationalized enterprises workers' control is exercised by submitting all declarations and decisions of the Factory or Shop Committee, or of the control commission, to the Economic Administrative Council for approval". "Not more than half the members of the Administrative Council should be workers or employees".

During the early months of 1918 the Vesenka had begun to build, from the top, its "unified administration" of particular industries. The pattern was informative. During 1915 and 1916 the Tsarist government had set up central bodies (sometimes called "committees" and sometimes "centres") governing the activities of industries producing commodities directly or indirectly necessary for the war. By 1917 these central bodies (generally composed of representatives of the industry concerned and exercising regulatory functions of a rather undefined character) had spread over almost the whole field of industrial production. During the first half of 1918 Vesenka gradually took over these bodies (or what was left of them) and converted them - under the name of *glavki* (chief committees) or *tsentry* (centres) into administrative organs subject to the direction and control of Vesenka. The "chief committee" for the leather industry (Glavkozh) was set up in January 1918. This was quickly followed by chief paper and sugar committees, and by soap and tea "centres". These, together with Tsentrotekstil, were all in existence by March 1918. They

> could scarcely have come into being except on foundations already laid before the revolution or without the collaboration of the managerial and technical staffs... A certain tacit community of interests could be detected between the government and the more sensible and moderate of the industrialists in bringing about a return to some kind of orderly production.[390]

This raised a question of considerable theoretical interest. Marxists have usually argued that revolutionaries could not simply seize the political institutions of bourgeois society (parliament, etc.) and use them for different purposes (i.e. for the introduction of socialism). They have always claimed that new political institutions (Soviets) would have to be created to express the reality of workers' power. But they have usually remained discreetly silent on the question of whether revolutionaries could "capture" the institutions of bourgeois economic power and use them to their

---

389   *Sbornik dekretov i postanovlenii po narodnomu, khozyaistvu* (1918), pp. 311–15.

390   Carr, *op. cit.*, II, pp. 86–7.

own ends – or whether these too would have first to be smashed, and later replaced with a new kind of institution, representing a fundamental change in the relations of production. The Bolsheviks in 1918 clearly opted for the first course. Even within their own ranks this choice was to give rise to foreboding that all energies would now be directed to the "reinforcement and development of productive capacity, to organic construction, *involving a refusal to continue the break up of capitalist productive relations and even a partial restoration of them*".[391]

March 6–8
Seventh Party Congress.
Heated deliberations during this very short Congress centred on the signing of the Brest-Litovsk Peace Treaty.

March 14–18
Fourth All-Russian Congress of Soviets.

MARCH
"Left" Communists (Osinsky, Bukharin, Lomov, Smirnov) ousted from leading positions in Supreme Economic Council – partly because of their attitude to Brest-Litovsk – and replaced by "moderates" like Milyutin and Rykov.[392] Immediate steps taken to shore-up managerial authority, restore labour discipline and apply wage incentives under the supervision of the trade union organizations. The whole episode was a clear demonstration that "lefts" in top administrative positions are no substitute for rank-and-file control at the point of production.

March 26
Isvestiya of the All-Russian Central Executive Committee publishes Decree (issued by the Council of Peoples Commissars) on the "centralization of railway management". This decree, which ended workers' control on the railways was "an absolutely necessary prerequisite for the improvement of the conditions of the transport system".[393] It stressed the urgency of "iron labour discipline" and "individual management" on the railways and granted "dictatorial" powers to the Commissariat of Ways of Communication. Clause 6 proclaimed the need for selected individuals to act as "administrative technical executives" in every local, district or regional railway centre. These individuals were to be "responsible to the People's Commissars of Ways of Communication". They were to be "the embodiment of the whole of the dictatorial power of the proletariat in the given railway centre".[394]

March 30
Trotsky, appointed Commissar of Military Affairs after Brest-Litovsk, had rapidly been reorganizing the Red Army. The death penalty for disobedience under fire had been restored. So, more gradually, had saluting, special forms of address, separate living quarters and other privileges for officers.[395] Democratic forms of organi-

---

391   *Ibid.*, II, p. 95.
392   *Ibid.*, II, p. 91.
393   Lenin, *Selected Works*, VII, Explanatory Notes, p. 505.
394   *Ibid.*

zation, including the election of officers, had been quickly dispensed with. "The elective basis", Trotsky wrote, "is politically pointless and technically inexpedient and has already been set aside by decree".[396] N. V. Krylenko, one of the Co-Commissars of Military Affairs appointed after the October Revolution, had resigned in disgust from the Defence Establishment as a result of these measures.[397]

April 3

The Central Council of Trade Unions issued its first detailed pronouncement on the function of the trade unions in relation to "labour discipline" and "incentives".

The trade unions should "apply all their efforts to raise the productivity of labour and consistently to create in factories and workshops the indispensable foundations of labour discipline". Every union should establish a commission "to fix norms of productivity for every trade and category of workers". The use of piece rates "to raise the productivity of labour" was conceded. It was claimed that "bonuses for increased productivity above the established norm may within certain limits be a useful measure for raising productivity without exhausting the worker". Finally if "individual groups of workers" refused to submit to union discipline, they could in the last resort be expelled from the union "with all the consequences that flow therefrom".[398]

April 11–12

Armed detachments of Cheka raid 26 anarchist centres in Moscow. Fighting breaks out between Cheka agents and Black Guardsmen in Donskoi Monastery. Forty anarchists killed or wounded, over 500 taken prisoner.

April 20

The issue of workers' control was now being widely discussed within the Party. Petrograd District Committee publishes first issue of *Kommunist* (a "left" Communist theoretical journal edited by Bukharin, Radek and Osinsky, later to be joined by Smirnov). This issue contained the editors' "Theses on the Present Situation". The paper denounced "a labour policy designed to implant discipline among the workers under the flag of 'self-discipline', the introduction of labour service for workers, piece rates, and the lengthening of the working day". It proclaimed that "the introduction of labour discipline in connection with the restoration of capitalist management of industry cannot really increase the productivity of labour". It would:

> diminish the class initiative, activity and organization of the proletariat. It threatens to enslave the working class. It will arouse discontent among the backward elements as well as among the vanguard of the proletariat. In order to introduce this system in the face of the hatred prevailing at present among the proletariat against the "capitalist saboteurs" the Communist Party would have to rely on the petty-bourgeoisie, as against the workers.

---

395 For years Trotskyist literature has denounced these reactionary facets of the Red Army as examples of what happened to it "under Stalinism". They were in fact first challenged by Smirnov at the Eighth Party Congress, in March 1919.

396 L. Trotsky, "Work, Discipline, Order", *Sochineniya*, XVII, pp. 171–2.

397 N V. Krylenko, Autobiography in *Ency. Dict.*, XLI–1, Appendix, p. 246.

398 *Narodnoye Khozyaisto*, no.2, 1918, p. 38.

It would "ruin itself as the party of the proletariat".

The first issue of the new paper also contained a serious warning by Radek: "If the Russian Revolution were overthrown by violence on the part of the bourgeois counter-revolution it would rise again like a phoenix; if however it lost its socialist character and thereby disappointed the working masses, the blow would have ten times more terrible consequences for the future of the Russian and the international revolution".[399] The same issue warned of "bureaucratic centralization, the rule of various commissars, the loss of independence for local Soviets and in practice the rejection of the type of state-commune administered from below".[400] "It was all very well", Bukharin pointed out, "to say as Lenin had [in *State and Revolution*] that each cook should learn to manage the State. But what happened when each cook had a commissar appointed to order him about?"

The second issue of the paper contained some prophetic comments by Osinsky:

> We stand for the construction of the proletarian society by the class creativity of the workers themselves, not by the ukases of the captains of industry…if the proletariat itself does not know how to create the necessary prerequisites for the socialist organization of labour no one can do this for it and no one can compel it to do this. The stick, if raised against the workers, will find itself in the hands of a social force which is either under the influence of another social class or is in the hands of the soviet power; but the soviet power will then be forced to seek support against the proletariat from another class (e.g. the peasantry) and by this it will destroy itself as the dictatorship of the proletariat. Socialism and socialist organization will be set up by the proletariat itself, or they will not be set up at all: something else will be set up - state capitalism".[401]

Lenin reacted very sharply. The usual vituperation followed. The views of the "left" Communists were "a disgrace", "a complete renunciation of Communism in practice", "a desertion to the camp of the petty bourgeoisie".[402] The left were being "provoked by the Isuvs [Mensheviks] and other Judases of capitalism". A campaign was whipped up in Petrograd which compelled *Kommunist* to transfer publication to Moscow, where the paper reappeared first under the auspices of the Moscow Regional Organization of the Party, later as the "unofficial" mouthpiece of a group of comrades. After the appearance of the first issue of the paper a hastily convened Petrograd Party Conference produced a majority for Lenin and "demanded that the adherents of *Kommunist* cease their separate organizational existence".[403] So much for alleged factional rights…in 1918 (i.e. long before the Tenth Congress officially prohibited factions - in 1921)!

During the following months the Leninists succeeded in extending their organizational control into areas which had originally backed the "lefts". By the end of May the predominantly proletarian Party organization in the Ural region, led by Preobrazhensky, and the Moscow Regional Bureau of the Party had been won back

---

399   K. Radek, "Posle pyatimesyatsev" (After Five Months), *Kommunist*, no. 1 (April 1918), pp. 3–4.

400   "Tesisy o tekushchem moment" (Theses on the Current Situation), *Kommunist*, no. 1, p. 8.

401   Osinsky, "O stroitelstve sotsializma" (On the Building of Socialism), *Kommunist*, no. 2 (April 1918), p. 5. It was already obvious to some, *in* 1918, in which direction Leninist economic policy was leading. Those who, today, claim to be both "Leninists" and "state capitalists", please note!

402   V.I. Lenin, "Left–Wing Childishness and Petty–Bourgeois Mentality", *Selected Works*, VII, p. 374.

403   V. Sorin, "Partiya i oppozitsiya" (The Party and the Opposition), I, *Fraktsiya levykh kommunistov* (The Fraction of Left Communists) (Moscow, 1925), pp. 21–2.

by the supporters of the Party leadership. The fourth and final issue of *Kommunist* (May 1918) had to be published as a private factional paper. The settlement of these important issues, profoundly affecting the whole working class, had not been

> by discussion, persuasion or compromise, but by a high-pressure campaign in the Party organizations, backed by a barrage of violent invective in the Party press and in the pronouncements of the Party leaders. Lenin's polemics set the tone and his organizational lieutenants brought the membership into line.[404]

Many in the traditional revolutionary movement will be thoroughly familiar with these methods!

April 28

Lenin's article on "The Immediate Tasks of the Soviet Government" published in *Isvestiya* of the All-Russian Central Executive Committee. "Measures and decrees" were called for "to raise labour discipline" which was "the condition of economic revival". (Among the measures suggested were the introduction of a card system for registering the productivity of each worker, the introduction of factory regulations in every enterprise, the establishment of rate-of-output bureaux for the purpose of fixing the output of each worker and payment of bonuses for increased productivity.) If Lenin ever sensed the potentially harmful aspects of these proposals he certainly never mentioned it. No great imagination was needed, however, to see in the pen-pushers (recording the "productivity of each worker") and in the clerks (manning the "rate-of-output bureaux") the as yet amorphous elements of a new bureaucracy.

Lenin went even further. He wrote:

> We must raise the question of piecework and apply and test it in practice...we must raise the question of applying much of what is scientific and progressive in the Taylor system[405]...the Soviet Republic must at all costs adopt all that is valuable in the achievements of science and technology in this field...we must organize in Russia the study and teaching of the Taylor system.

Only "the conscious representatives of petty-bourgeois laxity" could see in the recent decree on the management of the railways, "which granted individual leaders dictatorial powers", some kind of "departure from the collegium principle, from democracy and from other principles of soviet government":

> The irrefutable experience of history has shown that the dictatorship of individual persons was very often the vehicle, the channel of the dictatorship of the revolutionary classes.

> Large-scale machine industry - which is the material productive source and foundation of socialism - calls for absolute and strict unity of will... How can strict unity of will be ensured? By thousands subordinating their will to the will of one.

> *Unquestioning submission* [emphasis in original] to a single will is absolutely necessary for the success of labour processes that are based on large-scale machine industry...today the Revolution demands, in the interests of socialism, that the masses *unquestioningly obey the single will* [emphasis in original] of the leaders of the labour process.[406]

---

404   Daniels, *op. cit.*, p. 87.

405   Before the Revolution Lenin had denounced Taylorism as "the enslavement of man by the machine" (*Sochineniya*, XVII, pp. 247–8).

406   Lenin, *Selected Works*, VII, pp. 332–3, 340–42.

The demand for "unquestioning" obedience has, throughout history, been voiced by countless reactionaries, who have sought moreover to impose such obedience on those over whom they exerted authority. A highly critical (and self-critical) attitude is, on the other hand, the hallmark of the real revolutionary.

MAY

Burevestnik, Anarkhia, Golos Truda and other leading anarchist periodicals closed down.

Preobrazhensky, writing in *Kommunist* warns: "The Party will soon have to decide to what degree the dictatorship of individuals will be extended from the railroads and other branches of the economy to the Party itself".[407]

May 5

Publication of *Left-Wing Childishness and Petty-Bourgeois Mentality*. After denouncing *Kommunist*'s views as "a riot of phrasemongering", "the flaunting of high-sounding phrases", etc, etc, etc, Lenin attempted to answer some of the points made by the "left" Communists. According to Lenin "state capitalism" wasn't a danger. It was, on the contrary, something to be aimed for:

> If we introduced state capitalism in approximately six months' time we would achieve a great success and a sure guarantee that within a year socialism will have gained a permanently firm hold and will have become invincible in our country.

> Economically, state capitalism is immeasurably superior to the present system of economy...the soviet power has nothing terrible to fear from it, for the soviet state is a state in which the power of the workers and the poor is assured [because a "Workers' Party" held political power].

The "*sum total* of the necessary conditions for socialism" were "large-scale capitalist technique based on the last word of modern science...inconceivable without planned state organization which subjects tens of millions of people to the strictest observance of a single standard in production and distribution" and "proletarian state power". (It is important to note that the power of the working class *in production* isn't mentioned as one of the "necessary conditions for socialism".) Lenin continues by pointing out that in 1918 the "two unconnected halves of socialism existed side by side like two future chickens in a single shell of international imperialism". In 1918 Germany and Russia were the embodiments, respectively of the "economic, productive and social economic conditions for socialism on the one hand, and of the political conditions on the other". The task of the Bolsheviks was "to study the state capitalism of the Germans, to spare no effort at copying it". They shouldn't "shrink from adopting dictatorial methods to hasten the copying of it". As originally published[408] Lenin's text then contained the interesting phrase: "Our task is to hasten this even more than Peter hastened the adoption of westernism by barbarian Russia, not shrinking from the use of barbarous methods to fight barbarism". This was perhaps the only admiring reference to any Tsar, in any of Lenin's writings. In quoting this passage three years later Lenin omitted the reference to Peter the Great.[409]

407   *Kommunist*, no. 4.
408   Lenin, *Sochineniya*, XXII, pp. 516–17.

"One and the same road", Lenin continued, led from the petty-bourgeois capitalism that prevailed in Russia in 1918 to large-scale capitalism and to socialism, through one and the same intermediary station called "national accounting and control of production and distribution". Fighting against state capitalism, in April 1918, was (according to Lenin) "beating the air".[410] The allegation that the Soviet Republic was threatened with "evolution in the direction of state capitalism" would "provoke nothing but Homeric laughter". If a merchant told him that there had been an improvement on some railways, "such praise seems to me a thousand times more valuable than twenty Communist resolutions".[411] When reading passages such as the above, it is difficult to understand how some comrades can simultaneously claim to be "Leninists" and claim that the Russian society is a form of state capitalism to be deplored. Some, however, manage to do just this.

It is crystal clear from the above (and from other passages written at the time) that the "proletarian" nature of the regime was seen by nearly all the Bolshevik leaders as hinging on the proletarian nature of the Party that had taken state power. None of them saw the proletarian nature of the Russian regime as primarily and crucially dependent on the exercise of workers' power *at the point of production* (i.e. on workers' management of production). It should have been obvious to them, as Marxists, that if the working class did not hold economic power, its "political" power would at best be insecure and would in fact soon degenerate. The Bolshevik leaders saw the capitalist organization of production as something which, in itself, was socially neutral. It could be used indifferently for bad purposes (as when the bourgeoisie used it with the aim of private accumulation) or good ones (as when the "workers' state" used it "for the benefit of the many"). Lenin put this quite bluntly. "Socialism", he said, "is nothing but state-capitalist monopoly made to benefit the whole people".[412] What was wrong with capitalist methods of production, in Lenin's eyes, was that they had in the past served the bourgeoisie. They were now going to be used by the Workers' State and would thereby become "one of the conditions of socialism". It all depended on who held state power.[413] The argument that Russia was a workers' state *because of* the nationalization of the means of production was only put forward by Trotsky…in 1936! He was trying to reconcile his view that "the Soviet Union had to be defended" with his view that "the Bolshevik Party was no longer a workers' party".

May 24 –June 4

First All-Russian Congress of Regional Economic Councils held in Moscow. This "economic Parliament" was attended by rather more than a hundred voting delegates (and 150 non-voting delegates) drawn from Vesenka, its *glavki* and centres, from regional and local Sovnarkhozy, and from the trade unions.

The Congress was presided over by Rykov - a man of "unimpeachable record and colourless opinions".[414] Lenin opened the proceedings with a plea for "labour

409   *Ibid.*, XXVI, p. 326.

410   Lenin, *Selected Works*, VII, pp. 360–66.

411   Carr, *op. cit.*, II, p. 100.

412   V. I. Lenin, *The Threatening Catastrophe and How to Fight It*.

413   For a fuller analysis of this concept of means and ends — and of what it led to — see Paul Cardan, *From Bolshevism to the Bureaucracy* (Solidarity Pamphlet 24).

414   Carr, *op. cit.*, II, p. 101, n. 4.

discipline" and a long explanation for the need to employ the highly paid *spetsy* (specialists).

Osinsky stood uncompromisingly for the democratization of industry. He led an attack on "piece rates" and "Taylorism". He was supported by Smirnov and a number of provincial delegates. The "opposition" urged the recognition and completion of the *de facto* nationalization of industry which the Factory Committees were bringing about and called for the establishment of an overall national economic authority based on and representing the organs of workers' control.[415] They called for "a workers' administration…not only from above but from below" as the indispensable economic base for the new regime. Lomov, in a plea for a massive extension of workers' control, warned that

> bureaucratic centralization…was strangling the forces of the country. The masses are being cut off from living, creative power in all branches of our economy.

He reminded the Congress that Lenin's phrase about "learning from the capitalists" had been coined in the 1890s by the quasi-Marxist (and present bourgeois) Struve.[416]

There then took place one of those episodes which can highlight a whole discussion and epitomize the various viewpoints. A sub-committee of the Congress passed a resolution that *two-thirds* of the representatives on the management boards of industrial enterprises should be elected from among the workers.[417] Lenin was furious at this "stupid decision". Under his guidance a Plenary Session of the Congress "corrected" the resolution and decreed that no more than *one-third* of the managerial personnel of industrial enterprises should be elected. The management committees were to be integrated into the previously outlined complex hierarchical structure which vested veto rights in the Supreme Economic Council (Vesenka) set up in December 1917.[418]

The Congress formally endorsed a resolution from the Trade Union Central Council asserting the principle of "a definite, fixed rate of productivity in return for a guaranteed wage". It accepted the institution of piecework and of bonuses. A "climate of opinion rather than a settled policy was in the course of formation".[419]

May 25

Clashes between government forces and troops of the Czech Legion in the Urals. Anti-Bolshevik uprisings throughout Siberia and South-Eastern Russia. **Beginning of large-scale civil war and beginning of Allied intervention.** (Those who wish to incriminate the Civil War for anti-proletarian Bolshevik practices can do so from now on.)

June 28

Council of Peoples' Commissars, after an all-night sitting, issues *Decree on General Nationalization* involving all industrial enterprises with a capital of over one

---

415   Osinsky, in *Trudy pervogo vserossiiskogo s' yezda sovetov narodnogo khozyaistva* (Proceedings of the First All-Russian Congress of Economic Councils) (Moscow, 1918), pp. 61–4.

416   *Ibid.*, p. 75.

417   *Ibid.*, p. 65.

418   *Polozheniye ob upravlenii natsionalizirovannymi predpriyatiyami* (Regulations for the Administration of Nationalized Enterprises), *ibid.*, pp. 477–8.

419   Carr, *op. cit.*, II, pp. 119–20.

million rubles. The aims of the decree were "a decisive struggle against disorganiza-
tion in production and supply".

The sectors affected, whose assets were now declared the property of the
Russian Socialist Federal Soviet Republic, were the mining, metallurgical, textile, elec-
trical, timber, tobacco, resin, glass and pottery, leather and cement industries, all
steam-driven mills, local utilities and private railways, together with a few other
minor industries. The task of "organizing the administration of nationalized enterprises" was entrusted "as a matter of urgency" to Vesenka and its sections. But until
Vesenka issued specific instructions regarding individual enterprises covered by the
decree "such enterprises would be regarded as leased rent-free to their former owners, who would continue to finance them and to draw revenue from them".[420]

The legal transfer of individual enterprises to the state was easily transacted.
The assumption of managerial functions by appointees was to take a little longer but
this process was also to be completed within a few months. Both steps had been
accelerated under the threat of foreign intervention. The change in the *property relations* had been deep-going. *In this sense* a profound revolution had taken place. "As
the Revolution had unleashed Civil War, so Civil War was to intensify the
Revolution".[421] But as far as any fundamental changes in the relations of production
were concerned, the Revolution was already spent. The period of "War Communism"
- now starting - was to see the working class lose what little power it had enjoyed
in production, during the last few weeks of 1917 and the first few weeks of 1918.

July 4–10
Fifth All-Russian Congress of Soviets.

Throughout the first half of 1918 the issue of "nationalization" had been the
subject of bitter controversy between the "left" Communists and the Leninists. Lenin
had been opposed to the total nationalization of the means of production, immediately after October. This was not because of any wish to do a political deal with the
bourgeoisie but because of his underestimation of the technological and administrative maturity of the proletariat, a maturity that would have been put to an immediate test had all major industry been formally nationalized. The result had been an
extremely complex situation in which some industries had been nationalized "from
above", (i.e. by decree of the Central Government), others "from below" (i.e. where
workers had taken over enterprises abandoned by their former owners), while in yet
other places the former owners were still in charge of their factories - although
restricted in their freedom of action or authority by the encroachment of the Factory
Committees. Kritzman, one of the ablest theoreticians of "left" Communism, had criticized this state of affairs from an early date. He had referred to the "Workers'
Control" decree of November 14, 1917, as "half-measures, therefore unrealizable":

> As a slogan workers' control implied the growing but as yet insufficient power of
> the proletariat. It was the implied expression of a weakness, still to be overcome,
> of the working-class movement. Employers would not be inclined to run their
> businesses with the sole aim of teaching the workers how to manage them.

420   *Ibid.*, II, p. 105.
421   Daniels, *op. cit.*, p. 92.

Conversely the workers felt only hatred for the capitalists and saw no reason why they should voluntarily remain exploited.[422]

Osinsky, another "left" Communist, stressed another aspect. "The fate of the workers' control slogan", he wrote,

> is most interesting. Born of the wish to unmask the opponent, it failed when it sought to convert itself into a system. Where, despite everything it fulfilled itself, its content altered completely from what we had originally envisaged. It took the form of a decentralized dictatorship, of the subordination of capitalists, taken individually, to various working-class organizations acting independently of one another... Workers' Control had originally been aimed at subordinating the owners of the means of production... But this co-existence soon became intolerable. The state of dual power between managers and workers soon led to the collapse of the enterprise. Or it rapidly became transformed into the total power of the workers, without the least authorization of the central powers.[423]

Much "left" Communist writing at this time stressed the theme that early nationalization of the means of production would have avoided many of these ambiguities. Total expropriation of the capitalists would have allowed one to proceed immediately from "workers' control" to "workers' management" through the medium of some central organism regulating the whole of the socialized economy. It is interesting that Lozovsky, although at the time strongly opposed to the viewpoint of the "left" Communists (because he felt that the Revolution had only been a "bourgeois-democratic" revolution), was later to write: "It was soon to be proved that in the era of social revolution, a constitutional monarchy in each enterprise [i.e. the previous boss, but only exercising limited power (MB)] was impossible and that the former owner - however complex the structure of a modern enterprise - was a superfluous cog".[424]

A split occurred a little later among the "left" Communists. Radek reached an agreement with the Leninists. He was prepared to accept "one-man management" in principle (not too hard a task for a non-proletarian?) because it was now to be applied in the context of the extensive nationalization decrees of June 1918. In Radek's opinion these decrees would help ensure the "proletarian basis of the regime". Bukharin too broke with Osinsky and rejoined the fold. Osinsky and his supporters however proceeded to form a new oppositional tendency: the "democratic centralists" (so-called because of their opposition to the "bureaucratic centralism" of the Party leadership). They continued to agitate for workers' management of production. Their ideas, and those of the original group of "left" Communists were to play an important role in the development, two years later, of the Workers' Opposition.

With the Civil War and "War Communism" the issues appeared, for a while, to become blurred. There was little production for any one to control:

> The issues of 1918 however were only postponed. They could not be forgotten thanks to the left communists' work of criticism. As soon as the military respite permitted, left-wing oppositionists were ready to raise again the fundamental question of the social nature of the Soviet regime.[425]

---

422   I. Larine and L. Kritzman, *Wirtschaftsleben und Wirtschaftlicher Aufbau in Soviet Russland, 1917–1920* (Hamburg, 1921), p. 163.

423   N. Osinsky, *O stroitelstve sotsialisma* (The Building of Socialism) (Moscow, 1918), p. 35 et seq.

424   A. Lozovsky, *The Trade Unions in Soviet Russia* (Moscow: All-Russian Central Council of Trade Unions, 1920), p. 654.

425   Daniels, *op. cit.*, p. 91

AUGUST

High point of Volga offensive by the Whites.

The Civil War immensely accelerated the process of economic centralization. As a knowledge of previous Bolshevik practice might have led one to expect, this was to prove an extremely bureaucratic form of centralization. The whole Russian economy was "reorganized" on a semi-military basis. The Civil War tended to transform all major industry into a supply organization for the Red Army. This made industrial policy a matter of military strategy. It is worth pointing out, at this stage, that we doubt if there is any *intrinsic* merit in decentralization, as some anarchists maintain. The Paris Commune, a Congress of Soviets (or a shop stewards' committee or strike committee to take modern analogies) are all highly centralized yet fairly democratic. Feudalism on the other hand was both decentralized and highly bureaucratic. The key question is whether the "centralized" apparatus is controlled from below (by elected and revocable delegates) or whether it separates itself from those on whose behalf it is allegedly acting.

This period witnessed a considerable fall in production, due to a complex variety of factors which have been well described elsewhere.[426] The trouble was often blamed by Party spokesmen on the influence of heretical "anarcho-syndicalist" ideas. Mistakes had certainly been made, but what had been the growing pains of a new movement were now being attributed to the inherent vices of any attempt by the workers to dominate production. "Workers' control over industry carried out by the Factory and Plant Committees", wrote one government spokesman, "has shown what can be expected if the plans of the anarchists are realized".[427] Attempts at control from below were now being systematically suppressed. Proletarian partisans of the individual Factory Committees tried to resist but their resistance was easily overcome.[428] Bitterness and despair developed among sections of the proletariat (and by no means "backward" sections). Such factors must also be taken into account - but seldom are - in discussing the fall of production, and the widespread resort to "anti-social activities" so characteristic of the years of "War Communism".

August 25–September 1

First All-Russian Conference of Anarcho-Syndicalists meets in Moscow. The industrial resolution accused the government of

> betraying the working class with its suppression of workers' control in favour of such capitalist devices as one-man management, labour discipline and the employment of "bourgeois" engineers and technicians. By forsaking the Factory Committees - the beloved child of the great workers' revolution - for those "dead organizations", the trade unions, and by substituting decrees and red tape for industrial democracy, the Bolshevik leadership was creating a monster of "state capitalism", a bureaucratic Behemoth, which it ludicrously called socialism.[429]

Volny Golos Truda (The Free Voice of Labour) was established as the successor to *Golos Truda* (closed down in May 1918). The new paper was itself closed down

---

426   See for instance I. Deutscher, *The Prophet Unarmed* (Oxford University Press, 1959), pp. 1–14.

427   I. I. Stepanov-Skortsov, *op cit.*, p. 24.

428   M.. Dobb, *Soviet Economic Development since 1917* (New York, 1948), pp. 89–90.

429   Avrich. *op. cit.*, p. 191.

after its fourth issue (September 16, 1918). This had contained an interesting article by "M. Sergven" (?Maximov) called "Paths of Revolution". The article

> made a remarkable departure from the usual condemnation of the Bolsheviks as "Betrayers of the Working Class". Lenin and his followers were not necessarily cold-blooded cynics who, with Machiavellian cunning, had mapped out the new class structure in advance to satisfy their personal lust for power. Quite possibly they were motivated by a genuine concern for human suffering… .But the division of society into administrators and workers followed inexorably from the centralization of authority. It could not be otherwise. Once the functions of management and labour had become separated (the former assigned to a minority of "experts" and the latter to the untutored masses) all possibility of dignity or equality were destroyed.[430]

In the same issue Maximov slammed the "Manilovs"[431] in the anarchist camp as

> romantic visionaries who pined for pastoral utopias, oblivious of the complex forces at work in the modern world. It was time to stop dreaming of the Golden Age. It was time to organize and act.

For these principled yet realistic views Maximov and the anarcho-syndicalists were to be viciously attacked as "anarcho-bureaucratic Judases by other tendencies in the anarchist movement".[432]

AUGUST

A government decree fixes the composition of the Vesenka to thirty members nominated by the All-Russian Central Council of Trade Unions, twenty nominated by the Regional Councils of National Economy (Sovnarkhozy) and ten nominated by the All-Russian Central Executive of the Soviets (V.Ts.I.K.). Current Vesenka business was to be entrusted to a Presidium of nine other members, of whom the President and his Deputy were nominated by the Council of People's Commissars (Sovnarkom) and the others by the V.Ts.I.K. The Presidium was officially supposed to implement the policies decided at the monthly meetings of all 69 of the Vesenka's members. But it soon came to undertake more and more of the work. After the autumn of 1918 full meetings of the Vesenka were no longer held. It had become a department of state.[433]

In other words within a year of the capture of state power by the Bolsheviks, the relations of production (shaken for a while at the height of the mass movement) had reverted to the classical authoritarian pattern seen in all class societies. The workers *as workers* had been divested of any meaningful decisional authority in the matters that concerned them most.

September 28

The Bolshevik trade-union leader Tomsky declares at the **First All-Russian Congress of Communist Railwaymen** that "it was the task of the Communists firstly to create well-knit trade unions in their own industries, secondly to take possession of these organizations by tenacious work, thirdly to stand at the head of these

---

430   *Ibid.*, pp. 192–3.
431   Manilov was a day–dreaming landowner in Gogol's *Dead Souls*.
432   Avrich, *op. cit.*, pp. 196–7.
433   Carr, *op. cit.*, II, p. 180.

organizations, fourthly to expel all non-proletarian organizations and fifthly to take the union under our own Communist influence".[434]

OCTOBER

Government Decree reiterates the ruling that no body other than Vesenka "in its capacity as the central organ regulating and organizing the whole production of the Republic" has the right to sequester industrial enterprises.[435] The need to publish such a decree suggests that local Soviets, or perhaps even local Sovnarkhozy were doing just that.

November 6–9
Sixth All-Russian Congress of Soviets.

November 25 - December 1
Second All-Russian Conference of Anarcho-Syndicalists meets in Moscow.

DECEMBER

A new decree abolished the regional Sovnarkhozy and recognized the provincial Sovnarkhozy as "executive organs of Vesenka". The local Sovnarkhozy were to become "economic sections" of the executive committees of the corresponding local Soviets. The *glavki* were to have their own subordinate organs at provincial headquarters. "This clearly represented a further step towards the centralized control of every branch of industry all over the country by its *glavk* or centre in Moscow, under the supreme authority of Vesenka".[436]

Second All-Russian Congress of Regional Economic Councils.

Molotov analyzed the membership of twenty most important *glavki* and "centres". Of 400 persons concerned, over 10 per cent were former employers or employers' representatives, 9 per cent technicians, 38 per cent officials from various departments (including Vesenka)…and the remaining 43 per cent workers or representatives of workers' organizations, including trade unions. The management of production was predominantly in the hands of persons "having no relation to the proletarian elements in industry". The *glavki* had to be regarded as "organs in no way corresponding to the proletarian dictatorship". Those who directed policy were "employers' representatives, technicians and specialists".[437] "It was indisputable that the Soviet bureaucrat of these early years was as a rule a former member of the bourgeois intelligentsia or official class, and brought with him many of the traditions of the old Russian bureaucracy".[438]

---

434 *Vserossiiskaya konferentsiya zheleznodorozhnikov komunistov* (First All-Russian Conference of Communist Railwaymen) (Moscow, 1919), p. 72.

435 *Sbornik dekretov i postanovlenii po narodnomu khozyaistvu* (1920), ii, 83.

436 Carr, *op cit.*, II, p. 183.

437 *Trudy vtorogo vserossiiskogo s'yezda sovetov narodnogo khosyaistva* (Second All-Russian Congress of Regional Economic Councils) (n.d.), p. 213.

438 Carr, *op. cit.*, II, p. 190.

1919

January 16–25
Second All-Russian Congress of Trade Unions.

Throughout 1918 the trade unions had played an important role in industrial administration. This had vastly increased when the government, afraid that privately-owned industry wouldn't work for the needs of the Red Army, speeded up the nationalization programme, "at first as a matter of military rather than of economic policy".[439] What Lenin called the "state functions" of the unions had increased rapidly. Party members in the trade-union leadership (such as Tomsky, Chairman of the All-Russian Central Council of Trade Unions) enjoyed considerable power.

The relation between the union leaderships and the rank and file were far from democratic however. "In practice the more the trade unions assumed the administrative functions of a conventional managerial bureaucracy, the more bureaucratic they themselves became".[440] A Congress delegate, Chirkin, claimed for instance that "although in most regions there were institutions representing the trade union movement, these institutions were not elected or ratified in any way; where elections had been conducted and individuals elected who were not suitable to the needs of the Central Council or local powers, the elections had been annulled very freely and the individuals replaced by others more subservient to the administration".[441] Another delegate, Perkin, spoke out against new regulations which required that representatives sent by workers' organizations to the Commissariat of Labour be ratified by the Commissariat:

> If at a union meeting we elect a person as a commissar – i.e. if the working class is allowed in a given case to express its will – one would think that this individual would be allowed to represent our interests in the Commissariat, would be our commissar. But, no. In spite of the fact that we have expressed our will – the will of the working class – it is still necessary for the commissar we have elected to be confirmed by the authorities… The proletariat is allowed the right to make a fool of itself. It is allowed to elect representatives but the state power, through its right to ratify the elections or not, treats our representatives as it pleases.[442]

The unions – and all other bodies for that matter – were increasingly coming under the control of the state, itself already in the exclusive hands of the Party and its nominees. But although there had already been a very definite shift of power in the direction of the emerging bureaucracy, working class organization and consciousness were still strong enough to exact at least verbal concessions from Party and union leaders. The autonomous Factory Committees had by now been completely smashed but the workers were still fighting a rearguard action in the unions themselves. They were seeking to preserve a few residual shreds of their erstwhile power.

---

439   Deutscher, *Soviet Trade Unions, op. cit.*, p. 25.

440   Waldemar Koch, *Die Bolshevistischen Gewerkshaften* (Jena, 1932), pp. 81–2.

441   *Vtoroi vserossiiski s'yezd professionalnykh soyuzov: stenograficheski otchet* (Second All-Russian Congress of Trade Unions: Stenographic Report) (Moscow: Central Trade Union Press, 1919), I, p. 34. (Henceforth referred to as Second Trade Union Congress).

442   *Ibid.*, p. 103.

The Second Trade Union Congress "sanctioned the arrangements under which the unions had become at once military recruiting agents, supply services, punitive organs, and so on".[443] Tomsky for instance pointed out:

> that at a time when the trade unions determined wages and conditions of work, strikes could no longer be tolerated. It was necessary to put dots on the i's.

Lenin spoke about the "inevitable stratification of the trade unions". (The pill was coated with talk about the function of the unions being to educate the workers in the art of administration and about the eventual "withering away" of the state.) Lozovsky, who had left the Party, spoke as an independent internationalist against Bolshevik policy in the unions.

A resolution was passed demanding that "official status be granted to the administrative prerogatives of the unions". It spoke of "statization" (*ogosudarstvlenie*) of the trade unions, "as their function broadened and merged with the governmental machinery of industrial administration and control".[444] The Commissar for Labour, V.V. Shmidt, accepted that "even the organs of the Commissariat of Labour should be built out of the trade union apparatus".[445] (At this stage the membership of the unions stood at 3,500,000. It had been 2,600,000 at the time of the First Trade Union Congress, in January 1918, and 1,500,000 at the July Conference of 1917.)[446]

The Second Congress finally set up an Executive vested with supreme authority between Congresses. The decrees of this Executive were declared "compulsory for all the unions within its jurisdiction *and for each member of those unions*":

> The violation of the decrees and insubordination to them on the part of individual unions will lead to their expulsion from the family of proletarian unions.[447]

This would of course place the union outside the only legal framework in which the Bolshevik regime would permit unions to exist at all.

March 2–7
First Congress of Comintern (Third International).

March 18–23
Eighth Party Congress.
The Ukraine and Volga regions had now been reoccupied by the Red Army. A short period of relative stability followed. Later in the year, the advances of Denikin and Yudenich were to threaten Moscow and Petrograd respectively.

A wave of left criticism surged up at the Eighth Congress against the ultra-centralist trends. A new Party programme was discussed and accepted. Point 5 of the "Economic Section" stated that

> the organizational apparatus of socialized industry must be based primarily on the trade unions...Participating already in accordance with the laws of the Soviet Republic and established practice in all local and central organs of industrial administration, the trade unions must proceed to the actual concentration *in their*

---

443   Deutscher, *Soviet Trade Unions, op. cit.*, p. 26.

444   Second Trade Union Congress, I, p. 97.

445   *Ibid.*, p. 99.

446   Zinoviev, *Desyaty s'yezd RKP (b): Protokoly* (The Tenth Congress of the RCP (b): Protocols) (Moscow: IMEL, 1933), p. 188. (Henceforth referred to as Tenth Party Congress.)

447   Second Trade Union Congress, I, p. 127.

own hands [my emphasis] of all the administration of the entire economy, as a single economic unit... The participation of the trade unions in economic management and their drawing the broad masses into this work constitutes also the chief method of struggle against the bureaucratization of the economic apparatus.[448]

This famous paragraph was to give rise to heated controversies in the years to come. The conservatives in the Party felt it was going too far. Ryazanov warned the Congress that "we will not avoid bureaucratization until all trade unions...relinquish *every* right in the administration of production".[449] On the other hand those Bolsheviks who had voted for the incorporation of the Factory Committees into the structure of the unions – and belatedly seen the error of their ways – were to hang on to this clause as to a last bastion, seeking to defend it against the all-pervasive encroachments of the Party bureaucracy. Deutscher describes the famous Point 5 as "a 'syndicalist' slip committed by the Bolshevik leadership in a mood of genuine gratitude to the trade unions for the work performed by them in the Civil War".[450] He describes how Lenin and the other Bolshevik leaders "would soon have to do a lot of explaining away in order to invalidate this promissory note which the Party had so solemnly and authoritatively handed to the trade unions". The interpretation is questionable. Lenin was not in the habit of making "slips" (syndicalist or otherwise) or of being influenced by such considerations as "gratitude". It is more probable that the relation of forces, revealed at the Congress – itself only a pale reflection of working-class attitudes outside the Party – compelled the Bolshevik leadership to beat a verbal retreat. The clause was anyway surrounded by a number of others, partly invalidating it.

The programme proclaimed that "the socialist method of production could only be made secure on the basis of the comradely discipline of the workers". It assigned to the trade unions "the chief role in creating this new socialist discipline". Point 8

urged the unions to impress upon the workers the need to work with and learn from the bourgeois technicians and specialists – and to overcome their "ultra-radical" distrust of the latter... The workers could not build socialism without a period of apprenticeship to the bourgeois intelligentsia... Payment of high salaries and premiums to bourgeois specialists was therefore sanctioned. It was the ransom which the young proletarian State had to pay the bourgeois-bred technicians and scientists for services with which it could not dispense.[451]

We cannot here become involved in a full discussion on the role of "specialists" after the revolution. The problem is not an exclusively Russian one, although the specific conditions of Russian development doubtless resulted in a particularly marked divorce between technicians and industrial workers. Specialized knowledge of a technical nature will clearly be required by the Workers' Councils but there is no reason why those who now possess it should all find themselves on the side of the bourgeoisie. This knowledge does not of itself, however, entitle anyone either to impose decisions or to enjoy material benefits.

---

448   *Vosmoi s'yezd RKP (b): Protokoly* (The Eighth Congress of the RCP (b): Protocols) (Moscow: IMEL, 1933), Resolutions, I, p. 422. (Henceforth referred to as Eighth Party Congress.)

449   *Ibid.*, p. 72.

450   Deutscher, *Soviet Trade Unions, op. cit.*, p. 29.

451   *Ibid.*, p. 31

These problems have been exhaustively discussed in a number of publications - but nearly always in terms of either crude expediency or of immutable "basic principles". The theoretical implications have only recently been explored. According to Limon management is partly a technical question.[452] But the historical circumstances in which the working class will be compelled to undertake it will make it appear to them as primarily a political and social task. At the everyday, down-to-earth and *human* level the workers at the time of the socialist revolution will almost inevitably see the technicians and specialists not as human beings (who also happen to have technological know-how) but exclusively as the agents of the exploitation of man by man.

The capitalist world is one of fetishism, where *interpersonal* relationships tend to disappear behind relationships between *things*. But the very moment when the masses revolt against this state of affairs, they break through this smoke screen. They see through the taboo of "things" and come to grips with *people*, whom they had "respected" until then in the name of the all-holy fetish known as private property. From that moment on the specialist, manager or capitalist, whatever his technical or personal relationship to the enterprise, appears to the workers as the incarnation of exploitation, as the enemy, as the one with whom the only thing they want to do is to get him out of their lives. To ask the workers, *at this stage*, to have a more "balanced" attitude, to recognize in the old boss the new "technical director", the "indispensable specialist", is tantamount to asking the workers - at the very moment when they are becoming aware of their historical role and of their social power, at the very moment when at last confident in themselves they are asserting their autonomy - to confess their incompetence, their weakness, their insufficiency, and this in the area where they are most sensitive, the field encompassing their daily lives from childhood on: the field of production.

The bureaucratization of the Party itself provoked pointed comments at the Congress. Osinsky declared: "It is necessary to enrol workers into the Central Committee on a broad scale; it is necessary to introduce there a sufficient quantity of workers in order to proletarianize the Central Committee".[453] (Lenin was to come to the same conclusion in 1923, at the time of the so-called Lenin Levy !) Osinsky proposed that the Central Committee be expanded from 15 to 21 members. It was extremely naive, however, to expect that this introduction of proletarians into the higher echelons of the administrative machine could somewhat compensate for the fact that the working class had by now almost totally lost the power it had briefly held *at the point of production*.

The decline in the Soviets was also discussed at the Congress. The Soviets were no longer playing any active role in relation to production - and very little role in other matters either. More and more of the decisions were being taken by the Party members serving in the "Soviet apparatus". The Soviets had become mere organs of ratification (rubber stamps). The theses of Sapronov and Osinsky - according to which the Party should not seek to "impose its will on the Soviets" - were decisively rejected.

The Party leaders made minor concessions on all of these issues. But the process of tightening up control, both in the Party and in the economy as a whole, continued at an unrelenting pace. The Eighth Congress established the Politbureau,

---

452 Limon, *op. cit.*, p. 79.
453 Osinsky, Eighth Party Congress, pp. 30, 168.

the Orgbureau and the Secretariat, technically only sub-committees of the Central Committee, but soon to assume tremendous power. The concentration of decision-making authority had taken a big step forward. "Party discipline" was strengthened. The Congress ruled that each decision must above all be fulfilled. Only after this is an appeal to the corresponding Party organ permissible:[454]

> ...The whole matter of posting of Party workers is in the hands of the Central Committee. Its decisions are binding for everyone.[455]

The era of political postings - as a means of silencing embarrassing criticism - had begun in earnest.

APRIL
Highpoint of Kolchak's offensive in Urals.

JUNE
Decree introducing "labour books" for workers in Moscow and Petrograd.

OCTOBER
Highpoint of Denikin's offensive in South Russia. Yudenich's drive on Petrograd.

December 2–4
Eighth Party Conference.

The Eighth Conference worked out a statute which rigidly defined the rights and duties of Party cells (fractions or *fraktsya*) and elaborated a scheme calculated to secure for the Party a leading role in every organization. "The Communist trade unionist was thus a Communist first and only then a trade unionist, and by his disciplined behaviour he enabled the Party to lead the trade unions."[456] As the Party degenerated this "leadership" was to play an increasingly pernicious role.

December 5-9
Seventh All-Russian Congress of Soviets. (There had been two such Congresses in 1917 and four in 1918). Resolution passed in favour of collective management of industry.[457] At the congress, Sapronov attacked the unpopular *glavki*, arguing that they represented an attempt to substitute "organization by departments for organization by Soviets, the bureaucratic for the democratic system". Another speaker declared that if people were asked "what should be destroyed on the day after the destruction of Denikin and Kolchak, 90 per cent would reply: the *glavki* and the centres".[458]

---

454 A pathetic echo, nearly fifty years later, is to be found in the "Perspectives for I.S.", submitted in September 1968 by the Political Committee of *International Socialism*. Point 4 ran: "Branches must accept directives from the Centre, unless they fundamentally disagree with them, in which case they should try to accord with them, while demanding an open debate on the matter".

455 Eighth Party Congress, Resolutions, I, p. 444.

456 Deutscher, *Soviet Trade Unions, op. cit.*, p. 33.

457 Preobrazhensky, *Devyaty s'yezd RKP (b): Protokoly* (The Ninth Congress of the RCP (b): Protocols) (Moscow: IMEL, 1934), p. 72. (Henceforth referred to as Ninth Party Congress.)

458 Carr, *op. cit.*, II, p. 184.

December 16

Trotsky submits to Central Committee of the Party his "**Theses on the Transition from War to Peace**" (dealing in particular with the "*militarization of labour*"), intending them, for the time being, to go no further.[459] The most fundamental decisions, affecting the material conditions of life of millions of ordinary Russian workers, had first to be discussed and decided behind closed doors, by the Party leaders. The following day, *Pravda*, under the editorship of Bukharin, published Trotsky's theses "by mistake" (in reality as part of a campaign to discredit Trotsky). For those who can see deeper than the surface of things, the whole episode was highly symptomatic of the tensions within the Party at the time.

At this stage Lenin wholeheartedly supported Trotsky's proposals. (A whole mythology was later to be built up by Trotskyists and others to the effect that "Trotsky may have been wrong on the militarization of labour" but that Lenin was always opposed to it. This is untrue. *Lenin was only to oppose Trotsky on this question twelve months later, at the end of 1920, as will be described shortly.*)

Trotsky's proposals let loose "an avalanche of protests".[460] He was shouted down at Conferences of Party members, administrators and trade unionists.[461] A comment is perhaps called for at this stage concerning the attitude of revolutionaries towards "drastic measures" needed for the salvation of the Revolution. Throughout history the masses have always been prepared to make enormous sacrifices whenever they felt really fundamental issues were at stake. The real problem is not, however, to discuss whether this or that suggestion was "too drastic" or not. The problem is to know from whom the decision emanated. Was it taken by institutions controlled from below? Or was it taken by some self-appointed and self-perpetuating organism divorced from the masses? Party members opposing the measures being proposed at this stage were caught in an insoluble contradiction. They denounced the *policies* of the Party leaders without really understanding the extent to which their own organizational conceptions had contributed to what was happening to the Revolution. Only some members of the Workers' Opposition of 1921 (to a slight degree) and Myasnikov's Workers' Group of 1922 (to a greater extent) began to sense the new reality.

DECEMBER 27

With Lenin's approval the government sets up the Commission on Labour Duty, with Trotsky (still Commissar for War) as its President.

1920

JANUARY

Collapse of Whites in Siberia. Blockade lifted by Great Britain, France and Italy.

Decree issued by Sovnarkom laid down general regulations for universal labour service "to supply industry, agriculture, transport and other branches of the national economy with labour power on the basis of a general economic plan". Anyone could be called up on a single occasion or periodically for various forms of work (agricul-

459   Deutscher, *The Prophet Armed*, op. cit., p. 487.

460   *Ibid.*, p. 492.

461   *Ibid.*, p. 492.

ture, building, road-making, food or fuel supplies, snow clearance, carting and "measures to deal with the consequences of public calamities"). In an amazing aside the document stated that there was even cause to "regret the destruction of the old police apparatus which had known how to register citizens, not only in towns but also in the country".[462]

January 12
Meeting of All-Russian Central Council of Trade Unions.
At the gathering of the Bolshevik fraction Lenin and Trotsky together urge acceptance of the militarization of labour. Only two of sixty or more Bolshevik trade-union leaders support them. "Never before had Trotsky or Lenin met with so striking a rebuff".[463]

January 10–21
Third Congress of Economic Councils.
In a speech to the Congress Lenin declares:

> the collegial principle [collective management]…represents something rudimen-tary, necessary for the first stage, when it is necessary to build anew… The tran-sition to practical work is connected with individual authority. This is the system which more than any other assures the best utilization of human resources. [464]

Despite this exhortation, opposition to Lenin and Trotsky's views was steadily gaining ground. The Congress adopted a resolution *in favour* of collective manage-ment of production.

FEBRUARY
Regional Party Conferences in Moscow and Kharkov come out against "one-man management". So did the Bolshevik faction of the All-Russian Central Council of Trade Unions (ARCCTU) at its meetings in January and March.[465] Tomsky, a well-known trade-union leader and a member of the ARCCTU presented "Theses" ("On the Tasks of the Trade Unions") which were accepted despite their implicit criticism of Lenin's and Trotsky's views.

Tomsky's theses claimed that

> the fundamental principle guiding the work of various bodies leading and admin-istering the economy remains the principle now in existence: collective manage-ment. This must be applied from the Presidium of the Vesenka right down to the management of the factories. Collective management alone can guarantee the participation of the broad non-Party masses, through the medium of the unions.

The matter was still seen however as one of expediency rather than basic principle. "The trade unions", Tomsky claimed, "are the most competent and interested organ-izations in the matter of restoring the country's production and its correct function-ing".[466]

---

462 *Sobraniye Uzakonenii, 1920*, no. 8, Art. 49. Also *Treti vserossiiski s'yezd professionalnykh soyuzoz* (Third All–Russian Congress of Trade Unions) (1920), I, Plenumi, pp. 50–51. (Henceforth referred to as Third Trade Union Congress).

463 Deutscher, *The Prophet Armed, op. cit.*, p. 493.

464 V. I. Lenin, "Speech to Third Congress of Economic Councils", *Sochineniya*, XXV, p. 17.

465 Carr, *op. cit.*, II, p. 193.

466 Tomsky, *"Zadachi prosoyuzov"* (The Tasks of the Trade Unions), Ninth Party Congress, Appendix 13, p. 534.

The adoption of Tomsky's theses by a substantial majority marked the high-point of opposition, within the Party, to Lenin's views. Resolutions however were unlikely to resolve the differences. Both sides realized this. A more serious threat to the Party leadership came from the efforts of Party dissidents in industry to establish an independent centre, from which to control the Party organizations in the trade unions. Friction had developed between the Party and trade union authorities over assignments of Party members to trade union work. The Party fraction in the All-Russian Central Council of Trade Unions, dominated by "lefts"

> was claiming direct authority over the Party members in the various industrial unions. Shortly before the Ninth Congress the Party fraction in the ARCCTU passed a resolution which would confirm this claim, by making all Party fractions in the unions directly subordinate to the Party fraction in the ARCCTU, rather than to the geographical organizations of the Party. This literally would have created a Party within the Party, a semi-autonomous body embracing a substantial pro-portion of the Party's membership... The mere existence of such an inner sub-party would be contrary to centralist principles, to say nothing of the prospect of its domination by leftist opponents of Lenin's leadership... It was inevitable that the unionists' demand for autonomy within the Party would be rejected and when the resolution was submitted to the Orgbureau this is precisely what hap-pened.[467]

The whole episode had interesting repercussions. Confronted with a conflict between democracy and centralism, the "democratic centralists" proved that on this issue - as on so many others - centralist considerations were paramount. They pro-posed a resolution, passed by the Moscow organization of the Party, to the effect that "Party discipline in every case takes precedence over trade union discipline".[468] On the other hand the Southern Bureau of the ARCCTU passed a resolution on autonomy for Party trade unionists similar to that drawn up by the parent organiza-tion - *and got it passed by the Fourth Ukrainian Party Conference.*

MARCH

Second All-Russian Congress of Food Industry Workers (under syndicalist influence) meets in Moscow. Censures Bolshevik regime for inaugurating "unlimited and uncontrolled dominion over the proletariat and peasantry, frightful centralism carried to the point of absurdity...destroying in the country all that is alive, sponta-neous and free". "The so-called dictatorship of the proletariat is in reality the dicta-torship over the proletariat by the Party and even by individual persons".[469]

March 29–April 4
Ninth Party Congress.
The Civil War had by now almost been won. The people were yearning to taste, at last, the fruits of their revolution. But the Congress foreshadowed the continua-tion and extension into peacetime of some of the methods of War Communism (conscription of manpower, compulsory direction of labour, strict rationing of con-sumer goods, payment of wages in kind, requisition of agricultural produce from the

---

467   Daniels, *op. cit.*, p. 126.

468   Theses of the Moscow Provincial Committee of the RCP, Ninth Party Congress, Appendix 15, p. 542.

469   *Vmesto programmy: rezolyutsii I i II vserossiiskikh konferentsii anarkho-sindikalistov* (Berlin,1922), p. 28.

peasants – in the place of taxation). The most controversial issues discussed were the "militarization of labour" and "one-man management" of industry. The proposals put to the Congress may be taken as representing the views of Lenin and Trotsky concerning the period of industrial reconstruction.

On the question of direction of labour, Trotsky's views were heavily influenced by his experiences as Commissar for War. Battalions awaiting demobilization had been used on a wide scale for forestry and other work. According to Deutscher "it was only a step from the employment of armed forces as labour battalions to the organization of civilian labour into military units".[470] "The working class", Trotsky announced to the Congress:

> cannot be left wandering all over Russia. They must be thrown here and there, appointed, commanded, just like soldiers.

> Compulsion of labour will reach the highest degree of intensity during the transition from capitalism to socialism.

> Deserters from labour ought to be formed into punitive battalions or put into concentration camps.

He advocated "incentive wages for efficient workers", "socialist emulation" and spoke of the "need to adopt the progressive essence of Taylorism".[471] In relation to industrial management Lenin and Trotsky's main preoccupations were with "economic efficiency". Like the bourgeoisie (both before and after them) they identified "efficiency" with individual management. They realized however that this would be a bitter pill for the workers to swallow. They had to tread carefully.

"Individual management", the official resolution delicately proclaimed,

> does not in any degree limit or infringe upon the rights of the working class or the "rights" of the trade unions, because the class can exercise its rule in one form or another, as technical expediency may dictate. It is the ruling class at large [again identified with the Party (MB)] which in every case "appoints" persons for managerial and administrative jobs.[472]

Their caution was justified. The workers had not forgotten how at the First Trade Union Congress (January 1918) a resolution had proclaimed that "it was the task of workers' control to put an end to autocracy in the economic field just as an end had been put to it in the political field".[473]

Various patterns of industrial management were soon outlined.[474] In drawing these up it is doubtful whether Lenin and Trotsky were encumbered by any doctrinal considerations such as those of Kritzman, the theoretician of "left" Communism, who had defined collective management as "the specific, distinctive mark of the proletariat…distinguishing it from all other social classes…the most democratic principle of organization".[475] Insofar as he had any principled view on the matter Trotsky was to declare that collective management was a "Menshevik idea".

At the Ninth Congress Lenin and Trotsky were opposed most vehemently by the Democratic Centralists (Osinsky, Sapronov, Preobrazhensky). Smirnov, obviously

470 Deutscher, *Soviet Trade Unions, op. cit.,* p. 36.
471 L. Trotsky, *Sochineniya* (Works), XV, p. 126.
472 Ninth Party Congress, p. 128.
473 First Trade Union Congress, pp. 269–72.
474 Deutscher, *Soviet Trade Unions, op. cit.* p. 35
475 L. Kritzman, *Geroicheski period russkoi revolyutsii* (The Heroic Period of the Russian Revolution) (Moscow and Leningrad, 1926), p. 83.

ahead of his time, enquired why if one-man management was such a good idea it wasn't being practised in the Sovnarkom (Council of People's Commissars). Lutovinov, the metalworkers' leader, who was to play an important role in the development of the Workers' Opposition later that year, asserted that

> the responsible head of each branch of industry can only be the production union. And of industry as a whole it can only be the All-Russian Central Council of Trade Unions - it cannot be otherwise.[476]

Shlyapnikov called explicitly for a three-way "separation of powers" between Party, Soviets and the trade unions.[477] Speaking for the Democratic Centralists, Osinsky endorsed Shlyapnikov's idea. He observed a "clash of several cultures" (the "military-soviet" culture, the "civil-soviet" culture and the trade-union movement which had "created its own sphere of culture"). It was improper to apply to all of the cultures certain particular methods (such as militarization) which were appropriate to only one of them.[478] This was a clear case of being caught in a trap of one's own making.

On the question of "one-man management" the Democratic Centralists also had a position which was beside the real point. A resolution, which they had voted through the earlier Moscow Provincial Party Conference, minimized the matter:

> The question of the collegial system [collective management] and individual authority is not a question of principle, but a practical one. It must be decided in each case according to the circumstances.[479]

While correctly grasping that collective management had *of itself* no implicit virtues they failed to recognize that the real problem was that of the relation between management (individual or collective) and those it managed. The real problem was *from whom* the "one" or the "several" managers would derive their authority.

Lenin was not prepared for any concessions on the matter of trade-union autonomy: "The Russian Communist Party can in no case agree that political leadership alone should belong to the Party and economic leadership to the trade unions".[480] Krestinsky had denounced Lutovinov's ideas as "syndicalist contraband".[481] At Lenin's instigation the Congress called on the unions "to explain to the broad circles of the working class that industrial reconstruction can only be achieved by a transition to the maximum curtailment of collective administration and by the gradual introduction of individual management in units directly engaged in production".[482] One-man management was to apply to all institutions from State Trusts to individual factories. "The elective principle must now be replaced by the principle of selection".[483] Collective management was "utopian", "impractical" and "injurious".[484] The Congress also called for a struggle "against the ignorant conceit of...demagogic elements...who think that the working class can solve its problems without having recourse to bourgeois specialists in the most responsible posts":

476 Ninth Party Congress, pp. 254–5.

477 *Ibid.*, p. 564, n. 32.

478 *Ibid.*, pp. 123–4.

479 *Ibid.*, p. 571, n. 75.

480 "To the organizations of the R.C.P. (b) On the Question of the Agenda of the Party Congress", *ibid.*, Appendix 2, p. 474.

481 *Pravda*, March 12, 1920.

482 *Po voprosu o professionalnykh soyuzokh i ikh organizatsii* (On the Question of the Trade Unions and Their Organization), Ninth Party Congress, Resolutions, I, p. 493.

483 "The Trade Unions and their Tasks" (Lenin's Theses), Ninth Party Congress, Appendix 12, p. 532.

484 Ninth Party Congress, pp. 26, 28.

There could be no place in the ranks of the Party of scientific socialism for those demagogic elements which play upon this sort of prejudice among the backward sections of the workers.[485]

The Ninth Congress specifically decreed that "no trade-union group should directly intervene in industrial management" and that "Factory Committees should devote themselves to the questions of labour discipline, of propaganda and of education of the workers".[486] To avoid any recurrence of "independent" tendencies among the leaders of the trade unions those well-known proletarians Bukharin and Radek were moved on to the All-Russian Central Council of Trade Unions to represent the Party leadership and keep a watchful eye on the ARCCTU's proceedings.[487]

All this of course was in flagrant contradiction with the spirit of the decisions taken a year earlier, at the Eighth Party Congress, and in particular to the famous Point 5 of the Economic Section of the 1919 Party Programme. It illustrates quite clearly how vulnerable the working class was to become, once it had been forced to relinquish its real power, the power it had once held in production, in exchange for a shadowy substitute - political power represented by the power of "its" Party. The policy advocated by Lenin was vigorously to be followed. In late 1920, of 2,051 important enterprises for which data were available, 1,783 were already under "one-man management".[488]

The Ninth Party Congress also saw changes relating to the internal Party regime. The Congress had opened to a storm of protests concerning this matter. Local Party Committees (at least democratic in form) were being made subservient to bureaucratically constituted local "political departments":

> With the institution of such bodies all political activity in the plant, industry, organization or locality under their jurisdiction was placed under rigid control from above… This innovation…taken from the Army…was designed to transmit propaganda downward rather than opinion upward.[489]

Verbal concessions were again made - amid repeated pleas for unity. Both at the Congress and later in the year:

> the dissidents made the mistake of concentrating on attempts to rearrange top political institutions, to reshuffle the forms of political control or to introduce new blood into the leadership - while leaving the real sources of power relatively unaffected… Organization, they naively believed, was the most effective weapon against bureaucracy.[490]

The Ninth Congress finally gave the Orgbureau (set up a year earlier and composed of five members of the Central Committee) the right to carry out transfers and postings of Party members without reference to the Politbureau. As had happened

---

485 *Ibid.*

486 At the Eleventh Congress in 1922, Lenin was to say: "It is absolutely essential that all the authority in the factories should be concentrated in the hands of management… Under these circumstances any direct intervention by the trade unions in the management of enterprises must be regarded as positively harmful and impermissible (Resolutions I, pp. 607, 610–612).

487 V.I. Lenin, Ninth Party Congress, p. 96.

488 Kritzman, *op. cit.,* p. 83.

489 Daniels, *op. cit.,* p. 114.

490 *Ibid.,* pp. 115, 117.

before – and was to happen again repeatedly – retrogressive changes in industrial policy went hand in hand with retrogressive changes in internal Party structure.

APRIL

Trotsky given Commissariat of Transport as well as his Defence post. "The Politbureau....offered to back him to the hilt in any action he might take, no matter how severe".[491] Those who peddle the myth of an alleged Leninist opposition to Trotsky's methods *at this stage*, please note.

April 6–15
Third All-Russian Congress of Trade Unions.

Trotsky declared that "the militarization of labour...is the indispensable basic method for the organization of our labour forces":

> Is it true that compulsory labour is always unproductive?...This is the most wretched and miserable liberal prejudice: chattel slavery too was productive.

> Compulsory slave labour...was in its, time a progressive phenomenon.

> Labour...obligatory for the whole country, compulsory for every worker, is the basis of socialism.

"Wages...must not be viewed from the angle of securing the personal existence of the individual worker" but should "measure the conscientiousness, and efficiency of the work of every labourer".[492] Trotsky stressed that coercion, regimentation and militarization of labour were no mere emergency measures. The workers' state normally had the right to coerce *any* citizen to perform *any* work, at *any* time of its choosing.[493] With a vengeance, Trotsky's philosophy of labour came to underline Stalin's practical labour policy in the thirties.

At this Congress Lenin publicly boasted that he had stood for one-man management from the beginning. He claimed that in 1918 he "pointed out the necessity of recognizing the dictatorial authority of single individuals for the purpose of carrying out the Soviet idea"[494] and claimed that at that stage "there were no disputes in connection with the question [of one-man management]". This last assertion is obviously untrue – even if one's terms of reference are restricted to the ranks of the Party. The files of *Kommunist* are there to prove the point!

JUNE–JULY

By the middle of 1920 there had been little if any change in the harsh reality of Russian working class life. Years of war, of civil war and of wars of intervention, coupled with devastation, sabotage, drought, famine and the low initial level of the productive forces, made material improvement difficult. But even the vision had now become blurred. In the "Soviet" Russia of 1920 the industrial workers were "subjected again to managerial authority, labour discipline, wage incentives, scientific man-

---

491   Deutscher, *The Prophet Armed, op. cit.,* p. 498.

492   *Treti vserossiiski s'yezd professionalnykh soyuzov: stenograficheski otchet* (Third All-Russian Congress of Trade Unions: Stenographic Report) (Moscow, 1920), pp. 87–97. (Henceforth referred to as Third Trade Union Congress.)

493   Deutscher, *The Prophet Armed,* op. cit., pp. 500–07.

494   *Trade Unions in Soviet Russia* (Labour Research Department and ILP Information Committee, November 1920) (British Museum Reading Room: press mark 0824–bb–41).

agement – to the familiar forms of capitalist industrial organization with the same bourgeois managers, qualified only by the State's holding the title to the property".[495]

A "white" professor who reached Omsk in the autumn of 1919 from Moscow reported that

> at the head of many of the centres and *glavki* sit former employers and responsible officials and managers of business. The unprepared visitor to the centres who is personally acquainted with the former commercial and industrial world would be surprised to see the former owners of big leather factories sitting in Glavkozh, big manufacturers in the Central textile organizations, etc.[496]

Under the circumstances it is scarcely surprising that the spurious unity achieved at the Ninth Congress a few months earlier did not last. Throughout the summer and autumn differences of opinion on such issues as bureaucracy within the Party, the relations of the trade unions to the State and even the class nature of the State itself were to take on a very sharp form. Opposition groups appeared at almost every level. In the latter part of the year (after the conclusion of the Russo-Polish war) repressed discontent broke into the open. In the autumn Lenin's authority was to be challenged more seriously than at any time since the "left" Communist movement of early 1918.

July

Publication of Trotsky's classic **Terrorism and Communism** (just before the Second Congress of the Communist International). This work gives Trotsky's views on the "socialist" organization of labour in their most finished, lucid and unambiguous form:

> The organization of labour is in its essence the organization of the new society: every historical form of society is in its foundation a form of organization of labour.[497]

> The creation of a socialist society means the organization of the workers on new foundations, their adaptation to those foundations and their labour re-education, with the one unchanging end of the increase in the productivity of labour.[498]

> Wages, in the form of both money and goods, must be brought into the closest possible touch with the productivity of individual labour. Under capitalism the system of piecework and of grading, the application of the Taylor system, etc., have as their object to increase the exploitation of the workers by the squeezing out of surplus value. Under socialist production, piecework, bonuses, etc., have as their problem to increase the volume of the social product…those workers who do more for the general interest than others receive the right to a greater quantity of the social product than the lazy, the careless and the disorganizers.[499]

> The very principle of compulsory labour is for the Communist quite unquestionable…the only solution to economic difficulties that is correct from the point of view both of principle and of practice is to treat the population of the whole country as the reservoir of the necessary labour power – an almost inexhaustible

495 Daniels, *op. cit.*, p. 107.

496 G. K. Gins, *Sibir, Soyuzniki, Kolchak* (Peking, 1921), II, p. 429.

497 L. Trotsky, *Terrorism and Communism*, (Ann Arbor: University of Michigan Press, 1961), p. 133.

498 *Ibid.*, p. 146.

499 *Ibid.*, p. 149.

reservoir - and to introduce strict order into the work of its registration, mobilization and utilization.[500]

The introduction of compulsory labour service is unthinkable without the application, to a greater or lesser degree, of the methods of militarization of labour.[501]

The unions should discipline the workers and teach them to place the interests of production above their own needs and demands.

The young Workers' State requires trade unions not for a struggle for better conditions of labour - that is the task of the social and state organizations as a whole - but to organize the working class for the ends of production.[502]

It would be a most crying error to confuse the question as to the supremacy of the proletariat with the question of boards of workers at the head of factories. The dictatorship of the proletariat is expressed in the abolition of private property in the means of production, in the supremacy over the whole soviet mechanism of the collective will of the workers [a euphemism for the Party (MB)] and not at all in the form in which individual economic enterprises are administered.[503]

I consider that if the Civil War had not plundered our economic organs of all that was strongest, most independent, most endowed with initiative, we should undoubtedly have entered the path of one-man management in the sphere of economic administration much sooner and much less painfully.[504]

AUGUST

Due to the Civil War - and to other factors less often mentioned such as the attitude of the railway workers to the "new" regime - the Russian railways had virtually ceased to function. Trotsky, Commissar for Transport, was granted wide emergency powers to try out his theories of "militarization of labour". He started by placing the railwaymen and the personnel of the repair workshops under martial law. When the railwaymen's trade union objected, he summarily ousted its leaders and, *with the full support and endorsement of the Party leadership*

> appointed others willing to do his bidding. He repeated the procedure in other unions of transport workers.[505]

EARLY SEPTEMBER

Setting up of Tsektran (Central Administrative Body of Railways). Very much Trotsky's brainchild, it was brought into being as a result of a compulsory fusion of the Commissariat of Transport, of the railway unions and of the Party organs ("political departments") in this field. The entire railroad and water transport systems were to fall within Tsektran's compass. Trotsky was appointed its head. He ruled the Tsektran along strictly military and bureaucratic lines. "The Politbureau backed him

---

500   *Ibid.*, p. 135.
501   *Ibid.*, p. 137.
502   *Ibid.*, p. 143.
503   *Ibid.*, p. 162.
504   *Ibid.*, pp. 162–3.
505   Deutscher, *The Prophet Armed, op. cit.*, pp. 501–2.

to the hilt, as it had promised".[506] The railways were got going again. But the cost to the image of the Party was incalculable. Those who wonder why, at a later stage, Trotsky was unable to mobilize mass support for his struggle, within the apparatus, against the "Stalinist" bureaucracy should meditate on such facts.

September 22–25
Ninth Party Conference.

Zinoviev gave the official report on behalf of the Central Committee. Sapronov presented a minority report on behalf of the "Democratic Centralists" who were well represented. Lutovinov spoke for the recently constituted Workers' Opposition. He called for the immediate institution of the widest measures of proletarian democracy, the total rejection of the system whereby appointments from above were made to nominally elected positions, and the purging of the Party of careerist elements who were now joining in droves. He also asked that the Central Committee refrain from its constant and exaggerated interventions in the life of the trade unions and of the Soviets.

The leadership had to retreat. Zinoviev evaded answering the main complaints. A resolution was passed stressing the need for "full equality within the Party" and denouncing "the domination of rank-and-file members by privileged bureaucrats". The resolution instructed the Central Committee to proceed by means of "recommendations" rather than by appointments from above and to abstain from "disciplinary transfers on political grounds".[507]

Despite these verbal concessions the leadership, through their spokesman Zinoviev, succeeded in getting the September Conference to accept the setting up of Central and Regional Control Commissions. These were to play an important role in the further bureaucratization of the Party – when the early incumbents (Dzerzhinsky, Preobrazhensky and Muranov) had been replaced by Stalin's henchmen.

OCTOBER
Signature of Peace Treaty with Poland.

November 2–6
Fifth All-Russian Trade Union Conference.

Trotsky points out that the parallelism between unions and administrative organs, responsible for the prevailing confusion, had to be eliminated. This could only be done by the conversion of trade (*professionalny*) unions into production (*proizvodstvenny*) unions. If the leadership of the unions objected, they would have to be "shaken up" as the leaders of the railway unions had been. The "winged word" (Lenin) had been uttered!

November 14
General Wrangel evacuates the Crimea. End of Civil War.

---

506   *Ibid.*, p. 502.
507   *Isvestiya* of the Central Committee, October 12, 1920.

NOVEMBER
Moscow Provincial Party Conference.
Opposition groups within Party shown to be growing rapidly. The recently formed Workers' Opposition, the Democratic Centralists and the Ignatov group (a local Moscow faction closely allied to the Workers' Opposition and later to merge with it) had secured 124 delegates to this Conference against 154 for supporters of the Central Committee.[508]

November 8–9
Meeting of Plenum of Central Committee.
Trotsky submits a "preliminary draft of theses" entitled "The Trade Unions and Their Future Role", later published on December 25 - in slightly altered form - as a pamphlet, *The Role and Tasks of the Trade Unions*: "It was necessary immediately to proceed to reorganize the trade unions, i.e. to select the leading personnel" (Thesis 5). Dizzy with success, Trotsky again threatened to "shake up" various trade unions as he had "shaken up those of the transport workers".[509] What was needed was "to replace irresponsible agitators [sic!] by production-minded trade unionists".[510] Trotsky's theses were put to the vote and defeated by the narrow margin of eight votes to seven. Lenin then "bluntly dissociated himself from Trotsky and persuaded the Central Committee to do likewise".[511] An alternative resolution proposed by Lenin was then passed by ten votes to four. It called for "reform of the Tsektran", advocated "sound forms of the militarization of labour"[512] and proclaimed that "the Party ought to educate and support…a new type of trade unionist, the energetic and imaginative economic organizer who will approach economic issues not from the angle of distribution and consumption but from that of expanding production".[513] The latter was clearly the dominant viewpoint. Trotsky's "error" had been that he had carried it out to its logical conclusion. But the Party needed a sacrificial goat. The Plenum was "to forbid Trotsky to speak in public on the relationship between the trade unions and the State".[514]

December 2
Trotsky, in a speech to the enlarged Plenum of Tsektran declared that

a competent, hierarchically organized civil service had its merits. Russia suffered not from the excess but from the lack of an efficient bureaucracy.[515]

The militarization of the trade unions and the militarization of transport required an internal, ideological militarization.[516]

---

508   Tenth Party Congress, p. 829, n. 2.

509   Deutscher, *The Prophet Armed, op. cit.*, pp. 502–3.

510   Deutscher, *Soviet Trade Unions, op. cit.*, p. 41.

511   Deutscher, *The Prophet Armed, op. cit.*, pp. 502–3.

512   Lenin, *Selected Works*, IX, p. 30.

513   G. Zinoviev, *Sochineniya* (Moscow,1924–6), VI, pp. 599–600.

514   Deutscher, *The Prophet Armed, op. cit.*, pp. 502–3. This sanction was to be lifted by the Central Committee, at its meeting of December 24, which also decided that the whole matter ought now to be openly discussed.

515   *Ibid.*, p. 503.

516   Trotsky, *Sochineniya*, XV, pp. 422–3.

Stalin was later to describe Trotsky as "the patriarch of the bureaucrats".[517] When the Central Committee again rebuffed him:

> Trotsky fretfully reminded Lenin and the other members of how often they had privately urged him...to act ruthlessly and disregard considerations of democracy. It was disloyal of them...to pretend in public that they defended the democratic principle against him.[518]

December 7

At a Plenum of the Central Committee Bukharin had produced a resolution on "industrial democracy". The terms were to infuriate Lenin. They were "a verbal twist", "a tricky phrase", "confusing", "a squib":

> Industry is always necessary. Democracy is not always necessary. The term "industrial democracy" gives rise to a number of utterly false ideas.[519]

> It might be understood to repudiate dictatorship and individual management.[520]

> Without bonuses in kind and disciplinary courts it was just empty talk.[521]

The strongest opposition to Trotsky's schemes for the "militarization of labour" came from that section of the Party with the deepest roots in the trade unions. Some of these Party members had not only dominated the Trade Union Council up to this time but "were also the direct beneficiaries of the doctrine of autonomous trade union responsibility".[522] In other words they were already, in part, trade union bureaucrats. It was partly from these elements that the Workers' Opposition was to develop.

By now, however, the leading politico-economic apparatus was quite different from the one we saw emerging in 1918. In just over two years the Party apparatus had gained undisputed political control of the State (through the bureaucratized Soviets). It had also gained almost complete control of the economic apparatus (through trade-union officials and appointed industrial managers). The various groups had acquired the competence and experience necessary to become a social category with a specific function: to manage Russia. Their fusion was inevitable.

December 22–29

The **Eighth All-Russian Congress of Soviets** was held in Moscow. It provided an opportunity for a public airing of the diverging viewpoints on the trade union question which had developed within the Party and which could now no longer be contained within its ranks. The degree of opposition which had developed to official Party policy can be gauged by the contents of Zinoviev's speech:

> We will establish more intimate contacts with the working masses. We will hold meetings in the barracks, in the camps and in the factories. The working masses will then...understand that it is no joke when we proclaim that a new era is about to start, that as soon as we can breathe freely again we will transfer our political

---

517   J. Stalin, *Sochineniya*, VI, p. 29.
518   Deutscher, *The Prophet Armed, op. cit.*, p. 503.
519   Lenin, *Selected Works*, IX, p. 12.
520   *Ibid.*, p. 53.
521   *Ibid.*, p. 26.
522   Daniels, *op. cit.*, p. 125.

meetings into the factories… We are asked what we mean by workers' and peasants' democracy. I answer: nothing more and nothing less than what we meant
by it in 1917. We must re-establish the principle of election in the workers' and
peasants' democracy… If we have deprived ourselves of the most elementary
democratic rights for workers and peasants, it is time we put an end to this state
of affairs.[523]

Zinoviev's concern for democracy did not carry much weight, being factionally
motivated (it was part of a campaign to discredit Trotsky). At that time public orators
in search of laughs could usually get them by carefully chosen quotations from
Zinoviev on the subject of democratic rights.[524]

December 30

Joint meeting of the Party fraction to the Eighth Congress of Soviets, of Party
members on the All-Russian Central Council of Trade Unions, and of Party members
in various other organizations, held in the Bolshoi Theatre, Moscow, to discuss the
"trade union question". All the main protagonists were on hand to state their respective cases. The various viewpoints, as stated at the meeting (or outlined in articles
written at the time or within the next few weeks) can be summarized as follows.[525]

Trotsky and particularly Bukharin later amended their original proposals in
order to constitute a bloc at the Congress.

For *Lenin* the trade unions were "reservoirs of state power". They were to provide a broad social basis "for the proletarian dictatorship exercised by the Party", a
base that was badly needed in view of the predominantly peasant nature of the
country. The unions were to be the "link" or "transmission belt" between the Party and
the mass of non-Party workers. The unions could not be autonomous. They could
not play an independent role either in the initiation or in the implementation of policy. They had to be strongly influenced by Party thinking and would undertake the
political education of the masses along lines determined by the Party. In this way they
would become "schools of Communism" for their seven million members.[526] The
Party was to be the teacher: "The Russian Communist Party, in the person of its
Central and Regional organizations, *unconditionally* guides as before the whole ideological side of the work of the trade unions".[527]

Lenin stressed that the unions could not be instruments of the State. Trotsky's
assumption that the unions need no longer defend the workers because the State
was now a workers' state was wrong: "Our state is such that the entire organized

---

523   *Vosmoi vserossiiski s'yezd sovetov: stenograficheski otche*t (Eighth All-Russian Congress of Soviets:
Stenographic Report) (Moscow, 1921), p. 324.

524   L. Schapiro, *The Origin of the Communist Autocracy* (New York: Praeger, 1965), p. 271.

525   These summaries are based on Deutscher's detailed accounts in *Soviet Trade Unions, op. cit.*, pp. 42–52. In
the course of the pre-Congress discussion a great number of factions and groups emerged, each with its own
views and "thesis" on the trade unions. The differences between some of these groups were very subtle indeed,
and nearly all groups referred to so many common principles that sometimes the object of the debate seemed
almost unreal. Only three motions were finally presented to the Congress: Lenin's *(The Platform of the Ten)*, the
Trotsky-Bukharin motion and the proposals of the Workers' Opposition. Deutscher points out that "a compari-
son between these motions tends up to a point to obscure rather than throw into relief the issue with which the
Congress tried to come to grips because, for tactical reasons, the authors of every motion incorporated passages
from their opponents' motions and thereby blurred the real differences".

526   According to figures given by Zinoviev at the Tenth Party Congress, union membership was 1.5 million in
July 1917, 2.6 million in January 1918, 3.5 million in 1919, 4.3 million in 1920 and 7 million in 1921.

527   "*O roli i zadachakh profsoyuzov*" (On the Role and Tasks of Trade Unions), Tenth Party Congress,
Resolutions, I, pp. 536–542 ff.

proletariat must defend itself: we [sic] must use these workers' organizations for the defence of the workers from their state *and for the defence of our state by the workers*". (The words in italics are often omitted when this famous passage is quoted.)

According to Lenin, militarization was not to be regarded as a permanent feature of socialist labour policy. Persuasion had to be used as well as coercion. While it was *normal* [sic!] for the state to appoint officials from above (a long, long way had been travelled since the statements recorded under the heading of May 20, 1917) it would be inexpedient for the trade unions to do the same. The unions could make recommendations for administrative-economic jobs and should co-operate in planning. They should inspect, through specialized departments, the work of the economic administration.

Wage-rate fixing was to be transferred to the All-Russian Central Council of Trade Unions. In relation to wages the extreme egalitarianism of the Workers' Opposition had to be fought. Wages policy was to be designed so as to "discipline labour and increase its productivity".[528] Party members had

> chattered enough about principles in the Smolny. Now, after three years, they had decrees on all points of the production problem.[529]

> The decisions on the militarization of labour, etc., were incontrovertible and there is no need whatsoever to withdraw my words of ridicule concerning references to democracy made by those who challenged these decisions...we shall extend democracy in the workers' organizations but not make a fetish of it...[530]

Trotsky reiterated his belief that "the transformation of the trade unions into production unions...formed the greatest task of our epoch":

> The unions ought permanently to assess their membership from the angle of production and should always possess a full and precise characterization of the productive value of any worker.

The leading bodies of the trade unions and of the economic administration should have between one-third and one-half of their members in common in order to put an end to the antagonism between them. Bourgeois technicians and administrators who had become full members of a union were to be entitled to hold managerial posts, without supervision by commissars. After a real minimum wage had been secured for all workers there should be "shock competition" (*udarnichestvo*) between workers in production.

Bukharin's views had been evolving rapidly. What he now advocated was an attempt to build a bridge between the official views of the Party and those of the Workers' Opposition. There had to be "workers' democracy in production". The "governmentalizing of the unions" had to go hand in hand with the "unionizing of the state".

> The logical and historical termination [of this process] will not be the engulfment of the unions by the proletarian state, but the disappearance of both categories

---

528　Deutscher, *Soviet Trade Unions, op. cit.*, p. 51.

529　Lenin, *Selected Works*, IX, p. 6.

530　*Ibid.*, p. 76

- of the unions as well as of the state - and the creation of a third: the commu-
nistically organized society".[531]

Lenin was to seize upon Bukharin's platform as "a full break with Communism and
a transition to a position of syndicalism".[532]

> It destroyed the need for the Party. If the trade unions, nine-tenths of whose
> members are non-Party workers, appoint the managers of industry, what is the
> use of the Party?"[533]

"So we have grown up", he added ominously, "from small differences to syndicalism, signifying a complete break with Communism and an unavoidable split in the
Party".[534] Other attacks by Lenin on Bukharin's views are to be found in his famous
article censuring Trotsky.[535]

The views of the *Workers' Opposition* were put to the Moscow meeting by
Shlyapnikov, a metalworker (and were later to be developed more fully by Kollontai
and others). Explicitly or implicitly these views postulated the domination of the trade
unions over the state.

The Workers' Opposition referred of course to Point 5 of the 1919 Programme
and charged the leadership of the Party with violating its pledges towards the trade
unions…the leadership of the Party and of Government bodies had in the last two
years systematically narrowed the scope of trade union work and reduced almost to
nil the influence of the working class… The Party and the economic authorities, having been swamped by bourgeois technicians and other non-proletarian elements
displayed outward hostility to the unions… The remedy was the concentration of
industrial management in the hands of the trade unions.

The transition should take place from below up: "At the factory level, the Factory
Committees should regain their erstwhile dominant position". (The Bolshevik trade
unionists had taken a long time to come round to this viewpoint!) The Opposition
proposed more trade union representation in various controlling bodies. Not a single person was to be appointed to any administrative-economic post without the
agreement of the trade unions. Officials recommended by the trade unions were to
remain accountable for their conduct to the unions, who should also have the right
to recall them from their posts at any time. The programme culminated in the
demand that an "All-Russian Producers' Congress" be convened to elect the central
management of the entire national economy. National Congresses of separate
unions were similarly to elect managements for the various branches of the economy. Local and regional managements should be formed by local trade union conferences, while the management of single factories was to belong to the Factory
Committees, which were to remain part of the trade union organization… "In this
way", Shlyapnikov asserted, "there is created the unity of will which is essential in the
organization of the economy, and also a real possibility for the influence of the initiative of the broad working masses on the organization and development of our

---

531   Bukharin, *"O zadachakh i strukture profsoyuzov"* (On the Tasks and Structure of the Trade Unions), Tenth
Party Congress, Appendix 16, p. 802.

532   Lenin, *Selected Works*, IX, p. 35.

533   *Ibid.*, p. 36.

534   V.I. Lenin, *"Krisis partii"* (The Crisis in the Party), *Pravda*, January 21, 1921.

535   V.I. Lenin, "Once Again on the Trade Unions, the Present Situation and the Mistakes of Comrades Trotsky
and Bukharin", *Selected Works*, IX, pp. 40–80.

economy".[536] Last but not least the Workers' Opposition proposed a radical revision of the wages policy in an extremely egalitarian spirit: money wages were to be progressively replaced by rewards in kind. Within the Party, it was clearly on the shoulders of the Workers' Opposition that, at this late stage, fell the task of endeavouring to maintain the revolutionary ideals of *State and Revolution*, with respect to the autonomous and democratic involvement of the masses in the functions of economic decision taking.

1921

JANUARY

"Official" campaign, preparatory to Tenth Congress, launched by the strongly Leninist Petrograd Party Committee (in Zinoviev's hands). Even before the Congress, many administrative measures were taken to ensure the defeat of the Opposition. So irregular were some of these that the Moscow Party Committee at one stage voted a resolution publicly censuring the Petrograd organization "for not observing the rules of proper controversy".[537]

January 13

Moscow Party Committee denounced "tendency of the Petrograd organization to make itself a special centre for the preparation of Party Congresses".[538] The Leninists were using the Petrograd organization as a base from which to apply pressure to the rest of the Party. Moscow Committee urged Central Committee "to ensure the equitable distribution of materials and speakers...so that all points of view should be represented".[539] This recommendation was to be flagrantly violated. At the Congress, Kollontai stated that the circulation of her pamphlet had been deliberately impeded.[540]

January 14

Publication of the **Platform of the Ten**(Artem, Kalinin, Kamenev, Lenin, Lozovsky, Petrovsky, Rudzutak, Stalin, Tomsky and Zinoviev). This document gave a more finished form to Lenin's theses for the Congress.

January 16

Pravda publishes the Bukharin platform, described by Lenin as the "acme of ideological disintegration".[541]

---

536   Shlyapnikov, *"Organizatsiya narodnogo khozyaistva i zadachi soyuzov"* (The Organization of the Economy and the Tasks of the Unions), Tenth Party Congress, speech of December 30, 1920, Appendix 2, pp. 789–93.

537   L. Trotsky, *"Otvet petrogradskim tovarishcham"* (Answer to the Petrograd Comrades), Tenth Party Congress, pp. 826–7, n. 1.

538   Tenth Party Congress, p. 779, Appendix 6.

539   *Ibid.*

540   A. Kollontai, Tenth Party Congress, p. 103.

541   Lenin, *Selected Works*, IX, p. 35.

January 21

In an article in *Pravda* on the Party crisis, Lenin writes:

> Now we add to our platform the following: we must combat the ideological con-
> fusion of those unsound elements of the opposition who go to the lengths of
> repudiating all "militarization of economy", of repudiating not only the "method
> of appointing" which has been the prevailing method up to now, but all appoint-
> ments. In the last analysis this means repudiating the leading role of the Party in
> relation to the non-Party masses. We must combat the syndicalist deviation
> which will kill the Party if it is not completely cured of it.

A little later Lenin was to write that "the syndicalist deviation leads to the fall of the
dictatorship of the proletariat".[542] In other words working class power ("the dictatorship of the proletariat") is impossible if there are militants in the Party who think the
working class should exert more power in production ("the syndicalist deviation").[543]

January 24

Meeting of the Communist Fraction during **Second Congress of the Miners'
Union**. Kiselev, a miner, put the case for the Workers' Opposition which got 62 votes
– as against 137 for the Leninist platform and 8 for Trotsky's.[544]

January 25

Pravda publishes the Workers' Opposition's 'Theses on the Trade Unions'.
Alexandra Kollontai publishes *The Workers' Opposition* which develops the same
ideas at a more theoretical level.[545]

For all the political storm unleashed by the Workers' Opposition there is little
reliable documentation about this tendency. What information there is comes mainly from Leninist sources.[546] The virulence of the attacks against the Workers'
Opposition suggests it enjoyed considerable support among rank-and-file factory
workers and that this caused the Party leadership serious alarm. Shlyapnikov (the
first Commissar of Labour), Lutovinov and Medvedev, the leaders of the metalworkers, were its most prominent spokesmen:

> Geographically it seems to have been concentrated in the South-Eastern parts of
> European Russia: the Donets Basin, the Don and Kuban regions and the Samara
> province on the Volga. In Samara the Workers' Opposition was actually in con-
> trol of the Party organization in 1921. Before the Party shake-up in the Ukraine, in
> late 1920, the oppositionists had won a sympathetic majority in the republic as a
> whole. Other points of strength were in the Moscow province, where the
> Workers' Opposition polled about a quarter of the Party votes and in the
> Metalworkers' Union throughout the country.[547]

---

542 *Ibid*, p. 57.

543 Lenin here poses quite clearly the question "power of the Party" or "power of the class". He unambiguously
opts for the former – no doubt rationalizing his choice by equating the two. But he goes even further. He not
only equates "workers' power" with the rule of the Party. He equates it with acceptance of the ideas of the Party
leaders!

544 Lenin, *Selected Works*, IX, p. 79.

545 The full text was published as Solidarity Pamphlet 7.

546 See for instance K. Shelavin, *Rabochaya oppozitsiya* (The Workers' Opposition) (Moscow, 1930).

547 Daniels, *op. cit.*, p. 127.

When Tomsky was to abandon the trade unionists and rejoin Lenin's camp later in 1921, he was to "explain" the appeal of the Workers' Opposition in terms of the metalworkers' ideology of industrialism and syndicalism.[548] It should be remembered that these same metalworkers had formed the backbone of the Factory Committees in 1917.

FEBRUARY

During the pre-Congress discussion the Leninist faction made full use of the newly established Control Commission. They ensured the resignation of both Preobrazhensky and Dzerzhinsky (judged unduly "soft" in relation to the Workers' Opposition and to the Trotskyists respectively) and their replacement by hardened apparatchiks such as Solts who proceeded to berate the divided Party leadership for its weakness in curtailing the "ultra left". The Leninists whipped up a noisy campaign and played relentlessly on the themes of unity and of the internal dangers confronting the Revolution. Again and again they took refuge in the cult of Lenin's personality. All other tendencies were labelled "objectively counter-revolutionary". They succeeded in getting control of the Party machine, even in areas with a long tradition of support for the Opposition.

So "successful" were some of these "victories" that there is serious doubt as to whether they were not achieved by fraud. On January 19 for instance a Party Conference of the Baltic Fleet is said to have given a 90 per cent vote to the Leninists.[549] Yet within two or three weeks a strong Fleet Opposition was to develop and widely distribute leaflets proclaiming:

> The Political Department of the Baltic Fleet has lost all contact not only with the masses but with the active political workers too. It has become a bureaucratic organ without authority... It has annihilated all local initiative and reduced all political work to the level of secretarial correspondence.[550]

Outside the Party, even harsher things were being said.

March 17
The Kronstadt Rebellion.

This key event which had a profound effect on the Congress which opened a few days later has been analyzed in detail elsewhere.[551]

March 8–16
Tenth Party Congress.

This was to prove one of the most dramatic assemblies in the whole history of Bolshevism. But in a sense the arguments used and the battles fought out there were only a distorted reflection of the much deeper crisis in the country as a whole. Strikes had broken out in the Petrograd area towards the end of February and Kronstadt

---

548 Tomsky, Tenth Party Congress, pp. 371–2.

549 *Pravda*, January 27, 1921.

550 Quoted in A.S. Pukhov, *Kronshtadtski myatezh v 1921 g.* (The Kronstadt Revolt of 1921) (Leningrad, 1931), p. 52. Ida Mett's pamphlet, *The Kronstadt Commune*, gives a good idea of the "disaffection" rampant in Petrograd at the time.

551 For useful documentation, see Ida Mett, *The Kronstadt Commune* (Solidarity Pamphlet 27) and Victor Serge, *Kronstadt, 1921* (Solidarity Pamphlet (reprinted from Solidarity, I, 7 [1961])).

was up in arms. Both were but the visible portions of a much larger iceberg of sub-merged discontent and disaffection.

From beginning to end the apparatus was in full control of the Congress. An atmosphere of near hysteria, such as had not been seen before at Bolshevik gatherings, pervaded the proceedings. It was now essential for the Party leadership to suppress the Opposition which whether it knew it or not - and whether it wanted to do so or not - was making itself the mouthpiece of all these frustrated aspirations. It was above all necessary to expunge the image of Kronstadt as a movement which defended the principles of the October Revolution against the Communists - the idea of the "third revolution" - which was exactly what the Kronstadters were proclaiming. "We fight", the rebels proclaimed, "for the genuine power of the working people while the bloody Trotsky and the glutted Zinoviev and their band of adherents fight for the power of the Party…"[552]

> Kronstadt has raised for the first time the banner of the uprising of the Third Revolution of the toilers… The autocracy has fallen. The Constituent Assembly has been dispatched to the region of the damned. Now the commissariocracy is crumbling…[553]

At the Congress Trotsky rounded on the Workers' Opposition:

> They have come out with dangerous slogans. They have made a fetish of democratic principles. They have placed the workers' right to elect representatives above the Party. As if the Party were not entitled to assert its dictatorship even if that dictatorship temporarily clashed with the passing moods of the workers' democracy!

Trotsky spoke of the "revolutionary historical birthright of the Party":

> The Party is obliged to maintain its dictatorship…regardless of temporary vacillations even in the working class… The dictatorship does not base itself at every given moment on the formal principle of a workers' democracy…

The physical attack on Kronstadt - in which over two hundred delegates to the Congress participated - was accompanied by a massive verbal onslaught against the Workers' Opposition and similar tendencies. Although leading members of the Opposition were to fight against the Kronstadters (because they still retained illusions about "the historical role of the Party" and because they were still trapped in old organizational loyalties), Lenin and the Party leaders were fully aware of the deep affinities between the two movements: "Both attacked his leadership for having violated the spirit of the revolution, for having sacrificed democratic and egalitarian ideals on the altar of expediency and for inclining to bureaucratic concern with power for its own sake".[554] In relation to real issues their demands also overlapped in a number of areas. The Kronstadters - among whom were many dissident Party members - had proclaimed that

> the Soviet Socialist Republic can only be strong when its administration belongs to the toiling classes, represented by renovated trade unions… Thanks to the policy of the ruling party the trade unions have had absolutely no opportunity to be purely class organizations. [555]

---

552   *Isvestiya vremennogo revolyutsionnogo komiteta* (News of the Provisional Revolutionary Committee), March 10, 1921.

553   *Ibid.*, March 12, 1921.

554   Daniels, *op. cit.*, pp. 145–6.

555   *Isvestiya vremennogo revolyutsionnogo komiteta*, March 9, 1921.

Down to the fetishism of the unions, the language was the same.

The Congress opened with a virulent speech by Lenin appealing for loyalty to the Party and denouncing the Workers' Opposition as a threat to the Revolution. The Opposition was a "petty-bourgeois", "syndicalist", "anarchist" strand "caused in part by the entry into the ranks of the Party of elements which had still not completely adopted the Communist world view".[556] (In fact the Opposition was the very opposite. It was the reaction of the proletarian base of the Party to the entry of hordes of such elements.) The basic arguments of the Opposition were not dealt with in any depth. What argument - as distinct from invective - there was, was often confused. For instance, apart from being (a) "genuinely counter-revolutionary" and (b) "objectively counter-revolutionary", the Workers' Opposition was also "too revolutionary". Their demands were "too advanced" and the Soviet Government still had to concentrate on overcoming the masses' cultural backwardness.[557] According to Smilga the extreme demands (of the Workers' Opposition) disrupted the Party's efforts and raised hopes among the workers which could only be disappointed.[558] But, most important, the demands of the Workers' Opposition were revolutionary in a wrong (anarcho-syndicalist) way. This was the ultimate anathema. "If we perish", Lenin said privately

> it is all the more important to preserve our ideological line and give a lesson to our continuators. This should never be forgotten, even in hopeless circumstances.[559]

Gone were the brief days of the 1917 honeymoon. Gone was the rhetoric of *State and Revolution*. Out came the skeletons of the split in the First International. The cardinal crime of the Opposition was that elements among it (and more particularly among its fringes, such as Myasnikov and Bogdanov) were beginning to raise really awkward questions. In a clumsy and still fumbling manner some were beginning to question the primacy of the Party - others the class nature of the Russian State. As long as criticisms dealt with the "bureaucratic deformations or distortions" of this or that institution - or even in the Party itself - the Party could cope (it had in fact become quite practised in the matter!). But to raise doubts about these other absolutely basic matters could not be tolerated.

The threat was serious, even if at the moment only implicit in the Opposition's thinking. Ignatov's theses had warned of the likely effects of "the mass entry into the ranks of our Party of people from bourgeois and petty-bourgeois strata" combined with "the heavy losses sustained by the proletariat during the Civil War".[560] But one thing led to another. Shortly after the Congress Bogdanov and the *Workers' Truth Group* were to claim that the revolution had ended in a "complete defeat for the working class". They were to charge that:

> the bureaucracy, along with the NEP men had become a new bourgeoisie, depending on the exploitation of the workers and taking advantage of their disorganization. With the trade unions in the hands of the bureaucracy the workers were more helpless than ever.

556   *"O sindikalistskom i anarkhistskom uklone v nashei partii"* (On the Syndicalist and Anarchist Deviation in Our Party), Tenth Party Congress, Resolutions, I, p. 530.

557   Tenth Party Congress, pp. 382–3.

558   *Ibid.*, p. 258.

559   Trotsky, Letter to friends in the USSR, 1930 (Trotsky Archive T 3279).

560   Ignatov Theses, Tenth Party Congress.

> The Communist Party…after becoming the ruling Party, the party of the organiz-
> ers and leaders of the State apparatus and of the capitalist-based economic
> life….had irrevocably lost its tie and community with the proletariat.[561]

This kind of thinking threatened the very basis of the Bolshevik regime and had ruthlessly to be expunged from the minds of working people.

"Marxism teaches us", Lenin said,

> that only the political party of the working class, i.e. the Communist Party, is in a
> position to unite, educate, organize…and direct all sides of the proletarian move-
> ment and hence all the working masses. Without this the dictatorship of the pro-
> letariat is meaningless.[562]

"Marxism" of course taught other things too. It emphasized that "the emancipation
of the working class was the task of the working class itself"[563] and that "the
Communists do not form a separate party opposed to other working-class parties".[564] What Lenin was now preaching was not in fact "Marxism" but the crude
Leninism of *What Is To Be Done?* (written in 1902), the Leninism which had asserted
that the working class left to its own devices could only develop a trade union consciousness and would have to have political consciousness injected into it from the
outside, by those "vehicles of science" the petty-bourgeois intelligentsia.[565] In the
minds of the Bolsheviks the Party embodied the historical interests of the class
whether the class understood it or not – and whether the class wanted it or not.
Given these premises, any challenge to the hegemony of the Party – whether in action
or only in thought – was tantamount to "treason" to the Revolution, to a rape of
History.

"Unity" was the all-pervasive theme of the Congress. Given the threat from without and the "threat" from within it didn't prove very hard for the leadership to get
draconian measures accepted. These were still further to restrict the rights of Party
members. Factional rights were abolished:

> The Congress prescribes the rapid dispersal of all groups without exception
> which have formed themselves on one platform or another…failure to execute
> this decision of the Congress will lead to immediate and unconditional expulsion
> from the Party.[566]

A secret provision gave the Central Committee unlimited disciplinary rights, including expulsion from the Party and even from the Central Committee itself (for which
a majority of two-thirds would be required.)

These measures, an organizational turning-point in the history of Bolshevism,
were overwhelmingly endorsed. But not without certain misgivings. Karl Radek stated:

> I had a feeling that a rule was being established which left us uncertain as to
> whom it might be applied against. When the Central Committee was chosen, the
> comrades from the majority composed a list which gave them control. Every

561   N. Karev, "O gruppe 'Rabochya Pravda'" (On the "Workers' Truth" Group), *Bolshevik*, July 15, 1924, pp. 31 ff.

562   Tenth Party Congress, Resolutions, I, p. 531.

563   K. Marx and F. Engels, *Manifesto of the Communist Party*, in *Selected Works* (Moscow: Foreign Languages
Publishing House, 1958), I, p. 28.

564   *Ibid.*, p. 46.

565   But even then they were material of dubious value. The first Russian edition of *What Is To Be Done?* had carried
on its frontispiece Lasalle's famous aphorism, "The Party strengthens itself by purging itself".

566   "On the Unity of the Party", Tenth Party Congress, Resolutions, I, pp. 527–30.

comrade knew that this was done at the beginning of the dissension in the Party. We do not know…what complications may arise. The comrades who propose this rule think it is a sword aimed against differently thinking comrades. Although I am voting for this resolution I feel that it may even be turned against us.

Stressing the dangerous situation confronting both Party and State, Radek concluded, "let the Central Committee at the moment of danger take the sternest measures against the best comrades, if it finds this necessary".[567] This attitude, or rather this mentality – the Party can't be wrong in relation to the class, the Central Committee can't be wrong in relation to the Party – was to explain many subsequent events. It was literally to prove a noose around the necks of thousands of honest revolutionaries. It helps one understand both Trotsky's public denials of 1927 that Lenin had ever left a political testament, and the "confessions" of the Bolshevik Old Guard during the Moscow Trials of 1936–38. The Party, as an institution, had become reified. It now epitomized man's alienation in relation to revolutionary politics.

In relation to these political shifts – or rather to this emergence of what had always been some of the underlying strands of Bolshevism – the actual "discussions" of the Conference were of less significance. They have therefore deliberately been left to the end. Still operating within the ideological framework of "the Party" Perepechko, a member of the Workers' Opposition, identified bureaucratism (in the Party) as the source of the cleavage between the authority of the Soviets and the soviet apparatus as a whole and the broad working masses.[568] Medvedev charged the Central Committee with "deviations in the direction of distrust of the creative powers of the working class and concessions to the petty-bourgeoisie and to the bourgeois official castes".[569] To offset this tendency and preserve the proletarian spirit in the Party, the Workers' Opposition proposed that "every Party member be required to live and work for three months out of every year as an ordinary proletarian or peasant, engaged in physical labour".[570] Ignatov's theses called for a minimum of two-thirds of each body to be composed of workers. Criticism of the leadership was more bitter than it had been for years. A delegate raised a storm by calling Lenin "the greatest *chinovnik*" (hierarch of the Tsarist bureaucracy).[571] The leadership played its usual game. A long resolution on the trade unions, drawn up by Zinoviev was passed by 336 to 50 (for Trotsky's position) and 18 (for the Workers' Opposition):[572]

> Zinoviev took pains in this document to claim absolute continuity with the trade-union doctrine…stated by the First Trade Union Congress and in the Party programme of 1919. This was the familiar device of generating a smokescreen of orthodoxy to cover a change of course.[573]

The document which spoke a lot about "workers' democracy" went on to stress in unequivocal terms that the Party would guide all trade union work.

On the penultimate day of the Congress, at the end of a session, without any previous discussion in the Party and after a number of delegates had already left, Lenin made his famous proposals concerning the New Economic Policy. He pro-

---

567 Radek, Tenth Party Congress, p. 540.

568 Tenth Party Congress, p. 93.

569 *Ibid.*, p. 140.

570 "Resolution on Party Organization Proposed by the Workers' Opposition", Tenth Party Congress, p. 663.

571 Yaroslavsky, Tenth Party Congress, reporting statements by Y. K. Milonov.

572 Tenth Party Congress, p. 828, n. 1.

573 Daniels, *op. cit.*, p. 156.

posed the substitution of a "tax in kind" for the forced requisitioning of grain from the peasants, one of the most hated features of "War Communism". There would be an end to Government control of the grain supply and, by implication, a free trade in grain. This momentous proposal was followed by four ten-minute contributions from the floor. The official report of the Tenth Congress runs to 330 pages, of which a bare twenty are devoted to the NEP![574] The main preoccupations of the Congress had clearly been elsewhere!

Internal tightening up now proceeded with a vengeance. A resolution was voted to the effect that "the most immediate task of the Central Committee was the stringent effectuation of uniformity in the structure of Party committees". The membership of the Central Committee was raised from 19 to 25 – of whom five were to devote themselves exclusively to Party work (especially visiting provincial committees and attending provincial Party Conferences).[575] The new Central Committee immediately imposed a radical change in the composition of the Secretariat. The Trotskyists (Krestinsky, Preobrazhensky and Serebriakov), judged lukewarm in their support of the Leninist line, were dropped from the Central Committee altogether. Radical changes were also brought about in the Orgbureau and in the composition of a number of regional Party organizations.[576] "Disciplined", "safe" mediocrities were being installed at all levels. "The organizational shifts of 1921 were a decisive victory for Lenin, the Leninists and the Leninist philosophy of Party life".[577] The Party having willed the end was now willing the means.

EPILOGUE

May 1921
All-Russian Congress of Metalworkers' Union.
This union had proved the backbone of the 1905 events. It had been won over by the Bolsheviks as early as 1913. It had animated the Factory Committees and provided many detachments of Red Guards. It was now deeply influenced by the idea of the Workers' Opposition. Its leader, Medvedev, was an active member of the Opposition. His grip on the union had to be broken.

At the Metalworkers' Congress the Central Committee of the Party handed down to the Party fraction in the union a list of recommended candidates for *union* [sic!] leadership. The metalworkers' delegates voted down this list, as did the Party fraction in the union (by 120 votes to 40). Every conceivable pressure was then brought to bear against them. The Opposition had to be smashed. The Central Committee of the Party disregarded every one of the votes and appointed a Metalworkers' Committee of its own.[578] So much for "elected and revocable delegates". Elected by the union rank and file and revocable by the Party leadership!

May 17–25
Fourth All-Russian Congress of Trade Unions.

---

574   Schapiro, *op. cit.,* p. 308.

575   Tenth Party Congress, Resolutions, pp. 522–6.

576   Daniels, *op. cit.,* pp. 151–2.

577   *Ibid.,* p. 152.

578   *Isvestiya* Ts. K., no. 32 (1921), pp. 3–4. See also Schapiro, *op. cit.,* pp. 323–4.

This was to discuss the role of trade unions in the new, privately owned, sector sanctioned by the NEP. Tomsky, as president of the All-Russian Central Council of Trade Unions, was entrusted by the Central Committee of the Party with the preparation of the appropriate "theses" and with getting them accepted first by the Party fraction and later by the Congress as a whole. All went smoothly until by 1,500 votes to 30 the Congress also accepted an inoffensive-looking motion proposed by Ryazanov on behalf of the Party fraction, which was to precipitate a major scandal. The key section of the resolution stated: "the leading personnel of the trade union movement must be chosen under the general guidance of the Party, but the Party must make a special effort to allow normal methods of proletarian democracy, particularly in the trade unions, where the choice of leaders should be left to the trade unionists themselves".[579]

The Central Committee was furious. It came down on the Congress like a ton of bricks. Tomsky, who had not even supported the maverick resolution, had his credentials as representative of the Central Committee to the Congress immediately withdrawn. He was replaced in this position by such noted trade unionists as Lenin, Stalin and Bukharin – whose task it was to curb the fractious fraction. Ryazanov was barred from ever engaging in trade-union work again.

A special commission, headed by Stalin, was set up to "investigate Tomsky's behaviour". Its investigation completed, it decided to reprimand him severely for his "criminal negligence" (in allowing the Congress to express its own wishes). Tomsky was relieved of all his functions on the All-Russian Central Council of Trade Unions. As for the Party fraction, it was "talked into" reversing its decision of the day before. There is no record of how the hundreds of others fared who had supported the resolution. But who cared? In 1917 it had been proclaimed that "every cook should learn to govern the State". By 1921 the State was clearly powerful enough to govern every cook!

CONCLUSION

The events described in this pamphlet show that in relation to industrial policy there is a clear-cut and incontrovertible link between what happened under Lenin and Trotsky and the later practices of Stalinism. We know that many on the revolutionary left will find this statement hard to swallow. We are convinced however that any honest reading of the facts cannot but lead to this conclusion. The more one unearths about this period the more difficult it becomes to define – or even to see – the "gulf" allegedly separating what happened in Lenin's time from what happened later. Real knowledge of the facts also makes it impossible to accept – as Deutscher does – that the whole course of events was "historically inevitable" and "objectively determined". Bolshevik ideology and practice were *themselves* important and sometimes decisive factors in the equation, at every critical stage of this critical period. Now that more facts are available self-mystification on these issues should no longer be possible. Should any who have read these pages remain "confused" it will be because they want to remain in that state – or because (as the future beneficiaries of a society similar to the Russian one) it is their interest to remain so.

The fact that so many who have spent a lifetime in the socialist movement know so little about this period is not really surprising. In the first flush of enthusiasm for the "victorious socialist revolution" of 1917 it was almost inevitable that the viewpoint

---

579   Ryazanov, Eleventh Party Congress, pp. 277–8. Also Schapiro, *op. cit.*, pp. 324–5.

of the victors should alone have achieved a hearing. For many years the only alternative appeared to be the hypocritical laments of social democracy or the snarls of
open counter-revolution. The voice of the revolutionary-libertarian opposition to
Bolshevism had been well and truly smothered.

"*Vae victis*", said Brennus the Gaul in 390 BC as he threw his heavy sword on to
the scales that were weighing the ransom, to lift the siege of Rome. "Woe to the vanquished" has indeed been the immediate judgement of history throughout the ages.
This is why so little was heard about those revolutionaries who didn't wait till 1923
but who as early as 1918 saw the direction in which Russian society was moving and
proclaimed their opposition, often at the cost of their lives. They, and their very memory, were to be obliterated in the great bureaucratic upsurge of the ensuing decades,
euphemistically described as the "building of socialism".

It is only in recent years, when the fruits of the "victorious" revolution began to
be reaped (in Hungary, Czechoslovakia and elsewhere) that widespread doubts have
emerged and real questions at last been asked. It is only now that serious work is
being devoted to the real nature of the rot (the Bolshevik attitude to the relations of
production) and attention redirected to the prophetic warnings of the "vanquished".
An enormous amount of valuable material relating to those formative years still
remains to be restored to the revolutionary movement, to whom it rightly belongs.

Fifty years after the Russian Revolution we can see in sharper focus some of the
problems that were being so heatedly discussed between 1917 and 1921. The libertarian revolutionaries of 1917 went as far as they could. But today we can speak from
real experience. Hungary 1956 and France 1968 have highlighted the problems of
modern bureaucratic capitalist societies and shown the nature of the revolutionary
oppositions they engender, in both Eastern and Western contexts. The irrelevant and
the contingent have been swept aside. The key questions of our epoch are now
increasingly seen as man's domination over his environment and over the institutions he creates to solve the tasks that face him. Will man remain in control of his
creations or will they dominate him? In these questions are embedded the even more
fundamental ones of man's own "false-consciousness", of his demystification in relation to the "complexities" of management, of restoring to him his own self-confidence, of his ability to ensure control over delegated authority, and of his re-appro-
priation of *everything* that capitalism has taken from him. Also implicit in this question is how to release the tremendous creative potential within every one of us and
harness it to ends which we ourselves have chosen.

In the struggle for these objectives Bolshevism will eventually be seen to have
been a monstrous aberration, the last garb donned by a bourgeois ideology as it was
being subverted at the roots. Bolshevism's emphasis on the incapacity of the masses to achieve a socialist consciousness through their own experience of life under
capitalism, its prescription of a hierarchically structured "vanguard party" and of "centralization to fight the centralized state power of the bourgeoisie", its proclamation
of the "historical birthright" of those who have accepted a particular vision of society (and of its future) and the decreed right to dictate this vision to others – if necessary at the point of a gun – all these will be recognized for what they are: the last
attempt of bourgeois society to reassert its ordained division into leaders and led,
and to maintain authoritarian social relations in all aspects of human life.

To be meaningful the revolution to come will have to be profoundly libertarian.
It will be based on a real assimilation of the whole Russian experience. It will refuse

to exchange one set of rulers for another, one bunch of exploiters for another, one lot of priests for another, one authoritarianism for another, or one constricting orthodoxy for another. It will have to root out all such false solutions which are but so many residual manifestations of man's continued alienation. A real understanding of Bolshevism will have to be an essential ingredient in any revolution which aims at transcending *all* forms of alienation and of self-mystification. As the old society crumbles both the bourgeoisie and the bureaucracy will have to be buried under its ruins. The real roots from which they grew will have to be understood. In this gigantic task the revolution to come will find its strength and its inspiration in the real experience of millions, both East and West. If it is even marginally assisted by this little book our efforts will have been well worthwhile.

SOLIDARITY BOOK, 1970

AK Press Books, CDs and DVDs

Books

MARTHA ACKELSBERG—Free Women of Spain

KATHY ACKER—Pussycat Fever

MICHAEL ALBERT—Moving Forward: Program for a Participatory Economy

JOEL ANDREAS—Addicted to War: Why the U.S. Can't Kick Militarism

PAUL AVRICH—Modern School Movement, The

ALEXANDER BERKMAN—What is Anarchism?

ALEXANDER BERKMAN—Blast, The

HAKIM BEY—Immediatism

JANET BIEHL & PETER STAUDEN-MAIER—Ecofascism: Lessons From The German Experience

BIOTIC BAKING BRIGADE—Pie Any Means Necessary: The Biotic Baking Brigade Cookbook

JACK BLACK—You Can't Win

MURRAY BOOKCHIN—Anarchism, Marxism, and the Future of the Left

MURRAY BOOKCHIN—Post Scarcity Anarchism

MURRAY BOOKCHIN—Social Anarchism or Lifestyle Anarchism: An Unbridgeable Chasm

MURRAY BOOKCHIN—Spanish Anarchists: The Heroic Years 1868–1936, The

MURRAY BOOKCHIN—To Remember Spain: The Anarchist and Syndicalist Revolution of 1936

MURRAY BOOKCHIN—Which Way for the Ecology Movement?

DANNY BURNS—Poll Tax Rebellion

CHRIS CARLSSON—Critical Mass: Bicycling's Defiant Celebration

JAMES CARR–Bad

NOAM CHOMSKY—At War With Asia

NOAM CHOMSKY—Language and Politics

NOAM CHOMSKY—Radical Priorities

WARD CHURCHILL—On the Justice of Roosting Chickens: Reflections on the Consequences of U.S. Imperial Arrogance and Criminality

WARD CHURCHILL—Speaking Truth in the Teeth of Power

HARRY CLEAVER—Reading Capital Politically

ALEXANDER COCKBURN & JEFFREY ST. CLAIR (ed.)—Dime's Worth of Difference

ALEXANDER COCKBURN & JEFFREY ST. CLAIR (ed.)—Politics of Anti-Semitism, The

ALEXANDER COCKBURN & JEFFREY ST. CLAIR (ed.)—Serpents in the Garden

DANIEL & GABRIEL COHN-BENDIT—Obsolete Communism: The Left-Wing Alternative

EG SMITH COLLECTIVE—Animal Ingredients A–Z (3rd edition)

VOLTAIRINE de CLEYRE—Voltairine de Cleyre Reader

HOWARD EHRLICH—Reinventing Anarchy, Again

SIMON FORD—Realization and Suppression of the Situationist International: An Annotated Bibliography 1972–1992, The

YVES FREMION & VOLNY—Orgasms of History: 3000 Years of Spontaneous Revolt

DANIEL GUERIN—No Gods No Masters

AGUSTIN GUILLAMON—Friends Of Durruti Group, 1937–1939, The

ANN HANSEN—Direct Action: Memoirs Of An Urban Guerilla

WILLIAM HERRICK—Jumping the Line: The Adventures and Misadventures of an American Radical

FRED HO—Legacy to Liberation: Politics & Culture of Revolutionary Asian/Pacific America

STEWART HOME—Assault on Culture

STEWART HOME—Neoism, Plagiarism & Praxis

STEWART HOME—Neoist Manifestos / The Art Strike Papers

STEWART HOME—No Pity

STEWART HOME—Red London

STEWART HOME—What Is Situationism? A Reader

JAMES KELMAN—Some Recent Attacks: Essays Cultural And Political

KEN KNABB—Complete Cinematic Works of Guy Debord

KATYA KOMISARUK—Beat the Heat: How to Handle Encounters With Law Enforcement

NESTOR MAKHNO—Struggle Against The State & Other Essays, The

SUBCOMMANDANTE MARCOS—¡Ya Basta!

G.A. MATIASZ—End Time

CHERIE MATRIX—Tales From the Clit

ALBERT MELTZER—Anarchism: Arguments For & Against

ALBERT MELTZER—I Couldn't Paint Golden Angels

RAY MURPHY—Siege Of Gresham

NORMAN NAWROCKI—Rebel Moon

HENRY NORMAL—Map of Heaven, A

HENRY NORMAL—Dream Ticket

HENRY NORMAL—Fifteenth of February

HENRY NORMAL—Third Person

FIONBARRA O'DOCHARTAIGH—Ulster's White Negroes: From Civil Rights To Insurrection

DAN O'MAHONY—Four Letter World

CRAIG O'HARA—Philosophy Of Punk, The

ANTON PANNEKOEK—Workers' Councils

BEN REITMAN—Sister of the Road: the Autobiography of Boxcar Bertha

PENNY RIMBAUD—Diamond Signature, The

PENNY RIMBAUD—Shibboleth: My Revolting Life

RUDOLF ROCKER—Anarcho-Syndicalism

ROY SAN FILIPPO—New World In Our Hearts: 8 Years of Writings from the Love and Rage Revolutionary Anarchist Federation, A

ALEXANDRE SKIRDA—Nestor Makhno—Anarchy's Cossack

ALEXANDRE SKIRDA—Facing the Enemy: A History Of Anarchist Organisation From Proudhon To May 1968

RON SAKOLSKY & STEPHEN DUNIFER—Seizing the Airwaves: A Free Radio Handbook

VALERIE SOLANAS—Scum Manifesto

CJ STONE—Housing Benefit Hill & Other Places

ANTONIO TELLEZ—Sabate: Guerilla Extraordinary

MICHAEL TOBIAS—Rage and Reason

JIM TULLY—Beggars of Life: A Hobo Autobiography

TOM VAGUE—Anarchy in the UK: The Angry Brigade

TOM VAGUE—Great British Mistake, The

TOM VAGUE—Televisionaries

JAN VALTIN—Out of the Night

RAOUL VANEIGEM—Cavalier History Of Surrealism, A

FRANCOIS EUGENE VIDOCQ—Memoirs of Vidocq: Master of Crime

GEE VOUCHER—Crass Art And Other Pre-Postmodern Monsters

MARK J WHITE—Idol Killing, An

JOHN YATES—Controlled Flight Into Terrain

JOHN YATES—September Commando

BENJAMIN ZEPHANIAH—Little Book of Vegan Poems

BENJAMIN ZEPHANIAH—School's Out

HELLO—2/15: The Day The World Said NO To War

DARK STAR COLLECTIVE—Beneath the Paving Stones: Situationists and the Beach, May 68

DARK STAR COLLECTIVE —Quiet Rumours: An Anarcha-Feminist Reader

ANONYMOUS —Test Card F

CLASS WAR FEDERATION —Unfinished Business: The Politics of Class War

MUMIA ABU JAMAL—All Things Censored Vol.1

MUMIA ABU JAMAL—Spoken Word

FREEDOM ARCHIVES—Chile: Promise of Freedom

FREEDOM ARCHIVES—Prisons on Fire: George Jackson, Attica & Black Liberation

JUDI BARI—Who Bombed Judi Bari?

JELLO BIAFRA—Become the Media

JELLO BIAFRA—Beyond The Valley of the Gift Police

JELLO BIAFRA—High Priest of Harmful

JELLO BIAFRA—I Blow Minds For A Living

JELLO BIAFRA—If Evolution Is Outlawed

JELLO BIAFRA—Machine Gun In The Clown's Hand

JELLO BIAFRA—No More Cocoons

NOAM CHOMSKY—American Addiction, An

NOAM CHOMSKY—Case Studies in Hypocrisy

NOAM CHOMSKY—Emerging Framework of World Power

NOAM CHOMSKY—Free Market Fantasies

NOAM CHOMSKY—New War On Terrorism: Fact And Fiction

NOAM CHOMSKY—Propaganda and Control of the Public Mind

NOAM CHOMSKY—Prospects for Democracy

NOAM CHOMSKY/CHUMBAWAMBA—For A Free Humanity: For Anarchy

WARD CHURCHILL—Doing Time: The Politics of Imprisonment

WARD CHURCHILL—In A Pig's Eye: Reflections on the Police State, Repression, and Native America

WARD CHURCHILL—Life in Occupied America

WARD CHURCHILL—Pacifism and Pathology in the American Left

ALEXANDER COCKBURN—Beating the Devil: The Incendiary Rants of Alexander Cockburn

ANGELA DAVIS—Prison Industrial Complex, The

JAMES KELMAN—Seven Stories

TOM LEONARD—Nora's Place and Other Poems 1965–99

CASEY NEIL—Memory Against Forgetting

CHRISTIAN PARENTI—Taking Liberties: Policing, Prisons and Surveillance in an Age of Crisis

UTAH PHILLIPS—I've Got To know

DAVID ROVICS—Behind the Barricades: Best of David Rovics

ARUNDHATI ROY—Come September

VARIOUS—Better Read Than Dead

VARIOUS—Less Rock, More Talk

VARIOUS—Mob Action Against the State: Collected Speeches from the Bay Area Anarchist Bookfair

VARIOUS—Monkeywrenching the New World Order

VARIOUS—Return of the Read Menace

HOWARD ZINN—Artists In A Time of War

HOWARD ZINN—Heroes and Martyrs: Emma Goldman, Sacco & Vanzetti, and the Revolutionary Struggle

HOWARD ZINN—People's History of the United States: A Lecture at Reed College, A

HOWARD ZINN—People's History Project

HOWARD ZINN–Stories Hollywood Never Tells

DVDs

NOAM CHOMSKY—Distorted Morality

ARUNDHATI ROY—Instant Mix Imperial Democracy

Online at:

www.akpress.org / www.akuk.com

CDs

THE EX—1936: The Spanish Revolution

MUMIA ABU JAMAL—175 Progress Drive